The
ENLIGHTENED ECONOMY

THE NEW ECONOMIC HISTORY OF BRITAIN
General Editor: David Cannadine

Already published:

Making a Living in the Middle Ages: The People of Britain, 850-1520
Christopher Dyer

Earthly Necessities: Economic Lives in Early Modern Britain
Keith Wrightson

The

ENLIGHTENED ECONOMY

An Economic History
of Britain 1700–1850

JOEL MOKYR

YALE UNIVERSITY PRESS
NEW HAVEN AND LONDON

THE NEW ECONOMIC HISTORY OF BRITAIN
General Editor: David Cannadine

Published with assistance from the Annie Burr Lewis Fund

For information about this and other Yale University Press publications, please contact:
U.S. Office: sales.press@yale.edu   www.yalebooks.com
Europe Office: sales@yaleup.co.uk   www.yaleup.co.uk

Set in Garamond by the author
Printed in the United States of America

Library of Congress Cataloging-in-Publication Data

Mokyr, Joel.
    The enlightened economy : an economic history of Britain, 1700-1850/Joel Mokyr.
        p. cm. (The New economic history of Britain)
    Includes bibliographical references and index.
    ISBN 978-0-300-12455-2 (cloth : alk. paper)
    1. Great Britain–Economic conditions–18th century. 2. Great Britain–Economic
    conditions–19th century. 3. Industrial revolution–Great Britain. 4. Enlightenment–Great
    Britain. I. Title.
    HC254.5.M59 2009
    330.941'07–dc22
                                                                    2009014236

A catalogue record for this book is available from the British Library.

10 9 8 7 6 5 4 3

מוקדש לה,
היחידה שיודעת
כמה אני באמת חייב לה

The same age, which produces great philosophers and politicians, renowned generals and poets, usually abounds with skilful weavers and ship carpenters. We cannot reasonably expect, that a piece of woollen cloth will be wrought to perfection in a nation, which is ignorant of astronomy, or where ethics are neglected.

David Hume, 'Of Refinements in the Arts,' 1752

Contents

Acknowledgments

Books such as this are not written alone, even if only one name appears on the title page. During the six years of its writing, I have drawn on the minds and erudition of more scholars than I will ever be able to recall.

A number of names, however, stand out. Among my many dear friends in economic history, none has had a bigger impact on my thinking and research for this book than my life-long *vriendin*, Deirdre N. McCloskey, who read the manuscript in an earlier version, and gave me a generous dose of her original and unconventional economics, together with the optimal amount of tough love. I have equally learned an enormous amount from Margaret C. Jacob, a brilliant social historian of science and technology. My former student and now friend, colleague, and rabbi, Avner Greif, has left a large mark on the development of my thinking and research as an economic historian. Among the many other people whom I count both as personal friends and as kind but relentless critics of this project, I must mention Robert C. Allen, Maxine Berg, Maristella Botticini, Gregory Clark, Nicholas Crafts, Jack Goldstone, Murat Iyigun, Douglass North, John Nye, Amira Ofer, Cormac Ó Gráda, Nathan Rosenberg, Joachim Voth, and Jan Luiten van Zanden. All of them have provided me with valuable suggestions and advice over the years as well as the emotional support that is indispensable over long projects. They have been with me for the duration of the journey, and no one can imagine better fellow-travelers. Gillian Hutchinson, a life-long friend, provided important advice at the final stages of the editorial process. Many others have read half-baked chapters from this book and/or made valuable suggestions, among them Ken Alder, Alice Amsden, Joerg Baten, Dan Bogart, Stan Engerman, the late S.R. (Larry) Epstein, Karla Hoff, Jeff Horn, Tim Leunig, John Lyons, Sarah Maza, David Mitch, Ed Muir, Alessandro Nuvolari, Maarten Prak, Christina Romer, Johan Schot, the late Kenneth Sokoloff, and Larry Stewart.

At Northwestern, many of my friends and colleagues in both my home departments have enriched me with advice, comments, and suggestions. Among them, of course, are the permanent members of the economic history seminar Louis Cain, Joe Ferrie, Regina Grafe, David Haddock, Lynne Kiesling, Hilarie Lieb, and Chiaki Moriguchi. It is a special delight to mention the many graduate students who went through either the economics or the history department at Northwestern and consequently have had to listen to incoherent and preliminary versions of this work and improved it with their many suggestions. I have benefited to no end from their minds and research. Among them, I must single out Ran Abramitzky, Fabio Braggion, Joyce Burnette, Mauricio Drelichman, Haggay Etkes, Kripa Freitas, Tom Geraghty, Elise Lipkowitz,

Jason Long, Ralf Meisenzahl, Lyndon Moore, John Parman, and Tuan-Hwee Sng. Gergely (Gergo) Baics read the entire manuscript and hugely improved it with many insightful and wise suggestions. Alexandru Rus appeared on the scene late in the writing, but made many helpful last-minute suggestions. Last but certainly not least, I owe a huge debt to the endlessly resourceful and energetic Marianne Hinds Wanamaker, who has set new global standards for graduate research assistance.

No work like this could ever hope to be completed without undergraduate research assistance. Many talented and eager young women and men have suffered from the afflictions of Enlightenment research, and I am grateful to them all: Elizabeth Brown-Inz, Chip Dickerson, Paul Isaac, Hillary King, Aslam Rawoof, and Margaret Schumacher. A special debt is owed to Michael Silver, whose prodigious editorial talents and capabilities made me regret all the more that he chose to become a lawyer.

Special thanks to the Mercatus Center at George Mason University for organizing a special conference discussing the draft of this ms. in June 2008 in Arlington, Va. Every one of the scholars who attended this conference contributed materially to making this a better book. Those not already mentioned who attended the conference were my admired former teacher, Peter Temin; a friend and fellow Chicagoan for many years, Daniel Headrick; as well as Peter Boettke, Philip Hoffman, Claire Morgan, and John Wallis.

For a decade and a half I have been associated with the various programs in economics sponsored by the Canadian Institute for Advanced Research. The many conversations I have had there with some of the best economists on the planet, among them Daron Acemoglu, George Akerlof, Tim Besley, Elhanan Helpman, Roger Myerson, and James Robinson, have influenced my thinking more than I dare to admit.

Financial support from Northwestern University and the Searle Foundation is gratefully acknowledged. The original idea of writing this book was proposed to me by Simon Winder of Penguin books, and while what was produced does not quite match what he suggested that fateful day, I hope he is satisfied after all. Beth Humphries and Rosamund Howe edited the manuscript thoroughly and with great competence. Robert Baldock and Candida Brazil at Yale University Press in London were voices of sanity and reason in the later stages of the book.

As I have for the past seventeen years, I carry with me fond memories and the intellectual imprint of my unforgettable late colleague Jonathan R.T. Hughes. I suspect he would have liked this book, but I will never know for sure.

Finally, those who can read the dedication and those who cannot all know to whom I owe the biggest debt of all.

1 Counties of Great Britain, 1850

Coalfields

— Major canals

• Cities with population of over 250,000

Major industries
- Ⓘ Iron
- Ⓣ Tin
- Ⓢ Shipbuilding
- Ⓒ Cotton
- Ⓦ Wool

Lewis

SCOTLAND

Skye

NORTH SEA

Islay

Ⓢ • Glasgow   • Edinburgh
Ⓒ

Newcastle Ⓢ
Ⓘ   Ⓢ

Leeds & Liverpool Canal

Isle of Man

IRISH SEA

Ⓦ Ⓦ
Ⓒ • Bradford   • Leeds   • Hull
Ⓒ • Manchester
Liverpool Ⓒ
Ⓢ   • Sheffield

IRELAND

Trent & Mersey Canal

• Stoke   Ⓘ   • Nottingham
Ⓘ   • Leicester
Ⓘ Ⓘ
Ⓘ   • Birmingham

WALES   E   N   G   L   A   N   D

Ⓘ   *Oxford Canal*
Ⓘ Ⓘ   Ⓦ   *Grand Junction Canal*
Swansea   Ⓦ
• Bristol   Ⓦ   Ⓢ • London
Ⓦ   Ⓢ

Ⓦ   Ⓦ

Ⓦ   *Isle of Wight*
Ⓣ   Ⓣ
Ⓣ Ⓣ

ENGLISH CHANNEL

2 Industrial Britain, 1850

Ideology, Knowledge, and Institutions in Economic Change

Economic change in all periods depends, more than most economists think, on what people believe, and this was very much true for the economic development of the British economy between the Glorious Revolution and the Crystal Palace exhibition. This book is a personal interpretative essay on the factors that led to the emergence of modern economic growth in what became "the industrialized world" in which, by all accounts, the British economy played a pivotal role. It provides an account of economic developments in Britain during the century and a half after 1700. It is not a balanced account: given the magnitude of the literature on this period, any survey needs to pick priorities and I have done so shamelessly. It argues, in short, that in addition to standard arguments such as geographical factors and the role of markets, politics, and society, the beginnings of modern economic growth depended a great deal on what people knew and believed, and how those beliefs affected their economic behavior. The eighteenth century was the Age of Enlightenment—and the economic ramifications of that fact need to be fully confronted. Thought and philosophy, as Hegel pointed out, inspired a world of reality that people constructed, and the French and American Revolutions demonstrated this amply (Himmelfarb, 2004, p. 7). But what about economics?

Do ideology and "culture" affect economic outcomes? The question is as old as economics itself. Both Marx and modern free market economists have felt that beliefs adjust themselves to economic interests that themselves are largely determined by deeper forces of technology, demography, geography, and so on. Most economists, ironically enough, share with Marx a historical materialism which holds that ideology is basically endogenous to economic environments and does not shape them. At the other end of the continuum there have always been those who felt with John Maynard Keynes, in a famous paragraph, that "the power of vested interests is vastly exaggerated compared with the gradual encroachment of ideas ... soon or late, it is ideas, not vested interests, which are dangerous for good or evil" ([1936] 1964, pp. 383–84). I will argue that in historical reality the two interacted in complicated ways. Under the right circumstances, as they occurred in eighteenth-century Britain, this interaction produced a positive feedback loop that created the greatest sea-change in economic history since the advent of agriculture: the Industrial Revolution and the emergence of sustained economic growth.

The way this interaction between what people believed and knew on the one hand and their economic actions on the other took place was historically contingent. By this I mean that it was the result of a confluence of circumstances that was in no way inevitable. It seems natural to infer that the beliefs of rulers and policy makers, those who wrote the rules and regulations by which the economic game was played, were crucial. But in the Industrial Revolution the beliefs and ideas of intellectuals, scientists, skilled mechanics, inventors, and entrepreneurs may have mattered more. Of course, ideas do not rain down from heaven. Commercial and urban societies, which could afford to sustain a substantial number of people living by their wits rather than having to toil in the fields, were necessary if intellectual ideas were to be created. Those people whose main occupation was to think and analyze competed in a marketplace for ideas (Mokyr, 2007). Some ideas proved victorious, others did not. From this competitive natural selection process, changes in the intellectual environment emerged, with far-reaching consequences for the creation of "modern" polities and economies.

There are no simple answers to the question of why some ideas won out and became a "dominant paradigm." Some ideas will succeed when the "circumstances" are right, and at other times the circumstances seem propitious but the ideas are not forthcoming or fail. Just as in evolutionary biology we can never know precisely why some highly fit species emerged and others, just as fit, did not, there is a baffling indeterminacy in history. Good timing and contingency explain outcomes. Surely, those ideas that proved amenable to strong economic interests had an advantage. But was there an autonomous logic to the evolution of the ideas held by the elites whose beliefs proved so important to economic development? Was rhetoric entirely marginal to the outcome? It would be simply wrong to believe that ideologies were simply a reflection of economic interests and that *persuasion* itself did not matter at all. Many influential intellectuals in history were traitors to their class, none more so than that great believer in historical materialism, Friedrich Engels. The *philosophes* who created the Enlightenment were, on the whole, very good at persuading, and slowly imbued the social and economic elites of their time with a new set of values and beliefs. The question "in whose interests" is always a good first place to look for answers as to why policies are made the way they are. But it should never be the final stop. Looking just for the answer to the *cui bono* issue overlooks the obvious fact that economic interests were often opposed by other economic interests. Alliances were formed, deals were made, and persuasive rhetoric about what was best "for the nation" must be taken into account. Reformers were met every inch of the way by incumbents and reactionaries, with the outcome indeterminate. There was nothing predetermined or inexorable about these outcomes, but once they took place, it is impossible to explain the transformation of the British economy without them.

There is a lot to explain. This was an economy that changed profoundly in a century and a half. By 1850, Britain had a population more than three times as large as in 1700. Furthermore, a far larger proportion (45 percent compared to 18 percent) of that population lived in towns. People purchased many more of the goods and services they consumed from strangers, and worked increasingly in large establishments that were separate from their homes and which demanded discipline and punctuality. They moved around their country in trains rather than in stagecoaches and their "sailing" across the seas was relying less and less on sails. The division of work within the household had changed, and so had the economic relations of individuals with their neighbors and communities. Markets, while already omnipresent in 1700, were dominant in 1850. People not only bought their daily bread, clothing, and houses, but also sold their labor and invested their savings through markets, in all aspects of economic life dealing increasingly with strangers. The clothes they wore were made of cotton rather than wool or linen, and while the changes in the quality of homes in which they lived and the food they ate were not all that dramatic, careful examination reveals shifts even there. Accounts of these changes tend to expose themselves to the charge of "teleology," meaning that we tell the tale of change as if everything that happened was somehow meant to bring about the outcome we observe at the end. Economic accounts of this period have tended to describe this transformation as a success story, opening themselves up to charges of "triumphalism." I will make a conscious effort to avoid such pitfalls in this book, but I will probably fail to some extent. The dilemma that a historian asked to describe this process faces is obvious: can one and should one tell this tale without stressing that by most criteria – not least those of people living at the time – this was an astonishing success story? The fact remains that by the time of the famed Crystal Palace exhibition (1851), Britain had become the undisputed economic leader of the world, enjoying a newly found (if ephemeral) political prestige and hegemonic power, and had become capable of providing permanently higher living standards for most members of a large and growing proportion of its population. Luxuries that had once been reserved to the very rich and powerful (or had been unknown altogether) were becoming routine consumption for ever-larger segments of the British population.

Historians of every nation are disproportionately interested in what happened in Britain in the eighteenth and early nineteenth centuries because it was not, in the end, a strictly British affair. The changes in the British economy were shared by other nations in Europe and eventually overseas as well. This is the era in which modern economic growth was "invented"—a phenomenon unprecedented in human history, which lifted a majority of the people above the minimum consumption needed to survive and provided them with comfort, security, leisure, and material satisfaction that in previous ages had been confined to a few. Whether one considers the rise of commercial industrialism, financial capitalism, urbanization, and the achievements of technology a blessing or a curse, there can be no doubt that they took place. The period in which the plant of prosperity germinated and first blossomed is the period under discussion here, and the place in which it happened was Britain. At the center of it all was the Industrial Revolution.

If any consensus among historians, economists, and historically inclined social scientists is to be found regarding the economic history of the world, it is that what is regarded today as modern economic growth started in Britain as a result of the Industrial Revolution. Whereas many of the details of timing, causes, and effects have remained in dispute, historians and economists have sensed that at some point after 1750 something deep and irreversible happened in the British Isles, that eventually spread to most of Western Europe, North America, and other areas influenced by the West. In 1700, economic growth was not entirely new to the world, and certainly not to Britain: few scholars would disagree that by the Glorious Revolution of 1688, when a first quantitative picture of the British economy was sketched by Gregory King ([1688], 1936) material life and economic institutions had changed a great deal since the Norman conquest, and that consumption patterns and aggregate output had grown in the long haul. And yet by modern standards change had been extremely slow. "A matter of degree," some might say, but degree is everything in economic history and the acceleration in the rate of economic change is the central event that needs to be explained.

All the same, it would be misleading to call British economic history of the period under discussion "the age of the Industrial Revolution," as if the period before it was but a prelude to the Industrial Revolution and the decades following it the aftermath. The event looms large to the modern economist because in retrospect it had huge repercussions on global economic history. Much of the economic history of the nation, however, can be described, analyzed, quantified and even modeled without reference to the subsequent emergence of modern economic growth. In the period 1700–1850, a great deal happened in the British economy that was in no way or only tangentially related to the Industrial Revolution. Just because the Industrial Revolution took place does not imply that everything before and during it inevitably "caused" or even facilitated it or that everything after it was caused by it.

Yet economic growth will continue to fascinate economists, and historians will not be able to avoid it. Before the Industrial Revolution economic growth, such as it was, was not only slower but qualitatively different from what economists today would regard as "normal" economic growth. Growth in our age relies heavily on technical advances and the accumulation of improved capital goods and new skills and competences that embody and enable innovations. Such advances, although present in the pre-1750 world, played only a secondary role in bringing about economic change. Although this hypothesis is difficult to quantify, it seems that until the Industrial Revolution, economic growth, such as it was, constituted primarily what is often known as "Smithian growth." Such growth was based on the expansion of commerce, the growth of markets, and improvements in the allocation of resources. As Adam Smith observed and economists have taught ever since, when two regions or economies trade with one another, both gain due to the benefits of specialization. The volume of trade increased prodigiously between 1450 and 1750, and Western Europe especially benefited. Much of the increase in trade was itself due to a growth in useful knowledge: improvements in ship design and navigation, the growth in geographical knowledge, and the discovery of new trade routes and trading partners. Moreover, trade was facilitated by improved institutions that strengthened the "rule of law." Institutions that eliminated piracy, improved enforcement of contracts and property rights, reduced risk and provided credit, insurance, information, and the reasonable assurance that trading partners would meet their commitments were a major factor in Smithian growth.

As a consequence, in the centuries before the Industrial Revolution, markets got better at the allocation of resources. Economics teaches that if labor or capital is reallocated from low- to high-productivity uses, overall output rises. Such improvements in allocation can be brought about by improving the institutional framework and the markets in which economic activity takes place. At one time or another, northern Italy, the Low Countries, southern Germany, and England were the beneficiaries of what is now known as "Smithian growth" and created considerable wealth. Commercial flourishing was often associated with industrial and technological change: the Dutch economy in its seventeenth-century golden age was rich in part because of shipping and commerce, but also because it relied on industries that catered to or depended on international trade, such as sailcloth weaving, papermaking, and sugar refining, and was able to increase productivity and compete through innovation. But such developments were normally driven by the engines of commerce and institutional improvement, with technology providing the auxiliary source of power. Around 1750 all this began to change. The best definition of the Industrial Revolution is the set of events that placed technology in the position of the main engine of economic change.

Many historians and economists describe the pre-Industrial Revolution economies as being dominated by Malthusian mechanisms, in which population pressure prevented income per capita from growing. One view of the modern age, especially popular among economists but also quite common among historians, is that modern economic growth consisted of overcoming these demographic negative feedbacks. The significance of the Industrial Revolution was that the race between babies and resources was won, resoundingly, by re-sources. How did this happen? In part, available resources expanded at an ever faster rate, as people became better and better at exploiting things they had possessed all along but had been unable to take advantage of. Three funda-mental factors brought this about. The first is ingenuity. The Malthusian model describes an "organic economy" based on plants and animals, supplemented here and there by water and wind power (Wrigley, 1987, 1988, 2004a). The Industrial Revolution is said to have shifted the material and energy basis of the economy firmly to minerals and fossil fuels, thus augmenting the *effective* resour-ces at the economy's disposal. Iron and later steel replaced wood, and coal re-placed animal and human energy. This view may understate the dependence of the pre-1700 economy on non-organic resources such as wind- and water power, but grosso modo it is an apt description. The supposedly fixed supply of land was stretched to yield ever more food, energy, and materials. The greater exploitation of natural resources in the eighteenth century came about not because of demand-side pressures, but because the knowledge needed to extract, transport, and utilize mineral was growing. Second, Britain learned to rely more and more on imported resources. Minerals could not be eaten, but food could be purchased overseas from nations that had more or better land and could therefore produce it more cheaply than Britain ever could. To pay for this food, Britain exported manufactured goods and minerals. Thirdly, people eventually decided to have fewer babies. The population of Britain—excepting Ire-land—kept expanding, but in the nineteenth century the rate of income growth began to exceed the rate of population growth by a larger and larger margin. When fertility began to decline, the gap between the two grew rapidly.

It has often been remarked that Malthus wrote his famous and highly influential *Essay on Population* (1798) at just about the time that it became irrelevant. Perhaps so—yet there are some reasons to believe that even before that time, his model was a rather rough approximation at best. Its most famous implication, the "iron law of wages" held that all per capita growth was doomed in the long term because population growth would undo it. In part that account is simply belied by the evidence: in the very long run, the economy was growing, if at a very slow rate by modern standards. Productivity in farming, mining, and shipping increased, and the range of consumer goods available to the average Briton by 1700 was far wider and richer than it had been in 1400. Most estimates of the rate of growth before 1750 are of the order of 0.2–0.3 percent per year (Snooks, 1994; Maddison, 2002, pp. 46, 90). At that rate income per capita doubled every two and a half to three centuries.

Moreover, fluctuations in population seem to have been governed by forces more powerful than income per capita: the incidence of diseases and epidemics seems to have followed its own dynamic, and might be chalked up to exogenous microbiological events as much as to what Malthus called "positive checks"

—that is, endogenous responses of mortality to overpopulation (Goldstone, 1991). Fluctuations in climate, too, had a substantial impact on productivity. Moreover, some economists, such as the Danish economist Ester Boserup, have criticized the classical Malthusian model by arguing that in the long run Malthus's idea that population increase would lead to diminishing returns and thus to lower income per capita (which in the Malthusian story would bring population increase to a halt) underestimates society's capability to adapt to population pressure by using its relatively scarce resources more intensively and effectively.

It seems, therefore, that just breaking out of the Malthusian "regime" through better technology does not constitute the entire story of the transformation of the British economy. In recent years, more and more economic historians, inspired by the pioneering writings of Douglass C. North, have begun to pay serious attention to institutions, that is, to the rules by which the economic game is played and the beliefs that generate these rules and people's adherence to them. For much of recorded history, the arch-enemy of economic growth was not population pressure so much as predators, pirates, and parasites, often known euphemistically by economists as "rent-seekers," who found it easier to pillage and plunder the work of others than to engage in economically productive activities themselves. Whether they were the King's or the Bishop's tax collectors, highwaymen, corrupt officials, greedy local monopolists, guilds that tightly controlled entry and production, or invading neighboring armies, aggressive rent-seeking often led to the end of the economic activity that brought about growth. In this way growth, in truly dialectical fashion, created the conditions that led to its own demise. Wealthy towns such as Milan, Antwerp, and Magdeburg raised the envy and greed of strong neighbors, who besieged, sacked, and taxed them. Only a few areas with unusual geographical characteristics such as Venice or the maritime provinces of the Dutch Republic could avoid the worst of these ravages, but even they had to devote a large proportion of their economic surplus to defense.

Britain was unusually lucky in two respects. One was that as it was an island, the threats to its security were less pressing. They were not absent altogether, as the Spanish Armada attests, and certainly being an island was not a sufficient condition to keep out foreign occupiers and plunderers (as Ireland and the Philippines found out to their misfortune), but all the same it was an advantage. However, keeping out foreign marauders was insufficient, because much of the rent-seeking was carried out by local notables and home-grown bullies. In the seventeenth century, British society became unusually good at restraining the greatest local bully of them all, namely the King. The principle that Britons would not be taxed unless they agreed to be, embodied in Article 4 of the Declaration of Rights of 1689 (stating that "levying money for or to the use of the crown, without grant of Parliament ... is illegal"), should be regarded as an important step toward constraining this one form of rent-seeking (North and Weingast, 1989). Yet rent-seeking was alive and well in eighteenth-century Britain: there were still many ways in which rules, regulations, and restrictions siphoned off wealth from those whom we would regard as "productive," and redistributed it to others with political influence or traditional privileges.

Much of the economic history of Britain during the period under discussion here cannot be properly understood without realizing that after the middle of the eighteenth century redistributive activities, inimical to economic development, were on the retreat. The attacks on mercantilism—which was the formal manifestation of rent-seeking—by liberal economists were one front on which this battle was fought. The term "mercantilism" post-dates the age in which it predominated in much of European commercial policies, although Adam Smith wrote scathingly of the "mercantile system." In much of Europe around 1700, governments had created alliances with economic interests that provided each with something they badly wanted. Governments were provided with much-needed tax revenues; special interests gained protection and other exclusionary rents. But in Britain, more than anywhere else, the legitimacy of government regulation, monopolies, privileges, and the rent-seeking they implied in the foreign and colonial trades, came under criticism on account of the growing abhorrence felt for monopolies, workers' combinations, and other encumbrances to the free and uninhibited exercise of economic activity. The groups in power increasingly decided to curb ancient privileges, including the misnamed "freedoms" (i.e., privileges), which gave certain groups the right to exercise a monopoly in incorporated towns, and the tight regulation of apprenticeships.

Economic liberty based on the loosening of economic regulations and their enforcement was only one element in a wider set of changes in eighteenth-century Britain. On the Continent, of course, these changes were inextricably mixed up with the French Revolution and its diffusion to other countries on the bayonets of Napoleon's soldiers; in North America, with the American Revolution and the emergence of the institutional foundations of American economic growth. In Britain, there were fewer dramatic events, and not all of them point unambiguously in the direction of liberalization. All the same, this was a society that drifted hesitantly and slowly toward more openness, higher competitiveness, and more unfettered economic choices. By the time of Queen Victoria's ascent to the throne, it had become as much of a laissez-faire economy as can be expected on this earth, and rent-seeking in Britain was approaching extinction. Instead, it placed its faith—excessively in some views—in the one institution whose wisdom it had learned to appreciate: the free market. This transition, the mother of all institutional changes, needed to take place before economic growth was to become the norm rather than the exception.

A successful economy depends on good institutions to create the right incentives for commerce, finance, and innovation. Yet there is no set of institutions that we could design as universally "optimal." As the circumstances change, institutions need to adapt. What matters therefore is for institutions to have the agility to change as circumstances change. It needs not only rules that determine how the economic game is played, it needs rules to change the rules if necessary in a way that is as costless as possible. In other words, it needs *meta*-institutions that change the institutions, and whose changes will be accepted even by those who stand to lose from these changes. Institutions did not change just because it was efficient for them to do so. They changed because key people's ideas and beliefs that supported them changed (Greif, 2005; North 2005). Much as some economists may be suspicious of cultural beliefs underpinning economic change, we cannot avoid facing changing ideology and institutions when discussing the eighteenth century.

And yet by itself institutional change would not have been enough. There was another element that held back pre-Industrial Revolution economies and prevented sustained growth. Their technological options were limited. The simple truth is that in many of the relevant fields of human productive activity, people did not know enough to make techniques work effectively and to solve bottlenecks that kept productivity low. This is not to say, of course, that before the Industrial Revolution technology was stagnant. By 1700, Britons and other Europeans made high-quality steel without understanding the basic metallurgy of steel; brewed beer without understanding the modus operandi of yeasts; bred animals without understanding genetics; and mixed elements and compounds without understanding basic chemistry. They manipulated power without understanding thermodynamics and fertilized their fields without soil chemistry. New techniques emerged as a result of trial and error and serendipity, and at times the progress they wrought was remarkable. But just as strikingly, people at times got it rather astonishingly wrong (especially in medical and agricultural technology). The growth of useful knowledge is at the center of any story of modern growth. As we shall see, the movement from the knowledge of nature to technology was a two-way street, with the movement going as much from practice to theory as it was going in the other (and more widely discussed) direction.

This is not to argue that the Industrial Revolution and economic growth were driven primarily by scientific breakthroughs. Scholars are still divided on the issue of how much technological progress during the Industrial Revolution *really* depended on scientific expertise (Landes, 1969; Musson and Robinson, 1969; Jacob, 1997). The impact of science on solving technological issues differed a great deal from problem to problem and from industry to industry. Many of the "wave of gadgets" that we associate with the classical Industrial Revolution—steam power being the most notable exception—could have been easily made with the knowledge available in 1600. What is beyond question is that the relative importance of science to the productive economy kept growing throughout the late eighteenth and nineteenth centuries, and became indispensable after 1870, with the so-called second Industrial Revolution. Much knowledge codified in books and articles as well as tacit knowledge that passed on between individuals would not qualify as "science" in its modern incarnation, but was of critical importance. Engineering, mechanics, the natural regularities involved in crop rotation, the location and extraction of minerals, the construction of instruments used in surveying and navigation, and the manufacture of material-intensive products such as potter's clay, paper, and metals became increasingly reliant on useful knowledge embedded in printed sources or obtained from experts. The essence of the Enlightenment's impact on the economy was the drive to expand the accumulation of useful knowledge and direct it toward practical use.

Explaining the Industrial Revolution and the origins of modern economic growth thus involves at least two separate problems, as Deirdre McCloskey (1994, p. 242) has pointed out. One of them is the "big problem": why did Western Europe succeed in doing something that no society in history had ever done, that is, break through the confining negative feedback barriers that had kept the bulk of people who had ever lived before 1800 at a level of poverty that is by now practically unknown in the West? Despite their formidable scientific and technological achievements in years past, neither the Ottoman world, nor China, nor India, even came close. Answers to this question have ranged from the bizarre (climate, race, religion) to the plausible-but-hard-to-prove such as culture, society, empire, and politics. Most of the answers, however, are explanations of the "big question." In what follows, I will address the "little problem": why was it *Britain* that took the leadership in the movement that turned the European Industrial Enlightenment into lasting economic prosperity?

The importance of the "little" question for the understanding of the history of Europe and the world is hardly marginal: by the mid-nineteenth century Britain had become the workshop of the world, the unquestioned technological leader, a source of economic and political power that was instrumental in implementing the Pax Britannica, that consolidated the British Empire, and that created the Victorian age that was, in retrospect, the true Golden Age of Great Britain. It was much on the minds of contemporaries. Concerned Frenchmen regarded Britain's leadership as a reversal of the normal state of things (which, they felt, was French leadership). Economic success led to a smugness and self-congratulatory mood in Victorian Britain that took many decades to fade. It also established Britain as the first nation dominated by factories and later by railroads, a nation that developed the first large industrial urban proletariat. The Industrial Revolution helped establish the financial hegemony of the City of London, which for many decades dominated the international banking scene. Moreover, it caused the demise of domestic industries, in which manual workers throughout Europe fought an increasingly desperate rearguard battle against the ever cheaper mass-produced factory products. In every conceivable manner economic growth changed the way in which people lived their lives. The British Industrial Revolution influenced the economic structure of the young American Republic by creating the demand for raw cotton that transformed the economies of the Southern States and gave slavery a new lease of life.

If the basic premise that the Industrial Revolution was the outgrowth of the social and intellectual foundations laid by the Enlightenment and the Scientific Revolution is correct, it was a European, not a British, phenomenon. In that sense, the "big question" and the "small question" are impossible to separate. Britain's leadership by itself was probably not essential to economic growth in the West. Without it, another Western economy could have led, and the process might have been delayed and differed in details. Britain's position of leadership increasingly shaped the Western world in the decades leading up to 1850, when it reached its zenith, but this hegemony was not a long-term equilibrium, and other economies had the wherewithal to emulate Britain and modernize their economies. This is not to say that they slavishly adopted the British model of steam and cotton; different economies, facing a variety of local circumstances, found their own "paths to the twentieth century." Yet to admit these differences is not to deny the enormous influence that the British example had on the decisions and choices that faced the entrepreneurs and engineers in Germany, France, Belgium, or Scandinavia. Everyone in Europe between 1820 and 1860 recognized Britain's economic leadership.

It makes little sense to think of the rest of Europe as "slow" or "backward." Each continental country had its own specific constraints and obstacles that needed to be removed or overcome before it could do what Britain did, and follow its own variation on the theme of industrialization and the modernization of production. Some of them chose a different path in terms of the techniques and forms of industrial organization adopted. Many of them required a political revolution to clear away the institutional debris, from restrictive craft guilds to internal tariffs to serfdom, that had accumulated over centuries of predatory rule and rent-seeking. It took another full generation for the Continent after 1815 to pull even, but clearly none of the British advantages were especially deep or permanent. They explain Britain's position as the lead car in the Occident Express that gathered steam in the nineteenth century and drove away from the rest of the world, but they do not tell us much about the source of power. Was Britain the engine that pulled the other European cars behind it, or were Western Europe and its offshoots on an electric train deriving its power from a shared source of motive energy?

The French Revolution violently swept away much of the institutional remains of the *ancien régime* and laid the foundation for the economic success of many continental nations. By the end of the period under discussion here, 1850, they had on the whole not quite caught up. By 1914, however, they had, and Britain was demoted from "leader" to "one of many." Implicit in this formulation is the notion that had it not started in Britain, it would have started somewhere else in Western Europe. It would probably have been a bit later, and the exact pattern would have been different in many details, but it would have occurred nonetheless. Europe, not Britain, was the entity that was unique in this interpretation. And yet within Europe, Britain played an undoubted leadership role, and why and how it came to play this role is a second and somewhat different question.

The answers to both questions in the end need to be sought in the realms of knowledge and institutions, not geography. The economic game is played at two levels: the level of a game against Nature (technology), and a game of interacting with other people (institutions). Stripped to its barest essentials, the game against nature is not a social game—though in any practical historical situation it was of course mixed up with social elements. Technology is always and everywhere about utilizing natural phenomena and regularities to extract from Nature something she does not willingly give us. Production involves harnessing these regularities to further human material needs. In principle, even Robinson Crusoe faced this kind of problem, providing for food, shelter, clothing, transportation, and medicine. In practice, this distinction has its limits. Useful knowledge was distributed, shared, and communicated, and social relations such as trust and authority were at the core of market relations and at the center of economic development. In eighteenth-century Britain, a sophisticated market economy, institutions and technology interacted at many levels. It is in this complex of interactions that the answers to the big historical questions must be sought: what was special about Britain to account for the unique role it played as the cradle of industrial capitalism and the prosperity of the nineteenth century?

When thinking about such questions, it is important not to succumb to "hindsight bias." By this I mean that when we know that a certain event occurred, we tend to view it as more or less inevitable and reinterpret all prior conditions as facilitating the outcome. After all, a lot of outcomes occur despite some prior conditions. Many of the institutions in eighteenth-century Britain were still hostile to economic development and this hostility somehow had to be overcome. On the eve of the Industrial Revolution it was in many ways still a protectionist and regulated economy. If Britain succeeded more than other European nations, it was because at that time she was better situated and equipped by comparison. But such differences were of degree, not essence, and they were fluid. The age of the Industrial Revolution was a golden age for British technological hegemony and all that flowed from it; yet, like all economic leadership, it was ephemeral.

CHAPTER 1

The British Economy in 1700

At the beginning of the eighteenth century, many decades before the Industrial Revolution, Britain was already a rich and sophisticated economy by the standards of the time. The usual measure economists use for this is income or GDP per capita, but perhaps the data and accounting difficulties are such that these comparisons by themselves do not make the case entirely persuasive. Angus Maddison's (2002) estimates have Britain in 1700 close to the top of the ranking with an income per capita of $1,405 (1990 prices), behind the embarrassingly rich United Provinces at $2,110 but already well ahead of France, Germany, and Spain. Some skeptics feel that the use of GDP per capita statistics in 1990 prices for 1700 relies on too many heroic assumptions to be taken at face value. Relying on very different kind of data (and other, equally strong, assumptions), Graeme Snooks (1994) has computed that the English economy (per capita income) grew by a factor of 5.75 over the 600 years between the Domesday Book (1086) and Gregory King's numbers (1688). This is tantamount to an average annual rate of growth of 0.29 percent, which was not significantly exceeded until 1800. There is no real way to make sure that such numbers are "correct"—the idea of GDP and national income accounts cannot really accommodate many of the developments of an economy over so many years, such as the appearance of new goods, the improvement of quality, and the replacement of self-sufficiency by market transactions. But it is telling that many of the most knowledgeable contemporaries were amazed at how rich England was, how high its wages, and how extensive and sophisticated the markets. Daniel Defoe, widely regarded as the best-informed writer on the state of pre-Industrial Revolution Britain, wrote with pride on the wealth of his country, even if he was concerned about its future. Adam Smith, half a century later, had no doubt that "the annual produce of the land and labour of England ... is certainly much greater than it was a little more than a century ago at the restoration of Charles II (1660) ... and [it] was certainly much greater at the restoration than we can suppose it to have been a hundred years before" ([1776], 1976, pp. 365–66).

Beyond income per capita, there are other measures we can examine to persuade ourselves that by the standards of the time this was an economy that had made considerable progress compared to the dismal picture often painted of pre-modern economies as poor and miserable societies in which everyone toiled from childhood to death to scrape out a wretched existence. For one thing, this was an economy in which a large number of people lived in urban centers. London was already an astounding metropolis of 575,000 in 1700 and other towns such as Bristol (25,000), Exeter (14,000), Norwich (29,000), and Edinburgh (40,000) were becoming more substantial even if they were dwarfed by London's huge size (De Vries, 1984, pp. 270–72). The sizable villages of the West Riding of Yorkshire such as Halifax and Leeds, by the time of Daniel Defoe's visits, were bustling centers of wool manufacturing, where most people purchased rather than grew their food (Earle, 1977, p. 115). Large urban populations were found in economies that could produce enough food surplus to sustain people who engaged in commercial, industrial, or administrative occupations, which in turn were often associated with higher living standards. In terms of the proportion of the population living in large towns (exceeding 10,000 people), Britain was still considerably below the Low Countries: only 13.3 percent of its population lived in such towns, compared with 34 percent in the Netherlands and 24 percent in the area that is today Belgium (De Vries, 1984, p. 39). But this was soon to change, and this figure ignores the large number of people living in British provincial market and manufacturing towns such as Birmingham (7,000) Worcester (9,000), and Cambridge (9,000).

The sectoral distribution of labor points in a similar direction. The proportion of non-agricultural workers in an economy is a decent, if not infallible, indicator of its wealth. Here, too, Britain looks impressive in 1700. The proportion of people in farming was estimated at between 30 percent and one-third (Lindert, 1980). This is a lot higher, of course, than in any modern industrialized nation, but it was substantially better than, for instance, Spain or Russia where, as recently as 1900, two-thirds or more of the (male) labor force was still employed in agricultural activities. What made this possible was, of course, the high productivity of British agriculture, which by 1700 had already reached the levels of output per worker attained previously only in the highly productive Low Countries.

What did Englishmen and women do for a living around 1700? For many generations, historians have had to rely on the estimates of Gregory King, whose famous tract *The Natural and Political Observations and Conclusions upon the State and Condition of England* was published in 1688. King's numbers showed an England that was far less industrialized and commercialized than one would infer from other sources: only about 110,000 adult males (or 8 percent) were either merchants or artisans. Peter H. Lindert (1980) used samples from parish records to demonstrate the fragility of King's estimates, and claimed that the true figure for these groups may have been in the neighborhood of 400,000, almost four times higher than King's estimate. In a set of further revisions,

Lindert and Williamson (1982) estimated the number of shopkeepers, traders, and artisans at 384,000, or about 28 percent of households. Their numbers suggest that agriculture proper only accounted for about 227,000, plus another 285,000 defined as "laborers." Even if we assume that three-quarters of those laborers were full time or largely in agriculture, we still have only about 32 percent of the labor force in agriculture in 1700, an astonishingly low figure for a "pre-industrial" economy, and not many more than were in commerce and manufacturing. A sharp distinction between merchants and artisans may be rather difficult to make, because many craftsmen sold their own goods. Data for women are harder to come by, but almost all who provided an occupation were "servants"—presumably domestic servants. The vast majority, in all likelihood, were wives and widows and were occupied in the market and non-market activities within their households.

It is rather striking that early eighteenth-century Britain was no longer a "traditional economy" in that it had by now a substantial number of people who might, with some license, be called "middle class," or in the language of the time, "the middling sort." Historians have defined this group as yeomen and farmers who had managed to augment their holdings, merchants and craftsmen who had benefited from the spread of a commercial economy, and some professionals (Smail, 1994, p. 26). One important thing about these people was that they lived substantially above the level of subsistence, and provided the main source of the surge in demand for middle-class consumer goods that appeared as luxuries to contemporaries. Living standards in Britain in 1700 were significantly higher than they had been in the early Middle Ages and they were higher than elsewhere in the West, excepting the North American colonies and the Dutch Republic. In the previous century the range of goods had expanded considerably, with colonial goods and other imports becoming increasingly common. More and more people drank tea and chocolate, sweetened them with sugar, smoked pipes, ate spicier mutton and beef from ceramic plates, and dressed in fancier clothes made from imported fabrics. The consumer revolution, as it has been called, clearly preceded the Industrial Revolution and has been attributed to a growth in household earnings stimulated by the new and desirable goods that were coming on-line in the seventeenth century and which prompted people to work more to generate the cash that made them accessible (De Vries, 2008). Comparisons of real disposable income with that of our own time, so beloved by economists, make little sense. Most of the goods consumed in the twenty-first century were unavailable in 1700 and thus such comparisons are more or less meaningless. The comparison involves asking implicitly how much a person in 1750 would have been willing to pay for a machine that played movies or for a liver transplant. Similarly, the comparison between 1700 and, say, 1100 means little. But the range and quality of goods had undoubtedly increased.

Contemporary accounts from the early eighteenth century are consistent with a substantial class that enjoyed high living standards in Britain in the first half of the eighteenth century. A Swiss traveler, César de Saussure, found the British to be "large eaters; they prefer meat to bread ... and consume a great quantity of dairy products" as well as great consumers of fruits and vegetables "and an abundance of every kind of salt and fresh water fish." Most fish consumed was dried or pickled, since the preservation of fish remained a difficult technical problem. Housing, too, was of better quality than elsewhere. Saussure also noted that the British lower classes "are usually well dressed, wearing good cloth and linen ... the poorest individuals never go with naked feet ... even the English peasants are comfortably off ... they are well-fed and well-dressed" (de Saussure, [1726], 1902, pp. 133, 171, 112–13, 219–20). Josiah Tucker, writing in the late 1750s thought that "the English have better conveniences in their houses and affect to have more in quantity of clean, neat furniture and a greater variety such as carpets, screens, curtains, chamber bells ... than are to be found in any other country in Europe, Holland excepted" (Tucker, 1758, p. 26). The quantitative study of probate records and other sources has prompted historians to conclude that the increase in consumer durable goods such as clocks, furniture, toys, books, rugs, carriages, jewelry, flatware, coffee and tea paraphernalia, paintings and other domestic decorations, peaked between 1680 and 1720 (Weatherill, 1988; Shammas, 1990; Styles, 1993). Most of these goods remained primarily within the confines of the middle class—indeed they may have been the signs that *defined* the middle class. Yet in the eighteenth century they kept trickling down to working-class people, if not, perhaps, to the unskilled poor, cottagers and paupers, who constituted the bottom 20 percent of the income distribution.

Moreover, it seems that a trend had been under way to make the average Briton a healthier person. Demographic data suggest that by two of the most widely used measures, Britain was already in much better shape than most other countries. Life expectancy at birth around 1700 was approximately 37 years. In the early decades of the eighteenth century it declined somewhat, but it recovered after 1740. Infant mortality at that time was of the order of 190 per thousand. These statistics are of course frightful by the standards of our age but are very respectable by the standards of the time. By comparison, French life expectancy in 1740 was about 28 years, and infant mortality around 280 per thousand. In countries like Russia and Spain, the numbers were in all likelihood even worse.

Famines and epidemics, which had filled the hearts of Britons with fear since time immemorial, were abating. Bubonic plague, the bane of the late Middle Ages, had vanished after a final visitation to Britain in 1665, and truly devastating famines were becoming increasingly rare, in part because in years of scarcity Britain could import food from surplus regions elsewhere in Europe. Defoe remarked in 1709 that "we know not in England what belongs to Famine ... It amounts to no more than this, that your fine Flower, your Manchet Bread, in short your Wheat is dear" (1704–13, issue of Oct. 20, 1709). Surges in mortality rates still occurred in the eighteenth century but they were less severe and more infrequent. From the fragmentary statistical evidence we have, it seems that in some of the more revealing biological indicators of living standards, the British were better off than most other European and Asian nations of the time, with the exception—oddly—of Japan. Britain was unusual in that while it was quite wealthy, it was still rural compared to its Dutch neighbors, with London being the only truly large city. Because urban areas in the pre-modern age were death traps with very high mortality rates, this accounts for Britain's relatively better performance. Mortality in London, especially child and infant mortality, was indeed significantly worse than for the rest of Britain (Wrigley, 1987, p. 137).

The growth of this middle class holds the key to subsequent economic development. The almost hackneyed theme of the eternal "rise" of the bourgeoisie or middle class in the historiography of the era has in recent years been justly criticized and dated as late as the second third of the nineteenth century (Wahrman, 1995). As a conscious political entity, or even an organizing concept of cultural identity, the middle class may well be a disputable category in eighteenth-century Britain. But the eighteenth-century writers (such as Daniel Defoe and David Hume) who identified it knew of which they spoke when they referred to the "middling sort." They viewed it as a segment of the population that followed certain common practices in production and consumption, and that shared certain values and beliefs, The large size of the British middle class in the early eighteenth century indicates that Britain had a comparatively equal (or at least less *un*equal) income distribution. Societies that were highly unequal to the point where they consisted of a mass of poor peasants and laborers whose efforts sustained a small group of leisurely and wealthy aristocratic drones were probably less amenable to subsequent economic development than more equitable economies. In part this is because the goods that the middle class purchased were increasingly produced by skilled artisans or imported, and thus created the demand for a set of skills and a trading infrastructure that were part of what a more modern economy required. But a middle class or "bourgeoisie" consisted of people with a different mentality, one of acquisitiveness, a desire for social upward mobility, and a willingness to invest in the education and well-being of their children (Doepke and Zilibotti, 2008). As a result, perhaps, more of the middle-class children survived to maturity by the late seventeenth century, and this led to a slow swelling of their ranks (Clark and Hamilton, 2006). But these values were also followed and emulated by others, aspiring to join the better life of the bourgeoisie.

Another measure of the economic "progressiveness" (not quite the same as wealth, but a close relative) of Britain in 1700 was the importance of markets in economic life. Well-functioning and extensive markets meant specialization and gains from trade, a more efficient deployment of resources, and the cushioning of local negative supply shocks such as bad harvests or epizootics. Such markets worked at three levels. One was the local level: people bought their bread from the local baker, had their shoes repaired by the cobbler, and their roofs fixed by thatchers. They usually paid for these transactions with cash. The second was the national level: a large and increasing number of goods were traded and transported all over Britain: buckles, guns, toys, and other metalware from Birmingham, flatware from Sheffield, pottery from Staffordshire, coal from Wales and Newcastle, silk goods from Spitalfields and many other goods subject to regional specialization that had emerged in the sixteenth and seventeenth centuries. These goods were shipped and traded throughout the country, as the travel journals of Daniel Defoe and many other contemporaries amply attest, despite the poor roads and the hard-to-navigate rivers. Britain's geography favored coastal shipping, and the absence of internal toll barriers, the bane of trade on the Continent, favored the emergence of a national market.

Third, by 1700 there was a great deal of trade at the international level, much of which had emerged since the death of Queen Elizabeth in 1601. The great geographical discoveries—as they were viewed in Europe—had created long-distance trade where there had been none before. Goods like sugar, spices, tea, tobacco, cod, indigo, rice, and cotton, to name but a few, came from thousands of miles away. Equally important, eighteenth-century Britain could rely on grains from France, the Baltic, and other parts of the Continent when its own harvests fell short, and although food prices still fluctuated, even in years of severe scarcity disastrous excess mortality was rare. Its shipping industry depended on naval stores and timber imported from the Baltic and its textiles on imported raw wool, linen, silk, and cotton. While it may be an exaggeration to call this a "world system" or "globalization" as many scholars in Wallerstein's (1976, 1980) tradition have done, at the time of the Glorious Revolution in 1688 Britain was surely part of a more integrated world economy than it had been in 1485.

Exact statistical evidence on the growth of international trade in the two centuries before 1700 is hard to find, but what little we know strongly suggests a rapid expansion: between 1622 and 1700 both imports and exports just about doubled, and a new commercial activity, re-exports, had emerged. By 1700, long-distance trade had been extended to the Caribbean, North America, and Asia. This trade would grow a great deal in the following century and a half. Whether Britain was truly at the "core" of a "world system," as followers of such interpretations would have us believe, is a matter of interpretation. Trade took place in a large number of commodities, but by necessity it was confined to goods that had high value-to-weight ratios. True "globalization" in which an economy depended on imports for its daily food supply and essential raw materials did not really take place till the late nineteenth century. Some have argued that "market integration" (as measured by the correlation of prices) cannot be observed before 1820 (O'Rourke and Williamson, 2002b), although the world was becoming more integrated in the standard sense of the word, in that the level of international trade was increasing faster than income, and new areas were drawn into trade networks.

Globalized or not, the gains from trade were real enough, and contemporaries well understood them: " Our *Foreign Trade* is the ... living Fountain from whence we draw all our Nourishment," crowed William Wood (1718). "Trade is so Noble a Master, that it is willing to entertain all Mankind in its Service ... all the Happiness and Glory of England depends upon the Encouragement and good Management of Trade and Navigation," added Thomas Baston (1728). Trade created wealth in many ways, not all of which were fully understood by contemporaries, and quite a few still bought into the mercantilist belief that trade was necessary above all because "we have no other means to get Treasure but by foreign Trade, for Mines we have none, and how this money is gotten in the Management of our Trade is already shewn, that it is done by making our Commodities which are exported, to over-ballance in Value the foreign Wares which we consume" (A.Z., 1754, p. 18). The standard economic story on which all undergraduates are feasted is the concept of the Ricardian gains from trade, in which it is triumphantly shown how each of two economies (or regions, villages, or individuals), which were both previously on their own, gains from engaging in trade. Eighteenth-century Britain provided the canonical example of such gains from trade. Ricardo formally showed in 1817 what many political economists and their students had realized intuitively for many decades, namely that free trade was normally beneficial to both sides. Over the course of the eighteenth century, access to imported goods filtered down from the rich to middle-class consumers and widened from a few goods such as spices and dyes to a much wider array of consumer non-durables (tea, sugar, tobacco) and even durables such as chinaware and upscale textiles (O'Rourke and Williamson, 2002a). But openness had many other blessings besides these static gains. It reduced the risks of famine, it exposed Europeans to new goods such as maize, turkeys, cocoa, and potatoes, or goods that had been hitherto known but unaffordable to most consumers such as sugar, spices, and cotton goods. It provided the British with new ideas about what could be done. Chinaware inspired the potters of Staffordshire to make better and more sophisticated earthenware, and the importation of calico from India suggested the opportunity of making better yarns from cotton. The British were rarely coy about utilizing foreign ideas or about reverse-engineering imported inventions. Trade created so-called *exposure effects*, inspiring imitation and innovation through the observation of what foreigners could do.

The ruling economic doctrines of the time were apparently oblivious to the rather obvious advantages of an open economy, fully transparent to the modern economist, and unfettered foreign trade was continuously under attack. In part this was because trade was invariably mixed up with politics, with trade often becoming a tool or victim of war (Nye, 2007). But above all, people simply had the wrong kind of notion of what trade did. It was believed that if Britain bought French wine, the gold used to pay for it would help the French kings threaten British interests. It was also believed that imports displaced domestic employment and that banning imports would extend the local tax base and prevent riots. This mercantilist outlook led to endless tariffs, duties, prohibitions, Navigation Acts, and other trade-restricting measures. Worse, during war time a popular and trusted weapon was privateering, essentially a government-sponsored form of piracy, that was undoubtedly lucrative to its practitioners, but turned out to be costly to the economy at large in the longer run. Commercial policy was continuously subject to special interests seeking some kind of tariff or subsidy that would increase the size of their slice, even if it reduced the size of the national pie and thus was a form of rent-seeking (Ekelund and Tollison, 1997). Their slow retreat over the period 1700–1850 was an essential ingredient in the recipe for long-term growth.

At times, however, such policies could alter the course of history in irreversible ways. The British tariff on French wine finalized in 1713 made wine so expensive that Britain became a nation of ale and whisky drinkers, with French wines (known as clarets) confined largely to the privileged few. The 1703 Methuen Treaty favored Portugal over France, hence the favorable treatment of heavy Portuguese wines known as port (Nye, 2007). The Calico Act of 1721, which banned the consumption of Indian-made printed cloth, encouraged the British to engage in the cotton-printing industry for re-exports (Wadsworth and Mann, 1931, p. 144). Militant mercantilism created the need for a large navy, and thus for the instruments and skills that would help navigate these ships and for the iron used to make the cannon that would protect them. Whether or not these efforts had substantial technological spillover benefits or whether they should be regarded as the wasteful cost of a misguided policy is still subject to debate, but they were not neutral.

Britain at the end of the seventeenth century was no longer a traditional static economy. There was growth, but by modern standards it was slow, uneven, and often reversed. Economists have long been wondering about the reasons why economies before the nineteenth century could not grow faster and improve the life of people at a more rapid rate. The answers are instructive, since clearly these factors changed during the decades that followed 1700. Part of the answer is what might be called Malthusian negative feedback. An increase in living standards in a Malthusian economy, in this theory, would lead to an increase in population, either through a decline in mortality or through a rise in birth rates, or both. Such an increase in population would increase the supply of labor and by the principle of diminishing returns cause a decline in income per capita, thus constituting in effect a negative feedback mechanism. Some modern economic historians and growth economists have eloquently restated the fundamentalist position that this doomed all long-term growth in the pre-modern economy (Galor and Weil, 2000; Clark, 2007). Even if the pre-1750 growth picture was not quite as bleak as all that, there can be little doubt that Malthusian negative feedback was an important factor.

A different negative feedback was rooted in the institutions of pre-modern economies. When some region or economy grew rich, it invited stronger and poorer neighbors to try to expropriate this wealth, either through outright plunder and piracy, or through more subtle means such as tariffs, Navigation Acts, and trade restrictions. Even when foreign invaders were eventually driven off, the costs of doing so and the taxes to pay for these costs could sap the economic power and energies of the economies. This is to a large extent what happened to the United Provinces in the eighteenth century. Internally, too, there was always the danger of powerful individuals trying to redistribute the wealth in their favor through taxes, monopolies, or other means. Such efforts, when taken to the extreme, could lead to the killing of golden-egg-laying geese and thus constituted an alternative form of negative feedback.

Finally, technology was another binding constraint. The pre-modern economies were at times capable of creating radical inventions, but such advances tended to settle down rather quickly into a new dominant design largely because most inventions were arrived at through trial and error and hit-and-miss procedures. Systematic research and development based on something we would recognize today as scientific rigor was still highly uncommon. The continuous improvements, tweaking, and refinement of new techniques that we are accustomed to in the modern age, and that have yielded most of the productivity gains, were far slower and soon tapered off.

These three factors, population, institutions, and inadequate knowledge, held back every economy before the Industrial Revolution, but some economies were showing signs that the age-old constraints were starting to crack. Britain, by all assessments, was one of the first nations in which a new economy was trying to break out of its shell. These signs are at first hard to discern, and there is not much evidence that many Britons in 1700 had much of an idea that such a radical transformation was imminent.

Although it was no longer a subsistence economy, many of the characteristics of traditional economies were still in place in 1700. At the beginning of the eighteenth century, the majority of Britons still lived in villages or small towns, and agriculture was a dominant activity. One of the more important findings of modern research has been to distinguish between a "rural" and an "agricultural" sector. By 1700 a large number of men and women who lived on the land were no longer full-time farmers. Agriculture had always been a highly seasonal activity, in which all available hands were activated during a few periods of feverish activity, while at other times, especially during the winter months, there was not all that much to do on the fields. In many regions of Britain, especially in the West Country and parts of the Midlands, rural industry, or "the domestic system" as contemporaries referred to it, was becoming an off-season occupation. In the eighteenth century an unprecedented flourishing of these cottage industries occurred, only to decline disastrously in the nineteenth. Weaving, spinning, nail-making, and the manufacture of baskets, brooms, and other simple industrial products became important off-season activities. For that reason, the word "industrialization" is not an apt description of this period. Indeed, the percentage of people associated with manufacturing in 1700 was little different from that in 1850. Some people worked most of the year on their farms, devoting themselves to the loom or the forge for only a few weeks or months; others were more or less full-time cottage-industry workers, who joined in the effort to bring in the harvest in the fall months. The far-reaching specialization of labor that we observe in more modern societies had not fully taken hold.

Economic life in 1700 was seasonal even outside agriculture. Transportation depended on roads that often turned impassable during hard rains. When transportation was disrupted, the wheels of commerce ground to a halt. Sources of power were also subject to the vicissitudes of nature: water mills could run dry, windmills depended on enough wind, and even animal power depended on supplies of fodder that might run out if harvests had been poor. Lighting was costly and poor; the winter months lent themselves much less to productive activity after dark. Seasonal unemployment was one of the main causes of low incomes in societies with poor transportation and communication facilities, and much of the concern of eighteenth-century writers with idleness and indolence was based on the observation that the state might be able to alleviate this problem by improving the infrastructure.

One product that helped the British protect themselves from the seasons was coal. At the beginning of Queen Elizabeth's rule, British annual coal consumption was about 177,000 tons. By 1700, it had increased to close to 2.5 million tons, most of which was still used for home-heating, but by that time it also had found many industrial uses, such as brickmaking, glass, ceramics, soapboiling, lime burning, forging, distilling, and brewing (Nef, 1933). It should be stressed that the use of coal by itself in no way "signals" the coming of the Industrial Revolution. John R. Harris (1988) has pointed out that the switch from wood or charcoal to coal-based fuels in the iron industry in the second half of the eighteenth century is often believed to be the first such transition whereas in fact it was virtually the last.

Pre-modern economies were not technologically static. By the early eighteenth century, Britain had experienced a considerable number of technological innovations. Many of these were importations or adaptations of new ideas first explored elsewhere. The so-called "New Draperies," a textile industry based on worsted (combed, as opposed to carded, wool, producing a finer yarn and thus a lighter fabric), had started in East Anglia and had expanded throughout northern England in the seventeenth century. The new draperies became a major export industry and by 1700 the woolen industry constituted one of the pillars of British international trade. The knitting frame and the ribbon- (or Dutch) loom were among the other innovations introduced in the decades before 1700. Farming, too, had advanced considerably. Yet the years around 1700 also witnessed important original innovations. The most remarkable of all was the Newcomen steam engine, first completed in 1712. Three years before Newcomen, Abraham Darby, the founding father of the great iron works in Coalbrookdale, destined to become one of the paradigmatic enterprises of the Industrial Revolution, had succeeded in melting iron ore with coke instead of charcoal, although it would still take decades for coke smelting to become profitable and widely diffused in Britain. Yet many of the most influential writers of the eighteenth century—Daniel Defoe and Adam Smith included—had little sense of the significance of what was happening in the area of technology in their time, let alone a premonition of what was to come.

Innovativeness in the decades around 1700 was not confined to factories or the few other large-scale enterprises such as shipyards or mines. Even the cottage industries, where production took place in workers' homes, were capable of technological progress (Berg, 1994), and many of the inventions we associate with the factory system were first tried in small-scale workshops. In textiles, the flying shuttle was invented in 1733. Yet it is important to realize that an economy in which there are innovators is not one in which all or even most people are inclined to experiment or to take risks, much less to express their disrespect for the wisdom of their teachers and ancestors by declaring the new to be better. The obstacles to any kind of technological innovation for an artisan or farmer around 1700 are almost unimaginable to a reader in the twenty-first century. Any concept similar to modern systematic research and development was absent. Inventions were made by inspired and obsessive individuals, mostly working on their own. The risks associated with invention were large, and the likelihood of technical (much less economic) success was vanishingly small. Yet the dynamic of a competitive economy such as Britain's in the eighteenth century was such that a small number of courageous and brilliant innovators was sufficient to gradually infiltrate and then take over one sector after another.

Another area in which the economy of 1700 shows signs of dynamism is in its capital markets. A few pockets of sophisticated niches in which assets were being traded had emerged, none more than in Exchange Alley, off Lombard Street in London, where shares of joint-stock companies and government bonds were bought and sold by specialists. This was a new development. None of these activities had existed at the time of Cromwell. Goldsmith bankers, the traditional backbone of the financial markets, had been joined by a new institution, the Bank of England, which was still struggling to keep rivals out, but was already establishing itself as a major actor in the financial affairs of both the public and private sectors. Both public and private credit were increasingly a matter for markets to decide, no longer a private bilateral arrangement between a King and a rich citizen.

Despite the importance of markets in economic life, Britain in 1700 was a pre-modern economy in one important aspect: the vast majority of the labor force still worked in or near their homes, and the people who worked for and with them were most often members of their own families. Non-family employees, such as servants and apprentices, often lived with the families and thus became members of the household. To be sure, for some occupations such as sailors, coachmen, miners, and even a few workers in manufacture, this was not the case even then and they were forced to work away from home. All the same, the sharp distinction we make today between household and firm, one the locus of consumption, the other the locus of production, did not apply in Britain—or anywhere else—in 1700.

Nonetheless, what some may call capitalist relations of production, in which one person hires another's labor, were common in the early eighteenth century and had been for a long time. This was true not only in urban areas where artisans employed apprentices and servants, but also in rural areas, in which the so-called "putting-out" system emerged. By 1700 Britain had a labor market, to some extent regulated and controlled by law and guild regulations but much less encumbered than on the Continent. Although craft guilds still existed in many areas and professions, the traditional restrictive and regulatory powers of guilds in controlling training and procedures, barring new entries, and enforcing quality codes and standards had over the previous centuries been increasingly replaced by markets. The majority of workers continued to work for themselves, but if their little business was unsuccessful, they could opt to work for someone else. A growing number of domestic workers were employed by so-called merchant-manufacturers, who managed and controlled a network of cottage-industries. It is now estimated that perhaps 30 percent of British laborers in the early eighteenth century were at some point employed in a formal labor market, where they received a money wage. But the majority of workers do not fall into the neat categorization of self-employed vs. wage-labor; instead the nature of the work fluctuated over the seasons of a given year, as well as over the life cycle of individual workers, who received wage income as a teenage servants or laborers, and later farmed or worked for themselves.

In short, by the standards of the time the British economy at the start of the eighteenth century was sophisticated, prosperous, commercial, and productive —a success story by all accounts. It was not the only such economy in Europe at the time, and there certainly was nothing inexorable about the economic advances of the next century and a half. It would perhaps be helpful if economic historians could show unambiguously that it was an economy whose institutions were, in some definable sense, progressive and conducive to economic progress. Some scholars, such as Douglass C. North and Mancur Olson, have indeed maintained that the Glorious Revolution of 1688 and its aftermath prepared much of the ground for eighteenth-century economic growth in that it established a firm set of ground rules by which the state would define and protect property rights. There is some truth in this view, but as always history is a complex and difficult tale. Whereas Britain had some institutions that fostered and encouraged growth, many others were more of an obstacle to than a support for economic development. Not all institutional elements in Britain worked to promote economic and technological development. Although the eventual outcome was unprecedented growth, this took place *despite* rather than *because* of some of the institutional preconditions.

To be sure, Britain was a land in which property rights were regarded above all. The various institutional changes culminating in the Bill of Rights of 1689 severely restricted the ability of the Crown to rule the country arbitrarily. It was a land in which the rule of law was at least respected if not always followed. Britain's day-to-day government in 1700 was decentralized and mostly run by local magistrates such as unpaid Justices of the Peace whose competence obviously varied a great deal. Contracts were enforced, and the power of the state protected assets—above all landed property. Adam Smith ([1776], 1976, Vol. 2, p. 49) noted that the "security which the laws of Great Britain give to every man that he shall enjoy the fruits of his own labour is alone sufficient to make any country flourish." There is some doubt about the extent to which law and order depended on government enforcement of formal rules, and I shall return to this issue repeatedly below. Be that as it may, people felt increasingly comfortable about transacting with others whom they did not know well, given the likelihood that the deal would be carried out, since both sides knew that reneging on promises would be penalized.

The view of many scholars influenced by Douglass North's interpretation is that by 1700 Britain had resolved what is known as the "commitment problem," that is, it had created a society in which the state had a virtual monopoly on violence to protect its citizens, yet most citizens could be reasonably sure that the state would not abuse this monopoly (Dam, 2005, p. 84). The age-old query "who shall guard us from the guardians?" had been resolved. Property rights had to be defended abroad as well as at home. The British Hanoverian government aggressively protected the property of its citizens from foreigners. This effort involved investing heavily in a military (that is, the all-powerful Royal Navy) that protected the colonial interests of large companies and fought ferocious wars against competing nations, above all France. By 1700, this policy had yielded considerable dividends in the early years of what was to become a British Empire in North America, the Caribbean, Asia, and elsewhere. While economic historians are divided about the overall economic effects of Empire (rightly urging us to consider the costs as well as the benefits), it seems hard to deny that the Crown felt that it was its duty to protect its citizens and their property overseas and that this stimulated and supported long-distance trade in exotic commodities. Its policies opened markets and generated profits, especially for domestic and colonial businesses benefiting from the Navigation Acts, privateering, and naval procurements.

The Enlightenment view that it was the role of the state to enhance prosperity and growth and to encourage the formation and dissemination of useful knowledge ripened slowly in the eighteenth century, but its institutional manifestations can be traced to earlier times. Monopolies, of which patents were an example, were primarily a fiscal tool that the Crown sold to interested parties in exchange for cash. Britain's patent law, dating from 1624, was an example of such a monopoly. Over the eighteenth century it evolved into a recognition that inventors are entitled to the fruits of their efforts and that they should be allowed to have an exclusive right to exploit this knowledge before it reverts to the public realm. Gradually it dawned on people that by awarding protection to inventors, society actually stimulated and encouraged potential inventors to engage in the risky activity of trying to create a new technique.

At times the government asserted its powers when it felt the need to correct something important in the economy or to redistribute resources from one group to another. When it was believed that companies with limited liability might foster speculation and possibly social unrest, the government passed the famous Bubble Act, which prohibited the formation of such companies without an Act of Parliament (1720). The mercantilist state in Britain had many other laws on the books that had the effect of redistributing income, such as Navigation Acts, usury laws, laws that regulated labor practices, and laws regulating the quality of many consumer goods. Other Acts of Parliament were passed to protect British commerce and manufacturing from foreigners. These included Acts that prohibited the exportation of machinery and the emigration of artisans (first passed in 1695 and repeatedly amended in the eighteenth century). Reality on the ground was often quite different. There were many exemptions to the restrictive laws and regulations, and many regulations were rarely enforced consistently and perhaps were not even meant to be. Important restrictions on economic activity such as the usury laws and the statutes of apprentices probably still constituted serious impediments to the conduct of business, although they were hard to enforce. Some firms obviously had to comply. Hoare's bank, a small London private bank catering mostly to the well-off, had to change its lending practices quite drastically when the British government lowered the maximum interest rate from 6 to 5 percent in 1714 (Temin and Voth, 2008a).

Some of the seventeenth-century trade with the colonies had been exclusively limited to companies such as the East India Company and the Hudson Bay

Company, monopolies that were enforced by the government. Yet from 1689 on, the great trading monopolies were on the defensive and by 1720 their control of much of British foreign trade was over. Indeed, the enlightened notion that "freedom" meant the freedom to *enter* a branch of economic activity rather than the freedom to exclude others was taking root in the early eighteenth century. By the late seventeenth century, a great number of foreigners, including Britain's erstwhile arch-rivals, the Dutch, participated in the British maritime and financial sectors (Ormrod, 2003, pp. 92–5). Yet the growth of the notions of free entry and their extension to the entire economy was very slow, and had not fully caught on even by 1800.

The British mercantilist state helped turn London into a commercial multi-functional center of international economic activity, overtaking Amsterdam in the closing decades of the seventeenth century and never looking back. All the same, the more extreme forms of mercantilism we observe on the Continent—always excepting the Netherlands—such as state-run factories and government-mandated and managed enterprises, were absent in Britain. An instinctive trust in the marketplace and a sense that the economic system is best left to its own devices was already taking shape many decades before *The Wealth of Nations* was published. This ideology, then as now, had continuously to struggle with many interest groups and "distributional coalitions," a term coined by Mancur Olson (1982) to describe groups that used the coercive mechanism of the state to redistribute resources to its members. States, by their very nature, redistribute resources, through exclusions, subsidies, price controls, and many other mechanisms. The institutional structure of the state helps determine whether incentives and payoffs are properly lined up to direct efforts toward productive or redistributive activities, and the fate of the economy is often determined by this structure (Baumol, 1993, 2002).

In 1700, powerful vested interests could and did lobby for special dispensations, regulations, and restrictions that enriched them at the expense of the consumer. After it had definitively seized the bulk of discretionary power in 1688, Parliament's regulatory powers spawned lobbies that sought rents at the expense of the general population. In 1722, for example, it prohibited the use of cloth buttons in order to support the silk and mohair industries, which made a competing product. Landlords were voted bounties on agricultural exports, colonial interests lobbied for and received protection and favorable regulation. Labor relations were regulated by law, to the advantage of some. But as so often was the case in eighteenth-century Britain, the letter of the law was one thing, reality another. Moreover, even a government that was susceptible to lobbying and persuasion by economic interests could make decisions that enhanced the performance of the economy, even if it did so in an awkward way, and even if these decisions were slow and often incomplete. In Britain, Parliament often passed laws that benefited some group at the expense of others (or the consumer at large), but at times it instinctively recognized failures in the operation of the market system and tried to set it straight. The Bankruptcy Act passed in 1706 helped streamline the enforcement of contracts and was meant to reduce cheating and opportunistic behavior, and Queen Anne's Act of 1710 regulated the rights of authors to their written work. There is no a priori presumption that in a parliamentary system, where lobbying is formalized, legislation will be necessarily more salutary for technological progress or economic performance than in an absolutist regime. It just happened to work that way in eighteenth-century Britain.

In general, the British economy around 1700 displays a hodgepodge of economic freedoms and restrictions. Many people were barred from access to rights we would consider normal: non-Anglicans were barred from official positions, women were excluded from universities and many occupations as well as from elementary legal rights. The poor, of course, had limited access to education and the law and could neither vote nor serve on juries, much less have access to credit. At the same time it had clearly become a more diverse and tolerant society; decades of senseless bloodshed over metaphysics had transformed into a more live-and-let-live attitude. It was far from an emancipated country, and yet as John Locke noted in 1689, "Toleration has now at last been established by law in our country. Not perhaps so wide in scope as might be wished for by you and those like you who are true Christians and free from ambition or envy. Still, it is something to have progressed so far" (Locke, 1976, Vol. 3, p. 633). It was in no way a democracy, much less a free-market economy. However, it was a nation in which freedom of expression, of occupational choice, of residence, and of association were exercised, in which the economic status quo had less power to suppress novelty, and in which experimental economic ventures using new techniques or manufacturing new products were becoming more common. As Hoppit (2000, p. 8) has put it well, in the early eighteenth century it became increasingly clear that heterodoxy no longer signaled chaos. People who begged to differ from the Anglican consensus were allowed to stay and pursue their business, and many refugees from less fortunate areas—Huguenots, Jews, Palatines—showed up in Britain and brought with them rare skills as well as the immigrant's customary determination to do well. It was also a society in which the uncertainty and riskiness of economic life had been reduced to the point where economic fluctuations no longer threatened the physical survival of large numbers. In part, this was because of poor relief. By 1700 the poor relief system was already well established in England, though it was to be transformed and changed many times over the next century and a half.

Whether in 1700 Britain was a "modern" or a "traditional" economy is a moot point. It combined some elements of modernity with many relics of earlier ages that no longer were consistent with a developing economy. Many—but not all—economic transactions, especially in labor and capital markets, were still based on personal relationships and reputations. The impersonal markets that became the hallmark of industrial society were still many decades in the future. While not quite as urbanized as the Netherlands and not as well educated as the Lutheran societies in Northern Europe, the economy in the British Isles contained many elements consistent with economic growth. Although contemporaries did not always recognize it, it was a society that held great promise. Yet history is full of examples of great promises that were disappointed. The real miracle is that in this case they were fulfilled, and thus changed not only Britain's economy but that of the entire world.

CHAPTER 2

Enlightenment and Economy

The Enlightenment was a phenomenon that set Britain and north-western Europe apart from the rest of the world in the eighteenth century. A huge amount of scholarship has been devoted to what it was and where it came from. Oddly enough, however, few have attempted to link it with subsequent economic development. Not much of the Enlightenment literature is concerned with the effect it had on economic change, not only during the eighteenth century but equally after 1815. The Enlightenment was an intellectual movement, a set of beliefs and values about both positive (what the world is) and normative matters (how the world ought to be). It emerged in a European, not a British context, though Britain was very much part of it. It is striking that the two gigantic literatures, that of the Enlightenment and that of the Industrial Revolution, have been almost entirely disjointed, despite the rather obvious connections. The Enlightenment project, writes a leading modern philosopher for instance, consisted of two projects, a political one that would create a better society and a philosophical one that would replace religion with rational thought and an understanding of nature (Rorty, 2001, p. 19). There was a third project, however, namely to make the economy produce more wealth and thus to increase what economists today would call economic welfare. Of the three projects of the Enlightenment, the third has been by far the most successful even if on a global scale it is as yet incomplete. The impact of the Enlightenment on the economy was slow and subtle. It would be impossible to discern its influence in the fields and shops of Britain in the eighteenth century. To repeat Kant's famous characterization made in 1784, it was an age of Enlightenment but not an enlightened age. But if the effects on the economy were slower, they penetrated more deeply and were impossible to undo.

If ideas affected economic outcomes, where did they come from, and how do they become sufficiently accepted to make a difference? As I have argued elsewhere (Mokyr, 2006c, 2007), intellectual innovation could only occur in the kind of tolerant societies in which sometimes outrageous ideas proposed by highly eccentric men would not entail a violent response against "heresy" and "apostasy." By our standards, Britain in the eighteenth century may not seem very tolerant. But after 1680 or so, few Britons got into serious trouble because they proposed new ideas about theology that some regarded as blasphemous, or chemistry that went against the grain. Britain's intellectual sphere had turned into a competitive market for ideas, in which logic and evidence were becoming more important and "authority" as such was on the defensive. In the marketplace for ideas, economic factors played a role in both the demand and the supply side, but they alone did not determine outcomes. Issues of ideology and knowledge are decided by the rhetorical criteria that society sets up for persuasion: what kind of evidence and logic are permissible, what kind of experiment is decisive, when a proof is "correct," and what is meant by a "true statement." These decisions were to play a growing role in the history of knowledge in the eighteenth and nineteenth centuries.

The literature on the Industrial Revolution to date has paid little heed to the Enlightenment, in large part because scholars trained in the hard-nosed facts of the beginnings of economic growth in Europe were reluctant to deal with phenomena that were hard to measure and explain, such as beliefs and ideas. The other reason why economic historians have shied away from drawing a connection between intellectual changes in the age of Enlightenment and the economics of the Industrial Revolution is that it is often believed that the Enlightenment was primarily a French affair, whereas the Industrial Revolution was British. Both of these statements are misleading. Indeed, many of the most important and influential Enlightenment ideas came out of the Scottish universities, and The *Wealth of Nations* itself was the culmination of decades of progressive and heterodox thought by such giants of the Scottish Enlightenment as David Hume, Lord Kames, and Francis Hutcheson. Indeed, the role of Scotland in the success of Britain is remarkable. The Scottish tail was beginning to wag the English dog, one historian has remarked, and there were areas in which Scotland was not England's equal but its superior (Colley, 1992, pp. 122–23). Scotland was a small open country, and it had excellent intellectual connections to the European Continent. Until late in the eighteenth century Scottish intellectuals may have been more familiar with Paris and Amsterdam than with London. Moreover, the most influential politician in Scotland was the third Duke of Argyll, an enlightened and secular-minded lawyer and intellectual, under whose patronage many of the most creative minds of the Scottish Enlightenment flourished (Emerson, 2003). It was no accident that Scotland brought to the party not only a disproportionate number of Enlightenment *philosophes* but also an astonishing number of inventors, engineers, chemists, mathematicians, and physicians.

But England, too, had an Enlightenment and not all of it was imported (Porter, 2000). Spadafora (1990, p. 3) notes that it seems implausible that the country that built the foundations of the Enlightenment such as "a constitution widely hailed at home and abroad" and the technological marvels of the Industrial Revolution would have merely *borrowed* the idea of progress. England had a different kind of Enlightenment because many of the relics of the ancient regime were already gone, and its precocious modernity did not so much pre-empt an Enlightenment, as John Robertson (2000a) has argued, so much as gave it a different character. Its Enlightenment was oddly flavored with a religious revival in the late eighteenth century and the preservation of many conservative values. In England, as Roy Porter put it, Enlightenment took place within rather than against Protestantism (2000, p. 99). A rather liberal Christianity resulted from this blend, in which religion was used as a justification to pursue one's self-interests. As it turned out, this religion was perfectly consistent with the cultural values of an industrial society. Yet the Enlightenment, while it could coexist with religion, did not need it to make its point, and religion became a matter of moral choice rather than intellectual foundation. For the economic historian these differences are in the end of second order, significant as they may be for the intellectual historian. The Enlightenment planted the seeds of economic progress in every country in which it was prevalent, but British soil proved to be the most fertile and the one in which they sprouted first. The challenge is to identify the sources of this precocity.

The argument whether the Industrial Revolution was "British" is more complex. In a narrow sense, and for a limited period, the statement is appropriate. But in a wider sense it is misleading: Britain owed a great deal of new technology to the rest of Europe; and even more so the knowledge on which the techniques rested. Without Britain's technological leadership, Europe would have had an Industrial Revolution: slower, later, and different in some important details, but sustained economic growth would have taken place in the nineteenth century all the same. Much like the new technology, the Enlightenment was a European, not a specific national movement. There is some value in placing it in a national context (Porter and Teich, 1981; Teich and Porter, 1996), but such an approach can easily lose sight of the fact that people, ideas, knowledge, and skills moved readily across borders. Nations and governments as well as individuals looked over their shoulder to see what other nations were doing and constantly learned, imitated, and adapted where they could (e.g., Robertson, 1997).

Of course, historians of the Enlightenment differ markedly in their interpretations of what the Enlightenment was, where and when it actually was located, and what is left of it today. The wide range of often contradictory attitudes, sensibilities, concerns, and hopes that Enlightenment writers have displayed makes any single statement about the movement close to meaningless. The ideas that constituted the Enlightenment were heterogeneous, and it is sometimes difficult to find a common denominator among the many *philosophes*, social and moral thinkers, and scientists active in the eighteenth century. Yet its impact on the character of modern society cannot be overestimated. Porter's notion that the Enlightenment's claims should be taken first and foremost as "propaganda" (Porter, 1990b, p. 22) is suggestive of the main purpose of the intellectuals of the Enlightenment, which was not just to describe the world but to reform and improve it. The amazing fact for the economic historian is that they were successful, probably beyond their own wildest dreams.

Some post-modern and radical writers have adopted the cantankerous attitudes of the Frankfurt School to the Enlightenment, that it was a prelude to barbarism, controlling, manipulative, and dominating, to be dismissed, in the words of Eric Hobsbawm (1997, pp. 253–65) as "anything from superficial and intellectually naive to a conspiracy of dead white men in periwigs to provide the intellectual foundation for Western Imperialism." Those who can find no fault in the thinking of Michel Foucault or the *Dialectic of Enlightenment* (Horkheimer and Adorno ([1947], 2002) may dismiss the opinion of an economist looking to it for the roots of modern economic prosperity and wealth as "Whiggish." All the economic historian can respond is that these roots have to be found *somewhere*, because the eventual outcome is there for all to see. Whether we regard the Industrial Revolution as the triumph of virtue and ingenuity over poverty or as the victory of perfidious capitalist exploitation, there is no denial that it changed history fundamentally and irreversibly. What is new here is not an argument that the Enlightenment changed history, for better and/or worse, but that its economic effects on the wealth-creating capabilities of the affected societies have been overlooked. Even Himmelfarb (2004), who has made an eloquent plea for its rehabilitation, does not connect it explicitly to the Industrial Revolution, to economic development, or to the technological and institutional progress that brought them about.

What, then, was the Enlightenment and why did it matter to the development of the economy in the long run? It has been defined in many ways by many scholars, but Roy Porter's (1981) pithy summary as a gradual switch from asking "how can I be good?" to "how can I be happy?" captures perhaps something essential. It made research and reflection on the human condition increasingly material and pragmatic. Above all, it was a movement that believed in social progress and the improvability of mankind. The belief in growth and improvement, and the specific notion that innovations and the growth of useful knowledge were the way to bring them about and thus a source of hope and excitement, were central to the entire Enlightenment movement. As Peter Gay has put it, in the century of Enlightenment, the word *innovation*, traditionally a term of abuse, had become a word of praise (Gay, 1969, p. 3, emphasis in original). The actual phenomenon of progress, in the sense of a trend toward social improvement for the majority of people, was not new in the Western world, but a conscious belief in the possibility of continuous betterment of society and a detailed set of prescriptions for how to bring it about were innovations associated with the Enlightenment. It stands to reason that such a belief interacted in many ways with the actual facts on the ground, both in terms of technological advances and institutional changes. In that regard the British case does represent something different. It was the English Enlightenment that spawned the "greatest happiness principle"—generally attributed to Jeremy Bentham, but by Bentham's own admission developed independently by Joseph Priestley (Schofield, 1997, p. 208).

Not all Enlightenment writers shared the ideas that I regard as "enlightened" and there were profound differences among the writers who were part of the Enlightenment on many issues. But what they shared was a belief that in some definable sense human and social progress was possible and desirable. They differed on their assessment of the likelihood of such progress actually occurring in their lifetime. Equally important, they had concrete ideas on how to bring it about and were determined to implement this agenda. Different societies had different needs, and the road to a better life was interpreted differently by different writers. Yet it is this "dominant mood," wrote a pre-eminent historian of eighteenth-century Britain, that was a necessary condition for Britain to become "the first society dedicated to ever-expanding con-sumption" (Plumb, 1982, p. 316). Defining the Enlightenment as the "age of reason" is a historical distortion, but Hampson may be close to an apt characterization when he defines it as an age not of reason but of reasonable-ness (Hampson, 1968, p. 157). But what does this mean?

At the heart of social progress was the expansion of useful knowledge. Kant's definition of the Enlightenment was "dare to know," roughly translatable as the modern bumper-sticker wisdom "question authority" (Kant, 1784). In 1760 David Hume wrote in his "Of Refinements in the Arts" about "the spirit of the age" which, in his view, "roused the minds of men from their lethargy and put them into a fermentation ... to carry improvement into every art and science" (Hume, [1777], 1985, p. 271). Joseph Priestley, the most articulate and distinguished English proponent of Baconian optimism, felt that "all things (and particularly whatever depends on science) have of late years been in a quicker progress toward perfection than ever ... in spite of all the fetters we can lay upon the human mind ... knowledge of all kinds ... will increase. The wisdom of one generation will ever be the folly of the next" (1771, pp. 253, 265). In this rosy view, the ability of people to command and control nature would not only lead to them having a life that was more easy and comfortable, but also mean that they would "grow daily more happy" (ibid., p. 6). Richard Price, a dissenting minister, mathematician, demographer, and well-known English Enlightenment figure considered his own age (1785) to be one of "increased light" and thought that technological advances such as the lightning rod and "aerostatic machines" (balloons) were only harbingers of "many similar discoveries" and that the "progress of improvement will not cease until it has excluded from the earth most of the worst evils" (Price, 1785, pp. 4–5). The personification of the Anglo-American Enlightenment, Benjamin Franklin, summarized this ideology in his 1743 call for a Philosophical Society in the colonies: "To ... men of speculation, many observations may occur, which if well-examined, pursued and improved, might produce discoveries to the advantage of the British plantations or mankind in general" (1887, Vol. 1, p. 480). Useful knowledge was often seen as raising productivity that would stimulate commerce and employment. Such was the thinking for instance of Malachy Postlethwayt. Yet he, too, recognized the mutual reinforcement of useful knowledge and economic performance: "when trade and industry administered wealth and honour, then was encouragement given to letters: in return for which, learning and science have contributed to the general advancement of trade and commerce" and he realized that "the commerce and navigation of this nation principally depend on the daily improvements made by our artificers" (1774, p. vi; entry on *Artificers*).

As many recent writers have stressed following Foucault's famous formulations, knowledge implied *power* at a variety of levels. There can be no doubt that knowledge has been used to acquire power over others, and in that regard the age of the Enlightenment was no different than the rest of human history. Where things were different was, above all, in the idea of *useful knowledge* which gave people power over *nature* and not (just) over *other people*. It is this kind of power that the entire historical literature inspired by Foucault's approach to the Enlightenment studiously ignores, and yet it is at the very core of what increasingly mattered in this period.

Useful knowledge was central to the British Enlightenment. While I will refer to it as knowledge of natural phenomena and regularities that had the potential to affect technology, the Enlightenment concept of "usefulness" involved both practical uses (that is, technology) and a moral and intellectual improvement of humanity so that people would be taught more virtuous lives. The courses taught in Scottish universities claimed to do both (Wood, 2003) under the assumption that the two reinforced one another. The importance of practical applications of science and mathematics grew over the eighteenth century. There was a great deal of self-serving propaganda in natural philosophers in search of patronage "playing the improvement card," as Paul Wood (ibid., p. 103) has put it, but if science had not delivered on its promises, the disillusionment would eventually have put an end to this part of the Enlightenment.

But useful knowledge, that is, science and technology, was not all there was. Another way that progress would be attained was through the perfection of institutions. Enlightenment thinkers thoroughly rethought the role of the state in society, and formulated proper rules for government and law based on such ideas as a "social contract" and "civil society" (the latter term was introduced by the Scottish writer and contemporary of Adam Smith, Adam Ferguson). Many felt that in this regard, too, they already lived in an age of improvement. Religious philosophers, such as Edmund Law (1703–87) and John Gordon (1725–93) felt that lives and property were more secure than ever. Priestley, writing in the 1780s, felt similarly that "the science of civil government was gradually improving" (Spadafora, 1990, p. 239).

The more ambitious of these writers such as the Frenchman Jean-Antoine-Nicolas de Condorcet or the English physician and psychologist David Hartley (1705–57) pushed the idea of progress further and expressed hope that individuals and institutions could be reformed through education because individuals, they thought, were perfectly malleable (Locke's *tabula rasa*) and thus in some way improvable. The most influential early thinker in this respect may have been Shaftesbury, who suggested that logic and ridicule would make people abandon extreme positions and bad behavior. This kind of optimism, the belief that human practices and social institutions could be improved through reason and knowledge, appears naive today and indeed the more sophisticated later Enlightenment writers such as Adam Smith, David Hume, Voltaire, and Diderot tempered their hopes for social progress with a great deal of sober realism. Hume in "Of Commerce" for instance worried that economic growth would increase the power of the state so that the price of prosperity would be reduced liberty (Hume, [1777], 1985, p. 262). Many of the most creative minds of the Enlightenment fully realized that progress was neither assured nor rapid nor costless. The French mathematician d'Alembert, for instance, thought that "men hardly acquire any new knowledge without undeceiving themselves about some agreeable illusion, and our enlightenment is almost always at the expense of our pleasures ... Still, we would not want to exchange our enlightenment for the ignorance of ... our ancestors" (cited by Gay, 1969, p. 102).

In retrospect, those who thought that individuals and their institutions could be perfected by better knowledge underestimated the potential of human beings to make stupid and cruel decisions even when they were better informed. They also failed to appreciate fully that suspicion and fear might lead people to self-enforcing bad equilibria, in which they behave opportunistically or "cheat" because they fear that others are doing so. Social perfection of the kind some Enlightenment thinkers dreamed of was and remains a chimera. Yet things that cannot be made perfect or fine-tuned with precision can still be improved, even if progress is fumbling and bumbling, even if every two steps forward are followed by a step back. In terms of the advance of the "useful arts," even the most optimistic and exuberant Enlightenment author did not dare hope for the economic miracles that were to follow. In retrospect, the economic historian finds herself agreeing with the rather obscure economist Lord Lauderdale who in 1804 criticized a skeptical David Hume for neglecting the "unlimited resources that are to be found in the ingenuity of man ... [and] capital laid out in roads, canals, bridges and inclosures" (1804, p. 299).

The Enlightenment of the eighteenth century shared certain basic principles, but of course these ideas were locally expressed and their manifestations varied considerably over space (Withers, 2007, p. 75). The Enlightenment in Britain (itself an uneasy compound of the English and Scottish Enlightenments) was different from the Continent's in nuances and emphases. The exchange and circulation of ideas emerging in different regions—itself a foundational principle of the eighteenth-century Republic of Letters—meant, however, that such differences could erode over time. The chemistry of Paris and that of Edinburgh or the medicine of London and that of Glasgow might vary, but they read one another's books and articles, and with time consensuses on many topics emerged. All the same, it seems fair to say that the English Enlightenment had a somewhat different character than that of the Continent. It placed a large premium on empiricism, pragmatism, and individual utilitarianism (Porter, 1981). The Scottish Enlightenment provided a deeper philosophical and scientific rationale for economic and social progress and the idea of a civil society. However, the Scottish Enlightenment, too, had a strong commitment to economic progress through political economy and the application of useful knowledge that could be incorporated into a Baconian program (Robertson, 2000b; Sher, 2000). It thus had practical implications, and progress was to believed to occur through technological activities that were theoretically grounded (Campbell, 1982, pp. 9–11; Macdonald, 2000, p. 199). The Enlightenment in Britain, whatever else it was, created an ideological background on which technological progress could flourish as it had never done before in history.

Within the Enlightenment paradigm, many ambiguities remained unresolved. One was the attitude toward non-Europeans. Eighteenth-century Enlightenment thought, on the whole, was anti-Imperial, and regarded non-Europeans with a certain respect that seems to have eroded in the decades after 1830 and turned into a new wave of colonialism. Another was transnationalism. The Enlightenment was originally explicitly cosmopolitan and pacifist, but it existed in a world of national and local rivalries that at certain junctures were clearly stronger than the Enlightenment instincts. The Republic of Letters consisted of spontaneous networks of individuals across political boundaries who were interested in similar topics and corresponded and collaborated on those issues (Withers, 2007, p. 47). Yet the nation state would not go away, and in some areas on the Continent, Enlightenment thought blended with nationalism. Efforts to improve "society" could never quite separate themselves from efforts to strengthen the nation. The Enlightenment never quite extinguished nationalism, and the political economist Malachy Postlethwayt, for example, in his introduction to the fourth edition of his amended and enlarged translation of Savary des Brûlons' massive *Universal Dictionary* advocated extending useful knowledge explicitly so that "the labour and ingenuity of our people, being inferior to those of no other state and empire, the kingdom may not dwindle into poverty and ignominy; and from being the greatest nation in the world, we may not become the least and the most contemptible" (1774, Vol. 1, p. x).

Especially after 1793, this conflict led to serious setbacks in the program for progress, and it is a testimony to the power of the idea that it was resumed after the fall of Napoleon and maintained, more or less for a century. Enlightenment thinkers realized the contradictions in the "European System" of competitive states in which suppression of innovation would be hard, but whose rivalry might degenerate into armed conflict. David Hume noted that "the divisions into small states are favourable to learning, by stopping the progress of authority as well as that of power" ([1777], 1985), p. 120.

Another ambiguity was the question of *whose* interests would be served by the drive to improvement, that is to say, who was included in concepts such as "the nation" and "the people." Shaftesbury, who placed "people" at the center of his thought, defined them as "the free citizens of the commonwealth, such as have seen the world and informed themselves of the Manners and Customs of several nations." Enlightened elites had mixed feelings about the lower classes, often patronizing, even condescending. The people, wrote the reverend John Brown (1715–66), who otherwise was a critic of Shaftesbury's philosophy, were "landed gentry, beneficed country clergy ... considerable merchants and men of trade" (cited by Porter, 2000, pp. 367–68). While the elite felt it was responsible for the well-being and improvement of the vulgus, clearly they felt a large social gap between themselves and the working poor. Dr. Johnson, in some ways an enlightened conservative, felt that "where a great proportion of the people ... languish in helpless misery, that county must be ill-policed and wretchedly governed; a decent provision for the poor is the true test of civilisation" (Boswell, 1793, Vol. 1, p. vii). At the same time the French radical *philosophe* Baron d'Holbach spoke for many colleagues when he surmised that "it would be a vain enterprise to write for the vulgar, we write only for those who read and reason ... the (common) people do not read and reason even less" and thus the masses would be enlightened only very slowly (d'Holbach, 1786, p. 295).

In economic matters some ambiguities are equally perplexing. Free trade was generally regarded as beneficial, but there was always hesitation and concern about possible exceptions. While blatant forms of exclusionary rent-seeking such as guilds and state-sponsored monopolies were widely condemned, not all forms of redistribution were regarded similarly, and concern for the poor and working classes and what to do about relief remained a topic of dispute. The difficulty of separating the deserving poor from able-bodied workers and resolving the standard issues of moral hazard in social policies was not—could not be—resolved by eighteenth-century writers. The same was true regarding property rights, where the rights of the property owner had often to be weighed against the interests of society at large. In general, the liberal political economy that the Enlightenment spawned had to struggle with the question of where to draw the boundary between the private and the public in an economy that was changing rapidly. Against the intuition that laissez faire was the best default policy, there was a growing realization, already present in Adam Smith, that there were too many exceptions and market failures to design hard and fast rules. Another perplexing issue was the economic and social status of women, on which eighteenth-century thinkers were hopelessly divided. In many areas of economic life, then, Enlightenment thought had no clear answer. All the same, its impact on the long-term development of the societies affected by it was enormous.

It is reasonable to query how big a part of the population was influenced by Enlightenment thought. The answer must be, whatever the numbers, that it was a relatively small minority, consisting of people who were not only literate but actually spent time reading and communicating with others about intellectual matters. One suggestion is to divide the country into those who paid poor rates and those who were exempted and might be candidates for relief (Langford, 1989, p. 63) but that divide, too, was often crossed in both directions and differed between counties. Modern historians often refer to the class susceptible to enlightened ideas as "polite society," which is not quite the same as middle class but overlaps with it. These were people who became members of literary societies, who attended lectures and concerts. Most of them were quite religious but, by the standards of the time, open-minded and tolerant. They would of course include intellectuals and professionals, but also well-to-do farmers, landed gentry, merchants, engineers and other skilled craftsmen. Coming up with a number for such people implies a firm separating line that did not exist, but somewhere between 10 and 15 percent of Britain's population may not be far off the mark. Using Mathias's (1979, pp. 166-67) reworking of the 1760 estimates by Joseph Massie, those families earning more than £ 50 per annum amounted to about 14. 2 percent of all families. It is not very surprising that the great economic changes of the modern age were brought about by a relatively small minority, as long as this is not interpreted as a return to the "heroic" view of invention, in which a few key persons were held responsible for profound historical changes. From the ranks of the British middling sorts came the men and (a few) women who shaped institutions, determined the agenda of research and experimentation, and decided on investment flows. Their impact on the direction of the economy was self-evident.

Of course, persuasion is a dynamic force. Ideas trickled down and percolated up in intricate and devious ways. Critics have rightly noted that the Enlightenment was an elite movement, and that much of its thinking served class interests. It was an ideology designed to protect private property from the masses and create the conditions for it to expand. It was neither egalitarian nor democratic in the modern sense of the word. All the same, much of the Enlightenment agenda was directed at improving society as a whole, whether it was motivated by nationalistic, Christian, or utilitarian motives.

CHAPTER 3

Useful Knowledge and Technology

The Enlightenment's long-term impact on technological practices and through these on economic performance is something that economic historians have neglected at their peril. This neglect is perhaps because it was a relatively amorphous and hard-to-define intellectual movement, perhaps because the Enlightenment was believed to be primarily French whereas the Industrial Revolution was British, and most plausibly because the connections between beliefs and intellectual conventions on the one hand and economic events on the other are poorly understood. Economists reasonably like to explain economic events through other economic events, making growth "endogenous." But at times there is room to introduce matters of the mind into long-term economic change.

I have proposed the term "Industrial Enlightenment" to describe this aspect of eighteenth-century society (Mokyr, 2002). The Industrial Enlightenment refers to that part of the Enlightenment which believed that material progress and economic growth could be achieved through increasing human knowledge of natural phenomena and making this knowledge accessible to those who could make use of it in production. It was believed that social progress could be attained through the "useful arts," what we today call science and technology, which should inform and reinforce one another. This belief spawned what has been called "the Baconian program." The program consisted of three components. First, research should expand humanity's knowledge and understanding of the universe by accelerating the pace of research into natural phenomena that had been of interest for a long time, armed with better research equipment and scientific method. Second, the research agenda should be directed to areas where there was a high chance of solving practical problems—in medicine, manufacturing, navigation, and so on. Third, the access costs to this knowledge should be made as low as possible, not only by dissemination but also by organizing and classifying what was known (Mokyr, 2005a).

The name is apt: the influence of Francis Bacon was central to the Industrial Enlightenment. The material aspect of Enlightenment beliefs followed in the footsteps of Bacon's idea of understanding nature in order to control her, although its parentage was of course more complex than that. Bacon's idea of the role of science was, in his own words, as "a rich storehouse, for the Glory of the

Creator and relief of Man's estate" (Bacon, 1996, p. 143). In the decades following the writing of these words, relief of the human condition became increasingly important, while the glory of the Creator took a back seat. As Bacon noted in a 1592 speech entitled "In Praise of Knowledge," "the sovereignty of man lieth hid in knowledge ... now we govern nature in opinions but we are thrall unto her [dependent upon her] in necessity; but if we would be led by her in invention, we should command her in action" (Bacon, 1850, Vol. 1, p. 80). That was, perhaps, the essence of the significance of the Enlightenment for the economy. In the words of one scholar, "The major purpose of Baconian natural philosophy is to produce innovations of which nature unaided is not capable" (Zagorin, 1998, p. 97). The program that Bacon suggested to attain material progress through technological progress consisted of the application of inductive and experimental method to investigate nature, the creation of a universal natural history, and reorganization of science as a human activity (Gillispie, 1960, p. 78).

The enormous influence of Baconian thought on British scientific activity is well known. The so-called invisible college in the 1650s brought together a number of the leading intellectuals of the time, and after the restoration they founded the Royal Society (1660), an organization that was explicitly inspired by Bacon's idea of a scientific academy he called Solomon's House. By 1671 Robert Boyle (1744, Vol. 3, pp. 153–55) had refined and elaborated the ideas of Bacon and had fully described the critical interaction between propositional and prescriptive knowledge and the huge hope it held for the future. The reason the economy had not lived up to its potential, he pointed out, was that tradesmen (artisans) "have really dealt with but very few of nature's productions in comparison of those they have left unimployed" (p. 155). If only men were better informed, he noted, they might discover new techniques they had never suspected and imagined, and physical knowledge would be "teeming with profitable inventions ... the fruitful mother of divers things useful" to mankind as a whole and the inventor himself.

These notions formed the core of the British Industrial Enlightenment, as well as deeply influencing the beliefs of Denis Diderot and other continental *philosophes*. Benjamin Franklin's editor spoke for many when he surmised that experiments showed that electricity was perhaps the most formidable and irresistible agent in the universe (Franklin, 1760, p. ii). A decade later Priestley reflected in purely Baconian terms on the history of knowledge that it is here that "we see the human understanding to its greatest advantage ... increasing its own powers by acquiring to itself the powers of nature ... whereby the security and happiness of mankind are daily improved" (Priestley, 1769, p. iv). Their admiration for Bacon—the first philosopher to clearly lay out a technological program for economic expansion—permeates the writing of many eighteenth-century thinkers and scientists. The Scottish social theorist and legal scholar John Millar could pay no bigger compliment to Montesquieu than to describe him as the "Lord Bacon" of the study of man and society, while Adam Smith was "the Newton" (cited by Chitnis, 1976, p. 93). The profound belief that advances in natural philosophy would eventually pay off royally remained part of the conventional wisdom, despite a lack of results. An American physician (as well as historian and congressman), David Ramsay, reflecting in 1801 in rather overly optimistic terms on the medical achievements of the eighteenth century, felt that he had witnessed the birth of rational medicine based on the principles of Lord Bacon, "the father of all modern science" (cited by Gay, 1969, p. 23). It is telling that when Michael Faraday observed the mining safety lamp that his mentor Humphry Davy had invented, he noted that it "was an instance for Bacon's spirit to behold" (cited by James, 2005, p. 175). The payoff to the research begun by the Baconians of the eighteenth century was delayed for many decades, but in the end it was huge. It does not seem absurd to suggest that Francis Bacon would have been delighted by what he saw in the workshops and mines of Britain around 1820.

To be successful, the knowledge generated by the Baconian program had to meet three criteria concerning useful knowledge (that is, knowledge concerning the physical world): it had to be *cumulative, consensual,* and *contestable* (Mokyr, 2007). The cumulativeness seems obvious: unless mechanisms are designed that transferred knowledge from generation to generation and stored it in accessible devices, there was a danger that it would be lost (Lipsey, Carlaw, and Bekar, 2005, p. 260). Consensus means that knowledge was to be made tighter in the sense that if there were competing hypotheses or techniques, criteria existed or were designed to test them and choose between them whenever possible. Contestability meant that there were no sacred cows and that nothing would be accepted on authority alone, and that, moreover, doubts and criticism of conventional wisdom would not be penalized. The Enlightenment did a great deal to advance on all three fronts. All three were strongly affected by access costs: the costs paid by someone to find and obtain knowledge that he or she had not possessed previously (Mokyr, 2005a). After all, it is not enough for knowledge to "exist" in the sense that someone, somewhere, possesses it. It has to be accessible in the sense that an individual who needs it and can exploit it can readily learn first that this knowledge exists, where it is to be found, and finally acquire it at a fairly low cost.

A great deal of confusion has emerged from the fact that discussions of the role of science in the Industrial Revolution have employed a modern notion of science, only to discover and rediscover that the chemistry and physics—to say nothing of the physiology and pathology—of the time were not up to the challenges posed by the needs of industry and agriculture (Mathias, 1979). As we shall see, the connections between science and industry in this age were multiple and often roundabout. To infer, however, that useful knowledge in general had no effect on the long-term development of production technology and that progress was on the whole coincidental, the unintended by-product of the daily work of artisans, is simply to misunderstand what was happening at the frontier of production. The legitimization of systematic experiment as a scientific method carried over to the realm of technology. Experimentation is, of course, necessary because it is a way of accumulating an empirical body of knowledge and inferring regularities in a deductive fashion, without necessarily understanding the underlying mechanism. Yet the accumulation of such knowledge was at the heart of technological change in the period 1700–1850.

The eighteenth century thus spent an enormous amount of intellectual energy on describing what it could not understand. We tend to think of science as more "analytical" than descriptive. The three Cs—counting, classifying, cataloguing—were central to the Baconian program that guided much of the growth of useful knowledge in the century before the Industrial Revolution. Heat, energy, chemical affinities, electrical tension, capacitance, resistivity and many other properties of materials from iron to bricks to molasses were measured and tabulated before they were "understood." Measurement itself was not novel in the eighteenth century, but the accuracy, thoroughness, reliability, the scope of phenomena and quantities being measured, and the diffusion of this knowledge surely were (Heilbron, 1990). As an example, consider steam power. Six years after the establishment of the first working Newcomen engine, in 1718, Henry Beighton published a table entitled *A Calculation of the Power of the Fire (Newcomen's) Engine shewing the Diameter of the Cylinder, for Steam of the Pump that is Capable of Raising any Quantity of Water, from 48 to 440 Hogsheads an Hours; 15 to 100 Yards.* The paper was published in a magazine he edited, implausibly entitled *The Ladies' Diary.* It gave a highly accurate measure of the power of the engine as the diameter of the cylinder was varied. Beighton's tables were reproduced in John Theophile Desaguliers' *Course of Experimental Philosophy*, the most widely read book on applied science in the first half of the eighteenth century. Desaguliers (1683–1744) remarked that "Mr. Beighton's table agreed with all the experiments made ever since 1717" (1763, Vol. 2, p. 534). Neither Beighton nor Desaguliers (nor, for that matter, Watt or Smeaton) fully "understood" (whatever that exactly means) the science behind the steam engine, but they all knew that in order to utilize it better they had to measure and quantify it. The great effort of naturalists such as Carl Linnaeus to find a classificatory scheme was very much in the spirit of the Enlightenment: minute description and measurement. It may not have been a substitute for "understanding," but it was a common thread throughout the Enlightenment world. His belief that skillful naturalists could transform farming was widely shared and inspired the establishment of agricultural societies and farm improvement organizations throughout Europe. By the second half of the eighteenth century, botany, horticulture, and agronomy were working hand in hand through publications, meetings, and model gardens to introduce new crops, adjust rotations, improve tools and better management. To be sure, these natural history people catered to only the narrowest of the farming elites, but if the techniques were seen to work better, they would eventually be imitated.

Enlightenment intellectuals were often guided by their belief in rationality and efficiency, and as part of their efforts to measure economically important natural phenomena, made a serious attempt to measure human work and effort, so as to increase its efficiency. Eighteenth-century scientists, the best known of whom were Desaguliers himself or the Frenchmen Charles A. Coulomb and his colleague Jean-Charles de Borda, repeatedly tried to measure the amount of work that people could perform, and establish a reasonable amount of work that could be performed this way (Ferguson, 1971). In the nineteenth century, Charles Babbage famously anticipated Frederic Winslow Taylor in his attempt to compute the efficiency of a laborer shoveling earth. It was the spirit of rationality and the efficiency of human beings driven ad absurdum, and it was perhaps one of the reasons why later generations took exception to some of the cultural attitudes associated with the Enlightenment. There was a stream in it that regarded people and work in an overly mechanistic way even as the technology of the age was slowly making brute strength increasingly irrelevant as a measure of productivity. The capacity to bring about human progress was constrained, and it took many decades after the Enlightenment to find out what exactly these constraints were. Indeed, the project is still very much ongoing.

Beyond pure empirics, there was always the hope that the deeper foundations of why certain techniques worked could be understood in the same elegant and encompassing way that Newton had been able to explain the movements of heavenly bodies. There was a growing belief that the discovery of general scientific principles would help in some way in the design and operation of mechanical devices, chemical processes, navigation, medicine, and other areas in which material progress was envisaged. In other words, even if much knowledge was still untight and in dispute, Newton's work held the promise of tightening over time through both experimentation and mathematical logic, so that at the end of the day consensus would be reached on the basic principles that made the world work. Thus Colin MacLaurin idealized Newton as having "a particular aversion to disputes" and "weighed the reasons of things impartially and coolly" in order to reach a consensus (MacLaurin, 1750, pp. 13–14).

How such principles would be discovered was itself a matter of debate, but the growth of an experimentalist-quantitative approach, based on careful observation, was widely believed to hold the key to progress of knowledge. Some of that work turned after 1720 into the "gentrified experimentalism of the Royal Society" (Stewart, 1998, p. 273) and remained rather aloof from the day-to-day needs of the economy. But engineers from Smeaton and Watt to the hundreds of anonymous craftsmen in Britain's mines, mills, and forges performed experiments to see what worked and what did not, and then told the world about it. Such a concerted effort was not entirely novel in the eighteenth century, but its degree and extent were far larger than anything seen before and while it was not limited to Britain, the British excelled at it.

The Industrial Enlightenment project enjoyed support from the authorities in some European countries, but it was by and large a movement of individuals in the private sector, who communicated and cooperated across national boundaries in what they thought of as the "Republic of Letters." Before 1789, knowledge flowed within and between private networks, which did recognize national boundaries. It was a community that played by its own rules and presents the historian with an unusual example of private-order institutional progress driven by a shared set of axioms. It is striking, indeed, how spontaneous the movement was in Britain. The British authorities were little involved with the nitty gritty of technological progress and confined their role to focusing attention on a few clear-cut problems the solution of which was deemed clearly in the national interest, such as the measurement of longitude at sea; to rewarding a few inventors who had made inventions that were deemed to be particularly useful but who for one reason or another did not profit from their invention; and to making sure that those who resisted innovation would not sabotage it by illegal means.

The formal institutions supporting the expansion of useful knowledge took the form of enforcing, to some degree, intellectual property rights that protected inventors through the patent system. When it came to intellectual property rights, however, the new ideology found itself painfully torn between conflicting views (Machlup and Penrose, 1950). One was their visceral opposition to monopolies and restrictions of any kind on free entry, tempered by doubt as to whether a patent was really a true monopoly. This instinct was reinforced by the Baconian notion that useful knowledge should be shared and that its accumulation was a fundamentally cooperative endeavor. In such an ideal world, a patent system that limits usage is not desirable. Yet this view clashed with another set of Enlightenment axioms: first, the belief that ideas were "owned" and thus fell within the sanctity of private property; second, the concept that natural justice demands that people who perform a service to society be rewarded; third, the notion that technological progress was desirable and that patents provided high-powered incentives to engage in research and encouraged full disclosure of the results, thus contributing to the reduction of access costs. All of these were challenged: did an invention really constitute "private property" or was it knowledge to be shared with as many others as possible? To what extent was progress in useful knowledge sensitive to incentives and were patents the best way to encourage innovation? Private property itself was considered a natural law, a fundamental human right, and its extension to intellectual property found its way into a declaration made by the French National Assembly in 1790 and the United States Constitution a few years earlier. Moreover, the *philosophes* had to confront the notion that if a society wished to promote technological change, it needed to create the economic incentives for inventive activities to take place. An uncomfortable clash between what seemed "just" and what was necessary if progress was to be attained was recognized.

In some ways, the Industrial Enlightenment was the logical continuation of the Scientific Revolution by other means. But it was more concrete and more pragmatic. Behind the scenes was the growing conviction that the purpose of natural philosophy, beyond satisfying curiosity and illustrating the greatness of the Creator, was to advance the useful arts and the improvement of material conditions. In other words, useful knowledge had pragmatic as well as epistemic objectives. In the preface to the third edition of his *Course of Experimental Philosophy* (1st edn., 1734–44), Desaguliers wrote that the business of science was to contemplate the works of God and the distinguish causes from their effects, but, he added immediately, "to make Art and Nature Subservient to the Necessities of Life by Skill" (1763, Vol. 1, p. iii). Thus, practical handbooks, technical dictionaries, encyclopedias, descriptions of how to manufacture items, of what worked best, and of how natural philosophy could be applied to technology accumulated in the eighteenth century at a dazzling rate. In Britain a true rage for writing such books had emerged by the 1780s, and books in foreign languages were translated almost as soon as they appeared overseas. An analysis of the topics of the books published in the eighteenth century (based on a classification provided by ECCO, Eighteenth Century Collection Online) presented in table 3.1 shows that the proportion of books published on "Science, Technology and Medicine" increased from 5.5 percent of the total in 1701–1710 to 9 percent in 1790-1799. As the absolute number of books published in the British Isles tripled over this period, this implies a quintupling of the total number of such books.

If the paradigmatic book of the Scientific Revolution was Newton's *Principia*, that of the Industrial Enlightenment was the great French *Encyclopédie*, full of detailed illustrations of technical matters in addition to politically radical ideas. Engineers and skilled technicians learned from scientists about careful and detailed reporting of experiments and observations. In the late seventeenth and eighteenth centuries, Enlightenment culture glorified and codified the arts and crafts of artisans, farmers, chemists, instrument makers, surveyors, navigators, and others as never before. Of course, a few felt that such reporting would endanger the source of their income and tried to keep their knowledge private. But the eighteenth century witnessed a veritable explosion of scientific and technical dictionaries, compendia, and periodicals, publishing articles on diverse topics in medicine, farming, manufacturing implements, pumps, water mills, electricity, bleaching, and such.

Economic historians are not in agreement on the significance of such written works. It is not entirely clear who actually read these writings, much less how readers benefited from them. Books and periodicals, moreover, contained "codified" knowledge, and it is clear that in order to carry out production, more knowledge is needed than can be gleaned from written works, no matter how lavish and detailed the technical illustrations. This "tacit" knowledge required personal contact, such as a master–apprentice relation or a meeting place where tacit knowledge was passed between two individuals. The cutting edge of technology

Table 3.1: Number of books published annually in the British Isles, by decade and topic (averages and percentages)

Decade	Total	Hist. and geog.	Fine arts	Social science	Medic., science, and tech.	Litera-ture	Relig. and philos.	Law	Gen. refe-rence
1701–10	1045.1 (100)	72.6 (6.9)	11.5 (1.1)	217.1 (20.8)	58 (5.5)	193.1 (18.5)	399.1 (38.2)	72.8 (7.0)	20.9 (2.0)
1711–20	1179.3 (100)	82.2 (7.0)	9.3 (0.8)	289 (24.5)	61.4 (5.2)	240.3 (20.4)	415.8 (35.3)	58.9 (5.0)	22.4 (1.9)
1721–30	1003 (100)	89.8 (9.0)	18 (1.8)	162.5 (16.2)	92.5 (9.22)	259.1 (25.8)	308.2 (30.7)	46 (4.6)	26.9 (2.7)
1731–40	1065.7 (100)	85.3 (8.0)	22.2 (2.08)	166.7 (15.6)	80.7 (7.6)	311.7 (29.2)	311 (29.2)	57.5 (5.4)	30.6 (2.9)
1741–50	1184.6 (100)	107.2 (9.0)	16.9 (1.4)	220.2 (18.6)	95.3 (8.0)	301 (25.4)	349.7 (29.5)	67 (5.7)	27.3 (2.3)
1751–60	1355.6 (100)	124 (9.1)	26.8 (2.0)	219.6 (16.2)	108.9 (8.0)	375.2 (27.7)	345.2 (25.5)	120.3 (8.9)	35.6 (2.6)
1761–70	1666.1 (100)	152.8 (9.2)	39.9 (2.4)	234.8 (14.1)	123.1 (7.4)	481.7 (28.9)	345.8 (20.8)	248.5 (14.9)	39.5 (2.4)
1771–80	1823 (100)	193.5 (10.6)	44.2 (2.4)	278.2 (15.3)	162.4 (8.9)	609.6 (33.4)	381.1 (20.9)	88.8 (4.9)	65.2 (3.6)
1781–90	2153.4 (100)	242.9 (11.3)	56.7 (2.6)	403.2 (18.7)	190.7 (8.9)	686.5 (31.9)	412.4 (19.2)	98.4 (4.6)	62.6 (2.9)
1791–1800	2978.5 (100)	309 (10.4)	58.1 (2.0)	648.1 (21.8)	268.5 (9.0)	853.7 (28.7)	625.9 (21.0)	129.7 (4.4)	85.5 (2.9)

Source: computed from database ECCO, Eighteenth Century Collections Online, compiled by Thomson-Gale.

required interaction between the top inventors and engineers of the time and the best that "natural philosophy" had to offer. For that reason, the technical publications that diffused codified knowledge were supplemented by social organizations and academies that reflected the demand for tacit knowledge. The idea of such societies goes back, in a way, to Bacon's famous notion of a "House of Solomon" in which specialists would come together in a kind of research institute and together catalog and experiment. After Bacon's death, informal groups emerged such as the circle around Samuel Hartlib, a selected group of scholars and enthusiasts strongly influenced by Baconian ideas. This group, including John

Dury, William Petty, and John Evelyn, was focusing directly on economic progress. A classic essay (Houghton, 1941, p. 39) put it best: their main debt to Bacon was in "the inspiration to apply knowledge to the immediate and practical needs of middle-class society." The Royal Society at first explicitly tried to follow this model and Bishop Thomas Sprat, one of its founders, wrote in 1667 in his *History of the Royal Society*: "I shall mention only one great man, who had the true Imagination of the whole extent of this Enterprize, as it is now afoot, and that is the Lord Bacon" (Sprat, [1667], 1702, p. 35).

In the eighteenth century, the Enlightenment spawned a proliferation of provincial "philosophical" societies, which, their name notwithstanding, spent much of their meetings discussing practical and technical issues, listening to lectures discussing pumps, textile machines, chemistry, crop yields, and similar matters. Such societies were organized spontaneously by private interests, without much government support or encouragement. The Royal Society began with boundless enthusiasm for practical technical matters. "The business and design of the Royal Society is to improve the knowledge of naturall things, and all useful Arts, Manufactures, Mechanick practises, Engines, and Inventions by Experiments" (cited by Lyons, 1944, p. 41). Robert Hooke added in the preface to his *Micrographia* that the Fellows of the Royal Society "have one advantage peculiar to themselves, that very many of their number are men of converse and traffick, which is a good omen that their attempts will bring philosophy from words to action, seeing men of business have had so great a share in their first foundation" (cited by Lyons (1944), pp. 41–42). After 1700 the Society lost some of its fascination with practical matters to concentrate on more abstract subjects. But other organizations were established in the eighteenth century, many of them in the smaller towns that were soon to rival London as the center of activity in technological advance. Despite the huge size of London, the Industrial Enlightenment and the intellectual activities it spawned were distinctly provincial events, located in institutions such as the scientific societies in smaller English towns or the Scottish universities of Glasgow and Edinburgh. These institutions were often located near centers of industry and often served as clearing houses for useful knowledge between natural philosophers, engineers, and entrepreneurs.

In Scotland, where eighteenth-century intellectual life was on the whole more lively than in England, the first society (the Rankenian Club, named after the Inn where it met) dates from 1716. It was followed by the significantly named Society of Improvers in the Knowledge of Agriculture in Scotland (1723) and the Glasgow Political Economy Club (founded in 1743), and the Literary Society (1752), where Joseph Black first expounded his views on the theory of latent heat. The Edinburgh *literati*, a group of Edinburgh intellectuals, took a leadership role in their declared goal of the improvement of Scottish society, but because they became reconciled to the idea of the Union, their impact eventually extended south of the border and exerted a disproportionate influence on the Industrial Enlightenment in Britain (Herman, 2001).

Less famous societies came into existence in smaller provincial British towns in the eighteenth century, as they did throughout Western Europe. Towns like Coventry, Norwich, Bath, Newcastle, Bristol, and York had such societies around the middle of the century (Elliott, 2003, pp. 377–78). The Northampton Philosophical Society's most famous member, William Shipley, called it a "Royal Society in Miniature" and described its members as "addicted to all manner of Natural Knowledge" (cited in Allan, 1979, p. 169). Many of these societies carried out the Baconian program to establish "public science" through activities such as lectures on technology and public experiments. Not all these societies were exclusively devoted to the serious pursuit of the useful arts; some were little more than political meeting places and drinking clubs. Even the ones formally dedicated to useful knowledge were in many cases more social meeting places than organizations that practiced scientific research; that would be too much to expect. But we should not discount the social aspect: through these meeting places, the *savants* and the *fabricants* carried out a discourse between what Bacon had called "luciferous" and "fructiferous" knowledge. Those involved in production signaled their needs and problems, and those involved in science could refer producers to the best-practice knowledge on a variety of subjects (which often was not very good in eighteenth-century Britain). Yet the very fact that these organizations stressed the practical utility of their activities is a tell-tale sign of the spirit of the times.

Of the formal English societies, the most famous were the Birmingham Lunar Society, the Manchester Literary and Philosophical Society, and its successor in London, the London Chapter Coffee House. The Lunar Society provides the best-known example of this kind of organization. Its members were scientists such as Joseph Priestley and Erasmus Darwin, as well as industrialists such as Matthew Boulton and Josiah Wedgwood. In between the two spheres moved engineers such as James Watt or chemists like James Keir who could support this bridge. These and similar organizations provided a forum for discussions on natural philosophy, while more concrete topics of mutual interest in engineering, machinery, and chemistry could be discussed elsewhere once a relationship had been established. Their function as a facilitator of the Industrial Revolution must therefore be taken with a grain of salt. The Manchester Literary and Philosophical Society (the oldest surviving one) was founded in 1781, but a fair amount of informal networking between the various protagonists of industry and science had already taken place in the city in the preceding decades. It embodied many of the Industrial Enlightenment's hopes and ideals. It also had interesting social functions. As Arnold Thackray (1974) has shown, interest in science in Manchester was a means for the upstart commercial and manufacturing class to assert and legitimize itself. Because science was a natural rather than a moral discourse, it provided a neutral common ground where otherwise hostile subgroups of the urban elite could communicate and express "cultural solidarity and social cohesion" to set them apart from both the working class and the landed elite (p. 693). Also of note is the Spitalfields Mathematical Society, founded in 1717, a "from the bottom up" organization of artisans (many of them Huguenot refugees from France) fascinated by natural philosophy, especially electrical and chemical phenomena. It met in pubs and taverns in London's East End, and its rules are a shining symbol of the beliefs of the age of Enlightenment. Anyone who had been taught by a fellow member was obliged to become a tutor himself. A quaint system of "peppercorn fines" meant that when a fellow member asked a question, others had to look for the answer or be fined. Similar societies were established in Manchester and Oldham, catering to artisans, especially weavers (O'Day, 1982, p. 212). Knowledge was useful, and its dissemination was to be encouraged in every manner possible. Many of the members of the Spitalfields Society eventually became fellows of the Royal Society and published in respectable outlets such as *Nicholson's Journal* (Stewart, 1998, pp. 289–92). Scientific societies were complemented by the diffusion of provincial libraries, which spread rapidly in the early years of George III's reign. Thus Leeds acquired one in 1768, Bradford in 1774, and Hull in 1775. The libraries were supplemented by school and church libraries and so-called book clubs. Those who wanted access to existing knowledge they might find useful discovered that it was becoming easier and easier to find.

Before and during the emergence of these organizations, much interaction took place in more informal settings. The English coffee-houses that emerged in the second half of the seventeenth century became focal points for an intellectual elite known as "virtuosi"—gentlemen with cultural and intellectual proclivities, who sought the company of like-minded men to exchange ideas. John Houghton (1645–1705), a pharmacist and early writer in the best of the traditions of the Industrial Enlightenment, wrote in 1699 "coffee-houses improve arts, merchandize, and all other knowledge; for here an inquisitive man, that aims at good learning, may get more in an evening than he shall by books in a month" (cited by Cowan, 2005, p. 99). Lectures on technological and scientific topics took place in taverns and Masonic lodges, and the public was often willing to pay substantial fees to attend. The most famous of the lecturers before 1750 was the above-mentioned John T. Desaguliers, the son of Huguenot immigrants, whose lectures were bankrolled by the Royal Society. Margaret Jacob (1997, p. 113) has noted that Desaguliers was the first to stress that steam power could increase profits by saving labor costs, an obvious point to us perhaps, but one that shows an early sense of the importance of economic rationality paired to technological progress. A prominent figure of English intellectual life of his time and a technical consultant much in demand, he was a founding member of the British Freemason movement. There is no claim that Desaguliers was much of a scientific pioneer himself. He was a man who helped diffuse ideas rather than generate them, although in the experimental culture of the times, he investigated and helped codify some of the observed regularities of technology, such as the advantages of over-shot water mills compared to undershot ones (Hills, 1970, p. 98). Exactly in that way, men like him embodied what mattered most to the Industrial Enlightenment: the dissemination of and access to the best that useful knowledge had to offer.

Desaguliers was far from alone: William Whiston, one of Newton's most distin-guished proponents and his successor at Cambridge, "entertained his provincial listeners with combinations of scientific subjects and Providence and the Millen-nium." James Jurin, master of Newcastle Grammar School, gave courses catering to the local gentlemen concerned with collieries and lead mines (Stewart, 1992, p. 147). Adam Walker, whose course of twelve lectures included "mechanics, hydrostatics, pneumatics, chemistry, optics, electricity and the general properties of matter," and who carried a huge apparatus on his lecture tours, charged a guinea for gentlemen and half a guinea for ladies (Musson and Robinson, 1969, p. 105). Other British lecturers of note were James Ferguson, a Scottish instrument-maker and polymath, Peter Shaw, a chemist and physician, his partner the instrument maker Francis Hauksbee, the instrument-maker Benjamin Martin, Stephen Demainbray (Desaguliers' protégé), who lectured both in France and England and later became Superintendent of the King's Observatory at Kew, and the Reverend Richard Watson at Cambridge whose lectures on chemistry in the 1760s were so successful that he drew a patronage of £100 for his impoverished chair (Stewart, 1992). Britain had no shortage of well-rounded men of knowledge spreading their wisdom for a fee, even at a local level. Richard Kay, a Manchester surgeon, kept a diary between 1737 and 1751, which provides an interesting insight into this kind of experience, showing that people were willing to pay a guinea for a set of lectures covering mechanics, electric attraction, pneumatics, and astronomy (O'Day, 1982, p. 211). The demand for such lectures depended to some extent on the local eco-nomy and the position that useful knowledge occupied in it. In an economy focused on hardware and mechanics, such as Birmingham, it was easier to recruit a fee-paying audience for a lecture than in commercial Bristol (Jones, 2008, p. 73).

The sources of demand for public science in eighteenth-century Britain were diverse. Social historians influenced by Jürgen Habermas' (1991) interpretation of the social history of the age of Enlightenment have maintained that it was part of a new "public sphere." Public science was part of the commercialization of leisure. For middle-class people, especially in provincial towns, it was also a component of a polite culture, in which one signaled one's civility and politeness by displaying or faking an interest in science. "Individuals could 'buy into' the Enlightenment rationality and advertise their membership of the club of public rational discourse" (Elliott, 2003, p. 366). Little is known about who attended, and less about what the audience took away from these lectures. It would be absurd to argue that for the vast majority of the audience attending these events inspired much technological insight. Yet for a small minority, this method of diffusing knowledge may have been useful, and it would be rash to dismiss the possibility that some pragmatic individuals encountered knowledge, ideas, or equipment that might have proven useful to their business pursuits, technological or otherwise. After all, public science involved a great deal of useful knowledge, and was replete with the demonstration of new equipment and models of devices, and there can be no question that somebody was persuaded that acquiring it was useful. Public science underlined the mood of improvement, the fundamental Baconian belief that useful knowledge could be applied to make life better and that to do so was virtuous. It can be seen as one of the many bridges erected in the eighteenth century to connect craftsmen who made things, and natural philosophers who tried to understand why the techniques used by the craftsmen worked and how they could be improved. Polite middle-class society had accepted the notion that improvement and progress were respectable and even prestigious subjects. Thinking and conversing about mundane subjects such as engines and chemicals had become something that was fitting to a gentleman and, by extension, those who did this kind of work were dignified. In that sense, the triumph of the Enlightenment was astonishing. One could imagine that similar effects for polite society might have been attained through listening to string quartets, but the thirst for this kind of knowledge set the agenda.

Of particular significance is the Society of Arts, founded in 1754, which explicitly aimed at the dissemination of existing technical knowledge as well as at its augmentation through an active program of awards and prizes, and encouraged the exchange of ideas between its members through correspondence, the publication of periodicals, and the organization of meetings. William Shipley, its founder, viewed its purpose as follows: "Whereas the Riches, Honour, Strength and Prosperity of a Nation depend in a great Measure on Knowledge and Improvement of useful Arts, Manufactures, Etc. ... several [persons], being fully sensible that due Encouragements and Rewards are greatly conducive to excite a Spirit of Emulation and Industry have resolved to form [the Society of Arts] for such Productions, Inventions or Improvements as shall tend to the employing of the Poor and the Increase of Trade." The purpose of the Society reflects the ambiguity of the Enlightenment about its final goals: was it to improve the lot of humanity or to compete better with France? Among its most active members was Stephen Hales, one of Britain's most eminent eighteenth-century scientists and a leading physiologist. Although such effects are hard to measure, there can be little doubt that the Society helped to stimulate invention by increasing the social standing of inventors in Britain and improving communications between creative and knowledgeable people.

The conviction that such institutions were needed to spread useful knowledge and to establish channels of communication between the people who investigated nature and those who applied their findings to daily life became stronger as the products of their activity were becoming noticeable. In 1799, two paradigmatic figures of the Industrial Enlightenment, Sir Joseph Banks and Benjamin

Thompson (Count Rumford), founded the Royal Institution, devoted to research and charged with providing public lectures on scientific and technological issues. In the first decade of the nineteenth century, these lectures were dominated by the towering figure of Humphry Davy, in many ways a classic figure of the Industrial Enlightenment. A few years later the Royal Institution was followed by the founding of the Geological Society, the Institution of Royal Engineers, and similar bodies. The Royal Society, the oldest and most prestigious of these institutions, had by the second half of the eighteenth century lost much of its enthusiasm for technology. It was fearful that its reputation would be exploited by unscrupulous businessmen, and preferred a more limited role of paternalistic advocacy of material improvement, without actually getting commercial dirt under its fingernails. But British institutions were agile enough, and when one organization would not perform, others would be created that did.

A striking example of this ability of British institutions to reinvent themselves when the old ones would no longer do was the founding of the British Association for the Advancement of Science in 1831, when it was increasingly felt by leaders of the scientific community that the Royal Society had become too exclusive and that monopolies, even in this area, were undesirable. It embodied Whig values of moderate Anglicanism and it specifically aimed to coordinate the collection of data and information by the various scientific societies dispersed all over Britain. Its founding father, the Scottish scientist and academic entrepreneur David Brewster (1781–1868), insisted that the annual meetings should be held in a different location every year. The organizer and secretary of the BAAS, William Harcourt (1789–1871), was an admirer of Francis Bacon. Its Section G (mechanical science, established in 1836) delivered papers on such topics as the technical issues involving railways and iron ships, and counted some of the most illustrious engineers of the time as its members. Although the intricate politics of the BAAS made mechanical sciences subordinate to theoretical knowledge, it was, in the words of the historians of the Association, "an emblem of the material progress of the early Victorian period ... and fulfilled Bacon's dream of applying knowledge to the benefit of mankind, proclaiming that the superiority of British capitalist industry could be maintained by a union of theory and practice" (Morrell and Thackray, 1981, p. 266). The Whig spirit of reform and renewal was reaching everywhere.

Not all these institutions had a significant direct impact on actual technological progress. But the overall picture is of a strongly felt need for learning and teaching, and a demand for the diffusion of useful knowledge, which was a hallmark of the Industrial Enlightenment. What all this amounted to was a decline in access costs. William Godwin noted in 1798 that "Knowledge is communicated to too many individuals to afford its adversaries a chance of suppressing it. The monopoly of science is substantially at an end. By the easy multiplication of copies and the cheapness of books, everyone has access to them" (Godwin, 1798, pp. 282–83).

The Industrial Enlightenment then created a set of bridges between intellectuals and producers, between the *savants* and the *fabricants*. All in all, these channels of communication were the most obvious way in which "culture" affected technology and, in the long run, economic progress. In Scotland, the universities played this role. Unlike the English universities, the Scottish institutes of higher learning dedicated themselves to research in the useful arts such as medicine, chemistry, physics, and political economy. These universities were still controlled by powerful politicians, and Scotland's Enlightenment was focused on sciences and medicine because its patrons had decided that this was the correct course to take; obviously, they themselves had been influenced by Enlightenment thought (Wood, 2006). Glasgow's professors met businessmen and engineers in the inappropriately named Glasgow Literary Society, which for instance brought chemistry professor Joseph Black in contact with the young instrument maker James Watt. Such organizations were neither open nor democratic: they were strictly private affairs, and admitted only men of similar interests and social standing. Yet the exchange of knowledge that took place in them was of an unprecedented intensity, and was geared toward economic improvement. John Anderson, a Professor of Natural Philosophy at Glasgow, was a great believer in the dissemination of science to the general public, and established a set of "toga-less lectures," which were well attended by mechanics and artisans. Their main effect on the economy was imponderable and subtle: it consisted of the interaction of men of different interests and backgrounds, swapping and comparing knowledge and by synergy creating more. The institutions of eighteenth-century Britain provided the vessel in which these ingredients were translated into economic performance.

The Industrial Enlightenment, like all cultural movements, was a human creation although each individual took the spirit of the age as given and adjusted to it, thus reinforcing it. In that sense it may be regarded as an institution. Economists view institutions as "self-reinforcing" equilibria attained by the uncoordinated actions of rational actors, but there were clearly individuals who embodied the spirit of the time more than others. The motives propelling these men were not simple. None of them can be described by the simple income-maximizing calculus of introductory economics. The active ingredients in the process were four pervasive human motivators. *Curiosity* was the most elusive component of technological progress, and it seems at first glance a universal trait and not necessarily motivated by a drive for material progress. A second motivator was *ambition*: the desire to impress one's peers with one's ability and qualities. This was surely true for some of the great entrepreneurs and inventors of the age. When coupled to *greed*, however, curiosity and ambition had the potential to channel technical creativity into increasingly productive directions. Finally, some of the key persons were motivated by *altruism*, the desire to improve society, often supported by deep religious or nationalist convictions.

Popular beliefs and hagiographic biographies celebrate the lives of technological "superstars" such as James Watt, Richard Arkwright, Josiah Wedgwood, John Harrison, the Stephensons, and similar famous inventors. But the spirit of mechanical improvement through better access to knowledge is symbolized by many other figures whose mechanical aptitude and ability to tease every drop of economic value out of what they knew never ceases to astonish us. One of the prodigious inventors of the Industrial Revolution whose genius is not sufficiently appreciated is John Smeaton, widely regarded as the de facto founder of civil engineering as a profession. Smeaton, perhaps more than any other figure in the eighteenth century, personified what the Industrial Enlightenment was all about. Unlike his more famous colleague and friend James Watt, he never made a spectacular breakthrough that would enshrine his name in high school textbooks. Yet he made contributions to harbor engineering, bridge construction, water mills, steam engines, canals, and lighthouses. Although Smeaton was originally trained as a lawyer and was an empiricist par excellence, he also informed himself of pertinent scientific developments of his age, and read the mathematical works of Colin MacLaurin and Antoine Parent. As soon as he moved to London, in 1750, he started to attend the meetings of the Royal Society. He founded a society of engineers in 1771, eventually named after him. In addition, he personified the transnational nature of the Industrial Enlightenment: he traveled to the Low Countries to study their canal and harbor systems, and taught himself French to be able to read the theoretical papers of French hydraulic theorists despite his conviction that all theoretical predictions had to be tested empirically. He was one of the first to realize that improvements in technological systems can be tested only by varying components one at a time, holding all others constant. In such systems, progress tends to be piecemeal and cumulative rather than revolutionary, yet Smeaton's improvements to the water mill increased its efficiency substantially even if his inventions were not quite as spectacular as those of James Watt. The Smeatonian Society included as members all the kinds of people who needed to network if the Baconian project was to succeed: professional engineers such as Smeaton himself and his successor William Jessop; businessmen with a strong interest in technological matters such as Matthew Boulton and Josiah Wedgwood, and actual skilled craftsmen such as instrument makers, surveyors, and similar technical experts.

Like Watt and other engineers active in Britain at that time, Smeaton realized that in order to make breakthroughs in technology, it was not enough to know something about natural phenomena. There must also be some kind of economic motivation, based on the belief that such knowledge may enhance efficiency and raise profits. Practical engineering, he noted, must have an interest in scientific disputes because errors tend "to mislead the practical artist in works that occur daily and which require great sums of money in their execution." The Industrial Enlightenment developed a new set of criteria by which projects and devices were

judged: efficiency and commercial viability. Markets, rather than government officials or aristocratic aesthetes, were to be the ultimate arbiters. In that regard, the
British engineers differed from their continental colleagues, where elegance, sophistication, and usefulness to the state often came before usefulness in industry.
The British Industrial Enlightenment was characterized above all by a deliberate
attempt to make useful knowledge flow from natural philosophers (scientists) to
engineers and technicians. Institutional support for such channels was needed,
however, and Smeaton's career illustrates the emergence of such phenomena by
creating the figure of the "consulting engineer."

Scotland, as has often been recognized, was especially productive of individuals
who personify the Industrial Enlightenment. One of the lesser-known figures was
the Scottish farmer and essayist James Anderson (1738–1809), who wrote practical
essays on topics as wide ranging as chimneys, the planting of trees for timber, the
state of agriculture of Aberdeen country, and the high cost of colonies to the
motherland. He invented a two-horse plough, which he used on his farm, and was
close to Jeremy Bentham whose writings he strongly influenced. In his most
detailed book on political economy (Anderson, 1777) he made a reasonable case
for balanced growth arguing that the growth of manufacturing was a major
stimulant to more traditional sectors.

Another paradigmatic figure capturing the spirit of the Industrial Enlightenment was Erasmus Darwin, grandfather of the discoverer of natural selection.
Darwin was one of the founding fathers of the Lunar Society, and a remarkable
figure in his almost religious belief in technological progress and its ability to advance humanity. He wrote voluminous poetry in its celebration. He viewed progress as a natural phenomenon, but it was the progress of knowledge that would
ensure the continued progress of mankind. Darwin's confidence in this process
was based not on a providential view of history, but on the evidence of innovation
he saw about him (McNeil, 1987). Despite his closeness to the industrialists of
Birmingham and Scotland, he also published a major book on agriculture entitled
Phytologia (1800).

Within the Lunar Society and other societies, a main objective was the creation
of channels through which existing useful knowledge could flow to those who
were best situated to use it productively. William Small, a Scottish physician with
an active interest in all matters technological, was at the social center of the Lunar
Society until his premature death in 1775. He taught for a few years in America at
the College of William and Mary, where one of his students, Thomas Jefferson,
wrote of him that "it was my great good fortune, and what probably fixed the
destinies of my life that Dr Wm. Small of Scotland was then professor of
Mathematics, a man profound in most of the useful branches of science, with a
happy talent of communication correct and gentlemanly manners, & an enlarged
& liberal mind" (cited by Chandler, 1934, p. 305). Small conducted a scientific
correspondence with among others Benjamin Franklin, and introduced James

Watt and Matthew Boulton to one another, an act that was to have important consequences in the annals of technology.

These examples illustrate something of substantial importance: the Industrial Enlightenment was not the realm of a few heroic inventors and engineers, but neither was it a mass phenomenon that included the working class. It was a minority affair, confined to a fairly thin sliver of a technological elite of well-trained and often literate men (women were, as yet, of limited importance to this movement). A few famous inventors who clawed their way up from working-class origins notwithstanding, most of them clearly were members of a class of educated and privileged men (Khan and Sokoloff, 2005). Of course, only the biographies of the most successful and notable individuals have been preserved, but there is no reason not to regard their lives and motives as representative of those whose actions and writings have not been preserved.

To understand the full importance of the Industrial Enlightenment it should be recalled that in most of recorded history, the communication between intelligent, educated, literate people who knew things and the working people in the fields and workshops had been weak or non-existent. Separated by social class, political power, and often language and legal status, it rarely occurred to either that they could learn a great deal from one another. Hellenistic astronomers who gazed at the stars were unaware of or uninterested in the navigational difficulties that their knowledge could have solved. Arab opticians writing about light never stumbled on the possibility of applying their knowledge to make spectacles. Whether we look at classical civilization in Greece and Rome, the Chinese Empire under the Song and Ming, or the Islamic world, natural philosophers and artisans lived on different planets, so to speak.

In Britain, the Industrial Enlightenment ended that state of affairs once and for all, though the exact relation between theorists and practical artisans remained controversial. The Scottish chemist Joseph Black was not inclined to give much credit to those philosophers who shut themselves in their studies in retirement and seldom made discoveries that were of use to mankind. On the other hand, he thought, even a farmer who studies soil types and improves ploughs should be called "a Philosopher, though perhaps you may call him a rustic one" (cited by Jacob and Stewart, 2004, p. 117). Joseph Priestley (1768, p. 22) felt that "the politeness of the times has brought the learned and the unlearned into more familiar intercourse than they had before" and Humphry Davy wrote in 1802 that "in consequence of the multiplication of the means of instruction, the man of science and the manufacturer are daily becoming more assimilated to each other" (Davy [1802], 1840, Vol. 2, p. 321). Not everyone felt that way, of course, and progress was slow. Mandeville ([1724], 1755, p. 121) still thought that "they are very seldom the same sort of people, those that invent Arts and Improvements in them, and those that enquire into the Reason of Things," but Adam Smith in the "early draft" of his *Wealth of Nations* ([1757],1978, p. 570) stressed that "ingenious artists" were capable of applying known techniques up to a point, but that the discovery of techniques that were altogether unknown "belongs to those only who have a greater range of thought and more extensive views of things than naturally fall to the share of a meer artist." Count Rumford noted impatiently in 1799 that "there are no two classes of men in society that are more distinct, or that are more separated from each other by a more marked line, than philosophers and those who are engaged in arts and manufactures" and that this prevented "all connection and intercourse between them." He expressed hope that the Royal Institution he helped found in 1799 would "facilitate and consolidate" the union between science and art and would direct "their united efforts to the improvement of agriculture, manufactures, and commerce, and to the increase of domestic comfort" (Rumford, 1876, pp. 743–45).

Rumford was being overly pessimistic. By this time a market for useful knowledge had emerged, in which technical expertise and advice were bought and sold. Many leading manufacturers and engineers saw it as a matter of routine to consult the best and the brightest that science had to offer and scientists were in many cases all too happy to provide industrialists with their advice. A good example is the Cornwall mathematician Davies Giddy (later Gilbert) who consulted to the many engineers who tried to weaken Boulton and Watt's stranglehold over the steam engine industry and testified as an expert witness in one of the cases that Watt brought against a competitor. The clock and instrument maker John Whitehurst, a charter member of the Lunar Society, was a consultant for every major industrial undertaking in Derbyshire, where his skills in pneumatics, mechanics, and hydraulics were in great demand; Joseph Priestley worked as a paid consultant for his fellow "lunatics" Wedgwood and Boulton (Schofield, 1963, pp. 22, 201; Elliott, 2000, p. 83). Henry Cort, by no means a well-educated man, whose invention of the puddling and rolling process was no less central to the Industrial Revolution than Watt's separate condenser, also consulted the Scottish scientist Joseph Black during his work (Clow and Clow, 1992). Another well-known consulting engineer was Peter Ewart, a cousin of the Edinburgh natural philosopher John Robison, who worked for a number of entrepreneurs, including Samuel Oldknow and Samuel Greg. Ewart had started as Boulton and Watt's representative. Boulton and Watt, indeed, consulted to practically every firm that used their equipment, sending out engineers to install and maintain machinery.

Communication and the dissemination of existing knowledge were just as important to enlightenment thinkers as the increase in knowledge and the better understanding of nature. This was not just because it was felt that scientists and mathematicians possessed some applied knowledge that might be of benefit to artisans, but also because the Baconian program was inherently a collective enterprise, in which specialists were to focus on particular issues and then share the discoveries with each other. In that sense, it practiced a "division of knowledge" much like the division of labor that Smith made part of the vocabulary. Smith

([1757],1978, p. 570) argued outright that "speculation in the progress of society
... like every trade is subdivided into many different branches ... and the quantity
of science is considerably increased by it." The idea caught on. Dugald Stewart,
Adam Smith's popularizer and epigone, noted in an article in the 1815 *Encyclopedia
Britannica* that "the progress of knowledge must be wonderfully aided by the effect
of the [printing] press in multiplying the number of scientific inquirers, and in
facilitating a *free commerce of ideas* all over the civilized world; effects ... proportioned
to the powers of the increased number, combined with all those arising from the
division and distribution of intellectual labour" (1854, Vol. 1, p. 504). Scientists
saw it the same way. Joseph Priestley wrote in 1768 that "If, by this means, one art
or science should grow too large for an easy comprehension in a moderate space
of time, a commodious subdivision will be made. Thus all knowledge will be subdivided and extended, and knowledge as Lord Bacon observes, being power, the
human powers will be increased ... men will make their situation in this world
abundantly more easy and comfortable" (Priestley, 1768, p. 7). The Industrial Enlightenment thus not only represents a utopian belief in a more comfortable and
secure world thanks to the increase of useful knowledge, but was quite specific in
its recipe as to how such a world was to be achieved, namely through specialization and the division of knowledge.

The striking fact remains that, at least in the short run, the Baconian program
was not a success. Hopes for a quick technological payoff to scientific research
were, on the whole, disappointed in the eighteenth century. The chasm between
science and the mundane details of production in most economic activities that
mattered could not be closed in a few decades or even a century. One can, of
course, find a few examples in which scientific insights did enrich the knowledge
of key actors in the Industrial Revolution. The scientific milieu of Glasgow in
which James Watt lived contributed to his technical abilities. He maintained direct
contact with Black and his colleague John Robison, and as Dickinson and Jenkins
note in their memorial volume, "one can only say that Black gave, Robison gave,
and Watt received" ([1927], 1969, p. 16). Black's theory of latent heat helped Watt
compute the optimal amount of water to be injected without cooling the cylinder
too much. More interesting, however, was Watt's reliance on William Cullen's
finding that in a vacuum water would boil at much lower, even tepid temperatures,
releasing steam that would ruin the vacuum in a cylinder. That piece of knowledge
was essential to Watt's realization that he needed a separate condenser (Hills, 1989,
p. 53). Other cases can be cited. The introduction of chlorine bleaching and the
solution of the longitude problem depended, to some extent, on prior advances
in science; bleaching depended on the discoveries of the Swedish chemists Karl
Wilhelm Scheele and the Frenchman Claude Berthollet; measurement of longitude
at sea required a fair understanding of astronomy and mathematics. Formal
hydraulics contributed to advances in water power (Reynolds, 1983, esp. pp.
233–48). But, with some notable exceptions, science in the eighteenth century was

better at explaining why techniques that were already in use worked, than at suggesting techniques *de novo*. In the long run, this turned out to be invaluable because these explanations led to a sequence of improvements, adaptations, and extensions that were the backbone of the increase in productivity.

All the same, most of the technological advances we associate with the first Industrial Revolution needed little more than the mechanics that Galileo knew, and the bulk of innovation in manufacturing and agriculture before 1800 advanced without science providing indispensable inputs. The Scottish chemist William Cullen's self-serving prediction that chemical theory would yield the principles that would direct innovations in the practical arts remained, in the classic metaphor of the leading expert on eighteenth-century chemistry, "more in the nature of a promissory note than a cashed-in achievement" (Golinski, 1992, p. 29). Cullen and his best student Joseph Black were in many ways representative of the best and the worst of the Industrial Enlightenment. Cullen viewed the function of knowledge as economic improvement, meting out advice in agriculture, geology, and manufacturing, and in the best traditions of the Baconian program preached the need to improve the underlying science if technological practice was to advance (Donovan, 1982). They also trained and advised many of the leading engineers and chemists of the time. Yet the results were slow in coming. Best-practice chemistry did little to help manufacturers who needed to know why colors faded and why certain fabrics took dyes more readily than others (Keyser, 1990, p. 222). In medicine, metallurgy, and agriculture, to name a few areas, the situation before 1800 was not much different. Even in steam power, where popular belief still connects development to formal science, the direct connections are often tenuous.

The world turned out to be messier and more complex than the early and hopeful proponents of the Baconian program realized, as H.F. Cohen has memorably suggested (2004, p. 123). Between Newton and Lavoisier, no blinding new insights emerged. Scientists did not know enough and lacked the tools to learn quickly. Tacit artisanal *savoir-faire*, experience-driven insights, trial and error, and serendipity drove many of the eighteenth-century inventions, especially in mechanical engineering and iron and coal, far more than any solid scientific base. J.R. Harris and others have insisted that experience and practical knowledge were especially important in those industries such as woodworking and fuel-based processes, where the raw material was heterogeneous and small differences required adjustments that could only be learned informally. In puddling, the iron-refining technique perfected in the 1780s, workers learned "by doing, not by talking, and developed a taciturnity that lasted all their life" (Gale, 1961–62, p. 9). Experience, dexterity, imagination, and intuition created new technology more than science.

And yet, the belief that systematic useful knowledge and natural philosophy were the keys to economic development not only did not fade as a consequence of such disappointments, it continued to expand in Enlightenment Europe, and especially in Britain. Nothing exemplifies this more than the study of electricity, a true obsession for many scientists at the time (Home, 2003, pp. 234–37). It had few tangible results apart from the lightning rod, yet the research continued, unshaken in its belief that at the end of the process there would be economic benefits, even if these were not yet known. The Baconian program was built on two unshakeable axioms: that the expansion of useful knowledge would solve social and economic problems, and that the dissemination of existing knowledge to more and more people would lead to substantial efficiency gains. It was also understood how this was to be brought about. On its own, artisanal knowledge would be insufficient. Without the work of natural philosophers, who would infuse it with new knowledge and connect different industries, an artisanal economy would eventually revert to a technologically stationary state.

As Adam Smith noted, to attain a radical breakthrough often required an outsider, either a scientist or a clever man from a different background. A barber, a clockmaker, and a clergyman were responsible for the three dramatic break-throughs of the cotton industry. To be sure, without good artisans who could realize their design, maintain it, repair it, and see how it could be made to work marginally better, the new insights might have ended up like Leonardo's wonderful machines, none of which were ever built. Rather than posing the question of whether it was theorists or practical people who brought about technological pro-gress, we need to see the fundamental complementarity between them. It was precisely their presence together and their ability to interact and produce some-thing larger that has the power to explain Britain's technological successes.

To what extent was the Enlightenment a "cause" of the Industrial Revolution? Some of the inventions we associate with the Industrial Revolution would have occurred without the transformation of the intellectual climate. As Campbell (1982, p. 22) notes, the economic impact of the Enlightenment depended on the connection between intention and realization, and at least in the eighteenth century there were many slips between those two. But his suggestion that the economic advances that occurred during the Enlightenment were a coincidence and were not causally related to it seems short-sighted. For one thing, some of the inventions were inspired by science or made by scientists, and an essential principle of the Industrial Enlightenment was the close collaboration between the two. Moreover, inventions took place in a world of declining access costs, which, too, was a defining tenet of the Enlightenment. This meant not only that they diffused rapidly, but also that knowledge of them was available to other inventors who could further improve them or recombine them in new applications. The mecha-nics, ironmongers, and chemists who were responsible for the technological ad-vances of the age were by no means all intellectuals, much less "enlightened," but they moved in a milieu in which the effects of the Enlightenment were pervasive. Not *all* inventors can be shown to have been influenced by the cultural and social changes that the Enlightenment implied, but their numbers were rising steadily.

For that reason, the Enlightenment was the reason why the Industrial Revolution was the beginning of modern economic growth and not another technological flash in the pan. In previous ages, new techniques, even revolutionary ones, soon crystalized around the dominant designs that emerged and after a while progress fizzled out. Invention before the Industrial Revolution had been an event, an efflorescence, rather than a continuous process. We can imagine a counterfactual world in which the economies of Western Europe reached a new equilibrium around 1800 or 1810, with the new cotton spinning mills, low-pressure steam engines, and puddling furnaces becoming the dominant designs to crystalize into a new but stable industrial set of techniques. Instead, technology continued to expand. Sustained advances affected new industries and sectors, from sailing to printing, from chemicals to metals, from food preservation to paper making. The Industrial Revolution marks the first time that technological advances and refinements were continued and sustained. The intellectual and ideological changes of the eighteenth century turned a few key inventions into a macroeconomic sea change.

CHAPTER 4

An Enlightened Political Economy

In addition to its effect on technology, the Enlightenment had another impact that is hard to quantify: it affected the institutional structure of society, and indirectly the way income was distributed and resources allocated. To summarize the argument: Enlightenment thought was all along deeply concerned with political economy. In the second half of the eighteenth century, most important intellectuals became increasingly hostile to what modern economists would call *rent-seeking*, namely the use of political power to redistribute rather than create wealth. The influence of this movement affected the long-term evolution of the British economy in that it redirected creativity and energy away from rent-seeking and toward activities that increased national prosperity and social welfare.

Much of the literature regarding institutional change focuses on economic interests and the political power to ensure an income distribution favorable to one group or another, and hence focuses on issues such as the ability of a group in society to commit to certain promises it makes to another group and the capacity of interest groups to overcome collective bargaining issues (Acemoglu, Johnson, and Robinson, 2005a). While there is no question that such issues are historically important, they leave little room for ideology. Yet the history of the European Enlightenment demonstrates Douglass North's (2005) argument that what people believed about the world in which they lived and the principles they thought governed their societies played a crucial role in shaping these institutions. It is true, as Acemoglu and Robinson (2006) argue, that self-interest guides the choice of institutions. People, they feel, have preferences over institutions because institutions imply a certain allocation of resources and distribution of income, but this is not the entire story. People also have a view of the way society ought to work, of what institutions make sense to them and what appeals to their notions of fairness and logic. In the end, these beliefs help determine what kinds of institution are chosen and which survive. Beliefs, however, are not constant: people are open to learning, to persuasion, to new methods of understanding reality. Ideas, in the eighteenth century as much as in the twentieth, competed in a market for ideas, in which intellectual innovators provided new products to a public of educated consumers. The largest product "sold" in the eighteenth century to the literate elite was the Enlightenment. How did ideology affect institutions, and how did institutional change affect economic performance?

By the start of the eighteenth century, the British state was still firmly wedded to mercantilist principles, which were in many ways a justification of rent-seeking (Ekelund and Tollison, 1981). Enlightenment thought challenged the basic assumption of the mercantilist world, namely that the economic game, and above all the commerce between nations, was zero-sum such that the gains of any agent or any economy inevitably came at the expense of another. Adam Smith commented on this view scathingly: "nations having been taught that their interest consisted of beggaring their neighbours. Each nation has been made to look with an invidious eye upon the prosperity of all the nations with which it trades, and to consider their gain as its own loss" ([1776], 1976, Vol. 1, p. 519). In the mercantilist way of thinking, wealth generated power, because it built ships and hired mercenaries, while at the same time it was believed that power generated wealth, because military strength could force competitors out of markets. This kind of world-view made perfect sense if all other nations behaved similarly, and even Adam Smith, who fully realized that such legislation as the Navigation Acts reduced international trade and thus was costly to the economy, accepted them as necessary for defense, inevitable in a hostile world (ibid., p. 484). But the entire system was coming under attack in the eighteenth century. It was regarded as a self-serving policy that benefited a few merchants and manufacturers but harmed the economy as a whole, and a self-fulfilling prescription for ever more costly wars and trade barriers. Josiah Tucker thought that nothing was so absurd as going to war for the sake of getting trade. "Trade will always follow cheapness, not conquest," he argued (1763, p. 41). In its stead, Enlightenment writers proposed the concept of *doux commerce*, gentle trade, a concept popularized by Montesquieu in which a peaceful, mutually advantageous exchange in a "civilized consortium of nations" enriched and improved all participants (Howe, 2002, p. 195). Indeed, Montesquieu believed that "Peace is the natural effect of trade. Two nations that trade with one another become reciprocally dependent; for if one has an interest in buying, the other has an interest in selling; and thus their union is founded on their mutual necessities" (1768, Vol. 2, pp. 238–40). The hope was that calculated interests would overcome the passions of war (Hirschman, 1977, pp. 79–80).

Such beliefs were in the end inconsistent with eighteenth-century British commercial policies, which were based on the idea that commerce was a "kind of warfare" as the seventeenth-century economist Josiah Child (1630–99)—a rather moderate mercantilist—put it (Gay, 1969, p. 346). Even as sensible an observer as Daniel Defoe was committed to the zero-sum approach and thought that "by how much the trade, and consequently the wealth of France is encreased for the past 150 years past, by so much the trade and wealth of England, Holland, Spain, Flanders, and the rest of trading Europe has decreased ... the conquests made by the French upon our Trade, tho' they do not make an equal Noise in the World; yet, like a flow Poison, they are equally Fatal to our Prosperity, with the greatest Victories they obtain" (Defoe, 1705, Vol. 1, p. 385). Many policies implemented in the seventeenth century by the various Navigation Acts and other mercantilist measures limited the extent of and otherwise constrained foreign trade. British mercantilism was rooted not so much in deep analytical economic thought as in the needs of foreign policy in combination with special rent-seeking interests. The British fought wars with other nations over colonies, trade routes, and commercial monopolies. Enlightenment thinkers developed a growing conviction that wars over foreign resources and colonies often made little sense (Adam Smith was scathing about colonial adventures). Instead, the concept of free trade took root. Lord Mansfield, the influential Lord Chief Justice, was a free trader to the point that he supported trade with the enemy (Oldham, 2004). The dominant idea was that free trade between nations, unregulated and unfettered labor markets, the abolition of monopolies and various so-called "freedoms" (in reality, special deals), free markets in grain and other necessities, and other reforms were the key to economic prosperity. These pathbreaking notions took a long time to take hold and had to overcome powerful resistance. But slowly, with many reversals and setbacks, these ideas became established in Britain, and the continued growth of the British economy cannot be imagined without them.

The institutional reforms inspired by the Enlightenment were crucial to continued growth. Before detailing them, two points should be made. First, Britain in the eighteenth century still contained many elements of a rent-seeking and mercantilist society. Enlightened thinkers, especially Adam Smith, complained bitterly about the various economic practices prevalent at his time. Yet it should be kept in mind that mid-eighteenth-century Britain was, in many ways, ahead of its continental rivals in establishing the kind of free and open market economy that Enlightenment thinkers were supporting and that the overall dimensions of redistribution were fairly limited. It already had free internal trade, weak guilds, a relatively effective fiscal system, and a state that was firmly committed to the protection of property. Second, the Enlightenment movement was a European movement, not a British movement. Many of the reforms that French revolutionaries had to storm a Bastille for were in fact, and often in law, already the practice in Britain. The transition to a more "enlightened" set of institutions was therefore a lot less costly in Britain than elsewhere. Many further reforms were still needed, in part in response to technological progress as much as its facilitator. But Enlightenment ideas provided the reformers with the intellectual and rhetorical tools they needed; they were all, in one way or another, influenced by the ideas of liberal Political Economy, the Enlightenment's proudest offspring. The work of Adam Smith was of course central to this movement. The *Wealth of Nations*, one authority believes was the "cardinal document of the Enlightenment ... far beyond Scotland, in the German states and the American republic, economists wrote treatises and statesmen made policies in its name" (Gay, 1969, pp. 360, 368). However, Adam Smith was the culmination of half a century of Enlightenment thought that included

Montesquieu, Turgot, the physiocrats, Italian intellectuals such as Pietro Verri, and a long line of Scottish thinkers such as Lord Kames and David Hume.

The period of the Industrial Revolution was as remarkable for what did *not* happen in Britain as for what did. Britain was practically the only European nation that was not deeply and directly affected by the political and social disruptions that started with the French Revolution in 1789 and ended with the Battle of Waterloo in 1815. These events significantly affected the economic and technological development of the Continent and may have set it back by many years, which helps to explain Britain's head start. The costly wars were only one part of the disruption. The careers of many of the most talented inventors and scientists in France and elsewhere were disrupted or redirected to public service. The best-known example is the execution of Antoine Lavoisier, the greatest scientist of his time (for reasons that had nothing to do with his science), but many other examples of highly talented people who were distracted by politics and military affairs can be cited. What we do not know is how many resourceful and ambitious young persons, who in a more tranquil age would have chosen careers in manufacturing or commerce, ended up in leading positions in the military or political hierarchies. Moreover, the political shocks seriously set back some of the economies of the most advanced parts of the Continent such as the Netherlands, even as they favored a few others such as Flanders and Alsace. Economic warfare (privateering and later blockades) disrupted international trade, and while the British economy suffered from those as well, its naval superiority assured an asymmetric distribution of these costs. Within the country, taxes and the cost of living rose steeply and political freedoms suffered a setback, but there was no fighting on British soil, and the stability of the regime was never seriously threatened.

The absence of revolution in Britain is significant. It could be said that Britain did not have a violent political revolution when the rest of Europe did, because it could manage without one. Relative to French post-1789 radicalism it was a conservative society, yet it was a nation that had developed the unique ability to adapt its institutional structures without much violence and turmoil, always excepting the difficulties in Ireland. The election and franchise laws, the economic organization and distribution of land ownership, and the revocation of the right to trade in and own slaves are primary examples of deep institutional changes that caused other nations to slide into turmoil and violence, whereas in Britain the changes were brought about largely by peaceful deliberation. It is easy to mistake the divisions between radicals, Whigs, liberal Tories, and "high" Tories as a lack of consensus. On the main issues, however, there was agreement, or at least an agreement on how disagreements should be decided. Government should rule frugally and responsibly, getting rid of privileges and patronage, at least in part to disarm their increasingly vocal radical critics (Harling, 1996). Boyd Hilton notes that even groups apparently at opposite poles of the political spectrum, such as utilitarians and evangelical Christians, agreed on many issues, even if the former wanted to maximize happiness and the latter were mostly concerned with salvation (Hilton, 2006, pp. 332–33).

As the Industrial Revolution moved into a higher gear, Parliament gradually dismantled old institutional structures to adapt to the needs of a more industrial and technologically complex society: the Statute of Artificers was abolished in 1814, the enumeration clauses (that forced British colonial goods to be shipped to third markets through Britain) in the Navigation Acts were abolished in 1822, the law prohibiting the emigration of artisans was repealed in 1824, the export prohibition on machinery was weakened in 1824 and repealed in 1843, the Bubble Act in 1825, and trade liberalization slowly advanced, beginning in the early 1820s and culminating in the abolition of the Corn Laws in 1846 and what remained of the ultra-mercantilist Navigation Acts in 1849. Usury laws, a particularly atavistic restriction, were finally repealed as late as 1854 but rarely enforced long before—bills of exchange had already been exempted from it in 1833.

In other areas, too, liberal ideas were translated into policy changes. By the end of the eighteenth century monopolies were roundly condemned. Adam Smith ([1776], 1976, Vol. 1, p.165) called them the "great enemy of good management" and writers from William Godwin to Josiah Tucker treated them as an unmitigated social evil. The monopoly of the East India Company was weakened to the point that after the 1857 rebellion it lost its *raison d'être* altogether. In the 1830s the old Poor Law, long a thorn in the side of pro-business liberal thinkers, was thoroughly reformed, Catholics were emancipated, and the electoral system and local government structure were overhauled. Scottish serfdom, a quaintly anachronistic institution in the eighteenth century that involved miners and salters, was abolished in 1774 (the last traces were removed as late as 1799). These Acts, declared Parliament, would "remove the reproach of allowing such a state of servitude to exist in a free country" (cited by Smout, 1969, p. 406). A striking piece of legislation was the abolition of the slave trade in 1807; Enlightenment writings had increasingly expressed themselves against slavery, and the Act of 1807 brought the profitable trade of British slavers to an abrupt end (Cuenca, 2004, p. 46). In 1833, slavery was formally abolished throughout the British Empire. On purely economic grounds the anti-slavery policy of the British government is puzzling. It was an ideological shift in the mind-set of legislators, first and foremost, and hard to explain by a "who benefited?" argument.

It should be stressed that Enlightenment ideas did not mean a wholesale replacement of existing ideas about how the state was to be run. The motives for political action remained very similar. The landed and commercial interests in power were first and foremost looking out for themselves and were concerned with Britain's interests and standing in Europe and the world. But they shifted their beliefs on how and by which means these interests should be pursued. Their implicit and perhaps subconscious idea of the kind of world they wanted to make was influenced by the teachers, books, and social interactions that shaped the beliefs and attitudes of the ruling classes. As Harling (1996, pp. 162–63) noted, the post-1815 reform politicians were complex individuals who believed that a moral society would be created by stripping away privileges and the power to redistribute resources. By any modern standard Britain during the Industrial Revolution was neither liberal nor a democracy. But it was slowly beginning to move in those directions, faster toward liberalism than toward democracy. Moreover, the nation was able to change and adapt to changing circumstances and beliefs while maintaining much of the basic set-up of the rule of law and the political power structure. To be sure, political stability is not necessarily a positive factor in economic development: when based on a reactionary, backward-looking, and repressive regime such as Russia in much of the nineteenth century, stability may not have been a good thing.

Not everything was enlightened in Britain's political system in the late eighteenth and early nineteenth centuries. Britain's taxes were regressive and high (and became a lot higher during the expensive Napoleonic Wars), yet they were never perceived to be as much of a burden and a nuisance as the ineffectual and distorting taxation systems prevalent on much of the Continent. Britain's government enjoyed good credit, and its interest payments were thus lower even when it had to borrow heavily. The years of the French and Napoleonic Wars were difficult. Britain experienced inflation during the war years, the disruption of international trade, Combination Acts (prohibiting the organization of workers into labor unions), quite severe political repression, and the introduction of an income tax. However, these were temporary emergency measures. The Combination Acts were repealed in 1824 (and a wave of strikes followed). Britain did not need to outlaw guilds, abolish internal tariff barriers, or eliminate the "privileges" enjoyed by ruling classes on the Continent, legislate freedom of movement or occupational choice, release serfs, wholly reorganize the set-up of property rights over land to allow the rationalization of farming, and unify bewildering sets of different local weights and measures, to say nothing of laws and litigation procedures and hundreds of encumbrances, small and large, on the free exercise of commerce and industry. Moreover, as noted, the revolutionary and Napoleonic periods were even harder on the Continent. In addition to the obvious costs of warfare and trade disruptions, many areas experienced serious infringements of property rights, such as widespread confiscation of land, the institution of military conscription, and economy-wide inflation. None of this is to suggest that Britain had a society that was perfectly designed for economic growth and technological progress. Yet compared to the rest of Europe, its advantages seem obvious in this regard.

In Britain, then, if someone made money, he or she could expect to keep most of it and spend it. There was much that money could buy: the array of luxuries had expanded in the eighteenth century and Georgian-style country homes were built in massive number, decorated with paintings, expensive furnishings, and fancy tableware. Moreover, in Britain money, even "new money," could buy that most elusive and desirable of all commodities: social prestige. Adam Smith's *Theory of Moral Sentiments* (1759) had already noted that "the advantages of 'bettering our condition' ... were being the subject of attention and approbation" (ch. 2)—that is, social recognition and approval. In the view of Fred Hirsch (1976), society produces material goods whose supply can be augmented by increased productivity, and "positional" goods which are based on one's "relative income" and standing in society. The latter are, by definition, in very inelastic supply (and in some interpretations may be a zero-sum game). In eighteenth-century England, money made in commerce and industry could buy one a coveted position among the aristocratic elite: a country home, a noble title, and all the social trimmings associated with being a member of the upper class. That great parvenu entrepreneur, Richard Arkwright, who started his career as a barber and wigmaker in Preston died a wealthy country squire, a respected member of the country's landed elite. Some of the most influential politicians in nineteenth-century Britain, such as Peel, Disraeli, and Gladstone, came from such *nouveaux riches* families.

The doctrines of Smith and similar free-trade thinkers such as Hume, Josiah Tucker, and Jacob Vanderlint (d. 1740) were thus a decisive influence on many outstanding British statesmen in the post-1780 years, despite the serious setbacks to Enlightenment-inspired policy after 1793, and the stubborn resistance of mercantilist doctrines. The influence of *The Wealth of Nations* on policy-makers all over Europe is obscured by the repressive policies resorted to by the Pitt government in the 1790s, triggered by the events in France after 1789. But these should not distract from their longer-run impact. Dugald Stewart was a leading proponent of early nineteenth-century "Whiggery," and an enormously effective and eloquent teacher at Edinburgh. His lectures turned Smith's thought into the fountainhead of all economic theory. Stewart "made the book virtually Holy Scripture to generations of Edinburgh-educated thinkers, economists, and politicians who in turn spread its influence to Oxford, Cambridge, London, and the rest of the English-speaking world" (Herman, 2001, pp. 229–30; see also Rothschild, 2001). Among Stewart's pupils were two future prime ministers, Palmerston and John Russell, as well as other senior officials. Young Harry Temple, later Lord Palmerston, actually boarded with Stewart. The prominent Whig political economist and MP Francis Horner wrote that "Lord Bacon and Dugald Stewart have made me a little of a visionary" (cited by Chitnis, 1986, p. 71). Another student, Henry Cockburn, a Scottish Whig judge and politician, recollected many years later about Stewart that "without genius or even originality of talent, his intellectual character was marked by calm thought and great soundness ... within his proper sphere he was uniformly great and fascinating ... to me his lectures were like the opening of the Heavens" (Cockburn, 1856, pp. 29, 30, 32). Stewart was not the only Smith epigone to be influential: John Millar, a Whig Professor of Law at Glasgow, was a close friend of Smith's and his highly effective lectures reflected the master's thought. His students, too, included many powerful politicians, such as William Lamb, Lord Melbourne, who was a Whig prime minister between 1834 and 1841 (Chitnis, 1986).

The influence of Adam Smith and his colleagues in the Scottish Enlightenment on politicians was thus one identifiable channel through which Enlightenment thought affected public policy. William Pitt himself was known to have a deep admiration for Smith, though he did not abandon some of his mercantilist views and still thought that the Navigation Acts, for instance, were "necessary to the grandeur and prosperity of the whole empire." There is a possibly apocryphal story of Pitt telling Smith during a London visit, "Sir, we will stand till you are first seated, for we are all your scholars" (Ross, 1998, p. xxv; Ross, 1995, 375–76). Two years after Smith's death, Pitt referred in the House of Commons to "the writings of an author of our own times, now unfortunately no more, (I mean the author of a celebrated treatise on the Wealth of Nations,) whose extensive knowledge of detail, and depth of philosophical research, will, I believe, furnish the best solution to every question connected with the history of commerce, or with the systems of political economy" (Pitt, 1808, Vol. 1, pp. 357–59). The chief clerk of the Committee of Trade, George Chalmers, and his colleague Charles Jenkinson (later Lord Liverpool and father of the PM) were also deeply influenced by Smith's nuanced but clear-cut liberal ideas (Crowley, 1990, p. 341). Lord Shelburne, another ardent reformer and free-trader of the 1780s and Pitt's predecessor and mentor, recounted late in life in a 1795 letter to Dugald Stewart that as a young man he had traveled with Smith to London, a journey that made "the difference between light and darkness through the best part of my life. The novelty of his principles, added to my youth and prejudices, made me unable to comprehend them at the time, but he urged them with so much benevolence, as well as eloquence, that they took a certain hold, which, though it did not develope itself so as to arrive at full conviction for some few years after" (Ross, 1998, p. 147). Shelburne, sometimes thought of as "the first liberal statesman," was personally ineffective but had considerable influence over Pitt's economic policies (Hilton, 2006, p. 117), and was a friend of Richard Price's, a radical intellectual. Not surprisingly, Shelburne turned out a classic proponent of the Industrial Enlightenment and great friend of the new manufacturers's political lobby in Westminster. He maintained a forty-year correspondence with Samuel Garbett, a Birmingham manufacturer who founded the first successful political lobby in London. William Grenville, Pitt's cousin and Foreign Secretary, was strongly influenced by Smith's teaching and opposed price regulation of flour, pointing out that it would lead to scarcity. He repeatedly lectured the prime minister on the virtues of free trade, and had a strong impact on younger Whig MPs such as Francis Horner, Henry Brooke Parnell, and David Ricardo, whose own influence on the reform movement of the 1820s and 1830s was decisive. Smith's work, through his students and disciples, is an example of how the Enlightenment movement changed realities through the persuasion of powerful people.

The dominant figure in the "liberal Tory" government of Lord Liverpool in the 1820s was William Huskisson, an avowed Smithian – most famous among economic historians for being apparently the first person ever killed by a moving train on the opening day of the Manchester and Liverpool Railway – who passed a series of tariff reductions and was instrumental in re-energizing the reform movement in the 1820s. The Enlightenment inspired the more extreme radical reform movement of the 1820s, in which ideologues like Joseph Hume, John Wade, and Francis Place fought for reform legislation informed and inspired by political economy as they interpreted it. The astonishing historical fact is not that such radicals were tolerated (though Place was dubbed "a bad man" for his outrageous advocacy of contraceptives; he himself sired sixteen children), but how successful they eventually proved to be in implementing their liberal programs.

The ideological background of the post-1820 economic reforms should not be oversimplified. We can distinguish at least three Enlightenment-inspired reform movements that were quite different in emphases and goals. Political economy and ideology differed not only on how and when mercantilism should be dismantled, but also on the fate of colonies and internal regulation. In addition to the pure Smithians, whose main guiding principle was the strong complementarity of peace, prosperity, and free trade, there were the so-called Christian political economists, who combined the logic of Enlightenment with the evangelical religion that was making a comeback in Britain. This religious movement, an odd intellectual but very British development, managed to combine an essentially mechanistic view of the world with a return to devoutness, creating a "theological utilitarianism" (Hilton, 2006, p. 314). In the view of one scholar, this school helped convert the landed elite to a belief in freer trade, even if their world-view was more national-istic and cyclical than the eighteenth-century Scottish Enlightenment movement had hoped for (Howe, 2002). Boyd Hilton (1977) has maintained that beside En-lightenment there was "atonement," a religious reaction to Jacobinism that inspi-red some writers to support free trade for its intrinsic moral view. On their left were Ricardians and Benthamites, whose belief in free trade was more extreme and who implied that the landed aristocracy, on whose behalf the Corn Laws had been passed, was essentially parasitic. Even more radical were intellectuals such as Thomas Hodgskin, who believed that all technological innovation emanated from working-class ingenuity, and that if the laborers could only acquire such knowledge as the middle class possessed, they would no longer need the masters. Accordingly, he published in the 1820s the successful *Mechanics' Magazine*. The Enlightenment belief in the liberating power of useful knowledge was thus driven to its logical ex-treme. Liberal Tories such as Huskisson and Peel believed that rent-seeking was the main enemy of progressive society and that "if one could only strip away monopolies and pensions and other manifestations of control, society would regu-late itself" (Hilton, 1979, p. 607). Peel, whose position was critical in the repeal, clearly saw "free trade as conducive to sound economic progress" (ibid., p. 606).

Yet in the end these ideas were all elaborations of eighteenth-century Enlightenment thought, and the emergence of the ideology of a liberal market economy and the political economy that supported it in the first half of the nineteenth century cannot be imagined without the influence of Hume, Smith, and their followers.

The effects of changing ideology on British policy and institutions were slow in unfolding. The golden age of the great trading monopolies, excepting the East India Company, was largely over by 1720, but the notion that free entry into an industry or an occupation was a natural right gained acceptance very slowly. The Bubble Act of 1720, requiring parliamentary approval of the establishment of joint-stock enterprises, was used as a rent-seeking restriction. Ron Harris points out (2000, p. 135) that the main barrier to entry into joint-stock enterprise was not so much the difficulty of persuading Parliament to vote a private incorporation bill, as acquiring the money needed to overcome the resistance of incumbent firms or other vested interests. During much of the eighteenth century there was still ample opportunity for various groups to pass special-interest legislation that benefited the few at the expense of the many. Political pressure and rioting (or the threat thereof) often led to such legislation. A notorious case in point was the passage of the Calico Acts of 1700 and 1721, which followed the so-called Calico riots, and which prohibited the importation and sale of printed white calicoes. Passed at the behest of artisans in the woolen and silk trades, it was repealed in 1774. By another law, passed in 1666, all Britons had to be buried clothed or wrapped in shrouds made of wool fabrics, a measure passed on behest of the industry. It was abolished in 1814, although its enforcement must have been spotty at best.

By the late seventeenth century the seeds of change had already been planted: in international trade, monopolistic practices increasingly came under fire and Lockean ideas of natural law and personal liberty were in the air after 1688, though the battle for free trade would continue through much of the eighteenth and nineteenth centuries (Ormrod, 2003, pp. 126–27; Nye, 2007). Locke himself was still clearly in the mercantilist camp, but in the eighteenth century anti-mercantilist views gradually grew in influence. After 1770, the long-term trend in British economic policy was to create a more open and competitive society, although the triumph of Enlightenment thought was dealt a setback in the 1780s and 1790s when the *philosophes* were viewed as having allied themselves with American revolutionaries and French Jacobins.

Yet after 1820 the trend toward a growing influence of Enlightenment ideas unmistakably resumed. One of the most egregious examples of imperialist rent-seeking was the East India Company. The resentment of the rent-seeking "nabobs" reflected the changing ideological winds of the eighteenth century. The Company's autonomy was weakened by the East India Act of 1773, which established the principle that the Company was subject to the Crown, and Pitt's East India Acts of 1784 and 1786, which made the appointment of the Governor-

General the responsibility of the Crown and reserved all important policy decisions to a special committee controlled by the government. The Company's formal monopoly was ended by two parliamentary Acts in 1813 and 1833. After 1820, it became almost impossible to discern any monopolies in Britain, with the obvious exception of the Bank of England, which increasingly became an arm of the government.

Where the success of liberal thought was most complete was in the political economy of technological change. From about 1750 on, the government took an uncompromising position in support of new technology and stood firm against the incumbent interests that tried to protect their position through legislation. In the textile industries, by far the most significant resistance occurred in the woolen industries. Cotton was a relatively small industry on the eve of the Industrial Revolution and therefore had relatively weakly entrenched power groups. Wool, however, was initially a far larger industry and had an ancient tradition of professional organization and regulation. Laborers in the wool trades tried to use the political establishment for the purposes of stopping the new machines. In 1776 workers petitioned the House of Commons to suppress the jennies that threatened the livelihood of the "industrious poor," as they put it. Time and again, groups and lobbies turned to Parliament requesting the enforcement of old regulations or the introduction of new legislation that would hinder the machinery. Parliament refused. The old laws regulating the employment practices of the woolen industry were repealed in 1809, and the 250-year-old Statute of Artificers was repealed in 1814. Rent-seeking of any kind had fallen on hard times. As Paul Mantoux put it well many years ago, "Whether [the] resistance was instinctive or considered, peaceful or violent, it obviously had no chance of success" (Mantoux, [1905], 1961, p. 408). Challenges to law and order that could not be settled by local authorities were dealt with effectively and harshly. It could be maintained that the harsh Combination Acts passed in the 1790s acted in the same direction, although it is perhaps hard to think of that repressive legislation as "enlightened." When in 1826 a number of Bolton powerloom mills came under attack from mobs due to the sharp economic crisis, the government acted swiftly and brought in artillery and cavalry to make sure that in all the manufacturing towns peace and property were secure (Lewis, 2001, pp. 72–73). In the 1830s, a coalition of coach owners, canal companies, turnpike trusts, and eccentrics lobbied strongly against the railroads, to no avail.

For much of the period under discussion, the British state was in the hands of men of landed property and commercial wealth who were committed to a program of progress through advances in useful knowledge. Workers, the most likely victims of such changes, did not vote and had few options. Enlightenment thought in most cases was as yet little concerned with their interests, and believed that if progress took place, a rising tide would lift all ships. As it turned out, it did not; a large number of the small vessels were shipwrecked or stranded. The idea that capitalist production may produce a conflict between workers and employers was a later insight, and the British state before 1850 clearly supported capital over labor.

To be sure, Enlightenment thought was not unequivocally united behind technology as the driving force behind human progress. There was a stream in eighteenth-century thought, inherited by European intellectuals from Rousseau, that there was something unnatural and alien about technology, and that progress and improvement in society should look backward rather than forward. This strand of thought, associated with later radical writers in the traditions of romanticism such as Cobbett and Carlyle, viewed industrialization as dangerous at best and evil and destructive at worst. Other Enlightenment thinkers realized that technological change was often disruptive and could lead to social tensions, and as time moved on they were gradually forced to come to grips with the fact that markets might fail and not invariably deliver the kind of outcomes they hoped for.

In the late eighteenth and early nineteenth centuries, moreover, the belief in the possibility of progress was dented, if only temporarily. The two events that triggered this setback were the French Revolution and its subsequent wars, and a growing belief in Malthusianism. The French Revolution and the growing revulsion it caused in Britain led to serious doubts in some of the most dearly held beliefs of Enlightened thinkers (Rothschild, 2001). Free speech and the right to association were seriously limited in Britain by Pitt's anti-terror legislation, including for example the suppression of the academic societies in Leeds and Preston. Enhanced and more liberal trade with France, which had loomed briefly on the horizon during the 1780s was reversed and during the height of the Napoleonic Wars old practices such as privateering and blockades were revived and economic warfare was elevated to new levels. Moreover, the Enlightenment notion that intellectuals belonged to a single, transnational Republic of Letters that trumped national loyalties—always a fragile and somewhat naive concept—had to make room for serious questions of national interests and *raisons d'état*. The belief advanced by Lavoisier and others that "the sciences are never at war" seems ingenuous today. The state of war between Britain and the Continent between 1793 and 1814 seriously disrupted the exchange of information and the flows of technology, to the detriment of both sides (Lipkowitz, 2008). Mercantilism in its cruder forms may have been defeated, but nationalist notions that advanced one nation at the expense of others turned out to be far more resistant. All the same, after 1815, the transnationalism of the Republic of Letters returned with a vengeance and became the routine way of doing science in the Western world. The British Association for the Advancement of Science in the 1830s made a point of inviting foreign scientists, as an illustration of its ideology that in science there are no geographical boundaries, a classic Enlightenment concept that had become part of conventional wisdom. Yet the transnationalism was not entirely cooperative and an element of competition with foreigners was always present in debates about the utility of useful knowledge. Unfavorable comparisons of British institutions with those of foreign countries were made in debates about scientific priorities (Morell and Thackray, 1981, pp. 379, 385).

These doubts and ambiguities in the Enlightenment program found support from an unlikely corner, namely political economy itself. In the eighteenth century, the Enlightenment program had believed, with some exceptions, that economic progress was possible if nations would reform their institutions, adopt more peaceful and liberal attitudes toward one another, and avoid wars. But that optimistic outlook was challenged by the growing pessimist influence of Malthusianism. Political economy changed: it remained committed to free trade and sensible policies to minimize rent-seeking, but it lost some of its optimism and its belief in long-term progress as a likely outcome. Instead, the concept of a "stationary state" dominated economic thought just as it was becoming an increasingly less apt description of the British economy.

The fiercest debate was, of course, on foreign trade. The move toward free trade and more liberal policies occurred throughout a part of the world that had been exposed to the Enlightenment, though not without a struggle and far from uniformly. Free trade had support in much of Western Europe, and its adoption elsewhere facilitated its victory in Britain rather than the other way around (Nye, 2007). While its triumph was partial and short-lived in most other countries, Britain was one economy that remained loyal to it until 1931. Support for free trade came from people who had been persuaded by political economists that free trade was economically rational for the British economy as a whole as well as from those who felt with Cobden that free trade would "have the tendency to unite mankind in the bonds of peace" (cited by Grampp, 1987b, p. 252), or those who hoped that it would weaken the landowning classes to the point where the franchise could be (again) extended.

However, the position of Enlightenment thinkers was not as unequivocally supportive of free trade as might be thought. The Enlightenment advocated a "civilized consortium of nations" (Howe, 2002, p. 195), and disapproved of any kind of commercial policy motivated by what Hume called "the Jealousy of Trade." Most Enlightenment writers realized with David Hume that the policy of trade and that of war followed very different logics and that while trade was a positive-sum game, wars inevitably left winners and losers (Hont, 2005, p. 6). Smith and Hume realized full well that they lived in an imperfect world, in which the harsh realities of international politics and commercial interests often clashed. To be sure, Enlightenment writers were never unanimous on commercial policy (Irwin, 1996). Francis Hutcheson, a great believer in economic freedom, did not manage to project this idea to foreign trade. David Hume himself, while certainly no mercantilist, was of two minds about it, noting that a "tax on German linens encourages home manufactures and thereby multiplies our people and our industry" (Hume, [1777], 1985, p. 98). Unlike Smith, Hume did not feel that the advantages of free trade were universal and based on a general argument, and that if free trade was advantageous at some point, this was not invariant but a function of development. In other parts of Europe the doubts about free trade were even more pronounced, with Neapolitan writers, for instance, wondering whether the advantages of free trade would hold for relatively small city-state economies without overseas empires (Robertson, 1997). On the other hand, Edmund Burke, still reviled by some as the counter-Enlightenment thinker par excellence, was an enthusiastic supporter of free trade and free markets.

It cannot be seriously argued that the *only* reason why mercantilism was dismantled in the first half of the nineteenth century was the influence of the Enlightenment and the liberal ideology it spawned. Empirical work by quantitative political scientists and economists on the abolition of the Corn Laws in 1846 has shown that the move to free trade was prompted by the growth of a strong self-interest lobby against it as well as by the growing ability of landowners to diversify into non-agricultural assets, which safeguarded them against the decline in rents (Schonhardt-Bailey, 1996). The development of asset markets broke the nexus between incumbency and the reluctance to support new technology and institutional reform. Incumbents did not have to beat the new sectors, they could join them fairly easily by investing in turnpikes, canals, cotton mills, and later railroads. Powerful theoretical and historical objections have been raised against the ideological explanation of the abolition of the Corn Laws (Anderson and Tollison, 1985; McKeown, 1989). The dispute between those who feel that liberal reforms were the result of Enlightenment ideology and liberal political economy and those who feel it was nothing but a power play by the newly dominant industrial bourgeoisie seems to draw a false dichotomy. Persuasion was key to the victory of the free-traders, but persuasion involves both the rhetorical conventions of theory and evidence employed by both sides and the proclivities of the parties to believe those theories that happened to serve their interests. The point, then, is not that economic interests did not play an important role in determining policy, but rather that ideology and interests were complements rather than substitutes. Almost any policy change had groups that stood to lose as well as gain. The struggle was over those who had little direct stake in the issue, or who could somehow be persuaded to vote against their pocketbook. The outcome of that struggle could not but be influenced by prevailing beliefs (Grampp, 1987a).

The main problem for those who would dismiss any role for ideology in liberal legislation is that the repeal of the Corn Laws was only one of the last moves in a decades-long project that reduced and refocused the role of the state from that of a redistributive agency to a more benevolent one that corrected market failures and injustices. Had the Corn Laws been the only measure at stake in the years between 1815 and 1850, the arguments against a serious impact of Enlightenment ideology might have been more convincing. As early as 1820, Parliament had voted a statement of principle supporting the idea of free trade, a statement that had wide support from both parties. Policy-makers such as Lord Liverpool were demonstrably influenced by "economic ideas" coming from Hume, Smith, and their followers. These were the ideas on which politicians said they acted, "and by all appearances they actually did" (Grampp, 1987a, p. 87). Some of the key players started off as protectionists and then eventually were persuaded to the free trade cause. James Deacon Hume, the secretary of the Board of Trade who was one of the moving spirits of free trade reform, was converted after first having supported the Corn Laws. Robert Peel's sudden and abrupt change of mind was even more crucial to the repeal: originally a supporter of the Corn Laws (which he regarded as an exception to the general case for free trade), he changed his mind in the mid-1840s, though more as a result of pragmatic policy considerations than by abstract reasoning (Irwin, 1989). How much of this can be attributed to men in power being persuaded of (or educated in) the "enlightened" idea that trade was normally beneficial to both sides and any encumbrance of it costly to society, and how much was due to the narrow economic interests of an increasingly powerful industrial class, is hard to determine. It seems that both were necessary, and that without one part, the other might not have prevailed.

A significant and not often recognized effect of the changes in European ideology due to Enlightenment thinking is the Pax Britannica, that prevailed in Europe in the century following the fall of Napoleon. Britain had emerged from the French Wars as the most powerful nation in Europe, yet now it rarely used these advantages to impose its will and hegemony on its European neighbors. Predatory wars, such as were fought in the eighteenth century, were becoming rare in Europe. It did not have to be this way: Britain was probably powerful enough to impose its economic will on other European countries, but it had concluded that its interests were best served through peaceful commerce. The hard-fisted policies of Hanoverian Britain, in which a combination of naval power and foreign mercenaries defended narrow economic interests, were increasingly replaced with a liberal belief in peaceful market competition.

Of course, it could be objected that such a policy was attractive to Britain because it had become the technological leader, the "workshop of the world," that could out-compete other economies through lower prices and superior products. It was a self-serving credo. Liberal trade policies were supported by nations that were in a position of leadership; the emulators were those who felt they needed protection. But while this was true for those products most closely associated with the Industrial Revolution, such as textiles and machinery, it was less true for other products. Yet policy-makers, intellectuals, and entrepreneurs were increasingly inclined to let the market set the terms at which it traded and not rely primarily on gunships, unless it felt that other nations were refusing to play by these rules. In other words, the competitive game should be played in competitive and free markets with productivity as the main control variable. No heavy government hand to support these efforts was necessary.

To summarize: social and economic progress led to growth through the twin concepts of the expansion of useful knowledge and the rational reform of institutions. It is important to stress what is being argued here. The Enlightenment and eighteenth-century science were only partly responsible for the first Industrial Revolution. Most of the great macroinventions of the 1770s and 1780s were the result of the dexterity and ingenuity of British mechanics and not of the Baconian program. But the Enlightenment must be credited for turning these technical breakthroughs into a sustained stream of innovations and the eventual launching of a new world of continuous economic growth. It could also take credit for the fact that no institutional feedback occurred to negate the effects of technological progress. One might speculate that if the British economy had experienced just one of these effects of the Enlightenment but not the other, nineteenth-century growth would eventually have been stunted.

An example of a society with successful commercial institutions and flourishing (internal) trade is eighteenth-century China; yet it lacked anything remotely like an Industrial Enlightenment. While in earlier times the Chinese had shown enormous scientific and technological capabilities, by the time of the British Industrial Revolution it had become technologically stagnant and by the time of the Opium Wars of 1840 (British "enlightened" foreign policies clearly were confined to Europe), the gap in capabilities had become clear for all to see. In 1792 Britain made a bona fide attempt to "export" the Industrial Enlightenment to China in the form of the embassy of Lord George Macartney, who was sent to China to display the wonders of the age of Enlightenment and to pry open the Chinese market for British products. The Chinese on the whole rejected the opportunity and Macartney did not do for China what Admiral Perry was to do for Japan sixty years later. It is possible that the attempt was botched: Macartney brought with him mostly scientific instruments, and not many of the cheap and high-quality industrial products that manufacturers such as Boulton had wanted him to carry were displayed in the end (Berg, 2006). But by that time, the Chinese leadership lacked the aggressive curiosity of the Europeans. No Chinese envoys were sent to Britain to examine its innovations. Even when European goods and techniques were purchased and imitated in the nineteenth century, importing the political ideology associated with the Enlightenment was an altogether different matter.

Furthermore, without institutional reform, technology by itself could not have turned the economy into the kind of growth-producing engine that it became. In their different ways, the experience of Latin America and Russia have demonstrated to the world that access to modern science and technology without first changing the institutions that set incentives and define the rules of the economic game will not inevitably lead to the kind of economic growth experienced by the richest industrialized countries. The Enlightenment thus created a synergy of two sets of transformation that supported and reinforced one another. It is in that synergy that the roots of modern economic growth can be found.

CHAPTER 5

Enlightenment and the Industrial Revolution

The Industrial Revolution has figured so prominently in the economic historiography of eighteenth-century Britain that the literature seems at times to read as if there was little else going on in the British economy in those years. Every topic discussed in the literature of the economic history of this period, whether agriculture, finance, or commercial policy, has been discussed in the context of the Industrial Revolution or even endowed with a "revolution" of its own. Nothing could be more misleading. Daily material life in Britain, outside a few key areas and regions, proceeded more or less as it had in the past, and the average Briton in 1800 was probably only dimly if at all aware that something very large was brewing on the horizon. Economic historians have argued that there is little in the writings of political economists, including the "big three" (Smith, Malthus, and Ricardo), that indicates much awareness of an impending sea change. Perhaps economists were not the best equipped to sense big changes in economic reality, and perhaps they were too involved with other matters such as the nature of money, prices, value, and exchange to notice that the most important economic change, namely the acceleration and routinization of technological progress, was happening right under their noses. But their oversight was understandable, because whatever we might identify as "revolutionary" was confined at first to a few localities and industries, and it is only with hindsight that we realize its full implications.

Some highly informed and intelligent observers, however, sensed that the world was changing more rapidly than before. Certainly some involved manufacturers did. Josiah Wedgwood, the very epitome of an enlightened manufacturer, wrote in 1767 to his friend and, later, partner, the merchant Thomas Bentley, that a "revolution was at hand" and urged him to "assist in, proffitt by it" (Wedgwood, 1973, Vol. 1, pp. 164–65). Wedgwood was writing about the one industry he knew, pottery. By the end of the Napoleonic period, some informed observers realized what was happening throughout much of the industrial sector. The Scottish merchant and statistician Patrick Colquhoun (1815, pp. 68–69) in a famous quote declared that "It is impossible to contemplate the progress of manufactures in Great Britain within the last thirty years without wonder and astonishment. Its rapidity ... exceeds all credibility. The improvement of the steam engines, but above all the facilities afforded to the great branches of the woolen and cotton manufactories by ingenious machinery, invigorated by capital and skill, are beyond all calculation." At about the same time, the manufacturer and philanthropist Robert Owen ([1815], 1927, pp. 120, 121) added that "The general diffusion of manufactures throughout a country generates a new character in its inhabitants ... This change has been owing chiefly to the mechanical inventions which introduced the cotton trade into this country ... the immediate effects of this manufacturing phenomenon were a rapid increase in the wealth, industry, population, and political influence of the British Empire." Scientists sensed the same. Humphry Davy reflected in 1802 that, "we look for a time that we may reasonably expect, for a bright day of which we already behold the dawn." By 1830, Thomas Babington Macaulay predicted that a century hence Britons not only would be better fed, clad, and housed but also that they would number fifty million, on account of "machines constructed on principles yet undiscovered" (cited by McCloskey, 1994, p. 243). For most of the best-informed people in Britain the Whiggish message of improvement and advance had become self-evident by the early decades of Queen Victoria's rule.

It seems unlikely, however, that most Britons at the time saw themselves as living in an age of profound economic transformation. There were few signs of industrial change in the pastoral areas in the south of England where Jane Austen lived. The Industrial Revolution then was in its first stages a local phenomenon. As economic historians have stressed the limits of macroeconomic change at the time of the Industrial Revolution, some scholars have called for the concept to be abandoned altogether. The Industrial Revolution, it was argued, was neither industrial nor a revolution, it did not lead to economic growth, it could boast only a few very limited technological achievements, and thus we should not use the concept.

This call has not resonated with most scholars working in the area. In part this is because terms seem to acquire their own life and inertia and once they are accepted, it takes more than just a few apostates for the entire community to abandon them altogether. Similarly, terms like "the Middle Ages" and "the Scientific Revolution" could be and have been criticized but they have nonetheless stuck. At the same time, economic historians have felt and continue to feel that something deep and important changed in Britain between 1760 and 1830 (the "classic" period of the Industrial Revolution defined by T.S. Ashton). Whereas earlier emphases on technological discontinuities, to say nothing of radical macroeconomic changes, may have been overblown, there still was a sea change in those years that created an irreversible transformation in the way the British economy produced goods and services. The exact content of the idea of an Industrial Revolution may thus have changed, but the usefulness of the concept as a way of organizing our thinking has not been reduced.

What was the Industrial Revolution? Scholars have found different ways to define it, depending on the environment in which they were writing and the issues that interested them. But three or four "schools" stand out, and while they do not exclude one another, they differ in emphasis and in the aspects of the economy they stress most. One school has focused on technological change: the Industrial Revolution was a sequence of successful innovations like no other period before. Within a comparatively short time, a number of industries had been revolutionized by what I have called "macroinventions," that not only dramatically reduced prices and created new products, but also triggered a continuous flow of secondary and incremental inventions and improvements that made the new techniques work better, applied them to new industries, reduced accidents, down-time, and fuel consumption, and made products more attractive, durable, reliable, and user-friendly. First in cotton and then in other textiles, in iron and other materials such as glass and ceramics, in energy generation and their applications, and in a host of other and smaller industries these inventions came, often in clusters. As the widely cited remark by Alfred North Whitehead has it, the greatest invention of the nineteenth century was the invention of how to invent, but the second was to develop, improve, and tweak these inventions so that they could actually affect productivity and economic welfare (Mowery and Rosenberg, 1998, pp. 1ff.).

The Industrial Revolution has meant different things to historians interested in the business firm, the labor force, and the economic organization of production. For some, the Industrial Revolution was not so much the dawn of modern economic growth as it was the age of the creation of the factory system, the emergence of an industrial proletariat, the urban manufacturing centers with their grimy streets, crowded tenements, children and women working long hours in smokestacked mills. The Industrial Revolution in this view was the age that put an end to most domestic industry and turned independent and free artisans into an army of wage-laborers, a disenfranchised and exploited urban proletariat subject to discipline and a rigid schedule that had been previously unknown. It was the age of reification and alienation, in which people were thought to have lost their individuality and become part of undifferentiated industrial labor. For others, the same process has been described as the triumph of economic mobility, free markets, and a more efficient allocation of resources, an age that increasingly rewarded resourcefulness and hard work, in which entrepreneurs and innovators, and with them the mass of consumers, could reap the rewards and blessings that human ingenuity coupled to well-functioning markets bestowed upon them. Either way, to economists interested in the microeconomics of the firm the rise of the factory system has remained the central event of the Industrial Revolution.

A third approach has viewed the Industrial Revolution primarily as a process of economic growth. This "aggregative" view has come under increasing criticism. To be more exact, this view of the Industrial Revolution holds that a rapid acceleration of technological progress after 1760 led to productivity gains in key sectors that were the backbone of a sudden spurt or "take-off" in investment and economic growth. Yet at the end of the day there is more or less a consensus that the Industrial Revolution meant first and foremost that the engine of growth was to be found increasingly in technology, and that technology alone can propel a process that does not run into some kind of upper bound. Many of the great inventions in textiles, iron, energy, and other industries have been the topic of detailed investigations and are associated in the popular mind with the essence of the Industrial Revolution. Yet when we come down to it, these macroinventions were confined to a limited, if growing, sector of the economy. Cotton, for instance, was still a marginal industry in 1760, quite small compared to wool. The rapid advances in the spinning, printing, carding, and later weaving of cotton had turned it into the backbone of the British textile industry by the middle of the nineteenth century. However, in the closing decades of the eighteenth century its impact on the economy as a whole was proportional to its relative size, which was still small. The same is true for other "modern" industries in which the rate of innovation was high, such as steam, pottery, glass, iron, machine tools, and so on.

This engine of growth started in first gear and at first movement forward was slow and difficult. The impact of technological changes on aggregate variables was delayed and fully felt only decades after their first appearance. Only when the new technology has been improved and developed, has found new applications and new combinations with existing and other new techniques, and has started to spread to previously stagnant industries, and a large enough number of new machines embodying the new technique have been produced, can we start observing the impact of new technology on the economy at large. Steam power, a classic example of what economists call today "General Purpose Technology," eventually became a major source of growth and productivity increases, but much of this took place after 1850 (more than a century after the first steam engine was brought on-line), and the application of steam to transportation did not occur in earnest until the 1830s (Von Tunzelmann, 1978; Crafts, 2004). Many other major inventions show similar delays in their effect, such as Abraham Darby's use of coke for iron smelting (1712) and Edmund Cartwright's power loom (1785). The causes of such delays were varied, but they usually required further micro-inventions (improvements and adaptations) for a good idea to be implemented on a large scale, or they needed the development of complementary inputs such as competence to operate and maintain new equipment.

To be effective, most new techniques needed to be "tweaked" subsequent to their invention, adapted to local environments and requirements, debugged, and made to conform with the capabilities of labor and management. Often, a technique could only be exploited profitably after a complementary technique had been perfected. Thus Darby's coke-smelting required better air-bellows and the power equipment that drove them before it could be fully workable. These came a full half-century after Darby's first use of coke. Improvement and refinement of new techniques were usually slow in this period because often the underlying knowledge (or "epistemic base") was still quite limited in the early stages of the Industrial Revolution. The rate of improvement of production techniques depended in part on the extent to which people understood how and why the techniques really worked. Around 1800, such an understanding, in the majority of processes, was still limited. As we have seen, this was true for agriculture, and it was equally true for a much wider range of industries including food processing, chemistry, steelmaking, fine machinery, and medicine, as well as for traditional industries such as construction and apparel-making. In most of these industries, best-practice knowledge in the eighteenth century was simply inadequate to make rapid progress. But a great deal of useful knowledge in the early stages of the Industrial Revolution simply consisted of experience, systematic experimentation, a long catalog of techniques that worked, reports on how certain materials behave at different temperatures, how to find defects in machines and fix them, lists of optimal times, pressures, and shapes to use without a unifying principle that explained why they worked best. This process, however, became more efficient when the scientific underpinnings of the techniques in use were better understood. The continuous stream of small, incremental innovations, on which sustained productivity growth depended, demanded a better understanding of the underlying natural forces that made them work.

Some problems were simply hard and took many decades to solve because society as a whole did not know enough. Some of these were purely mechanical: sewing machines, to choose one example, were a hard technical problem, and workable machines were not produced until the 1850s. Cotton-picking machinery was not really perfected till the twentieth century despite the obvious need for it. The same is true for fully interchangeable parts, which required a higher degree of accuracy and uniformity than most machine tools could deliver before the mid-nineteenth century. Some were constrained by what people knew about the underlying process: synthetic dyes and the industrial and domestic use of electricity, for instance, required more understanding of chemical and physical processes than had been attained by 1850, the strenuous efforts of the best minds of the era notwithstanding. Medicine made little progress before the triumph of the germ theory in the last third of the nineteenth century. The requisite knowledge to solve problems quickly and adapt to changing circumstances in most production techniques that involved the manipulation of energy, materials, and living beings was only emerging slowly.

Growth and productivity change were thus quite modest in the early stages of the Industrial Revolution, and by some calculations barely registered (Antrás and Voth, 2003). The Industrial Revolution was above all a beginning. It cannot be judged on its own grounds without considering what it led to. What is truly significant is not the wave of great inventions made in the years between 1765 and 1800, but the fact that this process did not subsequently fizzle out. Some societies, in Europe and Asia, had witnessed previous clusters of macroinventions, leading to substantial economic changes. Thus the great inventions of the fifteenth century in shipping, the printing press, the casting of iron, navigation, and gunpowder use had wide-ranging effects on society and economic activity. But the innovative push slowed down eventually, and additional improvements in any of those activities become increasingly hard to discern after the limited knowledge base was exhausted. In contrast, the Industrial Revolution went into a higher gear after 1800, not only continuously improving those inventions that had started the movement, but also continuously finding entirely new avenues of innovation. If the first decades had been dominated by cotton-spinning, iron, and stationary steam engines, the second stage extended the wave of inventions to other textiles, to gas lighting, more advanced mechanical engineering and the sophisticated tools that made the machines, high-pressure steam engines, and later the telegraph, ship design, chemicals, and many other areas. The "classical" Industrial Revolution in the eighteenth century was not an altogether novel phenomenon. In contrast, the second and third waves in the nineteenth century, which made continuous technological progress the centerpiece of sustainable economic growth, were something that had never before been witnessed and that constituted a sea change in economic history like few other phenomena ever had. But what was it that made it so?

While the macroeconomic impact of the Industrial Revolution was inevitably slow and delayed, some microeconomic data indicate a marked acceleration if not a discontinuity after 1750. A number of seemingly unrelated series of significant variables seem to "take off" at some point after the middle of the eighteenth century. Patents taken out in Britain show an unmistakable breakpoint around 1757 (Sullivan, 1989). The average number of patents taken out annually had been 8.5 in the 1740s and 9.9 in the 1750s, but in the 1760s it was 22.1 and in the 1780s it was up to 51.2 (Mitchell, 1975, p. 438). The raw number of books published per year had hovered around 1,000 during the first half of the eighteenth century, but reaches 3,000 in 1790 (see table 3.1). The number of (successful) turnpike trust petitions, at 25 in the 1730s and 38 in the 1740s, suddenly leapt to 170 per decade in the 1750s and 1760s (Bogart, 2005b, p. 457). The explosion of the number of country banks from about ten in 1750 to close to four hundred by 1800 is another case in point. The annual number of bankruptcies in Britain between 1711 and 1760 was quite stationary, averaging 209 per year, but then started to rise rapidly and reached 539 in the 1780s, followed by the financial panics of the 1790s, which caused an even sharper rise (Hoppit, 1987, p. 45). A rather striking series is the number of civil engineering (mostly hydraulic) projects and their costs between 1700 and 1820, summarized in table 5.1. These data, too, show a remarkable discontinuity around 1760. The use of each of these series as a measure of change can be criticized in its own right: patent statistics do not properly reflect the rate of invention because only a minority of important inventions were patented, and the propensity to do so changed over time; the number of books published may reflect demand and/or supply factors, and does not obviously have any short-term impact on the economy; turnpike trusts reflect a specific set of institutional factors that may be quite independent of technological change; civil engineering projects were political decisions as much as economic ones, and the series shows high volatility. Yet these series jointly, precisely because they are so different, reflect a consistent set of mid-century discontinuities that are hard to ignore. Those who feel that the Industrial Revolution is an event largely invented by economic historians blinded by the exponential growth of iron and cotton and that it meant "minor changes of degree for the great majority of men" (Clark, 1985, p. 66), need to realize that, while it was not the entire economy that was subjected to change, it was much more than cotton and metals.

The Industrial Revolution must be understood in the light of its intellectual and institutional background as much as in the light of its economics. Whether one chooses to think of the Enlightenment as a cultural watershed or in terms of continuity, there can be little doubt that the preceding changes in the mental world of the British economic and technological elite were the background of the Industrial Revolution. New modes of thinking fell upon the fertile ground of a society in which opportunities to innovate and succeed in business had been increasingly a key to personal prosperity. The changing intellectual environment, above all, created communications between those who knew things and those who made things. Of course, this was not entirely new, nor was it confined to Britain. Precedents can be tracked to the Middle Ages, where medieval monks were the "first intellectuals to get dirt under their fingernails," as noted by Lynn White, the great historian of medieval technology (White, 1968, p. 65). In the sixteenth and seventeenth centuries, this gap closed further. Scientists grew more interested in pragmatic questions, especially in astrology and alchemy, two fields that absorbed a great deal more mental effort than they could show results for.

To the economist interested in changes in production, however, it is clear that the full force of this phenomenon was not felt until after 1750, when progressive manufacturers and engineers included a growing number of curious and progress-minded men, often well versed in mechanical science and chemistry such as they were. The Manchester cotton spinner George A. Lee, the owner of the first mill to introduce gas lighting, was described by none other than Robert Owen as "one of the most scientific men of his age" (Musson and Robinson, 1969, p. 99). Thomas Bentley, Wedgwood's partner, was a genuine intellectual who spoke fluent French and Italian and was a founder-trustee of the celebrated Warrington dissenting academy. William Strutt, the eldest son of the legendary Derby cotton master Jedediah Strutt, serves perhaps as another model of an enlightened factory master. He was not only well educated and widely read but a skilled architect, the designer of fire-resistant buildings with a particular interest in heating engineering. Among his friends were Erasmus Darwin, the Bentham brothers, and Robert Owen. His achievements led to his election to the Royal Society in 1817, an unusual honor for a manufacturer. Even lesser-known Industrial Revolution figures such as Charles Wolley Bage, himself a pragmatic nuts-and-bolts kind of engineer (who among others designed a fire-resistant textile mill in Ditherington near Shrewsbury), came from a highly enlightened family and must have been exposed to Enlightenment

Table 5.1: Civil engineering projects, 1700-1829

Decade[a]	Number of projects	Total costs (nominal 1000's of £)[b]	Decade	Number of projects	Total costs (nominal 1000's of £)[b]
1700–09	3	3	1770–79	27	1,288
1710–19	4	105	1780–89	23	1,237
1720–29	13	193	1790–99	47	8,778
1730–39	13	409	1800–09	29	5,440
1740–49	3	9	1810–19	34	9,868
1750–59	12	281	1820–29	47	6,631
1760–69	35	1,693			

[a] Calculated as projects starting in a year in that decade
[b] The few projects for which no cost was provided were assigned the average project cost for that decade.

Source: computed from Skempton et al., (2002), App. II.

values and beliefs. His father Robert Bage was an accomplished radical intellectual and novelist and friend of Erasmus Darwin and the Birmingham historian William Hutton, in addition to being a paper manufacturer. Whether or not at this time there was a philosopher "beneath the skin of the engineer and the entrepreneur" (Stewart, 2008, p. 25), the value of useful mechanical and chemical knowledge was increasingly appreciated and respected by this age. This, indeed, was one mechanism by which the age of Enlightenment led to the age of modern economic growth.

Enlightened industrialists also knew what they did not know and solicited scientists for advice, whether useful or not. We have already noted the unique eighteenth-century phenomenon of scientific societies and informal meeting places, which brought together people with different qualifications and backgrounds. But what counted especially were informal relationships and correspondences in which producers sought access to the best knowledge available at their time. If the Enlightenment, as modern scholars have argued, was first and foremost about communication, this is the kind of communication that was most significant to long-term economic performance.

Communication between those who knew things and those who made things could take the form of partnerships. Some of those relationships are famous, such as the friendship between Watt and Joseph Black, mentioned above. Black was a professional applied scientist who acted as consultant to potters, manufacturers of tar, lead miners, and distillers on matters as diverse as water analysis, indigo dyes, and sugar-boiling. Equally indicative of the role of science was Watt's relationship with James Keir, another Scottish professional chemist, whom he hired as a consultant for the Soho works. Keir went bankrupt at the age of 45, then went into business applying his practical knowledge of chemistry and ended up owning Britain's most successful alkali factory near the Birmingham canal. The Scottish physician and chemist William Cullen was retained by Scottish manufacturers to help them solve a variety of problems and worked on issues such as salt extraction, the use of lime in bleaching, and the manufacture of textile dyes. The mine viewer and engineer John Buddle teamed up with Humphry Davy to work on the safety lamp. Telegraph pioneer William Cooke worked closely with London physics professor, Charles Wheatstone. The leading engineer William Fairbairn teamed up with the mathematician Eaton Hodgkinson and Robert Stephenson, and together they worked out the materials used in the construction of the great tubular Britannia bridge that carried the railroad over the Menai straits in Wales. William Rankine, the noted Scottish physicist and engineer, worked closely with the Glasgow shipbuilder James Robert Napier on engine development. The correspondence and writings of many of the early industrial tycoons such as pottery manufacturer Josiah Wedgwood, wool spinner Benjamin Gott, his fellow citizen of Leeds the flax spinner John Marshall, and ironmasters Richard Crawshay and William Reynolds shows how keen they were on communicating with men of science, whether by letter or personal meeting. Even relatively practical engineers and manufacturers such as Richard Trevithick, the inventor of high-pressure steam engines and Henry Cort, the inventor of the puddling and rolling process, communicated with people they believed to be experts and asked them for advice. Such well-documented relationships were but the tip of the iceberg, most of which will never be fully known to us. But it is striking to observe the willingness of scientists to come off their Olympian heights, and engage industrialists, such as the astronomer William Herschel who took his son John to visit Watt's Soho works in 1810. Many enlightened scientists were determined to roll up their sleeves, and help solve problems in engineering and machinery. The determination of the industrialists who needed advice to actively seek it and use it whenever they could was symbolic of the Industrial Revolution. This is not to say that the advice given was usually sound and productive. All the same, in the closing decades of the eighteenth century, the Baconian program was finally experiencing a few of the first fruits of many decades of hard work and fervent hopes.

In other cases, creative and dexterous natural philosophers tried their hand at invention themselves. Many of them, such as Humphry Davy, Claude Berthollet, and Benjamin Franklin, refused to exploit these inventions for their financial profit and contributed them to improve others' lives (although they were often quite insistent to be awarded credit and recognition). In other cases, their entre-preneurial competence fell short of their knowledge and imagination. The Earl of Dundonald, an eccentric but brilliant scientist, who patented a chemical process to produce coal tar, exhausted his family's resources on trying to promote his in-vention unsuccessfully though the product would eventually become a great success. James Watt's first business partner, John Roebuck, who pioneered the manufacture of sulphuric acid using lead chambers, also went bankrupt. Trained in Edinburgh in medicine and chemistry, Roebuck's indomitable drive to improvement through useful knowledge paired with his incompetence as a busi-nessman, was typical of one kind of person who helped to bring about the tech-nological breakthroughs of the age: his optimism, energy, belief in progress, and competence almost entirely benefited the society in which he lived and not him-self. The Carron ironworks he helped found but had to withdraw from eventually became one of the most successful enterprises in the British iron industry.

Even in societies in which markets were relatively free and developed, there was rarely any proportionality between the contribution of an innovator and the re-wards he or she reaped. At least in that sense, the situation then was not different from what it is today: Nordhaus (2004) has estimated that in modern America only 2.2 percent of the surplus of an invention is captured by the inventor him/herself. Things surely looked no better for inventors in the eighteenth century. A few, like Watt, Arkwright, Strutt, Keir, and Peel, died rich and presumably satisfied men; other inventors, even when they found fame, rarely found fortune next to it. Knowledge was not yet a commodity to be bought and sold at market prices, and even when it was traded, its prices rarely reflected its benefit to society. If ever there was a divergence between social and private net benefits, the Industrial Revolution was it. The impact of the technological elite on the rest of the eco-nomy was thus vastly larger than proportional to their size. Big historical changes are often made by small groups.

Yet the Industrial Enlightenment was successful because beneath the giants operated a much larger contingent of scientific writers, tinkerers, engineers, lec-turers, machinists, and experimental philosophers, who may not have been quite in the class of a Joseph Priestley, a John Dalton, or a Michael Faraday, but who could stand on those giants' shoulders. These people spread the culture and values of the new gospel of useful knowledge and impressed upon natural philosophers the need to make their knowledge available to those who could make use of it. They should not necessarily be identified with a new industrial bourgeoisie or a capitalist mentality, although they may have had such connections. Rather, what characterized them was a firm belief in progress, and in the ability of useful knowledge to advance the state of mankind, provided it was diffused and popularized. A typical example of such a person was William Nicholson

(1753–1815). Nicholson started off working for Josiah Wedgwood. He made some original contributions: he was one of the first to realize the potential of the voltaic pile (invented in 1800) for chemical research and to discover electro-chemical reactions, an experimental area in which Humphry Davy made his reputation. He took out a number of important patents, including for a cotton-printing machine and a hydrometer, which could measure the density of liquids. But his main fame rests on his contribution to making others' work accessible. He translated into English the work of two of the leading post-Lavoisier French chemists, Jean-Antoine Chaptal and Antoine-François Fourcroy, arranging them into "a General System of Chemical Knowledge." He was a member of one of London's many informal scientific societies, the Chapter Coffee House Society (whose membership overlapped with that of the Birmingham Lunar Society) and eventually became its secretary. He was a patent agent, representing other inven-tors, and around 1800 ran a "scientific establishment for pupils" on London's Soho Square. According to the school's advertisement, "this institution affords a degree of practical knowledge of the sciences which is seldom acquired in the early part of life" and its weekly lectures on natural philosophy and chemistry were "illustrated by frequent exhibition and explanations of the tools, processes and operations of the useful arts and common operations of society." Above all, Nicholson was the founder and editor of the first truly scientific journal, the *Journal of Natural Philosophy, Chemistry, and the Arts* (more generally known at the time as *Nicholson's Journal*), which commenced publication in 1797. It published the works of most of the leading scientists of the time, and played the role of today's *Nature* or *Science*, that is, to announce important discoveries in short communications. In it, leading scientists including Dalton, Jöns Berzelius, Davy, Rumford, and George Cayley communicated their findings and opinions. Nicholson was driven by curio-sity and ambition, but if economic motives played a role in his work, he did not succeed and as Golinski (2004) put it, he never prospered financially, suffering "the common fate of projectors": continual labor without material reward. Yet it is people such as him who created a new world in which useful knowledge was made accessible, in which the search for profitable innovations was routine, and in which the agenda of science became increasingly geared toward the economi-cally useful. The Enlightenment idea of reducing access costs was pursued with vigor in Victorian Britain. An example is the weekly publication *The Athenaeum*, founded in 1828, which was inexpensive and enjoyed a wide circulation. Under the editorship of Charles Wentworth Dilke, it combined literary criticism with detailed surveys of developments in science and technology written for a lay audience (including essays by Lord Kelvin).

A somewhat different aspect of the Industrial Enlightenment was provided by one Friedrich Accum, a German-born chemist who migrated to London at an early age, and made his living as a supplier of scientific apparatus, a translator of scientific texts, and as a consultant for another German immigrant, F.A. Winsor (né Winzer), one of the pioneers of gas lighting in Britain. Accum was close to Nicholson and often published in his *Journal*. In 1820 he published his sensational *Treatise on Adulterations of Food and Culinary Poisons* in which he used his chemical knowledge to expose the practices of British brewers, bakers, grocers, and other food processors who routinely diluted their products and added a variety of noxious chemicals to them. Although the campaign ended disastrously for Accum (he was seen tearing pages from a library book, and left Britain in disgrace, to the delight of his many enemies), it was an early example of the realization of Enlightenment thinkers that free and unfettered markets can at times produce socially undesirable and even dangerous results.

An important cultural feature of the European West, prominent in Britain but by no means confined to it, is the way useful knowledge was placed in the public realm. Since the great breakthroughs of the seventeenth century, it was expected that new scientific knowledge would be published and placed in the public domain. In earlier centuries natural philosophers had often kept knowledge under a cloak of secretiveness, believing that such knowledge somehow conveyed power or gave the owner an edge in some deep and mysterious way (Eamon, 1994). Such habits surely impeded its diffusion and access by others. The culture of secretiveness had begun to abate long before 1700, and by that time open science based on "credit by priority" was well established, as the famous quarrel between Newton and Leibniz on the origins of calculus attests. Scientific discoveries of any kind were to be published, communicated, and placed in the public realm. When an unusual case occurred of an eccentric scientist refusing to comply (e.g. John Flamsteed, the first Astronomer Royal, or the pathologically shy Henry Cavendish, a leading chemist of the second half of the eighteenth century), others would take exception.

Open science was not run primarily by idealistic altruists who wanted humanity to be enriched by their knowledge: it was run by ambitious and hard-working people who had clear objectives in mind. Yet the standard pecuniary incentive system was supplemented by a more complex one that included peer recognition and the sheer satisfaction of being able to do what one desires. Credit would be given in terms of fame and patronage such as university- or court-related appointments, and sometimes a pension from a ruler or a rich citizen (David, 2004). Scientists who discovered matters of significant insight to industry, such as Count Rumford, Joseph Priestley, or Humphry Davy, usually wanted credit, not profit. Berthollet willingly shared his knowledge of the bleaching properties of chlorine with some savvy Scots, who soon were able to turn his discovery into a profitable venture."When one loves science," wrote Berthollet to one of those Scots, James Watt, "one has little need for fortune which would only risk one's happiness" (cited by Musson and Robinson, 1969, p. 266). The only invention of Michael Faraday's ever to be patented was his design for an improved chimney for lighthouses, which he made over to his brother Robert. William Wollaston took out two patents, neither of which related to his main line of research on rare metals. Bowler and Morus (2005, pp. 320–21) refer to a class of "gentlemanly specialists," men who led the development of useful knowledge but did not make their living from it and were suspicious of anyone who did. At the same time, those who were not independently wealthy needed to find patronage either as university professors or from government, industry or wealthy individuals. Gentleman-inventors, who regarded invention as an amusing pastime, rarely bothered to patent. Richard Lowell Edgeworth, for instance, took out only one patent in his entire life and preferred to submit his inventions to the Society of Arts which awarded him with a variety of medals given out only to unpatented inventions. More unexpectedly, some entrepreneurs, too, refused to take out patents on principle. The great engineers of the Industrial Revolution such as John Rennie and John Smeaton largely stayed away from the patent system. Abraham Darby II declined to take out a patent on his coke-smelting process, allegedly saying that "he would not deprive the public from such an acquisition" (cited by MacLeod, 1988, p. 185), and Richard Trevithick, a century later, likewise failed to take out a patent on his high-pressure engine. It was important for engineers and entrepreneurs to be seen as financially disinterested philosophers and as bound by a gentlemanly code of conduct (Miller, 1999, p. 191). This ideal of a gentleman was a central feature of British society that created enough trust to make the economy more dynamic and efficient, but also to facilitate the accumulation of useful knowledge.

The economics of the accumulation of useful knowledge might be compared to what is now known as an "open source" system in which individuals work on components of a larger endeavor, trying to make significant contributions and thus a name for themselves. Such reputations were quite useful in that they were correlated with patronage, but the rewards were not in true proportion to the net contribution that the discoveries made to society (David, 2004). The environment that determined one's reputation was the college of one's peers and colleagues, and it was for them that publications, lectures, correspondence, and scientific meetings took place. Yet the Industrial Enlightenment also featured individuals whose mission was to popularize the findings of the august scientific elite, and diffuse it to those who could make use of it.

The diffusion of strictly *technological* knowledge (what I have called prescriptive knowledge) is more complex because inventions had the potential of making a great deal of money in the right circumstances, but such income would be compromised if everyone had access to it. Establishing property rights to technical knowledge was regarded by many as a partial solution to this dilemma, but, as we have seen, this was controversial. Patents were not the only way to secure a flow of income from an innovation. Even without a patent, the inventor had a lead time on his competitors, a first-mover advantage that depended among others on the ease with which the invention could be reverse-engineered. Secrecy was the obvious alternative way to extend this lead time. A few desperate attempts to keep production techniques secret are known, especially that of Benjamin Huntsman, the inventor of the crucible technique of making high-quality steel (1740). Josiah Wedgwood's habit was to keep his workers ignorant of procedures in other departments and to isolate new workers until it could be determined that they were not industrial spies. But such secrecy only worked if the product could not be reverse-engineered, and even then was widely understood to be a hazardous strategy. Historians have shown that the reason coke-smelting was so slow to diffuse was not because Darby successfully kept it secret but because other smelters could not realize the cost advantages the Darbys had. Huntsman, too, in the end became a victim of industrial espionage: Samuel Smiles, the Victorian biographer of the pioneers of technology, recounts the (possibly apocryphal) story of a competitor who, disguised as a beggar, abused the pity of Huntsman's employees when he was admitted on a stormy night into the carefully guarded steelmaking premises to warm himself near the furnace.

Be that as it may, secrecy was clearly insufficient to protect intellectual property rights. Richard Roberts, one of the leading engineers of the first half of the nineteenth century, felt that "no trade secret can be kept very long; a quart of ale will do wonders in that way" (Great Britain, 1864, p. 81). By filing for a patent, an inventor could maintain some hope of extracting the income that would compensate him for his efforts. Patents also provided an inventor with time. If the invention needed further development, this could best be done without being rushed by competition into bringing to the market a half-cocked product. Matthew Boulton lobbied for (and got) a private bill through Parliament that extended the patent on Watt's machine to twenty-five years. It expired in 1800. The case of the Watt–Boulton patent illustrates the social cost of patents as well: work on high-pressure steam engines was terminated by Watt's stubborn refusal to experiment with these engines or to let others do so. Watt in his turn was thwarted by another person's patent on the use of crank-type mechanisms in steam engines, although in this case the restriction steered him into another invention, namely his "sun-and-planets" mechanism. In the years immediately after the expiration of the Watt patent, work on high-pressure engines resumed and led to the machines that powered Stephenson's locomotives in the 1820s.

By taking out a patent, however, the inventor placed the specifications and technical details of the invention in the public realm. The original statute made no such requirement, but after about 1734 some specifications became customary in patent filings. Specifications were made mandatory from 1778, when Justice Lord Mansfield, in *Liardet vs. Johnson*, decreed that they should be sufficiently precise and detailed to fully explain the invention to a technically educated person. For a fee and some hassle, anyone could read a full and detailed description of any patented invention even if they could not exploit it. In nineteenth-century debates on the patent system, it was often argued effectively that in its absence many new inventions would be kept secret and their knowledge unavailable to the public at large, thus possibly slowing down the entire process of innovation. It was never quite clear, however, what precisely should be included in such descriptions, and inventors could try to manipulate the descriptions by either including too much (and thus widening the area on which they would have monopoly rights), while at the same time not giving away some critical detail to avoid infringement. Hence the quality of the descriptions varied a great deal (Robinson, 1972).

There were, however, many other places where a curious and enterprising person could go to obtain technical knowledge. The Industrial Enlightenment created a whole set of what we could somewhat anachronistically call search engines, large and comprehensive volumes that were meant less to be read from cover to cover than to be used selectively for looking up a fact or number. The most general of these were encyclopedias, which ordered their material alphabetically. Such encyclopedias were not a British monopoly, but were found all over the Continent. The first encyclopedia devoted to the useful arts was John Harris' *Lexicon Technicum* (1704), which dealt with a host of technical issues. Its most prominent successor in English was Ephraim Chambers' *Cyclopedia,* published in 1728, which went through many editions. The political economist Malachy Postlethwayt (c.1707–67) published between 1751 and 1755 his *Universal Dictionary of Trade and Commerce* (much of it pilfered from an earlier compendium in French). In it, he states that his purpose for the book was "throughout to raise the spirit of universal art and industry in this nation" (1774, p. x).

These works were perhaps the prototype of a device meant to organize useful knowledge efficiently: weak on history and biography, strong on brewing, candle-making, and dyeing. They contained hundreds of engravings, cross-references, and an index. A good example is Thomas Croker's three-volume *Complete Dictionary* (1764–66) which explicitly promised its readers that in it "the whole circle of human learning is explained and the difficulties in the acquisition of every Art, whether liberal or mechanical, are removed in the most easy and familiar manner." The *Encyclopedia Britannica*'s first edition came out in 1771 (in a modest three volumes), and was dwarfed by the massive *Grande Encyclopédie* published by Diderot and d'Alembert in the 1750s. Pirated copies of this paradigmatic Enlightenment opus were much in demand in Britain.

Specialized technical manuals were in high demand in the second half of the eighteenth century. Here, too, the French seem to have put in the greater effort. Manuals of practically every craft known at the time were represented in the eighty volumes of the *Descriptions des arts et métiers* produced by the French Académie Royale des Sciences at the instigation of a scientist who embodied many of the great virtues of the Industrial Enlightenment, René Réaumur. Many of these volumes were translated into English, others were read by Britons in the original language. Manuals and books of instructions, often with excruciating detail and endless diagrams and minute descriptions of implements and processes, were published in every field. Linguistic and national boundaries amounted to little where the Industrial Enlightenment was concerned; the knowledge flowed to whoever wanted it in Europe and was willing to invest in reading and understanding it, or to hire someone who already did.

The precise impact of such codified knowledge-flows on technological practices is hard to estimate and was in all likelihood small in the short run. The nature of the demand for these works is not always easy to establish. Much of that demand was probably little more than the hobbies of curious and intelligent businessmen, rentiers, and landlords. Some of it may have been, in the words of one scholar, the "intellectual voyeurism" of a bored nouveau riche bourgeoisie. Encyclopedia essays were often already out of date by the time they were published. It is, without question, the case that many of the businessmen and manufacturers of the time seriously overestimated what best-practice knowledge could do for them. Yet the evidence that access to organized and codified knowledge at times informed and inspired key persons cannot be ignored. Smeaton and Wedgwood consulted French authorities when they ran into problems. Two of the most important figures of the later Industrial Enlightenment, the mathematician and physician Thomas Young (1773–1829) and the chemist and physicist Michael Faraday, were inspired by encyclopedia articles to pursue their subsequent work.

Moreover, access costs mattered because much invention takes the form of analogies to and combinations of existing techniques, or combined knowledge from diverse fields in what we might call technical hybrids or recombinations. Inventors who set their sight on a particular technological problem had to be familiar with a wide array of practices elsewhere, since they could never be sure in which unexpected corner the solution might be found. This phenomenon was already realized a century before the Industrial Revolution: Joseph Moxon wrote in the 1670s that "The Trades themselves might, by a Philosopher, be Improv'd ... I find that one Trade may borrow from many Eminent Helps in Work of another Trade" (Moxon, [1677], 1703, preface). Such inventions were more likely to take place if useful knowledge in other areas was readily accessible. The paradigmatic example is that of Henry Cort, the inventor of the puddling and rolling process, one of the pivotal breakthroughs of the classic Industrial Revolution (1785). He combined known processes in just the right way to obtain the desired effect, following earlier attempts by others to apply reverberatory furnaces (used in the glass industry). Another example is Samuel Crompton's appropriately named mule (1779), that combined the advantages of two prior inventions, the spinning jenny and the throstle. In the early nineteenth century, there are the first signs of the emergence of specialized professional inventors. These were often outsiders, who had no previous connection to the industry, a point made famous by Adam Smith who alleged that inventions were often made by "men of speculation, whose trade is not to do anything but to observe everything" ([1776], 1976, p. 14). Henry Bessemer, a century later, still agreed (Jewkes, Sawers and Stillerman, 1969, p. 96). It has been calculated that between 1790 and 1830 about half the patented inventions in the British textile industry were made by people who were not textile manufacturers or artisans (Dutton, 1984, p. 123). When Richard Roberts was asked to build an electro-magnet for the city of Manchester (a subject on which he had no prior experience), he had access to a host of well-organized written sources as well as to experts and colleagues with whom he rubbed shoulders in the Manchester Literary and Philosophical Society. For outsiders, whose unique ability was "to observe everything," access to knowledge was crucial.

*   *   *

The Industrial Revolution, as noted, was mostly a local phenomenon, leaving much of Britain unaffected at least until the coming of the railway. A debate has evolved among economic historians as to whether it was essentially confined to a handful of lucky industries in which fortuitous opportunities for mechanization created limited pockets of technological advance and productivity growth, or whether the phenomenon was, even in its early stages, too widespread in the economy to be dominated by a single or a small number of more or less accidental inventions. As Deirdre McCloskey (1981, p. 118) once put it, "the Industrial Revolution was neither the age of steam, nor the age of cotton, nor the age of iron. It was the age of progress." A similar point has been made by Temin (1997). As I will argue below, this point of view is more consistent with a full integration of the Industrial Revolution with the age of Enlightenment. The commitment to progress involved technological efforts along a broad front that included agriculture, medicine, energy, communications, and materials. Yet many processes that needed to be altered and technological bottlenecks that required resolution involved complex and messy natural phenomena that were poorly understood, and many resisted easy solutions. Progress occurred where such resistance was relatively weak, for instance in the cotton industry, or where knowledge had advanced sufficiently to make improvements within reach, as in hydraulics. In areas where the problems were difficult to solve, such as medicine, agriculture, and the more difficult to mechanize industries in the textile sector (such as wool-weaving and carding), progress was slow. But such outcomes are ex post, not ex ante. The attempts to achieve technological progress were widespread.

In the last four decades of the eighteenth century, most of Britain's industry was still located outside the modern sector and hardly experienced any technological change. Computing precisely how many workers were in the modern sector is difficult because the numbers changed rapidly over time, many workers spread their annual labor time over more than one activity, and the classification of some industries is in dispute. Moreover, in many products the old and the new collaborated and practiced a division of labor. As a consequence some industries in the traditional economy actually benefited from the technological advances that created the early factories. Nowhere was this more obvious than in textiles, where spinning and carding were mechanized in the 1780s, but weaving remained for decades a domestic industry, carried out by independent handloom weavers. After the power loom was perfected in around 1820, however, the factories gradually put the handloom weavers under pressure and their decline describes one of the most dramatic tragedies of the Industrial Revolution (Bythell, 1978). But even by the middle of the nineteenth century, the finishing trades in textiles, shoe- and glove-making, the "toy" (small metalware) and belt industries, and similar branches remained largely in the domain of small-time artisans, whose workshops employed at most a few servants or apprentices, were often attached to their homes, and rarely used mechanized devices. Steam power was introduced in more than just textiles, but as late as 1830 about equal quantities of power were derived from steam and water power (about 165,000 hp each) and even by 1850 it was by no means general. It has been calculated that in 1841 around two-thirds of all workers in cotton were employed in factories, but only half in woolen and worsteds and a third in the metal trades.

The so-called traditional sector was quite capable of change and expansion. In the eighteenth century parts of Europe underwent a rapid expansion of rural cottage industry. This expansion is sometimes known as "proto-industrialization" and tended to be located in areas of high population density or relatively low-quality soils, where labor was comparatively less productive in agriculture, especially in the off-season. This created an opportunity for low-skill manufacturing to expand, and led to a proliferation of rural spinners, handloom weavers, nailers, knitters, button-makers, basket weavers, and similar occupations. The advantages of this system are transparent. First, because of the seasonal nature of agricultural work, it could take advantage of the labor time available in the off-season, which had few other uses. Second, its location in the countryside freed it from the various constraints that urban institutions could still impose in some of the older British boroughs. Third, other family members could be recruited in a household-level mini-enterprise.

How large was the rural industrial sector on the eve of the Industrial Revolution? Any figures are fragile if only because so many rural workers were only part-time industrial workers, due to the seasonal nature of the demand for agricultural labor. What is more certain is that rural industry practiced a local specialization: the West Country specialized in woolen cloth, Lancashire in cotton, the area around Birmingham in hardware, and Leicestershire in framework knitting (stockings). A large proportion of these occupations, especially in cottons and worsteds, were organized and coordinated by so-called putting-out entrepreneurs, who paid the workers a piece rate and supplied them with the raw materials and the tools and then saw to the marketing of the finished product, much of which was shipped overseas. The pre-Industrial Revolution merchant manufacturer was the nodal point, connecting the dispersed producers with even more dispersed customers. He supplied the circulating capital and the marketing. But as François Crouzet (1985) has insisted, he was not sensu stricto an industrialist. The Industrial Revolution, it may be said, witnessed the emergence of industrialism, but not industry. Not all of the cottage industry sector was managed by these merchant-manufacturers. Artisans and workers, above all small-scale domestic clothiers in the wool industry, survived until deep into the nineteenth century and maintained some level of independence, being only partially employed by such entrepreneurs. The existence of widespread cottage industries in the countryside should serve, however, as a reminder that the Industrial Revolution was not industrialization per se, but was rather the gradual transition of workers from their cottages into centralized workshops and factories.

It is hard to quantify this proposition, because if industrialization means the shifting of workers into manufacturing, we face the problem that before the factory, most of these rural industrial workers were part-time farmers, who often cultivated small garden plots, worked as agricultural laborers in the busy seasons, and carried out manufacturing activity in the off-season. Should we wish to count them as part-time manufacturing workers, we would need to know what percentage of their time they spent on average in that activity. Eighteenth-century sources are largely silent on that matter. What seems clear is that these cottage industries provided a large pool of workers who could be recruited into the factories. They were at least to some degree familiar with industrial products, were experienced with tools and equipment used in manufacturing, and had been exposed rather intensively to markets, either directly peddling their wares or through the intermediation of a merchant-entrepreneur. The children and women of these proto-industrial families were often the first to end up in the factories.

Some of the skills acquired in the cottage industries could be transferred to the early factories, which used simple tools and equipment side by side with the new machines. Many early factories, indeed, amounted to little more than a group of workers concentrated in one large room, doing more or less what they had been doing at home. Proto-industry also involved "capitalist institutions" such as merchants and entrepreneurs familiar with markets and suppliers, and an infrastructure of services such as finance, transport, overseas connections, and supporting artisans that could have been a factor in the transition to the factories. Moreover, even after factories became more common, they often contracted out large portions of their work to domestic workers in the neighborhood, and many industrial entrepreneurs in the early stages of the Industrial Revolution employed factory workers and putting-out workers at the same time. Some areas in which proto-industry was substantial, especially in Lancashire, Cheshire, and the West Riding of Yorkshire, witnessed a neat transition from one to the other. One observes a similar correlation on the Continent (albeit a bit later), in the Swiss highlands, the Flemish lowlands, the Rhineland, and the Bohemian provinces of the Austrian Empire. These were all regions where significant concentrations of cottage industry accounted for a cheap (and elastically supplied) labor supply, deep market penetration, and the presence of local merchant-entrepreneurs who had marketing skills and capital, thus providing a local advantage.

And yet, not all areas that were well known for proto-industry made the transition: in wool, for example, the industry in 1750 was divided between Yorkshire and the West Country. The wool factories tended to be overwhelmingly concentrated in Yorkshire, with the West becoming slowly de-industrialized. This lack of full correspondence has led Donald Coleman (1983) and others to dismiss proto-industrialization as "one concept too many," but others have begged to differ and feel that there is a logical and historical nexus here, even if the pre-existence of cottage industry was perhaps neither a sufficient nor a necessary condition for modern industry to emerge.

CHAPTER 6

The Origins of British Technological Leadership

The technological revolution that created the modern industrial age cannot be fully understood without its intellectual underpinnings. All the same, inventions and improvements by informed and ingenious minds opened doors but could not force a society to walk through them. To understand the Industrial Revolution and why Britain played the leadership role in it that it did, we need to dig deeper into the economic roots of progress. Britain was not unique in its Enlightenment movement—the Enlightenment was a Western European phenomenon, and after 1750 it reached into Central and Eastern Europe as well, even if it left the Ottoman world and much of southern Europe unaffected. Nor did Britain monopolize technological creativity. Although it did lead in some of the most prominent areas of technological progress such as steam power, cotton-spinning, and iron production, many of the other inventions that made the Industrial Revolution a success, especially in chemicals, were imported from France and other places. In industries such as paper, food-processing, chemicals, and even some textiles such as linen and silk, Britain was a student rather than a teacher. But whereas Britain did not have a monopoly in invention, for many decades it dominated in developing inventions made at home or elsewhere, putting new ideas to successful commercial use, and finding new applications for them. French inventions such as chlorine-bleaching, the wet-spinning process of flax, gas lighting, food-canning, and the Jacquard loom, introduced to Britain after 1820, found widespread application in the British silk industry. Implementation meant economic success, and made Britain the envy of Europe. So why was Britain the leader? What did Britain have that others did not?

It stands to reason that Britain's advantages were primarily on the supply side, not the demand side of the economy. After all, the Netherlands was richer, France was larger, and Spain had more colonies, all of which should have given these economies an advantage on the demand side. More fundamentally, economies do not grow just because they want to consume more. Indeed, the desire for more income is shared by all economies; the ability to satisfy it is what makes all the difference. Of course, at a lower level of abstraction, demand factors and market size help determine how resources are to be allocated, and the rate of technological change may depend on these factors as well.

Some of the advantages can be read off a simple map. Britain as an island nation was more difficult to invade and has not been attacked successfully since 1066 (not counting the Glorious Revolution, which was more of a domestic coup d'etat than a hostile foreign invasion). One might counter reasonably that people living at the time could not know this and had to take costly protective measures, but it still is the case that in contrast to, say, the Low Countries, Britain's economy was less directly affected by martial activities. Island status meant a large maritime economy, shipbuilding and ancillary industries, as well as relatively cheap transportation in the form of coastal shipping. Britain was lucky to have a large supply of coal and iron in reasonable vicinity of one another. Moreover, Britain had more natural resources than coal and iron: she had substantial quantities of non-ferrous metals such as copper, zinc, and lead, as well as fuller's earth, high-quality fireclay, and materials needed to make mordants such as alum (Harris, 1998, p. 557).

Energy, more than anything else, is believed by many scholars to be at the core of long-term economic development (Malanima, 2006). Output of coal increased at a dazzling rate: total output in 1700 was about 3 million tons per year; by 1775 this had increased to almost 9 million, 15 million in 1800, and by 1850 annual output was over 60 million tons. Output thus grew twenty-fold in a century and a half. Many scholars (e.g. Pomeranz, 2000; Wrigley, 2004a, 2009) have pointed to the fortunate presence of coal in Britain as the pivotal difference between a successful industrializer such as Britain and an unsuccessful one such as China. Coal was more efficient and cheaper than wood, and also economized on land use since it allowed Britain to reduce its woodlands and use them in other ways. Moreover, its use stimulated new techniques, both in the extraction and the utilization of coal. As table 6.1 shows, coal was spread over a large part of Britain, and no single region dominated its production.

Yet here, too, both theory and evidence plead against too ready an acceptance of the belief that geography was destiny. Besides steam engines and iron smelting and processing, radical new uses for coal during the Industrial Revolution were not that many. Most of the uses of coal, both in home heating and in industrial applications, pre-date the Industrial Revolution. The main technological bottleneck solved during the Industrial Revolution was the problem of ore smelting. Since iron ore contains a great deal of oxygen, it needs to come into direct contact with pure carbon, so that the carbon gets burned and the oxygen is removed as carbon dioxide, leaving (more or less) pure iron. Before 1709 the only fuel that could serve this purpose was charcoal, which depended on wood supply and was difficult to transport. The coal derivative that replaced charcoal, coke, was first used as a fuel in this process by Abraham Darby in 1709, and caught on wholesale during the years of the Industrial Revolution after 1760.

More fundamentally, coal provided heat. But mechanization and other industrial activities required work. Converting one into the other through engines at ever

Table 6.1: The growth of coal output in Britain, 1700–1850, by region

	1700	1750	1775	1800	1815	1830	1850[a]
Scotland	450	715	1,000	2,000	2,500	3,000	8,100
Cumberland	25	350	450	500	520	560	900
Lancashire	80	350	900	1,400	2,800	4,000	9,600
N. Wales	25	80	110	150	350	600	1,400
S. Wales	80	140	650	1,700	2750	4,400	10,600
Southwest	150	180	250	445	610	800	1,400
E. Midlands	75	140	250	750	1,400	1,700	3,400
W. Midlands	510	820	1,400	2,550	3,990	5,600	10,900
Yorkshire	300	500	850	1,100	1,950	2,800	6,700
Northeast	1,290	1,955	2,990	4,450	5,395	6,915	15,200
Total	2,985	5,230	8,850	15,045	22,265	30,375	68,400

[a] pertains to 1850–55.

Sources: Flinn (1984, p. 26); Church (1984, p. 3).

more efficient rates was one of the great achievements of the Industrial Enlightenment. Progress could be measured here in very concrete terms of fuel efficiency.
A long series of first-class minds, from Christiaan Huygens and his assistant Denis
Papin all the way to Sadi Carnot, Lord Kelvin, and Rankine in the mid-nineteenth
century devoted themselves to this question. That this research took place largely
in Britain was in part attributable to the presence of abundant and cheap fuel
(Allen, 2009). It stands to reason that coal-using techniques would emerge in an
economy in which coal was plentiful, but whether that mechanism is powerful
enough to be a plausible explanation of the entire Industrial Revolution remains
to be seen, and I will return to the question in chapter 12. Lancashire was indeed
blessed with coal, but its iron ore was of low quality and limited in amount
(Timmins, 1998, p. 101).

Steam power, to be sure, was a dramatic change, but the Industrial Revolution
did not absolutely "need" steam (and for a long time manufacturing in many areas

continued to rely on water power), nor was steam power absolutely dependent on coal (peat and wood could be and were used in engines, even though their physical efficiency per pound of fuel was of course lower). Moreover, minerals and materials could be imported. Raw cotton, after all, could not grow in Britain and was shipped in, first from Asia Minor, then increasingly from North America. High-quality iron ores were shipped in from Sweden and Spain. Raw wool, silk, and flax were also imported—yet the British technological lead in textiles was as clear as it was in iron and steam. The Netherlands, which did not have much coal, relied to a great extent on imports from British ports and the price of coal in Amsterdam was not much higher than in London. Switzerland, which had no coal either, specialized in industries that could do without.

In a recent paper, Clark and Jacks (2007) take a fresh look at the role of coal in the Industrial Revolution. They conclude that the mining sector was largely a passive factor, and that its productivity increased only little between 1710 and 1869. Output increased largely because demand grew, not because of any major shock to the ability of the coal industry itself. Clark and Jacks may be understating some of the technological progressiveness of the sector, especially compound ventilation introduced by John Buddle in about 1810. This produced fresher air underground and reduced the hazards from ventilating furnaces and within a few years it was in general use throughout the north-east (Heesom, 2004). It seems plausible that technological progress in extraction technology helped offset the inevitable rise in coal prices that would have occurred once the lowest-hanging fruits in the coal seams had been picked clean. Of course, an elastic supply of coal still meant that Britain did not run into an energy shortage, but it is important to realize that other options were possible. Britain could have been more thrifty in its use of fuel, specialized in lower-energy industries, and tapped alternative sources such as Baltic timber and more efficient water and wind power. These alternatives would have been more expensive, but Clark and Jacks show that this difference would not have imposed a dramatic cost on the economy (in the order of 2 percent of GDP). Whatever the precise counterfactual chosen, the inference "no coal, no Industrial Revolution" seems untenable.

This is not to say that geography was not, all other things being equal, an advantage in that a favorable resource base made the transition from a (mostly) organic economy to a (mostly) mineral one advance faster and go deeper than it would otherwise have done. However, geography and trade were (and are) substitutes whereas trade and technology were complements. Most important, of course, is that natural resources and technology were complements. Coal and iron, the main elements of the mineral economy, had been in the British ground since the beginning of history. What made natural endowments all of a sudden so strategic in some sectors was not geography but changes in knowledge that increased the demand for coal and permitted its exploitation. To be sure, the need to pump out water from collieries exerted a powerful focusing influence on the emergence of steam power, but that was equally true for the copper and tin mines in Cornwall. The earliest steam engines were so inefficient that they could only operate near coal mines, and so the actual historical trajectory was dominated by coal mine location. All the same, it was not coal-use in and of itself that led to growth in the knowledge of converting fossilized energy into work, but the other way around.

The same principle applies to another important element of the mineral economy, salt, an ancient commodity. But its use changed in the eighteenth century: as early as 1736, French chemists discovered that common salt was, in some way, the "base" of soda (sodium carbonate), a key raw material in the glass and soap industries. Until the late eighteenth century soda was made from "organic" sources (kelp) but in the closing decades a feverish search to distill alkalis from salt took place. In 1785 Nicolas Leblanc discovered how to react salt with sulfuric acid, to produce a raw material that yielded soda after further processing (Multhauf, 1978, pp. 140–43). Science, however imperfect, had inspired and informed a vastly improved use of a mineral, and thus stimulated its production and lowered input prices in a host of soda-using industries. Continental science often combined with British competence and favorable institutional environment to produce rapid progress in Britain. The Leblanc process was adapted by a Liverpool chemist, James Muspratt (1793–1886), to become a profitable if noisome industry. Muspratt's own knowledge of chemistry was no more than fair, but he supplemented it with that of his partner, Josias C. Gamble (1775–1848), an Irishman trained in Glasgow.

As technology advanced and a movement toward freer trade became established, the tyranny of distance was progressively weakened and thus whatever role we assign to geography is reduced. The fortuitous presence of natural resources remained of some importance, but as an explanation of British economic leadership it was at best a second-order factor. If nobody had possessed coal, Britain would have had to find an alternative source of energy, and surely water- and wind power would have played a bigger role. The presence of fossil fuels thus had significant economic and environmental consequences, but did not "cause" economic growth. Ingenuity did.

It is often argued that the growing use of coal and the development of coal-using techniques were determined by the exhaustion of timber supplies. Had Britain not been fortunate enough to find itself located on top of a mountain of coal, it is believed, its economic history would have looked quite different. Britain was, throughout the period, a heavy user of timber, and there is no doubt that contemporaries were concerned that it was running out of trees. However, the evidence on the price of timber, as Michael Flinn has shown, does not suggest a serious timber scarcity in the eighteenth century (Flinn, 1959, 1978; see also Hammersley, 1973). Charcoal in Britain was not getting much more costly in the half century prior to Abraham Darby's first commercial use of the coke-smelting process in the eighteenth century and fell in the following half-century, and hence its rising price could not have stimulated the use of coke as a substitute (Malanima, 2003, p. 96). Had such a scarcity become truly felt, rising prices of timber would have induced British farmers to plant more trees than they already did, or imports of timber from the Baltic region would have been much larger. William Marshall (1745–1818), the late eighteenth-century expert on the rural economy, noted that "had it not been for foreign supply, scarcely a timber tree at this day would have been left standing upon the Island" (Marshall, 1785, p. 2). With about two million wooded acres, Britain was one of the least wooded countries in Europe. Yet elementary economics suggests that this was not necessarily a crisis: precisely because the growing of local timber supplies was not profitable, British landowners diverted the use of land to other crops whenever possible. In the absence of coal, the price of timber would have risen more steeply (depending on how much and at what prices timber could have been imported from overseas), and British land use would have shifted to a higher proportion of trees. Wrigley (1988, pp. 54–55; 2009, pp. 92–94) has calculated that in order to produce as much energy from wood as it consumed from coal, Britain would have to have 13 percent of its land covered by woodlands in 1750, and by 1850 woodlands would have had to exceed its surface by 50 percent if it were to supply the energy used in that year. But such calculations ignore the possibility of using more energy-saving techniques or rearranging the composition of output toward less energy-intensive goods in a counterfactual coal-less world with expensive fuel, and do not allow for increases in imports of timber. To some extent, this is what happened: the value of timber imports increased almost 11-fold between 1784-86 and 1854-56, and grew from 4 percent to 6.4 percent of imports (Davis, 1979, pp. 110-11, 124-25). Just as Britain depended on American cotton, it could have industrialized using more Baltic and Canadian timber—at a cost, to be sure, but not a prohibitive cost.

Forestry, like every other sector, was affected by the enlightened economy, which suggests that in the absence of coal, timber-growing technology could have developed a great deal more than it did. New specimens imported from other parts of the world were introduced, and at the progressive estate of Thomas William Coke in Holkham, Norfolk, no fewer than two million seedlings of forty-nine varieties were introduced between 1781 and 1807. The origins of the increase in the use of coal are thus to be sought not only in a putative timber supply crisis, but above all in the improving technology of transporting and using the much more efficient fuel. Note, however, that just by being more physically efficient (in terms of calories per pound), coal did not automatically become more economically efficient. That depended on the costs of alternative fuels as well.

A slightly different way of thinking about the role of geography and its importance is to eschew such terms as a switch from an "organic" to a "mineral" economy, and to see how geographical accident focused the creative energies and attention of the innovative classes in certain directions. Useful knowledge was channeled into some trajectories and not others in part because of the demands of the physical environment. Coal mines, for instance, were not important just because they supplied a cheap high-quality fuel. In the eighteenth century mining should be regarded as one of the high-tech sectors of the British economy, attracting and creating engineering talents and spreading positive technological spillovers to other sectors, above all of course steam power. Newcastle's mines began adopting Newcomen engines in the 1710s, although they only became common after 1740. Coal viewers and engineers were the technological whizkids of their time, and often advised owners on their investment decisions. The most prominent among the viewers, such as Durham's John Buddle (1773–1843), became consultants with a nationwide clientele and rose to considerable prominence and prosperity. It was no accident that many of the early railroad engineers came originally from the mining sector.

Mines tended to flood, requiring constant pumping. Pumps are devices that by definition need to be built with a high degree of engineering accuracy and with high-quality materials, and that lent themselves to the application of the earliest steam engines. As such, mines operated as focusing devices, which directed the ingenuity of Britain's engineers towards a specific problem that needed solving. A few of these engineers then had the genius to recognize that the solution to the problem of flooding mines could be applied more generally to the problem of industrial power by converting the reciprocal motion that early steam engines provided into rotative motion and increasing the efficiency of engines sufficiently to allow them to operate in places other than at the pithead of coal mines. In other areas, too, the search for minerals directed the growth of useful knowledge, and prospecting was placed on a more rigorous basis by recognizing the regularities of stratigraphy and the creation of geological maps (Winchester, 2001).

Geographical accident also accounted for Britain's maritime economy, which created shipyards and high-quality carpentry, and stimulated ancillary industries such as sailcloth weaving, nail-making, and sawmills. It also stimulated instrument-making for navigation through a happy marriage of the precision of clockmakers and the computations of astronomers. The path-dependent nature of technology suggests that such coincidences can be at times quite fateful. The physical environment, then, should be seen as a steering mechanism rather than an engine of economic growth. But, as every driver knows, where one ends up and how quickly one gets there depend as much on steering as on the reliability and power of the engine. Without the engine, however, no amount of careful steering will do much good. Ireland, for example, was as close to the ocean as Britain, yet it never developed a maritime sector with the concomitant spillover effects.

Next to the ingenuity and single-mindedness of many of the successful British industrialists and entrepreneurs came their ability and willingness to learn from the ideas of others and put them to good use. Whatever vices one may accuse the Hanoverians of, cultural arrogance in the tradition of "not invented here" was not one of them. Many of the great insights and ideas that drove technological progress in this age came from the European continent. The silk-throwing mill of Thomas Lombe in Derby, patented in 1718 and erected in 1720, was a case in point, as it was based on techniques "borrowed" from Italy. In this age, of course, intellectual property rights were not enforced across national boundaries, and Britain shamelessly copied techniques it observed elsewhere just as others did hers. Its skilled craftsmen and mechanics then invariably experimented in further improvement and refinement. Jean Ryhiner, a Swiss manufacturer visiting Britain, remarked in 1766 that for a thing to be perfect it has to be invented in France and worked out in England (cited by Wadsworth and Mann, 1931, p. 413). In this, he may have been echoing a common view: Daniel Defoe had made the same point earlier, noting that "the English ... are justly fam'd for improving Arts rather than inventing" and elsewhere in his *Plan of English Commerce* that "our great Advances in Arts, in Trade, in Government and in almost all the great Things we are now Masters of and in which we so much exceed all our Neighbouring Nations, are really founded upon the inventions of others" (Defoe, [1726–27], 2001, p. 162). David Hume pointed out that "every improvement which we have made [in the past two centuries] has arisen from our imitation of foreigners ... Notwithstanding the advanced state of our manufacturers, we daily adopt, in every art, the inventions and improvements of our neighbours" (Hume, [1777], 1985, p. 328). These statements should be taken with a pound of salt. British manufacturers led in some of the cutting-edge techniques of the period such as the use of coal, steam, metals, and textiles, but lagged in other areas, above all in chemical knowledge, glass, paper, and high-end textiles.

When it did not lead, however, Britain displayed an uncanny ability to recognize the discoveries of others, make them work by eliminating the bugs and problems, and then exploit them profitably. When it imported an invention, such as the Leblanc's soda-making process, continuous paper-making, food canning, or chlorine bleaching, it improved it by a sequence of microinventions. An earlier example is that of the reverberatory furnace, first described by Vanoccio Biringuccio in 1540 in glassblowing, and adopted in Britain in the early seventeenth century. By 1700, this device had been adapted successfully to non-ferrous metals by unknown British skilled workmen before its famous adaptation to iron-puddling. Even the Lombe mill, cited above, relied on domestic competence for its finer details. The Derby engineer George Sorocold, much experienced in the construction of water works and one of the most active engineers of the first half of the eighteenth century, was involved in its construction. A century later, British textile mechanics absorbed and improved two of the most important French inventions in the textile industry, De Girard's wet-spinning process of flax, and Jacquard's loom.

In part the explanation of British leadership is simply that in the crucial years between 1780 and 1815 the Continent was thrown into turmoil, while British society kept the peace (albeit not without some harsh measures), its government staunchly supported innovators against technological conservatism, and its institutions provided a more effective (if far from watertight) system to reward enterprising and ingenious individuals. Moreover, the British system made it easier for ingenious and enterprising individuals to use the market to exploit their ideas. The weakness of craft guilds, controlling and constraining how individual craftsmen could exercise their skills, coupled with personal freedom and mobility, provided opportunities for resourceful and ambitious young individuals.

Effective use of knowledge, however, required not only access and incentives to create and access new technology, but also the *competence* to make use of it and to carry out the "instructions" contained in the blueprint of the technique. Much of the knowledge employed by artisans and engineers was "tacit," that is, not formally written down in the "recipe" used for production, but little tricks and know-how based on experience or imitation. John Harris (1992, p. 33) describes tacit skills as "unanalysable pieces of expertise, the 'knacks' of the trade," a point made long ago by Michael Polanyi (1962). Harris' view may have been conditioned by his knowledge of the coal and iron industry, but much of the same was true in hardware, textiles, instrument-making, and engineering. He notes that such skills at the time were taken for granted at home and thus noted mostly by foreign visitors, including industrial spies (ibid., p. 26; see also Harris, 1998). Harris singles out the competence of the British puddler, requiring not only skills but experience and "almost artistic judgement." He adds that foreigners would have a hard time importing this competence, because the British skilled worker was the repository of the knowledge. He absorbed the skills needed to work with coal and iron "with the sooty atmosphere in which he lived" and would find it hard to know even what needed to be explained (Harris, 1992, pp. 28, 30). John Kennedy, a Manchester cotton manufacturer, wrote in 1824 that it was impossible to use machinery "without having at hand people competent to its repair and management" (cited by Jacob and Reid, 2001, p. 293).

On the eve of the Industrial Revolution, Britain could rely on a comparatively large number of skilled mechanics and technicians, people who had been selected for their dexterity and mechanical gifts and trained as apprentices. Of course, other countries could count on such people as well, but Britain seems to have been particularly well endowed with them. Continental Europeans felt envious and frustrated, reflecting Leibniz's prophetic words, written in 1670: "It is not laudable that we Germans were the first in the invention of mechanical, natural, and other arts and sciences, but are the last in their expansion and betterment" (cited in William Clark, 1991). The French political economist Jean-Baptiste Say, a keen observer of the economies of his time, noted in 1803 that "the enormous wealth of Britain is less owing to her own advances in scientific acquirements, high as she ranks in that department, as to the wonderful practical skills of her adventurers in the useful application of knowledge and the superiority of her workmen" (Say,

[1803], 1821, Vol. 1, pp. 32–33). A Swiss visitor, César de Saussure, had noticed the same seventy-five years earlier: "English workmen are everywhere renowned, and justly. They work to perfection, and though not inventive, are capable of improving and of finishing most admirably what the French and Germans have invented" (de Saussure, [1726], 1902, p. 218, letter dated May 29, 1727). The great engineer John Farey, who wrote an important treatise on steam power, testified a century later that "the prevailing talent of English and Scotch people is to apply new ideas to use, and to bring such applications to perfection, but they do not imagine as much as foreigners" (Great Britain, 1829, p. 153). He added that this was the case because "the means of executing and applying inventions abroad are so very inferior to ours." Perhaps a more accurate assessment would be that foreigners—at least in the North Atlantic economies—did not imagine less than the British, but that the economic environment in which they operated did not provide the opportunities and incentives found in Britain.

What provided the opportunities was the large number of competent skilled craftsmen in Britain. Josiah Tucker, a keen contemporary observer, pointed out in 1758 that "the Number of Workmen [in Britain] and their greater Experience excite the higher Emulation, and cause them to excel the Mechanics of other Countries in these Sorts of Manufactures" (Tucker, 1758, p. 26). A volume (originally written by a Frenchman but updated by an Englishman) published in the mid-eighteenth century crowed that "None has more improved the mechanic arts ... here [in England] are made the best *Clocks, Watches, Barometers, Thermometers, Air Pumps and all sort of Mathematical Instruments* ... they have invented the use of cane chairs and several engines for printing stuffs and linen &c. Glass, Tin, Copper, Brass, Earthen and Hornware, they have improved to admiration ... they excel all nations in polishing iron and making many useful and bright utensils thereof" (Miège, [1701], 1748, p. 136).

A few of these highly skilled industrialists, engineers, and artisans are justly famous, even if they did not quite become national celebrities like James Watt and Richard Arkwright. We should mention above all the Darbys of Coalbrookdale in Shropshire, ironmasters, who supplied the cylinders for many Newcomen engines and built the great Iron Bridge over the Severn that opened in 1781, one of the most prominent technological "events" of the Industrial Revolution. There was John Wilkinson, whose Bradley works pioneered new boring machines that were able to produce the cylinders Boulton and Watt needed for their engines with unrivaled accuracy and who was one of the first to install an industrial steam engine to drive his bellows. There was Charles Gascoigne, who took over the failing Carron ironworks in Falkirk (Scotland) in the 1760s and rescued it through relentless improvement and prudent management. Gascoigne ended up running an ironworks in Russia, but the Carron works had turned into the largest iron-works in Europe in 1814, employing over 2,000 workers, and making the famous cannon known as *carronades* that helped defeat Napoleon. We should also mention

Arthur Woolf, the Cornish engineer and inventor of the compound steam engine, and Bryan Donkin, famous for his improvements to the mechanized papermaking machine, who was also the inventor of the tachometer, a steel nib pen, and the metal tin for canned food. In the machine industry, most notable were the mechanics Joseph Bramah and his gifted apprentice Henry Maudslay, often regarded as the fathers of British machine tool industry.

Some other skilled craftsmen, not quite as famous, were important or inventive enough to have left a record. Among them were mathematically sophisticated instrument makers such as the optician John Dollond (1707–61), who started off as a silk weaver and amateur optician, and ended up winning the Copley medal (1761) for his work on achromatic lenses; Francis Hauksbee (1688–1763), who was active as an instrument maker as well as a scientific lecturer and entrepreneur; John Hadley (1682–1744), a mathematician who built a new and more accurate navigational instrument named Hadley's quadrant (or octant); Thomas Yeoman, a civil engineer, millwright, and instrument maker whose technical competence helped make Stephen Hales' invention of the ventilator a reality; Jesse Ramsden (1735–1800), a top-notch instrument maker who designed surveying and measuring instruments of unprecedented accuracy and user-friendliness; and Edward Troughton (1753–1835) who became the best instrument maker in London after Ramsden's death. John Whitehurst was a member of the Lunar Society and later the keeper of stamps and weights in London. William Murdoch was Watt's trusted lieutenant and an extraordinary engineer. His inventions include, beside gas lighting and iron cement, major improvements to steam power and air-compressed pumps. Finally, consider Benjamin Outram, a Derbyshire engineer and entrepreneur, whose fame is based on his advocacy of iron rails as means of transportation, to the point where it was erroneously believed that the word "tram" was derived from his name. These persons were examples of the second layer on which the Hall of Fame inventors could rely.

An impressive degree of competence was achieved by millwrights. British (and especially Scottish) millwrights were often highly sophisticated engineers. William Fairbairn, himself trained as a millwright, noted that eighteenth-century British millwrights were "men of superior attainments and intellectual power," and that the typical millwright would have been "a fair arithmetician, knew something of geometry, levelling and mensuration and possessed a very competent knowledge of practical mechanics" (cited in Musson and Robinson, 1969, p. 73). John Rennie (1761–1821), who introduced the sliding hatch to the waterwheel and built some of London's greatest bridges, began his career as a millwright, as did his apprentice Peter Ewart (1767–1842), a millwright who worked for Boulton and Watt and later for the cotton spinner Samuel Oldknow, and who ended his career as Chief Engineer in His Majesty's dockyards. William Hazledine (1763–1840), a pioneering Shropshire ironmaster, whose works supplied large iron castings for structures, and Andrew Meikle, the Scottish inventor of the threshing machine, were also trained as millwrights.

Below them was a much larger third layer, an army of mostly anonymous artisans and mechanics, the unsung foot soldiers of the Industrial Revolution whose names do not normally appear in biographical dictionaries but who supplied that indispensable workmanship on which technological progress depended. These were craftsmen blessed by a natural dexterity, who possessed a technical *savoir-faire* taught in no school, but whose experience, skills, and practical knowledge of energy and materials constituted the difference between an idea and a product. They were mechanics, highly skilled clock and instrument makers, metalworkers, woodworkers, toymakers, glasscutters, and similar specialists, who could accurately produce parts of the precisely correct dimensions and materials, who could read blueprints and compute velocities, and who understood tolerance, resistance, friction, lubrication, and the interdependence of mechanical parts. These were the applied chemists who could manipulate laboratory equipment and acids, the doctors whose advice sometimes saved lives even if nobody yet quite understood why, the expert farmers who experimented with new breeds of animals, fertilizers, drainage systems, and fodder crops.

A few of these artisans have been rescued from their undeserved obscurity by diligent scholarship; one example is Alexander Chisholm, who served for three decades as the technical assistant of the itinerant lecturer William Lewis and then placed his skills as an experimental chemist and factory assistant at the service of Josiah Wedgwood (Stewart, 2008). A large number of these engineers and mechanics have been immortalized by Skempton et al. (2002) and these biographical compilations illustrate the unusual and impressive supply of dexterous and able men that Britain could count on. In a few cases, we can look into the management of a firm, to provide us with a glimpse of this phenomenon. When Newcomen came to the Midlands to install his steam-powered engine, he and his assistant were "at a loss about pumps, but being near Birmingham and having the assistance of so many ingenious and admirable workmen, they soon came to methods of making the pump-valves, clacks, and buckets" (Desaguliers, 1734–44, Vol. 2, p. 533). At the Boulton and Watt workshop in Soho, on which a fair amount is known, the highly skilled "turners" and the equally skilled "fitters" would require many years of apprenticeship and work as assistants before allowed to operate the equipment on their own (Roll, [1930], 1968, pp. 181–83). One example is John Southern, an able draftsman and mechanic, who worked his whole life for Boulton and Watt, where he was Watt's right-hand man (Crouzet, 1985, pp. 132–33). James Lawson was another trusted Soho employee given many important tasks despite poor health (Griffiths, 1992, p. 114). Reflecting on the supply of the craftsmen he employed, Watt noted in 1794 that many of them had been trained in analogous skills "such as millwrights, architects and surveyors," with the practical skills and dexterity spilling over from occupation to occupation (cited by Jones, 2008, pp.

126–27). The British economy, with its absence of restrictions on labor mobility, was unusually well suited to take advantages of these opportunities.

Britain was thus fortunate to possess a class of able and skilled people, larger and more effective than anywhere else. Techniques could not be realized without subcontractors who could supply parts and materials made accurately to specifications, and workers sufficiently "good with their hands" to be able to carry out plans from blueprints not just once but over and over again. In addition, the best of these anonymous but capable workers produced a cumulative flow of small, incremental, unrecorded, but indispensable microinventions that adapted inventions to local needs and circumstances and made them work better. Without them, Britain would not have become the workshop of the world. Not all of these artisans were in any observable way affected by the Industrial Enlightenment, of course. Many were interested in the technical details of their trade and little else. Much as in our own time, engineers were rarely intellectuals. Others were poorly educated craftsmen who became well known through their prodigious practical skills. Matthew Murray, one of the most brilliant mechanical engineers of his age and James Watt's arch-rival, was described as "structurally illiterate" (Skempton et al., 2002, p. 462) but he was probably an exception (Allen, 2009, p. 260). Competence and new ideas were complementary, the country needed both. And yet a surprising number of the people who did the heavy lifting in production were well educated and published articles on a variety of topics. John Kennedy (1769–1855), one of the most successful cotton manufacturers of Lancashire in the first decades of the nineteenth century and a skilled and inventive engineer himself, was an active member of the Manchester Literary and Philosophical Society and published among others a paper on the Poor Law and the effect of the cotton industry on the working classes.

The difference between Britain and other nations was not only in the level or prevalence of mechanical skills but in their *allocation* as well. On the Continent, the state (primarily the military) absorbed the lion's share of engineering talent. The crucial elements of Britain's technological leadership were both the presence of people of technical competence and their agenda. The British state did not usually take an aggressive position on what such persons should be doing. On much of the Continent, engineers served above all the state in the military, the civil service, teaching, and administration. An "engineer" in France was a military man. In Britain, men of comparable interests and abilities had to find employment in the private sector, designing more efficient mills and lighthouses, making more accurate watches, more efficient spinning machines, and looking for seams of coal. British science and scientists occupied a different position in society. The contrast between pragmatic scientists in the tradition of Bacon in Britain and the theoretical and abstract bent of French science in the Cartesian tradition is still considered valid by some historians (Kuhn, 1977, p. 137; see also Inkster, 1991, p. 42). Such generalizations are inevitably hazardous: many French intellectuals and scientists, above all the great Denis Diderot, admired Bacon and his work. By 1750 the empirical tradition advocated by the Anglophile Voltaire and his followers was triumphing everywhere in Europe, even if national styles differed. The commitment of French scientists such as Réaumur, Laplace, and Lavoisier to experimental and applied work renders such generalizations about national differences in scientific style questionable.

To sum up: in Britain the high quality of workmanship available to support innovation, local and imported, helped create the Industrial Revolution. It was especially in their competence, in the application, adaptation, and tweaking stages of invention, that Britain's skilled mechanics and engineers excelled. These skills were often tacit and could not be readily transferred from country to country. The French scientist and industrialist Jean-Antoine Chaptal noted that in many branches of manufacturing the British had become dominant, but that even after importing the machinery the French could not compete and sold at twice the price of the British because they lacked the immense details, the customs, and the "turns of hand" (dexterity) and that while the slow progress of industry could be accelerated by learned men, there was no substitute for experience (Chaptal, 1819, Vol. 2, pp. 430–31).

The supply of skills, moreover, seems to have been sufficient to cope with the increased demand for skills that the many new machines and mechanical devices required. If the Industrial Revolution was what economists call skill-augmenting, that is, the new techniques required more skills, and the supply of these skills had been limited, we would have observed a sharp increase in the so-called skill premium in the wages commanded by highly trained workers. The problem is of course that without estimating a complete model of the market for skills, the historical course of that ratio cannot be readily attributed to demand or supply factors. If, however, we assume that technology was the prime mover in this market and we keep in mind that the supply of skills will at best lag considerably behind a rise in wages (since the acquisition of skills takes time), it would stand to reason that if the Industrial Revolution led to a net increase in the demand for skilled labor, an increase in the skill premium at that time should have been observed. Yet what is known about the ratio of the wages of skilled workers to unskilled ones indicates clearly that the skill ratio declined fairly significantly between 1750 and 1850 (Clark, 2005, 2007). Indeed, research into the wage premium has established that it changed little over the long haul between 1450 and 1900, yet it was much lower in Western Europe than in either Southern and Eastern Europe or Asia, indicating perhaps that Europe was more capable of generating the kinds of skills and abilities we associate with human capital in an age in which literacy mattered less (Van Zanden, 2009). This was true a fortiori in Britain. Clearly, the supply of "skills" as a factor of production was quite elastic, but it is also consistent with an interpretation that British inventors and engineers were able to design equipment that front-loaded the ingenuity in the design and the tasks of a small number of highly trained workers, whereas the majority of operatives could be unskilled (see Mokyr, 2005b for details).

One key to British technological success, then, was that its rich endowment of competent skilled artisans gave it a comparative advantage in the adoption of new techniques and their improvement through microinventions. This may seem unorthodox to those who think of the Industrial Revolution in terms of macroinvention milestones reached by James Watt, Richard Arkwright, and Henry Cort, but it should be recalled that it is possible to have an absolute advantage in both areas and yet a comparative advantage in one, although it is not altogether clear whether Britain had an absolute advantage in macroinventions. A test of the hypothesis that Britain had a comparative advantage in microinventions is the establishment of net trade directions. Economies tend to specialize in the areas in which they have a comparative advantage. The British economy, roughly speaking, was a net importer of macroinventions and exporter of microinventions and minor improvements, often embodied in the many hundreds of British skilled workers and technicians who found their way to the Continent (Henderson, 1954) and in the many spies that continental nations sent to Britain in the eighteenth century to learn the fine details of industrial processes (Harris, 1998). After 1815, a stream of German and French visitors arrived in Britain, visiting industrial sites such as the Soho works in Birmingham. They were especially impressed by the sophisticated Portsmouth dockyard, designed during the war by one of Britain's master practical engineers, Henry Maudslay. This specialization is no more than a central tendency, but in broad lines the distinction stands up. Britain took its major inventions where it could find them, but whatever it borrowed it improved and refined. When continental economies in turn emulated Britain, they would often find their ideas vastly improved, refined, debugged, and made operational and economical.

As in all cases of international movement of goods, factors, and knowledge, there was imperfect specialization. Especially in the eighteenth century, a number of foreign inventors and craftsmen arrived in Britain just as British technicians and mechanics went to the Continent. The exchange of useful knowledge was always bi-directional, as one would expect in a trading area in which partners were not too dissimilar. Some of the foreign inventors and engineers who wound up in Britain indicate the nature of the migration: many of them arrived in Britain just before or during the revolutions in Europe, when they found the environment in their homelands less than conducive to their pursuits. Among those, the best known are the Swiss Aimé Argand, whose revolutionary lamp failed to interest Parisians and who went to Britain in the 1780s, where commercial fortune eluded him as well, despite his association with Matthew Boulton and the success of his invention. John Jacob Holtzappfel, born in Alsace, settled in London in 1787 and built a successful business making and selling lathes. The Swedish engineer and inventor John Ericsson came to Britain in 1826 and stayed until 1839 before leaving for the

United States. We could also mention John-Joseph Merlin, a Walloon, whose many patents included roller-skates, musical instruments, a rotisserie, and a wheelchair, and who was the technical genius behind James Cox's "Mechanical Museum" that opened in 1772 in Spring Gardens near Charing Cross, displaying various wondrous inventions. The Saxon coachbuilder Rudolph Ackermann (1764–1834), who perfected the steering mechanism of coaches, settled in Britain in 1787, where he built innovative carriages and pioneered colored plate books using advanced lithography. The most important imports from France were the Brunels, a father and son dynasty. Marc Isambard, the father, escaped France in 1793 (he had royalist sympathies and an English wife) and settled in London in 1799. While he found the freedom and opportunities to engage in a large number of innovative projects and became quite eminent, he did not become rich, and depended for income on his wife and later his son Isambard Kingdom Brunel, arguably the leading civil engineer of his age. In short, although Britain was a prime producer of technical knowledge, it also imported it when it had a chance to. But the net flow of skilled artisans went in the other direction, with a large number of British craftsmen finding positions in Continental firms as managers, engineers, and consultants.

But whence Britain's advantage? To understand the British advantage we need to understand how manufacturing was carried out in Europe before the Industrial Revolution. The bulk of it was produced by artisans catering largely to a local market—bakers, millwrights, tailors, blacksmiths, thatchers, shoemakers, carpenters, traditional craftsmen who carried out their trades in traditional Europe between the Vistula and the mountains of Donegal. Another class of skilled craftsmen such as drawloom operators, perfumers, watchmakers, potters and porcelain-makers, mirror and glass producers, wigmakers, confectioners, and armorers had traditionally catered to the rich and powerful, the military, and the most fortunate of them to the courts. By 1700, however, their clients were increasingly drawn from a broader, less elite population. These skilled workers were carefully selected and well trained through long apprenticeships and embodied the state-of-the-art industrial human capital of the age.

By the early eighteenth century, Britain had raised a class of craftsmen with skills that turned out to be of great importance later on. Three sectors in particular were of central importance. One group was clock and instrument makers, many of whom had emigrated to Britain from France after the revocation of the Edict of Nantes in 1685 (which abolished religious freedom for French Protestants), courtesy of religious bigotry and political idiocy. Huguenot artisans played an important role in eighteenth-century inventions (Landes, 1983, p. 219). Clock- and instrument makers were trained to be accurate and use the appropriate materials; they understood cogs, springs, pulleys, and levers, and learned the fine art of the possibilities and constraints of mechanics. Some of the great inventors of the eighteenth century were trained as clockmakers, including James Watt himself, John

Kay (not to be confused with his namesake who invented the flying shuttle) who provided critical technical assistance to Richard Arkwright, and Benjamin Huntsman, who developed the crucible steelmaking technique in 1740 that made Sheffield the world center of steelmaking for the next century. Most notable, no doubt, was John Harrison, whose marine chronometer (developed between 1735 and 1762) solved the problem of longitude at sea. Yet again, the ingenuity of one brilliant figure would have had no long-term consequences had it not been for the competence of less-known figures, who could carry out the winning design not once but over and over again, while introducing further improvements, and thus manufacture a reliable product at affordable prices. In the case of the marine chronometer, Harrison's prototypes were taken further by two clockmakers, Thomas Earnshaw and John Arnold, whose spring detent escapement mechanisms (invented between 1779 and 1783) made it possible to produce marine chronometers on a large scale. Another cluster of mechanics, as already noted, was created around Britain's ever-growing shipping industry: sawyers, shipwrights, carpenters, sail- and ropemakers, and makers of navigational instruments. That industry was protected by the Navigation Acts and buoyed by the rising level of commerce. A third industry, as already noted, was mining, which required specialized engineers, pumps, and iron rails as well as land surveyors. Mining, in the words of Donald Cardwell (1972, p. 74) concentrates some of the most difficult technological problems, such as water control, earth-moving, prospecting, chemistry, the cutting and fitting of wooden and metal parts, and the use of powerful machinery for hoisting, conveying, and so on. The seminal idea of moving carts on smooth rails (first made of wood, then iron) originated in mines. Miners and iron masters, thus, provided a large supply of skilled craftsmen. The successful adoption of Boulton and Watt steam engines in Cornwall after 1777 despite the high price of coal suggests that the binding constraint on the diffusion of these engines was the presence of local competence. The Cornish mining engineers, at first properly supervised by high-ranking personnel from Birmingham, rapidly learned to handle the engines and soon generated improvements that adapted them to local circumstances.

The pre-existence of such skills was essential if the machine was to become a serious competitor with human and animal strength, and if mass production of standardized goods was to take off. Louis Simond, a French-born American visitor at the beginning of the nineteenth century observed that "the English are great in practical mechanics, in no country in the world are there, perhaps, so many applications of that science" (Simond [1815], 1968, p. 123). These industries provided the kinds of skills that were essential during the Industrial Revolution. Britain's position as a technological leader in Europe before 1850 depended to a very large degree on the presence of these artisans. Even in Britain, where there were more of them than elsewhere, the very best artisans were highly prized, and successful employers—most notably Boulton and Watt—jealously protected them from would-be poachers, and the laws purporting to prevent their emigration reflected this perception.

These supply factors explain much. Yet the development and transmission of these skills were also dependent on the existence of adequate demand. In a very poor or extremely unequal society, where the vast bulk of the population lives dangerously close to the margin of subsistence and spends most of its income on food, shelter, and bare necessities, one would not expect a class of clockmakers or fine pottery makers to emerge. What set Britain apart was the emergence of a substantial middle class before the Industrial Revolution, a large group of merchants, professionals, well-to-do farmers, and artisans who would vaguely fall into the modern notion of a middle class. These people consumed more consumer durables and other "middle-class goods" that demanded a high level of precision skills, from clocks to music boxes to porcelains to tapestries, and thus provided for the cadres of craftsmen (themselves equally middle class) whose abilities were essential if the innovative ideas of inventors were actually to be realized and to work as designed. The demand for consumer durables in the century before the Industrial Revolution shifted from an emphasis on the quality of the materials to an emphasis on workmanship (De Vries, 2008, p. 146). To satisfy this demand, a high level of skills had to be present among Britain's top artisans. James Watt, the ultimate instrument maker, advertised his ability as the maker of "all sorts of mathematical and musical instruments, with a variety of toys," which in Glasgow in the 1760s must have had a constituency (cited by Hart, 1949, p. 63).

Some modern scholars feel that artisans could have carried out most of the changes in technology needed for economic change (Berg, 2007; Hilaire-Pérez, 2007). Artisans were an essential ingredient in the growth of useful knowledge, and they were a large part of Britain's advantage. All the same, by themselves they were unlikely to generate an industrial revolution. What was needed was just the right combination of useful knowledge generated by scientists, engineers, and inventors with the existing supply of skilled craftsmen and an institutional environment that produced the correct incentives for entrepreneurs. A purely artisanal-knowledge society will eventually revert to a technological equilibrium in contrast to a society where the world of artisans is constantly shocked by infusions of new knowledge from outsiders. The history of steam illustrates this. Newcomen was by all accounts an artisan, and his ability to create a revolutionary device having been apprenticed as an engineer in Exeter struck contemporaries. J.T. Desaguliers, while giving Newcomen and his assistant John Calley full credit for getting their machine to work, added condescendingly that although "not being either philosophers to understand the reason, or mathematicians enough to calculate the powers and to proportion the parts, very luckily by accident found what they sought for" (Desaguliers, 1734–44, Vol. 2, p. 533). Steam became more than a pump only after better-trained minds like Smeaton and Watt turned to the task of improving it, and the continued exchange between technique and science gradually picked up momentum.

Improvements often depended on generalizations based on wide (and not just deep) knowledge, or an insight drawn from a very different area, which was unlikely to emanate from specialized craftsmen. William Lewis, a lecturer specializing in chemical experiments, noted that "all the arts have common principles but it would be in vain to expect the knowledge from those who exercise these arts, each of whom knows only the application of those principles to his own art ... 'Tis only by bringing the arts as it were to approach one another that we can make advances toward perfections." Moreover, he wrote, "the discoveries and improvements made in one art and even its common processes are generally little known to those employed in another, so that the workman can seldom avail himself of the advantages which he may receive from the correlative arts" (Lewis, 1763, pp. xiii–xiv). Postlethwayt (1774, entry on *Arts*) felt that "the greatest improvements in manufactural and mechanical arts, have been more owing to the real inventions of the learned ... than to the mechanics, manufacturers, and artificers themselves." Adam Smith heartily agreed. Artisans in the standard sense of the word were indispensable to inventors by building designs to specification and making complex mechanisms work, and work better. In that sense, there was a deep complementarity between competence and the growth of "useful knowledge" and it is the access to both that made Britain the technological leader of Europe.

Competence was a resource that was subject to considerable depreciation, as skilled artisans aged and died. The transmission of their skills from generation to generation in eighteenth-century Britain was carried out primarily by the apprenticeship system. Skilled artisans produced not only high-quality goods, but also more skilled artisans. Skills and other forms of human capital are odd economic entities. The market for them suffers from a number of difficulties that each generation has to solve. In part the problem has to do with credit markets; young people were in a poor position to borrow unless they could use their future earnings or services as collateral, which is what indentures did. Another problem is that while it was the youngster's fate that was being decided, the parents or guardians were normally the ones who made the decision. When parents were deceased or incompetent, the child's future was endangered. For that reason, British local authorities felt responsible for the so-called pauper apprentices, who could be placed with householders even against their will. Pauper apprentices were child-laborers, and were unlikely to receive much training. Justices of the Peace had a fair amount of authority over these children, as did Poor Law guardians, and the typical British institutions of poor relief and apprenticeship thus overlapped. Finally, the terms of the contract between the apprentice and the master could not be fully specified, the items exchanged were hard to measure, and the exchange was not contemporaneous, so that hold-up problems and apprentices absconding or masters not properly treating or training a boy after receiving a fee from the parents were all too common. Wallis (2008) has shown that a large number of apprentices left their masters before completing their term. Many of these early separations, he points out, were probably by mutual consent and may mean little more than that the seven-year rule imposed by the statute was irrelevant. Training took place as much by example and imitation as by any kind of systematic instruction. In other countries, powerful craft guilds often helped enforce the rules of master–apprentice relations. In Britain, in most trades, guilds were losing or abandoning this responsibility in the eighteenth century. We might expect, therefore, that this system would have seriously misfired and that the supply of skilled artisans in the British economy would be deficient. In fact, as we saw, the reverse was the case. Apprenticeship did not need guilds to be enforced, and may in fact have been a more efficient training tool in the absence of guilds.

Some scholars (e.g., Humphries, 2003; 2009, ch. 8) have maintained that the system of British apprenticeship was one of the institutions that set Britain apart and that explains the unique concentration of "practical skills" and dexterous craftsmen who helped make the Industrial Revolution. British law required that a formal contract had to be drawn up between an apprentice (or his parents) and the master who taught him the trade (needless to say, these contracts were subject to a stamp tax). Such a contract was fraught with difficulties, and in practice complaints about violation of the contract were rampant as the cases apprentices and masters brought against one another attest (Rushton, 1991). In fact, however, it is possible that the sources tend to highlight the atypical. Mitch (2004, p. 340) estimates that in 1700 more than a quarter of all males aged 21 had completed an apprenticeship. Another estimate is that in the eighteenth century no fewer than two-thirds of all boys completed their apprenticeships (Humphries, 2009, ch. 9, table 9.1). These estimates are very rough, but they suggest all the same that the institution was highly functional. Humphries (2003) has argued that the terms of the contract were in the interest of both master and apprentice; in other words, the contract was self-enforcing. As much as was possible, the arrangement provided good incentives for both sides to honor their agreement, and although a substantial proportion of apprenticeships were abrogated, the institution still served its purpose as the main channel through which artisans transferred their know-how to the next generation. In this regard, at least, modern scholarship has reversed the views of Adam Smith who thought the long apprenticeships "altogether unnecessary" ([1776], 1976, Vol. 1, p. 139).

As noted, a respectable tradition in economic history has maintained that the guild system was central to ensuring that skills were transmitted across generations. It is not easy to find much support for this view in the British experience. L.D. Schwarz has remarked that the British guilds' control over apprenticeship withered away, but that the institution of apprenticeship remained (Schwarz, 1992, p. 218). It is hard to say when this took place precisely, and it clearly differed from town to town and from trade to trade (Berlin, 2008). Snell (1985) has noted that there are few other historiographical topics in which such a wide variety of contradictory views prevails over the basic facts as the decline of British guilds in the eighteenth century. More than anything else, the reduction in their power to exclude others was hastened by mobility; many of the activities that urban craft guilds controlled could and did move out of their geographic sphere to the countryside or to towns free from guild control. New trades and most rural areas were rarely covered by guild regulations, and thus the existing arrangements favored innovation. Formal guilds were often replaced by informal associations of artisans that tried to guarantee quality standards by means of voluntary compliance.

British guilds were far from uniformly hostile to technological progress, and even when they tried to they often failed to stem the progress they feared. The desperate attempts of provincial tailors' guilds in Britain to prevent the diffusion of ready-made clothing in the early eighteenth century, often among its own members, is evidence of their growing inability to enforce the exclusionary restrictions that stifled economic change elsewhere in Europe (Lemire, 1997, pp. 44–49). Some historians who believe in the "proto-industrial model" have argued that much of the rise of rural domestic industry was prompted by an attempt to escape the stranglehold of urban guild regulations. It seems more plausible that industry moved away from the cities in search of cheap labor and space, and this weakened the guilds. The London guilds, known as "livery companies" saw their powers erode when economic activity moved to the suburbs such as Whitechapel and Spitalfields. All the same, these guilds had remarkable staying power and like many British institutions displayed a remarkable agility and a capacity to change with the times.

Some guilds required an apprentice to complete his term before he was admitted to membership. If the apprentice was anxious to stay in the same location, this arrangement would indeed spur him to make the effort to complete his term. This stricture was repealed in 1814, but the institution of apprenticeship survived and adapted well to the changes in economic circumstances in the nineteenth century. Apprenticeship contracts seem to have worked quite well in locations in which there were few guilds, such as Birmingham. In such locations the contract was informal and usually based on verbal agreements and trust. The institution continued to survive deep into the nineteenth century when guilds had for all practical purposes disappeared from the scene. Clearly, it was an example of the kind of well-functioning informal, private-order institution, on which much of the British economy depended.

By the second half of the eighteenth century, the inherent flexibility and responsiveness of British institutions to changing circumstances can be observed as apprenticeship was changing as the needs of the economy changed. Apprentices were "bound" by law to their masters for seven years, and their masters were expected to teach them the mysteries and tricks of a craft but also to imbue them with moral and religious values. The institution of indentured apprenticeship, in which an apprentice had to work for his master after the completion of his training, indicates that this was a valuable investment in human capital. The parents often paid extra for room and board when the apprentice was "indoor." After 1750 such arrangements declined, and in urban areas more and more apprentices remained with their parents. Especially in urban areas, "clubbing-out" apprenticeships became a more common form in the late eighteenth century. Apprentices started to receive some wages toward the end of their term, to induce them to stay with the master. Other potential rewards that induced them not to renege on the contract included marriage with a relative of the master and by the eighteenth century even becoming a partner. Those apprentices who stayed with their master and completed their term would acquire a local reputation as "trustworthy," a valuable asset in an economy in which such a reputation was a key to commercial success. They would also gain "settlement," a form of local citizenship in a parish that entitled them to poor relief if needed.

As larger enterprises emerged in the eighteenth century, the best apprentices could be promoted within the firm, as happened at such modern enterprises as Boulton's Soho works or Wedgwood's Etruria pottery. On the other hand, in industries that required few skills, the rules were little enforced. In 1777, fewer than 10 percent of calico printers were trained this way; it simply was no longer necessary. On the other hand, some apprentices were trained by multiple masters if their skills required it. Thus Watt's advice that a lad training to be a civil engineer should be "put out to a Cabinet Maker when he is 14 to learn to use his hands, and practice Geometry ... at the same time he should work in a smith's shop to learn to forge and file" (cited by Robinson, 1962, p. 196). The length of the apprenticeship declined sharply in the second half of the eighteenth century (Snell, 1985, p. 235).

To some extent, then, the presence of these skills in Britain was a historical contingency, to some extent the result of a well-functioning private-order economic institution, the apprenticeship system. Whatever it was, the capabilities of Britain in the age of the Industrial Revolution were determined by historical realities and by the institutions governing its economy in the previous century. Yet the old institutions that had worked so well in the past were being replaced as part of the new economy. New entrants in the market for skills threatened the venerable institution of indentured apprentices (nominally for a fixed term of fourteen years), and skills were increasingly imparted in other ways than the traditional formal apprenticeship mechanism. Growing concerns among vested interests about this threat to the status quo led to some half-hearted attempts to strengthen the moribund institutions of the past. The Spitalfields Act of 1773, for instance, prohibited London silk weavers from engaging more than two apprentices (Clapham, 1916). Such restrictive legislation, however, flew in the face of an increasingly predominant liberal economic ideology, and the Spitalfields Act was revoked in 1824, under the influence of David Ricardo and William Huskisson. By the middle of the nineteenth century in many industries the difference between "apprentices" and "workers" had become negligible (Kirby, 2003, pp. 66–67). To be sure, in the absence of high-quality vocational and technical schools to teach advanced skills, the mechanics and the engineers on whom the British manufacturing sector relied were still instructed in the old-fashioned way. But the distribution of skills became more and more skewed, and for a growing number of industrial workers the skills required for employment were less important than attitudes and behavior.

Over the eighteenth century, British manufacturing became increasingly tolerant of and hence more conducive to innovation. In these years some people were becoming specialized inventors, worthy precursors of Henry Bessemer and Thomas Edison. John Wyatt, famous for the first spinning machine, is also known for having invented a gun barrel boring machine and other contraptions. His spinning machine (patented jointly with Lewis Paul in 1738) did not yet work properly, but it was a harbinger of things to come. Obviously a large number of people were concerned with the problem of mechanical spinning. The same can be discerned in the iron industry: in the decades before Henry Cort, a large number of iron masters were at work in trying to refine pig iron into wrought iron, the process of "potted iron" becoming quite successful through a string of inventions made by a variety of now mostly forgotten ironmasters (such as the Cranage brothers employed by Richard Reynolds and Abraham Darby III at Coalbrookdale) who improved the wrought iron process before it was eventually replaced by Cort's (Hyde, 1977). The concept of a full-time inventor who took it upon himself to solve a problem became a feature of British industrial society. John Kay, the inventor of the spectacularly successful flying shuttle (which he failed to protect against patent-encroachers), invented among other things a windmill for raising water and a method for making salt "without much fire." Samuel Crompton, the inventor of the mule, wrote that he spent "four and a half years at least wherein every moment of time and power of mind as well as expense which my other employment would permit were devoted to this one end" (cited by Baines, 1835, p. 199). Crompton never took out a patent for his invention, and was later compensated by Parliament in recognition of his contribution. By the end of the eighteenth century, the Industrial Enlightenment lent such persons both respectability and employment.

It is important to stress that the Industrial Revolution was the creation of an elite, a relatively small number of ingenious, ambitious, and diligent persons who could think out of the box, and had the wherewithal to carry out their ideas and to find others who could assist them. This is not to return to the heroic interpretations of the Victorian hagiographers such as Samuel Smiles and credit a few famous individuals with the entire phenomenon. As Lucas (2002, p. 170) notes, "a small group of leisured aristocrats can produce Greek Philosophy or Portuguese navigation but that is not the way the Industrial Revolution came about." The great British inventors stood on the shoulders of those who provided them with the tools and workmanship. All the same, even these pivotal people were a minority, perhaps a few tens of thousands of elite workers, well trained through apprenticeships supplemented sometimes by informal studies. In the machine industry, a few firms such as Boulton & Watt, Maudslay & Field, and Matthew Murray & Woods (in Leeds) attracted many of the most talented apprentices, and clearly were of substantial importance to the generation and dissemination of innovations. Henry Maudslay's workshop in London has been called the "Mecca of aspiring young engineering" (Musson, 1980, p. 90).

In this sense, too, the history of technology appears much like an evolutionary system. It is the exception, the deviant, the aberration that is the agent of change. Rare events and unusual individuals get amplified and become critical elements in the process of change. Much as it may go against our democratic instincts, the bulk of British workers in the period may not have mattered much to the Industrial Revolution. The average "quality" of the majority of the labor force – in terms of their technical training—may thus be less relevant to the development and adoption of the new techniques than is commonly believed. The distribution of knowledge within society was highly skewed, but as long there was enough action in the upper tail of the distribution and as long as access costs to knowledge were sufficiently low, such a skewness would not impede further technological progress. There is evidence that contemporaries realized this: the Leeds machinery maker, Peter Fairbairn (younger brother of the more famous engineer William Fairbairn) testified in 1841 that the subdivision of labor he practiced enabled him to use inferior workers along with a "good many very superior men" (Great Britain, 1841, p. 211, q. 3113).

To sum up: Britain became the leader of the Industrial Revolution because, more than any other European economy, it was able to take advantage of its endowment of human and physical resources thanks to the great synergy of the Enlightenment: the combination of the Baconian program in useful knowledge and the recognition that better institutions created better incentives (Mokyr, 2006b). The British Enlightenment, being on the whole more practical and pragmatic, may have given it some advantage over other economies. Such differences are hard to measure, and their overall impact is unclear. What is clear is that in Britain the Enlightenment was able to find a more peaceful accommodation with the political status quo. The cartoon of Enlightenment intellectuals as a determined and coherent band of intellectuals struggling against the *ancien régime* was nowhere more absurd than in Britain. In Britain these intellectuals rarely took extreme radical positions, mostly accepted and even embraced religion, and managed to get reforms instituted from within. On the Continent, to be sure, many Enlightenment intellectuals, too, were hardly operating as underground subversives. Many of the leading *philosophes* were comfortable and influential. Even when they ran afoul of the regime, relations rarely degenerated into hostility. This "cosy fraternizing with the enemy," as Gay (1966, p. 24) put it, led to attempted reforms before 1789, but most of these ran into powerful opposition and failed (Scott, 1990). The point is that in Britain the state was not the enemy, at least not before the Jacobin scares of the 1790s. Ideas circulated freely, and they affected culture, institutions, and daily life in myriad ways. The difference, then, was that Britain got there earlier than its European competitors, and did not get sidetracked nearly as much between 1789 and 1815. But eventually other nations saw what had worked for Britain, found their own ways to implement a similar program, and caught up. The Anglophilia of the continental Enlightenment reflected the realization that Britain had something going for it that other nations lacked. The French mathematician Charles Dupin (1784–1873), who visited Britain in the 1810s, wondered about the sources of British prosperity which "behoves us to know as Frenchmen for the advantage of France." He pointed out that "the successes obtained in the government of the arts, [are] similar to the successes in the government of men" (Dupin, 1825, Vol. 1, p. xi).

CHAPTER 7

Technological Change in the Industrial Revolution

The Industrial Revolution was not confined to a single industry and affected a significant number of products and processes. However, change was uneven, with some parts of the manufacturing sector or even some processes in the same industry subject to mechanization and technological progress at different rates and times. By 1850, a substantial number of industries had been transformed. Some had moved early, whereas others were but lightly affected by the changes around them. The full modernization of industry moved into high gear during the so-called second Industrial Revolution, which is generally reckoned to have started around 1860 or so. The industries affected by the second Industrial Revolution were steel, electricity, chemicals, mass-produced interchangeable-parts production engineering. The possibilities that improvements in these areas held for the economy were already perceived in the first half of the nineteenth century, but they were still out of reach in 1850. All the same, it is conceivable that these advances could have been realized without the foundations laid before 1850.

In the popular mind, the Industrial Revolution of the eighteenth century is most widely associated with steam power. This is both correct and misleading. It is correct, because the steam engine was one of the most revolutionary inventions ever made by humans, and one that was to have enormous consequences in later years. It was seen as such by contemporaries, and its symbolic significance is wholly deserved. The great French scientist Sadi Carnot, widely regarded as the founder of the science of steam power (now known as thermodynamics), wrote in 1824 that "to take away England's steam engines today would amount to robbing her of her iron and coal, to drying up her sources of wealth, to ruining her means of prosperity and destroying her great power" (Carnot, 1824, p. 4). The steam engine was an Enlightenment machine par excellence. It was a spectacular device. It demonstrated the power that could be harnessed thanks to the control that people could exercise over nature, and it stimulated the popular imagination by its force, its noise, and the sheer novelty it represented. With the benefit of nineteenth-century physics we can acquiesce: it constituted the first controlled conversion of heat into work and opened up an unprecedented opportunity for harnessing minerals that supplied motive power to production instead of just heat.

Very little in human history comes close in terms of its sheer impact on the human material condition.

The steam engine, then, remains in our mind the defining invention of the Industrial Revolution. It had the power to relieve workers from the drudgery of hard, repetitive, physical labor as well as make the people who introduced it more prosperous. Consumers, facing lower prices and eventually better goods and services, may have secured the greatest benefits. In the very long run, there can be little doubt that they did so, as steam helped drive much of large-scale manufacturing as of 1850, as well as an increasing proportion of transport. It is important to stress, however, that during the classic years of the Industrial Revolution the immediate impact of steam power on industry and productivity was fairly limited. Much of what steam did before 1830 could have been (and to a large extent was) readily carried out by alternative sources of inanimate power, especially water power. Calculations measuring the so-called social savings (the net economic benefit of steam compared to the next best technology) have shown that the impact of steam power on the overall economy was slight before 1830 (von Tunzelmann, 1978; Crafts, 2004).

These statements are only contradictory if we expect technological progress to consist of radical innovations that have a major impact on a wide segment of the economy. Such "General Purpose Technologies" are rare, but when they occur they tend to affect much of the economy because they can be combined with a large number of existing techniques in addition to spawning many novel uses. The best example is perhaps the microprocessor, which has entered our lives in a myriad ways, whether as consumers or producers. Some historians have thought of steam as such a technology. Steam was definitely a multi-purpose technology, used in a number of industries (mining, textiles, pottery, sawmills, and food processing) and later in railroads and steamships. But it did not enter consumers' homes, and left much of the economy such as agriculture, construction, and most manufacturing untouched. Its impact, of course, grew over time. As late as 1770, the wasteful Newcomen machines were almost exclusively used for pumping water out of coal mines in places where coal was very cheap. The improvements introduced by Watt and others after 1769 turned it into a source of industrial power. Watt's famous improvements—the separate condenser, double-acting, steam-jacketing, and the sun-and-planet gears—greatly increased the steam engine's efficiency, versatility, and reliability, and made it easier to install, maintain, and repair. Eventually high pressure, compounding, and other improvements made steam a source of power in transport as well, but the first railroads date from 1830 and steam power on the oceans only became truly significant in the mid-1850s with the development of the screw propeller and the compound marine steam engine built by Glaswegian John Elder, in close cooperation with William Rankine.

Although its full economic effects were slow to be realized, steam power still became an inexorable force in determining the shape of modern society. Steam power could not have come into existence without the very rudimentary scientific discoveries that underlay it, many of them developed on the Continent (including the first model of a steam engine, built by Denis Papin). Its main achievement was to convert heat (thermal energy) into controllable work (kinetic energy), which is what any engine does. This idea is one of the most remarkable technological achievements humanity has ever made. It was bandied about in the last third of the seventeenth century, but not fully realized until the completion of Thomas Savery's "Miner's Friend" of 1705 (less of an engine than a steam-driven vacuum pump) and more importantly Thomas Newcomen's famous Dudley Castle machine completed in 1712, a spectacular achievement, clumsy and inefficient as it may seem today. Our planet provides us with large amounts of energy, and harnessing it is in large part what production technology is all about. What steam power and its descendants, internal combustion, diesel engines, and the turbine, all did was to utilize stored-up energy in coal and oil, and turn it into work. Before, people had been able to harness heat (by burning) and work (by utilizing animals, water, and wind), but not convert one into the other. The idea was so radical that it took many years for physicists and engineers to fully realize the enormity of their achievement. Subsequent engineers such as Smeaton, Watt, Woolf, and Trevithick worked long and hard to make engines more efficient and more versatile and to convert the reciprocating motion of early engines into the rotary motion that industrial processes required. The full theoretical understanding of what an engine was, how steam power worked, and how one form of energy was transformed into another, however, did not become clear until the middle of the nineteenth century. As late as 1827 John Farey, the best contemporary expositor of the mechanical details of the steam engine, still regarded the steam engine as a vapor-pressure engine rather than a heat engine. Ten years later the French engineer François Marie Pambour wrote his *Théorie de la machine à vapeur*, which became the standard work and was translated into German and English under the same premise.

All this changed by the middle of the nineteenth century. In 1843 the Mancunian James Prescott Joule published a famous paper showing the equivalence of heat and work, and by the late 1840s the ideas of thermodynamics took shape and finally straightened out what the engine really did. The efficiency (or "duty," measured as pounds of water raised one foot through the burning of one bushel of coal) of steam engines rose from 28 million lbs in 1820 to 80 million lbs in 1859 (Hills, 1989, p. 131), but the capital costs of steam power remained more or less constant in the 1830s and 1840s, and only in the second half of the nineteenth century did steam power have measurable effect on productivity in the British economy. Crafts (2004) estimates that the social savings due to steam engine improvements were still only 0.3 percent of GDP a year in the years 1830–50 and less before that, but jumped to 1.2 percent in the decades 1850–70.

The effects of technological innovation, as Arthur Clarke once said, are overrated in the short run but underestimated in the long run.

Yet steam was only a part of the energy revolution. Perhaps one of the best clues to the nature of the Industrial Revolution is that the technology that most closely competed with steam, water power, also improved immensely during these years, and for much the same reasons: people with scientific interests, mathematical skills, and the ability to experiment, compute, and make inferences, became interested in understanding what water mills did and what determined their efficiency. Their findings were eventually translated into improved machinery. In Britain, the most important improvements in water power were due to two engineers, John Smeaton and John Rennie. They designed the so-called breast wheel that combined the advantages of the more efficient overshot waterwheels with the flexibility and adaptability of the undershot waterwheel. The increased use of iron parts and the correct setting of the angle of the blades also increased efficiency. The French engineer Poncelet designed the so-called Poncelet waterwheel using curved blades. Theoretical hydraulics gradually merged with the practical design of waterwheels. The desire for improvement through experimentation and careful analysis of data backed whenever possible by formal reasoning, the essence of the Enlightenment, was the driving force behind the improvement of *all* power technology. Water power was perhaps not a winner, and in the long run lost out to engines that burned fossil fuels, yet it could be and was improved in an age that improved whatever could be improved. Even wind power, despite its general unsuitability to industry, was experimented with. Smeaton built a wind-powered oil mill in Wakefield in 1755, and the British adopted a few wind-driven paper mills from the Netherlands, and a wind-powered spinning mill existed in Stockport in 1791. Wind power could not provide the constant speed required for textile mills and was eventually abandoned as a source of industrial power (Hills, 1994, pp. 177, 190, 210), but at the time it seemed worth investigating.

The other industry most widely associated with the Industrial Revolution was cotton. Unlike energy or chemicals, textile machinery involved little complex science requiring mathematical formulation, and the new technology required no principles that "would have puzzled Archimedes" as Donald Cardwell (1994, p. 186) once put it. But here, too, improvements involved a familiarity with techniques used in other activities, a reliance on experimentation, manual dexterity, and a belief that things could be made better and that personal advantages could be secured if an improvement turned out to be a success. Spinning was of course an ancient skill, but despite the introduction of spinning wheels and some other advances in the Middle Ages, it still was a manual activity, in which the human fingers were essential in imparting the "twist" that made the yarn. Three names will remain forever associated with the breakthrough that liberated spinning from its digital dependence. First, Richard Arkwright, the inventor of the so-called throstle, which used rollers to draft out the fibers, realizing (as Wyatt had not) that he needed two pairs of rollers spaced at a proper distance. The distance between the rollers had to be adjusted to the length (or "staple") of the cotton. Arkwright also used lead weights on the rollers to prevent uneven drawing of the cotton. The strong yarns produced by these machines were suitable for the warp of the cotton fabric, a substantial improvement. The second was James Hargreaves, the inventor of the famous jenny that twisted the yarn by rotating spindles that pulled the rovings from their bobbins, with metal draw bars playing the role of human fingers guiding the spun yarn onto the spindles by means of a so-called faller wire. The jenny was a small and cheap machine that was used by small producers and the smaller models easily fitted in the cottages of domestic spinners: by 1811 over 150,000 of them were in use (Hills, 1970, pp. 58–59). Third, Samuel Crompton, who in 1779, after many years of hard work, combined the two in the aptly called mule which provided the optimal combination of the high-quality yarn made by the throstle and the speed of the jenny. The mule became one of the most famous inventions of all time and competed with steam power for the title of paradigmatic invention of the Industrial Revolution. It was at once a *process* innovation, that allowed the production of cotton yarn at far lower costs than before, and a *product* innovation in that the quality of the product (fine yarn) was such that Britain's cotton industry could out-compete the very fine Indian yarns known as muslins. Between 1779 and 1850, scores of incremental improvements were introduced in the mule, and endless mechanical problems in its operation were resolved by ingenious mechanics and technicians, most of whom remain obscure.

Yet cotton-spinning, much like steam, was only the first among equals. Improvement was spread throughout the cotton industry—and in other textiles as well—and new machinery was introduced, some of it improving and rivaling the cotton-spinning machines, some of it complementing them and resolving technological bottlenecks in production. In the temporal order of preparing textiles, spinning comes after carding and before weaving. Carding is the process in which cotton is combed and wound on rovings on which the fibers are strung out parallel to one another. Six years after patenting his throstle, Arkwright patented a carding machine. Cotton also required weaving, bleaching, and printing, as well as the ginning of the raw material; in all of those processes, advances were made before the eighteenth century was out. Weaving turned out to be the most difficult to mechanize, and as spinning machines turned out ever larger supplies of yarn to be woven, handloom weavers for a few decades experienced a golden age of high demand for their services. Handlooms were improved, for instance, by the introduction of the dandy loom in 1802 invented by Thomas Johnson, a good example of the kind of highly competent and ingenious mechanics that gave Britain a comparative advantage in microinventions. Johnson, "an ingenious young man" who was known as "the conjuror" by his fellow mechanics, worked for William Radcliffe in Stockport, and another invention, the dressing machine allowed the warp to be dressed before it was put on the loom, increasing the productivity of a handloom weaver by as much as 50 percent (Day and McNeil, 1996, pp. 386, 583; Timmins, 1998, p. 130). Such inventions did not lead to large-scale steam-powered fully mechanized factories, but they demonstrate the ability of well-focused research efforts to solve recognized bottlenecks. When the technical problems involved in the power loom—first conceived by Edmund Cartwright in 1785—were gradually resolved after 1815, in large part due to the brilliant work of Richard Roberts, the mechanization of the cotton industry became inevitable. Cotton production grew at an astonishing rate, and it was transformed from an exotic but marginal fabric to the centerpiece of the British textile industry.

The precise causes of the spectacular success of the British cotton industry seem to be reasonably well understood. O'Brien, Griffiths, and Hunt (1991) have suggested that despite the Calico Act, the cotton industry in Lancashire and Derbyshire (supposedly producing only mixed fabrics such as fustians) was sufficiently large to make experimentation in cotton worthwhile. In the 1736 Manchester Act, Parliament explicitly watered down the Calico Act to allow the wearing of fustians and other printed mixed fabrics, thus creating enough of an opening for cotton yarn to make experimentation on mechanical cotton spinning worthwile (Ormrod, 2003, p. 172). However, it is hard to see how the *passing* of these laws rather than their *weakening* were instrumental in stimulating the mechanized cotton industry after 1760.

In any event, by the middle of the eighteenth century, cotton was still a marginal industry compared with wool. What accounted for its success was not so much the protection provided to local industry (which would have been more consistent with a huge expansion of the fustian industry, which the Calico Act was supposed to protect) as the special characteristics of cotton fibers that made its mechanical spinning an easier (though not easy) problem to solve than for linen or wool. Cotton had to be imported, but was elastically supplied from North America, the result of the large reserves of suitable land in the south of what was to become the United States, the cotton gin, and the presence of a large slave population in exactly those areas suitable for cotton cultivation. On the demand side, cotton could be dyed, printed, and laundered easily and was felt to be comfortable and fashionable. As we have seen, the ingenuity of skilled British engineers and craftsmen was a main reason why this industry took off in Britain before it did anywhere else. Its access to overseas raw materials was also a contributing factor. Yet we should not succumb to the "hindsight bias" that would lead us to believe that just because these problems were solved in Britain, they could not have been solved elsewhere; continental inventors, after all, made major contributions to textile technology in all other fabrics and there was little that Crompton or Cartwright did that was beyond the capability of the best continental mechanics.

Other textiles could not but be influenced by what happened in cotton, but because the physical properties of wool, linen, and silk differed from those of cotton, the rate at which technical bottlenecks were resolved differed from material to material and from process to process. Thus in the worsted (combed wool) industry the cotton-spinning machinery worked well, but the combing process itself turned out to be a difficult technology to mechanize. Mechanical weaving of woolen fibers was difficult and handloom weaving in wool survived longer than in cotton. The problem for woolen manufacturers was that due to the falling prices and improved quality of cotton goods, the other textiles were increasingly substituted by cotton cloth. By 1850, however, the spinning of wool and linen had to all intents and purposes been mechanized, and home production in textiles had retreated to a few niches. Many of the inventions came from abroad, such as the De Girard wet-spinning process of linen and the Heilmann wool-combing machines. The only area to resist the onslaught of technological change was apparel-making: tailors and seamstresses, working from homes and small workshops, continued to produce clothing made from factory-made fabrics.

One of the most original and interesting inventions of the Industrial Revolution was the Jacquard loom, perfected in France in 1804. Although it produced mostly for the upscale market of expensive silks and fine worsteds, it resembled steam power in that it used a revolutionary technological principle whose full potential was not realized until much later. Joseph-Marie Jacquard, building on earlier work by Jacques de Vaucanson and others, programmed looms to weave patterns into the cloth. The programs were written onto punch cards, and represent the first application of binary coding of information. The Jacquard loom was very different from the traditional drawloom, which had previously been used to weave patterns into cloth, not only because it eliminated the drawboy (a second worker assisting the weaver by selecting and pulling the warp threads through which a particular weft was going), but also because the pattern could be changed in a few minutes, and the Jacquard could produce figures, effects, and colors unattainable by drawlooms. British weavers adopted the Jacquard loom on a large scale in the 1820s and 1830s. Moreover, Charles Babbage was inspired by this technique to build his famous analytical machine, the first attempt to build a computer.

The third area of "great inventions" of the Industrial Revolution was iron. Iron could claim to be, if not a General Purpose Technology, at least a general purpose material: almost anything that needed to be harder and stronger than wood had to be made out of iron. In the eighteenth and nineteenth centuries, there were no substitutes for iron in the majority of the many uses to which it was put. Before the Industrial Revolution, blast furnaces produced a substance known as pig iron which was high in carbon and thus hard, rigid, and fragile. Coke-smelting, which was introduced in the first decade of the eighteenth century but did not become widely used until the 1750s, reduced the cost of pig iron, and allowed the use of cast iron in many more applications. One of the lesser-known achievements of the age was the beginning of the use of cast iron as a construction material. The Shrewsbury engineer and architect Charles Woolley Bage (1751–1822) built

Ditherington flax mill in 1796–97, the first major building ever to use a cast-iron frame. The construction with iron was prompted not so much by cost as by the increased fire hazards caused by increasing use of steam power in textile mills. The innovation was significant above all because it augured a method that would produce high-rise construction in the later nineteenth century.

The bottleneck in the iron industry was refining pig iron into the more malleable low-carbon wrought iron that was needed for many purposes. For centuries, this process, carried out by mostly small forges, had been costly and time-consuming. Henry Cort, in 1785, solved the problem by combining the reverberatory furnaces used in glass-making with grooved rollers that had been used for some purposes, and by employing coke (purified coal) as a fuel. It is not easy to think of Cort as an Enlightenment figure. Joseph Black wrote to his friend James Watt that Cort was "a plain Englishman, without Science" whose discovery was due to "a dint of natural ingenuity and a turn for experiment" (cited by Coleman and MacLeod, 1986, p. 603). Yet Cort took the trouble to consult him, recognizing that if Black might know things that were relevant, it made sense to ask him. More importantly, Cort must have had access to a wide array of industrial practices in his time, since he was able to recombine them into a technique that solved a well-known problem, while avoiding some pitfalls. After a few further improvements and tweakings, the Cort puddling and rolling technique took the British metallurgical world by storm. The supply of wrought iron changed dramatically, marked both by a decline in price and an improvement in quality. Advances continued in the nineteenth century. James Neilson's "hot blast," perfected in 1829, which reduced the fuel consumption of blast furnaces by two-thirds, turned west central Scotland into the most efficient pig-iron producer of Britain (Whatley, 1997, p. 33). The puddler Joseph Hall discovered (to his surprise) that by adding old iron or rust to the puddling process, he could get the metal to boil quite strongly, yielding a superior product. This "wet puddling," adopted at his works in Tipton in the Black Country in the 1830s, constituted a significant improvement to the puddling and rolling process that was rapidly adopted throughout the industry. Hall arrived at this technique by trial and error, but by that time, increasingly, formal knowledge prepared the minds that Fortune favored (Gale, 1961–62, p. 5).

Much as the progressiveness of the textile industry was most remarkable in its leading branch, cotton, but eventually infected the other industries with its spirit of improvement, so the technologies of extracting, processing, and using non-ferrous metals advanced even if they are less well known than those of iron and steel. The copper industry was dominated by Thomas Williams (1737–1802), who became the richest man in Wales. While no inventor himself, he surrounded himself with the best minds he could find and he did take out a patent in 1778 for extracting arsenic from the ore with less trouble and expense than the common process. In the early 1780s his workers solved the problem of making hard cold-rolled copper bolts, and this invention helped solve the problem of corrosion through galvanic action between metals in copper-sheathed ships (J.R. Harris, 1966; 2004). The innovation turned out to be of major significance to shipping: the proportion of copper-sheathed merchant ships went from nothing in 1777 to 3.25 percent in 1786 and 18 percent in 1816 (Rees, 1971, p. 87). *The* Welsh method of copper refining adopted by him used reverberatory furnaces that smelted the ore in six stages using coke. The drive toward technical improvement even reached into the use of fairly rare metals. William Wollaston (1766–1828) attacked the rather formidable task of making platinum malleable and useful in a range of industries such as gunmaking and laboratory equipment. Unlike most accomplished scientists who applied their skills to industry, Wollaston kept his procedures a tight secret, yet seems to have benefited handsomely from his enterprise.

Not all such problems could be solved at the time: steel, a form of iron chemically intermediate between pig iron and wrought iron, could not be made cheaply enough throughout the period under discussion. Steel's properties of hardness and elasticity made it essential for many products but the high price of the best quality had always been an obstacle. Benjamin Huntsman, a Sheffield clockmaker, perfected in 1740 the so-called crucible process, which made it possible to make high-quality steel in reasonable quantities. Huntsman used coke and reverberatory ovens to generate sufficiently high temperatures to enable him to heat blister steel (an uneven material obtained by heating bar iron with layers of charcoal for long periods) to its melting point. In this way he produced a crucible (or cast) steel that was soon in high demand. Huntsman's process was superior in that it produced not only a more homogeneous product (important in a product such as steel, which consisted of about 2 percent carbon mixed in with the iron) but also removed impurities better because it created higher temperatures. Huntsman's product remained too expensive for many industrial uses, and attempts to make steel not only good but also cheap had to wait until the second half of the nineteenth century. Nevertheless, Huntsman's process, one of the early pathbreaking inventions of the eighteenth century, is worth mentioning as an important advance. Steel was essential in the production of machine parts, cutting tools, instruments, springs, and anything else that needed a material that was resilient and durable. Crucible steel is one important technological catalyst that economic historians have tended to overlook. The quality of crucible steel was such that it was produced in considerable quantities in Sheffield long after the nineteenth-century methods of producing cheap bulk steel had been introduced. Huntsman worked in a world of tacit knowledge, with an instinctive feel for what worked based on experience and intuition, data-driven rather than based on a scientific analysis. The fuller understanding of what steel was and how best to make it was very much part of the Enlightenment project and particularly fascinated continental scientists. By the 1820s and 1830s, the chemical nature of steel as an alloy of pure iron and small quantities of carbon was becoming known, and it is hard to envisage the subsequent advances in steelmaking without it.

The same was true for much of what we would call today the chemical industry. Textiles had to be dyed, but the vegetable substances used to make these dyes such as indigo, woad, and madder were costly to grow and process. But devising man-made substances that would replace them turned out to be beyond the capabilities of the age. The one bottleneck that the chemistry of the age of Enlightenment succeeded in solving was bleaching. Bleaching had always been a tricky problem, because it required the interaction of sunshine with certain acids, in a process known as grassing—yet sunshine was one resource Britain could neither boast nor import. The process of chlorine bleaching was therefore the leading invention in the chemical finishing processes of textiles, and nicely illustrates the international nature of the Industrial Enlightenment as well as the features of British society that allowed it to be the first to exploit the invention. The invention itself was made on the Continent: chlorine was discovered by a Swedish chemist, Carl-Wilhelm Scheele, in 1774, and its bleaching properties were realized by Claude Berthollet, one of Lavoisier's star students. When news of the invention reached Britain, its best engineer, James Watt, and its most successful entrepreneur, Watt's partner Matthew Boulton, traveled to Paris in 1786 and had Berthollet demonstrate the technique. British industrialists (including Watt's father-in-law, the bleacher James McGrigor) then set to the task of turning the invention into a viable industrial technique, a process that took a fair amount of "development" in our terms. In 1799 the Scottish bleacher Charles Tennant combined chlorine with slaked lime to produce bleaching powder and its success was phenomenal —grassing disappeared within a few years. "For the first time in History," wrote Berthollet in 1790, "an experiment has succeeded in four years to produce great manufactures" (cited by Musson and Robinson, 1969, p. 337). It is not quite accurate, of course, that this invention was an example of "science in the service of technology." Science and scientists helped, but chemical knowledge was highly imperfect and much of the actual implementation still depended on the trial-and-error evolutionary process of technological development in which inspiration and perspiration accounted for a lot more than scientific understanding.

The ceramic industry represents another successful breakthrough in the push for material progress. The precise chemical reactions that yielded porcelain (invented by the Chinese in the first millennium) were not well understood, so European advances came mostly through trial and error. Wedgwood's celebrated invention of colored Jasper, termed the most significant innovation in ceramic history since the Chinese invention of porcelain (Reilly, 1992, p. 153), came after thousands of experiments. Yet progress in this area clearly was no longer confined to the random stumblings of inspired artisans. Wedgwood sought the advice of the best scientists of his time, and himself was the inventor of a pyrometer that earned him his election to the Royal Society in 1783. His arch-enemy, the Cornish apothecary William Cookworthy, was a polymath intellectual, friendly with both John Smeaton and Joseph Banks. Not all the science was quite effective in advancing the industry. Cookworthy's belief in the ability of divining rods to locate deposits of metallic lodes serves as an example of the many pockets of superstition and ignorance that useful knowledge still needed to clear. There is little doubt that this industry in 1800 had progressed a great deal since Saxon porcelain-making techniques were first introduced into Britain in the 1740s. Advances in the use of materials other than iron were, however, widespread. Another example is the use of papier-mâché, patented by the Birmingham manufacturer Henry Clay in 1772. When subjected to a process of varnishing by a dark substance, known as "japanning," it became substantial enough to become a versatile material used for furniture and houseware.

The British manufacturing sector thus experienced at many levels signs of the "age of progress" that signaled the capability of human ingenuity and knowledge to control nature and improve the material condition of humanity, just as Francis Bacon had believed. But innovations in manufacturing were far from all there was to innovation. Some of the more spectacular innovations of the period of the Industrial Revolution constituted radical new solutions to age-old problems outside the realm of industry that people had faced since days immemorial, and illustrate the determination of the Industrial Enlightenment to break through the constraints of nature by the application of useful knowledge. Consider the problem of human flight, a subject of human dreams since the days of Daedalus. In 1783, observation, ingenuity, and a rudimentary understanding of physics produced the first defeat of gravity when on November 21 two French daredevils, Pilâtre de Rozier and the Marquis d'Arlandes, flew in a Montgolfier balloon. Ballooning did not attain economic significance until a century later, when it could be coupled with lightweight engines to produce airships. But its psychological effect should not be underestimated. Balloons were used to entertain at fairs and feasts, and new flight records made for good newspaper copy. Their capability of gathering huge crowds, amusing them, and filling them with a feeling of awe and wonderment at technology and its achievements helped persuade the public of the endless potential of the human mind to improve the human condition.

Another case in point was the solution to the longitude problem. Since the middle of the fifteenth century European ships had explored the world. One of the tools that allowed them to do this was a set of instruments that determined the latitude of the point of observation by measuring the angle of the sun or the stars. This technique provided one coordinate. The other, longitude, turned out to be far more difficult to establish in practice even if the theory behind measuring it was reasonably well understood by 1700. One technique was the construction of the Nautical Almanacs, detailed tables that allowed sailors to calculate their longitude from the position of certain stars, a method pioneered by the German astronomer Tobias Mayer in 1755. Nevil Maskelyne, the Astronomer Royal, designed tables put together by highly numerate "computers" that would allow seamen to compute with accuracy their location at sea in thirty minutes using this idea rather than the four hours required by Mayer's original suggestions (Croarken, 2002). The other option was to have a clock on board that gave the precise time at a given fixed point. By comparing that time to the time at the location of the ship (determined by the height of the sun), the longitude could be calculated. The difficulty was to construct a clock of sufficient accuracy to operate on the unstable sailing ships of the time. The Board of Longitude, a special body set up to solve the problem in 1714, promised the huge sum of £20,000 to "such person as shall discern the longitude at sea." After decades of experimentation, a clock accurate enough to solve the problem (known as H4) was completed by John Harrison in 1760, though it took another fifteen years and appeals to the King and Lord North for him to be paid the reward. Although a copy of H4 was actually used by Captain James Cook on his second and third voyages to the southern hemisphere, the early clocks were still expensive. When by the end of the century further improvements by British clockmakers reduced their price and they became more widely used, shipwrecks caused by mistaken location fell sharply. It was another triumph, not just of the ability of mechanical ingenuity and experimentation combined with just enough theoretical knowledge and mathematics to solve hard problems, but also of the promise that high degrees of technical precision and mathematics would be of great utility to society at large. Accuracy and reliability became the new catchwords. For clocks, pumps, scientific instruments, and chemical compounds, the old world of "more or less" would no longer do. That, too, was one of the principles of the Industrial Enlightenment (Heilbron, 1990).

A further example of useful knowledge being applied to solve a technological problem is found in the age-old issue of lighting. Modern observers might be astonished by how little progress there had been over the ages in lighting technology, given the universality of the problem of needing to see at night. If ever there was a counterexample to the misleading cliché that necessity is the mother of invention, this was it. The primitive oil lamps burned rapeseed oil and similar fuels, and provided a smoky and strongly colored flame. Tallow candles, widely used because of their low price, also provided fairly low-quality light. Wax candles were superior, but much more expensive. The true sea change came about two decades later. The notion that gas could be burned for useful purposes such as illumination and heating was an eighteenth-century insight. It became understood at around 1730 that coal could be broken up into components, one of which was a flammable gas. Most experiments with burning coal gas were, however, motivated by the need to get rid of the gas rather than produce it from coal and utilize the energy. Eventually it was realized that gas could be burned in a controllable fashion, giving a steady and clean flame, and turned to useful purposes. In about 1780, Archibald Cochrane, the Earl of Dundonald, lit the gases above his tar ovens mostly to amuse his friends. Yet much of the original insight into how to implement the insight in a practical way came again from the Continent, and a Frenchman named Philippe Lebon took out a patent in 1799 of a process in which he distilled gas from wood, cooled it, and proposed to burn the gas in a glass device known as a thermolamp in which gas and air were separately introduced, and the heavier by-products of the wood gas were collected in a special receptacle. In Britain, one of the leading entrepreneurs in the gas industry was a German, Friedrich Winser, and the first technical textbook on the industry was written by another, Friedrich Accum. Much as in the case of chlorine, however, it took British acumen and dexterity to take the idea to the finish line. William Murdoch, one of James Watt's most able employees, improved the technology (in part by using coal gas, a by-product of coking, rather than wood derivatives), and gas lighting became a reality, first in factories and theaters, then in streets and homes. By the middle of the nineteenth century the great majority of towns with over 2,500 inhabitants, and not a few smaller ones, had gas lighting (Falkus, 1967, p. 500). It was a quiet and unsung revolution, the most literal way in which the Industrial Enlightenment movement dispelled darkness. In the spirit of the age, morality was seen as enforcing utility. *The Times* exclaimed that nothing so important had been invented in the British realm since navigation (cited by Falkus, 1982, p. 226). The economist will recognize an improvement in material conditions when he or she sees it regardless of whether it shows up in the formal estimates of GDP, since sharp quality improvements are often inadequately reflected in such data (Nordhaus, 1997). Gas light was cheaper than any previous technology, easier to use, the light steadier and brighter, the fire hazards much reduced, and its price kept falling, from about £3,000 per million lumens/hour in 1820 to £500 in 1850 (Fouquet and Pearson, 2006, p. 158). The advent of gas lighting was hastened by the availability of government surplus musket barrels after the Napoleonic Wars, which were used as service conduits for gas. By 1829, two hundred public gas companies, as well as private installations, were in existence, and the idea of gas cooking had emerged, although adoption was slow (Chaloner, 1963, pp. 128–29).

What is striking is that side by side with a radical new technology, the old one kept improving as well. In 1782, a Frenchman named Aimé Argand invented a vastly improved lamp, but one that still burned oil. It used a round wick with a hollow air supply and a chimney, so it had excellent oxygen supply and emitted little smoke. Argand's invention involved ingenuity but little or no formal science, although he had studied with Lavoisier. This changed in the early nineteenth century. The French chemist Michel Eugène Chevreul's discoveries on the nature of fatty acids led to the emergence of a harder and purer fatty acid (stearine), the basis of candles, that burned longer and more brightly, with little smoke or smell. The real cost of candle light is estimated to have declined from £15,000 per million lumens-hour in 1760 to below £ 4,000 in constant prices in the 1820s (Fouquet and Pearson, 2006, p. 153).

In other industries, too, this was the age of progress. They were too many to sustain arguments that the Industrial Revolution was confined to so few industries that it was negligible, but too few to have major macroeconomic effects before 1830. In many activities promising advances were made in the technology, but actual implementation could take years and decades, until all the bugs had been removed and a cumulative set of improvements had made the new idea practicable. One industry which fits this pattern is that of food preservation. As in so many others, the original idea came from France: Nicolas Appert, attracted by a 12,000 franc reward promised by the Directoire in 1795, worked on the problem for a decade and received the prize in 1809. Although he never took out a patent, his British emulators did, and by 1813 a firm named Donkin, Hall, and Gamble was established that produced food in sheet-iron "cases" supplied to customers such as the Royal Navy and later Arctic explorers. For decades, the product remained too expensive and of too poor a quality to become mass-consumed, but as an illustration of the belief in making an improvement that would be both remunerative and socially beneficial, food-canning is paradigmatic of the age.

Or consider a very different product: cement. In 1756, John Smeaton began a series of experiments to see which forms of lime settle rapidly under water and discovered empirically that this was correlated with their content of clay. By adding small pebbles (known oddly as "aggregate") and finely ground bricks, he created "hydraulic cement," now known as concrete. In the 1820s a Leeds bricklayer, Joseph Aspdin, achieved the high strengths needed in high-quality construction by burning finely pulverized lime with clay at high temperatures. The new product became known as Portland cement (patented in 1824). A trained chemist, Isaac Charles Johnson, introduced some considerable improvements in the process in the 1840s, and while perhaps not lauded as one of the central advances of the Industrial Revolution, Portland cement quite literally became one of the building-blocks of the construction industry. In window (plate) glass, technological leadership was firmly in French hands before the Industrial Revolution. The St Gobain company had learned to cast plate glass when producing the windows for the Versailles palace in around 1688. The British started a similar process in 1776 in St Helens in Lancashire, but only after the firm was taken over by two brothers named Pilkington in 1826 did the firm become truly successful. Modern techniques were also used by their competitors, the Chance brothers in Smethwick (founded in 1824).

Substantial progress also took place during this period in paper-making. In the eighteenth century the only major innovation introduced into Britain's paper industry was the "Hollander" invented in about 1680, in which the time needed in the preparation of rags was shortened due to a roller equipped with knives or teeth, widely adopted by the British after 1750. Paper output between 1738 and 1800 increased by a factor of four, and much of this higher output is ascribed to higher productivity (Coleman, 1958, p. 111). Steam power was introduced in paper-making as early as 1786, when a 10hp Boulton and Watt engine was installed at a mill near Hull, though water power remained a viable source of power. The mechanical breakthroughs came at the end of the eighteenth century, and again originated in France, where in 1799 Nicolas-Louis Robert received a patent for continuous paper-making, in which sheets of paper were cut from a long roll of paper made on an endless belt of woven wire. It elegantly mechanized tasks formerly carried out by hand. The machine was much improved by the endlessly ingenious engineer Bryan Donkin and became known as the Fourdrinier machine after a London publisher who originally funded it and subsequently went bankrupt in 1810. But mechanization marched on, and over the next two decades mechanized paper gradually came to dominate the industry and by 1850 handmade paper had been reduced to a niche, accounting for no more than 10 percent of all paper in Britain. The very top-quality paper was still made by hand, but paper for everyday uses such as printing, wrapping, and writing had not only fallen in price but also experienced a "marked improvement in finish, strength, and regularity" (Coleman, 1958, p. 205).

Mechanization was at the center of the Industrial Revolution, and as Rosenberg (1976, pp. 9–31) has observed in the American context, mechanization was made possible by better machine tools and the skills of those who made them. As in other industries, Britain was well served by the advanced skills and broad practical knowledge of its mechanical engineers, in an age in which dexterity and experience could still substitute for a formal training in mathematics and physics. It had outstanding tool makers, the best-known of which was the famed Peter Stubs of Warrington, the maker of superb metal files inscribed with his initials (and inevitably counterfeited). Mechanical engineering, as MacLeod and Nuvolari (2009) stress, was a core activity of the Industrial Revolution, generating a disproportional share of innovations. Rolt has emphasized that progress in engineering was constrained by the ability of machine shops to turn inventions into hardware and that accuracy and high-quality materials were essentially self-propagating (1970, p. 94). The operators of lathes and cutting machines learned to make power-driven machinery that could then be applied in other industries by workers with fewer skills than themselves. Many machine tools, however, did not replace the skills and steady hands of trained mechanics but complemented them by allowing them to do things that nature had decreed they could not do by themselves. Lancashire's cotton industry generated a number of outstanding manufacturers of advanced textile machinery, prime examples of British competence in this area such as Henry Platt (1793-1842) whose specialty was carding machines, the partners Isaac Dobson and Peter Rothwell who manufactured mules in Bolton, and Samuel Lees, who produced rollers and spindles in Holt (Timmins, 1998, p. 104).

Much of this equipment was standardized. Standardization, of course, was an idea that came out of the Enlightenment movement's interest in the rationalization and coordination of weights and measures. In production it was not easy to bring about, because it required high degrees of accuracy and exacting tolerance. The key to progress was special-purpose tools; much like the division of labor, mass production required a specialization in the design of machine tools. Presses, drills, pumps, cranes, and many other forms of mechanical equipment were produced in large series. Manchester, close to the best customers for these machines, became a center of this industry. Perhaps the paradigmatic examples of a British engineer in this tradition were Henry Maudslay and his apprentice Joseph Whitworth. While Maudslay was obsessive in his attempt to standardize bolt heads and screw threads within his own works, Whitworth helped modernize mechanical production by standardizing them nation-wide and thus laid the foundation of modern mass production through the modularity of parts. As Musson (1975) and others have argued, the widespread belief that Britain fell behind in this area of technology and eventually ceded mass production to the United States is simply inaccurate. By 1841, a parliamentary committee could proudly report that the implements after 1820 were "some of the finest inventions of the age" and that by their means "the machinery produced by these tools is better as well as cheaper ... tools have intro-duced a revolution in machinery and tool-making" (Great Britain, 1841, p. vii). The influence of the machine-tool industry on the advance of manufactures, in the somewhat biased opinion of one of its leaders, had been comparable to that of the steam engine (Nasmyth, 1841, p. 397). By replacing the human hand in holding the tools of cutting metal by "mechanical contrivances," they achieved an accuracy hitherto unimaginable, using far less skilled labor. Through the early stages of the Industrial Revolution, mechanical engineers worked primarily in small workshops, sometimes serving in a hub and spokes kind of outsourcing network with larger manufacturers (Cookson, 1997, p. 5).

Britain's successful mechanical engineering sector is a useful example to illus-trate the key to British technological leadership. It relied for its best practitioners on a system of highly informal training, some of it through apprenticeships or other affiliations with known centers of excellent such as Henry Maudslay's workshop in London, and some of it on self-taught skills and a natural manual dexterity. George Stephenson, whose *Rocket* won the Rainhill Trials, was entirely self-trained in engineering skills, and had very little math and almost no writing skills. Many others in this industry, similarly, had informal training, and even Smeaton described himself, not entirely accurately, as "self-taught" and regretted his lack of formal training in practical "mechanical philosophy" (Skempton et al., 2002, p. 624). It was a sector that could still rely to a great extent on mechanical intuition and a high degree of competence. Its connections with formal science and mathematics, while not absent altogether, were still tenuous before the middle of the nineteenth century. Given that Britain's system of informal education and cooperation at the artisanal level served it much better than its formal schools and universities, its successful mechanical engineering sector should surprise no one.

How much of the technological progress of the age of the Industrial Revolution depended on scientific knowledge? This question seems ill-posed, since there was no linear causality of any kind. Instead, what we call science and technology interacted and fertilized each other in many ways. Engineers and mechanics often learned from scientists, but the reverse was equally true. Moreover, the nature of the interaction differed from industry to industry and from product to product. The Industrial Enlightenment emphasized the generation and dissemination of useful knowledge, whether it was theoretical, experimental, or practical.

An illuminating example of how the Enlightenment affected the economy can be found in the rapid growth in geological research. Organizations intended to promote the diffusion of knowledge sprung up everywhere in the late eighteenth century, all the way from local societies in Newcastle and Cornwall to the more lofty Geological Society in London (Marsden and Smith, 2005, pp. 33–35). This society, explicitly committed to a Baconian program of cooperative fact-gathering, prepared an extensive geological database to be used in surveying and mapping (Laudan, 1990, p. 316). This effort was a classic example of the Enlightenment's "three Cs," as any clear-cut understanding of how geological strata were constructed was still in the future. The Newcastle Literary and Philosophical Society (founded in 1793), its name notwithstanding, spent much of its time on geological issues and it was there that George Stephenson first demonstrated his safety lamp in 1815. Its founder, the polymath Unitarian minister William Turner, is a good example of the impact that the English Enlightenment had on provincial culture. In addition to papers on coal mining, Turner gave lectures on metal, chemical, and glass manufactures (Musson and Robinson, 1969, pp. 161–62). The most important product of this movement was a set of "practical professionals," coal viewers and civil engineers, who combined competence as it was defined here with a detailed knowledge of the best-practice geological science of the time. It was mostly a pragmatic and empirical endeavor, much of it based on accurate observation, mapping, and looking for exploitable regularities, but in close cooperation with mining interests that recognized the potential profits it could make if the epistemic base of mining could be expanded, so that the search for mineral resources and their subsequent exploitation would be made more systematic and depend less on trial and error and experimentation without science. The most famous product of the new geology were the geological maps produced by William Smith in 1815, and the competing map published in 1820 by the Geological Society of London. It is no exaggeration to say that a reciprocal relationship developed between the young science of geology and the mining and transportation sectors in Britain. Geologists and surveyors such as Smith and Thomas Sopwith (1803–1879) consulted to these industries, while practical professionals made contributions to the study of geology (Veneer, 2006, p. 80).

To say that continued technological progress after the first decades of *sturm und drang* of the Industrial Revolution was spurred and supported increasingly by the cumulation of useful knowledge is not the same as saying that it somehow depended on *formal* science. In the rather stringent definitions we employ for science, its impact remained fairly limited. But the growing application of useful knowledge of any kind to production in more and more industries kept productivity growing in many of them in the first half of the nineteenth century. One example is the famous mining safety lamp, invented by Davy in 1815, which allowed the opening of many deep coal seams that without the lamp "would never have seen the light of day," as a prominent mine viewer, John Buddle, rather quaintly put it (cited by James, 2005, p. 212). It has been argued that Davy's considerable knowledge of chemistry was of no direct help in developing the lamp (ibid., p. 201). Yet if we expand our definition of useful knowledge to include, in addition to formal science, the growing catalog of tricks, gimmicks, and rules of thumb that worked and the better understanding of heat, resistance, lubrication, plasticity, and mechanics that had accumulated, it is clear that growing useful knowledge was behind many of the nineteenth-century technological advances. By that time, for example, a body of knowledge about heat and the way certain materials behaved under heat had been the subject of scrutiny for many years, and it seems simply implausible that none of this epistemic base was of any use to Davy (Jacob, forthcoming). This hypothesis is supported by the fact that George Stephenson, an engineer with few scientific pretensions, came up with a very similar device at about the same time but apparently independently (unleashing an ugly argument between him and Davy about priority). Such coincidences are best explained by the cumulation of background knowledge that made the invention possible at that time. The same holds for the work in applied chemistry by Charles Macintosh (1766–1843), which led to the widespread application of rubber and rubber products. Macintosh was not the first to see the possibility of using rubber to waterproof textiles (for raincoats), but his knowledge of the underlying applied chemistry was just a tad better than that of his competitors (Clow and Clow, 1992, p. 253). Macintosh's partner Thomas Hancock (1786–1865) discovered the vulcanization process of rubber in 1842 independently of the American Charles Goodyear.

The cumulation of useful knowledge also played a role in the development of the work of another Scot (and for some time Macintosh's partner), James Neilson. Neilson, too, was no trained scientist but a practicing and experienced engineer, and his invention was the result of trial and error far more than of logical inference. Yet he was inspired and informed by the courses in chemistry he took in Glasgow, where he learned of the work of the French chemist Gay-Lussac on the expansion of gases (Clow and Clow, 1952, p. 354). In the cement industry, an article in Rees' *Encyclopedia* in 1819 described in detail the chemical processes involved in the hardening of cement, a description deemed "remarkably acute" by a modern expert (Halstead, 1961–62, p. 43). To be sure, the full explanation of cement's hydraulicity was not put forward until the1850s, but this was an area on which the new chemistry had a lot to say. In the 1830s, furthermore, the many decades of research in electricity started to see their first payoff: the research of scientists such as Hans-Christian Oersted and Joseph Henry led to the development of the electrical telegraph.

The payoff to better and wider propositional knowledge after 1815 can also be seen in the iron and steel industry. The famous paper by Berthollet, Monge, and Vandermonde, "Mémoire sur la fer consideré dans ses differens états métalliques" published in France in 1786, explaining the scientific nature of steel may have been above the heads of British steelmakers. The immediate impact of the paper was not large. It was "incomprehensible except to those who already knew how to make steel" (Harris, 1998, p. 220). But five years later the British chemist and physician Thomas Beddoes published a paper that relied on it and by 1820 it was well known enough to be made into an article in the *Repertory of Arts, Manufactures and Agriculture* (Boussingault, 1821, p. 369), which noted that idea had been adopted by all chemists who had turned their attention to the subject. Further work by scientists, such as Michael Faraday's on the crystalline nature of wootz steel (high-quality steel made directly from ores), increased the understanding of the characteristics of ferrous materials. By the 1860s, two processes, Bessemer's and Siemens-Martin, had been developed to produce cheap steel. As C.S. Smith (1964, p. 174) noted, "with carbon understood, Bessemer found control of his process easy, though its invention was not a deduction from theory, as the Martins' probably was."

After 1800, then, the mutual reinforcement of technology and science came to dominate the process of innovation in the economy and eventually the entire economy (Mokyr, 2002). By 1848, John Stuart Mill thought that "the perpetual and unlimited growth of man's power over nature" was the natural result of the fact that "increasing physical knowledge is now [1848] converted, by practical ingenuity into physical power" and that "the most marvelous of modern inventions ... sprang into existence but a few years after the scientific theory which it realizes and exemplifies" ([1848], 1929, p. 696).

The historiography of the Industrial Revolution has tended to focus on "process innovation" in which costs fell due to growing efficiency. Yet it has been stressed by a number of economic historians, above all Maxine Berg (2005), that this is only part of the story. British manufacturers learned to make goods attuned to changing consumer preferences and yet were "branded" so that consumers knew what they were getting. An old chestnut in the literature has it that French manufacturers catered to "luxury tastes" whereas the British catered to price, producing large series of inexpensive cookie-cutter products without individuality, in order to take advantage of economies of scale in batch production. This is far too simplistic a picture. Technology included not only making things that worked well at a low price, but also designs that were aesthetically pleasing. In the eighteenth century there was a conscious and well-orchestrated attempt to wrestle away the traditional edge that French manufacturers were supposed to have in luxury goods. Product innovation in the form of decoration, ornamentation, coloring, catering to fashion in custom-made products (or mass-produced goods made to look custom-made) were very much part of the innovative effort. Besides the famous pottery produced by Wedgwood at his "modern" plant in Burslem, Britain witnessed a huge expansion in a wide array of "small products," each of which perhaps counts for little in the national accounts, but which together defined an improving standard of living for a swelling middle class: buttons, buckles, gloves, door handles, chandeliers, wallpaper, toys, printed calicoes and cottons, fancy furniture, cutlery, and watch-chains (Berg, 2005). The improvement in quality of these goods consisted in part of standardization, in part of catering to new fashions. But having sufficient agility to adapt quickly to the changing whims and demands of a set of reasonably well-off consumers is itself a mark of technological capability, broadly defined.

The changing capabilities of producers to attract and satisfy consumers are one answer to the question of where the demand for the products that the Industrial Revolution produced in ever growing quantities came from. These capabilities resulted in goods that were not just cheaper but better in demonstrable dimensions. Technology and organization were joined in that effort. Samuel Oldknow, an entrepreneur specializing in high-quality muslins and calicoes, whose customers included "mostly people of fashion," had each piece of cloth examined and maintained a sophisticated system of record-keeping so that each warp that suffered from bad workmanship could be traced back to those who had handled it. Quality control methods were also found in other industries, such as Wedgwood's pottery plant, Boulton and Watt's Soho plant (which ended outsourcing of engine components in 1795 because they could not guarantee their quality), and Archibald Kenrick's hardware foundry in West Bromwich (founded in 1791), which specialized in high-quality hollowware such as kitchen utensils. More attractive and durable commodities at reasonable prices reflected the capabilities of manufacturers to give consumers what they wanted, whether they knew it or not.

The significance of demand is deeper than just the satisfaction of physical needs. Consumption played a social role of signaling one's status and one's aspirations, and nowhere was this more true than for the cotton industry. To be sure, the distribution of the demand for textiles reflected to a large extent the distribution of income and the social hierarchy. But at the invisible seams of this hierarchy were the hopes of social advance and mimicking those just above one's status. By the mid-eighteenth century the importance of fashion was remarkable enough to be noticed by foreign visitors and to spawn a considerable fashion literature. The hierarchy of clothing was continuous, much like the distribution of income, and thus signaling progress in climbing the socio-economic ladder remained a desirable option. Signaling that one belonged to the gentleman class and "polite society" was of considerable value to the functioning of the commercial economy.

Cotton was ideal because it was flexible. It could be colored and patterned in any shape that fashion dictated, and thus provided a vehicle for emulating those ahead of one in the hierarchy as well as for keeping a distance from those behind. Yet price was of supreme importance. The idea of ready-made mass-marketed clothing, sold off the rack, emerged in the eighteenth century. Gowns, hats, petticoats, and similar items were already sold in the early part of the century, and the growth of cotton clothes clearly spurred this trend on (Lemire, 1991, pp. 161–200). Stylish but affordable ready-made clothing seems to be one of the less widely trumpeted innovations of the age of Enlightenment, but no less than the mechanized spinning machines that provided the raw materials for them did they herald a manufacturing system that was totally different from the custom-made woolen clothes of an earlier age.

*   *   *

Despite the protestations of some scholars who call it "a misnomer," the idea of the Industrial Revolution will remain an essential concept in the economic history of Britain and the world. It was, in a narrow sense, neither exclusively industrial nor much of a revolution. But it remains in many ways the opening act of the still-developing drama of modern economic growth coupled to far-reaching changes in society. And while Britain's role as a pioneer should not be mistaken for indispensability, it was in Britain that the important action took place between 1750 and 1850. By 1850, as we shall see in more detail below, it had become a very different economy. Yet the Industrial Revolution was not all there was to British industrial history (let alone economic history) in the period 1700–1850, and while in hindsight it seems like the towering event of the time, for contemporaries the importance of technological change was only becoming clear very slowly and it was by no means clear to all in 1850 that a new economic age had dawned.

CHAPTER 8

Britain and the World: An Open Economy

The issues of foreign trade and payments and the economics of empire were a major item on the agenda of the Enlightenment as well as that of earlier writers in the mercantilist tradition. Mercantilist and liberal economists agreed on the importance of international trade to the economy, but differed radically on the way commerce affected wealth and hence on the appropriate policy. Modern scholars have also been much concerned with it, but with a somewhat different emphasis. What was the exact role of foreign trade and what was the British Empire's role in its economic success? Was the Industrial Revolution the result of foreign trade? Britain was an open economy by the standards of the time, excepting some periods of war. Economies that are open to the rest of the world tend in general to be more dynamic and more prone to growth. And yet it is a long way from that view to an argument that growing foreign trade (whether due to colonial policies or other factors) in some way "caused" the Industrial Revolution, as some writers (most recently Inikori, 2002 and Cuenca, 2004) have maintained.

Was international trade the "handmaiden" of growth? The fact that modern industry and foreign trade grew together does not allow us to infer any causation, since it is likely that a great deal of trade was stimulated by technological change and productivity growth rather than the other way around. At some level, the counterfactual question of whether a closed economy would have been very different is trivial: at least for the supply of raw cotton, Britain depended entirely on imports. Cotton cloth exports, too, became crucial to the growth of the industry. The Industrial Revolution was trade-augmenting. The changes in spinning and other cotton industry techniques reduced prices, which led to a rapidly growing demand for raw cotton. Many of the products that experienced supply-side productivity growth or quality improvements could compete more effectively in world markets and were thus exported. Had the Industrial Revolution been nothing more than cotton, the argument that openness was essential is undeniable. But the Industrial Revolution was much more than just one industry (Temin, 1997). If there had been no cotton, there still would have been an Industrial Revolution, even if its exact shape would have differed.

How, exactly, did openness to the world help British economic success? A wholly open economy with unencumbered trade and mobility, of course, was an Enlightenment ideal. The Enlightenment's ideal was an economy that was cosmo-

politan, universalist, and progress-oriented. For most of the eighteenth century
Britain was, however, an imperial nation still dominated by mercantilist notions.
Trade increased resources through specialization and access to materials and
substances such as American cotton, Caribbean sugar, Canadian timber, Atlantic
codfish, and the high-quality iron ore imported by Britain from Sweden and later
Spain. Access to natural resources outside British borders is sometimes known as
"ghost acreage." On the demand side, the openness of the British economy to
trade with the rest of the world meant that the terms of trade (relative prices) of
manufactured goods declined much more slowly than they would have in a closed
economy. All the same, after 1815 they did decline, but not as rapidly as they
would have in a closed economy. How much difference did openness make in this
respect? Trade in the narrowest of senses prevented the prices of those goods in
which technological progress was the fastest from falling too rapidly, and this
effect by itself has led Harley (2004, p. 194) to conclude that self-sufficiency would
have cost Britain only about 6 percent of GDP. These estimates are minimalist
and may leave out some of the more interesting consequences of trade.

The change in the terms of trade meant, for one thing, that the benefits of
British ingenuity were shared with non-British consumers. It does not prove that
without foreign demand, there would have been no Industrial Revolution.
Decisions to innovate were made by individual entrepreneurs, not by the industry
as a whole. Each manufacturer had little or no control over prices, and just sought
to outbid his competitors. Innovation will occur in a closed economy much as it
will in an open economy if it is sufficiently competitive, even if profits in the inno-
vating sectors of a closed economy will be exhausted earlier and so these sectors
will attain smaller ultimate size. For that reason, having an open economy was
surely a positive factor in the innovativeness of Britain. Findlay and O'Rourke
(2007, p. 339) argue reasonably that had it not been for trade, the relative price of
manufacturing goods to agricultural goods would have fallen even faster than it
did, and might well have slowed down the process of growth to a fraction of what
it actually was, especially in the post-1815 decades. Something akin to a Malthusian
crisis might well have occurred. Recent counterfactual computations based on
Computable General Equilibrium models (Clark, O'Rourke, and Taylor, 2008)
confirm this. But we cannot infer that had Britain had to depend entirely on the
home market, there would have been no Industrial Revolution altogether. In an
open economy some of the benefits of technological progress are transferred to
foreign consumers in the form of lower prices, whereas in a closed economy they
are all kept for domestic consumers.

Openness enhanced British economic performance because the continuing
concern with foreign competition constituted a stimulus for enhanced efficiency.
In 1773 Matthew Boulton wrote that Birmingham manufacturers would defeat
their continental competitors by mechanization and by being more efficient
(Uglow, 2002, p. 212). The literary hostess Elizabeth Montagu wrote to him in

1771 to urge him "to triumph over the French in taste & to embellish his country with useful inventions and elegant productions" (cited by Berg, 2005, pp. 176–77). Boulton's fellow Lunar Society member, Josiah Wedgwood, wondered if they could "conquer France in Burslem." Whether in practice competing with foreign producers was different from competing with domestic ones is unclear, but the concern with foreign competition did affect government policies toward innovation.

However, in the long run the main channel through which openness affected economic progress was via the salutary effects of useful knowledge and ideas that came from overseas, from the new chemistry of Lavoisier to Philippe De Girard's wet spinning process, to the idea that inoculation with the blood of a smallpox patient can actually make a person immune to the disease (introduced in the 1720s from the Ottoman Empire). Trade created so-called exposure effects, the importation of foreign products such as calicoes and chinaware, which served as a focusing device, showing the local people what could be done. The British first copied, and then improved. Openness was more than trade, it was British citizens traveling overseas, reading foreign books in translation, hosting foreign visitors, all the while learning how foreigners made things. Lord Macartney, on the eve of his famous embassy to China in 1792, thought that while the Chinese had long known all the great inventions which now characterized British civilization, yet "a few practical men admitted among them would in a few years acquire a mass of information for which if placed in the industrious and active hands of English manufacturers the whole revenue of the Chinese Empire would not be thought sufficient equivalent" (cited in Berg, 2006, p. 276).

The willingness and ability of the British to adopt the ideas of others and rely on resources from overseas has led some scholars to claim that the Industrial Revolution was entirely the result of the efforts of others. Thus we learn of "the Chinese Origins of British Industrialization" in which Britain is depicted as a "derivative late developer" (Hobson, 2004, ch. 9). Such claims, in their zeal to unmask and denigrate what these authors consider to be "Eurocentricity," are exaggerated and in part based on misapprehensions. The British Industrial Revolution found technological inspiration everywhere, in China, South America, and Africa as well as in the rest of Europe. Yet the fact remains that by 1850 Britain had done far more with these ideas than their originators. John Farey pointed out with some pride that foreign inventions, after being improved in Britain, even when they were returned in improved state to the countries in which they originated, could not be worked as extensively and profitably as in Britain (Great Britain, 1829, p. 153). Moreover, many breakthroughs made in Europe were original. It is simply incorrect, for instance, to argue that the Chinese were on the verge of inventing a steam engine. While they may have had an intuitive sense of atmospheric pressure, there is nothing in the Chinese record to suggest that they had stumbled on the principles that made the Newcomen engine click (Deng,

2004). The scholar of Chinese technology, Joseph Needham, pointed out that "Newcomen ... appears more original, and also at the same time more European, than [was previously realized] ... he stands out as a typical figure of that modern science and technology which grew up in Europe" (Needham, 1970, pp. 136, 202). The guiding ideas of the Industrial Enlightenment suggested that it mattered less where the ideas came from than how they could be adapted and improved, and above all how they could be exploited to make money for the entrepreneur as well as bring about the "relief of Man's Estate."

A more subtle but persuasive mechanism between trade and long-term economic development of the British economy is based on the idea that the expansion of trade in the centuries after 1450 (ultimately resulting from the improvements in shipping and navigation technology) wrought profound social and economic changes in the European economies. Specifically, it is argued that in the Atlantic seaports and surrounding areas, trade gave rise to a rapidly growing middle class of merchants, artisans, and financial agents, whose long-term impact on ideology and political institutions had momentous consequences (Acemoglu, Johnson, and Robinson, 2005b). These merchants, shipbuilders, insurance brokers, financial agents, and similar middle-class people demanded political concessions and protection of their property, and wherever successful, changed the long-term politics. A different version of this argument is proposed by Allen (2009), who suggested that international trade helped raise British wages, which stimulated labor-saving technological change. I will return to this issue in chapter 12 below.

The existence of a largely urban middle class was central to the economic development of Britain after 1700, but the exact impact of long-distance trade on its growth still needs to be established. After all, France, Portugal, Spain, and the Netherlands all participated in the long-distance trade, and experienced the emergence of a middle class, yet the impact of this class was weaker. How much of the middle class and urbanization between 1500 and 1750 was the result of long-distance trade and how much was due to domestic factors such as agricultural change, internal trade, and technological progress in manufacturing? Moreover, commercial interests demanded special privileges, monopolies, and exclusionary rights. They might just as well have led to an equilibrium of a mercantile, rent-seeking economy that would have proven an economic dead end. Why did this not happen?

Openness, of course, was itself not predetermined by fate but a function of politics, culture, institutions, technology, and to some extent geography. The British government in the age of mercantilism followed a set of policies that to the modern economist seem rather inconsistent: it clearly supported long-distance trade, such as by maintaining a powerful navy to protect and if possible expand commercial opportunities by the use of force (Ormrod, 2003; O'Brien, 2006). At the same time, it was still committed to protectionist practices on behalf of domestic rent-seeking lobbies. Examples were the Navigation Acts (not finally abolished until 1849–54), and the prohibition on the emigration of artisans and exports of machinery (neither of which seems to have been very effective). The Corn Laws and other tariffs were implemented in part to protect local interests and in part as a political measure to distinguish between foes (usually France and the Netherlands) and friends. Muscular "blue water" policies repeatedly got Britain involved in military conflicts with the European continent and North America which disrupted the normal international flows of goods, though wars rarely led to the complete collapse of trade as it did in 1914–18. Did colonial policies, however, protect and stimulate trade, as mercantilists believed, or did they raise trading costs substantially and by so doing actually impede the flow of trade (Findlay and O'Rourke, 2007, p. 307)?

*   *   *

Foreign trade was the one area in which the state made a big difference in the period 1700–1850. Trade was regulated, controlled, and taxed. During much of the period of the Industrial Revolution Britain maintained a mercantilist mindset in its commercial policies. Did these stimulate industrialization? The growth in imports over the eighteenth and early nineteenth centuries masks the fact that much of the British increase in industrial output was in part "import substitution"—that is, goods that may well have been produced better or cheaper overseas but which were kept out through tariffs or non-tariff trade barriers. Among those were cotton cloth, linen products, silk, paper, glass, ceramics, and dyestuffs. Moreover, many tariffs supported local substitutes. Thus, the tax on French wines was strongly supported by local brewers (Nye, 2007). Economists starting with Adam Smith have in general tended to take a dim view of such policies, since they realized that, while they may favor a few industries and their owners, protectionist measures will in the end worsen the economic well-being of consumers and might well result in retaliatory actions by other nations.

Yet some historians, especially the late Paul Bairoch (1989), have taken the position that protectionism may have had a favorable effect on industrial development, and in the end it may have been a positive factor in the Industrial Revolution by guaranteeing the home market for innovative entrepreneurs. Such arguments are hard to prove: what would technological creativity have been like in the absence of protection? It seems that few would go so far as to argue that in a completely closed economy, the Industrial Revolution would have proceeded as fast as it did. If Britain wanted to export industrial products, it had to import as well. It could be argued that if the country allowed in raw materials such as duty-free cotton and prohibited the importation of cotton cloth, domestic manufacturers would produce more of a good that was highly susceptible to technological advances and learning-by-doing, and thus the country would experience more innovation than it would have in a perfectly free trade economy. But for many years, Britain had few competitors in cotton textiles, precisely because it was more efficient than other economies. The spectacular increase in the imports of raw cotton after 1790 were undoubtedly an effect, not a cause, of the developments in cotton technology.

At the same time, protection might have meant that domestic markets were less competitive and thus the pressures on producers to become more efficient (or innovate more) were less severe. For instance, did the Calico Acts, which prohibited the importation and wearing of Indian calicoes, lead eventually to the phenomenal growth of the British cotton industry by stimulating import substitutes, or would the great inventions in cotton have happened anyway and perhaps even faster if they had more competition from cheap Indian imports? The idea of spinning fine cotton yarn must surely have come from observing the hand-made fabrics imported from India. Protectionism not only keeps out the competition, it also keeps out ideas. In the event, the Calico Acts were repealed in 1774, in the early days of the cotton industry's mechanization, and there is no evidence that by that time it mattered much. The British machine-spun cotton yarn could out-compete anything that the Indians could make.

As we have seen, the significance of the Enlightenment to international trade was to slowly replace the mercantilist premise that trade was at base a zero-sum game with the realization that trade was a positive-sum game. Foreign trade had always been the pivot of mercantilist rent-seeking. The Corn Laws, first passed in 1670 and reinstated in 1815, were the crowning achievement of rent-seeking landowners. Many other tariffs had a straightforward rent-seeking motive: the transfer of resources to those who stood to benefit from them, at the expense of other producers or, more usually, the consumer. The Navigation Acts were meant to benefit British shippers and the industries catering to them, by forcing imports to be carried on British ships. A prime example of the rent-seeking nature of British commercial policy was the system of agricultural bounties, which had been part of the Corn Law system since the years of William and Mary. Through it, the British government subsidized its prime constituency, namely large landowners. The odd fact is that most calculations show that cereals in Britain were among the most expensive in Europe, and yet until 1760 Britain was a major grain exporter thanks to the subsidy, particularly to the Netherlands. Government subsidy distorted the operation of the market at the expense of British consumers, who paid higher prices for bread, and British manufacturers who had to pay higher wages to their workers. But it also hurt British distillers and brewers, since their Dutch competitors had access to subsidized British malt and barley. Most governments in Europe did the reverse: they tried to set maximum prices to prevent food riots in the cities (Persson, 2000), with equally distorting effects. Such were the follies of mercantilist policy.

In the eighteenth century and well into the nineteenth, some proponents of Anglo-Saxon "liberalism" advocated free internal trade with some continued protection for external trade. David Hume was quite clear on this, but many other Enlightenment thinkers, such as the Scotsman James Anderson (1739–1808), who strongly influenced Jeremy Bentham, played an important role. The later stages of the Enlightenment, inspired and informed by post-Smithian political economy, extended liberalism to foreign trade. To be sure, here too Smith and his followers could draw on many precursors, such as Nicholas Barbon (1690) and Jacob Vanderlint (1734) who subjected mercantilist ideas and policies to a devastating critique. The liberal triumph was, however, late in the making, and the move to free trade was slow and difficult (Nye, 2007). All the same, as we saw in chapter 2, the influence of Enlightenment thought on the free trade movement is undeniable. Different people had different reasons to support free trade. One was the support of a Jeffersonian "virtuous" republic, which in Britain had strong religious overtones. Another was the foundation of an economic world order based on peace and mutually advantageous exchange, leading to global prosperity and progress within a stable civil society, as in the thought of a man like William Huskisson. Tariffs and transport costs worked in symmetrical fashion: both were a cost of shipping goods overseas. For a given level of transportation and trading costs, a reduction in tariffs could be expected to lead to an increase in the volume of trade and an improvement of national welfare. This basic insight turned from a heterodoxy in 1750 to conventional wisdom after 1820.

None of this happened very quickly. The Revolutionary and Napoleonic Wars in many ways represented a setback in the advance of Enlightenment-inspired policies. In 1815 Britain emerged from the French Wars with very high tariffs and a rejuvenated Corn Law, and had to shake off the temporary resurgence of neo-mercantilist thinking prompted by the wars with France and the United States. Some special interests were still very powerful and refused to concede. Landlords were of course primary in this argument, and they maintained that the high prices of farm products during the wars had induced them to invest heavily in agricultural capital, entitling them to some protection. But landlords were not the only ones. From the late seventeenth century Britain had effectively kept out French wines by imposing a high tariff on wine (by volume, which affected the "light" French wines more than Spanish and Portuguese wines). The result had been that Britain had learned to drink beer and stronger beverages during the eighteenth century. In 1696 the purpose of the high tariffs had been to weaken France, as part of the mercantilist zero-sum view of the world. By 1815 this view had faded, but the brewers and distillers were still a force to be reckoned with. In the decades that followed, the free traders slowly and gradually emerged victorious and the tariffs were phased out, but not until the later Victorian decades did the "free trade economy" fully emerge (Nye, 2007).

Of course, economic interests played an important role as well in the eventual triumph of free trade. John Stuart Mill famously pointed out that a good cause seldom triumphs unless someone's interest is bound up with it. But conflicting interests had to fight it out in the corridors of power, and it is unwarranted to dismiss the effects of economic ideas and ideology to the status of unprovable and unquantifiable and therefore unimportant. Vested interests and the lobbies that represented them were always instrumental in changing institutions, but ideas and their rhetorical power help explain why one lobby defeats another by persuading the uncommitted. The British economy was torn between groups that favored free trade and a more laissez-faire economy, and those who believed that some measure of state intervention was essential. These groups were not mutually exclusive. Often some interest group ostensibly committed to free trade for others employed special pleading to seek an exception for itself, much as is the case today. Many supporters of free trade, such as Peel himself for much of his career, found practical reasons to make exceptions. The Enlightenment, overall, supported the rationalization of economic activity through free markets, but it did not always speak in one voice and its leaders—including Adam Smith—recognized the ambiguities of a laissez-faire economy and its incompatibility with a utilitarian-based rational economy.

To complicate matters further, tariffs served purposes other than the protection of politically well-connected industries and the enrichment of their owners. Even some "enlightened" leaders who had read their *Wealth of Nations* had to admit that customs were an effective way to balance the government books. Tariffs were an easy way to collect tax, and one that was politically less costly than regressive sales taxes or direct taxes on income or real estate. Indeed, the sharp shift to a high-tariff economy in 1700 was originally fiscal in purpose. How should Britain balance the principles of free trade with its fiscal needs? Moreover, Adam Smith himself recognized the need for protection in cases in which the national interest or a policy was at stake. For instance, the linen industry was protected from continental competitors after 1700 because the government wanted to foster the Irish linen industry owned by loyal Huguenots, and reduce dependence on the imports of "strategic goods" (linen sailcloth and hemp for ropes were crucial for the provisioning of warships). In short, tariff protection embodied the very essence of mercantilism: the confluence of fiscal needs and special interests. To that we may add the "beggar thy neighbour" motif: many mercantilist theorists believed that the economy suffered from structural unemployment, and advocated protection in the belief that exports provided jobs at home and imports reduced them. Given all that, it is perhaps astonishing that free trade ever had a chance at all. It is a testimony to the powerful rhetoric of Enlightenment thinkers that, despite all the forces supporting protectionism, they were able to implement a free trade program.

Before the end of the eighteenth century, Britain remained on the whole committed to protectionist and mercantilist doctrines, but a few kinks appeared in the armor of the protectionist juggernaut. Between 1786 and 1792, a brief blossoming of trade liberalization between Britain and France took place, soon to be interrupted for many years by the wars and blockades of 1793–1815. The wars were followed by a set of high tariffs, including the reinstatement of Britain's notorious Corn Laws. But after 1815 the new liberalism was slowly gaining ground, through a combination of the growing influence of post-Smithian political economy and the growing political power of the new industrial and commercial elite. In the 1820s, a cautious move toward freer trade was begun, but not until the late 1840s did the move become pronounced with the abolition of the Corn Laws and the Navigation Acts. Free trade, as we have seen, was a complex issue, involving fiscal considerations, national security issues, debates about income distribution, and concerns about food supply. The careers of Victorian free-traders such as Richard Cobden and John Bright and the liberal Tories of the post-1815 era represent the kind of mixture of economic interests and liberal ideology that eventually secured victory for free trade.

The progress of free trade, then, was slow and uneven. An early sign that economic thought might have an influence on policy-makers was Burke's Act of 1773, amending the Corn Laws. The Corn Laws had in some form been on the books since the fifteenth century, were extended considerably in 1672 by the addition of a "bounty" (that is, subsidy) to exporters, and made permanent in 1689. Burke's Act attempted to streamline them by cutting the bounty when home prices were sufficiently high (44s. per quarter) and reducing the import duty to a nominal 6d. per quarter if the home price was at 48s. per quarter. Commercial policy showed the first unambiguous sign of Enlightenment influence in 1786 with the Eden commercial treaty between Britain and France. This treaty points to the direction that British commercial policy and international economic relations might have moved into had it not been for the disruptions of the French Revolution. The great irony of European history, as has already been noted, was that events triggered by the Enlightenment triggered a serious setback for enlightened policies in Britain. Concern about Jacobin-inspired political turmoil and fears of a French invasion led to retreats on a number of fronts. The wars changed prices and hence allocations, and specifically caused British landlords to invest heavily in agriculture to take advantage of the high prices of farm products; following the wars, they demanded protection—as did their continental counterparts in the manufacturing sector. The result was the rejuvenated Corn Laws of 1815, which, for a while, turned the clock back toward the protection of a politically powerful sector. It did away with the subsidy to exports (which perhaps was the most objectionable piece of rent-seeking), but replaced it with a prohibition on imports if the price fell below 80s. per quarter. Yet this success was ephemeral; the law was weakened in 1822 by allowing importation above 70s., and in 1828, the prohibition was replaced by a complex system of graduated duties meant to keep domestic prices at about 70–80s. per quarter. This system was again modified by Peel in 1842, before it was abolished.

All the same, commercial policy is a good illustration of the complexities of the impact of ideology on policy. As John Nye (2007) has shown, by most reasonable criteria Britain was not a free trade nation for much of the nineteenth century, and its overall rate of tariff protection was considerably higher than France's. However, in and of itself, this is not a sufficient indication that Enlightenment ideas had no effect. To be sure, the average tariff rate (computed as total tariff revenues as a proportion of imports) was far higher in Britain than in France in 1815, but this was largely because Britain was heavily taxed and, as noted, found collecting revenues from customs convenient as the government was determined to pay off the national debt (McCloskey, 1980). Between 1820 and 1850 average tariffs fell from about 60 percent to 20 percent, so that by mid-century the two nations had similar rates of tariff. Mercantilist views and protectionist interests in Britain were still strong, and fought back, but in the long run they were doomed. Economists in the school of liberal political economy, following the influential writings of Smith and Ricardo, helped persuade politicians to abandon foolhardy mercantilist practices and expand openness. To be sure, protection and regulation were abandoned slowly and reluctantly. There were just too many vested interests at stake for them to be eliminated without someone putting up a fight. But the combined impact of the heritage of Enlightenment ideology and an increasing assertiveness of an industrial middle class became increasingly powerful in the decades after 1815, and the country slowly and at times reluctantly abandoned mercantilism and embraced the cosmopolitan policy of openness that the *philosophes* had dreamed about. By that time Britain had attained a position of dominance that was the object of respect and envy throughout the world.

The openness of the economy was thus an important part of the story. But the home market remained of central importance to the Industrial Revolution. British population grew after 1750, and while the average Briton may not have become appreciably richer until well into the nineteenth century, the rise in the raw number of consumers and their growing access to cash defined an expanding market without precedent. Eighteenth-century Britain had a well-developed transportation system, based not just on coastal shipping but increasingly on a well-functioning system of private roads and canals built by entrepreneurs and local notables with some government help. There is little doubt that this transport system helped in technological progress, not just in making the mobility of people and ideas cheaper and faster, but because more integrated markets multiplied the gains from innovation and because protecting technologically backward "niches" would become increasingly difficult. Integrated markets led to growing product and input standardization, and people increasingly learned to buy products from far-away manufacturers, whom they did not know personally (Szostak, 1991).

Some scholars (e.g., Inikori, 2002) have argued that rather than a nationally integrated market Britain consisted of regional and relatively insulated economies. Such a description is specious, because if anything seems to be true about eighteenth-century Britain it is regional specialization, supported by the growing importance of interregional trade as transport improved. Birmingham made metal wares, the West Country made woolens, Staffordshire made ceramics, and Leicestershire made stockings. Regional boundaries were permeable and the oversized city of London served as a national market for goods from all over the kingdom. Of course, the level of trade was highly dependent on transportation costs, so that heavy and bulky goods were largely traded only over short distances unless they could use coastal shipping. But regional boundaries began to matter less and less as transport improved after 1750. Moreover, as I shall show in chapter 10, transportation itself benefited from the expansion of useful knowledge like few other industries.

The British Isle became a legally integrated market when Scotland was fully incorporated into the British economy in 1707, with Ireland still treated as a colony until its full incorporation in 1800. There is some debate in the literature as to what extent domestic demand was more important to the Industrial Revolution than foreign markets (Mokyr, 1998a; Cuenca, 2004). Elementary economic analysis suggests that a British manufacturer would not care a whit if his customer was in Britain, on the Continent, or in the colonies. But for the economy as a whole the trading sector mattered a great deal. Given the importance of foreign trade and relations with overseas countries, the connection between the Industrial Revolution and international trade has been the subject of much discussion. Two issues exist here that should be kept separate. One is that the British Industrial Revolution was enhanced and strengthened by the fact that it took place in an open economy, that trading goods and services with both European and more remote partners spurred and accelerated the Industrial Revolution. The other is the question of the importance of the British Empire, that is, actual political control over some of those trading partners.

During the entire period in question here, foreign trade expanded faster than total product. Total imports and exports in about 1700 have been estimated at £5.8 million and £4.4 million respectively, as opposed to £12.7 million and £9.9 millions respectively in 1772–74. By 1851 this had increased to £67 million. These numbers are not strictly comparable, since they are measured in inconsistent ways, but adjustments to them do not materially change the picture. All the same, as noted in chapter 4, access to foreign markets meant that the relative price of goods in which technological progress was the most rapid declined at a slower pace than it would have in a closed economy. International trade was not indispensable to successful industrialization, but by cushioning the decline in the relative price of goods in which the supply curve shifted out the most, it surely helped.

The more than doubling of the volume of foreign trade in the 1700–70 period had little to do with the Industrial Revolution but much with growing Atlantic trade with British and other colonies. The reasons are in part associated with the organization and technology of long-distance trade. Although sailing ships remained predominant until 1850, the costs of shipping kept falling as ships were designed and run more efficiently, as better navigational equipment reduced wrecks and enhanced speed, and as institutions that facilitated information and finance became more effective. In part, the reasons were political: British policy was firmly and unambiguously pro-trade. A pro-trade policy did not mean "free trade"—quite the contrary. In the eighteenth century, it meant above all ruthless competition with Britain's main rivals, the United Provinces, Spain, and France. Strict enforcement of the Navigation Acts, first passed in 1651, helped the British gradually weaken Dutch dominance of the carrying trade. Eighteenth-century political and military activity was aimed to weaken first Dutch and then French competition, and the effectiveness of the British navy was an important factor in bringing this hegemony about eventually. The Board of Trade was permanently established in 1696 and became an instrument of colonial administration and control. The colonial trade and the European trade were closely interconnected. Timber and other naval stores from the Baltic were essential to the eighteenth-century colonial trade, and re-exports of colonial wares (made inevitable by the Navigation Acts which prohibited direct trade between British colonies and the European Continent) became an essential part of the international flow of goods. Some historians, such as David Ormrod (2003), believe that at least until the mechanics of economic growth changed dramatically with the Industrial Revolution, the limits to economic growth were set by geopolitics, by the ability of foreign policy and military power to achieve advantage over others in commercial rivalry.

*   *   *

Foreign trade was one thing, imperialism another. During much of the eighteenth century empire and the powerful military apparatus supporting it was viewed by mercantilists as essential to prosperity and commerce, the misgivings of deeper thinkers such as Adam Smith notwithstanding. Modern historians have often seen it the same way. The importance of the British Empire and colonial trade to the development of the British economy has been emphasized by a number of scholars as a central factor in eighteenth-century development and even a cause of the Industrial Revolution (Inikori, 2002; O'Brien, 2006). Yet for much of the eighteenth century, it is debatable if the British colonial venture was unambiguously dominant. The peace treaties of Utrecht (1713) and Paris (1763) did establish Britain's dominance in Southern Asia and America (including the *Asiento*, the right to sell slaves to the Spanish colonies), but that of 1783 set them back a great deal. In the Caribbean, the French remained arguably more successful, controlling until 1793 the fertile island of Saint-Domingue, the largest sugar-exporting colony. Between 1715 and 1784, France's foreign trade grew faster than Britain's. Spanish and Portuguese colonies in America provided larger markets than the British colonies, and the Dutch possessions in Asia—relative to the size of the mother country—compared favorably with British India. Control of empires, moreover, seems not to have triggered an Industrial Revolution elsewhere. Britain aside, Switzerland and Belgium, two non-imperial nations, were successful continental industrializers, whereas the Netherlands and Portugal, which controlled large and rich colonies, remained behind. In the eighteenth century colonial markets had not reached the size that would make them a sine qua non. In 1784–86 Asia (that is, primarily India) absorbed 13.3 percent of British exports, a share that remained essentially constant until 1854–56. Of course, British colonial policy turned out eventually quite successful. By the early nineteenth century France and the Netherlands had been reduced to minor players in the colonial trade, with the French losses of Canada, India, and Saint Domingue particularly painful. But none of that was easily predictable in 1760.

The British Empire, of course, did play an important role in shaping the British economy in the eighteenth century in some respects. It must be credited with the expansion of commerce, shipping, and certain branches of manufacturing catering to or depending on long-distance shipping. It generated considerable profits for entrepreneurs and important gains for consumers at large. It produced a host of consumer goods that by 1800 cost a minute fraction of their price in 1650. It was, until the Industrial Revolution, the main force in the growth of many British towns. Bristol and London owed their eighteenth-century growth largely to colonial trade; Glasgow's growth was equally due to colonial trade, as were the other shipbuilding centers in Newcastle, London and Bristol. Of particular interest are the Royal Dockyards in Woolwich and Portsmouth, where the naval ships were built. They were probably the largest single employer in Britain, and a significant locus of innovation as well.

We could distinguish between a weak and a strong interpretation of the role of the foreign sector in the development of the British economy. The "weak role" emphasizes that the British navy and its policies allowed Britain to import colonial and other foreign goods at better prices, with lower freight and insurance costs, and supplied more reliably, while at the same time finding more dependable markets for British manufactured goods, supplied ever more cheaply and at higher quality. The British navy provided a secure environment for long-distance trade, and cleared the oceans of pirates and privateers. The Atlantic waters were cleared of pirates in the 1720s, and a convoy system was used to protect sugar ships when necessary (Crowhurst, 1977, pp. 80, 150, 204–05). British gunboats often helped local rulers to respect the property of British merchants, to say nothing of the property of His Majesty's government. No economist needs to be convinced that some international trade is better than no trade and that free trade needs to be supported by enforcement mechanisms that the state can supply most efficiently. Blue water policies were based on the belief that a strong naval presence supported trade. And trade led to growth for all the reasons that Adam Smith and nineteenth-century political economy explained.

Some scholars have gone further than this and tried to link eighteenth-century British mercantilism and imperialism with subsequent economic growth, arguing that it maximized, somehow, "the gains from overseas trade and imperialism" (O'Brien, 2006, p. 387). Patrick O'Brien (1988, 1994, 2006) and David Ormrod (2003), and more recently Findlay and O'Rourke (2007) have maintained that the aggressive and effective foreign policies followed by Hanoverian Britain in the eighteenth century and its powerful navy and take-no-prisoners attitude to its rivals created an economic empire of global dimensions that had far-reaching consequences for long-term growth. This view is a variation on Eric Hobsbawm's (1968, p. 50) theme that Britain's policies in the eighteenth century led to the "greatest triumph ever achieved by any state," a position that seems at least debatable, and the belief that war tended to boost exports (by crippling the competition) for which no evidence was adduced. Beside a post-hoc-ergo-propter-hoc logic there is little to recommend this interpretation. It fails to realize that war and protectionist measures, the inevitable results of these aggressive policies, were themselves the main element that disrupted and endangered normal trade. It also fails to recognize what Adam Smith and countless economists after him have seen, namely that voluntary trade between nations or regions benefits all sides and that political control did not normally enhance the overall gains from trade unless it was required to enforce contracts and property rights. If the Enlightenment doctrine of international trade had one message, it was that it is a classic positive-sum game, in which both sides can gain, and where one party's profit is not the other party's loss. To be sure, it is possible for one side to try to secure a disproportionate share of the gains from trade through military domination, legislation, and fiscal measures. Such policies, by distorting prices, curbing flows of merchandise, and inviting retaliation in kind from other nations, may in the end hurt trade altogether. If mercantilist policies degenerated into outright war, the costs of these policies would be compounded.

In the British mercantilist world, a tripartite global priority ordering was apparent: the interests of England (after 1707, Britain) were paramount. Its colonies, including Ireland, were in an intermediate position, subservient to Britain's needs, but ranked higher than competitor nations. Britain's trade with Ireland was characterized by this kind of asymmetry to the detriment and chagrin of the Irish, but its attempts to impose similar measures on its North American colonies in the end blew up in its face. Finally there were the trading "partners," often regarded more as rivals and competitors than as parties with whom one should do business. This is not to argue that determined pro-trade policies had no beneficial effects. They reduced the inherent risks of trade, eliminated some transactions and private enforcement costs, and helped disseminate information. In that way the state's mercantilist policies may have had a positive effect on the growth of trade. Although the colonial trade may have contributed to the wealth and well-being of *some* eighteenth-century Britons, the case that it was beneficial on a national level, let alone that it somehow led to the Industrial Revolution, is unpersuasive. What is at stake is whether this spur offset the obvious and high cost of these policies, and whether it was more effective than a more liberal policy. Most of the wars fought by Britain in the eighteenth century were in large part wars about colonies or colonial trade, and turned Britain into the most heavily taxed nation in Europe. War disrupted the very trade it was supposed to protect, especially since both sides employed privateers (government-sponsored pirates who sank ships and captured cargoes) and later imposed embargoes and trade restrictions. Some scholars seem to forget that the huge expenses of the Hanoverian foreign wars were costs, not benefits. Men-of-war were exceedingly expensive, around £50,000 in the 1780s, far more than was required to set up a cotton mill. Even without the threat of violence to trading partners, trade could and did emerge. Yet the notion that the Industrial Revolution "grew out of commerce—and especially commerce with the underdeveloped world" proposed by Hobsbawm (1968, p. 54) seems to be inaccurate and incomplete. It disregards the Enlightenment and the deep sources of technological progress. The belief that empire was a crucial factor in the success of the British economy may in part be based on a confusion between empire and openness. Openness did not necessarily require political domination, and whereas control did provide the colonialist nationals with some trading advantages, these were paid for dearly. In the years after the Peace of Vienna in 1815, the Enlightenment idea that political domination by one party over another was not a necessary condition for mutually beneficial exchange between them to take place, was vindicated for all to see.

The logical dilemma for those who feel that the British Empire was the answer to the question "why Britain?" is that trade with the empire may have been of importance before the Industrial Revolution, but lost much of its primacy in the years after 1780, when it might have been needed the most (Cain and Hopkins, 1980, p. 474). The greatest foreign policy fiasco of the British Empire, the loss of the thirteen American colonies, occurred right in the early stages of the Industrial Revolution but does not seem to have done much to slow it down. Despite political independence, the young United States remained firmly in the British commercial sphere until complications in Europe drove the two apart again for a few short periods between 1807 and 1814 (and indeed, the main disruptions occurred because of Britain's harsh use of its naval superiority, which led to Jefferson's embargo of 1806–07). When economic relations between the two nations were disrupted briefly in 1812–15 and again in 1861–65, it caused both economies considerable economic pain.

Even without political control and without the support of the British navy, Britain would have been able to secure what it needed from the rest of the world as long as it could pay. The Industrial Revolution did not require the creation of British India or the control of Canada, nor did it depend on the cheap sugar from the Caribbean. Enlightenment thinkers were, on the whole, skeptical of colonialism. The more radical thinkers such as James Mill squarely supported its abandonment. Jeremy Bentham argued that Spain would be better off without its colonies. In return for benefits to a few, he felt, restrictive colonial trade misallocated resources, raised prices and lowered the nation's growth (Cain, 2006). If the colonies were given independence, the volume of Spanish trade with them would actually increase (cited by Engerman, 2004, p. 266). James Anderson, a Scottish political economist, felt the same way about Britain's colonies (1782, pp. 60–98). A case could be made that history proves him right. To be sure, Indian and Caribbean markets were flooded by cheap factory-produced British textiles, yet these markets did not become of great importance until after most of the technological successes had been attained. Imperial markets were significant for some industries and becoming more so over the course of the eighteenth century. However, they remained less important than foreign markets in non-Empire nations, and certainly less important than the home market. In 1726–30, colonial markets accounted for 16.2 percent of British exports; by 1781–85, this proportion had increased to 39.4 percent, but at least half of that went to what was just about to become the United States. In the 1840s colonial markets in Asia, Africa, and the West Indies accounted for 24.4 percent of all exports and 25.4 percent of manufacturing exports. In every period Europe and the United States absorbed more than half of British exports.

The specific counterfactual here matters to the argument: if Britain had not built an empire, and all its rivals had, perhaps it would have found itself at a disadvantage as hostile powers controlled shipping routes and essential raw materials. But given the imperial structure of the world in 1770, would a world of freer trade and fewer colonial and predatory wars not have been better suited to economic development and industrialization? There may have been some benefits associated with these wars, but did they cover the costs? And if these benefits were largely gained at the expense of other nations, would there not have been political repercussions that eventually helped make the costs even larger? On the path to a more modern economy driven by technological progress, empire was, on balance, a distraction, not a stimulus to progress, and the blue water policies were more atavism than path to economic development. Adam Smith ([1776], 1976, Vol. II, p. 110) was the first to point out that colonies diverted British commerce from other regions, and thus rather than creating more trade, colonial ventures distorted it. On the whole, Enlightenment thought realized that imperial wars did not justify the costs. The most eloquent expression of an Enlightenment thinker on this matter remains Benjamin Franklin's statement in a famous letter to Joseph Banks in 1783 that there never was a good war or a bad peace, adding the less well-known lament that "what vast additions to the conveniences and comforts of living might mankind have acquired if the money spent in wars had been employed in works of public utility!" ([1783], 1907, Vol. 9, p. 74). Many Enlightenment thinkers, led by Jeremy Bentham, agreed with this view.

Some scholars have pointed to the Caribbean slave and sugar trades as sources of immense profits, which they were. Commercial interests, shipbuilding, banking, insurance services, and industries catering to the triangular colonial trade prospered, and the towns of Bristol and Liverpool consequently grew. Yet the links between Liverpool and Manchester do not prove Manchester's "tremendous dependence on the triangular trade" as Eric Williams famously put it and recent work (Inikori, 2002) has not been very successful in substantiating Williams' famous claim that the profits from this trade "provided one of the main streams of that accumulation of capital in England which financed the Industrial Revolution" (Williams, 1944, p. 52). Indeed, the most recent examination of the Williams thesis (Findlay and O'Rourke, 2007, p. 337), although sympathetic, concludes that it "reflects an inappropriate theoretical framework." The sentiment that the exploitation of African slaves in the Caribbean region was important to the British economy may reflect our sense that it surely mattered to the slaves themselves, as it did to Africa, and to the areas to which slaves were shipped. Yet that does not necessarily mean that it mattered to the same degree to Britain and the other European economies that were the main beneficiaries of the triangular trade system. The West Indian sugar economy, especially the highly successful colonies of Jamaica and Barbados, was substantial, but Britain was by no means the only European economy that exploited Africans in the sugar plantations of the New World. How could sugar colonies explain why the Industrial Revolution occurred in Britain and not in France or in Portugal (Eltis and Engerman, 2000)? In the history of imperialism, there is an unjust and cruel asymmetry in the respective histories of the victim and the perpetrator, an asymmetry also illustrated by the economic relations Britain had with India and with Ireland. John Robert Seeley's widely cited 1883 statement that in the eighteenth century "the history of England is not in England but in America and Asia" (cited by Findlay and O'Rourke, 2007, p. 230) is thus nonsense as far as economic history is concerned.

Perhaps typical of the way the British treated the non-British world was their policy in Ireland. In 1699, at the instigation of special interests from the woolen-producing counties in the English south-west, the government prohibited it from exporting finished woolen cloth to Britain, and Irish raw wool could only be sold domestically. Britain decided that Ireland should be a linen-producing nation.

Throughout the period in question, Britain relied on Ireland as a low-risk source of supply of agricultural products and a market for its goods (Thomas, 1985). Yet despite the 1801 Act of Union, Ireland was never viewed by the British as really part of the same country. When push came to shove in the horrible famine of 1845–50, Ireland was largely left to its own devices. Callous and unconscionable these policies were, yet it is difficult to argue that they were, in and of themselves, a critical factor in the British Industrial Revolution.

The one element in the Atlantic trade that has been argued to have been essential to the Industrial Revolution was North American slavery (Inikori, 2002, ch. 8). Before 1780, most of the (modest) import of raw cotton came to Britain from the West Indies, but clearly the potential to grow it there was limited, and following the inventions in the cotton industry in the 1780s, the industry needed an elastic source of supply and came to depend increasingly on the southern United States. Simply put, without U.S. slave labor it is hard to see how the tremendous growth in the demand for raw cotton could have been satisfied. Some counterfactual scenarios come to mind: for instance, more white immigrant labor in the US South could have been employed, or more cotton imports could have come from the Middle East, but these would have made raw cotton far more expensive and other textiles might have held their own for longer. While certain processes in the supply of raw cotton could be mechanized (for example, the cotton gin, invented in 1793), the planting and picking of cotton in the fields of the Southern United States remained a manual, labor-intensive process, and as the demand for cotton increased, American plantations rapidly switched to raising this crop. The resulting increase in the demand for labor was met through the employment of slaves of African origin. It is here and not in the consequences of eighteenth-century triangular trade that slavery truly "mattered" for the Industrial Revolution. Yet this is true exclusively for the cotton industry. The many other technological advances, successful and not, did not depend nearly as much on empire. The reverse effect, of course, is far stronger: without the British Industrial Revolution, the history of black slavery in what became the Southern States would have been very different indeed. If American slavery did not by itself make the Industrial Revolution, the Industrial Revolution was largely responsible for the survival of American slavery after 1780.

Trade with more remote economies was of growing relative importance to British producers and consumers in the eighteenth century. By 1785, importation of non-European goods accounted for about one-third of British imports from all countries including Ireland, but that share went up substantially during the Napoleonic Wars. By the middle of the nineteenth century, the share of non-European imports was 70 percent, though by that time trade with Ireland was counted as "internal" (Davis, 1979, p. 93). Raw materials accounted for much of it. Producers depended on raw cotton and dyestuffs from America, timber from Canada, high-quality iron from Sweden, and naval stores from the Baltic.

Consumers bought sugar from the Caribbean, silks and other high-quality textiles from Asia (until British manufacturers learned to out-compete them). Tea, tobacco, furs, rum, rice, and fancy textiles were all traded in ever-growing volumes. Some of this was re-exported, but British consumers had increasing access to and desire for exotic products. To pay for this, Britain exported manufactured goods and shipping services. India was eventually to become a major market for British manufactures. There was also a great deal of "third-party hauling," including for the entire eighteenth century the highly remunerative slave trade, which helped build the city of Liverpool. In the nineteenth century, after the slave trade was suppressed, the British merchants found the opium trade increasingly remunerative. They sold opium grown in India to Chinese consumers and when the Chinese government objected, the British government used its gunboats to great effect against a helpless giant in the infamous Opium Wars of 1840–41. Mercantilist states of mind, obviously, survived the Enlightenment even if they were less and less often aimed against fellow Europeans.

To sum up, the "strong" argument which maintains that the large foreign sector and the aggressive mercantilist policies that supported it could also take credit for the Industrial Revolution and long-term technological changes that were at its core is difficult to support. The Industrial Enlightenment, the taproot of long-term progress, did not depend on colonial trade and mercantilist policies, even as the audiences of the scientific lectures were sipping their Indian tea sweetened with Caribbean sugar. On the contrary, mercantilism and the Enlightenment were in the long run incompatible, even if not all eighteenth-century *philosophes* were necessarily as far-sighted as Adam Smith. Imperial mercantilism, the hard-nosed and tough foreign policy that Britain pursued through much of the eighteenth century, was above all a rent-seeking system in which the British taxpayer and consumer paid for the infrastructure and support that made the profits of a fairly small number of merchants and "nabobs" possible. In exchange for military protection and policies that excluded others, the special interests that benefited from this system used some of the rents they accumulated to help pay for a part of the expenses of the state. The rest had to be paid by taxpayers. People of power and wealth benefited, but at the expense of consumers and foreigners. The national debt increased to pay for a navy that protected British interests abroad, but most of the benefits of empire accrued to a relatively small part of society. For sustained growth to reach its full potential, mercantilism had eventually to be dismantled.

A direct link leading from trade itself (as opposed to a more general openness to foreign ideas) to technological change, as would be required by the "strong" hypothesis, is even more difficult to establish. It is often maintained that the stimulus of foreign markets in some way triggered technological progress and thus created a positive feedback mechanism in which trade and constantly improving technology reinforced one another. The argument appears plausible: in a famous quote from 1769 Matthew Boulton wrote to his partner James Watt, "It is not worth my while to manufacture your engine for three counties only, but I find it very well worth my while to make it for all the world" (cited by Roll, [1930], 1968, p. 14). Yet overseas sales of steam engines remained limited for many years, not only because their transportation was naturally awkward, but also because of the law prohibiting the exports of machinery and the disruptions caused to world trade by political conflicts. Boulton had to be satisfied with the British Isles as a market for his engines—and the record suggests that it was quite adequate.

Indeed, the argument that technological progress was export-driven seems awkward precisely because the period 1776–1815, which covers most of the classical Industrial Revolution, was hardly a period of uninterrupted foreign trade. First the American Revolution, then more than two decades of war with the European Continent, with an American embargo of 1806 and then another war with the US, all played havoc with Britain's dependence on export markets. British merchants, expelled from their traditional European markets, "discovered" South America and between 1806 and 1808 sent large amounts of merchandise to Montevideo, Buenos Aires, and Rio de Janeiro. Yet the hapless merchants lost fortunes by having to sell their wares at bargain basement prices (Heaton, 1946). J.R. McCulloch described British merchants' pathetic attempts to send *skates* to Rio (1864, p. 272, emphasis in original). The disruptions of trade flows in those years were thus quite severe, and Britain was forced to abandon the gold standard in 1797. Privateers, blockades, and military actions made foreign markets unreliable and uncertain when it counted most, and statistics used to try to depict this period as one of commercial expansion (Cuenca, 2004) are questionable at best. Insurance and freight charges shot up. Yet the pace of technological progress seems hardly to have been affected and while Britain went through some hard years during the Napoleonic Wars, the *relative* position it occupied in world trade became stronger. After four decades of disruptions in foreign trade, sufficiently severe to make the great economist David Ricardo include an entire chapter on the "Sudden Changes in the Channels of Trade" in his *Principles of Political Economy* of 1816, Britain emerged from a quarter of a century of war and blockades the envy of its continental neighbors.

The logical difficulty in arguing for a strong causal link between growing world demand and technological innovation, then, is that elementary economic analysis suggests that the reverse is the more likely mechanism. The logic of technological progress was (and is) that to a large extent it created its own market. By increasing productivity, it increased real income and thus provided much of the domestic market, as it were pulling the economy up by its bootstraps. Higher productivity also meant lower prices, and these attracted more consumers, at home and abroad. The original existence of export markets cannot be held to have had more than a second-order effect. It is hard to think of a single invention of the period for which the domestic market alone would not have provided enough demand to cover the costs of development even if export markets helped prevent prices from falling subsequently. Cheaper and better products will be more attractive to consumers and will thus secure profits by driving out the competition. The more consumers, the more profits, but either way, the innovations will be introduced, unless there is an overhead investment required to switch to the new technology that is so large that the domestic market is inadequate. At the foundation of economic expansion lies the ability and willingness of society to extend and exploit the useful knowledge at its disposal and experience productivity growth. If it did so better and faster than its trading partners, it would thereby create the comparative advantage that drove Ricardo's trade model (Temin, 1997). There can be no question that this is precisely what happened in the textile, iron, and energy industries during the Industrial Revolution.

Of course, in some sense demand factors must have mattered: why would anyone engage in the effort, costs, and risks to develop a new technique unless he thought that the product could be sold at all? This seems at first glance a reasonable argument, but the British patent records of the time are full of ingenious devices that seem to us completely unsaleable, from life jackets made of iron cylinders to a variety of patented medicines purporting to cure kidney stones. There were many inventors whose sense of what could be sold was less dead-on than that of Boulton or Wedgwood. But the argument made by scholars such as Cuenca (2004), who stress the importance of export-led growth, claims more than that. Their argument implies that the domestic market would have been inadequate for these inventors, so that *only* the hope of selling the product abroad kept the inventive efforts alive. Such arguments may perhaps have been true for small economies such as the Netherlands and Switzerland, but for a large (and growing) population such as the British Isles, it seems implausible. The colonial and foreign markets were, of course, a bonus, but between 1776 and 1815, at least, these markets looked uncertain and a weak reed indeed to lean on most of the time.

The true taproot of British economic development was to be found among the cotton spinners of Lancashire, the mining mechanics of Cornwall, the scientists and mechanics of Glasgow, the potters of Staffordshire, and the instrument-makers of London. The great engineers such as the Stephensons and the Brunels who conceived of and then built the steam locomotives and the great ships had promoted and stimulated international trade more than all the mercantilist laws together. It was ingenuity and innovativeness that drove exports and trade, not the other way around. The great minds of the Industrial Enlightenment had shown how the useful knowledge they were accumulating could be used to improve, to rationalize, and to innovate. The rest is commentary.

*   *   *

The increasingly free trade between 1820 and 1860 and the growing reliance on foreign markets suggest how important it was for Britain to abandon mercantilism. In part, of course, the causality worked the other way: because Britain was palpably enjoying the benefits of world-wide specialization and exchange, abandoning mercantilism was regarded as a wise policy. The nation that led the world technologically did not have to contemplate "infant industry" arguments in the vein of Alexander Hamilton or Friedrich List. Yet we cannot dismiss the ideological component of the Enlightenment here. After all, other European nations such as Prussia became equally committed to free trade, even though they did not have Britain's colonial and naval power.

Indeed, economic historians have long argued (McCloskey, 1980; Irwin, 1988; for a dissenting view, see Nye, 2007) that because Great Britain was large and rich, it could have affected international commodities prices. Had British manufacturers and merchants been able to collude and coordinate their action through a government policy, they might have been able to improve the terms of trade at which Britain bought and sold goods by setting an "optimal tariff." The absence of that policy meant that British income could have been even higher. Such an optimal tariff, as it is known in economics literature, was in reality anything but. It simply would have been an act of rent-seeking on a global level, in which a tariff would have caused British incomes to have increased (perhaps), but Britain's citizens would have gained less than its trading partners would have lost, meaning that *overall* there would have been a welfare loss. Such considerations are not the only objection to such policies. Without knowing with some precision the elasticities involved, it was hard to get the optimal tariff just right. Moreover, as Nye points out, the level of tariffs in Britain in the first half of the nineteenth century was already such that their tariff levels may have been above the optimal level. Most seriously, the idea of an optimal tariff abstracts from the very real possibility that trading partners might respond with a retaliatory tariff, in the end reducing the overall level of trade and everyone's welfare (Irwin, 1988, 1159–60). In any case, whether it was for ideological reasons or not, Albion was magnanimous and allowed other nations to enjoy the benefits of its superior technology by buying British goods at lower prices.

Growing foreign trade remained the hallmark of the period 1700–1850, with notable setbacks during wars. Estimates of the ratio of foreign trade to income, or the ratio of industrial exports to aggregate industrial product are not easy to make or to assess, but the best ones we can muster are reported in table 8.1. Two things are clear: exports did increase as a proportion of aggregate output, yet surprisingly more in the period 1700–60 and the period 1830–50 than during the classical Industrial Revolution years. Second, the proportion of industrial output exported depends crucially on whose estimates of industrial output are used, and clearly it is premature to assess precisely how critical the growth of export markets was to the industrial sector. We can be more certain about the role of imports. The one

Table 8.1. Exports Growth, 1700–1851

Year	Total exports (£ millions)	Nominal GDP (England only)	Exports as a % of GDP	Industrial exports as a % of industrial product (Crafts)	Industrial exports as a % of industrial product (Cuenca)	
1700	3.8	65.4	5.8	24.4	13[a]	20[b]
1760	8.3	92.0	9.0	35.2	18	28
1780	8.7	116.6	7.5	21.8	25	33
1801	28.4	230.9	12.3	34.4	40	40
1831	38.9	372.4	10.4	21.9	49	45
1851	67.3	505.5	13.3	24.7	69[c]	n.a.

[a] Column using Crafts's estimates of industrial output.
[b] Column using Cuenca's estimates of industrial output.
[c] Actual point estimate (all other Cuenca data are 11-year averaged centered on date).

Sources: Computed from Davis (1979, pp. 88–89), Crafts (1985, p. 132), and Cuenca (1997, table 1). Nominal GDP figures (England only), Clark, private communication.

indispensable input to a key industry was raw cotton. There were other raw materials that Britain imported: wool and ores from Spain, raw flax from the Baltic, livestock from Ireland, grains from France and Eastern Europe in years of poor harvests. These data are summarized in table 8.2. It is striking how, even in the early stages of the Industrial Revolution, Britain's foreign trade is already heavily specialized, with manufacturing dominating exports, and the country depending on imports for food and raw materials (understated in the table, since it excludes imports from Ireland). The dependence on foreign raw materials is often associated with raw cotton, which was the largest single item. Yet even at its peak, the value of cotton imports did not account for more than a quarter of raw materials. The industrial sector was, as we have seen, a great deal more than just cotton. In any event, with Britain's growing specialization and population, it seems obvious that it would start to import agricultural goods—despite its efficiency in farming. To pay for it, Britain had to export.

Table 8.2: The composition of foreign trade (without Ireland), 1784-1846

	1784-86	1814-16	1844-46[a]
Imports			
Raw materials £s (%)	9,585 (47.0%)	36,408 (56.2%)	51,033 (62.2%)
Foodstuffs £s (%)	8,657 (42.5%)	27,602 (42.6%)	27,386 (33.4%)
Manufactured goods £s(%)	2,144 (10.5%)	731 (1.1%)	3,544 (4.3%)
Total	20,386 (100%)	64,741 (100%)	81,963 (100%)
Exports			
Raw materials £s (%)	867 (6.8%)	1,460 (3.3%)	5,177 (8.9%)
Foodstuffs £s (%)	1,165 (9.2%)	4,995 (11.2%)	1,809 (3.1%)
Manufactured goods £s (%)	10,658 (84.0%)	38,019 (85.5%)	51,434 (88.0%)
Total	12,690 (100%)	44,474 (100%)	58,420 (100%)

[a] Data include imports into Ireland.

Source: Davis (1979).

To deal with the economy at an aggregate level, in which international trade, factor accumulation, relative prices, distribution, and population are allowed to affect one another, economists need fairly complex models. One of the lessons of economics is that when some kind of change is imposed on a system, the initial response may be quite different than the ultimate new equilibrium, in which the various feedbacks, reverberations, and interactions have been fully played out. One method to go to the next step and analyze the complete causal quantitative relations between different variables in a rigorous way is what is known among economists as CGE or computable general equilibrium. The method allows different markets to interact in complicated ways as the result of some outside "shock" such as a war, a legislative act, a change in taxes or tariffs, or even a growth in productivity. Such analytic insights come at a cost: the analysis assumes away a variety of frictions and costs, and does not allow for unemployed resources. It makes a host of assumptions that historical purists will find difficult to swallow, but these simplifications are the price we pay for better insights. Subject to these caveats, the method can provide some insights that allow the economic historian to carry out logical inference that otherwise would have to rest entirely on obiter dicta and intuition.

Perhaps the most important feature of these models in their most recent incarnation is that they consider the British economy to be open. General equilibrium models depend crucially on whether we assume the economy to be closed or open; many things that are true in an open economy are no longer true in a closed one. One example is the role of agriculture in the industrialization process. Matsuyama (1992) has demonstrated rigorously an intuition long prevalent among economic historians, namely that the relation between agricultural productivity and the rate of industrialization depends on the openness of the economy. In a closed economy, manufacturing depends on productivity growth in agriculture and its capacity to produce a surplus that will permit the reallocation of resources from farming to industry and to provide a market for manufactured products. It used to be thought that a prior "agricultural revolution" was a necessary precondition for British industrialization. Yet in an open economy this is clearly false: food can be imported and paid for by industrial goods. In fact, in an open economy a highly productive agricultural sector signals to the economy that its comparative advantage lies in farming. In the short run, it would pay the economy to specialize in farm products, but if future demand growth or technological progress is slower in agriculture, the economy might forego the (unforeseen) advantages of industrialization. In a small, open economy such as the Netherlands after 1815, a highly productive agricultural sector got in the way of industrialization and delayed it by many decades (Mokyr, 1976). In Britain, high agricultural productivity notwithstanding, industrialization occurred because manufacturing became even more productive. Matsuyama's model implies, correctly, that in an open economy the Industrial Revolution occurred not *because* of but *despite* growth in agricultural productivity.

Yet such models may not always reflect the historical reality. In part that is because the British economy was neither perfectly open (with negligible transport costs) nor closed (with very high transport costs). It was not a *small* open economy but one that could and did affect world prices. Hence, as it bought more agricultural goods and sold more manufactured goods, the terms of trade (that is, the price of agricultural goods relative to industrial products) turned against it. Moreover, we have to take into account the effects on distribution and savings. Crafts and Harley (2004) use a CGE model to simulate what would have happened to the

British economy if agricultural imports had not been allowed to increase (and had remained fixed at the level of 1770, about 85 percent lower than they actually were in 1841), so that Britain would have had to feed itself (for example if agricultural tariffs had been raised even higher). This would have raised agricultural prices relative to industrial prices, and thus enriched landlords. Since landlords were high savers, the counterfactual capital stock in 1841 would have been 18 percent higher. Industrial exports would have fallen by a third, but precisely for that reason Britain's terms of trade would have declined much less than they actually did, and hence the rather disturbing conclusion is reached that in the presence of trade-inhibiting tariffs, GNP per person would have been higher. Crafts and Harley hasten to add that they do not *really* believe this result and that "in general the opposite is the case" (p. 96).

The sometimes surprising findings of CGE models are less counterintuitive to economists, who have long been trained to realize that second- and higher-order "rounds" often reverse the first effects that our intuition indicates. All the same, the finding that higher tariffs lead to higher incomes depends critically on the degree to which world prices respond to changes in British trade. The lower that response (that is, the smaller the share of Britain relative to the rest of the world), the more obviously a tariff will hurt the economy. Moreover, the Crafts–Harley model measures the impact of changes in Britain on Britain, without considering the impact on the rest of the world. A more complete model would take into account the "other" economy affected, namely the rest of the world. A reduction in British agricultural imports might have slightly increased British income, but not world income. The model takes into account the effect of changes in income distribution on capital formation, but it does not take into account the full complexities of the capital market discussed above. It stands to reason that much of the hypothetical additional savings of landlords might not have found very profitable projects to invest in, given that the intersectoral flow of funds was still as limited as we have seen. Such relaxation in the assumptions might affect the results materially.

CHAPTER 9

Agriculture in the Age of Enlightenment

The mundane world of farming seems to be rather remote from the intellectual sphere of ideas. But an economy cannot be enlightened unless it has enough to eat. Defining "enough" is of course a difficult task here, but it should be obvious that if British food supplies had run out at some point during the period under discussion, the entire process would have ground to a halt. The food supply, however, did not run out, to the surprise of many contemporaries, and the British agricultural sector clearly played a role in averting such a disaster. But what role? Was there an Agricultural Enlightenment, comparable to the Industrial Enlightenment?

The history of farming and agriculture in Britain is one of the areas in which a serious revision in the thinking among specialists has occurred in the past decades, and yet it has remained controversial. The traditional view of British farming for many years was that organizational and technological changes in the century or so before and during the Industrial Revolution, often referred to as the Agricultural Revolution, increased productivity to the point where the rural sector could shed large number of workers without reducing food production. These workers could then be employed in producing manufactured goods and services and thus help bring about economic modernization. This story was pleasing, and seemed consistent with theory and with the experience of other countries. The term "Agricultural Revolution" has been used widely for this account, and a number of scholars still cling to the idea that something that merits this term describes the development of British agriculture between 1700 and 1850. The problem is that it is simply not consistent with much of the available evidence and the majority of specialists have abandoned the concept. Yet data on the aggregate agricultural economy are sufficiently poor and scarce, and the difficulties in measuring total agricultural output and inputs sufficiently severe for learned and reasonable scholars to continue to differ deeply on the issue. The reason for the disputatiousness of a seemingly innocuous topic is not only that reliable and representative data are singularly hard to come by in this area, but perhaps deeper, that scholars recognized it as an age of improvement, one in which Enlightenment beliefs in progress clearly permeated agricultural practices, yet there were no spectacular technological breakthroughs of multiple-purpose techniques in farming that improved productivity of crops across a wide spectrum. Neither the growth of useful knowledge in farm practices nor the reforms in the institutions in the agricultural sector seem to have had any dramatic effects. All the same, there were advances, and they pale in comparison only with other sectors, not with agriculture's own past.

Detailed local studies of British farming before the eighteenth century have shown that the British were already quite productive in raising food and raw materials from the land long before the technological revolutions of the eighteenth and nineteenth centuries (Allen, 2004). This finding is consistent with the well-established fact that around 1700 only about a third of all Britons were making their living from agriculture. Leaving aside foreign trade, in effect one British farmer raised enough food for himself and two others. In an age without chemical fertilizers, insecticides, and agricultural machinery, without detailed knowledge of genetics, soil chemistry, and the biology of pests—the foundations of the increased agricultural productivity of the twentieth century—it is striking that British farmers were so productive, more so than many farmers elsewhere. A recent comparison of arable farming estimates that English farm output per worker in 1705 was twice what it was in France and farm output per acre 50 percent higher. By 1775, this gap had increased substantially, to a ratio of 4.3:1 in labor productivity and 2.5:1 in land productivity (Brunt, 2006a, p. 15). These numbers are not to be taken too literally, as the data are very fragile, but it seems clear that this gap reflects a clear-cut British agricultural superiority.

High productivity in British agriculture was maintained by a combination of techniques, suitable for different soil types. On the whole, it involved a close interaction of arable farming and animal husbandry. Animals were increasingly stall-fed with field crops; in return they were healthier and stronger, and produced more manure that could then be used to fertilize field crops. Better tools, implements, some new crops, and water control technology were all elements in this story. Yet at the center of agricultural progress were changes in the way crops were rotated. Rotation served a number of purposes, including the breaking of disease cycles and risk management. Above all, however, it helped to restore the mineral content of the land, and especially to restore the nitrogen content in its usable form (not all soil nitrogen can be used by plants). Two kinds of rotation mattered most. One was the famous Norfolk rotation in which clover and turnips were rotated with barley and wheat. The technique was introduced from the Netherlands in the mid-seventeenth century, and by 1710 half of all farmers were growing some turnips. Turnips aided the soil indirectly through animals, but clover was a miracle crop that deposited "mineralized" (that is, usable) nitrogen directly into the soil and thus enhanced fertility (Allen, 2008). The second technique was quite different: it was known as "convertible husbandry" and involved growing cereals on land for years and then switching it to pasturage for decades so that the nitrogen content could recover. This technique was still widely practiced in 1700, but then fell into disuse as more sophisticated rotations replaced it. When exactly these rotations were introduced and how common they were remains in dispute.

There is now some evidence suggesting that the high levels of agricultural productivity in Britain around 1700 were nothing new and date back to the Middle
Ages. The Ramsey manors in Huntingdonshire in the eastern Midlands, which
have left us a great deal of evidence, show that labor productivity in agriculture in
the first half of the fourteenth century was as high as it was to be in the early
nineteenth century (Karakacili, 2004). To be sure, Ramsey Abbey may have been
unusually productive, and the work of Campbell (1983) has suggested a great deal
of variation in medieval agricultural productivity. In a similar vein, however,
Campbell and Overton (1993) have found that land productivity of the 1300s was
not surpassed until about 1710 in Norfolk. As this area was at the cutting edge of
farming technology, it may not have been representative either. Comparing *best*-
practice farming in one period with *average*-practice farming in another will give
misleading results. All the same, by 1700 British farming was, on average, as good
as could be found anywhere at this time. The concept of an eighteenth-century
Agricultural Revolution, analogous to the Industrial Revolution, has become increasingly difficult to defend. Instead, modern research seems to indicate that
much of the output per worker and total factor productivity growth had started
in the seventeenth century, when British farmers learned to adopt agricultural
techniques that had previously been developed in the Low Countries and constituted one ingredient of the astonishing economic development of those regions
before 1700. They continued apace in the eighteenth century, and by 1800 progress had been by all accounts impressive. It seems unlikely, however, that scholars
will ever reach a consensus on whether the eighteenth century witnessed an
acceleration in productivity, much less its precise timing and magnitude.

What were the changes in British farming that took place in the century and a
half after 1700? There were many changes, and whether they amount to a
"revolution" is a matter of taste. For one thing, the period saw the final demise of
open-field agriculture in Britain. Medieval farming in Britain (and much farming
on the Continent as late as 1850) had been "open field," in which land cultivated
by different farmers was not fenced off, and reverted to common use after the
harvest (largely communal livestock grazing on the post-harvest stubble and other
common lands). Open fields often meant non-contiguous pieces of land—that is,
scattered plots. It required a fair amount of cooperation between farmers. By
Tudor times the system was already in decline, and enclosure of open fields
(turning the disjoint and scattered strips of land into contiguous farms separated
by fences or hedges and allocating the common lands for private cultivation)
gradually reduced the proportion of land cultivated in this fashion. By 1700, it is
estimated, only about 29 percent of all Britain was still open field. This percentage
declined to around 8 percent in 1850, so that during the period 1700–1850, over
20 percent of all land was enclosed. Enclosures had been almost exclusively
voluntary before 1760, but in the last third of the eighteenth century parliamentary
enclosures became necessary to finish the process in those areas (mostly in the

Midlands) where peasants had resisted it and where only coercion could bring about enclosures.

Although the first parliamentary enclosures occurred as early as 1604, few bills of enclosure were passed before 1730, whereas between 1760 and 1800 1,800 such bills were passed. They often involved a complete survey of the land in question, checked on titles and leases, and redrew the layout of the land. Parliamentary enclosures required a bill of enclosure, submitted by the landowners to request the procedure. Once granted, the Bill required Parliament to appoint special commissioners, who reallocated not only the open fields (often scattered into many small plots) but also wastes, common lands, and grazing lands. These commissioners were often full-time and skilled professionals, employing surveyors and legal experts. At the end of the process, the new plots had to be enclosed by hedges or fences, rental contracts and tithes were revised, and some lands reassigned. Because it was more costly per acre to fence a small plot than a large plot, and because the smallholders had made disproportionate use of the common lands, it was believed that the enclosure movement discriminated against the smallholders and "cottagers" and was turning them into a de facto rural proletariat. Parliamentary enclosures were a uniquely British phenomenon. Enclosures, thus, were thought to have been part of British exceptionalism. Much of the Continent was still struggling with the perplexities of open fields well into the nineteenth century. The enclosure movement is one example of Britain's unique ability to change its institutions when economic circumstances required.

Whether parliamentary enclosures represented an enforcement of property rights or a violation of them could be disputed. The problem was that in open-field agriculture "property rights" were not defined with the sharpness that they are today. A landowner could "own" land but a copyholder or freeholder had certain inalienable rights on the use of common or others' land as long as he paid his rents. Neighbors owned the right to have their animals graze on others' fields after the harvest was brought in. Insofar as such "legal rights" were extinguished, owners were always compensated. But when the rights were traditional, especially those pertaining to the use of common lands associated with a plot that a tenant held but did not formally own, they were often lost without compensation during the enclosure process. What is clear, however, is that enclosures involved winners and losers. The losers were primarily smallholders who had enjoyed customary informal rights, which were mercilessly extinguished, those asked to put up expensive fences around their holdings, and those who had been relying on the common fields and waste to supplement their income and fuel supply (primarily women).

For many years, it was thought that enclosures had been the key to the growth of British agriculture. On the surface, it may seem to economists that there is a good logic to this argument. Open fields appeared to imply inefficient property rights, rife with negative spillovers and neighborhood effects, constraining what each individual decision-maker could do by necessitating cumbersome negotiations with the owners of adjacent plots. Moreover, the scattering of open fields may have been in the way of exploiting significant economies of scale in many aspects of farming, including improvements, the acquisition of more sophisticated tools, and the supervision of labor. And yet, despite the economist's intuition and the enthusiasm for enclosures of some contemporaries such as Arthur Young, there is little hard evidence to support the hypothesis that enclosures were a necessary condition for the diffusion of better techniques or superior crops, or that they in some other way increased agricultural productivity dramatically. The more scholars study the open fields, the more they realize that open-field agriculture was quite capable of technological progress, efficient organization, and productivity growth (McCloskey, 1972; Turner, 1986; Allen, 1992). In contrast with the accepted wisdom of earlier research, modern scholars have concluded that the enclosures were not strictly necessary to increase farm production, or yields per worker, or to create a large contingent of redundant workers who had no choice but to leave the land and find employment in urban mills. The evidence carefully assembled by these economic historians suggests a far weaker conclusion, which is that enclosed lands were generally more versatile and capable of adopting improved cultivation techniques, but that the margin was not nearly as high as its enthusiasts claimed. What enclosures did, above all, was to change the geography of the land, the organization of agricultural production, and the social composition of the agricultural labor force. Those are certainly weighty changes, but they were gradual and local in their impact. It is questionable if they amounted to an "Agricultural Revolution."

As a result of enclosures and consolidation, the size of the average agricultural holding increased. In 1700, average farm size in open field lands was around 65 acres. By 1800 this had increased to 150 acres in the south of England and to perhaps 100 in the north. These larger amalgamated units were enclosed and run by professional managers on new, market-based principles. By the early nineteenth century, the peasant-proprietor (in Britain a yeoman freeholder or copyholder), a growing presence in France, West Germany, and the Low Countries, was on his way out in Britain. Replacing him was a capitalist system in which the land was owned by a landlord, who leased it out to a tenant-farmer, basically an entrepreneur, who in turn employed day-laborers to do the work, and supplied much of the know-how, livestock, and circulating capital. In this regard, British agriculture ironically came to resemble more the kind of large-estate farming units of Europe east of the Elbe than the independent peasantry of the western continent. The difference was that Britain's was a highly efficient system, using free wage labor and managed on the whole by intelligent and informed entrepreneurs rather than the lords or their stewards. By 1790, about three-quarters of British soil was cultivated by such tenants and the proportion of owner-occupiers had declined to 20 percent at the peak of the Napoleonic Wars prosperity (Chambers and Mingay, 1966, p. 132). The agricultural workforce consisted increasingly of adult males; the "family economy" in which children, women, and live-in servants supplied much of the labor was declining. One measure of this efficient management was that much labor was employed seasonally—it made no sense to pay wage-laborers during the slack season when there was little for them to do. While the causes of agrarian change were thus rather different than Marx thought, his view that British agriculture had shown a pattern of proletarianization in the centuries before he wrote is not wholly incorrect. Yet compared to the rest of Europe this was a wildly successful system, the cantankerous William Cobbett's (1821) remark that "when farmers become gentlemen, their labourers become slaves" notwithstanding.

If there was no agricultural revolution, the challenge is to explain how the British agrarian economy succeeded in feeding the rapidly growing population of Britain, an increase that began around the middle of the eighteenth century and continued unabated until the twentieth century. At one level, this is easy: it increased output. Various estimation techniques, summarized in table 9.1, differ a bit, but all indicate that farm output increased almost at the same rate as population, by 144 percent (1700–1831) in one estimate, 185 percent (1700–1850) in another (Overton, 1996b, p. 75). Labor productivity in agriculture just about doubled. The question of food supply is acute because there is considerable evidence that weather conditions deteriorated in the second half of the eighteenth century: between the terrible harvests of 1740/41 and the disastrous year of 1816/17, the frequency of harvest failures in Britain was unusually high. Volcanic activity in remote areas, from Iceland to the catastrophic explosion of the island of Tamboro in the Indonesian archipelago in 1815 that affected weather patterns world-wide, was partly to blame. And yet, despite the hardships caused by high prices, there is little evidence of actual starvation in Britain.

As has already been noted, Malthus, and two generations of political economists after him, believed that the inability of the agrarian sector to increase food supply at the same rate that population increased would in the end doom the entire economy to stagnation. It was thought that when the economy experienced some form of growth due to a favorable "supply shock," that is, an improvement in economic conditions, whether institutional, technological, or purely autonomous (e.g., an improvement in weather conditions), this would lead only to a temporary increase in average income. As people became richer, the model predicted, their form of growth due to a favorable "supply shock," that is, an improvement in economic conditions, whether institutional, technological, or purely autonomous (e.g., form of growth due to a favorable "supply shock," that is, an improvement in economic conditions, whether institutional, technological, or purely autonomous (e.g., an improvement in weather conditions), this would lead only to a temporary increase in average income. As people became richer, the model predicted, their numbers grew either because they were better fed, housed, and clothed and thus less susceptible to famine and disease, or because the higher

Table 9.1: Estimates of agricultural output, England 1700–1850 (1700 = 100)

	1700	1750	1800	1850
Population method	100	121	159	272
Demand method	100	143[a]	172	244
Volume method:				
Crops	100	129	188	303
Meat	100	124	166	253
Dairy	100	179	244	320
Total	100	127	191	285
Population	100	114	171	331
Per capita, demand method	100	106	93	82
Per capita, volume method	100	111	101	86

[a] 1760

Notes:

Population method: assumes fixed consumption per capita, taking into account imports and exports.

Demand method: infers output from population, corrected for changes in prices and income.

Volume method: based on contemporary estimates.

Source: Overton (1996, p. 75).

incomes permitted them to marry earlier and have more children. Either way, as numbers went up, population began pressing upon the land and other natural resources in fixed supply, such as clean water or timber, and eventually pushed incomes back down to where they had been prior to the supply shock. Whether through preventive checks (lower birth rates) or positive checks (a rise in mortality), population would stop growing. The numbers of mouths to be fed would just rise along with the number of mouths that *could* be fed. Economic historians have had a field day, over and over again, pointing out how wrong these predictions have turned out to be for the nineteenth century. But where, exactly did this dire prediction go wrong?

In some parts of Europe it turned out to be the case that new and more nutritious crops were introduced, the originals imported from overseas. Ireland and the Low Countries increasingly consumed potatoes in the eighteenth century, and given that potatoes could provide three to four times the calories per acre that cereals did (not to mention the additional nutritional benefits such as Vitamin C, of which contemporaries were unaware), the adoption of the crop made it possible to feed much larger populations on the same amount of land. Oddly enough, Britain by comparison was unenthusiastic about the potato. In 1800 only about 2 percent of crop land was under potatoes, although more potatoes may have been grown in small garden plots. It has never been explained satisfactorily why nineteenth-century Britain was so reluctant to adopt the potato. One possibility is that the British simply were rich and productive enough to afford to do so, as potatoes were widely regarded as a food for the poor (having a low income elasticity). In Britain even the poor ate bread (the infatuation with fish and chips was to come much later). How, then, did Britain feed its growing population?

Part of the explanation is that the amount of land was not actually fixed, as Malthus supposed. What mattered was not the overall size of the island but how much of it was cultivated and how intensively. Table 9.2 demonstrates that total arable land increased from about 11 million acres to 14.6 million acres between 1700 and 1850, and land in pasture and meadows from about 10 to 16 million acres in the same years. This increase took place at the expense of woodlands and waste and was in part a consequence of the enclosures. Another source of agricultural productivity growth was intensity of cultivation. It seems plausible that lands under communal ownership were less likely to be kept in a good state of cultivation. Once enclosure placed these lands under single ownership and control, it would pay to invest in the improvement of the soils. The total increase in acreage under cultivation was greater, however, than enclosures of wastes and commons could account for. What the growth of land area under cultivation explains is why agricultural employment did not decline in the eighteenth century: agriculture on balance became more land- and capital-intensive (using less labor per acre, especially labor other than adult male labor), but because the total amount of land under cultivation expanded, the absolute size of employment in agriculture remained roughly the same (though it constituted a declining proportion of the total labor force, as the latter grew rapidly after 1750).

Moreover, the land under cultivation was made more productive. Oddly enough, the evidence seems to indicate that per acre yields in wheat (the main food crop of Britain) rose little between 1700 and 1800 (perhaps because they were already quite high). During the entire eighteenth century wheat yields increased by 36 percent. Overton (1996a, pp. 5–6) points out, however, that this is not a good indication of overall productivity not only because the growth in output per acre

Table 9.2: Land, labor and capital in British agriculture, 1700–1850.

	1700	1800	1850
Land: (millions of acres)			
Arable	11	11.6	14.6
pasture and meadows	10	17.5	16.0
woods and coppices	3	1.6	1.5
forests, parks, commons	3		
waste	10	6.5	3.0
buildings, water, roads	1	1.3	2.2
Labor (thousands)			
men	612	643	985
women	488	411	395
boys	453	351	144
Capital			
structures	112	143	232
implements	10	10	14
farm horses	20	18	22
other livestock	41	71	85

Source: Allen (2004, pp. 104, 105, 107).

could simply be the result of more labor or other inputs, but also because of the selection of acres that were actually sown with this crop. The yields of other crops such as   such as beans, barley, oats, and fodder crops did continue to increase in the eighteenth and early nineteenth centuries (ibid., p. 6; Turner, Beckett, and Afton, 2001, pp. 162–66). The flexible combination of arable and pasturage increased productivity, and the use of clover between crops increased the fertility of the soil, since clover fixed nitrogen from the atmosphere and the introduction of beans and other legumes accounts for a substantial proportion of increased soil fertility in the long run (Allen, 2008). While this mechanism was not really fully understood until the nineteenth century, the empirical relationship between clover and soil fertility was well known.

This productivity growth resulted not only in a higher supply of food crops to people but, equally importantly, in the better nutrition of animals. Fodder crops such as improved grasses, clovers, vetches, turnips, and mangel-wurzels were increasingly cultivated, and British animals grew fatter and bigger—that, too, should count as productivity growth. Moreover, better-fed animals produced more fertilizer. Many of the fodder crops that convertible husbandry raised were especially suitable for light, sandy soils such as those of Suffolk and Norfolk. Before these innovations, which were diffused in the eighteenth century, many of these light soils were un- or undercultivated, because their fertility was low without large amounts of fertilizer. A further improvement in these areas was marling, the application of a dressing of clay marl that bound together the finely grained soils of the sandy regions. The root crops cultivated on the sandy soils often did not suit the heavier and more fertile soils of the west. The net result was that the productivity of agriculture increased the most where it had previously been lowest, thus raising the least effective of the soils to the levels of output previously experienced by the best lands. The effect on the aggregate was quite remarkable, although data on individual farms varied considerably.

Animals were a central part of the story of European agriculture, and nowhere more so than in Britain. Some world historians such as Jared Diamond (1997) have argued that the presence of large farm animals in Europe and parts of Asia is integral to any explanation of the economic success story of Europe. Animals were central to British agrarian life for a number of reasons. First, they supplied a set of valuable outputs, including meat, dairy products, and raw materials. Second, they provided motive power to agricultural implements (above all of course plows), and transportation to markets where farmers sold their goods. Third, as a source of supply of nitrogen they were an integral part of maintaining soil fertility: yard dung was by far the most effective fertilizer used in arable crops and helped increase yields by restoring nitrogen to the soil. Livestock were thus part output, part capital stock, and part intermediate product. An increase in the quality of animals through selective breeding, lusher meadows, and improved fodder crops reverberated through the entire arable sector and beyond. While the number of animals did not grow much over the period, the volume of animal products increased by 150 percent (Overton, 1996a, p. 13). Selective breeding of animals became an eighteenth-century success story and one of the most interesting technological breakthroughs of the period.

Estimating what happened to total British agricultural product between 1700 and 1850 is difficult, as there are no nation-wide statistics on agricultural output. The problem is much like putting together a jigsaw puzzle with most of the pieces missing. The main findings are summarized in table 9.1. One method, pioneered by Nicholas Crafts (1985), is to assume that demand for farm products moves with demand as determined by population, income, and preferences, and that although the supply is not observed, we can infer what happened to it by looking at prices. The logic of this exercise is a powerful application of economic analysis to a historical problem. We have a good idea of how many people lived in Britain in this period, and while we do not know what and how much they ate, if there had been serious scarcities—as in some years there were—these would have manifested themselves in higher prices. By postulating a relationship between prices and demand, we can form fairly reliable estimates of what happened to supply even if there was no government agency that collected data from every individual farm. In other words, instead of predicting prices from supply and demand as economists are apt to do, economic historians, having data on prices and making educated guesses at what demand might have looked like, infer the historical path of supply. Using this technique, it is readily shown that agricultural output grew very slowly in the eighteenth century (0.2 percent per year), and fell behind population growth. From 1800 to 1850, however, agricultural output accelerated and grew at a rate of 1.1 percent per year, slightly faster than population. These numbers suggest that the use of the term "Agricultural Revolution" to denote what happened after 1750 may seem excessive, but that the performance of this sector was more impressive than has recently been suggested.

This price-based approach is far from perfect. It is sensitive to other factors affecting price data, and indeed farm prices in the late eighteenth century were abnormally high because of a run of unusually poor harvests due to bad weather. Moreover, in an open economy, prices are not determined wholly domestically. They are also affected by events in other economies and by disruptions in international trade caused by wars and political turmoil. Hence it is possible that these figures underestimate the growth of productivity in agriculture in the second half of the eighteenth century. An alternative method is to take surviving farm records and to blow them up into output for the country as a whole. This, however, is subject to major problems of representativeness, and what economists think of as "survival bias"—it seems plausible that the best-managed (and thus the most productive) farms kept the most accurate and detailed records and that these records had the best chances of surviving to be used by economic historians. In addition, these figures are sensitive to output estimates at the beginning of the period, and have tended to overestimate the growth of farm output during the eighteenth century. It seems implausible, however, that such errors are large enough to overturn completely the record of growth. And it is telling that this "volume method" over the long haul produces results that are not too dissimilar to those obtained from the demand method.

In sum, agricultural output after 1750 kept pace with a rapidly growing population until the end of the century, even if it did not always do so in the short run. After 1800, however, it did fall somewhat behind, yet unlike what happened in

Ireland, where a single high-yield crop increasingly fed a growing population, Britain's food basket does not seem to have deteriorated. It was no mean achievement. The performance of British agriculture was in fact what made the difference between Britain and eighteenth-century China where the growing pressure on the land led eventually to ecological costs that set the Chinese economy back in terms of its ability to feed the population. Furthermore, although in Ireland it is hard to think of the potato blight of 1846 as an inevitable "Malthusian disaster"—after all, the blight that destroyed the harvest was an unpredictable fluke—it is clear that the dependence on potatoes ended up defining a very different agricultural society. Ireland was, in some sense, "gambling" on a single high-yield crop. Britain achieved its goal of feeding its population before 1850 without increasing the number of people who worked on the land, without gambling on a single high-yield crop, and without truly dramatic inventions that revolutionized agricultural technology, such as the chemical fertilizers, full-fledged mechanization, and pesticides that changed twentieth-century farming. Whatever gains in output were achieved were derived from improvements in labor productivity due to changes in scale, organization, and relatively incremental improvements in agricultural technology. When that did not suffice, the country relied on imports. Imports from the Celtic fringe and the European Continent helped make up the British food deficit (Thomas, 1985).

Labor productivity in agriculture, then, increased for three main reasons, as can be verified from table 9.2. One was the increase in the amount of land under cultivation, as noted above. At a fixed labor force, this means that the land/labor ratio in agriculture was actually increasing during a period of rapid population growth—exactly the reverse of what one would expect in a Malthusian model. Another was the increase of agricultural capital. With more capital per worker, labor productivity could rise. The third element was the growing efficiency of farm production. Such enhanced efficiency could take the form of simply raising more crops per unit of input, or the emergence of altogether new crops. The latter makes measurement and comparisons over time especially difficult, but they remained a fact of life: Britain's progressive agriculture was certainly receptive to new crops: fodder crops, pulses, cabbages, kale, and rootcrops such as kohlrabi and above all turnips were all used as "catch crops" on lands that previously were left fallow. Even if output per acre sown did not increase, the acres available were utilized more efficiently.

New tools, or redesigned old tools, or making old tools with better materials, also added to agricultural progress. The Rotherham plow was the first "standardized" agricultural implement, an iron-made device of Dutch origin usually without wheels. Not only did it turn over the soil much better than earlier designs, it required fewer draught animals and because of its hardness, the plowshare kept its sharpness even when worn out. This piece of equipment was made by highly skilled manufacturers such as Tugwell of Tetbury and Ransome of Ipswich rather than by local craftsmen. It was first patented in 1730, and by the last third of the eighteenth century it was widely used. The unlikely confluence of the Enlightenment and agricultural tools is embodied in the career of the Scottish plow maker James Small (c. 1740–1793) who built a much improved plough with a moldboard whose shape was optimized through long experimentation. Small felt that his invention should be made available to all, wrote a book describing it, and refused to take out a patent (Day and McNeil, 1996, p. 648). Recent reworking of the data collected by Arthur Young indicates that improvement in plow design was responsible for a considerable improvement in plowing over the period 1700–1850 (Brunt, 2003). Further improved plows with self-sharpening shares were developed in the early nineteenth century. Another improved implement that came into general use in the early nineteenth century was Jethro Tull's famous seed drill, which had been ignored for most of the eighteenth century. Among the other tools that advanced farms used were threshing machines, winnowing machines, chaff cutters, turnip slicers, land rollers, and fodder preparing machinery. Not every farm possessed all of these, but the best-practice technique set a high standard.

Growing efficiency may have been the result of changes in the social structure of the farm sector. This argument, made most emphatically by Robert Brenner (1985), has it that "peasant" agriculture is insufficiently competitive to assure high-efficiency farming, and that only capitalist modes of farming with their high level of competition and more effective farm management could bring about the high labor productivity levels attained in British agriculture. Modern research, however, has dispelled old prejudices about rigid and conservative "peasants," who have been shown to have had far more agility and sensitivity to market opportunities and prices than had been supposed. All the same, it stands to reason that the capitalist structure of British farming, including larger farms managed by professional tenants with wage labor, had, on balance, favorable efficiency effects. The "improving landlord" of eighteenth-century Britain was perhaps not representative of rural life, but he was becoming more and more common especially among the "gentry," the country gentlemen who owned relatively small estates but who between them controlled close to half the arable land of Britain. Many of these landowners insisted on comparing, collating, and spreading the knowledge of "better farming." Even when landlords were not directly involved in agricultural improvements, they were often savvy enough to hire those who were. More than ever before, eighteenth-century landlords were in it for the money. Agricultural improvements could lead to higher rents, and higher rents were what they wanted. One tell-tale sign of the importance of the age of Enlightenment for farming is that societies for agricultural and farming improvement sprung up everywhere in late eighteenth-century Britain.

Oddly enough, while both Scotland and Ireland had formal societies dedicated to the improvement of agriculture from the beginning of the eighteenth century,

England lagged behind in this respect. In Scotland at least fourteen such societies were founded between 1723 and 1784, and by 1834 there were 136. In England, from the 1770s on the movement took off, leading to a plethora of local voluntary organizations that ran shows, awarded prizes, and set up professional libraries for farmers. The Agricultural Enlightenment culminated in the founding of the Board of Agriculture in 1793. The Board commissioned surveys and reports about agricultural practices but mismanagement and lack of funds resulted in sub-par quality. Its first president was the eccentric but brilliant Scotsman, John Sinclair, to whom Erasmus Darwin dedicated his massive text on agriculture. While in the end the Board itself was a disappointment, it reflected a growing sense of solidarity among farmers and furthered their notion that they represented something we might call a "landed interest." Support for agricultural improvement and the exchange of technical ideas were its most important functions, and the Board paved the way for the founding of the Royal Agricultural Society in 1838. The Dishley Society, founded in 1783, and the Smithfield Club, founded in 1798, specialized in the breeding and raising of animals. The most active organization in English agriculture before that was probably the Society of Arts, which encouraged innovation and its diffusion in every area of farming, from improved implements to soil chemistry to the spread of potato cultivation. By 1835 there were over ninety such societies in Britain. It may well be that such societies were above all symbols of the belief in progress, demonstrating the role of science in bringing it about, but they also encouraged innovators and made useful knowledge and successful techniques more accessible. Improvers corresponded with one another, and wrote essays in Arthur Young's *Annals of Agriculture* and the *Farmer's Magazine* founded in 1800 in Edinburgh. Agriculture, not less than any other sector of the economy, showed the spirit of the search for useful knowledge and the belief in progress.

Agricultural knowledge, whether effective or not, accumulated and diffused at a faster rate than ever before after 1750. Formal and informal organizations, exhibitions, cattle shows, and fairs were organized, in which people with an interest in agriculture interacted and networked, compared notes, and exchanged the results of experiments and investigations. Some of these figures, such as Thomas Coke of Norfolk, became symbols of the age of improvement. Even King George III earned the nickname "Farmer George" because of his deep interest in farming and his experimental farm in Kew outside London. Periodicals, pamphlets, and books, announcing discoveries and summarizing existing knowledge in farming technology, were published throughout the eighteenth century, and their coverage and readership may not have been very large but it kept expanding. William Ellis's *Modern Husbandman or Practice of Farming* published in 1731 gave a month-by-month set of suggestions, much like Arthur Young's most successful book, *The Farmer's Kalendar* (1770). In the last decade of the eighteenth century, enormous amounts of information were assembled by the two towering figures of the age, Young and his nemesis William Marshall (1745–1818), who meticulously collected data and information, and conducted agricultural experiments. These efforts were almost entirely empirical and pragmatic, and while by some purist standards they may not qualify as "formal" science they were very much part of what qualifies as useful knowledge.

The faith that cooperation between men of action and men of knowledge could be highly fruitful to society had clearly penetrated into agriculture. Marshall, indeed, made his living in part as an agricultural consultant to some improving landlords and as an agricultural reporter to the *Monthly Review*. Organized and systematic knowledge about what worked in farming was in great demand even before the sciences of soil chemistry and plant physiology had developed to the point where they could guide further technological progress. In that sense, enlightened farming was very much part of British agricultural society in the eighteenth century.

In the eighteenth century, especially during the decades after 1750 when farm prices were on the rise, agriculture was placed on the scientific agenda of enlightened Europe. Like all other aspects of the Enlightenment, it was not confined to the British Isles. The French were obsessed by the possibilities of agricultural improvement and even coined the phrase *agromanie* to describe the growing interest in farming. The Russian Empress Catherine the Great, influenced by the French Enlightenment, invited the noted German agronomist J.C. Schubart to Russia to help spread his ideas of improved farming. However, the great practical writers of the era, whom everyone interested in enlightened farming read and admired, were predominantly British. What is striking about them is the increasingly tight connections they sought with natural philosophers. Young himself sought the help of the leading British scientist of the 1780s, Joseph Priestley, in preparing his experiments. Many leading scientists were deeply interested in farming. The eminent chemist Humphry Davy was commissioned to give a series of lectures on soil chemistry, resulting in his *Elements of Agricultural Chemistry* (1813), which became the standard text until replaced by Von Liebig's work in 1840. The creative Scottish chemist Archibald Cochrane, the ninth Earl of Dundonald, published in 1795 a treatise entitled *Shewing the Intimate connection that Subsists between Agriculture and Chemistry*. Most of these writings were empirical or instructional in nature. Davy had to admit that the field was "still in its infancy" and his work was largely empirical. A few, however, actually tried to provide readers with some systematic analysis of the principles at work.

As in other areas of advances in useful knowledge, many of the trailblazers were Scottish. One of those Scots was Francis Home who published *Principles of Agriculture and Vegetation* (1756). Another was Lord Kames' *The Gentleman Farmer: Being an Attempt to Improve Agriculture by Subjecting it to the Test of Rational Principles* (1776). Kames believed that if a board of agriculture were to be established to disseminate useful knowledge about farming (such as the best crop rotation, optimal farm size, opening up of wastelands, and so on), the consequence would be a growth in "population and industry ... with a great increase of the public revenue. England would become so prosperous and powerful, as to suffer little distress from the loss of its American colonies, should that ungrateful people succeed ultimately in a total defection" (1776, p. 378). The geologist James Hutton (1726–97), too, was a practicing agriculturalist, who wrote an unfinished (and unpublished) 1,000-page manuscript on the *Elements of Agriculture*. Scottish agricultural societies maintained close contacts with the universities and the land-owning class, thus in a way mediating between the demand and the supply of useful knowledge. Beside the voluminous agricultural writings of recognized experts such as Young and Marshall, other treatises, essays, magazine articles, manuals, agricultural encyclopedias, and technical dictionaries on farming appeared more and more frequently between 1750 and 1850. While there was a lull of interest during the agricultural crisis that followed the French Wars, activity revived in the 1830s and 1840s. The research at that time became more rigorous, more professional, and more formal science-based.

One might legitimately wonder whether all this written material actually helped improve productivity in farming. Francis Home (1756, pp. 2–3) argued that the gap between science and practice was still huge: "This art [husbandry] is, in general, carried on by those whose minds have never been improved by science, taught to make observations, or draw conclusions, in order to attain the truth" and then proceeded anyway to write a detailed book reporting his agricultural experiments. Voltaire in his famed *Philosophical Dictionary* (1816, Vol. 3, p. 91) caustically remarked that after 1750 many useful books on agriculture were read by everyone but the farmers. Charles Gillispie (1980, p. 367) concluded that the impact of information flows "beyond the circle of persons who wrote, printed, and read the books," was probably small. It would be wrong to search for any direct connection between the intellectual ferment and productivity growth. Few of the books were based on practical experience on the ground, and Arthur Young (1772, p. 158) bemoaned that what was missing was a "general and comprehensive treatise or directionary of husbandry that a young cultivator may find as sure an advisor as a company of neighbouring farmers." He then proceeded to devote his life to filling that gap, though the quality of his insights has been disputed by modern scholars (Allen and Ó Gráda, 1988). Marshall's work, based on more personal experience, is by now better regarded by scholars. All in all, it seems implausible that all this intellectual activity affected more than a small sliver of the agricultural sector, and that its effects on overall output, with some exceptions, were modest and late.

Yet such scepticism misses the true significance of the "Agricultural Enlightenment." It tells us perhaps as much about the demand as about the supply side of useful knowledge in the eighteenth-century British economy. The "enlightened economy" was not confined to the modern sector in manufacturing, transportation, or mining. Its most spectacular achievements may have been in manufacturing, but above all its essence was in seeking to apply useful knowledge to techniques that worked better regardless of sector or use. The agricultural enlightenment was significant in part because its leaders were large farmers and country gentlemen rather than the urban and industrial bourgeoisie often thought to be at the cutting edge of the application of systematic useful knowledge and science to production. There was a thirst for this kind of knowledge among many British farmers, reflecting the widespread conviction that such an improvement was indeed feasible. Even if for much of this period the cost of books on farming was beyond the means of the majority of farmers, they were increasingly made available through lending libraries and reading rooms run by farmers' clubs and agricultural societies. In the long run, it may not have mattered all that much that only a small minority of farmers took the trouble to read these books. Knowledge spread and filtered down through networks of personal contacts and other barely visible channels. The result was that the dire predictions of the political economists influenced by Malthus were not realized and that the explosion of knowledge in the later nineteenth century eventually led to the reverse problem for Western agriculture in a later time, namely overproduction.

But even for the years before 1830 it would be rash to dismiss the impact of the Agricultural Enlightenment altogether. In an activity such as farming it is easy to underrate the importance of knowing what others do and imitating them. Coke of Holkham encouraged people to visit his Park Farm "because it is from them I gain the little knowledge I have and derive the satisfaction of communicating improvements among my tenantry" (cited by Beckett, 1989, p. 572). Coke ran a model farm, with continuous experimenting and a relentless push for technological progress, and his visitors came to learn from him as much as the other way around. At the ceremonial sheep-shearing hosted by Coke, all the prominent agriculturalists of the age and some of its most distinguished scientists met and exchanged views. For over forty years these meetings were an annual social event, and at different times such eminent scientific figures as Humphry Davy and Joseph Banks were seen there. These gatherings and others like them were, as Beckett (1989) points out, in effect agricultural shows providing opportunities for participants to share experiences and knowledge.

These kinds of meetings embodied the Enlightenment conviction that practical people and more theoretically inclined ("philosophical") minds could learn something from one another, and that such interactions and exchanges were the taproot of the growth in useful knowledge. Francis Home even suggested that a five-person committee should be assembled out of the members of the Edinburgh society whose task would be to "receive single and detached experiments" to publish. In order to encourage submissions, Home proposed that the committee "grant one or more honorary or lucrative premiums to those who shall have delivered the most ingenious and useful experiments in agriculture" (1756, p. 177). Obviously the concern with access to knowledge was especially acute in farming, in which a great deal depended on local soil and topography. Many of the insights thus gained became the basis of high farming during the Victorian age. The historical irony here was, of course, that the payoff of the agricultural enlightenment was in the future, but that Britain's future was not in farming. As a token of the belief in economic progress and the growing realization of how it was to be brought about, however, it is quite significant.

Enlightened farming was deeply interested in and committed to economic progress and innovation, and was hell bent on improvements and rationalization based on a better understanding of the natural processes at work. The growth in eighteenth-century agricultural output, however, was not affected more and sooner by these efforts because much of the useful knowledge applied to agriculture in the eighteenth century remained in the nature of the cataloguing and listing of natural regularities and "what worked" more than anything we would recognize as formal science. In the absence of biochemistry, physiology, bacteriology, genetics, entomology, formal statistics, and other sciences that agricultural improvers needed to master in order to understand why some techniques worked better than others, the road to progress led primarily through trial and error and experimentation. Knowledge accumulated about what worked and what did not, but only rarely did anyone have a good notion of why this was so. As a consequence, even the most advanced agriculturalists often failed to realize what would not work, and sorting out the true from the false was often difficult. In 1805, the eminent natural philosopher, horticulturalist, and Enlightenment figure Joseph Banks wrote a booklet identifying mildew in wheat—one of the great scourges of the age—as a fungal disease, yet this diagnosis did not penetrate down to the farmers till the second half of the nineteenth century. Since no effective fungicides were available, it is not clear what good this insight would have brought anyway. However, it is striking how clueless contemporary science still was in understanding the most disastrous fungus of all, the one that cause the potato blight in Ireland in the 1840s.

The same is true for one of the most fundamental practices in farming, the use of manure to increase fertility. The great agronomist Arthur Young sighed hopefully in 1772 that while in his day the farmers were largely ignorant of the "peculiar biasses" of individual soils, perhaps "one day the nature of all soils and the vegetables they particularly affect will be known experimentally ... a desideratum in natural philosophy worthy of another Bacon" (1772, p. 168). Kames, too, was acutely aware of this: "Agriculture, though it depends very much on the powers of machinery, yet I'll venture to affirm, that it has a greater dependence on chemistry. Without a knowledge in the latter science, its principles can never be settled" (1776, p. 5). That kind of knowledge was quite beyond the capability of Young and his contemporaries, but the need for it was greater than ever before, and by the middle of the nineteenth century the work of a Frenchman, Jean-Baptiste Boussingault, of German organic chemists led by Justus von Liebig in

Giessen, and of John Bennet Lawes in Britain began to reveal the secrets of soil chemistry. Modern research on the use of off-farm manure in British agriculture has shown that farms purchased considerable quantities of manure in 1700, and that their inputs did not increase dramatically in the next century and a half. Interestingly enough, farmers purchased large amounts of manure that augmented the nitrogen levels of their soils appreciably, but also urban industrial waste products such as soot and ashes with low effectiveness. The supply of market-purchased manure barely kept up with the expansion of acreage, and although it prevented yields from declining, it did not contribute to an agricultural revolution (Brunt, 2007).

Much of the useful knowledge of the eighteenth century, whether "scientific" or otherwise, may seem to us nowadays bogus. Modern historians of science and technology are perhaps cautious in designating knowledge as "correct" or not, knowing full well that our ideas of what is "true" may seem to future generations to be mistaken, much as the scientific theories of three centuries ago seem to us. But some statements and beliefs led to recommendations that can be classified at least as "ineffective" in the sense that any techniques based on them would not work. Jethro Tull (1674–1741), an inventor and early agricultural improver, argued that air was the best fertilizer. Arthur Young, the great compiler of travel notes and data on farming practices throughout Britain, was convinced that open field farming was completely incapable of technological advance, although his own data—when properly analyzed—do not bear him out (Allen and Ó Gráda, 1988). And yet the history of British agriculture in the period 1700–1850, as much as that of industry and transport, illustrates the belief that extending and collecting useful knowledge could be the key to generating sustained material progress. If the knowledge was incorrect, it would be tested and amended if possible. If it was incomplete, it would be expanded. Even with the very partial—by modern standards—knowledge available, the achievements in some areas were quite impressive. Jethro Tull, trying to farm without help (he was quite suspicious of farm labor), decided to discover the optimal rate of sowing sainfoin, and in the process of continuous observation and experimentation he invented a seed drill that economized on seeds, for which he became famous (sainfoin seeds were expensive), and a horse-pulled hoe. Tull's famous book *The New Horse Houghing Husbandry* was published in 1731, and Tull himself was well regarded in the circles of progressive farmers, who were carrying out experiments with enthusiasm.

Nowhere is the culture of enrichment through improvement based on experience and experiment better illustrated than in the area of livestock breeding. The genetics of animal reproduction were of course not understood a century or more before Mendel, yet farmers knew that the characteristics of animals were not wholly determined by environment and accident, but were in some mysterious way related to the characteristics of the parents. Better-bred and better-fed animals produced more and better dairy and meat. Animals that ate crops inedible for humans that were important in crop rotations (e.g., turnips) improved the fertility of the soil through fertilizer and greater motive power that improved plowing and harrowing.

This activity will forever be associated with the name of Robert Bakewell (1725–95), although selective breeding was practiced by others as well. Breed selection was both difficult and costly: the technique essentially consisted of cross-breeding animals with desirable characteristics and mercilessly culling undesirable specimens. The successes of systematic breeders were indisputable: they improved the efficiency of animals. Since animals served more than one purpose, there were often trade-offs between different features. British sheep were bred for the dinner table rather than the shears. Thus Bakewell's New Leicester sheep were unusually fleshy, gained weight earlier in life and in the most desirable parts, though their wool was of a middling quality. Bakewell spent fifteen years experimenting till he managed to fix a population of high muscle-to-bone ratio which was desirable in a nation of mutton eaters. By 1780, he was able to charge 100 guineas for the procreative service of one of his rams. John Ellman's Southdown breed also matured early, and its fine and short wool was ideal for carding. The enthusiastic Joseph Banks, always with an eye to possible improvements, founded the Merino Society in 1811 with the purpose of rearing Spanish Merino sheep in Britain. In the end, this attempt proved unsuccessful, and Britain increasingly relied on imported wool for its industry.

Progress also took place in the breeding of cattle. The shorthorn, the product of a number of Yorkshire breeders, was a general-purpose animal suited for both dairy production and fattening and could be matured at an early age by feeding it on the fodder crops that mixed farming of the first half of the nineteenth century produced so abundantly. Bakewell and his colleague Robert Fowler produced a "butcher's beast," the longhorn, which matured early and maximized beef production, at the cost of reduced fecundity and milk production. Another breed developed in this period was the Hereford, whose advantage was its ability to subsist on grazing. In pigs, too, the same methods were used with considerable success to attain desirable characteristics. Even hunting dogs, hardly an important contributor to agricultural productivity but of considerable interest to the leisured classes of the time, were improved by selective breeding by the great foxhound breeder Hugo Meynell (1735–1808). Somewhat surprisingly, success was much more limited for horses, despite the dependence of farmers on horses for most of their heavy work. Farmers seem to have been willing to "settle for the nondescript and the mongrel" (Brown and Beecham, 1989, p. 351). Arthur Young complained in the 1780s about farmers having to work with light coach horses. All the same, the Suffolk breed developed in the late eighteenth century and the Black Shire horses as well were improved through careful breeding and Gerhold (1996a, pp. 501–02) has surmised that draft animals improved substantially and that the cost of horses for transport declined 20–30 percent between 1724 and 1816–21. Most horses were, however, passed from hand to hand and purpose to purpose during their life cycle, and were thus, unlike sheep and cattle, less bred for specialization. All in all, the successful breeding of animals between 1750 and 1850, given the very limited knowledge of the age of animal physiology, to say nothing of genetics, was quite impressive.

The same innovative energy permeated gardening, an activity usually ignored by economic historians but of paramount interest in Britain. New varieties of flowers and shrubs were experimented with, compared, swapped, and imitated. The number of cultivable garden plants that had been a few hundreds in the mid-sixteenth century had increased to 18,000 by 1839. In 1789 a Leicester seeds salesman offered sixteen different varieties of peas, thirteen varieties of beans, and much more. As J.H. Plumb (1982, p. 326) summarized the development of eighteenth-century horticulture, "people no longer expected flowers, vegetables, or trees, to be static objects in the field of creation, but constantly changing, constantly improving .... due to the experimental activity of man." To be sure, for much of the period these activities were confined to a fairly small class of leisured gentlemen who pursued gardening as a hobby. But as so often happened in this age, useful knowledge was created by a small minority, but as it was accessed, adapted, and applied by others who could make use of it, its economic role slowly increased. The experience of gardeners was made accessible through the work of such persons as the great gardener John Claudius Loudon (1783–1843), who published popular sets of books including the *Encyclopedia of Gardening* (1822), the *Encyclopedia of Agriculture* (1825), and the periodical *Gardener's Magazine* (from 1826). The innovative landscape gardener Humphry Repton (1752–1818) published a number of influential books and was successful as a landscape consultant, in effect selling knowledge.

To summarize, the amount of useful knowledge about plants and animals available in Britain in 1850 was many times larger than it had been in 1700. What needs explanation, then, was why its impact on agricultural productivity remained slim for so many decades. For one thing, the interest in improvement was by no means universal. A few British great landlords were deeply involved in long discussions about crops, seeds, animals, drainage, and of course the reorganization of agriculture and land use and the need to enclose open fields. It is possible to highlight these examples to support the hypothesis that concentrated ownership and relatively large farms were critical to a progressive farm sector. However, great improving landlords were not all that common. Most landlords confined themselves by and large to passive roles: appointing good stewards, providing their tenants with long leases so that they could be secure enough to introduce capital-intensive improvements, and at times lending them money to make those investments. In short, they created a favorable environment in which active improvers, with the best access to knowledge that could help farming be more efficient, would thrive. Despite some eminent exceptions, then, the most active improvers tended to be the smaller gentry, the large tenant-farmers, and the large owner-occupiers.

Furthermore, unlike in manufacturing, where improved techniques mercilessly drove out less efficient competitors, the diffusion of best-practice techniques in farming was constrained by an important difference between agricultural and manufacturing technology. Mechanical devices and chemical processes work by and large independently of the local environment. A steam engine, a candlemaker's vats, or a wool-comber's tools work wherever they are placed. In agriculture, small differences in soil conditions, topography, microclimates, and other local variations could determine whether a new technique worked well or not. The result was that technology in agriculture diffused at a painstakingly slow pace (Coke of Holkham said that "his improvements travelled at the rate of a mile a year") and that there were often large differences in technological practices even in a close proximity. The economist James Caird ([1852], 1967) made an investigative tour of British agriculture in 1850 and 1851, and described the enormous variety in sophistication and progressiveness in the agricultural methods in use. He noted with amazement that farms employing backward techniques were often right next to other farms using the most up-to-date implements and drainage systems (p. 499). Progress was slow, local, and uneven. In the felicitous words of one scholar, agricultural progress in this period was the net result of "a war of attrition between the forces of cautious, eclectic experimentation on the one hand and those of custom and inertia on the other" (Walton, 1984, p. 32). Advances on a broad front, such as the revolutionary inventions in iron-making and cotton-spinning, were absent in agriculture. By 1850, the experimental station of John Bennet Lawes at Rothamsted was in operation, but agricultural experimentation would have run into diminishing returns unless it was supported by more theoretical understanding of the mechanisms that made plants grow.

Moreover, agriculture was constrained by technical bottlenecks. Before the invention of lightweight engines in the late nineteenth century, the supply of motive power to the fields was confined to large animals, mostly horses. Many of the tasks of farming such as plowing and harvesting must be carried out in the field, and although steam power could be applied to certain activities such as threshing, in 1850 horses and humans still supplied most of the energy that did the hard work in situ. Mechanical (horse-drawn) reapers were only slowly being adopted in the United States at this time, and were not yet in widespread use in Britain where the terrain was more difficult (David, 1975b). Other arduous and labor-intensive tasks proved beyond the capability of the age, no matter how large the incentives. As late as 1879, the Royal Agricultural Society offered a prize to the inventor of an efficient milking machine—which attracted no entries.

What emerged in the early nineteenth century was a form of farming that contemporaries thought of as "high farming," basically best-practice technique in the lingo of modern economists. It was based on sophisticated, region-dependent crop rotations, heavy use of fertilizer, and a sophisticated interplay of arable and animal husbandry. It used improved implements, tools that were more durable, better-designed, more user-friendly, and often cheaper. The system of "high farming" aspired to be the best that could be done at the time and was open to new ideas, techniques, materials, and implements. By 1850, even more so than in 1700, British agriculture was commercial, capitalist, and capital-intensive, placed almost entirely in the context of a market economy, and run by informed businessmen whose main purpose was to make money. It was as close an economic system as one can find that can be described by the economist's paradigm of rational, informed, profit-maximizing agents operating in a competitive world using best-practice technology. And yet this system, ironically enough, was moribund.

The driving force behind changes in farming was money. A few improving landlords may have found the work intellectually challenging or morally satisfactory, but there can be little doubt that this was primarily a movement motivated by the desire for cash. The landlord's rent was the difference between the value of the crops and the total cost of producing it (including the farmer's profits and interest). Rents were the payment for the natural qualities of the land, but these qualities could be enhanced by improvements, and often the return on drainage, consolidation, and the improvement of wastes and commons was quite substantial to the landlord even if the contribution of these investments to total productivity was relatively modest. Rents, indeed, increased considerably in the period under question: recent research on rents per acre in this period places the rent-index at 15.7 in 1700–1724 (1825–49 = 100), implying a sixfold increase over the period (Turner, Beckett, and Afton, 1997, p. 165). Deflating these by prices shows that real rents declined during the period of rising prices between 1750 and 1815 and rose sharply afterward. This sensitivity of real rents to prices suggests that nominal rents could not always adjust quickly to changes, in large part because nominal rents were often fixed by contract or by custom.

Rising agricultural rents were the result of many different trends. Enclosures had a lot to do with it, not only because they may have increased the ability of the farmer to utilize land more effectively, but also because they involved the rewriting of rental contracts to bring rents up to date. But landlords also had political clout, and as we have seen, were able to pass tariff legislation that protected their income. By the middle of the nineteenth century, six-sevenths of all farmland in Britain was farmed by tenants, with only one-seventh in the hands of peasant proprietors. Caird and others wondered about the incentives that such tenants had to introduce improvements that were embodied in the soil, since in principle their landlords could expropriate these by not renewing their leases. The property rights in these improvements were rooted in informal contracts and implicit understandings based on trust. The striking fact is that, by and large, this arrangement seems to have worked. Tenant rights and very long leases did exist, but they were relatively rare. The relationship between the landlord class and the class of professional tenants and farmers in Britain was on the whole harmonious, unlike in Ireland.

Yet perceptions of land and landlords and their economic functions changed over time as the economy changed. Land was increasingly regarded as just another asset, something that was costly to acquire and therefore should yield a stream of revenue. It remained in the eyes of many something special, the ownership of which yielded social status or prestige, but it was also a business that should be managed rationally to produce income. In the eighteenth century, some landlords were regarded as technological experimenters, and it was the duty of the landlord to inform himself of techniques in use elsewhere and apply them to his lands, and to try to improve upon them. By the early nineteenth century that function was passing to specialists and the role of the landlord was to supply fixed capital if he had better access to long-term credit than his tenants, and to provide tenants, who were in charge of the day-to-day management of farming, with the long-term leases and contracts that would induce them to introduce improvements and maintain the fertility of the land. Traditional encumbrances on land ownership such as entail and primogeniture were increasingly criticized as inimical to capitalist and rational exploitation of the land.

To summarize, recent scholarship has passed a mixed verdict on the performance of British agriculture between 1700 and 1850. By 1700 (and possibly long before), British agriculture had reached very high levels of efficiency. It is therefore perhaps not all that surprising that while the eighteenth century was an age of feverish searches for improvement and progress, with the exception of certain regions, the achievements were modest. In large part this was because British farming had reached the limits of productivity, given what people knew at the time. The inability to bring mechanical power to the fields, the difficulty of constructing agricultural machinery, the lack of understanding of the way minerals interacted with soil chemistry in plant growth, and the inability to cope effectively with pests and epizootics limited the additional expansion of productivity in grain production. If there were no breakthroughs in agricultural technology such as in the cotton industry or steam power, it was not for lack of trying. Most of the technical problems were simply too difficult for eighteenth-century farmers to solve, even if they were aware of the best-practice science of their time. The work that "broke open" agricultural productivity in the nineteenth century was carried out between 1840 and 1880. By the end of that time, however, agriculture had irretrievably lost its central position in the British economy.

How, then, were the rapidly multiplying masses of British population fed in the period 1700–1850? There is no single answer to this question. First, population growth started in earnest only after 1750, and for the first half of the eighteenth century there was no population problem. Britain was self-sufficient in food supplies in normal years, and when the harvest fell short, it made up the deficit through imports. The years between 1760 and 1816, by contrast, were a time of frequent crises: rapid population growth was coupled with unusually poor harvests and weather, and a series of wars that at times made imports difficult. British farmers displayed a considerable capability to respond to favorable market conditions. Farmers living near large urban markets, with opportunities to sell high-value crops, found ways to make their farming more productive and more profitable. They did so by bringing into use land that had previously not been cultivated rather than by intensifying cultivation and raising per acre yields on the wheat crop. They reorganized considerable areas through the consolidation of holdings and enclosure and by improving seeds and animals, but all in all the rapid increase in demand for food and raw materials due to population growth and industrialization was sufficiently fast to outstrip the supply of agricultural products. Britain began to depend more and more on imports for its food supply not just in years of disastrously low harvests but also in years that looked more and more like average years. As Britain learned the hard way in 1914–18 and again in 1940–45, the disadvantage of following the dictates of comparative advantage and depending on imports for food is that in times of war, imports are vulnerable to hostile acts by the enemy.

The problem should not be overstated: even during war with France, imports of food to Britain from the Continent did not necessarily end. Napoleon did not want to starve Britain; his strategic interests dictated that he should sell food to her in years of need, so that less British gold would be available to subsidize hostile armies. Food was also imported from Germany and the Baltic regions. Furthermore, Britain imported large amounts of food from Ireland, where the potato's miraculous efficiency in extracting carbohydrates from the soil made it possible to export large agricultural surpluses, despite the nation's obvious poverty. In 1824–26, Britain imported 70 percent of its grains from Ireland. On a few occasions, especially in the difficult years of 1800–1801 and again in 1816–17, food supplies were menacingly low. On the whole, however, famines no longer turned into demographic disasters in Great Britain. Ireland, of course, was a very different story.

The argument about the performance of British agriculture is thus a classic case of a cup being half full or half empty. It is hard to find convincing evidence that by 1850 Britons were eating much better than they had in 1700, and in this sense a century and a half of farming enthusiasm, political maneuvering, and feverish discussions and writings on farming had yielded little. But it is also true that in that period the population of Britain had just about tripled from 6.5 million to around 21 million and that such a rapid and sustained demographic boom would have been unthinkable in the pre-modern economy with its comparatively low levels of international trade, and without the Enlightenment faith in the importance of useful knowledge. We could summarize the agrarian history of Britain in the long run as a tale in which an efficient and market-based local rural economy could provide a surprising security and quality of life to the average Briton, but it was eventually rational for the economy to do even better by relying on imports.

Despite its achievements, there is some reason to be cautious in viewing agriculture as an indispensable dynamic element of the development of the British economy. Before the late nineteenth century, notwithstanding the huge efforts of people like Arthur Young, William Marshall, and John Sinclair, and some impressive local successes, British agriculture did not experience a "revolution." It could not yet break through the barriers that had constrained traditional agriculture as had happened in energy, textiles, and transportation. In a long period of economic and technological progress, the most basic needs of humankind were the hardest to meet through radical improvements. Perhaps, then, we can assess the role of agriculture in the performance of the British economy in the age of Enlightenment and that of the Industrial Revolution in terms of the importance of what did not happen. Britain did not experience dazzling productivity increases due to a combination of innovation and organizational change, as some scholars in the 1950s believed. The traditional dynamic functions that economists have assigned to a successful agricultural sector, namely to release labor from farming to non-agricultural occupations, to provide ever cheaper food and raw materials, and to serve as a growing market for industrial products, seem all to be of rather limited importance. Instead, the emphasis should be on useful knowledge, openness, demographic change, and the evolution of economically effective institutions. An agricultural revolution was not a necessary "precondition" for economic development or industrialization. Agriculture did not "release" labor for factory industry (population growth and cottage industries did that), nor did the farm sector play a crucial role in generating the demand for manufactured goods and services that supposedly played such a big role in industrialization (lower prices and self-generating markets did that). Nor did British agriculture supply all of the raw materials for manufacturing (raw cotton and increasingly timber were imported). On the other hand, despite a rapid growth in demand, adverse weather conditions, and at times disruptions in international trade, British farms were able to keep up with a growing population and provide a more or less constant supply of food, and prevent real wages from falling in the long run. Malthus notwithstanding, Britain did not experience a serious famine; by this time its path had diverged sufficiently from its less fortunate neighbor in the west for it to be spared anything resembling the Irish disaster of 1845–50.

Furthermore, the growing non-farm sector demanded large amounts of inputs produced by the agricultural economy: wool, leather, and tallow, but also barley for brewing, straw for brushes and brooms. The transport sector needed horses, which by the later eighteenth century had almost entirely replaced oxen as draft animals. Horses needed oats; oats were the petroleum of the eighteenth century. In 1800, a third of all the land in cereals was growing oats, most of which were consumed by horses. The sharp increase in its output reflected the growing dependence of the British economy on *reproducible* sources of energy even though the Industrial Revolution is often depicted as a transition from reproducible to fossil sources of energy.

At the end of the day, despite a highly productive agriculture, farming was not an activity in which Britain had a comparative advantage. After 1850, the sector declined in size as Britain relied increasingly on imported food. This specialization made perfect economic sense, and might have been achieved even earlier, had it not been for protection and the high cost of transportation. Yet in appraising the British record in the period 1700–1850, the economic historian is struck by how good the British were at farming. It is one of the best examples of the difference between absolute and comparative advantage that the economics teacher can devise: Britain may by 1815 have had the most productive and advanced farming sector in the world, but it was *still* in its best interest to abandon all that and specialize in what it was best at, which was manufacturing and services.

CHAPTER 10

The Service Sectors: Commerce and Transport

The term "service sector" sounds vaguely anachronistic. The twenty-first century, often referred to as the post-industrial age, is one of the unmistakable dominance of service industries. The great economic historian R.M. Hartwell (1971) once lamented that the service sector was the "neglected variable" in the economic history of Britain at this time, and that our knowledge of what transpired with this variable during the Industrial Revolution was rather modest compared to the huge amounts written on manufacturing and agriculture.

The period 1700–1850 was hardly an age in which all production took place in the tangible sectors of agriculture and manufacturing. The service sector was already quite large in 1700 (estimated at 34 percent of national product in 1688, see Deane and Cole, 1969, p. 156) and kept expanding, though exact numbers are hard to take seriously given the ambiguities of the data and of the definition of what the sector includes. Lee (1986, pp. 9–11, 98–100) has computed that, with the exception of the years 1815–40, the contribution of services to aggregate growth was at least as large as that of manufacturing. The same is true for employment growth. To some extent, dividing the labor force into such sectors quantitatively ignores the difficult problem that many workers were doing part-time work in different sectors. The sectoral distribution of workers assumes a level of specialization that had not yet been attained. Yet it deserves attention despite the roughness of the estimates. For one thing, perhaps the most common single occupation of the British working population in the mid-nineteenth century was that of domestic servant, a profession that, save for a small minority, has passed away from the industrialized world. In 1841, however, there still were 984,357 "domestic servants" in Britain out of a total labor force of 16 million (Great Britain, 1844b, p. 283), the largest reported occupation by the 1841 census, slightly ahead of "labourers, agricultural" (960,382) and almost five times larger than "cotton manufacturers, all branches" (213,944). Transportation, too, was a major employer in 1841, with 33,867 adults employed as carters and wagoners and 45,915 sailors on shore (the ones at sea were missed by the census). Other service sectors that were still small compared to the dimensions they were to attain in our own time were education, finance, government, and health. Even if these sectors were still rather modest in size compared to, say, agriculture, they contributed disproportionately to the economy, much as a lubricant to a well-functioning engine. Above all, however,

Britain bore out the dismissive remark attributed to Napoleon that Britain was a "nation of shopkeepers." In fact Adam Smith had coined the phrase and Napoleon may have been familiar with it. It was a commercial nation, one in which trade, shipping, and transportation played roles of great importance. The basic Enlightenment concept of progress and enrichment through the systematic accumulation of useful knowledge and its rational application can be seen to play a major role in the service sectors as well, although it was not as palpable and concrete as it was in the production of textiles or hardware. Yet there was no automatic transition from a commercial nation to sustained technological progress and industrialization. What was the service sector's function in the creation of modern growth?

*   *   *

Gregory King ([1688], 1936) estimated that out of a population of 5.5 million, 180,000 people were shopkeepers or their families, and another 54,000 people were "Merchants & Traders by the Sea." Altogether, this would point to a total of 4.2 percent of the population in "commercial" activities. There were also 240,000 people in occupations he called "artizans & handycrafts"—and many of those must have spent some time selling the goods they made. Modern research (Lindert, 1980, pp. 702–03) has established that in 1688, about 9.6 percent of all males had occupations that can be classified as "commercial." For 1700, the corresponding number is 8.3 percent. In 1755 commercial occupations rise to 13 percent, but afterward the numbers seem to stabilize and even to decline slightly relative to the population. The census of 1811 reports only 5.9 percent of the population as part of the commercial classes, but the computations in Lindert and Williamson, 1982, suggest a total of 205,800 merchants and shopkeepers in 1801, which would be about 10 percent of households. The later and more reliable censuses of 1841 and 1851 make such computations cumbersome, because of their odd and inconsistent ways of classifying workers. Among the adult males surveyed in the 1841 census, we can add all occupations that were clearly mercantile, and find that 305,625 or 16.7 percent of employed males over 20 declared occupations such as "grocer," "dealer," and "broker." For adult women the number is 3.55 percent (largely because 45 percent of all women over age 20 were employed as "servants"). These numbers seriously understate the real number, because this estimate excludes a substantial number of people who classified themselves as having *both* a manufacturing and a commercial occupation, such as the 114 "pen-makers and dealers." Independent artisans sold their own wares, and some of those occupations were of course numerous (bakers and shoemakers alone accounted for 243,000 adult males). Long before the Industrial Revolution, Britain was a commercialized nation which relied on markets, where supply met demand, money changed hands, credit was widely used, and competition was often fierce.

All the same, commerce changed considerably in the period 1700–1850. Urbanization meant, inevitably, a growth in the number of customers who raised little or no food themselves and were entirely dependent on what they could purchase. But these were also years of growing occupational specialization, in which occupations began to mean more what they mean today: some people made things, others maintained and repaired them, still others sold them, and these functions were slowly becoming more separate although the process was far from complete by 1850. Foreign visitors were astonished by British stores. In 1706 the Frenchman de Souligné (probably a pseudonym) thought that ancient Rome had not "the Fourth part of Shops, Arts and Handicrafts as we have in London" (1706, pp. 100–01). In London "the magnificence of the shops and warehouses, which often extend without interruption the length of an English mile are peculiarly striking," wrote the German visitor J. von Archenholz ([1785], 1797, p. 145) in around 1780. Even within commerce, growing specialization began to occur, with wholesalers becoming distinct from retailers in some sectors. With the integration of markets and the rise of a "national market" in some commodities, more and more people ended up purchasing from strangers. If local carpenters and brushmakers had supplied most of the needs of the average family in the time of Elizabeth I, in the eighteenth century regional or national markets in many goods began to emerge. By the late eighteenth century Frederick Eden found that while in Elizabethan times husbandmen still wore coarse linen made at home, this held by his time only for the northern counties and Scotland. In the Midlands and southern counties the laborers purchased most if not all of their clothes from the shopkeeper whereas in the north there were still many respectable persons who never "wore a bought pair of stockings, coat, nor waistcoat in their lives" (Eden, 1797, Vol. 1, pp. 120–21, 554–55). The "moral economy," in which people traded primarily with people they knew personally, slowly gave way to a more sophisticated, complex, impersonal system. Many contemporaries decried this loss of innocence, suspecting middlemen of profiteering, and voiced their suspicion of the laws of supply and demand. Ideas now taught in every business school such as "marketing" and "advertising" slowly picked up. Special clothing halls to sell woolen products were opened, and traveling salespeople with their samples and drawings charged into expanding markets. Consumers were constantly told that the world of goods was a good world, the only world worth living for. In the eighteenth century trading cards issued by merchants became an effective means of bringing one's goods to the attention of customers as well as a gentle reminder to customers who owed a balance (Hubbard, 2009).

The notion of marketing was pushed furthest by the famed potter Josiah Wedgwood, whose appeals to snobbery and to the nobility-envy of the merchant and middle classes were an early example of what some might think of as consumer manipulation. Wedgwood's marketing strategies included a brazen display of goods targeted at the high and the mighty, to be imitated by the would-have-beens and even by the never-were. It is easy to exaggerate the representativeness of Wedgwood: he was in many ways a highly unusual individual, an entrepreneur of rare imagination and audacity, and few could measure up to him. But he did set an example, and aggressive marketing strategies can be discerned in other industries such as printing, cutlery, clocks, high-end textiles, and household implements, to say nothing of medical doctors and pharmacists selling miracle drugs. Advertisers shamelessly dropped the names of peers and royalty, whether honestly or not. Matthew Boulton mentioned the King's architect, clockmaker, cutler, and physician in his correspondence and clearly cultivated such relationships (Robinson, 1963, p. 50). Marketing became an industry. A well-known example is that of the razor salesman George Packwood whose advertising campaign in the mid-1790s was a "remorseless attempt to imprint the brand name on the public memory" (McKendrick, 1982, p. 148). Advertising revenues became an ever more important source of income for newspapers. Provincial newspapers teemed with advertisements, particularly appealing to the snobs by alerting them to "metropolitan tastes"—that of London, above all. Advertising may seem far removed from ideas of Enlightenment, but free competition, ingenuity, and the dissemination of information, all core values of the Industrial Enlightenment, were what advertising were all about. So, of course, were dissimulation and consumer manipulation.

  With declining transport costs in the late eighteenth century, more of London's consumer culture filtered down even to small provincial towns, who aped it wherever possible. Coffee-houses, opera companies, and lending libraries emerged all over provincial Britain. Theaters with names such as Drury Lane sprouted up in small cities. A visitor to Halifax in 1781 was astounded by the quality of the local bookseller. London may not have been an industrial and technological leader during the the Industrial Revolution, but it still set the tone of demand patterns. The wool industry, especially, increasingly catered to fashion, understood it, and manipulated it. The cotton industry's great success was in part based on the ability of cotton fabrics to absorb printed patterns and colors, which made them attractive to consumers, especially after 1783 when Thomas Bell perfected the technique of printing patterns on cotton cloth using copper cylinders. Dr Johnson sighed that "Promise, large promise, is the soul of advertisement. I remember a *Wash-ball* that had a quality truly wonderful; it gave an exquisite edge to the razor ... The vender of the Beautifying Fluid sells a Lotion that repels pimples, washes away freckles, smooths the skin, and plumps the flesh; and yet, with a generous abhorrence of ostentation, confesses, that it will not restore the bloom of fifteen to a Lady of fifty ... The trade of advertising is now so near perfection that it is not easy to propose any improvement" ([1759], 1800, Vol. 1, pp. 135–37). This may seem somewhat comical in the twenty-first century, yet clearly indicates that by this time commercial advertising was a common sight.

Retailers found new ways to reach customers. Samples were sent around with traveling salesmen, and displayed in country inns. Warehouses and display rooms were set up in places like Bolton (outside Manchester), although eventually much of this activity moved to the city itself. Some manufacturers opened permanent showrooms (e.g., the cutlery works of Rodgers & Sons in Sheffield). In Halifax, the cloth hall was opened in 1775, and had 300 rooms in which trading and the exchange of information could take place. Firms also increasingly employed overseas agents to help them market products abroad. Some manufacturers decided to do their own marketing, while others relied on wholesalers. Wholesale trade emerged slowly over the eighteenth century, but by 1850, the separation between it and retailing was already quite advanced. The result of the gradual expansion of marketing, new and better goods, more choice and lower prices was that in eighteenth-century Britain consumerism—some would say materialism—became a significant social force. It affected the choice every consumer had between market-produced goods and home-made ones, and helped shift preferences toward purchased goods. Yet in order to buy goods, households needed cash, that is, to work more outside the home or sell the products they made rather than consume them. This gave rise to what has become known as the "Industrious Revolution"—a growth in the market-oriented labor supply driven by a desire for consumer goods (De Vries, 1993, 1994, 2008).

*   *   *

Of the many "revolutions" that were supposed to have taken place in Britain between 1700 and 1850, the transportation revolution occupies a pivotal role, in that it affected all other sectors in subtle but pervasive ways, and was itself subject to the institutional and technological advances that changed the British economy. Transportation is a technology, but it also needs to be organized, coordinated, and financed in ways that are special. Transportation usually requires substantial overhead investment as well a physical layout as a network, in which complementary and rival lines are often very close to one another. The history of modern transportation was punctuated by the development of the railroad in the late 1820s, and some historians have viewed the railroad as the primary driving force of modernization and growth. There is more and less to this story than is thought: transportation development included much more than railroads, which, however, may not quite have had the dramatic impact believed by some in the period covered here. Much like the argument I made for agricultural and industrial steam power, the real factor that transformed the economy was the general drive for progress and not just its various manifestations. Long before the emergence of the steam locomotive, transport costs were declining. Thus, better-built roads and improved coaches sharply reduced internal travel time in the eighteenth century: the coach from London to Edinburgh still took 10–12 days in the mid-1750s, whereas in 1836 (just before being replaced by a railroad) it could cover the distance in 45½ hours.

Assessing the exact impact of transportation improvements on economic development is far from easy. The movement of goods and mobile factors of production *within* a country permits regional specialization, which, as economists never tire of explaining, makes *all* regions better off. Better transportation will lead to better allocations of capital and labor. Following the development of the transport network, British labor became more mobile. Workers could travel around looking for jobs, and in some cases work for periods in remote places without arduous and long trudges across the country. Even capital seems to have been sensitive to these developments and became more mobile in the eighteenth century (Buchinsky and Polak, 1993). Adam Smith's celebrated division of labor depended on tolerably low transport costs in the market: his idea of "the extent of the market" must be defined in the context of transportation capabilities. But there were more subtle and indirect effects as well: in much of the eighteenth century, Britain's regional diversity was still quite pronounced, and ideology, politics, and culture expressed local values and interests as much as national or universal ones (Langton, 1984). It is this kind of cultural heterogeneity that better transportation and communications tend to erase, though diversity is never quite eliminated. Indeed, specialization may have enhanced regional differences, not just between manufacturing and farming regions but also between, say, the textiles of Lancashire and the hardware industries of the Black Country.

Better transportation weakened and possibly eliminated local monopolies and forced producers and merchants to compete with one another, a process that enhanced efficiency and speeded up the diffusion of new techniques. By unifying large markets, good transport tended to encourage the creation of standardized products and through it mass production, and encouraged investment in marketing and management (Szostak, 1991). A good railroad is the mortal enemy of the monopsonistic employer in the "one-company-town," who could exploit his employees. More subtly and harder to observe, better transportation meant that ideas and knowledge could flow more easily across space and thus that they affected access costs. With the completion of the turnpikes, Boulton and Watt were able to travel from Birmingham to Paris in 1786 in the astonishingly short time of six days (Jones, 2008, p. 27). Ideas and information were carried by books, magazines, letters, and people, which could only move at the speed at which physical objects could move, a constraint that is easily forgotten in the age of the internet. As John R. Harris (1992) has argued, much of the tacit, crafts-based knowledge in the eighteenth century spread through the movement of skilled workers from one area to another, and "industrial espionage" remained an important part of the technology of access to knowledge. Specialists such as the consulting engineers needed for the maintenance of early steam engines and other machinery or coal viewers, the experts who assisted in the construction of deeper and more elaborate mines, could travel from site to site. Itinerant lecturers moved about in Britain and spread knowledge and techniques. Consultants and experts traveled about and helped diffuse technology. The roads between Cornwall and the southern Midlands were well traveled by Watt's employees. Books, magazines, pamphlets, and letters spread more easily and quickly. Technology improved faster when inventors and mechanics could have good access to techniques used elsewhere, could compare notes, and could combine different and disparate ideas into new forms. To do this, they needed good access—and that was what better transportation provided.

Before the coming of the railroad, transport took three forms: road transport, ocean transport, and internal waterways. All three modes had their own technological and organizational problems that needed to be solved, and the period in question saw a plethora of solutions. None of those were perhaps as dramatic and as spectacular as the railroad, but economic effects are sometimes most penetrating and pervasive when the changes are least visible on the surface. In the case of transportation, at least, the changes were visible and have been documented by historians.

Road transport in Britain improved a great deal in the century before the railroad. Like every other economic sector between 1700 and 1850, progress came not from a single spectacular breakthrough but from a variety of sources. Technology improved at a multitude of levels: roads were better constructed, and stronger animals hauled better-made carriages. But improved institutions and organizations were equally important. Firms running passenger and freight services got larger and more efficient, through learning-by-doing or economies of scale (Gerhold, 1996a, p. 502). The most important development, however, arose from the evolution of the turnpike trust. Road-building and maintenance had traditionally been the responsibility of local authorities (parishes). The dilemma was that the benefits of free-access roads accrued to a large extent to non-residents in transit or their customers, and unless there was a way to collect money from these customers, there would be no incentive for local authorities to spend resources on roads. The coordination problem here was quite obvious: when a road led through many parishes, each parish was in charge only of the segment running through it. There was little point in the local authorities improving it beyond what the neighboring parish would do. Thus the mean quality of roads would gravitate to the level of quality consistent with the poorest or stingiest parish on the way, what is known today as a "race to the bottom."

Turnpike trusts had emerged in the seventeenth century. A good example of institutional innovation, these trusts were established by Act of Parliament. Such Acts allowed local authorities to charge tolls from users in exchange for maintaining the quality of the roads. The tolls were regulated by Parliament, so this was hardly a free market, but it was a vast improvement on the chaotic system and poor-quality roads that the parishes had created. The first such trust was passed by Parliament in 1663, but in the seventeenth century these were largely confined to the London area. The decades 1750–70 witnessed the peak of the "turnpike boom" in which much of the rest of the country was turned into turnpikes. By the mid-1830s, about 22,000 miles of roads in Britain (about 17 percent of the entire road network, but including most of the important roads leading to big cities, including London) had been "turnpiked" and roads had improved significantly (Bogart, 2005a, 2005b). Using the best data available, Bogart has shown that the trusts reduced transport costs while improving quality, and that the effect of turnpike trusts came on top of the technological changes in road transport. The social savings methodology he employs indicates that around 1820, on the eve of the railroad age, turnpike trusts added around 1 percent to national income through lower transport costs, not counting the indirect and harder to measure spillover effects discussed earlier (Bogart, 2005a, p. 501). Furthermore, by comparing the roads that were turnpiked with those that remained under the traditional parish management (and adjusting for inevitable selection bias), Bogart (2005b) shows that turnpike trusts actually increased investment in road improvement and did not just replace funds that would have come from somewhere else. The quantitative evidence amassed by Bogart is complemented by evidence from firm records: turnpike roads were used to transport cotton goods in the 1780s and 1790s because they were faster and more reliable even if canals were less expensive (Freeman, 1980).

The turnpike movement coincided chronologically more or less with the Industrial Revolution. Its significance for an understanding of the era is that it cannot have been caused by the developments in cotton, steam, and iron, which were still in the future, nor was its impact on the economy large enough to account by itself for the technological developments. The only conclusion one can draw is that both were driven by a deeper phenomenon, which involved the ability to apply useful knowledge to practical problems as well as the political willingness to reform antiquated inefficient institutions to make the economy work more smoothly. The capability of British institutions to reinvent themselves and make the economy advance without bloodshed and political upheaval reform constituted an essential component of the success of the Enlightenment program in that country.

Institutional progress, even more than technological progress, was never linear and direct. As we have seen, the attempt to advance on many fronts ran into stubborn resistance in the form of "messy" technical problems that could not be readily solved with the knowledge base available. Even when they were solved, however, ex post concepts of progress could be misleading. Road travel and canals provide an example of how the relentless quest for improvements sometimes led to progress on fronts that eventually turned out to be a dead end. Stagecoach traffic through England increased rapidly during the eighteenth century. The number of public coaches leaving London each week (in the summer) was 465, of which 394 traveled less than 60 miles from the city. By 1783, this number had increased to 5,805, of which 3,735 traveled less than 60 miles (Austen, 1981, p. 26). The average speed of these coaches was slow, less than 4 miles per hour in the early 1760s, but by the early 1830s this had increased to about 8 miles per hour (Jackman, [1916], 1962, pp. 683–701; Bogart, 2005a, p. 484). The costs of travel did not fall much over the long haul, but costs were not everything in transportation: frequency, reliability, speed, and comfort all increased dramatically in the century before the first railroad was built. Stage-coaching, despite the costs and the discomforts, was very much the mechanism that provided Britons with the mobility on which so much depended, and one scholar, writing in about the 1830s, has remarked that in the industrializing areas the coaches provided the kind of communication that broke down barriers and gave these areas greater cohesion and unity than ever before. The idea of regular, reliable, and frequent passenger transport between towns was due to the stagecoach, not the railway (Dickinson, 1959, pp. 10–11). When the railroads came, passengers were ready for it, but the turnpikes lost their importance.

The age of Enlightenment was the age of improving communications and declining access costs. Much information was communicated through personal letters, and what a letter-writing age needed was a good postal service. In 1683, William Dockwra, a London armorer, set up London's Penny Post. In an age of rent-seeking, however, natural monopolies were confused with revenue-generating government enterprises, and the Crown revoked his patent and took over the enterprise. During the eighteenth century mail services gradually expanded through byway posts (cutting out the need to go through London). These byway posts were the brainchild of a Cornwall postal employee, Ralph Allen, one of the unsung successful entrepreneurs of the first half of the eighteenth century, who bought the rights to all byway post in Britain. By the time of Allen's death in 1764, most of England and Wales received mail daily (Headrick, 2000, p. 187).

The Post Office became a factor in land transportation with the introduction of mail coaches in 1784. The brainchild of John Palmer, the mail coach adopted an innovative design made by carriage maker John Besant in 1795 that used the famed "mail axle" that prevented the wheels from coming off accidentally. Palmer was a rather obsessive Bath theater owner, who became frustrated by the slowness of the mail, and single-handedly cowed and bullied the Pitt government into reforming the mail services. The mailcoaches carried passengers as well as mail, and although the share of passengers they carried remained small, the competition did the industry a lot of good, especially in long-distance travel. The process was completed in the mid-1780s. Mail coaches were a considerable improvement, with the emphasis on promptness, punctuality, and speed, traveling overnight and stopping only to change horses. They were absolved from turnpike tolls, and received priority over other vehicles. The postal system was wholly reformed, and Palmer was recognized as one of the most distinguished improvers of his age, and awarded a grant of £50,000 in 1813. In 1840 Rowland Hill established the national Penny Post, which became the standard of the efficient and accessible postal system that signifies the importance that Victorian society placed on good communications.

Better road-building technology added to these improvements. The period of the Industrial Revolution was famous for progress in the way roads were built. The "trio" of great road engineers consisted of John Metcalfe (1717–1810), most famous for his technique for draining rainwater on both sides of the road in ditches; Thomas Telford (1757–1834), who used uniformly sized stones for the foundation of his roads and small broken stones on the top, which got harder as horses' hooves and carriage wheels compacted them solid; and John Loudon MacAdam (1756–1836) whose idea of building slightly convex roads earned him immortality as "Macadamization" (covering roads with layers of broken stones) spread far beyond Britain. Gentler gradients, a central component of road improvement, helped reduce horse exertion. Surface durability and the ease of drainage, however, were only two technical aspects of these improvements. Other forms of progress were equally important. One example of the happy marriage between ever better informed and more sophisticated engineers and the transportation sector was the construction of more advanced bridges. Of these, the most remarkable was Telford's magnificent suspension bridge over the Menai Straits in Wales, completed in 1826.

With better roads came better-designed and lighter carriages, stronger and more efficient horses, and greater speed (Gerhold, 1996a). An index of productivity in road transport (measured inversely through costs), provided in table 10.1, shows that the efficiency of road transport on two selected and perhaps not typical routes (Leeds to London freight carrier, London to Exeter coaches) more or less tripled between 1700 and about 1830, with the greatest acceleration happening around the middle of the eighteenth century. Given that the truly discontinuous breakthroughs in road technology such as asphalt, pneumatic tires, and the internal combustion engine were still far in the future, this was a truly remarkable achievement. Improvements in internal transport were an important part of the continuous spread of knowledge and ideas essential to an enlightened economy. But beyond that, commodities needed to be moved around if economic efficiency was to be attained through competition and specialization. The improvements in roads were essential to an industrial town like Birmingham, which had neither a harbor nor a good river nearby. Its population tripled between 1700 and 1750,

Table 10.1: Productivity increase in road transport

	Cost index for Leeds–London carriers (1693–1702 = 100)	Cost index for London–Exeter coaches (1658 = 100)
1700–09	102.0	
1710–19	92.3	
1720–29	95.4	119[a]
1730–39	96.8	
1740–49	82.4	
1750–59	62.3	73[b]
1760–69	51.2	47[c]
1770–79	50.9	46.3[d]
1780–89	51.2	41.6[e]
1790–99	46.4	
1800–09	44	
1810–14	47.8	35.7[f]
1820	43.2	23
1825	36.2	
1838	30.9	

[a] 1728
[b] 1757
[c] average of 1760–67
[d] average of 1776–78
[e] average of 1786–88
[f] average of 1810–14

Source: Gerhold (1996a, pp. 494, 508).

and tripled again between 1750 and 1800, making it the third largest town in England after London and Bristol in 1775. It success as the hardware capital of Britain depended on its ability to ship its buttons and toys through the entire kingdom.

More than the manufacturing sector, transportation demonstrates how technological and institutional factors interacted and that any attempt to disentangle the effects of one or the other runs into what economists call "non-separability." Gerhold (1996a, p. 506) concludes that the savings in transport costs were not due to the turnpike trusts as such, and that without them, new techniques such as MacAdam's could have been adopted by some other form of road authority or even by the parishes. Yet Bogart's demonstration of the importance of trusts suggests the strong synergy between institutional change and technological progress. In that respect the transport sector was a microcosm of the enlightened economy.

The most ambitious and costly project of the years of the Industrial Revolution was the construction of canals. In many respects, internal waterways were unglamorous projects. The technology involved was, in the main part, old and unspectacular. Canals were mostly designed for bulky, slow-moving cargoes and served mostly local transport needs, the average haul estimated at 26 miles or less. Much like turnpikes, they required parliamentary approval. They were also expensive to build and maintain, with a great deal of engineering ingenuity invested in the construction of aqueducts, embankments, bridges, locks, and tunnels. The early canals were still set up by landowners, who accounted for over 40 percent of all investment in them, but by the years 1780–1815 their share had fallen to 22 percent and manufacturers accounted for 15 percent (Hawke and Higgins, 1981, p. 233).

A number of canals have become *causes célèbres* in the economic history of the Industrial Revolution, above all the famous Bridgewater Canal completed in 1759, which connected the coal mines of the Duke of Bridgewater in Worsley with Manchester. It was a fairly small, local affair despite its great publicity, though it halved the price of coal in Manchester, and sent a powerful signal regarding the profitability and feasibility of canals. Much more consequential was the Grand Trunk (Trent and Mersey) Canal, completed in 1777 at the initiative of Josiah Wedgwood. It connected the east and west coasts of England and was designed and built, like many of the eighteenth-century canals, by the great engineer James Brindley. The Birmingham Canal, authorized in 1768 and completed in 1772, was a success, and by 1800 Birmingham had become "the Kremlin from which canals radiated in all directions" (Jackman [1916], 1962, p. 370). The challenge to connect the network that had grown in the Midlands to London was taken up in 1793, through the Grand Junction Canal, completed in 1805, which reduced the distance by almost 60 miles. The Chester Canal could boast the two huge iron aqueducts built by the miraculous Thomas Telford at Chirk and Pontcysyllte in eastern Wales.

Canal barges were slow: they were pulled by horses along towpaths. But for the purposes of hauling bulky and heavy loads such as coal, bricks, limestone, salt, timber, clay, and ore, they were of substantial importance to the continuing development of the economy. Inland waterways' capacity almost tripled from about 1,400 miles in 1760 to almost 3,900 miles in 1830. The benefits were, of course, not evenly spread: canals were local affairs and served primarily local needs, and cooperation between adjacent companies was often lacking, to the annoyance of their customers. Canal companies were "extremely parochial" (Turnbull, 1987, p. 541). A contemporary author noted that "no towns have derived greater advantage of canals perhaps than Manchester and Liverpool" (cited by Harris, 1956, p. 158). All the same, their rather sudden surge in the closing decades of the eighteenth century was another mark of the determination of the age of improvement to apply the best useful knowledge they had in engineering to economic progress. Although the completion of a national network took decades, the gains of greater economic integration in the end accrued to the entire country. Indeed, it may well be questioned to what extent Britain could have taken advantage of its generous endowments of coal without the canal network.

A good example of the costs and benefits of canals was the construction of the Leeds–Liverpool Canal, commenced in 1770, which extended 127 miles across the Pennines. The project was interrupted when the company ran out of money between 1777 and 1790, and was only completed in 1816, although portions of the canal came into use as early as 1774. Under the inspired leadership of James Brindley and later his partner John Longbotham (another Smeaton pupil), it turned out a feat of engineering without precedent and amazed contemporaries. Because of the difficulty of the terrain, the canal required no fewer than 91 locks and a tunnel of 1,630 yards at Foulridge, yet it was highly successful and reduced transport costs between the two prime industrializing counties of England, Lancashire and Yorkshire, by as much as 80 percent (Baines, 1875). Like most canals, its costs were such that incorporation was required, but because the shares were large, only wealthy investors—mostly local landowners from Yorkshire – participated in the project and controlled its technical parameters.

The canal era was driven by the financial resources and entrepreneurial energies of local notables. They hired expert engineers such as Brindley, William Jessop, Thomas Telford, and James Green to design their canals, and overcame the often stubborn resistance of vested interests that stood to lose from the competition. The enormous technological advances that the engineering profession had experienced were epitomized in the magnificent Pontcysyllte aqueduct, which to this day is the longest and highest in Britain, built between 1795 and 1805 by Telford and Jessop, and the first such project to rely heavily on cast iron as a construction material.

British inland waterways went from triumph to triumph and many of them returned a healthy profit—until the trains came. With the arrival of the railroad, canal construction understandably slowed down and then stopped altogether. But economic historians have long seen canals as the "next best" alternative to railroads. They were slower, of course, froze over in cold winters, and lacked the technological excitement of the early trains. But speed mattered less for the cargoes that used the canals, and the notion that without the railroad industrial growth and economic progress would have ground to an early halt is no longer tenable. Canals, like turnpike roads, eventually turned out to be a costly dead end, though they long remained useful for some specific purposes. But the history of economic progress is inevitably studded with such "failures." In a world of technologically driven growth, the road was littered with could-have-beens, the unavoidable cost of progress.

Coastal shipping has been termed the "Cinderella of the transport world" (Armstrong, 1996). It, too, was distinctly unglamorous, and devoid of melodrama and heroes. Yet that does not mean it was unimportant to the British economy. John Armstrong (1987, p. 176) has calculated that as late as 1910, coastal ships carried 59 percent of all ton-miles of internal freight, with the railroad picking up 39 percent and canals only 2 percent. For the first half of the nineteenth century the size of coastal shipping cannot have been less, although good numbers are lacking. Needless to say, ton-mileage is not the best measure of transport intensity, but it underlines the importance of coastal shipping as a cheap mode of hauling heavy and bulky cargoes over relatively long distances. In terms of hauling bulky and heavy goods such as cereals, bricks, sand, iron ore, and above all coal, it provided by far the cheapest mode and helped make Britain an integrated economy, contributing to regional specialization and efficiency. Baldwin's *London Directory* published in 1768 listed no fewer than 580 places in England and Wales accessible by water—the majority of them being served by ports. Coastal shipping made energy-intensive industries, such as brewing, glass, bricks, and salt, possible in sites far removed from the mines, and it kept Londoners warm and London increasingly foggy by shipping in coal to be burned in private hearths. It was also one of the main sources of demand for the British shipping industry: in the first half of the eighteenth century the average annual shipment of coal from the northeastern ports such as Newcastle to London was around half a million tons a year, exceeding the total tonnage of Britain's two bulkiest exports, grain and coal. To be sure, coastal voyages were shorter, yet these ships had to be seaworthy in every respect.

Coastal and cross-Channel shipping was technologically no less progressive than deep-water vessels, and in some advances in shipping technology coastal ships were the pioneers. As soon as steam power became feasible, it was adopted by coastal shippers, to reduce their dependence on the whims of winds and tides: as early as 1821, there were 188 steamers occupied in the British coastal trade, and their tonnage increased by a factor of ten in the next century. While their navigational demands were perhaps different than transoceanic shipping, they were far from trivial. Until the railroads came, it is hard to see how on many routes the heavy loads of fuel and building materials that industrialization and urbanization demanded would have been hauled around in the absence of coastal shipping. Canals were better suited for short-distance hauls, and in any case coasters were more of a complement than a competitor to canals. Coastal shipping also carried considerable passenger traffic, especially in the northern parts of Britain. The trips were slow, but more comfortable and cheaper than road transport.

One of the typical transport improvements of the age was the renovation of London Harbor and the construction of a dock system in a feverish construction scheme during the first years of the nineteenth century. The moving force behind the improvements in the West India Dock were London merchants with strong Caribbean connections such as George Hibbert and Robert Milligan. Parliament itself passed the Bill to authorize the construction (in 1799) and appointed the civil engineer William Jessop, John Smeaton's star apprentice and protégé, and the chief engineer of the Grand Junction Canal, as the engineer in charge. John Rennie served as consultant to the project, and it employed one of the first high-pressure engines ever used in an engineering project for the dredging work, designed by Richard Trevithick himself (Burton, 2000, pp. 113–20). The smaller East India Docks were authorized in 1803, London Docks at Wapping were built between 1802 and 1805 (by Rennie as well), and the St Katherine Docks in the early 1820s, designed and supervised by Telford.

Railroads were the invention that par excellence defined modernity, both to contemporaries and to economic historians. Before the railroad, people had never been able to move at a speed exceeding that of a fast horse – and only a select few had experienced that. Travel by stagecoach was slow, expensive, and uncomfortable. Trains were faster, cheaper, and could reach places that previously were quite inaccessible. Like many of the other developments during the Industrial Revolution they were essentially democratic in that they made accessible services that previously had been confined to the rich and privileged. The majority of people who were to make use of passenger trains had had to walk to their destinations before 1830. The railroads, much like our own communication technology, shrunk the world—perhaps more so than any invention since the sailing ship. They were spectacularly visible and audible, and could be experienced at a low cost. The development of the railroad drove home, even to the most remote and peaceful rural regions of Britain, the message that the world was changing at an ever accelerating pace, and that in the long run no place would remain unaffected. But the railroads are equally interesting for the technological problems that they created and solved and the economic and institutional implications of the construction and operation of a project of unprecedented size and complexity.

Wooden tracks that minimized the friction created by pulling heavy cargoes on wheeled vehicles can be traced back to the early Middle Ages, and were quite widely used by British mines in the late eighteenth century. The idea of a smooth rail as a friction-minimizing surface for wheels had been used in coal mines since the eighteenth century, and Richard Reynolds (Abraham Darby II's partner) substituted iron rails for wooden ones as early as 1768, but the use of iron rails on a wider scale would not have been possible without the puddling and rolling process. By the first decade of the nineteenth century, decades before the first successful locomotives, Britain was estimated to have 300 miles of railway track (Bagwell, 1974, p. 90). The first "general-purpose" railroad (built by Jessop) was the Surrey horse-drawn iron railway completed in 1805, and the famed "Mumbles" railroad established in Swansea was the first one to haul passengers. While no financial success, they indicated what this form of transport could do. The first use of steam power was on the Stockton and Darlington railroad (mixed horse- and steam power) in 1825. The conventional start of the railway age, however, is taken as the opening of the Liverpool–Manchester route in 1830.

The railroad was the unmistakable child of the Industrial Revolution. Its two central technological components were the steam engine and the iron rail. Neither of these was entirely new in 1830, when the first steam railroad was officially opened. The steam engine that propelled the locomotives was a high-pressure engine, developed in the first decade of the nineteenth century by engineers such as Richard Trevithick and Arthur Woolf. There were different kinds of machine that used "strong steam" in the parlance of the day, and Trevithick's insight was to get rid of Watt's separate condenser, which made for a lighter and smaller device. This engine was adapted by a brilliant father and son team of engineers, George and Robert Stephenson, to the specific purpose of creating a steam loco-motive, using a revolutionary multi-tubular boiler. Other insights by engineers associated with new technologies also found their way into the complex tech-nological issues that railroads involved, such as brakes, gears, axles, gauges, couplings, and springs. But the railroad also posed entirely new problems, none larger than the need to communicate rapidly over large distances to coordinate the movement of trains. The telegraph, the first large-scale technique to rely on electrical phenomena and thus just as radical and momentous an innovation as the trains it announced, developed about a decade after the railroad. If ever there was a case of technological symbiosis, this was it.

The railroad was the climactic achievement of British engineering competence. It had not much science or even formal mathematics underlying it. It was mostly designed and built by people with little or no formal education, but who had mastered a profound if informal understanding of what did and did not work, through a combination of natural talent and access to the right masters. The first models were built by Richard Trevithick, whose education was mostly provided by his own father and uncle in the Cornish mines (Burton, 2000, p. 28). George

Stephenson had even less formal education, and he, John Blenkinsop (often credited with building the very first locomotive), and William Hedley, the designer of an intermediate proto-model of the locomotive known as "Puffing Billy," were all trained as practical mining engineers. Another railroad pioneer, Timothy Hackworth, similarly, was apprenticed to his father (a blacksmith) and he, too, worked at a colliery. The technical problems in the railroad were often hard and perplexing, but they were still of the kind that could be overcome with the traditional empiricist engineering skills that had stood British manufacturing in such good stead during the Industrial Revolution. It was, however, not a promising strategy for future technological advances.

The technical challenges of the railroad were matched by economic and institutional ones. For one thing, the construction of the network was by far the most costly and ambitious overhead investment project since the Pyramids. The questions of who could and would finance and manage it were raised in every nation that contemplated constructing a railroad network. Much like any other investment that has social overhead characteristics, there was an ambiguity about the role of the state. By the 1830s, Britain's commitment to liberalism made its government hesitant to follow the model of continental nations like Belgium and Prussia where the government participated actively in the financing and construction of the new project. British railroads were financed by securities sold to the general public. But clearly pure laissez-faire in this sector was unrealistic. Parliament still had to approve each company, and some limitations were imposed on the free operation of railroad companies in the famous Railways Act of 1844 (drawn up by the young William Gladstone, then President of the Board of Trade), which limited the prices that railroads could charge and imposed safety regulations that remained on the books till the twentieth century. Even when it seemed that necessary coordination could be dealt with through private means, government support was needed. A case in point is the Railway Clearing House, set up in 1842 by a few companies to compute the net balance of each company's dealing with others when passengers and freight were transshipped through more than one company. It also set technical standards that benefited all, such as the adoption of Greenwich Mean Time for railroad schedules and a variety of technical standards. In 1850 the members themselves had to initiate the Railway Clearing Act to compel some recalcitrant companies to participate in this scheme.

The railroad network turned out to be a huge investment project. To provide some context, consider this: in the 1820s, transport investment—roads, harbors, and canals—absorbed about 15 percent of British Gross Capital Formation, whereas in the late 1840s, the peak of the railroad boom, this figure jumped to a lower bound of 40–45 percent, with some of the higher estimates reaching 54 percent. Regardless of which estimate is more accurate, it was an order of magnitude above the already considerable costs of maintaining the existing superstructure. An analysis of the owners of the securities shows that a substantial number of these stocks and bonds were owned by merchants and landowners. Not necessarily the class that had been most active in leading the Industrial Revolution, but perhaps the one which indirectly had benefited most from it. The ability of the British economy to finance this huge project was truly impressive. Rates of growth of the railroad network are of course not very meaningful, - because it started from nothing: in 1830 Britain had less than 200 kilometers of railroad track. In 1850 it had completed 9,800 km, almost a third of the 30,000 km it ended up with in 1900. To carry out this project required a considerable reallocation of resources. In the feverish peak years of railroad construction, between 1845 and 1849, close to a quarter of a million men were employed, perhaps 4 percent of the male labor force (Mitchell, 1964, p. 323). Many of these workers were Irish immigrants; others may have been young males whose prospects in domestic manufacturing were bleak in the 1840s.

Part of the reason why the railway was so expensive was that the two leading engineers and builders, Robert Stephenson and Isambard K. Brunel, were both profligate with investor money. Stephenson had estimated that the London–Liverpool line would cost somewhat over £21,000 per mile, whereas the actual cost was over £50,000. Brunel had underestimated the cost of his London–Bristol line by a factor of 150 percent. A third engineer, Joseph Locke, was far more economical and was willing to build along steeper gradients, which saved costs. But until his approach became common practice, a lot of stockholder money was wasted. Moreover, railroad companies built extravagant, lavish, architect-designed stations, which cost far more than necessary. It may well be that those stations were intended to attract worried and reluctant passengers, but they added to the overall costs of construction (Rolt, 1970, ch. 1).

Other new institutional problems that emerged with the railroads had to do with the need to coordinate technical standards so that different railroads could connect to one another. Of these, the most notorious was the railroad gauge. Different railroad companies used different standards, with the obvious results that their trains could not use each other's tracks, and freights and passengers had to unload and re-embark at terminal points. Two gauge standards emerged, the gauge used by George Stephenson on his Manchester–Liverpool line opened in 1830 (4' 8½") and the wide gauge preferred by the Great Western Line owner, Isambard K. Brunel. Long debates, sometimes known as the "gauge wars" ensued on the relative merits of each of these gauges. It was believed that wider gauges provided more stability to trains, and no less an authority than Charles Babbage supported this view. But in the end it became clear that differences between the two standards were less important than the cost of incompatibility and Parliament had to impose a standard. In 1845, a special commission recommended adopting the narrow (Stephenson) gauge for all new railroads and the last of the wide gauges, the Great Western, converted to the standard in 1892. The actual Stephenson standard selected was more "in the nature of a random draw from a variety of practices" but in this case diversity was costly and inefficient, and coordination by a government agency was necessary (Puffert, 2009, p. 48). It was one of the first historical cases of network externalities, and it became clear, even to the most laissez-faire Victorian, that arbitrating such disputes could be more efficiently done by an impartial outsider than by the market (Siddall, 1969).

The exact quantitative significance of the railroads to the overall development of the British economy will remain a matter of dispute. The locational patterns of manufacturing had already been set in 1830, and the appearance of the railroad did little in the medium term to change that—indeed railroad construction was determined by existing locations of manufacturing centers. Economists have developed the concept of social savings, the total net gain to society from developing a new technique compared to the next best technique available. They point out that the marked alterations in landscape and to some extent lifestyle that the railroad wrought were the means by which such social savings were achieved, not an addition to them. Gary Hawke (1970) applied this technique to the compu-tation of the net social savings of British railroads in 1865, and estimated that the total savings came to 6–10 percent of GDP. In 1850 the net impact of the railroad on the economy was still not earth-shaking at around 2.5 percent of GDP (Gourvish, 1980, p. 34), with the bulk of the economic impact coming in the 1850s and 1860s. These numbers, however, are only as good as the assumptions made to compute them. The estimates depend rather crucially on the value placed on passenger comfort. Freight alone accounted for a social saving of only about 4 percent of GDP in 1865, while passenger services accounted for 1.5–6 percent depending on the value that passengers placed on comfort. The higher figure has been criticized quite effectively (Gourvish, 1988, p. 81). More recently, Foreman-Peck (1991) has revisited the 1865 computations by accounting for their impact on such second-round effects as enhanced labor mobility and higher capital formation, and found them to be more or less robust to any adjustments, though for the later decades the social savings may have been underestimated. Of deeper significance in revising these figures is research by Leunig (2006), who accounts for the time saved by passengers who could get to their destinations faster and more reliably, which he reckons at about 2 percent of 1865 GDP. Even that estimate could be argued to be a lower bound of the total economic welfare gain or "social surplus" created. If the passengers traveling third class had to walk before the time of the railroad, clearly the physical effort saved by traveling by train should have improved their well-being even more.

Ocean shipping was of course an ancient activity, but it, too, was wholly trans-formed in the period under discussion here. In 1700, Britain was still playing second fiddle to the Dutch as master of the oceans. The lucrative carrying trade (equivalent to the export of shipping services, an "invisible export") was gradually expropriated by the British thanks to an aggressive mercantilist policy as expressed in the Navigation Acts. In the early eighteenth century British ships gradually began to out-compete others in the North Sea and Baltic trade, as well as the Atlantic (Ormrod, 2003, pp. 60–66). Part of the British success on the high seas was due to the strength of the British navy protecting British interests, its effectiveness in using privateering to disrupt Dutch and French trade during wartime, and the growing efficiency with which the British maritime sector financed, insured, and organized its enterprise. The Royal Exchange Assurance and its sister company, the London Assurance, were founded in 1720 and from then on British insurers competed successfully with the Dutch. The expanding colonial Empire increasingly required the services of British vessels. It is telling, indeed, that Dutch capitalists invested heavily in British shipping, a testimony to their efficiency. Yet the success of British shipping also reflects in large measure the growing openness of the economy, the skills of its seamen, and the capability of its mercantile institutions to organize and finance sea voyages, notwithstanding the often destructive mercantilist meddling with and limitations on trade. The Navigation Acts made sure that British shipping interests benefited from the carrying of these goods, but it stands to reason that even without any favorable policy, the rising efficiency of the British maritime sector ensured that it would have expanded pari passu with the growth of long-distance commerce.

The technological revolutions reached the ocean shipping sector relatively late. The application of steam to ships was slow, perhaps slower than the early experimenters had envisaged. For decades after the first famous crossing of the Atlantic by the *Savannah* in 1819, the oceans were crossed by sailing ships with auxiliary steam engines. One difficulty was that paddle wheels, the obvious form of propelling a steam-driven ship, worked poorly on the open waters, and it took decades until screw propellers were perfected in the 1850s. Another technological hurdle was that high pressure in marine steam engines was unusually hazardous, as salt in the water used to run the boilers tended to corrode the cylinders and lead to explosions. The surface condenser, which separated the water that cooled the condenser and the water in it, was developed in the 1830s but turned out to be a difficult problem (despite the efforts of some of the best minds in Britain, including William Thomson, later Lord Kelvin), and the ultimate victory of the steam engine on the oceans was not complete until the 1860s. The earliest steamers thus relied heavily on sails and their engines were auxiliary in nature, a hybrid technology if there ever was one. Yet by the 1830s, paddle steamers ("steam packets") had established a regular service with the Continent and Ireland.

Although the full application of steam power to ocean navigation, then, did not occur until the second half of the nineteenth century, contemporaries saw its potential long before and used it as an illustration of the power of new technology to enforce the powers of enlightenment. Sadi Carnot wrote in 1824 that "The safe and rapid navigation by steamships may be regarded as an entirely new art due to the steam-engine. Already this art has permitted the establishment of prompt and regular communications across the arms of the sea, and on the rivers of the old and new continents. Steam navigation brings nearer together the most distant nations. It tends to unite the nations of the earth as inhabitants of one country" (1824, p. 4).

One striking feature of the entire transport sector is that, much as we saw in steam and water power, the "old technology" showed remarkable ability to reinvent itself not only because it was threatened by a competitor, but because the economy-wide phenomena of improved access to knowledge and better understanding of the details of the techniques in use affected traditional techniques such as sailing as well. Formal "science" was not yet the decisive factor, but improved engineering and materials, and the smoother flow of useful knowledge were. The fact remains that between 1820 and 1860, sailing vessels were completely redesigned after very slow change in the previous two centuries. By reducing the size of sails and increasing their numbers, sailing ships could be made more flexible and faster, and could be operated by fewer sailors, an important source of cost-saving. Metal replaced wood in fittings, copper sheathing was employed to prevent marine growth on iron hulls, and riggings were redesigned, and construction and operating costs declined. The best-practice knowledge of the day was applied to clear and well-defined technological problems. A typical advance in shipbuilding was John Scott Russell's "wave-form" theory of ship design proposed in the 1830s, which, while flawed and no longer accepted today, led him to build more streamlined and therefore more efficient ships than ever before. British shipbuilders successfully competed with technological American clipper ships, which by 1850 were the top of the line of sailing ships.

The decline in the prices of materials coupled with an improved knowledge of their properties led to a radical change in the materials from which ships were made. When the ironmaster John Wilkinson launched the first iron-made vessel into the Severn at Coalbrookdale in 1787, a large crowd was attending, expecting it to sink like a stone. The iron ships were at first built more like wooden ships, with transverse iron frames that did not take advantage of the inherent strength of iron plating. The entire art of building ships had to be relearned. By the middle of the nineteenth century iron had replaced wood as the main shipbuilding material. The use of iron (and later steel) in hull construction once and for all removed the constraints on the size of ships that wooden construction had imposed from the earliest days of shipbuilding. It has been estimated that ocean freight shipping costs fell by 0.88 percent per year between 1811/30 and 1852/58—and most of this took place through small technological improvements in the design of wooden sailing ships or through the improvement of harbor facilities or the greater reliance on tugboats (Harley, 1988, p. 861). The eventual disappearance of the great sailing ships from the oceans should not obscure the efforts and successes in improving old and ultimately "unsuccessful" designs. Techniques should not be overlooked even if the future was to determine that many of these old techniques were moribund. The wooden sailing ship, the design of which had changed but little between 1650 and 1850, all of a sudden underwent dramatic productivity change, as new knowledge was brought to bear on an old technology.

The consequences of the advances in ocean shipping and the concomitant decline in shipping costs were far-reaching. The growth in the volume of international trade before 1850—much faster than the growth in output—must be largely chalked up to the decline in transportation costs. But better ships had unexpected results not wholly reflected by shipping costs alone. At the beginning of the nineteenth century, it could take as long as two years for a letter from Britain to Calcutta to receive an answer, in part because the Hooghly river was hard to navigate upstream due to monsoon winds. By 1840, the one-way journey around Africa had been cut to six weeks, as auxiliary steam had solved the problem. At the same time a single steam-propelled gunboat, the *Nemesis,* and her unexpected ability to sail up the Yangtze river and blow away Chinese ships with her superior guns, determined the outcome of the Opium Wars and provided a painful illustration of the gap that by that time had opened between Western and Eastern technology.

CHAPTER 11

The Service Sectors: Finance and Personal Services

Finance and insurance were comparatively small parts of the economy as late as 1850 in terms of their employment and contribution to the overall economy. Needless to say, in and of itself this does not imply that they were unimportant. A number of historians have suggested, in fact, that the significance of the commercial and financial sectors in the British economy has been underrated, even if innovation was less spectacular and palpable than in manufacturing and in shipping. Nothing like the mule or the Newcomen engine can be observed in the financial industry, but that in and of itself does not demonstrate that innovation was absent. Indeed, financial innovation, while in some ways different from technological innovation, were another manifestation of the belief in progress. If finance was, as it was often argued to be, a lubricant more than a propellant, its role in economic development was not proportional to its weight in GNP or employment any more than the weight of engine oil relative to the total weight of a car tells us much about the function of oil. Financial institutions were widespread in Britain during the Industrial Revolution, and as we saw above, they were capable of rapid transformation when they were called upon to finance a long-term investment project such as the railroads (and canals before that). Formal financial institutions played a fairly modest role in the Industrial Revolution if we judge them by the narrow criterion of their contribution to the investment in plant and equipment needed by factories and their equipment. After 1815, the prevailing condition was one in which many industrializing areas were quite well supplied with capital, but the high risks meant that "the problem of the banker was not to find money but names with sufficient standing to entrust it to" (Chapman, 1979, p. 60). Many of Britain's most innovative firms were seriously credit-constrained in this sense, and overcoming the standard shortages of venture capital was the main difficulty, not the supply of capital in general.

Britain's banks were sharply segmented by location: city banks (located in London) and country banks (located in provincial towns and the countryside). City banks, already active in the early eighteenth century, primarily discounted commercial paper, provided credit for international commerce, and lent money to the politically well connected. Growth through self-finance was impossible, of course, when overhead investment demanded a large initial outlay before any revenues came in, as with projects as canals, turnpikes, and later railroads. Overhead investment, largely carried out by the private sector, relied heavily on the financial sector.

What, then, did banks do in the eighteenth and early nineteenth centuries? They had two primary functions: to connect savers and investors, so that funds would flow to those who needed them, and to help provide the system with liquidity to facilitate the exchange process. Banks provided those services to a considerable extent in this era, but it is hard to determine whether their operation was *essential* to modernization. In part this was because banks were seriously constrained in what they could and could not do: ordinary banks were not allowed to incorporate as limited liability entities or operate in the London area, where the Bank of England had a monopoly, except for the so-called private London banks.

The earliest financial institutions, London based, were the private merchant banks, institutions "like elephants, difficult to define but easily recognizable" (Davies, 2002, p. 345). These institutions, which grew out of the seventeenth-century goldsmiths, of which there may have been about fifty in London in the late eighteenth century, were networked internationally, and a large proportion of their business was overseas, much of it involving loans to foreign governments and infrastructural projects. Their business often involved as much intermediation, consulting, and political negotiations as it did lending, and often much of their business drew heavily on their own account. Many merchant bankers were foreigners, and a large proportion were Jewish. The most famous of the merchant bank houses were those of the Barings, who arrived in Britain in 1717 from Bremen, the Hopes who fled from the Netherlands in 1795, and the Rothschilds, who arrived from Frankfurt in 1798. The role of these institutions in supporting the financial aspects of Britain's growing overseas market was matched by their importance in supporting the export of British savings overseas. Yet, much like other financial institutions in the City, they seem to have had little interest in providing venture capital to Britain's technologically progressive industries and apart from serving as "correspondents," had little interest in the British provinces. Until recently, little was known about the activities of these private banks, but the research of Temin and Voth (2008b) has shed considerable light on one bank, Hoare's. They conclude that borrowing was largely confined to a privileged few, that the role of these banks in economic growth was at best quite modest, and that the heavy intervention of the state in capital markets in the early eighteenth century hindered rather than helped industrialization.

The dominant position occupied by London in early eighteenth-century banking led to the emergence of country banks, a typical English institution. The rather sudden rise of these banks in the second half of the eighteenth century illustrates the high degree of adaptiveness of private-order British institutions; they were not coordinated or supervised by some central authority, and no political revolution was necessary to bring them into existence. Yet once the circumstances were suitable and opportunities arose, these banks emerged almost ab nihilo. They replaced the informal activities of local merchants, notaries, and attorneys who intermediated in credit transactions. Country banks were still quite rare on the eve of the Industrial Revolution in 1750, perhaps no more than a dozen or so, but by 1775 there were already a hundred of them, 370 in 1800, rising to around 800 by 1815. Local merchants and businessmen, shopkeepers, artisans, and even publicans often gradually promoted their businesses into country banks, and most were small, local affairs. Around 1800 their mean size (in terms of capitalization) was in the order of £10,000. Every country bank maintained an agent or correspondent bank in London, which helped it handle and discount bills of exchange. Country banks were normally involved in many other businesses, and because of the legal prohibition on joint-stock and unlimited liability, they were quite vulnerable to business fluctuations and panics. They were subject to different rules than London banks. For instance, if they wished to issue notes, they could have no more than six partners, and they could not incorporate before the Country Bankers' Act of 1826. This Act permitted country banks to become joint stock, provided they were 65 miles or further from London, a bow to the monopoly of the Bank of England. Even then, full limited liability, the main feature of joint-stock firms, was still not allowed. In the crisis of 1825–26 many of them failed, but the number of joint-stock banks went from none to over 100 in the span of a decade.

Some of the functions that these banks fulfilled in lubricating the wheels of commercial capitalism in provincial Britain are clear enough. The issue of notes that circulated locally and complemented the rather poor supply of coins must surely count as their main contribution to the economy, and so was the credit they provided to facilitate the transactions between local manufacturers and merchants. In 1774, despite a minor trade depression, there was a burst of new bank creation, since it was the year in which guineas and half-guineas were recalled for recoinage, so that the means of exchange issued by country banks were in high demand (Ashton, 1955, p. 183). Their role in facilitating the transition to industrial capitalism is more problematic. Country banks in rural areas, which tended to act as banks of deposit, transferred their funds to London correspondents, who channeled the funds to country banks in urban areas as short-term loans, though this was probably a fairly minor contributor to industrial finance. Recent work (Brunt, 2006b) has argued that at least some of the country banks resembled modern venture capitalists in that they invested in high-risk industries (such as copper mining), on which they had some inside information. Elsewhere, in the textile industries in Lancashire and Yorkshire, local banks and entrepreneurs commingled, and supported one another. Many of them spanned both activities (Hudson, 1986, p. 20). This argument implies the possibility that the British banking system during the Industrial Revolution was less conservative than at the time of Queen Victoria. But the analogy seems otherwise strained, as today's venture capitalist firms can afford to invest in non-performing projects provided they earn exceedingly high rates of return on successful ones. This was not possible for country banks.

To be sure, some of these banks invested in high-tech industries. One tell-tale sign of their involvement in the modern sector is that many bankers who had invested in textile mills and other high-tech industries failed during crises, especially the panics of the 1790s and those of 1825–26 and 1837. Thus, for instance, a bank was opened in Manchester by Samuel Jones & Co., a family of tea merchants, to lend to the growing textile industry, but they ran into trouble in the crisis of 1793. Country banks were vulnerable precisely because the law prohibited them from becoming unlimited liability enterprises, and so one exposed partner could bring down the entire venture. Country banks were a paramount example of the heavily networked nature of Britain's entrepreneurial class. Many businesses took on bankers as partners, and many banks were partners in half a dozen enterprises. Indeed, many country banks emerged as a side-effect of other activities, not the other way around. Their connection with the Industrial Revolution remains somewhat tenuous. For example, country banks were relatively rare in Lancashire, where the center of gravity of the Industrial Revolution rested; one would surmise that if they had played a more central role in the modernization of textile manufacturing, this geographical pattern would have been different.

Another function of country banks was to provide liquidity for day-to-day transactions. A pervasive complaint in eighteenth-century Britain concerned the scarcity of money in small denominations, a weakness that may seem at first surprising for a sophisticated and monetized economy. The inadequacy reached the point where many industrialists had to issue their own token coins, or paper bills, which often circulated locally. Workers were often paid in goods, or were issued bills that could only be used in company stores, a system known at the time as the "truck system." Foreign coins too circulated widely. In this regard, the relatively small notes issued by country banks before 1775 (when notes below £1 were declared illegal) filled an important gap. The new law, driven by a concern about the soundness and stability of small banks, prohibited them from issuing smaller notes than £5 and ended their role as the source of small-denomination currency. The rules under which they operated were changed a number of times: in 1826, country banks away from London were allowed to incorporate and open demand deposits. Other than that, until the Bank Charter Act of 1844 they were subject to little regulation and supervision. The number of country banks in 1838 reached 1,100 and clearly they had become an essential part of the operation of the British economy.

Most of the activity of British banks concerned the discounting of bills; that is, banks accepted bills of exchange from merchants and manufacturers, and provided the seller with cash in the form of overdrafts. These operations provided the economy with a constant infusion of short-term credit, which was rolled over again and again. The significance of country and London banks to the commercial sector is obvious and immediate; without it long- and medium-distance trade would have been all but impossible. Their importance to manufacturing was primarily, as noted, in supplying circulating capital. Unless manufacturers could borrow to meet payrolls and pay suppliers of fuel and raw materials and meet the variable costs involved in trading in remote markets, they would have to provide that capital from their own sources, and there would have been less for investment in plant, fixed equipment, and machinery. But even in 1780 the number of manufacturers who needed large loans for fixed capital such as machinery was quite small, and for the rest the financial sector provided what they needed.

The lending of banks and other financial institutions to private borrowers was in most cases limited to short-term securities and they preferred liquid assets such as government consols. Depositors could withdraw their funds at short notice and there was no formal lender of last resort, thus all financial institutions were forced to maintain a high level of reserve liquidity. In the early stages of the Industrial Revolution, the capital requirements of industry remained small enough for these private sources to finance some fixed investments and machines. But their impact here remained marginal. One needs to be cautious, however, not to underestimate the role of banks in the industrialization process: research on the Yorkshire wool industry shows that at times manufacturers did secure considerable loans from local bankers—as long, of course, as such loans did not comprise too large a percentage of the bank's assets. This prudence was, however, sometimes overlooked when the banker himself or a relative was directly involved in the industry (Hudson, 1986, p. 219). The meaning of "too large" varied from bank to bank, and those bankers who got it wrong paid the price, as did their depositors. Yet throughout their history, most British banks remained conservative in their lending practices, confining themselves to discounting commercial paper and lending mostly to familiar customers. Such inside lending has sometimes been condemned as discriminatory and cronyist, but modern financial economics indicates that it is primarily a tool to overcome asymmetric information, that is, the basic fact that the borrower knows things about himself that the lender does not, and therefore makes the lender reluctant to engage in the transaction in the first place. Many decades later, at the end of the nineteenth century, the dependence on people of known reputation was still an important tool in capital markets (Braggion, 2006).

The bill of exchange, awarded legal status in 1697, became a prime financial instrument for large-scale commercial transactions, and discounting them constituted one of the main forms in which short-term credit was supplied to merchants. London banks specialized in bill discounting for overseas trade and operated as agents for country banks. These "discount houses," largely concentrated in Lombard Street in London, gradually became a strategic element of the British money market. Growth of this market, which was slow in the eighteenth century, accelerated in its closing decades, by which time some of the discount brokers had started to specialize in just that activity, gradually withdrawing from other banking activities. In 1826 the re-discounting of bank bills was restricted by law to specialized bill brokers. This led to the rise of the specialized discount market, which later became the heart of a national and eventually an international financial center.

The largest bank, of course, was the Bank of England, founded in 1694, primarily as an instrument to raise credit for the government. The brainchild of an enterprising Scot, William Paterson, it was demonstrably inspired by banking and financial practices that the British had observed in the Netherlands. In its early history it was hardly what we think of today as a central bank, that is, a government regulatory agency with a high degree of independence. Instead, it was a private financial institution that issued notes and maintained deposits in addition to its functions as the fiscal agent of the Crown. Its biggest asset was good connections with Parliament that helped it to ward off competition using political clout, in the best tradition of rent-seeking. Its early directors were predominantly members of the ruling Whig party, as were the majority of its shareholders. In 1697, at a critical juncture of the war against France, it raised a large sum and was able to hold Parliament up in return for a number of privileges that no other financial organization enjoyed, including full exemption from taxation, and capital punishment for counterfeiters of its notes (which placed them on a par with the King's coinage). In 1708 Parliament prohibited any banking activity by associations of more than six individuals. The South Sea Bubble of 1720, in which a Tory-led rival institution challenged its position as the main financial arm of the government, ended in fiasco and left the institution in an unassailable position. It was, until 1826, the only joint-stock bank in England, and it enjoyed many other monopolistic advantages. The distribution of banking in England during the Industrial Revolution was thus rather odd: one very large and powerful joint-stock bank, and many other scattered small private institutions (Grossman, 2009, pp. 174–218).

The Bank of England from the start was of critical importance to government finances, because of its ability to raise large amounts in a short time and lend these to the government at good terms. It could do so because it was able to establish an unprecedented guarantee that its loans to the government would be repaid: if revenues were insufficient, the Exchequer was mandated to allocate additional funds without the requirement of parliamentary approval. Thus it essentially implied a credible commitment that the British state would pay its debt, allowing the government to borrow at advantageous terms throughout the nineteenth century. The Bank of England took advantage of the government's financial emergencies by teasing privileges and special legislation from the authorities. Its charter was renewed nine times between 1694 and 1844, and on the whole these renewals occurred when the government needed more money (Broz and Grossman, 2004).

Soon it became the main banker to the government, with the government funds earmarked to pay interest on the debt going directly through the Bank of England. It was in charge of placing government securities with the public for a nice profit and on the side carried out other banking services from a privileged position. Whereas in private banking it had to compete with other banks, it was placed at an advantage by the various restrictions imposed on other banks concerning the issuance of banknotes. As the eighteenth century progressed, and the government's dependence on debt increased, the Bank expanded and its relations with the government tightened. Yet direct government borrowing from the Bank declined relative to other sources, and the functions of the Bank of England began to change after 1790.

Over the course of the eighteenth century, Bank of England notes slowly established their position as a formal means of payment. Before 1759, these notes were for large amounts (denominations ranging from £20 to £1,000), but then gold shortages due to war led gradually to the issue of smaller notes that enjoyed wider circulation. In the 1790s, first £5 and then £1 and £2 notes entered circulation These notes served as a means of exchange, and after the suspension of convertibility in 1797, the silver coins and notes that the Bank of England issued became the most widely used means of exchange. Other tokens and foreign coins circulated widely, but the Act of 1817 suppressed these tokens. The restrictions on other banks, which had protected the Bank of England in the eighteenth century, were lifted between 1826 and 1844. The Bank of England Act of 1833 decreed that Bank of England notes became legal tender for all notes above £5. This measure was a means of compensating it for allowing joint-stock banks within the 65 miles from London limit (even though these banks were not allowed to issue notes), and the elimination of various restrictions on the issuance of notes for less than £50.

The history of the Bank of England mirrors the institutional development of Britain between 1700 and 1850 from a mercantilist to a liberal economy. It started off primarily as a rent-seeking monopoly, relying on political clout to seek privileges and exclusionary rights. But the Enlightenment notion that such monopolies could not be justified unless they served a clear-cut public purpose and therefore became part of the state, grew in influence. Unlike other monopolies, the Bank of England survived in its protected position, but it slowly transformed itself into a public institution whose purpose was to lubricate the economic activities of others and to reduce the instability caused by free-market financial institutions. The history of the Bank of England, then, in some way reflects the impact of Enlightenment ideology. Privilege and rents were replaced by social responsibility and the sense of a need to create the institutions that supported a free-enterprise market economy. By 1844, however, the fundamentalist commitment to free markets had been tempered by the slow realization that in certain areas, especially money and financial markets, the free market system needed help. Among these areas were the supply of liquidity and the protection of the stability and reliability of the institutions that provided it.

The idea that one of the functions of the central bank was to regulate the liquidity produced by private banks because the banking sector had the potential to become an inherently destabilizing influence on the economy began to ripen in the early nineteenth century. In the crises of 1793 and 1797, the function of the Bank of England as a lender of last resort was still far from clear. In 1825, on the other hand, the Bank seemed to have accepted this responsibility (Grossman, 2009, p. 240). In 1825, Lord Liverpool's government persuaded the Bank of England to extend liquidity and prevent the crisis from becoming even worse. Dissatisfaction with the way the system worked led to the Bank Charter Act of 1844, which quite dramatically revamped the system, but limited the Bank's flexibility as a lender in time of crisis. As a result, the Act was suspended during the crises of 1847 and 1857, and the Bank of England assumed de facto the function of lender of last resort.

The question of the money supply was debated seriously by people who were genuinely concerned with the functioning of the economy and not primarily with padding their own pockets. The dispute was on the link between gold, the high-powered money supply, and the banknotes that performed much of the actual work as money. The issue was how to constrain the creation of paper money, something that the members of the so-called "Currency School" had been concerned about. They were opposed by more liberal economists, known as the "Banking School" (led by Thomas Tooke), who argued that the money supply should be allowed to expand naturally to accommodate the "needs of trade" and that there was no reason to be concerned with overexpansion. The Bank Charter Act of 1844, written mostly by Samuel Jones-Loyd (later Lord Overstone), a leader of the Currency School, established some elements of central banking: the Bank of England henceforth would establish a monopoly on issuing notes by restricting and constraining further note issues of other banks (though the extant notes of other banks continued to circulate for many decades). The Act stipulated that the issue of notes by the Bank of England would from now on be separate from its general banking business, recognizing it de facto as a public institution. While that did not give it much control over the monetary base (which under a gold standard was governed by the balance of payments and the world supply of gold), it meant that its notes alone would be legal tender and that it had a lot of control over the quantity of money in circulation. Ostensibly this seems like a victory for the Currency School, but appearances were misleading. Had the more restrictive ideas of the Currency School really been triumphant, the supply of liquidity might well have become a serious bottleneck for the British economy after 1844 and the ability of the Bank of England to function as a lender of last resort would have been impaired. In practice, the Bank Charter Act allowed far more monetary flexibility than was originally envisaged, in large part because the people who wrote it employed a confused and overly narrow definition of what money was. The rapid expansion of checking accounts (demand deposits) in the second half of the nineteenth century ensured the elastic supply of liquidity that the industrialized economy required. In any event, three years later, during the panic of 1847, the Act had to be suspended temporarily—evidence, perhaps, of legislation based on insufficient knowledge but also of the kind of institutional agility that was needed to correct such errors.

Apart from banks, the financial sector contained insurance and security markets. Insurance in this period covered only three contingencies: deaths, fires, and shipwrecks. The fire insurance industry, which has been researched extensively, shows in some ways remarkable growth, and its history surely does not justify the assumption, made by scholars trying to reconstruct the national accounts, that the growth in the service sector can be proxied by the growth of population (Pearson, 2005, p. 28). The volume of fire insurance grew rapidly at some periods, but oddly enough this growth does not match the periods we traditionally associate with the Industrial Revolution: the industry grew rapidly in the 1750s and 1760s, then slowed down till about 1810, after which the level of real assets insured increased from about £28 per capita to £80 per capita in 1850. This rapid expansion was fueled by urbanization and industrialization, which increased the fire hazard and the value of the property at risk. New industrial technologies raised dangers, such as boiler explosions and the combustion of depots of chemicals. Insurance employed mostly agents working on commission, and by 1850 about 13,000 people were employed as insurance salespersons. The exact dimensions of the sector cannot be fully measured, but Pearson estimates that by 1850 about half of all "insurable assets" in Britain were insured, though probably not for their full value.

Interestingly, the nineteenth-century fire insurance sector is notable for a feat of industrial organization that serves as a harbinger for capitalist societies. In the years after 1815, the industry was highly competitive, with cutthroat price-cutting and a consequent low level of profitability. To reduce this competition, the large firms colluded and engaged in an aggressive set of mergers and acquisitions. This process came together in the early 1840s in an agreement to fix prices in order to restore profitability. Eventually these companies formed a cartel-like organization, the Fire Offices Committee, that controlled the industry for over a century. This kind of action seems more typical of late nineteenth-century behavior, and as Pearson (2005, p. 364) notes, these tactics had a "particularly 'modern' look about them." At the same time, however, there was apparently little progress in the way the industry calculated risks, collected and processed data, and underwriting techniques changed remarkably little in the face of a rapidly changing economy, despite the growing understanding of statistics and probability in other areas. It is also striking that, despite a considerable level of property crime, there was no successful company that offered burglary insurance. Why fire insurance should be so successful whereas burglary insurance was absent remains a mystery.

Maritime insurance was much older than fire insurance and was widely transacted in medieval Italy. By the late seventeenth century, it was already thriving on London's Lombard Street. In the eighteenth century it was dominated in Britain by the rather unusual phenomenon of Lloyd's in London. Lloyd's coffee-house was first mentioned in 1688 and four years later the owner, Thomas Lloyd, moved to Lombard Street and soon started to publish *Lloyd's List*, a weekly compilation of shipping information. At these premises insurers would sign for the proportion of risk they were willing to cover; they signed their name at the bottom of the policy and thus established the term "underwriter." Most underwriters were individuals, though they had to compete with two "monopolistic" joint-stock companies, chartered in 1720 in exchange for a rather substantial contribution to the British treasury £300,000 apiece. The unincorporated insurance business was organized at Lloyd's, and increased steadily through the eighteenth century. There is no evidence that in its early history Lloyd's imposed any firm rules or regulations on the market, but it obviously saved in transactions and information costs. In the 1770s this informal set-up proved increasingly inadequate and in 1774 the market moved into new quarters at the Royal Exchange and created a more formal organization with standardized underwriting forms that lasted for many decades. The industry survived the difficult years of the Revolutionary and Napoleonic Wars (when losses and hence premia mounted). The opposition to barriers to entry and privilege, a product of Enlightenment ideology, increasingly prevailed. In 1825, after the abolition of the Bubble Act, a number of new joint-stock companies were created (Lloyd's itself was not incorporated until 1871). Unlike fire insurance, maritime insurance remained quite competitive, and throughout the nineteenth century provided an essential service to an economy increasingly dependent on its ships. Lloyd's of London remained the central organizing institution for this business, a uniquely British phenomenon that supported and underpinned the operation of a market, set the rules of the game, and yet was sufficiently flexible to have the capability of adapting to changing circumstances.

Life insurance was a thriving sector and one that went through considerable changes in the late eighteenth and early nineteenth centuries. The sum assured in 1800 was still only about £10 million, but by 1850 it had increased to £150 million. Its eighteenth-century growth has been associated with the rise of a bourgeois ethic of prudence and middle-class thrift. Yet a growing body of evidence casts doubt on this interpretation. Instead, it seems that life insurance in the early eighteenth century was, at least to some extent, a kind of gambling industry, in which people placed bets on the date of death of one of them, or a third person. The Life Assurance Act of 1774 (known as the Gambling Act) prohibited taking out a policy on a third person in which the insured had no direct interest. Over time, however, the industry changed, and life insurance increasingly became a part of the financial network, to collateralize loans and as a means of expanding the credit facilities among the wealthy and entrepreneurial classes. As the prospectus of a life insurance company in 1828 pointed out, these policies of life assurance afforded "means of certain indemnity against pecuniary loss, claim or inconvenience whatsoever, to which one individual may become subject by the death of another" (cited by Pearson, 1990, p. 242). Life insurance was not a mass product even by 1850; it was largely confined to landowners, professional people, and merchants. As an element in financial markets or a major form of savings it was as yet marginal.

Life insurance is, however, of considerable interest to the historical account proposed here. The idea that useful knowledge of any kind should be brought to bear on the production of goods and services and that it should therefore be applied to the insurance industry is typical of the age of Enlightenment. Formal mathematics and demographic statistics were important components of the epistemic base that supported the correct actuarial techniques in this industry. The mathematician Abraham de Moivre (1667–1754), a Huguenot refugee who spent his life in Britain and is famous for his development of the central limit theorem, also published a book entitled *Annuities upon Lives* (de Moivre, 1725), which went through four editions in his lifetime. In this he offered solutions to the mathematical problems of computing the value of contracts that depended on the rate of interest and the expected duration of life. An early example of the application of these ideas is found in the attempt to establish an insurance fund for widows and orphans of ministers of the Church of Scotland in the 1740s. Two sophisticated ministers and amateur demographers, Robert Wallace (1697–1771) and Alexander Webster (1707–84), started the scheme. Webster collected the data from the Scottish parishes and Wallace did the preliminary calculations, but both felt that more mathematical horsepower was needed, so they called in the mathematician Colin Maclaurin, who used calculus and probability theory to arrive at an actuarially correct insurance scheme. The success of the scheme led to its being imitated elsewhere, and demonstrated the potential of superior useful knowledge to affect efficiency in economic activities quite remote from manufacturing (Grabiner, 2004).

Other mathematicians worked to develop the principles of actuarial science. Among them was James Dodson (1705–57) whose work led to the founding of the Society for Equitable Assurance, a life insurance company, in 1762. In 1765 the radical philosopher and dissenting minister Richard Price (1723–91) was invited by the Society to compute the premia to be paid for reversions (insurance payments at death), based on his work in demography on life expectancy. His *Observations on Reversionary Payments*, published in 1771, became a standard in the industry and went through five editions in Price's lifetime. Unfortunately, Price was mistaken on many matters of fact, including his famous erroneous assessment that Britain's population in his age was declining. Price's suggestion to appoint his brother-in-law, William Morgan (1750–1833), as an actuary turned out to be good advice. Morgan's work turned Equitable into a huge success story; by 1829, it had issued over 8,800 policies valued at £12.4 million.

Among the new companies created in 1825 was the Alliance Assurance Company, and its history reflects some of the changes in the British economy that the Enlightenment had wrought. In part, this was because it was run by Jews, the brainchild of Nathan de Rothschild and Moses Montefiore. Actual management was in the hands of Benjamin Gompertz, whose parents were of Dutch extraction. Gompertz's career is interesting because it is marked by being on the seam of the transition to a more tolerant society. Denied entrance to the universities because of his religion (he was Jewish) and largely self-taught, he became a member of the Spitalfields Mathematical Society and could not be denied entrance to the Royal Society, to which he was elected in 1819. When he was denied a job at the Guardian Insurance Company, also on account of his religion, it helped prompt the founding of the new company in 1825 by irate Jewish businessmen. Gompertz was appointed manager of the Alliance Marine Insurance Company, as well as actuary of the sister life insurance company.

Gompertz, an accomplished mathematician, helped created the formal basis of the mathematics that underlies the insurance business. Among his most notable contributions to the field was a deeper understanding of life tables and the formal understanding of the empirical regularities on which they rest. Gompertz was not the only brilliant scientist who applied his talents to the insurance industry. One might also mention his colleague and collaborator Francis Baily, most famous for his work in astronomy. Baily, too, was a typical product of the late British Enlightenment, expressing his horror of American slavery after a tour of the United States as a young man and sympathizing with the radical views of Joseph Priestley. In a series of books published in the early 1800s, he placed commercial computation on a scientific basis. Thus, he showed how the present value of rent and annuities could be computed from annual flow data and life tables (Baily, 1808). In this case, improved useful knowledge was applied to a service industry rather than a physical process, and with considerable success. To be sure, the formal techniques developed by mathematicians were not adopted everywhere, and most of the life insurance companies only began to rely on more advanced actuarial methods after the mid-nineteenth century.

The formal security markets, where stocks and bonds were bought and sold, originated with the coffee-houses in the late seventeenth century. The most famous of these was Jonathan's in Exchange Alley, and the formal building in London known as the Stock Exchange was opened in 1773. Originally, this building was open to all traders, but from 1801 it became restricted to members only. The main financial assets traded in the eighteenth century were government securities, although some of the shares of the larger companies such as the Bank of England and the East India Company were also traded. The securities trade in the eighteenth century expanded enormously, in part because of the creation of low-risk government debt, especially a risk-free bond, the consol, in 1751. The market also adopted a number of important innovations, such as trading without the costly formal transfer of property, trading for fictitious partial low-denomination shares, and the trading in derivatives, both put and call options. British securities markets were also buoyed by the arrival of emigrants from the Continent who repeatedly found refuge in Britain. French Huguenots and Dutch financiers arrived in King William's entourage in 1688, and throughout the eighteenth century this trickle continued (including David Ricardo's father). In the 1790s the trickle grew into a torrent, when Dutch and German financiers, among them Henry Hope and Nathan de Rothschild, fled the disruptions of the European Continent and set up shop in Britain. The exact role of these securities markets in the economy remains a matter of some debate. It clearly was instrumental in financing government debt and a few large companies, but its effects on the most dynamic sectors of the British economy remained limited.

*   *   *

The other service sectors of particular interest to the economic historian are education and medical care. Formal education in Britain before 1850 was, with the exception of a very small minority, confined to what we would consider today an elementary education. It was entirely voluntary and private. For the most part, children went to school because their parents met three conditions: they felt that education was important to the future of their children, they could afford the school fees, and they did not need the children to work on the farm, in the factories or mines, or to look after siblings. Such individuals belonged predominantly to the middle class and as we have seen, Britain's middle class was already quite substantial in the early eighteenth century and kept growing throughout the period 1700–1850.

In the eighteenth century most of the grammar school system which provided a classical and traditional education to middle-class children, by all available evidence, seems to have contributed little to the economic development of England and Wales. Many schools saw it as their mission to educate "gentlemen" in the traditional sense of the word, that is, men without a well-defined occupation. Teaching jobs were often sinecures for corrupt and incompetent individuals, and even in schools that succeeded in teaching anything, the curricula consisted of the classics, languages, and other humanities. No wonder that the successful landscape gardener, Humphry Repton, wrote in his memoirs that he was removed from Norwich grammar school because his father " thought proper to put the stopper in my vial of classic literature, determined to make me a rich, rather than a learned, man" (1840, p. 5). Rather than invest in what we would today recognize as human capital, public education in eighteenth-century Britain was primarily destined, in the words of a distinguished justice, to "break the natural ferocity of human nature, to subdue the passions and to impress the principles of religion and morality ... of obedience and subordination" (cited by O'Day, 1982, p. 207). Some of these schools tried to adapt to the changing demand, but on the whole they experienced a period of decline in the eighteenth century as the middle classes shifted their interests from a classical and leisure-oriented education to demanding more practical skills. The great English engineers of the Industrial Revolution learned their skills by being apprenticed to able masters, and otherwise were largely self-taught. James Brindley, the canal engineer, was taught by his mother and, like many other pivotal figures in the Industrial Revolution, never went to a formal school. Many of the others were educated in Scotland.

This is not to say that there were no good schools: Kingston grammar school, under its famous headmaster Richard Wooddeson, trained some of the finest historians and scholars of the era including Edward Gibbon. Many of the best academies in Britain were run by Anglican clergymen, and while the quality of education they provided varied, there are sufficient examples of successful careers launched by these schools to give pause to those who would dismiss Britain's education altogether as a factor in the creation of human capital. Matthew Boulton acquired a lifelong respect for science and technology in addition to his business acumen at a school run by Reverend John Hanstead. George Stephenson, the early nineteenth-century engineer, regretted his own poor education and made sure to send his son Robert to a private school in Newcastle. Samuel Whitbread, the most successful brewer of the eighteenth century, went to such a school before he was apprenticed to a London brewer (although he sent his son to Eton). Islington Academy in London taught languages, arithmetic, double-entry bookkeeping, and mathematics, as well as dancing, music, and fencing. These schools were for-profit organizations, and they competed fiercely for the children of the well-to-do with one another as well as with private tutors. Most of them were short-lived.

Of considerable importance to the enlightened economy were the so-called dissenting academies, which were attended by lads denied entry to Anglican grammar schools and universities. These schools taught a great deal of heterodox religion, but also useful subjects such as geography, mathematics, and science. Among the teachers in such academies were scientific heavyweights like John Dalton (in Manchester) and Joseph Priestley (at Warrington). Priestley, faithful to his Enlightenment commitment to useful knowledge, revised the curriculum, introducing the study of chemistry, anatomy, and languages. Many of the industrial leaders of the age were graduates of these schools, including the ironmasters the Wilkinson brothers and the nineteenth-century engineer Joseph Whitworth. The majority of graduates ended up in commerce, medicine, and industry. These schools emphasized an experimental and pragmatic approach to science and mathematics, and their impact was a major reason why nonconformists played a disproportionate role in British entrepreneurship in the eighteenth century.

The other part of the kingdom where education was strong and valuable was in Scotland, which trained a disproportionate number of chemists, physicians, and engineers. Scottish grammar schools combined the obligatory Latin with mathematics, science, and commercial subjects. It is hard to imagine how the Industrial Enlightenment would have developed in Britain had it not been for the Scottish educational system. Originally set up to help convert the population to the Protestant Kirk, it became increasingly secular after 1660, a trend that accelerated after the Union of 1707. The Scottish elite believed that Scotland was designed to play a major role in improving the civilized world, but realized that they could not compete with England in commerce and manufacturing. The investment in human capital was at a level and of a quality that is nothing short of amazing given that in 1707 Scotland's population was not more than a million people. Eighteenth-century Scotland was too small and too poor to absorb all the human capital that it generated, and many of its most gifted and creative people found their way into England. Scottish education was practical and pragmatic far ahead of its time. "As the world now goes, the mathematical part of learning is a principal part of a gentleman's education," explained a teacher to the Ayr town council in 1729 (O'Day, 1982, p. 233). The University of Edinburgh, still a poor and provincial school in 1700, became world-renowned in the eighteenth century and a main center of the Scottish Enlightenment.

Adult education, too, had its roots in Scotland. John Anderson (1726–96), an eccentric and cantankerous Professor at the University of Glasgow and as famous for his popular lectures aimed at the general public as he was for suing and insulting his colleagues, provided in his will for the establishment of an educational institution in Glasgow that would provide such lectures to the general public, mostly to spite his colleagues at the university. The Andersonian Institute eventually became the University of Strathclyde, and inspired George Birkbeck (one of its first lecturers) and others to set up similar organizations throughout Britain.

If there was any real virtue in the British educational system in the eighteenth century it was that it was a free-entry private enterprise. It was highly diverse, messy, disorganized, competitive, lacking in standards and norms, with high entry and exit rates, ranging from conservative strict religious teaching to progressive Rousseauism. Such diversity was of course costly and wasteful, but it did enhance creativity and innovativeness, allowed well-to-do parents to choose the kind of education they wanted for their children and created opportunities for talented individuals, and these, in the end, were what counted.

For the children of the poor, such schools were of course not an option. However, a large number of charity schools existed (some of them sponsored by organizations such as the Society for the Promotion of Christian Knowledge). The charity school movement seems to have peaked in the 1720s and 1730s as a fashionable form of poor relief (in 1724, there were over 1,300 of these schools in the country), after which their numbers appear to have declined slowly. These schools were subsidized by philanthropists, and taught catechism, reading, and numeracy, though most of the efforts were directed to steering children towards industrial occupations and saving them from a life of vagrancy. Only 42 percent of all enrolled students in 1818 went to such subsidized schools, which implies that only a small proportion of the poor could attend. Girls attending such schools were often bound to domestic service and boys to work as cheap labor, mislabeled as "apprentices." In any case, it is hard to discover in these schools much that a modern economist would recognize as investment in human capital. The curricula of these schools was only in small part directed towards imparting children with human capital, that is, capabilities that would increase their skills as adult workers —the benefits would above all be godliness, sobriety, and subordination. John Evans wrote that "it is through education that the poor become acquainted with the duties they owe society" (cited by Porter, 1991, p. 165). The influential and deeply religious conservative publicist Hannah More spent much of her life furthering education for the working classes, and although she was often regarded as a conservative antidote to feminist writers, she too was a product of the Enlightenment, having been educated on Hume and Voltaire and confident that "reason and judgement could subdue the errors which the passions ... naturally led to" (Hilton, 2006, p. 180). Moral conduct, industry, piety, and virtue, rather than skills, were the priority of these schools.

Above the charity schools were grade schools which cost parents about £1 a year. By about 1800, around 5,000 children in London went to charity schools and 25,000 to grade schools (George, 1966, p. 218). The better ones did supply some skills that in the end contributed to economic performance, but it is difficult to identify in the schooling system anything that would explain Britain's economic precociousness in technological innovations. This is true a fortiori for the schools to which the children of the elite went, which taught primarily classics, leisure activities, style, and a sense of class superiority.

The universities added even less: Oxford and Cambridge taught little that was of value to a vibrant economy, and their enrollments declined in the eighteenth century. The number of freshmen admitted to Oxford, which had still been 460 per annum in the 1660s, had fallen to below 200 per annum in the 1750s (O'Day, 1982, p. 196). They catered to the military and clergy, and sent few of their graduates into business or the professions. Adam Smith ([1776], 1976, Vol. 2, p. 284) remarked sarcastically that at Oxford the dons had "long ago given up all pretence of teaching" and Joseph Priestley (1787, p. 32) compared the mainstream colleges (from which dissenters such as himself were excluded) to "pools of stagnant water." Yet his plea to open "the advantages of Oxford and Cambridge to us dissenters" betrays his view that they taught something useful after all. There were, indeed, some exceptions, especially in Cambridge where Richard Watson was "chiefly concerned with manufacturing processes rather than with the advancement of pure science" and John Hadley (1731–64, not to be confused with his instrument-maker and mathematician namesake) who showed a "noticeable interest in industrial-chemical processes" (Musson and Robinson, 1969, pp. 36, 168). His colleague in Magdalene College, John Rowning, was a mathematician who wrote a popular *Compendious System of Natural Philosophy* that went through eight editions between 1735 and 1779. The brilliant physician Thomas Beddoes taught chemistry at Oxford but was made to resign because of his sympathy with the French Revolution. All in all, the two universities show a bleak picture. The Scottish universities were better, but even here relatively few graduates went on to industry and commerce.

Formal higher education in this age was probably not very important to economic development. Birse (1983, p. 16) has collected data that show that out of 498 applied scientists and engineers born between 1700 and 1850, 91 were educated in Scotland, 50 at Oxbridge, and 329 (about two-thirds) had no university education at all. It is interesting to note that the proportion of notable engineers with no university education in the eighteenth century was 71 percent, whereas in the four decades 1820–59, it was 58 percent, a significant decline (but still quite high). Computations based on 680 eighteenth-century scientists and engineers mentioned in the *Dictionary of National Biography* shows that by the time of the Industrial Revolution the number of significant people trained in Edinburgh alone exceeded those trained in Oxford and Cambridge yet most did not get any formal university training at all. More recent research has confirmed the extent to which technological advances were disconnected from formal scientific education. Data assembled by Khan (2006) show that of the important inventors she has included in her prosopographical study only a minority had enjoyed a post-secondary education. Of the 244 inventors in her sample born before 1820, only 68 had enjoyed such a training.

How did this picture change over time? Many children who worked in early nineteenth-century factories did have the opportunity to attend Sunday schools, often subsidized by factory owners. These schools served a number of purposes. One of them was to provide at least the barest essentials of a secular education without impinging on the earning capacity of the children. A second was to indoctrinate children with religious values in an age in which piety was still equated with virtue, industry, and respect for authorities. A third was to imbue them with the new values that the factories required: docility, punctuality, and loyalty to their employers. Sunday schools, it seems, emphasized the latter the most, whereas day schools provided a broader secular education in terms of basic literacy and numeracy skills to those children fortunate enough to attend. David Mitch (1999) concluded that by the middle of the nineteenth century attendance in primary day schools had come to play a central role in how the English working classes learned to read and write. Moreover, recent research (Long, 2006) has shown that by the middle of the nineteenth century it made sense for parents to send their children to these schools. Long demonstrates that nineteenth-century children who went to such schools had a better chance of advancing to better occupations, and thus presumably to higher incomes. Toward the end of the period, the first engineering degrees were established at universities, among them the University of Durham (1838), Trinity College Dublin (1841), and King's College in London (founded 1829), which established a Department of Civil Engineering and Mining in 1838, in part as a response to the growth of the railway system and the need for more qualified engineers.

Measures based on formal definitions of human capital thus seem to a great extent irrelevant. This was a society that could provide a great deal of informal education to those who sought it. In the eighteenth century, learning was personal, uncoordinated, and mostly private. Inquisitive and intelligent children taught themselves or were taught by their mothers, or plundered their family's or neighbor's bookshelves. The eighteenth-century British printing industry supplied cheap tools, from cards that taught children to read, to cheap reprints of classics, teach-yourself-type books, and dictionaries, encyclopedias, and compendia of all sorts. The eminent scientist Thomas Young was inspired as a boy by a *Dictionary of Arts and Sciences* he discovered in the library of a neighbor. The way in which technological knowledge was passed on from generation to generation was not through "formal" education (i.e., schools) but through the teaching of apprentices. Every British baker, thatcher, glazier, printer, and cooper was a potential teacher as well as a craftsman. Human capital, in such a society, is produced jointly with commodities, by osmosis and imitation. Those members of the technically literate public who wished for further instruction could find it in the many books and periodicals on technical subjects published at the time. Private commercial schools taught bookkeeping, arithmetic, and formal business letter writing. Popular lectures and evening courses were inexpensive and widely attended by members of the commercial and skilled classes who wanted to improve their skills or widen their horizons. To what extent such lectures actually taught skills and competencies that had a real effect on productivity is difficult to say.

Yet it seems that contemporaries believed that the dissemination of useful knowledge was having real effects. Lectures by eminent scientists to a public of laypersons were regarded as highly beneficial. Rumford's Royal Institution was explicitly dedicated to that goal. Its stated purpose in its charter summarizes what the Industrial Enlightenment was about: it was established for "diffusing the knowledge, and facilitating the general introduction, of useful mechanical inventions and improvements; and for teaching, by courses of philosophical lectures and experiments, the application of science to the common purposes of life." The lectures given by Humphry Davy were so popular that the carriages that brought his audience to hear him so clogged up Albemarle Street in London that it was turned into the first one-way street of the city. Enlightened Whigs in the early nineteenth century, such as Henry Peter Brougham and George Birkbeck, took initiatives to establish a variety of institutions such as the Society for the Diffusion of Useful Knowledge founded in 1825.

Furthermore, there were the Mechanics Institutes. The first one was established by George Birkbeck in 1804 in London and then others spread through the rest of the country. Mechanics Institutes provided technical and scientific instruction to the general public. Their objectives were viewed differently: employers hoped that education would improve the quality of the workers, whereas well-meaning social improvers hoped that it would alleviate the misery and bad habits of the working classes. The institutes expanded a great deal in the first half of the nineteenth century and by 1850 there were over a thousand of them spread around the country, displaying a range of effectiveness and durability. Ian Inkster, the scholar who has studied them in detail, has conjectured that they and similar organizations may have had up to 400,000 members (Inkster, 1991, pp. 78–79). Their net effect on the economy maybe somewhat in question. Elaborate lectures that bored illiterate workmen with advanced and esoteric scientific subjects were of little value, but many lecturers taught more elementary topics (geometry, commercial subjects) to artisans with prior education and may have been quite beneficial to some individuals. The Leeds locomotive manufacturer James Kitson learned much of what he knew at the local Mechanics' Institution and Literary Society and admitted that before "he knew that steam caused the steam engines to work, but not how and why" (cited by Jacob, 2007, p. 202). Institutions such as the Mechanics' Institutes may have affected only a small percentage of their students, but it is precisely through those critical agents of change and innovation that the system was effective. The censuses of the middle of the nineteenth century confirm the image of widespread informal adult education. The importance of these institutes was that in the nineteenth century they spread to smaller manufacturing towns such as Sheffield, Nottingham, and Derby, where lectures were organized on topics such as hydrostatics, the steam engine, the philosophy of natural history, and chemistry (Inkster, 1976).

The belief in making useful knowledge available to as wide an audience as possible was stressed by the founders of the *Mechanic's Magazine* in 1823. One of those, the radical journalist Thomas Hodgskin, argued that if only useful knowledge could be made accessible to labor, it was destined to raise the economic position of workers, and that workers, because they alone possessed the practical tacit skills to actually implement the techniques, were in a unique position to make technical improvements. With a circulation of about 16,000, the *Magazine* obviously only reached a highly skilled labor aristocracy. Hodgskin (1825), without using the term, came closer than anyone to realizing the central role of human capital in economic growth and its complementarity with physical capital (Hodgskin, 1825, p. 16). The idea was basically that by investing in the education and skills of his workers, an industrialist would also increase the return on his physical capital. This point and its significance for the relationship between classes were subsequently ignored by Karl Marx, and revived by modern economists in modified form (Galor and Moav, 2006).

In any event, as far as formal human capital is concerned, Britain was obviously not in a leadership position. Literacy rates in England compared to the Continent were not particularly high and certainly do not point to a particular advantage. For the entire period between 1500 and 1800 literacy rose in all of Europe, and Britain was no exception. Measuring literacy rates in a consistent and comparable fashion is no minor matter, especially with the kind of pre-1800 sources available. Based on the ability to sign one's name in around 1800, this proportion is estimated at about 60 percent for British males and 40 percent for females, more or less on a par with Belgium, slightly better than France, but worse than the Netherlands and Germany (Reis, 2005, p. 202). However, Britain was considerably richer than those countries, and if we allow for the fact that literacy was in part a desirable good that people consumed more of when they became richer, Britain's lack of advantage is all the more striking (Mitch, 1992, 1999). Its ability or willingness to educate its young did not appreciably improve during the years of the Industrial Revolution. Britain could not boast anything like the French system of *grandes écoles* (the first of which was founded in the mid-eighteenth century) or the technical and engineering schools that began sprouting up on the Continent in the early nineteenth century. Literacy rates rose only slowly after 1800, and while the industrializing countries had slightly higher rates than the rest, the Industrial Revolution did not cause a spurt in education. By 1830, 28 percent of all lads aged 5–14 in England and Wales were enrolled in schools, a number that rises to 50 percent in 1850, significantly less than in Prussia where the percentages were respectively 70 percent in 1830 and 73 percent in 1850, and even behind France (39 percent and 51 percent) (Lindert, 2004, pp. 125–26). Data on British convicts arriving in Australia show some improvement in literacy after 1790, but by 1835 the rates had fallen back more or less to where they had been in 1790 (Nicholas and Nicholas, 1992). Even in the industries that were high-tech by the standards of the time, illiteracy did not decline much. In the metal industry, for instance, the male illiteracy rate was estimated at 22 percent in 1754–84, rising to 29 percent in 1785–1814 and then declining to 19 percent in the years 1815–44 (Schofield, 1973, p. 450).

Distinguishing between literacy, formal education, and human capital for this age is far from simple. If the critical component of British technological success was competence, the question is to what extent it required literacy. It may be exaggerated to argue that literacy was inessential, but many practicing engineers treated such skills with contempt, Brunel once remarking that he "would never employ a man who could read" (Palmer, 1978, p. 238). To understand the history of the evolution of human capital, we need to realize that reading and writing were desirable in their own right, that is, as consumption goods (inclusive of religious purposes), and they were not just parts of an investment process in which the rate of return on the margin would be equal to the interest rate. Indeed, it might well be that the causal direction is reversed here: many people decided for non-economic reasons to educate their children and then discovered that this education imparted economically useful capabilities. Mitch's view is that from a pure production point of view, if anything nineteenth-century Britain was overeducated. By this he means only that the amount of formal human capital exceeded that which was needed by the demands for production, but not that the supply of technical skills did not have a marginal product.

What counted for technological progress was numeracy as much as literacy. Numeracy research, based mostly on age-heaping estimates, is still in its early stages, but Britain's population appears not to have been more numerate than most of the nations of continental Western Europe, and there appears to be no evidence of improvement over the eighteenth century (A'Hearn, Baten, and Crayen, 2009, table 4). There are some tantalizing suggestions, however, that numeracy may have been improving among those classes that mattered for technological progress. One hint is the huge success of books that taught arithmetic, such as Francis Walkingame's *Tutor's Assistant*, which, between its first publication in 1751 and the death of its author in 1783, went through no fewer than 18 editions, each consisting of between 5,000 and 10,000 copies and which included mathematical methods employed by glaziers, painters, plasterers, and bricklayers, pointing to the applied and pragmatic nature of the mathematics the author taught (Wallis, 1963).

In any event, to the extent that the data available permit us to make any inferences, the notion that the Industrial Revolution depended a great deal on human capital as customarily defined is not sustained. Nicholas and Nicholas (1992) show that according to their data there was little difference in literacy rates between the industrializing north and the as yet mostly agrarian south. Urban convicts were somewhat more literate than rural ones, and understandably workers in "skilled" occupations were on average more literate than those in unskilled occupations. More unexpected are the differences between men and women: only 13.7 percent of all convict women were illiterate as opposed to 26 percent of all men, but almost half of them declared themselves as being able to read but not write. Even more surprising, their data suggest that the literacy rates among skilled workers were actually declining after 1800.

The modern theory of economic growth has reached something of a consensus on the importance of schooling and human capital to technological progress and economic growth. It must therefore face the problem that Britain's technological and economic leadership in the century before 1850 does not correspond with any obvious advantage in human capital as customarily defined. This paradox is in part resolved by noting that in the eighteenth century identifying human capital with formal schooling is misleading. To understand the role of education in this period, we should keep in mind that technology is a type of knowledge we may call imple-mentable. Much like original music, technology involves two types of skill: the originality and technical capability of the author of the instructions (the inventor), and the competence of the persons who actually carry out the instructions written down by the inventor. Such skills could be acquired in many ways, above all through being an apprentice in a skill-intensive industry, which created able and experienced mechanics or practical chemists who could apply and adapt existing techniques to new permutations and products, and often saw opportunities in the discoveries of scientists.

Yet the demand for the skills that were necessary to suggest innovations that worked and the demand for those that implemented them were not independent of one another, and their relationship flavors much of the technological history of the modern age. The precise nature of the invention determined the amount of skills need for their deployment. Steam power, iron working, and mining involved techniques based on tacit knowledge in which outside consultants were often re-quired; in the textile industries, most factory masters managed on their own. In-ventors could leave a great deal to the ingenuity of the worker, or they could try to dumb down the tasks, and relieve the user of the need to find skilled workers. During the Industrial Revolution, much inventive activity has been termed "de-skilling," that is, the ingenuity and cleverness was front-loaded in a user-friendly design that reduced the skills necessary for implementation. Such inventions supplied the employers with what Marx called the "weapons against the revolt of the working class" by reducing the specific skills (and thus the bargaining power) of workers. The classic and most-cited example is the invention of the self-acting mule by Roberts in 1825, which simplified the process of mule-spinning. But the machine tool industry in general was capable of creating devices in which the ingenuity was concentrated in their construction and not operation. The Com-mittee on the Exportation of Machinery concluded that thanks to the new machine tools, "machinery may be constructed by mere labourers much better than it was formerly made by first-class workmen" (Great Britain, 1841, p. vii). As a result, the demand for human capital became more skewed as the Industrial Revolution progressed: the economy demanded more highly skilled engineers and technicians, so as to reduce the demand for skills at the lower levels of the labor hierarchy. The role of educators and teachers in the development of the British economy was thus clearly circumscribed to produce highly competent mechanics and technicians, whereas the overall level of skills of most of the labor force may not have mattered all that much, as long as they were submissive and obedient. Adam Ferguson, Adam Smith's contemporary and friend, noted that "Many mechanical arts require no capacity ... ignorance is the mother of industry as well as superstition ... Manufactures, accordingly, prosper most where the mind is least consulted" (1767, p. 273).

*   *   *

The other service industry of interest in this period is medicine. Physicians worked in a free and competitive environment, without much quality control. Their ability to address most medical problems was limited. By modern standards, indeed, the practice of medicine before 1850 has traditionally been regarded as little more than quackery. Few medical doctors had much of an idea of what caused disease, and many of the ideas they had about disease often strike us as laughable. But modern standards could be regarded as misleading here. Medical care was eagerly sought by all who could afford it. Much like education, the best morsels were absorbed by the well-to-do while the poor received little, and what services they received were certainly of low quality. Yet doctors in this age did contribute to health in certain areas: they lanced abscesses, set broken bones, carried out Caesarean deliveries, performed simple surgery (without anesthesia), and prescribed many herbs and minerals, not *all* of which were positively harmful. To be sure, the endless bloodletting, purges, and emetics prescribed by the physicians of the time probably had few salutary physiological effects—but as modern medical researchers believe, they may still have improved the patient's condition through placebo effects. At the same time, however, physicians were powerless to combat the infectious diseases spread by food, water, air, and insects, which were the constant threat to life in this period.

Nonetheless, we may think of the late eighteenth century as an age of Medical Enlightenment, one in which people increasingly realized that knowledge could improve health and lengthen human life (Gay, 1969, pp. 12–23; Porter, 1982). The spirit of improvement permeated every industry and every service, and health was no exception. Medicine was, in a very precise sense, "philosophy at work," as Peter Gay put it. The actual effects of the Medical Enlightenment on health and life expectancy are, however, far from obvious. The idea that the road to the reduction of physical suffering and the extension of life led through improved knowledge was widely accepted by eighteenth-century writers, but they were constrained by the limitations of useful knowledge in what they could achieve. As in many other aspects of technology in the eighteenth and early nineteenth centuries, there was a large gap between what people thought they should know and what they actually knew. Perhaps this is true for all ages, including our own. But in the late eighteenth century this gap was acutely felt in the area of medicine when various medical grand theories rose and fell, and when competing schools and interpretations about questions such as "what is life?," "what causes disease?," "why do epidemics strike some and not others?," and "why do sick people have a fever?" were increasingly asked. The knowledge, such as it was, was untight, that is, it remained difficult to choose among competing answers.

Until the middle of the eighteenth century, at least the Holy Grail of medicine was the search for a single cause of all disease, for a Newton-like one-line answer to all medical puzzles. A Dutch doctor, Herman Boerhaave, who had a strong following throughout Europe, analyzed health in terms of a hydrostatic equilibrium, in which all diseases were classified as those of the solids and those of liquids. Another example of overarching medical theories was the bizarre career of John Brown (1735–88), who invented the "excitability" theory of medicine. This rather fanciful theory maintained basically that all diseases had their root in a state of either under- or overexcitement of the human body, and accordingly prescribed laudanum (an opium derivative) or alcohol for practically every ailment. Accordingly, he was as popular with his patients as he was disliked by his colleagues and competitors in Edinburgh. Yet Brown was no country quack. He had studied with the foremost teacher of the time (William Cullen in Edinburgh), and published his main treatise, *Elementa Medicinae,* in impeccable Latin. Even the far more level-headed physician John Hunter (1728–93) often made what seems to us egregious mistakes in his experimental work: after injecting a subject with pus from a patient with gonorrhea, the subject developed syphilis, upon which he concluded that the two diseases were one and the same (it must not have occurred to him that the subject might have been infected with both). No wonder that Voltaire is reported to have said that doctors were people who poured drugs of which they knew little to cure diseases of which they knew less into people of whom they knew nothing.

And yet things were not quite as bleak as Voltaire suggested. In the eighteenth century, Enlightenment ideas penetrated the conservative world of medical knowledge, intent on improving the human condition despite the lack of understanding of the nature of infectious disease (Ryan-Johansson, 2006). Empirical evaluation and the reliance on medical statistics suggested the efficacy of certain therapeutic procedures and drugs. These attempts go straight back to Francis Bacon and his concept of "ordered experience" (objective and systematic observations), and are a perfect example of the Enlightenment's belief in progress and its list of recipes on how to bring this about. An important figure by all accounts was the great medic Thomas Sydenham (1624–89), an admirer of Bacon's and friend of Locke's, who firmly supported the Baconian idea of collecting systematic data on diseases to buttress his view that specific medications cured specific diseases. Systematic collection of data in the hope of seeing patterns and being able to exploit them was a methodology inspired by Bacon and typical of eighteenth-century medical science. It was realized by Enlightenment thinkers that even if the underlying mechanism was not really within grasp, useful knowledge could be extracted and perhaps exploited by looking for empirical regularities and patterns, either by experimentation or by collecting datasets. Medicine was the field that fitted this insight as much as any.

A celebrated example of Enlightenment research in medicine is the work of James Lind, who in 1747 carried out his famous experiment on twelve sailors, six of whom received a treatment believed to be effective for scurvy. His conclusion that those who received two oranges and a lemon recovered much faster than the others represents a landmark in the empirical study of preventive medicine and the key to successful battle against scurvy, so critical in a seafaring nation. Another significant historical episode is the testing of the efficacy of smallpox inoculation, a procedure by which patients were deliberately infected with smallpox but in sufficiently small quantities to allow them in the majority of cases to recover quickly and without scarring. The procedure was introduced in the early 1720s. Lady Mary Montagu, the wife of the British Envoy in Constantinople and an enlightened and educated woman, observed its use for this purpose and made it her mission to introduce it into England, despite considerable doubts and resistance. Benighted clergymen such as Edmund Massey thundered that diseases were sent to mankind for the trial of their faith or punishment for their sins and that without them vice and iniquity would rule. By grabbing the right to interfere in diseases, he felt, inoculators "usurped an authority founded neither in the Laws of Nature nor of Religion" (1722, pp. 8, 12, 15). Such views were increasingly being rejected in many circles, and inoculation made considerable progress in the eighteenth century.

Certainly, Lady Montagu was already affected by the spirit of the Medical Enlightenment. Inoculation was a risky procedure, but contemporaries attacked the question of whether the risks were outweighed by the benefits head on. John Arbuthnot, a literary figure, and James Jurin, secretary to the Royal Society, were both strong mathematicians who persuaded themselves and then the public that on balance inoculation improved the odds of avoiding smallpox (Rusnock, 2002). By the end of the eighteenth century inoculation was widely practiced in Britain, although the narrowness of the epistemic base underlying the technique (nobody had any idea *why* it worked) meant that practitioners got some crucial details wrong. At first, British inoculators made incisions deeper than necessary, thus actually increasing the chance of contracting the disease. Modified inoculation, with much smaller incisions and using pus from a smallpox pustule at an early stage of development, was introduced in 1762 by Robert Sutton, a Suffolk country doctor (Hopkins, 1983, p. 88). With the Suttonian method, inoculation became less risky.

The quantitative tools that underlay this research became a useful tool in trying to sort out what worked, and while its full flourishing did not take place until after 1825, the public-health statistical movement of the nineteenth century had eighteenth-century roots. Among the founding figures of this statistically based Medical Enlightenment were such pioneers as John Millar (1733–1805, not to be confused with his contemporary the Scottish legal scholar), who used statistical tables to show that prevalent clinical treatments such as antimony and bleeding were ineffective. Another was William Black (1750–1829), who tried to create something like a "medical arithmetic" much like the earlier "political arithmetic" (Tröhler, 2000). In the absence of a firm epistemic base of infectious disease, clinical practitioners could still get it disastrously wrong, as in the notorious reintroduction of massive bloodletting in the early nineteenth century. But the promise of progress was in the air.

Where the medical profession had its most profound effect on the well-being of society, however, was in preventive medicine and public health. The idea that solid filth and polluted air were harmful to one's health was widely adhered to—even if the exact mechanisms were not wholly understood (Riley, 1987). It was felt that an enlightened society ought to be able to protect its citizens from the ravages of disease. The question was how. Much as was true for the Agricultural Enlightenment, real progress would be limited until a deeper understanding of the natural process at work emerged. But it was not for lack of trying. On the Continent, especially before 1789, the attempts to battle disease were inspired by a medical cameralism, hoping that the state could "sanitize society" (Porter, 1982, p. 50). Its proponents expounded and at times implemented the idea (first proposed by Johann Peter Frank, an advisor to the Habsburg Emperor Joseph II) of a "medical police." In Britain, the state played a less active role, but private and spontaneous voluntary organizations filled the void.

Hopes for a quick payoff of the Medical Enlightenment were thus disappointed. Thomas Beddoes (1760–1808), a typical Medical Enlightenment figure, serves as a case in point. Beddoes, a physician and chemist, was closely affiliated with the British Industrial Enlightenment, being the son-in-law of Richard Edgeworth (a member of the Lunar Society), a collaborator of James Watt's who helped him design his experimental instruments, and a mentor to the great scientist Humphry Davy in Bristol. His belief in the capability of bringing about unbounded progress in his field through more knowledge was ebullient: "I see no reason to doubt that, by taking advantage of various and continual accessions as they accrue to science, the same power will be acquired over living, as it is at present exercised over some inanimate bodies; and that not only the cure and prevention of diseases, but the art of protracting the fairest season of life and rendering health more vigorous, will one day half realize half the dream of Alchemy" (Beddoes, 1793, p. 29). Beddoes advocated what he called "pneumatic" (or chemical) medicine, which he believed would improve the health of the masses if guided by an enlightened and progressive medical leadership. Applying the spirit of experimentalism to the application of the new chemistry to medicine, he researched whether the inhalation of newly discovered gases such as oxygen and nitrous oxide (laughing gas) could cure lung diseases such as tuberculosis. At the same time he also stressed that social change and institutional improvement held the key to improved national health and for a long time supported the French Revolution. With the support of the members of the Lunar Society he opened a research hospital in Bristol called the Pneumatic Institute in 1799 to investigate his hypotheses, eventually changing its name into the Preventive Medical Institution for the Sick and Drooping Poor. Like many Enlightenment thinkers he was torn between his compassion for the unfortunate and his belief that rational adults were responsible for their own actions and fate. Yet eventually it became clear to him that his goals were not attainable in his age and that rapid social change might in fact be detrimental to health policy owing to the actions of irresponsible and opportunistic doctors and chemists, and he died a disappointed and embittered man in 1808.

The limits of medicine at this time are also well illustrated by the career of John Hunter whose life-long research in various aspects of surgery and anatomy helped transform surgery from a craft not much different from that of barbers into something that resembled an experimental science. Yet surgeons, until well into the nineteenth century, were still operating with unsterilized tools and without anesthesia, and thus largely limited themselves to non-invasive surgery. Even Caesarean sections were "a desperate measure" and there is no record of a mother in Britain surviving one before 1800. The constraint on what doctors and surgeons could contribute to society was not just access or money—it was the state of best-practice knowledge. The surprising thing is that the spirit of hope in medical progress persisted despite the lack of progress on most fronts.

The Medical Enlightenment in Britain developed further and flourished in the nineteenth century. No better example of what it stood for can be chosen than the career of Thomas Wakley (1795–1862), the founding editor of *The Lancet*. Wakley was in many ways a medical radical, close in his political views to such progressives as Cobbett. As a scientist he was aware of the blessings that improved medical technology could bring to the population. Under his leadership, *The Lancet* aimed at a wider audience, and often published verbatim transcripts of public lectures conducted in London. *The Lancet* exemplified one of the Enlightenment's most re-vered principles: the concept that knowledge should not be kept secret but spread and diffused so it could do the most good. In its first issue, it published the ingredients of twenty-four patent medicines, hitherto kept secret (Corfield, 1995, p. 139). It was equally dedicated to the other objective of the Enlightenment: insti-tutional reform. It launched frequent attacks on the medical establishment, espe-cially the oligarchic, self-perpetuating Royal College of Surgeons, a typical rent-seeking coalition of experts operating under the guise of protecting the public against quacks. In its early years *The Lancet* was an odd mixture of a scientific journal and a medical scandal sheet, but it was effective. Wakley's efforts and his tireless attempts at social reform brought him a great deal of conflict and many lawsuits. Yet in the long run he was successful as a publicist, a member of Parliament, and a coroner in London. He was instrumental in bringing about and passing a number of pioneering laws, including the 1848 Public Health Act and the Medical Act of 1858.

As noted, medical knowledge before the age of bacteriology depended a great deal on data collection, searching for empirical regularities that might point to the causes of diseases and the effectiveness of remedies in the absence of a more specific understanding of the nature of infectious diseases. By 1830 or so, it was widely agreed that statistical analysis of disease data held the key to medical progress. This view was held, for instance by Francis Bisset Hawkins, whose *Elements of Medical Statistics* ([1829], 1973) pioneered this approach. Hawkins felt that "a careful cultivation [of statistics] ... would materially assist the completion of a philosophy of medicine by ... pointing out the comparative merits of various modes of practice ... and afford the most convincing proofs of the efficacy of medicine" (pp. 2–3). While his numbers were on the whole suspect, Hawkins's methodology became widely shared in the following decades. What was needed, above all, was good information. Soon enough, better data led people like Edwin Chadwick and his circle to doubt Hawkins's conclusion that cities had become "more friendly to health" (p. 18). The question remained, of course: why were cities so unhealthy? Only better data could provide the answer.

The statistical movement picked up steam in the early nineteenth century. Statistical societies became almost the rage in the early 1830s, and they were much concerned with public health. What was becoming increasingly clear, following the pioneering statistical work of data-oriented investigators such as William Farr, James Phillips Kay, Neil Arnott, Thomas Southwood Smith, and above all Chadwick himself was that the suspicion of eighteenth-century doctors that disease and poverty were correlated was correct even if it was not entirely clear why. If poverty "caused" disease, public health could be improved by reducing poverty, even if public officials did not know what it was exactly about poverty that caused people to get sick. Concerns about public health clashed with liberal philosophy. Slowly it dawned on these researchers that free markets could not be relied upon as far as public health was concerned and the state should take a forceful position on these matters. Until this insight became more widespread, many of the public policies advocated by the sanitary movement were ineffective, not because they could not have worked at all, but because, given the limited resources at the disposal of government agencies, they had to be fine-tuned. This process had begun by 1850, and the early fruits of reform had already ripened, but it still had a long way to go—in large part because before the germ theory of disease almost any proposed measure and analysis of public health were disputed.

What about private clinical care? William Petty wondered in the late seventeenth century whether "of 100 sick of acute diseases who use physicians, as many die and in misery as where no art is used or only chance" (cited by Banta, 1987, p. 197). In a recent paper, Ryan-Johansson (2006) has made an eloquent case for considerable progress in medical best practice in the eighteenth century. She points to a number of concrete advances in medical knowledge, and notes the otherwise inexplicable increase in the life expectancy of the aristocracy and especially the royal family in the eighteenth century. A number of medical treatments were available if one could pay for them, and while they were by no means all beneficial and some were positively harmful, the very best doctors often treated some diseases sensibly. Even with the limited tools of the time, some advances were made. In the seventeenth century Sydenham had experimented with iron supplements for patients suffering from anemia, and recommended keeping fever patients in cool rooms. Other advances were the discovery, already noted, that fresh fruit and vegetables could prevent scurvy, the use of cinchona bark (quinine) to fight off the symptoms of malaria, the prescription of foxglove (now known as digitalis) as a treatment for edemas (first recommended by Dr William Withering, a member of the Lunar Society, in 1785), and the taking of cod liver to prevent rickets. Above all towers the miraculous vaccination against smallpox discovered by Edward Jenner in 1796. Jenner's discovery, in many ways, epitomizes the changes that had occurred in Europe in the preceding century: the legitimization of the application of new useful knowledge as an effective tool to the improvement of the material conditions of life. By that time, statistics and probability calculations had become part and parcel of scientific discourse, and Jenner's discovery had to be verified by more systematic minds. By 1806, the Royal College of Surgeons had data for over 164,000 vaccinations and could readily assess its efficacy. The practice spread like wildfire through Europe and beyond, and reduced the incidence of smallpox.

The eighteenth century also saw the rise of childbirth as a medical episode, in which male midwives known as *accoucheurs* gradually began supplying their services to those who could afford them. Equipped with surgical instruments such as the new forceps, the new obstetric professionals claimed to provide a better service than untrained (mostly female) midwives. They recommended a few procedures that still strike us as sensible, such as breast-feeding and to refrain from swaddling. William Hunter (1718–83), a famous physician and brother of the above-mentioned John Hunter, recommended for instance that mothers in his lying-in hospital begin nursing within a day rather than only after three or four days as had been the custom, which significantly reduced milk fever, a common ailment among new mothers (Sherwood, 1993, p. 37). The Bristol physician William Cadogan (1711–97) wrote a famous pamphlet entitled *An Essay upon Nursing and the Management of Children* published in 1748 in which he made many reasonable suggestions. It went through twelve editions in the next thirty-seven years and its insights and level-headed advice helped dispel some appalling practices in child care—at least among those who had access to it. Cadogan was the kind of intellectual we see a lot in the Enlightenment, contrasting his own "natural" and "philosophical" practices with the benighted customs of traditional society (Porter, 1982, p. 56). Even more popular was William Buchan's *Domestic Medicine*, a good example of how the decline in access costs affected the diffusion of medical knowledge. Between its first publication in 1769 and 1871, it went through 142 English-language editions, and was translated into numerous languages. It provided advice on both healthy living and the diagnosis and treatment of most diseases—with all the limitations thereof. Buchan's work was a "typical work of the Enlightenment" (Wear, 1993, p. 1297). Buchan felt that the poor could be made more healthy if their ignorance was relieved, so that they would have access to decent medical care and nursing, and be liberated from their prejudices and less victimized by quacks and impostors. "Diffusing medical knowledge among the people would not only tend to improve the art but likewise render Medicine universally more useful by extending its benefits to society" (Buchan, 1772, p. xxvii). It was Baconian thinking applied directly to medical practice.

The market for medical services, then as now, was characterized by highly asymmetrical information. The physician knows more than the patient, and so it is difficult for the patient to assess the quality of the product that is purchased. For that reason principles such as *caveat emptor* are extraordinarily hard to apply to this market. Yet government regulation was essentially absent, and the three professions that constituted the formal medical establishment (physicians, surgeons, and apothecaries) relied on self-regulation and reputational effects. In other words, in such markets trust was an essential component of every transaction, and until the mid-nineteenth century such trust was largely spontaneous. Physicians organized in local societies in which such reputations could be maintained. By 1832, there were forty local organizations, one of which became the British Medical Association in 1855 (Corfield, 1995, p. 160).

Other factors besides knowledge mattered to health. It is likely that the money and education of the propertied and middle classes bought them a lifestyle and a consumption basket, as well as access to information, that were on balance healthier, and that this is the main explanation of the gap in life expectancy between rich and poor. But such differences were limited. Given that the clinicians at the time did not realize that the vast majority of diseases were infections caused by microbial agents, they were clearly constrained in what they could diagnose, let alone cure.

Enlightened ideology and its medical manifestations did, however, find ways to trickle down to a wider social group. One late eighteenth-century phenomenon that fits this bill is the emergence of public dispensaries, essentially public-access clinics, the first of which was opened in London in 1770. By 1800, there were sixteen such dispensaries in London alone, handling over 50,000 cases a year. They provided free advice, outpatient services, and free medication to the poor. The moving spirit behind London's dispensaries was John Coakley Lettsom (1744–1815), an idealistic and enlightened Quaker, a physician and polymath and a typical example of the Medical Enlightenment in Britain. He founded Lettsom's Medical Society in London in 1773, in an attempt to enforce standards and share knowledge among physicians, surgeons, and apothecaries as well as the General

Dispensary of London in Aldersgate Street in London in 1770, the first of its kind. John Haygarth, a Chester physician and one of the initiators of the provincial fever hospital movement, could be thought of in similar terms. The dispensary movement was symbolic of the British Enlightenment: based on private, voluntary efforts of public-spirited individuals, it followed a detailed agenda of social improvement, but limited, for the time being, by the tight constraints on eighteenth-century medical knowledge.

*   *   *

The period under discussion here, 1700–1850, saw the rise of many other "white-collar professions" that would be classified today in the service industries. In 1700, very few Britons were engaged in such occupations as land agents, dentists, architects, surveyors, apothecaries, or even attorneys. Apart from the very top, most of these specialists were trained through an apprenticeship system rather than through the universities. Apothecaries served as general practitioners, but could not join the Royal College of Medicine in London, because that august body only recognized physicians trained in Oxford, Cambridge, or Dublin (never mind that the best medical school in Britain was in Edinburgh). Barristers had to be called to the bar, but attorneys were numerous, intermediating, arbitrating, and swapping information. In the early 1730s the total number of lawyers in England and Wales was 5,500 to 6,000 (Corfield, 1995, p. 79). In 1841 England and Wales had 11,763 men (no women) in the category "attorneys, solicitors, and law students" and another 2,103 classified as "barristers and conveyancers." By the middle of the nineteenth century a new white-collar middle class had emerged. There were 4,425 "accountants" and 48,806 "clerks, commercial" (to distinguish them from "clergymen"), 3,639 musicians, and 16,173 "surgeons, apothecaries and medical students" in addition to the 1,112 physicians.

No market economy can operate without an extensive service industry that supports trade and travel. As people moved about more, they needed more coaches, innkeepers, sailors, horse dealers, and eating places. England and Wales in 1841 had 15,441 hotel- and innkeepers, 37,805 "publicans and victuallers," and 5,629 beer-shop keepers. As Britons communicated more, they made heavier use of the postal service, which as we have seen was reformed repeatedly in the eighteenth and nineteenth centuries. Britain's market economy became more sophisticated and complex, and more and more resources had to be invested in those activities that reduced transaction costs in the economy. Above all, more knowledge had to be generated and disseminated for a sophisticated economy to function. The total amount of relevant knowledge in the economy was such that it had to be divided and subdivided over and over again, and specialists had to be in charge of distributing it, either directly (such as journalists, attorneys, and teachers) or by using it (brokers, jobbers, speculators, scriveners, and various merchants). Between 1700 and 1850 the market for information of all kinds grew enormously. The age of Enlightenment in many ways can be regarded as the age of communication, in which knowledge was placed in the public sphere, sometimes free of charge, sometimes sold (Headrick, 2000). The great irony is that economic growth was propelled by the growth of knowledge and the expansion of markets, but markets for knowledge themselves were problematic. Knowledge became valuable, but it turned out to be a slippery commodity, and property rights in it, in any form, turned out to be hard to establish.

Not only economic information became more complex: the same was true for technical information: consulting engineers, mechanics, and various professional experts were called in by manufacturers, farmers, and mine-owners to dispense what they knew. Agricultural specialists, surveyors, coal viewers, designers, road-building engineers—all became separate occupations. Some of these experts became famous for discovering something truly important (such as William Smith, the geologist who pioneered the methods of stratigraphy) or by meticulously observing existing practices, taking good notes, and thus leaving rich sources for economic historians, such as Arthur Young's meticulous notes on farming. Others, such as the mining "captain" of Cornwall, Richard Trevithick, one of the most celebrated inventors of his age, became consulting engineers. The founding father of the itinerant consulting engineers was the great John Smeaton. Some of the great civil engineers such as James Brindley, John Grundy, Thomas Telford, and the Brunels also made their living consulting. Among the great mechanical (later railway) engineers, the Stephensons, John Rennie, and Richard Roberts stand out with many others. John Rastrick, who had managed the famous engineering plant of Foster & Rastrick in Stourbridge, retired in 1830 to become a railway consulting engineer.

Expertise became a profession in chemistry as well, often combined with medicine: in the early eighteenth century, as noted above, the Scottish chemist and physician William Cullen was much in demand as a consultant by the bleachers and dyers of the time, the customers obviously hoping that his knowledge would solve various technical problems. Another chemist-physician was John Roebuck, an active inventor and businessman, a close associate of and advisor to James Watt in his early career. Wedgwood employed the experimental chemist Alexander Chisholm, but also relied on the advice of the Irish chemist Richard Kirwan. In Cullen's days, and even in the 1780s, when Wedgwood hired Chisholm, such advice was probably only modestly productive and largely the result of hit-and-miss experimentation; a century later, however, the value of expert knowledge had increased significantly. There was, in other words, a market for useful knowledge, because in an enlightened economy it is both demanded and supplied at ever in-creasing levels. Some chemists were able to exploit their knowledge for themselves. James Hutton, most famous for being the foremost geologist of his age, also set up a plant to manufacture ammonium chloride (used in the tinning of iron and brass) by collecting the soot from Edinburgh's chimneys as the raw material. The business, managed by his partner John Davie, flourished until the early nineteenth century (Clow and Clow, 1992, pp. 420–21).

But property rights in knowledge were always hard to define and harder to enforce. The idea that the author had inalienable or natural rights to the fruit of his labor as much as any other asset crystalized around 1700. This thus took place at the very beginning of the transition between the mercantilist idea of monopoly as a property right granted by a higher authority and the "emergent ideology of the market" (Rose, 1993, p. 33). The problem was, of course, that the public-good nature of new knowledge and the high cost of excluding others clashed with the incentive structure facing creative individuals. In the early 1700s, two of the most influential literary figures of the time, Joseph Addison and Daniel Defoe, developed the idea that writers had a natural right to the fruits of their labor much like artisans, rather than regarding copyright as a privilege granted by the King. The dilemma for subsequent Enlightenment thought on the subject was that this natural right appeared to conflict with the equally strongly held antipathy toward monopoly, already expressed by John Locke in the 1690s, and the Enlightenment view that useful knowledge should be disseminated as widely as possible if it was to have a salutary effect on society.

The central development in intellectual property law was what became known as Queen Anne's Act of 1710, which established the law of copyright. There was, as yet, little in the law that one could term "enlightened" despite its preamble, which stated that it was intended to "encourage learned men to compose and write useful books." It was in many ways a compromise, and it did not really resolve the hard questions about intellectual property rights that had just bubbled to the surface. Its attack on the monopoly of the Company of Stationers disguised its rent-seeking effect by spreading the rents of publications between a number of book-sellers, with little if any attention to the rights and needs of authors. Copyright was awarded normally for fourteen years, with the possibility of renewing it to double this length. This Act was far from waterproof, as it did not cover Ireland and the American colonies, where British books were printed freely. It was not consistent with the common law concept of perpetual owner's rights, and publishers kept on suing rivals who reprinted books that by the 1710 statute should be in the public domain. Yet the Enlightenment idea that supported the right of society to have access to useful knowledge in compromise with the right of individuals to be rewarded for their originality and creativity grew over the eighteenth century, and British institutions adapted. In a landmark decision, *Donaldson v. Becket* (1774), the House of Lords ruled that the common law ownership of property rights on written work held only for unpublished work; once published, the writer conferred the property rights to the publisher for a limited period. Once and for all, the idea of books lapsing into the public domain at some point became established. The Enlightenment idea that authors' creativity bestowed upon them a property right collided with the antipathy felt toward monopolies and the general conviction that knowledge should be as accessible as possible so as to maximize its social benefits (Rose, 2003). Ambiguity thus continued: copyrighted material was expected to permit "fair use"—yet exactly where fair use ended and plagiarism began was never made very clear. In 1842, finally, the copyright law (known as Talfourd's Act) was rewritten to last forty-two years (or for the duration of the author's life plus seven).

Whatever the intellectual property rights regime, the age of Enlightenment witnessed a fury of book-writing like no others. The number of books published annually in the British Isles between 1700 and 1799 just about tripled in the eighteenth century. Table 3.1 above presents a summary of the number of books published by decade and their subject matter. As is obvious, the average number of books published annually tripled in the eighteenth century, as compared to a population growth of 65 percent (in England and Wales). Moreover, as already noted in chapter 3, the proportion of books dedicated to what may be described roughly as useful knowledge increased from roughly 5.5 percent to 9 percent, while the proportion devoted to religion and philosophy fell from 38 percent at the beginning of the century to below 20 percent at the end. It is not clear if these changes were primarily demand-driven (due to rising income of the literate public, or a rise in literacy) or whether the falling price and greater accessibility of books were also factors. Reading was one of the few leisurely activities of the age, and as the leisured and literate middle classes expanded in Britain, so did their appetite for books. The most successful of the writers did well, often by securing nice advances. Dr. Samuel Johnson and David Hume received handsome advances for respectively their *Dictionary* ($£1,575$) and *History of Britain* ($£1,400$). Alexander Pope was said to have earned $£5,000$ from his translation of the *Odyssey*. A few writers and artists enjoyed the patronage of the rich and powerful, but such support could be unreliable and even arbitrary, as Dr. Johnson's bitter relationship with the Earl of Chesterfield attests. For every truly successful writer there were a hundred "hacks" (named after the London cabs called hackneys). In 1777 London had seventy-two booksellers, more than any city in Europe (Burke, 2000, p. 165). Publishing was a small industry and not a leading sector of course, but it symbolizes the difference that the Enlightenment made. Of the books that people read, as far as we can ascertain, only a small fraction concerned "useful knowledge." Even within natural philosophy, the percentage of actual writings that might have had a direct effect on technology was surely small. All the same, this small output, by helping to disseminate that part of knowledge that was codifiable, surely was of greater than proportional importance.

In the closing decades of the seventeenth century, the publication of commercial and financial information commenced in Britain. These publications were the seeds of what might be called somewhat anachronistically an "information industry." Consider one John Houghton (1645–1705), a London apothecary, and one of the first merchants to be admitted to the Royal Society. In the best Baconian traditions, he began publishing a monthly newsletter entitled *Letters for the Improvement of Husbandry and Trade* (1681–83), in which he discussed agriculture and methods to render farming more progressive and efficient, as well as popular science and technology. This was followed by a second series (1692–1703) in which he published information on current prices of commodities and financial assets, including the prices of the shares of fifty-two joint-stock companies, thus making his publication the first "financial" paper (Neal, 1990, pp. 22–23). Two other publications followed: John Castaing's celebrated *Course of the Exchange* that first appeared in 1697 and that continued, under various forms, to be published from the eighteenth century until today, and *Lloyd's List*, which listed the arrival and departure of merchant ships. To what extent this was a true "market" could be debated: Houghton sent his newsletter free of charge to anyone who supplied him with information (including prices).

Whether the service sector still deserves the epithet of a "neglected variable" could be debated. What is clear is that the impact of the Enlightenment was not confined to the few manufacturing sectors associated with the Industrial Revolution. Throughout the service sector, there are signs of a relentless push for progress and economic improvement through a better understanding of the natural regularities at work. Here, too, success depended on how difficult it was to solve the technical problems, given what people knew. Hence, for instance, the technology of road-building may have experienced more breakthroughs than in-fectious disease. But everywhere there was a belief that the road to material progress, if not salvation, led through more knowledge, and the dogged persis-tence in pursuing this knowledge paid dividends that were to have consequences on a global scale.

CHAPTER 12

Progress and Productivity

Many economists feel that economic growth summarizes much of what is happening in an economy and that changes in aggregate product can be represented and measured by national or sectoral income or output statistics. A summary of these statistics for the British economy is presented in table 12.1. In contrast to Deane and Cole (1969) and Hartwell (1971), who viewed the Industrial Revolution as a period of accelerated economic growth, Nicholas Crafts and C. Knick Harley (1992) have shown that aggregate growth was fairly slow during the Industrial Revolution and that even industrial output grew at a slower rate than was implied by anything truly discontinuous (like a "revolution"). There is no real mystery in this. The truism of growth in an economy with many sectors is that the impact of new technology on the overall economy is always proportional to the relative weight or share of the sectors affected by productivity growth in initial output or employment. Since those shares were small at the outset, by definition their impact on the overall economy could not be very large in the early stages. This arithmetical relationship is one fundamental reason why it is difficult for technological breakthroughs, no matter how pathbreaking and novel, to affect the overall performance of the economy in a "revolutionary" fashion. It could be debated whether the history of technology shows that "nature makes leaps" (Mokyr, 1990b), but it is clear that such leaps do not have large immediate effects on aggregate performance.

This does not mean that technological progress was unimportant in the eighteenth century; but it does mean that the effects of modern industries on the aggregate economy will be diluted by the sheer massive size of the slow-growing traditional sector. The onset of modern growth requires the technologically "progressive" industries to be a substantial part of the economy. Given the technological dynamism of the "modern sectors" and their seeming ability to "infect" the traditional sectors, this was inevitable, but it took decades. Even if the technological achievements of the era of the Industrial Revolution were impressive, it remains true that this was a period of relatively slow growth and that any obvious identification of the period with an acceleration in growth rates is mistaken. All the same, the connection between the Industrial Revolution and the sustained economic growth that Britain experienced after 1850 is undeniable.

Table 12.1: Estimated annual rates of growth of real output, 1700–1871 (in percentages)

Period	National income per cap. (Deane & Cole)	National income per cap. (Crafts)	Indust. product (Hoffmann)	Indust. product (Deane & Cole)	Indust. product (Harley)	Indust. product (Crafts)	Indust. product (Cuenca)
1700–1760	0.44	0.3	0.67	0.74	n.a.	0.62	--
1760–1800	0.52	0.17	2.45	1.24	1.6[a]	1.96	2.61[c]
1800–1830	1.61	0.52	2.70	4.4	3.2[b]	3.0	3.18
1830–1870	1.98	1.98	3.1	2.9	n.a.	n.a.	

[a] 1770–1815
[b] 1815–1841
[c] 1770–1801

Source: computed from Harley (1998); Hoffmann (1965); Cuenca (1994).

The Industrial Revolution was above all a period of transition, in which technological change both deepened and widened until the sectors that resisted rapid change became more and more isolated enclaves, and we can speak with confidence of a "modernized economy."

It turns out, then, that the "classical" period itself (that is, 1760 to 1830) was a period of very slow growth of per capita GDP. The best numbers we can produce, summarized in table 12.1, indicate that national income per capita grew in the years 1760–1800 at only 0.17 percent per annum, little more than half the rate of growth of the period 1700–60. Growth did pick up in the years 1800–40 to about 0.5 percent a year, but some of this must be viewed as recovery from the crises of 1800–15. It is only in the decades after 1830 that growth accelerated. All in all, adjusting for price movements, income per capita as estimated by Maddison (2007) was 86 percent higher in 1850 than in 1700, which amounts to an annual rate of growth of about 0.4 percent. To the modern eye, used to growth rates of close to 2 percent a year, this seems slow. It certainly is not much faster than the best performance that medieval economies were capable of. The critical difference was the ability of the enlightened economy not only to sustain this effort but to intensify it.

How slow is slow? A growth rate of about four-tenths of a percent for the entire period of the Industrial Revolution is about the same as in the pre-Industrial

Revolution years 1700–60. But without more details, it would be easy to draw misleading inferences from this fact. To start with, between 1760 and 1830 English population increased from 6.1 million to 13.1 million, whereas in the previous sixty years it had been more or less stagnant. One does not have to be a committed Malthusian to believe that a sudden increase in population growth might have affected income per capita negatively: just the need to accumulate enough capital and bring more land into cultivation to keep the capital/labor and land/labor ratios from declining required a considerable effort.

Behind output are relations known as production functions. Production functions mean that output is produced by inputs, and if an increase in output can be produced by a constant level of inputs it is possible that technological progress has taken place or that for some reason the inputs are deployed more efficiently. Such a phenomenon is known as a growth in total factor productivity. A growth in productivity is not logically a necessary or sufficient condition for economic growth to occur, since income per capita could increase on account of a rapid growth in the capital per worker ratio. In the long run, however, we expect the two to move together. More seriously, the assumption made by many economists that a growth in total factor productivity is indicative of the overall rate of technological progress is not warranted. An economy could easily experience one without the other. For instance, one could think of an economy with a fixed technology but in which political or institutional improvements led to the migration of low-productivity workers to areas or activities where they can be more productive—such a migration would be registered as an increase in total productivity. The same would be true if, for instance, workers were becoming more socially adjusted to factory work and the rate of turnover, absenteeism, and labor conflict diminished. Or consider an economy in which there was a reduction in crime, in which contracts became more enforceable as a result of better law and order, and thus property became more secure. On the other hand, important technological advances might never register on the total productivity scale. The introduction of anesthesia in surgery in the middle of the nineteenth century, an innovation few of us would do without, is undetectable in the national income statistics.

Moreover, even when technological progress takes place, it is often not easy to measure it exactly. In principle, the computation consists of taking the rate of growth of output and subtracting the contributions of the various inputs (measured as a weighted average of their rates of growth). What is left is that part of output growth that is *not* due to more inputs. How should we think of this residual? Part of the problem is simply the mathematics. As Richard Nelson (1973) showed many years ago, computing total factor productivity as a residual from production functions is only correct for relatively small changes in inputs because there is no clear-cut way to know to what extent technical advance offsets declining marginal products. The other problem is the economics. There are many assumptions underlying the measurement of total factor productivity, and this is not the place to discuss them. But to convey the flavor of the difficulties, consider what happens when technology improves to make a product *better* rather than (or in addition to) *cheaper*. The computation assumes that technological progress consists of process innovation; goods can be made with fewer inputs which are more productive and thus they will cost less. But what if the goods cost the same but are better, or if they cost *a little* more and are *much* better? Since "better" can mean many different qualities, a great deal more information is needed to adjust the quantities involved. Such information is rarely available for our own time—let alone for 1820. By failing to account for the fact that Arkwright's cottons, Donkin's paper, and Wedgwood's chinaware were, in some definable way, of higher quality than the products they replaced, we understate the rate of output growth and thus the growth of productivity.

Another problem involves the correct measurement of inputs. Thus, to measure the labor input in an economy, what we really need is not the size of the population or even the size of the labor force but the number of actual person-hours worked per year, preferably broken down by gender and age. Such data are simply unavailable for the time. Over the longer haul, as we shall see below, there is good reason to believe that participation rates in this economy changed, and using population data as a proxy for the labor input is rather precarious. There is, however, a deeper economic question here: an economy in which people work more hours, all other things being equal, will have a higher income, but are people better off? Put differently, should leisure be considered one of the outputs of the economy in productivity calculations? Another issue concerns natural resources, an input into the production function. By definition these resources are not produced within the system, so their quantity is fixed. But their availability to the economy depends entirely on knowledge: the knowledge that they actually exist (following discovery), the technical ability to extract and process them, and the technical knowledge necessary to take advantage of them.

Notwithstanding those concerns, economic historians have carried out the computation of total factor productivity for the period, and their findings are summarized in table 12.2. The main findings are that though British economic growth was slow in this period, what little there was seems to be explained by the residual. Ingenuity, not accumulation, drove economic growth in this period. Indeed, part b of table 12.2, based on output and factor prices rather than estimates of inputs, "over-explains" the growth in productivity in that it grows faster than per capita output before 1830. The precise assessment of the importance of TFP in the critical period 1770–1800 is difficult because it relies on the division of one small growth rate by another. A ratio of two numbers very close to zero rarely produces a robust result. Even a minor revision in computation procedures means a major difference in the conclusions: by changing some reasonable assumptions

Table 12.2: Estimates of total factor productivity

Part a: Total factor productivity, computed from product accounts

	Per capita growth	Contrib. of capital/ labor ratio	Contrib. of resources per capita ratio	Total contrib. of nonlabor inputs	Total factor producti- vity growth	Producti- vity as a % of total per capita growth
1760–1800	0.2	0.2*0.35 = 0.07	−0.065*0.15 = −0.01	0.06	0.14	70
1800– 30	0.5	0.3*0.35 = 0.105	−0.1*0.15 = −0.015	0.09	0.41	82

Source: computed from Crafts (1985, p. 81) and Crafts and Harley (1992, table 5).

Part b: Total factor productivity, computed from income accounts

"Preferred Estimates"							
	Per capita output growth	Total factor productivity growth					TFP growth
		Capital income	Labor income	Land income	Total private sector	Govern- ment	
1770–1801	0.2	−0.40*0.33 = −0.132	0.35*0.45 = 0.157	0.26*0.14 = 0.036	0.061	2.60*.08= .208	.27
1801–31	0.5	0.71*0.33= 0.234	0.25*0.45 = 0.112	0.76*0.14 = 0.106	0.452	1.11*.08 = .088	.54
1831–60	1.1	−0.21*0.33 = −0.069	0.68*0.45 = 0.306	0.48*0.14 = 0.067	0.304	0.31*.08 =.025	.33

Source: computed from Antràs and Voth (2003).

total factor productivity growth could be made to vary from 0.06 percent to 0.24 percent per annum, accounting for between 30 percent and 120 percent of per capita annual growth. The growth rate of per capita output is sufficiently small to be explained by almost anything. While the procedure does leave a lot to be desired, it still indicates that the economy was getting more efficient, and that if this increased efficiency did not help the economy to grow very rapidly, at least it prevented a decline of per capita income in the face of population growth.

The role of the traditional factors of production, capital and labor, has been widely discussed in the literature. A venerable theory, now mostly discarded, used to hold that the "take-off" into sustained growth coincided with a sharp increase in the proportion of aggregate output that was earmarked for investment. This view, associated with the writings of W.W. Rostow and W.A. Lewis (working in the 1950s and 1960s), maintained that this proportion doubled from around 5 percent of national income to over 10 percent in a fairly short time. As the somewhat mechanical "stages" theories have fallen into disrepute, economic historians have been critical of these generalizations, yet the best numbers we have today about the proportion of gross investment in GDP indicate that it increased from 8.6 percent in the 1760s to 13.3 percent in the 1840s, as can be seen in table 12.3. Although this increase was a bit more gradual than the proponents of the "take-off" believed, the increase in the investment ratio is consistent with the acceleration in the growth of the labor force (new workers needed more equipment and houses to live in), the emergence of a capital-intensive transport network, and the need for new technology to be embodied in new capital goods (that is, it is difficult to adopt steam power without renting or purchasing a steam engine).

*   *   *

The exact role of capital in the British economy in this era cannot be summarized easily because capital means different things in different contexts. Creating an investable surplus that could be used for some goal beyond the survival and reproduction of society had been possible in past societies, which built the Pyramids, medieval cathedrals, and the Spanish Armada. Economies that could afford such expensive projects clearly were in principle capable of saving. Directing such a surplus toward the accumulation of capital goods that increased output per capita was an altogether different thing. That effort depended, among other things on the productivity of capital, which itself depended on the rate of technological progress and the capability of the economy to deploy and exploit the new techniques. But it also depended on institutions and the ability of a capital market to channel the savings to where they had the highest return. New technology was uncertain and its success unknowable. As a result, venture capital, needed to build the equipment

Table 12.3: National expenditure (in percent), and consumption per capita, 1760–1850

Decade	Total net investment	Of which: fixed domestic capital formation	Govern-ment spending	Private consum-ption	Consum-ption per head (£ p. a., 1851–60 prices)
1761–70	8.6	7.0	7.5	83.9	9.6
1771–80	10.2	7.1	7.1	82.7	9.3
1781–90	13.1	9.9	7.2	79.3	9.5
1791–1800	14.2	10.8	11.2	74.6	9.8
1801–10	9.6[a]	10.2	15.5	74.5	10.5
1811–20	13.5	10.1	12.8	73.4	11.3
1821–30	14.4	10.2	5.0	80.6	14.6
1831–40	12.5	10.3	3.2	84.1	17.9
1841–50	13.3	10.8	3.5	83.2	19.4

[a] less than FDCF because of negative foreign investment.

Source: computed from Feinstein (1978, 1981).

and tools that embodied the new technology, could not access the same sources of capital that borrowers intent on spending on wars or residential buildings had available to them.

In an aggregate production context, "capital" means mostly capital goods: producer durables such as machines, buildings, tools, livestock, equipment, and inventories. But for most of the period in question, working or circulating capital was of greater importance. This capital lubricated production, because of the non-simultaneity of transactions, and the slowness of the transport and communications system. Eighteenth-century businessmen needed trade credit and this credit became one of the pillars of the operation of the British economy. Indeed, any neo-institutional analysis of the performance of the British economy after 1700 needs to analyze how this system operated. Some of it was supplied by "formal" lending institutions like bill-discount houses, or country banks. But much of that capital was in the form of book credit, inland bills of exchange, and other forms of short-term credit. As one scholar expresses it, "all businessmen were creditors and all businessmen were debtors" (Hoppit, 1986a, p. 66). What has not perhaps been emphasized sufficiently is how much credit went to consumers. Most economic historians have typically assumed that credit was used primarily for production and that consumers paid cash. Nothing could be further from the truth. Not only was the cash supply, especially that of small change, inadequate, but consumers were often deeply in debt for both durable and non-durable purchases, buying "on account," that is, using book credit (Finn, 2003). Consumer credit was a personal transaction, in which reputation counted for a lot.

As the Industrial Revolution proceeded, the ratio of fixed capital (buildings and equipment) to circulating capital (inventories, raw materials) increased as one would expect, not so much because the latter went down as because the former went up. The new technology increasingly demanded large outlays of fixed capital. In industry and commerce the ratio of total circulating to total fixed capital fell from 1.2 in 1760 to 0.39 in 1830 and 0.30 in 1860 (Feinstein, 1978, p. 88). Comparing the size of these two forms of capital is a tad misleading, a bit like comparing the number of gallons of motor oil to gallons of fuel: they met quite different needs. As transportation, financial services, and the supply of small-denomination legal tender coins all improved after 1800, the pivotal function of circulating capital and short-term credit diminished somewhat, but remained quite prominent. Furthermore, we need to keep in mind that in capital formation, as in employment and output, the "mechanized" or "modern" sectors were for most of the period under question still fairly small. In the decade of 1831–40, "manufacturing and mining" absorbed only 21 percent of total capital formation. Construction, transportation, and farming were still major targets of investment. Capital was essential to the Industrial Revolution, but it is hard to say that the reverse held to the same extent. In the most dynamic industry of the Industrial Revolution, the cotton industry, fixed capital relied mostly on self-finance. Yet from the finance point of view, there was substitutability: firms could borrow short term, and then roll the loans over and over to finance fixed capital outlays. Such practices solved some problems but created others, especially greater volatility in the economy, as we shall see below.

It has often been observed that the investment goods most closely associated with the Industrial Revolution were rarely financed by financial institutions. The initial amount of "venture capital" to start a new firm based on a novel technique or product, typically not a large amount, was scraped together from private sources, either relatives, in-laws, or so-called projectors with whom the inventor was acquainted and who often became partners in the firm. Once the firm had started, however, it usually expanded under its own steam. Much of the fixed capital used by the large "mills" of the Industrial Revolution was plowed back by its owners from previous profits. In that sense, too, the Industrial Revolution pulled itself up by its bootstraps. There are, however, quite a few examples of a few medium- and long-term investment projects financed by banks, even if these were unusual. Entrepreneurs and businessmen who needed additional funds, as noted, normally went through informal networks, marrying well or borrowing from friends, relatives, and neighbors. Taking in partners was another widely used way to raise capital. Yorkshire clothiers who owned land raised capital by mortgaging their real estate (Hudson, 1986, pp. 96–108). By and large through most of the eighteenth century capital was still a very personal thing, which most people wanted to keep under control. If one lent it out, it was only to an acquaintance or to the government. Even partnerships, which were frequently resorted to in order to raise capital while avoiding the costly process of forming a joint-stock company, were usually closely tied to family firms. The taking in of sleeping partners merely for the sake of getting access to their capital was relatively rare at first. This caution slowly dissipated during the Industrial Revolution, but active partners often bought out the others, and the advantages of partnership were as much in the division of labor as in the opportunity to raise credit.

Drawing a sharp boundary between formal and informal capital markets may be something of an anachronism anyway. Borrowing from acquaintances and from local bankers were not mutually exclusive: provincial business communities were often quite tight local networks in which people worked together and trusted each other. Country banks mostly transacted with local businessmen with whom the banker was acquainted socially. Indeed, as we shall see below, this feature of British society was a crucial ingredient in the success of Britain's entrepreneurial class.

As already noted, the main source of manufacturing fixed capital was self-finance, that is, profits plowed back into the firm. This was possible to a large extent because the minimum viable size of firms was still relatively small, so that an aspiring entrepreneur could start very small and then grow—if he was profitable—by purchasing new equipment from his own means. As technology became more sophisticated after 1830, the initial capital outlays increased, and it became increasingly difficult to rely on internal finance to start a business. For railroads this was of course out of the question. For existing industrial firms, retained profits, however, usually remained central to the accumulation of fixed capital. What this meant in effect was that the rate of growth of capital in the modern sector was constrained by the rate of profit.

Even in an economy in which most firms relied on retained earnings, however, an intersectoral capital market did function. Individuals who made their fortunes in farming, commerce, real estate, or the slave trade used these funds to diversify into manufacturing. There were some examples of capital accumulated in the commercial sector flowing into manufacturing. This flow occurred when merchant princes entered into modern manufacturing, such as was the case with Kirkman Finlay, an overseas merchant who entered cotton spinning between 1798 and 1806, and with the Wilson brothers who established the Wilsontown ironworks near Glasgow. On the whole, however, these cases were exceptional. The reverse was more likely: profits made in the most technologically dynamic sectors often flowed elsewhere to reduce risk. High profits in the Manchester cotton industry in the 1820s led to heavy investment of these funds in other industries such as insurance, gasworks, water supply, and later railroads (Pearson, 1991). The operation of the informal capital market can thus easily be illustrated with examples, but it is not known how important this form of finance was relative to other sources.

Many of the most famous characters in the Industrial Revolution had to resort to personal connections to mobilize funds. Richard Arkwright got his first loan from a politician friend, and James Watt borrowed funds from, among others, his friend and mentor, Joseph Black. Matthew Boulton was able to finance the construction of his Soho works by marrying well. François Crouzet, the foremost expert on the topic, has pointed out how exclusive and selective these personalized credit markets were: to have access to these informal networks one needed to be a member of them and be "known and well thought of in the local community" (1985, p. 96). The market for capital depended to a great degree on the market for information. After all, the main difficulty capital markets have to face is that the borrower inevitably knows more about his firm and his project than the lender.

An exchange economy depended on a means of exchange. In Britain, like anywhere else, transactions were paid for by some combination of credit and cash. Short-term credit, such as trade credit and bills of exchange, was an indispensable lubricant to this economy, as contemporaries were fully aware. In large part this was made necessary by the scarcity of small change, a problem that dogged British commerce throughout the eighteenth century. Contemporaries believed that credit financed the majority of transactions in Britain, and that it was more important than money for that purpose. Charles Davenant wrote in 1698 that "nothing is more fantastical and nice than Credit" (Davenant, [1698], 1771, p. 151), and many eighteenth-century writers felt that it was the "Jewel of Trade." However, credit needs to be settled eventually, and it depended to a great extent on beliefs and expectations. In times of pessimism and depression, credit often melted away and the economy needed to go back to hard cash. Credit also raised moral concerns about overextension, abuse, and exploitation, and it remained an ambiguous institution, essential but dangerous (Hoppit, 1990). Margot Finn (2003) has stressed that the eighteenth-century exchange economy depended greatly on private credit, which in some way was not a modern institution at all but harked back to a traditional economy "of obligation," as Muldrew (1998) has called it. Yet reputation mechanisms and the institutions that supported them underwent enormous changes in the eighteenth century, attesting to the institutional flexibility that was the strength of the British economy. The emergence of country banking, discussed above, from practically nothing to a dense if uneven network by 1815 is one example of this flexibility.

Yet above all, the importance of credit is testimony to the strength of Britain's "informal institutions," customs and rules of behavior that were less formal than laws but no less binding and certainly no less significant.These laws were enforced by reputational mechanisms, and modern institutional analysis has shown how critical they can be to the support of commerce (Greif, 2005). An illustration is the career of the Lancaster Quaker merchant William Stout (1665–1752), whose autobiography appeared in 1851. His economic success was largely fueled by his meticulous reputation for honesty and generosity. He covered the debts incurred by a dissolute apprentice as well as a nephew, and avoided pressing lawsuits to recover debts for "the preservation of my reputation" (Muldrew, 1998, pp. 171–72). Daniel Defoe, perceptive as ever, noted that "Credit is a consequence, not a cause ... it is produced and grows insensibly from fair and upright dealing, punctual compliance ... the Off-spring of universal probity" (Defoe, 1710, p. 9). Credit depended above all on a set of codes that defined gentlemanly conduct, and they determined a self-enforcing equilibrium. The importance of such reputational mechanisms was not new to the writers of the age of Enlightenment. Defoe was not the only one to emphasize how essential trade credit was to a merchant: "it is the choicest ware he deals in ... 'tis current money in his cash chest; it accepts all his bills, 'tis the life and soul of his trade." Yet reputation was everything here, and "a tradesman's credit and a maid's virtue ought to be equally sacred from evil tongues" (1738, Vol. 1, p. 197). He was particularly concerned about the possibility of malicious behavior and slander. Elsewhere he notes (ibid., p. 361) that a shopkeeper may borrow at better terms than a prince "if he has the reputation of an honest man." Davenant saw the same thing: "[Credit] very much resembles, and in many instances is near a kin to that fame and reputation that men obtain by wisdom in governing state affairs" (Davenant [1698], 1771, p. 151). Such credit arrangements required above all judgments about other people's honesty and ability to repay debts and judgments about the importance and value of reputations (Muldrew, 1998, p. 148). The social norms and institutions that supported this structure continued to evolve and adapt in the eighteenth century. Credit remained, in most cases, a personal transaction between people who knew one another or at least had acquaintances in common.

Others were concerned with the possibilities that credit lent itself to speculation, usury, and other poorly understood economic phenomena. Credit, in the self-righteous opinion of the age of Enlightenment, could be abused for immoral and speculative purposes. Laws were passed to prevent this: Barnard's Law of 1734 forbade options trading; the Gambling Act of 1774 forbade the taking out of insurance on third parties. Arguably, even if such legislation was hard to enforce, it was more than just pious moralizing: credit markets—much like all markets which operate at arm's length—required a certain kind of "morality" to function properly, otherwise they might be undone by wholesale opportunistic behavior. Britain's formal institutions confirmed and supported the social norms that supported credit markets, but in and of themselves they were inadequate to prevent large-scale fraud. Its courts and other officers were unable to deal with the complex relations between creditors and debtors. Credit, like the rest of the increasingly complex economy, relied on self-enforcing rules and norms more than on the coercive powers of the state. I shall return to this issue in chapter 16.

Traditional and informal sources of capital have been somewhat neglected in the literature because so much of the economic literature on the eighteenth century has been obsessed by the Industrial Revolution. Yet outside the modern sector, a mortgage market developed, in which so-called scrivening attorneys carried out functions that elsewhere in Europe were the responsibility of notaries, namely to intermediate between borrowers and lenders, using real estate or personal possessions as collateral and relying on their personal acquaintance with the parties. To be sure, some of these mortgages were taken out by the lavish and irresponsible scions of land owning families, but often they were used to expand the businesses of small artisans and to introduce improvements on landed estates (Brewer, 1982, pp. 204–05). A substantial demand for capital was generated by the enclosures: the fences and hedges that enclosures required were costly, and paid for by taking out mortgages. The advantage of local brokers, who often had personal familiarity with both mortgager and mortgagee, was considerable, and at least in Lancashire we have good evidence that their activities were of considerable importance to the functioning of credit markets (Anderson, 1972).

In the absence of hard data, it is hard to say a great deal with certainty about the aggregate rates of saving in the economy, but at least two facts are at this stage beyond dispute. One is that the vast bulk of savings were generated by relatively wealthy people, either landlords who had benefited from high farm prices supported by tariffs, or by merchants, bankers, and other people whose profits were a function of the growth of the service sector, or a growing number of successful industrialists. Workers and the lower middle class, artisans and small shopkeepers, saved little and contributed practically nothing to the aggregate supply of capital. The other is that Britain saved enough not only for itself but even for others. After 1776, Britain became a net creditor to the world, and while the flow of funds to foreign projects was small compared to the later nineteenth century, it indicates that Britain saved more than enough to finance its economic expansion. This applies particularly to two periods in which unusually large demands were made on British savers. One was the French and Napoleonic Wars, in which the government ran large deficits, yet there is little evidence that these led to a serious crowding-out of investment (Mokyr, 1987; Clark, 2001). The other was period of the railroad construction boom after 1830, which made unprecedented demands on the British capital market. It was a hugely expensive project: in the decades 1841–60, transportation consumed 35 percent of total fixed capital formation in Britain, compared to 20 percent in 1821–40 (Feinstein, 1981, p. 133). In railroad boom years, such as 1847, the percentage of Gross Domestic Fixed Capital

Formation invested in railroads was about 45 percent (Gourvish, 1980, p. 13). The ability of the British economy to finance this unprecedented project and still have funds left over to finance railroads overseas is a testimony to the thriftiness of Britain's citizens—at least those wealthy enough.

The railroad itself affected the way the capital markets worked. The sale of railroad securities to the general public took place through hundreds of so-called "jobbers" whose offices sprung up like mushrooms after rain in the 1830s, peddling railroad bonds and stocks often in small denominations—a remarkable example of institutional agility. They obtained the securities from "brokers," essentially wholesalers of railroad stocks and bonds. Securities were sold through a massive campaign of advertisement, including public meetings. Spackman (1845, p. 5) observed that the great bulk of society, "in fact, all classes, must have left their usual avocations and embarked their capital and their credit in the numerous avocations" of the railways. Demand for railroad securities spurred the creation of specialized publications and the emergence of provincial stock exchanges in Manchester, Leeds, and Glasgow. Railroad paper helped establish a secondary market for transferable securities, which enjoyed full limited liability protection and thus played a central role in the creation of a modern capital market. The investment in railroads before 1845 came primarily from merchants (45 percent) and landowners (28 percent), with manufacturing accounting for only 11 percent (Hawke and Higgins, 1981, p. 233). By 1845 forty-seven companies had been established, 118 lines and branches in the course of execution, and another 1,263 railways were projected (most of the latter, of course, never saw the light of day). In 1843, seventy railroad companies accounted for about 26 percent of all the capital quoted on the London Stock Exchange, as much as the entire banking sector, the East India Company, and the turnpike trusts together (Reed, 1975, p. 46).

*   *   *

The characteristics and history of the British labor force in this era, too, have been investigated a great deal in recent years. One of the more robust findings is that eighteenth-century Britain was a high-wage economy, relative to other European economies, to say nothing of Asian ones (Allen, 2009). These high wages pre-date the eighteenth century, and were well understood by the writers of the period. In a mercantilist context, high wages were a source of concern. First, it was feared that high wages would cause high prices, and in a world of fixed (metal-based) exchange rates, that would inevitably reduce competitiveness and thus exports. Second, employment might be unfavorably affected, and unemployment was much on the minds of the economists of the time. The mercantilists thought that on the one hand high wages would reduce the demand for labor, but on the other hand would also reduce the supply because, as one late seventeenth-century writer had it, "Wages hath proved an inducement to Idleness; for many are being Idle the oftner, because they can get much in little time ... Excessive Wages is a load upon a Nation" (Pollexfen, 1697, pp. 47, 83). It seems perhaps bizarre today that political economists should think that high wages were a bane on the economy rather than a symptom of success and high productivity. What is less clear is the effect that such wages had on the technological dynamism of the economy. It has been argued that high labor costs reduced profitability and thus slowed down industrialization and capital accumulation (Mokyr, 1976). However, such an interpretation fails to take into effect the impact that high wages could have on technological change. In the context of Britain in the eighteenth century this connection is particularly interesting because high wages were coupled with low fuel costs, and thus, it is argued, encouraged industrialists to generate techniques in which they could replace expensive labor with cheap coal (Allen, 2009).

The basic idea in this model, known as an "induced innovation" model, is that most inventions were labor-saving, and that high wages relative to energy costs would stimulate the search for such inventions. The relatively low price of British coal, at least near the areas where it was mined, stimulated the use of techniques that used it intensively and thus biased the direction of technological change. Induced innovation has a venerable lineage in economic history, going back to a highly influential book by H.J. Habakkuk (1962), culminating in Vernon Ruttan's magisterial work (2001). The gist of the model is concerned not so much with technical choice among known techniques as with the development of new techniques under the influence of relative factor prices. But the argument in its more extreme form has never quite caught on, and for good reason. While it is obvious that costly labor would make firms choose techniques that were intensive in non-labor factors, it is far from obvious that the same holds for the search for *new* techniques. The most cogent version of the argument was proposed by David (1975a), who linked static technical choice to dynamic technological progress through "local" learning by doing. Adapting David's account to the British Industrial Revolution would go something like this: British entrepreneurs chose relatively capital- and energy-intensive techniques because they faced high wages and enjoyed cheap energy. These techniques happened to be more amenable to further progress than labor-intensive manual techniques and so choosing them had the unintended consequence of increasing productivity at a faster rate than in a low-wage economy. Within a century, these capital-intensive techniques had become so efficient that even low-wage economies ended up adopting them. This framework may well apply to a few individual industries such as cotton spinning. Broadberry and Gupta (2009) use this model to explain the development of mechanized cotton spinning in high-wage Britain and not in low-wage India, which seems plausible. Even in this more sophisticated version, this account raises some legitimate doubts as an explanation of the Industrial Revolution as a whole.

For one thing, firms try to save all costs, not just those of relatively expensive factors. Indeed, if they can easily substitute factors, the costly factor may be little used to start with, and costs would be reduced most if the firm could find a way to deploy the intensively used factors more efficiently. Furthermore, one could question whether mechanization and steam power were as uniformly labor-saving as they are made out to be. The early steam engines, presented by Allen as a labor-saving device, actually replaced horses used to power pumps. At Darby's furnaces steam power was used to pump water up, so that the water mills that ran the bellows would not run dry. This hardly counts as labor-saving. Oddly enough for those who claim that *cheap* coal was driving the process, after the development of the Newcomen engine the main efforts went into making the engines more energy-efficient and saving fuel (which it used profligately), which would be capital-saving. Elsewhere, too, fuel-saving technological change was a central focus of research, as exemplified for instance in the work of John Smeaton. Only the adoption of steam power in the textile industry, seven decades after its invention, counts as labor-saving, although there, too, steam often replaced water power as well as labor. More generally, labor saving technological progress may have been important in some industries, but the Industrial Revolution was about more than just labor saving. Many of the most important breakthroughs of the age, such as the improvements in water power, gas lighting, food preservation, soda-making, and the use of digitally-encoded information in Jacquard looms had little to do with the relative price of energy to labor and everything with a wide search for improvement across the board.

Moreover, whereas coal was cheap in Britain near coal mines and later near canals connected to them, this was not a national parameter. Coal was considerably more expensive in areas remote from coal mines such as Cornwall. In the mid-1820s, for instance, the price of a ton of coal was around 30s. in London and about 20s. in Cornwall, as opposed to 10s. in Manchester and about 6s. in Leeds (von Tunzelmann, 1978, p. 96; Nuvolari and Verspagen, 2008, p. 28). The price of coal could easily double even if it had to be transported over a short distance (Turnbull, 1987). And yet London used coal heavily, both for heating and steam power. Cornwall adopted steam engines in large numbers in the second half of the eighteenth century, and while quite naturally it developed and adopted more fuel-efficient (high-pressure) engines, there seems to be little evidence that the vastly different cost of coal across Britain affected the *rate* of technological change. This is not to deny that relative costs fine-tuned the precise *direction* of innovation. When coal was truly abundant, such as the famous "ten-yard seam" in Staffordshire in the Black Country that yielded 20,000 tons per acre, it was used in wasteful ways (Rolt, 1970, pp. 85–86). John Farey complained about a "state of apathy as to the consumption of coal" outside Cornwall (where fuel-efficient Woolf engines were prominent) but, being an engineer, attributed this to the lack of "true knowledge" among those who might want to save fuel and not the lack of incentives (Farey, 1971, p. 307). On the other hand, when coal was dear, innovation would be biased to economize on it. As Nuvolari and Verspagen (2008, pp. 10–11) point out, the Cornish machines, stimulated by expensive coal and developed in a "highly favorable context ... and an institutional set-up that stimulated the rapid dissemination of technological knowledge," turned out to be best-practice technology.

To put it differently: the difficulty with a theory that attributes technological change to the cost of fuel relative to that of labor is that fuel costs are not exogenous. Mining technologies, from pumping to geology, were advancing at a number of fronts as part of the Industrial Enlightenment. The price of coal at any given location except pithead was a function of the improvements and investments in the transport system that a society hell bent on progress had made. To repeat: there was a fundamental difference between factors affecting the rate versus the direction of innovation. The low price of coal, rather than being a cause of the Industrial Revolution, was very much a consequence of it.

The Allen hypothesis appears at first glance to be supported, somewhat perversely, by the case of the missing mechanical sawmills in eighteenth-century Britain. Mechanical (wind-driven) sawmills appeared in the Netherlands in the eighteenth century but seem to be absent or at least to be quite rare in Britain until steam-driven mills were introduced in the early nineteenth century (Cooney, 1991, 1998). It is likely that other factors came into play here: there was violent resistance to the mechanical mills in Britain, and a sawmill built near London at Limehouse was destroyed in 1768 by an angry mob. Recent research, however, has explained this difference by factor prices. The induced innovation hypothesis is turned on its head here. In the Netherlands sawyers' wages were inordinately high and mechanical sawmills were introduced there in the seventeenth century, whereas in Britain, even though wages were high, the ratio between sawyers' and construction wages was lower than in the Netherlands. Thus differences in factor prices declared that mechanical sawmills would be introduced in the Netherlands and not in England until steam-powered engines became a reality (van Bochove, 2008, p. 173). At first glance, this seems an a fortiori argument in support of the induced-innovation hypothesis (even if Britain is the low-wage economy here). Van Bochove estimates, however, an internal rate of return of 85 percent on wind-driven mechanical sawmills in Britain, which still seems high under any assumption. Moreover, if British wages were high enough to spur the introduction of steam-powered sawmills, why would they not have been high enough to support wind-driven ones?

Allen's basic assumption that inventive activity was driven by a desire to make money is of course not controversial. Technological change depended on the expected payoff of invention and the costs of "research and development." But would-be inventors were constrained by what they knew and what knowledge of others they could access. Steam power and other high-tech eighteenth-century innovations depended on skilled people whose competence was essential to make advanced machinery work properly (Jacob, forthcoming). By the very nature of R&D, it is not always clear at the start of a research project whether the end-product of the research will save labor more than capital. Even so, it is far from clear that high wages and the need to save labor were as high on the priorities of inventors as Allen suggests. We can discover something about the motivations of inventors by examining the stated goals of inventions, as filed in their patent applications. To judge from these declared purposes of invention, labor-saving was a stated goal in only 4.2 percent of all patents taken out between 1660 and 1800, whereas capital saving was the goal in 30.8 percent of all patents. It could be argued that this number is seriously understated since saving labor might have been highly unpopular in an age obsessed with unemployment, but even if we adjust these goals by what the patent actually did, only 21 percent of all inventions can be said to have saved labor (MacLeod, 1988, pp. 160–71). This evidence is consistent with the macroeconomic record, questionable as it is, summarized by von Tunzelmann (1994, pp. 289–91). Apart from a short period during the Napoleonic Wars, there is little evidence that technological change in Britain as a whole was on balance labor-saving before 1830. Even after that year, when there is a clear-cut shift toward more labor-saving machinery, it was dampened by "the continuing labour-surplus of males" (ibid., p. 291).

One question that may shed light on the debate is to ask, why were British wages high in the first place? A plausible contributing factor causing a high-wage economy, suggested by Allen, was the involvement of the British economy in international trade, which tended to produce high wages in part because urban areas paid higher wages. They did so because the cost of living was higher in towns, and to compensate workers for the unhealthy living conditions there. An alternative explanation emphasizes the relation between high wages and labor productivity. A labor force that was on average healthy, skilled, and faced with the proper incentives would expect and receive higher wages. High wages do not necessarily imply dear labor if the labor is more productive, and thus the incentive to save labor may be illusory. One of the first to realize this crucial distinction was Daniel Defoe. He noted that a French worker may well be more diligent than his English colleague, but "the English Man shall do as much Business in the fewer hours as the Foreigner who sits longer at it" (Defoe, 1728, p. 38). It is interesting to note that eighteenth-century attempts to measure the physical output of humans consistently found that the energy output of people relative to that of horses was higher in England than on the Continent (Ferguson, 1971). As a possible explanation, Defoe pointed to the better nutrition of the English workman, which higher wages made possible. He thus anticipated what modern economists refer to as "efficiency-wages," that is, a world in which higher wages lead to more productive labor as well as vice versa. Desaguliers (1734–44, Vol. 1, p. 254) found that the strength of five Englishmen equaled that of a horse, as did the strength of seven

Dutchmen or Frenchmen. Other eighteenth-century observers noted the same thing: Arthur Young, writing in the late 1780s, notes that "labour is generally in reality the cheapest where it is nominally the dearest" (Young, [1790], 1929, p. 311). Of course, in the long run the physical strength of manual workers was becoming less of a measure of productivity as people were gradually being replaced in menial jobs by machinery, but this process was far from complete even in 1850.

In short, Britain's high wages as such were neither an obvious advantage nor a disadvantage, but revealed something deeper about the British economy. Higher wages in Britain may have reflected the higher level of skills and competence, due to better training, more able supervision, and a relatively high level of capital per worker. In any event, factor prices would not by themselves make an economy more technologically creative. As with the effect of the physical environment on the rate of technological progress, factor prices might have determined the *direction* of technological change, but the *power* and *intensity* of improvement were a function of technological capabilities and motives that had deeper causes.

But what if the labor supply curve were downward sloping and higher wages led workers to actually work less, because higher incomes meant that they could afford more leisure? This possibility was a major concern of mercantilist writings, but historians are skeptical. One fascinating hypothesis is that the Industrial Revolution was preceded by and coincided with what has been termed by Jan De Vries (1993, 1994, 2008) the "Industrious Revolution," referring to workers willing to work harder in large part because in the eighteenth century there were simply more things on the market to buy that they liked and could afford. The evidence marshaled by De Vries indicates that during the decades of the Industrial Revolution the working year increased by about 25 percent. Economics suggests that people will only work if the money they earn actually makes them better off than they would be if they simply took the time off. As people get richer, they may decide to take more of their income in the form of leisure, but the De Vries hypothesis implies that over the eighteenth century, with the proliferation of "luxury" goods and their growing accessibility to consumers, households decided to work harder to gain access to the new goods, both by spending more hours per year on work and by having more members work in cash-generating employment. Moreover, some of the goods that households consumed, such as apparel or schooling, could either be supplied by the parents or purchased from non-household members for cash. Such decisions are part and parcel of consumer economics. The industrious revolution hypothesis suggests that the period in question by and large coincides with the increase in market involvement and possibly more work, not only by adult males but also by their family members. In other words, income in cash was desirable because households could buy more market goods that people wanted, even if they had to work more and longer to get them. Such an observation is clearly inconsistent with a downward-sloping labor supply curve, where people work less as their wages go up. Leisure is not traditionally considered part of national income (although there is no compelling reason why not) and so the industrious revolution has serious implications for measured economic growth.

Changes in preferences as causes of economic change are not popular among economists and are hard to document. However, while an exogenous change in preferences cannot be ruled out, the kind of redeployment of household resources implicit in the industrious revolution hypothesis could also have come about as a response to technological changes. After all, better technology created and brought close to home some of the market-produced goods that the British consumer wanted to buy: cotton clothes, toys, belts and buckles, adornments, musical instruments, tableware, kitchen utensils, clocks, books, and so on (Berg, 2005). Non-durable consumer goods such as sugar, tea, and tobacco, which had entered consumption in the previous century, also had to be purchased in the market. Technological progress implied that at the same time the array of goods that the consumer could buy increased, their quality improved, the uncertainty of their characteristics declined with standardization, and their price fell. Under these conditions, consumers were more inclined to substitute cash income for home-produced goods. The factory and the workshop were of course the obvious loci of the specialization of labor, and were almost entirely dependent on cash transactions. But even those workers who remained at home found increasingly that they preferred to buy the goods they needed while producing for the market. In short, the industrious revolution may have been one of the factors behind changes in labor supply and economic growth during the eighteenth and early nineteenth centuries, but itself was not independent of technological change.

The actual evidence on how much people worked is very spotty indeed. We do have a good idea of the length of the labor week in factories and mines, that is, employers who employed workers in formal conditions. But even by 1850, many and perhaps most of people who worked in Britain worked in their home or in the home or attached workshop of their employer. Those who were paid by the piece often had the option to come and go as they pleased, which was desirable perhaps for them but makes it hard for the historian who is trying to estimate how many hours people worked. Recent research by Joachim Voth (1998, 2000) has lifted the veil on this matter just a bit, and indicates that in the second half of the eighteenth century many people in Britain worked harder than before; specifically, we know that the venerable institution of "St Monday" according to which people took the Monday off to rest after the delights of the weekend fell into disuse. Assuming that this change was not offset by lighter work on other days, it constitutes the best evidence we have that the industrious revolution triggered more hours of work. But there are complicating factors. It seems that on days on which an eighteenth-century laborer worked, he or she worked very long hours. However, much of the demand for labor in Britain was highly seasonal, and periods of idleness punctuated periods of long work days. As transportation improved, many of the local peaks of unemployment, caused by impassable roads for example, were attenuated. While we cannot be sure, then, whether a typical laborer worked more hours in 1850 than in 1700, it seems that work had become a little more regular.

One implication of a rising work-week is that the estimates of labor input that are based on a constant proportion of the population of working age *under*estimate the actual labor input and thus overestimate the rate of productivity growth in the economy. The same holds if the labor force participation rate was rising. It might be added that the macroeconomic concept of a participation rate is something of an anachronism: it requires each person to "declare" whether she or he was in the labor force. Such a decision would have sounded odd to most people living in Britain in 1760 and even in 1850. Many women and children lived in households in which they helped with the work when needed and were idle when not. Only with the rise of the "factory system" was a more rigid system of participants and non-participants created.

There is also considerable evidence of rising child labor in this age—although it is of course hard to know whether this was prompted by the industrious revolution or by an increase in the opportunities for child labor that machines and mines provided. Child labor was attractive because it was cheap, often outrageously so. Poor children were often treated little better than slaves. Children did not have the physical strength of adults, of course, but they were more obedient, and had not yet picked up bad habits of intemperance and pugnaciousness. Interestingly enough, in the early stages of the Industrial Revolution child labor was seen by many as a blessing. Saving children, especially orphans, pauper apprentices, and other "indolent" youths, from the dual menaces of poverty and sloth was a Christian duty. Only in the nineteenth century did people begin to feel that child labor might be socially costly and moved to do something about it. Parliamentary committees were established to investigate the phenomenon and suggested reforms, which remained largely ineffective before the middle of the nineteenth century.

The evidence on female labor force participation is equally difficult to interpret: the decline in the cottage industries after 1815 left many married women without much "work" (in the sense of earning cash) within the household. Unmarried women worked predominantly in factories or as domestic servants. There were considerable advantages for an employer to hire women: given their low opportunity costs, they tended to be cheaper, and on the whole more docile and malleable. In some sense the first half of the nineteenth century witnessed a peculiar historical phenomenon in which the Industrial Revolution created its own labor force: by flooding world markets with cheap textiles and other manufactured products, the new technology reduced the earnings that the hundreds of thousands engaged in cottage industry could secure by working at home, almost literally forcing them into the factories. For adult men, such as the fiercely independent handloom weavers, this was a very difficult transition to make, but their daughters and sons had little choice, and they either found employment in the mills or had to emigrate. The 1851 census, with its odd classification of occupations by the natural source of the raw materials being processed, reported that of the workers under age 20 in the four big textile manufacturing industries (linen, wool, worsted, and cotton), 128,653 were male and 171,114 were female. Among adults, the numbers were more balanced in favor of males, but barely so (278,522 males and 231,763 females). In 1851, too, 2.6 million women were classified as "wives with no occupation" and another 320,000 women aged 20 or over were classified as "daughters, sisters, nieces." How many of these women really worked at home in some cash-generating occupation is unknown, but it must have been a respectable proportion. Yet in the subsequent decades, the economy's reliance on labor other than that of adult males began to decline, as fewer children were formally occupied and married women tended to stay at home. I will return to the issue of child and female labor in chapter 14 below.

One of the more fascinating issues of the era is the question of unemployment. In the eighteenth century, the issue was quite prominent on the agendas of writers in political economy. This led modern writers on the issue such as John Maynard Keynes and scholars influenced by him to suspect that the pre-Industrial Revolution may have been similar in some ways to the depressed economies of the 1930s. Many eighteenth-century writers, such as Bernard de Mandeville, Malachy Postlethwayt, and Sir James Steuart wrote in a quaintly proto-Keynesian fashion as if an increase in aggregate spending and monetary and fiscal expansion would put people to work. Keynes himself, in his "notes on Mercantilism," claimed these writers as his precursors ([1936], 1964, ch. 23). On closer examination, it seems that such notions could be misleading. As noted above, much of the unemployment observed before 1850 was seasonal in nature, due to the rhythm of farm work and weather patterns. Moving workers from the land to other areas where they could be employed in the off-season was unrealistic. There was also a deep question of voluntary as opposed to involuntary unemployment. Many people who were "idle" may just have preferred leisure—though the nature of the industrious revolution was to reduce their numbers. Finally, pre-Industrial Revolution economies had a substantial number of people who were idle because they were *unemployable*: invalids, cripples, mentally retarded, as well as able-bodied vagrants and vagabonds, beggars and rogues, people on the fringes of society whose lifestyle and appearance frightened the more settled citizens. Whether an increase in aggregate demand would have done much to put such people to work is subject to serious doubt.

The great fear of contemporaries was technological unemployment; that is, workers being replaced by machinery. The acceleration of the rate of technological change had led the economy to *terra incognita*, and it seemed to many contemporaries that mechanization could threaten the livelihood of workers and throw substantial numbers of them out of work. This concern became known as "the machinery question." The economics of technological unemployment was still not well understood, and the idea that technological progress creates as many or more jobs than it displaced had not yet taken root. Some enlightened writers knew better. Josiah Tucker explained concisely and clearly that machinery and innovation complemented labor and increased its productivity, and thus led to lower prices for final products and increased the demand for labor (1758, pp. 31–38). But the message was not getting through to everyone. It is telling that working-class leaders, in Berg's view, resisted the machine because of the economic distress it caused, such as "technological unemployment, long hours of alienated factory labour, and the smoking blight of rapidly expanding industrial towns" (Berg, 1985, p. 17)—the former clearly being contradicted by the latter two. Yet in the short term there could be considerable pain. The danger here is one of over-aggregation: it is likely that compensating fluctuations in labor demand in different sectors spawned substantial friction even if total demand for labor was unchanged. The cost of making the transition was often non-negligible, and workers were likely to observe the decline in their own sector before they perceived better opportunities elsewhere. One interesting corollary is that the traditional domestic industry such as handloom weaving often served as the shock-absorbing buffer for the factory sector. Short-term fluctuations in economic activity would lead to large fluctuations in the demand for domestic workers, whereas employment in the capital-intensive mechanized sector was relatively stable (Nardinelli, 1986).

One issue that has received a fair amount of attention is the mobility of the labor force. Mobility can mean both geographical and occupational mobility. Both are essential if an economy is to allocate resources in an efficient way and if it is to adapt to shocks on either the demand or the supply side. In eighteenth-century Britain, there was much complaint about the Settlement Acts (dating from 1662), which in the view of some inhibited the free movement of labor. Adam Smith ([1776], 1976, p. 157) thought that "the very unequal price of labour which we frequently find in England in places at no great distance from one another, is probably owing to the obstruction which the law of settlements gives to a poor man who would carry his industry from one parish to another without a certificate." Twentieth-century historians agreed. Without much more than Adam Smith's authority as evidence, Karl Polanyi ([1944], 1985, p. 88) declared that people "were not free to choose their occupations or those of their children; they were not free to settle where they pleased." It is interesting to observe the attitude that the Settlement Acts revealed: the migration of workers, rather than being seen as a key to efficiency and growth, was viewed with concern. Residents wondered whether such workers would not become unemployed and a burden on "the rates." Above all, it was important for local magistrates to prevent others from "dumping" their poor and unemployable in their parishes. Yet it seems that over the course of the eighteenth century these attitudes changed, in part because of a growing realization that wage labor was needed to keep the local economy moving even if there were cyclical and seasonal disruptions in the level of economic activity. David Eastwood, among others, has argued that Smith's concerns about the impact of the Settlement Acts were "wildly exaggerated" (1994, pp. 25–26). Local authorities were quite able to distinguish between able-bodied and industrious workers and idle vagrants. In practice, these laws rarely amounted to more than a nuisance, and it seems unlikely that they seriously impeded mobility. Even if in the mid-eighteenth century some of the harassment of migrants seen as potential burdens on the poor rates was still taking place, by the late eighteenth century this phenomenon was subsiding, especially in rural areas (Landau, 1990). In any case, in 1795 the Poor Law Removal Act of 1795 (35 Geo. III (1795) c. 101) reformed the Settlement Acts, prohibiting the removal of paupers until they became chargeable, and placing the costs on the removing parish rather than the parish of origin. It may seem curious that in a period of political repression and Jacobin-phobia, the government would relax the laws of settlement to make migration easier (Redford, [1926], 1964, p. 87). The explanation is that by this time the 1795 reform was just formalizing existing practices and that, in Landau's words, it was no longer necessary to regulate migration because the new market economy made such regulation redundant (Landau, 1990, p. 571).

Even before 1795 the system was "by no means such a check on mobility of labour as some of the older writers ... supposed," because the option to evict was exercised in a haphazard and casual way (Styles, 1963, p. 62). Some contemporary opinion agrees with this finding. Sir F. M. Eden (1797, Vol. 1, pp. 297–98) argued that "the poor are no longer liable to be removed at the caprice of the parish officers on the grounds that they are likely to become chargeable ... there is no country in Europe where [man] changes his residence as often as in England." More to the point, Boyer's (1990) analysis shows that the overall effect of the Poor Law on labor mobility was small and that these laws were unlikely to have deterred able-bodied young males from emigrating to new industrial sectors. Migration statistics bear this out, even if they are but crude indicators: between 1750 and 1800, the net migration into Lancashire and the West Riding of Yorkshire came to about 355,000 people (Wrigley, 2009, pp. 113-14). While Settlement Acts remained on the books, authorities clearly felt it no longer necessary to use these laws to control and regulate the labor force.

To be sure, after 1795 the parishes still had the right to remove any person back to his or her "parish of settlement" if they became chargeable to their new parish, and before the law was changed in 1846 internal migrants faced the possibility of being sent back home during periods of economic slump. This, indeed, happened to a substantial degree in the 1840s, when non-able-bodied men, women, and workers in declining industries were "removed" disproportionately. Perhaps the primary mechanism by which the Settlement Acts discouraged migration was their sheer complexity and the uncertainty that irregular enforcement implied for anyone contemplating migration. Since migration was a risky undertaking under any circumstances, it is far from obvious to what extent the Old Poor Law made things worse. In any event, if all else failed, migrants could always *in extremis* return home, where relief was assured. Whether "removals" were really disastrous for their subjects is unclear, since the distances involved were fairly small. Many migrants moved back and forth between their parishes of settlement and parishes of residence. Temporary migration of any kind was quite common and underlines the relatively footloose character of the British labor force. Of course, mobility is purely a relative concept. In the middle of the nineteenth century British labor was relatively *immobile* compared with the United States, but it seems plausible that it was more mobile than most European nations (Long and Ferrie, 2010).

The impact of the railroad on the mobility of labor is worth revisiting. Travel costs work in a manner symmetric to legal restrictions: they raise the cost of moving. Before 1830, while carriages and stagecoaches were becoming better, faster, and more reliable, they were still beyond the means of the bulk of the labor force. Before the trains, the passengers who ended up traveling in third-class compartments with relative ease and speed, would either have walked or used slow-moving carts (Leunig, 2006, p. 641). The democratization of travel, which is what the trains amounted to, added a great deal to the ability of labor to move about for the best jobs, although most of these benefits came after 1850.

It is worth emphasizing how seasonal the demand for labor was in Britain. Farming, with its strong emphasis on grain production, was highly seasonal in Britain. Yet manufacturing, too, with its dependence on water power and transport on poor roads, was often disrupted for weeks on end by bad weather. In an important paper, Sokoloff and Dollar (1997) argued that the higher seasonality of British labor demand led to the rise of cottage industries in Britain but not in the United States. Cottage industries, as noted above, were a cushion that absorbed seasonal shocks but they did so imperfectly, and especially in the south of England other cushions were required. The extensive Poor Law provisions in these counties created exactly that. One of the great achievements of technological progress in the century after 1750 was to make the supply of labor more synchronized with the fluctuations in demand. Railroads helped shuttle workers around between different work sites even in the short term. The relative decline in agricultural employment, and the increase in the share of industries and services that were not as susceptible to seasonality also helped. The improvements in lighting technology made working in the winter months easier. Yet it is far from certain whether these improvements benefited the labor force as a whole, or whether they improved things for young and able-bodied men but much less for women and children.

CHAPTER 13

Demographic Transformation
in the Age of Enlightenment

I have already noted the rather astonishing growth in population that Britain experienced during the period in question. The essential data on the growth of British population are provided in table 13.1. The basic facts are not in doubt, although some details have remained controversial. At some point in the middle of the eighteenth century, British population abruptly began to surge at a rate far more rapid than ever experienced before. This phenomenon was not unique to Britain: in other countries in Europe, too, there were signs by 1750 that the Malthusian constraints were becoming looser. The early data are still somewhat conjectural and the experiences of different economies vary. In the Netherlands and Germany, for instance, population growth set in later, but once it had shifted into high gear, it was faster and continued for longer than in Britain. The French experience was the reverse: population did take off in the eighteenth century, but then its growth slowed down long before the British did. Even in the relatively backward southern and eastern parts of the Continent, the decades of the late eighteenth century and early nineteenth century mark a break in the "old demographic regime." Something truly dramatic changed in the population dynamics of the European Continent and the British Isles. The hard but ineluctable question is why it happened.

The evidence on the disintegration of the Malthusian model in Britain is perplexing because it is quite clear that it happened *before* there was any sign of the Industrial Revolution, to say nothing of sustained economic growth. A detailed test of a Malthusian model is not easy to carry out, but work by historical demographers suggests that already by the mid-eighteenth century British demographic behavior was no longer very sensitive to fluctuations in real wages or real income. A recent paper by Nicolini (2007) finds the impact of real wages on mortality to be weak after 1640 and that on fertility to disappear around 1740. The reverse impact, of birth and death rates on wages, was found to be "weak and sporadic" (p. 115). In other words, the negative feedback mechanism that was supposed to regulate population through the sensitivity of birth and death rates to living standards and real wages seems to have been de-activated before the Industrial Revolution. In this respect, Britain was a leader; in no other country was the connection between real wages and demographic variables so weak (Galloway,

1988; Post, 1990). Yet Britain was just like the rest of Europe: after 1750 the old demographic regime seems to have collapsed abruptly everywhere and, whether the economy was rich or poor, in the nineteenth century population just took off.

As table 13.1 shows, demographic growth in Britain in the period 1700–1850 went through four stages. During the first fifty years of the eighteenth century, English population grew quite slowly, at an average growth rate of 0.26 percent a year. In the following forty years, 1751–91, population growth rate almost tripled to 0.73 percent. In the next forty years, which included the hard years of the French Wars, growth peaked at 1.35 percent a year. In the two decades 1831–51 (and in the two subsequent decades as well), population growth slowed down marginally to 1.15 percent. Scottish population, less well documented, seems to have grown as well if somewhat slower: between 1700 and 1821 it went from about 1.1 million to 2.1 million, or at about 0.54 percent per year. Irish population grew as fast as England's until the Famine hit in 1845, after which Ireland's demographic history was unlike that of any other European country.

How did economic factors affect the rate of population growth? Simple models may not be able to do justice to this immensely complicated matter. To start with, all demographic change consists of three elements: births, deaths, and migration. International migration—Ireland always excepted—was still a relatively small factor in this era, so we are down to fertility and mortality. Yet both fertility and mortality were influenced by economic factors through a variety of channels and the connections are far from simple. Even in our own time, such connections are not easy to understand. The rate of population growth in industrialized Europe in the twentieth century has fallen steadily in the past decades and has reached (or is about to reach) negative rates in many countries—but demographers and economists are still not quite sure why. The microbial environment in which people lived clearly could affect population numbers. Each epidemic disease seems to have followed a logic of its own and can be taken in part as exogenous to the economic system. The role of AIDS in our own age is mirrored in the European past by the sudden appearance and disappearance of bubonic plague, syphilis, smallpox, and cholera. During the period under discussion here, bubonic plague (which had still devastated London in the famous outbreak of 1665–66) disappeared from the European scene, while cholera appeared mysteriously in 1831 and struck again in 1847.

The evolution of the birth rate is just as complex: does it make sense to speak of a "demand" for children, or were births just an inevitable by-product of married life? What variables determined the propensity to marry (both the percentages ever married and the average age at which people married for the first time)? And what determined the rate of marital fertility? How significant were births out of wedlock? At one end, many of these variables touched on the most intimate microdetails of human families and households, and at the other end they were

Table 13.1: Main population data, England and Wales, 1701–1850

	Total population (mid-year, 000s)	Crude birth rate (aver. per annum)	Crude death ate (aver. per annum)	Net population increase (aver. per annum)
1701–10	5,334	30.2	26.1	4.1
1711–20	5,428	30.6	27.4	3.2
1721–30	5,602	32.0	32.6	−0.6
1731–40	5,599	34.5	28.0	6.5
1741–50	5,782	32.2	27.9	4.3
1751–60	6,149	32.4	25.2	7.2
1761–70	6,448	33.7	28.0	5.7
1771–80	6,913	35.4	26.0	9.4
1781–90	7,434	35.9	26.5	9.4
1791–1800	8,256	36.4	25.4	11.0
1801–10	9,232	37.8	23.9	12.9
1811–20	10,628	39.4	23.4	16.0
1821–30	12,374	38.8	23.1	15.7
1831–40	14,100	35.7	22.4	13.3
1841–50	15,910	35.4	22.7	12.7

Source: computed from Wrigley and Schofield (1997, p. 614).

impinged on by the behavior of macro-variables such as real wages and prices, the terms of trade between agricultural and industrial goods, and social policies toward the poor. Nor is the distinction between birth- and death-related demographic change as neat as we would like: infant and maternal mortality, stillbirths, and the real dangers of abortion connected fertility and mortality rates. All the same, in what follows I will deal with the two topics separately, drawing the connections when necessary.

To start with, it is important to stress one matter that often is left implicit in most discussions of demographic change in the past. It is quite essential to grasp that the biology of birth, disease, and death was poorly understood by the people living at the time. As a result, the link between choices and outcomes was far more tenuous in the demographic area than elsewhere in the economy and certainly more tenuous than in our own time. I am not trying to argue that today we fully understand those mysteries. All the same, it seems impossible to deny that by comparison, the understanding of the biological mechanisms at work has allowed individuals in the modern age a great deal more control over their demographic fate than they had in 1750. This is certainly the case for fertility control and family planning, but even as far as morbidity and mortality are concerned, life in the eighteenth century was uncertain and short by today's standards. To be sure, even in the twenty-first century society is constrained in its control over life by budgets and by knowledge, but in eighteenth-century Britain such constraints held with much greater force. Poverty and ignorance interacted in complicated ways. The very rich and aristocrats lived longer than the poor because they lived in better hygienic conditions, could afford warmer homes in the winter, enjoyed better diets, and had better access to medical care, though the impact of the latter remains doubtful. Given how little was known about the causes of disease, it seems a bit of a stretch to argue that before 1850 education led to better all-around household management and thus avoided disease, but some effect of an emphasis on better hygiene and nutrition cannot be ruled out.

What killed far more people than anything else in this era was infectious disease, from ugly epidemics such as smallpox, typhoid, and (later) cholera, to the mysterious and much feared killer of young adults, tuberculosis (known as consumption to people at the time), to more mundane but still poorly understood afflictions such as influenza, pneumonia, and diarrhea. Medical science, whether formal as practiced by expensive doctors licensed by the Royal College of Physicians, or informal folk medicine practiced by quacks of various calibers, was essentially powerless to diagnose or treat infectious disease, because the role of microbes and their modes of transmission was not understood. The difference between formally trained medics and quacks, at least from the point of view of their effects, was not all that clear: the most celebrated patent medicine sold in the eighteenth century was Dr James' powder, sold by a Dr. Robert James, who had had formal training. The powder he peddled was based on antimony, a slow-working but relentless poison, that reputedly killed among others the prison reformer John Howard and the poet Oliver Goldsmith. Bloodletting, purges, emetics, the administration of addictive narcotics such as laudanum, and other widespread practices of questionable medical value remained the backbone of medicine until well into the nineteenth century, and surgery without either anesthesia or sterilized tools claimed far more lives than it saved. A similar lack of knowledge characterized human reproduction. Indeed, the modern idea of conception and the existence of a human egg fertilized by sperm was not fully worked out until 1827. People, of course, understood that sex led to pregnancy, but many of the details eluded even the most learned doctors, and as a consequence contraceptive techniques—for those willing to practice them —were imperfect and unreliable.

And yet society in the eighteenth century had developed mechanisms and tools that helped them control nature on this front as well. Even a little knowledge could at times be better than none at all, and more than once do we observe the odd phenomenon of people doing the right thing for the wrong (or at least irrelevant) reason, such as cleaning campaigns to fight miasmas believed to cause infectious disease (Riley, 1987). Medical treatment may have been effective if only because of the placebo effect, reinforced by the aura of learning and competence that medical doctors carried even if they were by our reckoning clueless. On a few occasions, as we have seen in chapter 11, they stumbled on a number of things that worked. Emphasizing what seems to us to be ignorance in the medical practices of the time runs the risk of attracting criticism of "Whiggishness" or even "triumphalism." Disdaining the wisdom of a previous generation is hazardous—as if our own age will not be the butt of derision and mockery by a future generation that knows more. The demographic statistics do not lie, however, and the conclusion that demographic change was caused at least in part by increases in certain forms of useful knowledge and best-practice clinical and public health techniques is not implausible. What I called before the Medical Enlightenment was in full swing by the early nineteenth century, and although its effects were still mostly limited to the rich and powerful, and to a few diseases, there were some important precedents to the medical revolution that materialized after 1900.

*　　*　　*

The tripling of the population of the British Isles between 1750 and 1850 was due to a combination of a rising birth rate with a falling death rate. The reconstruction of the demographic history by the Cambridge Group headed by E.A. Wrigley and R.S. Schofield (1981, 1997) has established, if not to everyone's full satisfaction, that the role of the birth rate in that transition in the eight decades after 1750 was about twice as large as that of falling mortality, so that fertility increase accounted for roughly two-thirds of the population growth.

Birth rates in the past were normally a function of the propensity to marry (assuming that illegitimate fertility was sufficiently low, which in 1750 is a good approximation). Marital fertility rates varied as well. In part they depended on the health and natural fertility of women. But, of course, married women may have wanted to control their fertility. If they wished to do that, and could do so effectively, marital fertility would become a choice variable and we can speak of the "demand" for children. The extent to which couples before 1900 could control their fertility has been the subject of a very large literature, and systematic data are for obvious reasons difficult to come by. The second volume of the Cambridge Group (Wrigley and Schofield, 1997), entirely based on the analysis of parish records and relying on advanced demographic techniques, concluded cautiously that fertility control in Britain before 1871 was not common enough to be demographically significant. Woods (2000) reached the same conclusion, attributing the Victorian decline in fertility to changing ideology, primarily "the desire or willingness to limit family size from the 1860s on" (p. 150) and suggests, more provocatively, that "the very question 'how many children should we have' was new to most Victorians" (p. 169). Before 1850 then, such behavior, by the best evidence, was insignificant. That does not, of course, mean that *nobody* practiced birth control at the time; all we can infer is that not enough people did so to make a palpable impact on marital fertility. The data cannot tell us whether this behavior derived from the fact that people were just uninterested in limiting fertility, whether they would have liked to do so but shied away from it for religious reasons, or whether they simply did not know enough about birth control to practice it effectively.

If contraception was not an important practice, it might seem that "economic" decision-making based on the costs and benefits of children (e.g., the money that they could earn for the family, or their value as old-age insurance for their parents) would be irrelevant. But such a conclusion would be rash. British society, like that of much of Europe, practiced a form of birth control that worked even if there was little or no fertility limitation within marriage; this was marriage delay. At least since the end of the Middle Ages, many European societies saw women marrying far later than their biological maturation (which in a pre-industrial age was around age 16, unlike our own age when this happens at about age 13). Wrigley and Schofield estimate that in the first quarter of the eighteenth century, the woman's age at first marriage was around 26. Marrying at this late age lopped off about ten years of the woman's fertile years and thus served as an effective means of contraception. To be sure, there was some illegitimacy and a large number of brides turned out to have been pregnant at their wedding (as witnessed by the time difference between marriage and the birth of the first child as recorded in parish records). All the same, if the age at first marriage of women declined, fertility rates should rise.

There is good evidence that this is precisely what happened. The decline in the age at first marriage of women during the eighteenth century was the driving force behind the rise in British fertility rates. The average age of first marriage of women was 26 in 1700, 24.9 in 1750, about 24.2 in 1800, and 23.2 in 1830 (Wrigley and

Schofield, 1997, p. 134). This trend was reinforced by trends in the proportion ever married. Not only did women in eighteenth-century Britain marry younger, more of them entered nuptials at all. In 1701 the proportion never married was still 11.2 percent; in the 1770s it was as low as 6.5 percent, though by 1806 it crept back up to 10 percent. The same is true for illegitimacy: one would have expected that in an age of late marriage, the pent-up sexual energies would have led to more illegitimacy, whereas in the later age with earlier marriages and fewer celibacies, the illegitimacy rate would fall. In fact the reverse seems to be the case—by the end of the eighteenth century no fewer than one-quarter of all *first* births were illegitimate and another quarter were pre-maritally conceived (Wrigley and Schofield, 1997, p. 195), as opposed to one-tenth at the start of the century.

The other surprising fact is that the data collected by Wrigley and Schofield (1997, p. 355) show little sign of rising marital fertility after 1700. Fertility within marriage depended on fecundity (that is, the *ability* of a woman to conceive, given her behavior) as well as on sexual behavior and, if present, contraception. Fecundity in turn depended not only on the level of nutrition and health of women, but also on lactation habits. Breast-feeding reduces the chance of healthy mothers becoming pregnant again. By the same token, given a certain regime of breast-feeding, an increase in infant mortality would increase fecundity purely for the mechanical reason that mothers would stop nursing when a baby died and thus would, all other things equal, become more fecund, while a decline in infant mortality would reduce it. This effect has been used ingeniously to infer the prevalence of breast-feeding in Britain: it turns out that a hypothetical fecundity function around a mean of 19 months till weaning produces an interval between births that resembles the patterns observed. Breast-feeding, thus, was quite universal and prolonged for many months after childbirth (Wrigley and Schofield, 1997, p. 491). This finding is of considerable significance, since breast-feeding may have been the most important single factor affecting fecundity and hence marital fertility before the growth of the use of contraceptives in the late nineteenth century. British mothers after 1750 tended to breast-feed their babies more than their continental neighbors, and this has been argued to be a main reason for their lower marital fertility and infant mortality. Compared to most European countries, British marital fertility rates were low (Flinn, 1981, p. 86). The Prussian von Archenholz ([1785], 1797, p. 327) noted that "English women of quality often suckled their own children; they do not consider the name nor the duties of a mother disgraceful." Modern experts seem to have accepted this view (Fildes, 1986, p. 106; McLaren, 1990, p. 163).

There is an interesting link between ideology and demographics here. Breast-feeding was an important item on the agenda of the Enlightenment. Rousseau's famous advocacy of breast-feeding was by no means the only influential voice supporting it (Linnaeus was another). These authors mainly popularized the writings of mid-eighteenth-century physicians. Realization of the salutary effects of breast-feeding, of course, was not new. What was uniquely a result of the

Enlightenment was the belief that "breast-feeding was a *technology* for producing an improved human being" (Sherwood, 1993, p. 27). Eighteenth-century doctors came to regard breast-feeding as a "natural" (and hence commendable) habit. Nature intended mothers to nurse, the enlightened medical literature reasoned, and when nature's command was disobeyed, "illness follows" (ibid., p. 32). What is of course unknown is to what extent the breast-feeding habits of the population at large were influenced by these writings. Highly popular and influential texts such as Buchan's *Domestic Medicine* (1772, pp. 3, 672) strongly supported it. A substantial segment of the population had some contact with the medical profession, and medical advice certainly filtered down even to those who did not. Whether the conscious understanding of the benefits of nursing extended to its contraceptive effects is unclear. There is some evidence that prolonged breast-feeding was understood to delay the resumption of menstruation and fertility. But not all physicians agreed, and a few ridiculed the folk wisdom that claimed a connection between breast-feeding and lower fertility, even suggesting that extended breast-feeding was dangerous to mothers. One of the more intriguing phenomena here is wet-nursing, the custom of upper-class women hiring another woman to breast-feed their babies. The diffusion of this custom to middle-class women may have helped to raise fecundity in the early eighteenth century, but later on the custom was broadly condemned and seems to have gone into decline, and in Britain it never reached the proportions it did in France.

Fertility also depended on intercourse frequency, which itself may have depended on certain social and economic factors: given that the physical discomforts and health risk of child-bearing and child-care costs were borne disproportionately by women, it stands to reason that men and women had different assessments of the costs of having sex and babies, and that what actually took place depended to some extent on the relative bargaining positions of husband and wife within the marriage and the threat point of the two partners (the point at which they can dissolve the household). Estimating such factors with any precision is of course impossible, but it seems implausible that they would remain totally unchanged for a century given the sea changes in the British economy and the changes in the economic position of women. It seems more likely that what we observe is the result of marital fertility being subject to contradictory forces that, to some extent, offset one another to create the appearance of constancy. Specifically, when economic forces favored female work, especially during the period of the early factory or in regions in which domestic work was still flourishing, women could earn decent incomes and would be in a better position to bargain with their husbands. As we shall see below (chapter 14), in the early nineteenth century the bargaining power of married women on the whole declined. Divorce was not a serious option, and the law made married women little more than possessions of their husbands. In any situation in which the partners disagreed on whether to have another child, the woman was less likely to carry the day.

The Wrigley–Schofield interpretation of British demographic history is that population growth after 1750 was driven in large part by nuptiality. The English experience was thus different from that of other European societies. In Sweden, for example, population growth was primarily driven by a decline in mortality, whereas in the Netherlands there was a surge in births after 1815 with only a moderate decline in death rates before 1850. In France, the experience was different again: fertility increased a little in the eighteenth century but then started to decline precipitously after 1815. Whatever population growth took place in France was largely the result of mortality change. The wide variety of experiences in Europe suggests that the mechanism that led to population growth was complex and operated differently in different countries. While the net results in the end were roughly the same—every European country experienced rapid population growth in the century between 1750 and 1850—clearly there was more than one factor at work.

Why did eighteenth-century nuptiality in Britain rise? Attempts to relate the propensity to marry to the behavior of real wages, through grain prices or other variables, have foundered on the rather undeniable fact that grain prices were low in the period 1700–1750—when population growth was slow—and high in the years of high fertility after 1750. If the high cost of living prevented people from starting families because they could not be sure they could feed the children that the union would produce, the actual pattern would be the reverse of what we observe. Population growth kept accelerating through the first decades of the nineteenth century (peaking around the expensive years during and right after the French and Napoleonic Wars), and just when real wages start trending upwards, in the 1840s, we observe a slowdown in nuptiality and birth rates.

A more sophisticated explanation relies on the changes in market opportunities for younger workers. In a world of farmers and artisans, a precondition for marriage was to get a hold of a piece of land, which required a young man to await the death of his father, or to be confirmed as a master of a craft, which required not only completing the various apprenticeship and journeyman requirements but also securing a workshop, the tools, and the customer connections. To be sure, those barriers would seem to constrain primarily *male*, not female ages of marriage, but if we make the not unreasonable assumption that the mean difference in the male and female ages at marriage reflected some social and biological constants, the two are correlated—as in fact they were. All the same, the difference between male and female ages at first marriage could have responded to economic conditions, and there seems to be no overwhelming reason why economic opportunities that primarily affected males should influence female behavior. Economic opportunities such as control of land or the right to exercise a craft were evidently household-wide factors, and thus affected the marriage ages of both genders in similar ways.

Some of the economic developments we have observed so far after 1700 and especially after 1750 indicate that these constraints were coming apart. The regulations that set up the strict requirements for craftsmen to undergo many years of apprenticeship were enforced less and less during the eighteenth century and more and more exceptions to them could be found. As was noted earlier, the mandated length of the period of apprenticeship was shortened. The nature of apprenticeship changed, and outdoor apprenticeship became more prevalent. Domestic industry expanded a great deal into low-skill full-time occupations, and permitted young couples to set up shop in a small cottage. This effect of proto-industrialization on demographic behavior was demonstrated in a famous study by David Levine (1977), who showed that in the village of Shepshed, Leicester-shire, where framework knitting was of considerable importance, women in the early nineteenth century married five and half years younger than their peasant ancestors in the seventeenth century. Others have made similar claims for other societies and have tried to connect eighteenth-century proto-industrialization with the demographic revolution (especially Mendels, 1972; Clarkson, 1985).

These models that linked cottage industries and demographic change were popular in the 1970s, but have come under criticism in recent decades. Some evidence has shown, for instance, that female lacemakers in Devon, who could earn cash by working at home, used their earnings to stay independent rather than commit to the earnings of a husband (Sharpe, 1991). In other parts of Britain, evidence suggests that the marriage age declined long before the eighteenth century, especially in the cloth-making areas. For young couples considering marriage, economic opportunities were all-important. Cottage industries, requiring little physical or human capital, provided one such opportunity. The availability of land, or steady agricultural employment, the decline of the strict limitations on apprenticeship, and the growing availability of employment for young lads that sufficed for them to eke out a living, all played a role in the decline in marriage age.

In the very long run the factory spelled the demise of domestic industry and when it declined and many formerly well-off rural workers fell on hard times, the demographic effects—at least among those who stayed in the countryside—must have worked in the direction of reducing marriage rates and fertility. However, paradoxically for the first decades of the Industrial Revolution, many cottage industries actually benefited from the technological changes in textiles and other industries. For every spinster displaced by a mule, there was a handloom weaver who benefited from cheap yarn and the booming demand for cotton cloth—as long as the power looms were still in their infancy. Cottage industries also provided an opportunity for young children to help generate cash by assisting their parents in their cottage industrial work, more than they could have in farming. The developments in agriculture reinforced this trend: the disappearance of yeomen —effectively peasant proprietors even if they did not formally "own" the land—and their replacement by an agricultural proletariat meant that any young lad and lass with the willingness and ability to work could reasonably hope to maintain a family with children. In Ireland, such opportunities were much more limited, but there the constraints on marriage were lifted by the diffusion of the potato and the subdivision of plots. A family could be sustained on a small plot of five to ten acres, which would produce enough potatoes to feed a family and maintain a pig or a cow that could then be sold off to secure the cash to pay the rent and purchase the few things the family needed from the market. Although the mechanism thus differed from that in England, both the Irish and the British experiences boiled down to a breaking down of the traditional economic constraints that had limited marriage. The hypothesis is often referred to as "proletarianization," as if that term meant something degrading and dehumanizing. But in fact it refers to a freedom and a set of options that a 20-year-old may not have had in 1600.

The factory system and the changes it implied reinforced this trend. Mines and mills employed youngsters from age 14 and often younger. By age 20 or so, they were fully trained and there was no reason they could not marry. Whereas marriage implied that the woman would have to leave gainful employment, this would soon be offset by the possibility of sending the children to work and to earn cash. It is unclear whether such anticipations actually encouraged people to marry younger than they otherwise would have. Industrialization led to urbanization, and people in cities tended to marry somewhat younger, but the differences in fertility behavior between urban and rural areas were not all that pronounced before 1850. Nevertheless, it seems probable that the money that children could generate played a role in parents' marriage behavior. This was even more pronounced, if conservative contemporaries are to be believed, in the effects of the Poor Law. Because the British Poor Law system from 1795 on provided relief that was specified in *real* terms (that is, payments were coupled to the price of bread), and in proportion to the number of persons in the household, Malthus and his followers thought that these laws created the poor they were supposed to maintain by encouraging behavior that was "imprudent and improvident." Their agitation was finally successful in 1834 with the reform of the Poor Law. Whether the effect of poor relief on fertility that Malthus so strongly believed in existed or not is still a matter of some dispute, but the econometric work of George Boyer (1990) has vindicated it, estimating that in the absence of the liberal poor relief, British population in the late 1820s might have been considerably smaller. It may or may not be a coincidence that the birth rate started to decline in the period after the Poor Law reform. In any case, it would seem odd if the poor and working classes paid no attention whatsoever to economic opportunities (whether employment or the dole) when making the decision to marry.

Economists have argued that technological change during the Industrial Revolution increased the rate of return on human capital and education. As we have seen, this may be true for some segments of the population, but it is far from obvious that it applied to all or even to most workers. If true, it implies that people would have preferred to have *smaller* families, in the parlance of economics, invest in the *quality* rather than the *quantity* of children: parents would choose to spend money on their children's education and training and on making sure that they were well fed and healthy (for example, Galor and Moav, 2002). Such theories seem plausible enough as a *long-run* consequence of the Industrial Revolution, but the trade-off between quality and quantity does require that families use birth control effectively, for which there is no evidence for the period in question, or use the marriage age as a substitute, which they obviously did not.

One of the most intriguing questions about the demographic behavior of British couples is the extent that contraception was practiced. Given human nature, in the absence of any fertility control the fertility rate depended on the age at marriage, the proportion of women ever married, and their fecundity. Fertility control allowed married couples to choose the number of children they preferred. Condoms were viewed primarily as a protection against venereal disease, and it attests to this age's embarrassment with them that they were called "French letters" in England and "la capote anglaise" in France. The willingness to use contraceptive devices was limited to sexual activity outside marriage, such as in brothels. Given the cost and the knowledge involved in practicing any kind of mechanical or chemical contraception, it was clearly confined to the better-off and educated class. Historians of contraception (e.g. McLaren, 1990, p. 154) have no doubt that Europeans understood the effectiveness of coitus interruptus, but there is simply little evidence whether it was used a great deal within marriage. One indicator that contraceptive technology did not expand all that much is a rise in the proportion of illegitimate births in the population. By the end of the seventeenth century only about 2 percent of all births were illegitimate; by the late eighteenth century this had tripled to 6 percent. It stands to reason that in extramarital intercourse the costs of an undesirable pregnancy were much higher so the incentives to prevent it were stronger. Of course, it could be the case that social customs and moral codes had changed to such an extent that even a tripling of illegitimacy is consistent with more contraception.

Some scholars, especially Edward Shorter (1971), have maintained that the age of Enlightenment was also the age of sexual liberation. Our knowledge of the population-wide behavior of Britons in this age has been enhanced a great deal by the work on parish registers, from which certain patterns can extracted with reasonable certainty. The assumption that has to be made to verify the conclusion, for instance, is that parents practiced "parity-dependent" fertility control, that is, that the number of children already present had a negative effect on fertility, given the parents' age. It is of course possible that fertility control took other forms, for instance uniformly widening the "spacing" between successive births. Ruling out the latter, the technique applied by Wrigley and Schofield allows them to conclude that family limitation was "restricted to a small minority of the population, if practiced at all" (Wrigley and Schofield, 1997, p. 461). The implications for formal economic models that depend on couples choosing consciously between quality and quantity are quite disturbing. Even couples who desired small families and high-quality offspring would have found it difficult to do so.

The role of rising birth rates in the demographic growth of Britain in this period had important implications for the operation of the economy. For one thing, it increased the number of "dependents" in the economy: in most economies of this time, the population aged 15–49 did most of the work, child labor notwith-standing. The higher the dependency ratio (the ratio of those not working to the total), the more infants, toddlers, and seniors depended on the labors of the people in the middle. The dependency ratio would be higher if population growth was "driven" by birth rates, since the incremental population all had to go through childhood, increasing dependency ratios. This ratio went from 815 in 1750 to a peak of 1,000 in 1826 and was still at 868 in 1850. Moreover, the higher nuptiality and birth rates imply that more women were pregnant, and while there is no pre-sumption that pregnant women were relieved of their duties, it seems plausible that their productivity was impaired around delivery and during nursing. The economic effects of a rise in the birth rates were compounded by the fact that for most of the eighteenth century there was little decline in infant mortality rates, with a dip only in the closing decades (Wrigley and Schofield, 1997, p. 215). Their failure to improve considerably, as we shall see below, was a result of urbanization and related phenomena.

*   *   *

The other part of the story of population growth is mortality. The most common and intuitive measure of the mortality rate of a society is life expectancy at birth. This measure is highly sensitive to changes in infant and child mortality and thus indirectly affected by the birth rate. In any case, life expectancy in England in the first half of the eighteenth century was already quite impressive by the standards of the time: the mean of the quinquennial observations computed by Wrigley and Schofield for the first fifty years of the eighteenth century is 34.2 years, less than half of what a person born in 2000 could expect, but better than what could be expected in Germany or Eastern Europe at the time, where life expectancy hovered around 30 years. Over the next half-century this figure did not move much, but by the 1820s it had reached about 40, where it stayed until the mid-1850s. Oddly, we see the same for death as we see for birth: the only period of real improvement are the hard decades of war and inflation between 1801 and 1821.

Demographic historians have provided a ready answer to this paradox: smallpox vaccination. The chance discovery of a country doctor in 1796 represented not only one of the more dramatic and discontinuous technological breakthroughs of the era of the Industrial Revolution but also a major demographic "event." Smallpox was primarily a major killer of infants and small children, but its demographic effects went beyond the raw number of people who died of it, since it weakened the immune system of those who recovered, and they often succumbed to secondary complications of other diseases (Mercer, 1990, p. 73). The London Bills of Mortality attributed more than 10 percent of all deaths in the 1760s and 1770s to smallpox, which had declined to 2.8 percent in the 1830s, while in Glasgow the proportion attributed to smallpox fell from 19.6 in the 1780s to 3.9 in 1807–12 (ibid., pp. 227, 230). All the same, the dilemma is real: if smallpox vaccination was such a dramatic event, why did infant mortality rates not decline more dramatically? One answer is that perhaps infant mortality would have *increased* had it not been for smallpox vaccination, due to urbanization and larger families. On the other hand, smallpox did not vanish altogether; vaccination was resisted by many doctors and religious leaders loath to introduce an animal substance into the sacred human body. Vaccinations were often administered incorrectly and the need for revaccination was not recognized. Consequently there were further outbreaks of the disease in the nineteenth century, and no comparable preventive technology for other infectious diseases was discovered for almost a century. Some "free riding" may have occurred: when a vaccination campaign is undertaken to stop a contagious disease, a single individual need not incur the cost and risk of being vaccinated if he supposes that enough others will be. Bavaria and the Scandinavian countries in fact made vaccination compulsory. In Britain, Parliament asked the Royal College of Physicians to organize vaccination and made it available free of charge. However, like so many of the technological breakthroughs of the time, the modus operandi of vaccination was not properly understood. All the same, the demographic impact of this one invention was highly significant.

Public health, however, had other trump cards up its sleeve even if they were not all aces. Before smallpox was conquered, Europe had successfully defeated the great medieval scourge, bubonic plague. By 1700, this disease had been eradicated in Britain, and its last appearance in Western Europe was in 1720 in Marseilles. The disease continued to appear in the Near East and in the Indian subcontinent, but in Europe tough public health measures, learned the hard way over many centuries, successfully eradicated it. The notions of public health and hygiene were becoming increasingly rooted in eighteenth-century British society. It may well be that many health-promoting habits became established for reasons other than conscious avoidance of disease. People may have wanted to have cleaner bodies and homes, learned not to spit in public, and to cook and eat healthier foods for reasons that had less to do with their impact on health than with social habits, mimicking the elite, or trying to look and behave differently from the lower classes. César de Saussure noted in 1726 that "English women and men are very clean: not a day passes by without their washing their hands, arms, faces, necks, and throats in cold water, and that in winter as well as in summer"(1902, p. 205). All the same, there seem to be clear signs that in the eighteenth century more and more people in Britain intuitively realized the possible connection between cleanliness and health and that efforts were made to improve public health as well. A leader in this movement was the Scottish military physician John Pringle (1707–82) who insisted on the importance of infection to the incidence of disease and the possibility to prevent infection by better hygiene (Riley, 1987). Physicians such as Pringle highlight one of the most interesting and potentially beneficial aspects of the Medical Enlightenment, namely a concern for public cleanliness and personal hygiene (Porter, 1997, p. 295). The problem was, as with so many of the policies aimed at improvement, that the details were not properly understood, and so many of the measures remained ineffective. The miasma theories of disease made some very helpful suggestions about sanitation, but also implied conveniently that it was in the public domain—streets, back yards, rivers, and sewers—that reform and regulation were most needed, and not the more difficult to penetrate sphere of the domestic homemakers. Sanitation and sewage disposal required engineering skills, and these Britain had like no other. In 1775 the first modern valve closet was patented, and the engineer Joseph Bramah perfected the water closet at about the same time. By 1830 toilets were widely used in London. Numerous problems had still to be overcome, but both the demand and the capability were there.

Yet clinical medicine and public health, like so many other technological avenues, were constrained by knowledge and money. The Enlightenment hope that life could be improved by better knowledge and by improved public policies and individual behavior based on it remained limited by best-practice under-standing of what made people sick. Before 1850, for instance, it was not under-stood that water that looked, tasted, and smelled clean could all the same be a carrier of deadly disease. Evil-smelling refuse had to be removed from people's yards, where its smell was believed to make them ill—so it was dumped into rivers from which people then drew their drinking water. The idea that it was insects and not bad air that carried the microscopic causes of malaria and typhus was not dis-covered until the 1890s.

There is at least one tantalizing piece of evidence suggesting that something beside money was a constraint. Studies of the life expectancy of the peerage, the rich elite of British society, and the royal family show that while in the sixteenth and seventeenth centuries, life expectancy for both rich and poor in Britain hovered between the mid- and upper thirties, by 1800 a gap of nine years had opened up between the two (Hollingsworth, 1977; Ryan-Johansson, 2006). Even a peer with unlimited financial resources could expect to live only to the age of about 48 in 1800. But the gap that had opened up is highly significant. It seems that by 1800 society as a whole had learned something about how to prevent a few of the worst diseases, but clearly the fruits of this knowledge, or the resources to take advantage of it, were largely confined to the rich.

This finding is corroborated by the large body of anthropometric research that tries to infer living standards and economic welfare from evidence on stature.

While the exact interpretation of height data is still a matter of some controversy, there is little doubt that young lads from rich families were substantially taller than those from working-class families (Floud, Wachter, and Gregory, 1990, pp. 163–75). This inequality was earlier attributed to better net nutritional intake, but by now it is well understood that differential susceptibility to disease was an important factor as well. It is also possible that the decline of pandemic diseases such as the plague and the transformation of some pandemic diseases into endemic ones (e.g., smallpox) implies that social and economic factors became more significant in avoiding disease and helped create an income gradient in morbidity and mortality (Kunitz and Engerman, 1992, p. 32). Whatever the case may be, there is no question that by 1800 having access to resources meant substantially improved health, and hence a longer life expectancy. The exact extent to which this difference can be attributed to differences in access to *knowledge* (either by the family itself or by consultants such as physicians and pharmacists) remains unknown, but it stands to reason that a better understanding of some factors associated with infectious disease emerged in this period, even if the exact mechanisms were still unknown. This knowledge started with the rich and the well-educated, and trickled down only very slowly to the working class.

By the end of the eighteenth century, the better-educated parts of British society had learned that infection was exacerbated by crowded living conditions and filth, that country living was healthier than living in urban areas, and that breast-feeding was healthier for babies than solid food. For the others who could afford it, hiring wet-nurses made life easy. Many of the ingredients of consumption that extended life, above all less congested housing and improved nutrition, were costly, and not an option for much of the working class. Clinical medicine was probably out of reach for the majority of the population; however, it remains in doubt by how much it would have increased their life expectancy had it been more widely available. To be sure, people had learned that a few medicines and procedures worked. The prescriptions implied by the growing awareness of the causes of diseases were, however, expensive, and thus confined largely to the well-to-do. Moreover, apart from smallpox vaccination (which was free), few of these had much impact on mortality, and some others such as the widely used "blue pills" of calomel (mercurous chloride) and a variety of antimony-based purgatives were probably outright toxic.

One of the many things that the English did in the eighteenth century that enhanced their health was to get addicted to tea. Tea is known to have certain bactericidal properties, but the main mechanism may have been that the water had to boil—thus killing many of the dangerous organisms that lived in the drinking water of Britain, unsuspected by most consumers. Yet observant contemporaries had an inkling that such may have been the case: Lord Kames wrote in 1788 that the decline of the great pestilences was caused by "the great consumption of tea and sugar, which I am told by physicians to be no inconsiderable antiseptics" (Kames, 1788, Vol. I, p. 324n). John Coakley Lettsom, who was more skeptical, actually conducted experiments examining the wholesome properties of tea. Others disagreed, but whether they were pro-tea such as Dr Johnson or anti (such as Arthur Young), all agreed that it was very widely consumed in all layers of British society, including the poor. The same is true, at least up to a point, for beer and ale, which were safer to drink than water despite their high costs, and contained hops, which had bacteriostatic properties (MacFarlane, 1997, p. 130). Other substances that higher incomes made affordable were far less salubrious: tobacco-smoking became firmly entrenched in the population, and the gin mania of the 1740s and 1750s, immortalized in Hogarth's famous engraving *Gin Lane*, is suspected to have contributed to the high mortality rates in London in the middle of the eighteenth century. One substance that was cheap enough to be used widely by the population at large was laudanum, an alcoholic tincture of opium. As it was not taxed and was highly effective as a palliative and anti-diarrhea drug, it became highly popular. Some well-known figures such as Coleridge and Byron were addicted to laudanum and its long-term effect on the health of the heavy user was quite harmful.

The idea that public health is one of those uncomfortable concepts that spans both the private and public spheres was slowly dawning on Britain during this period. The notion was uninformed as yet by either data or an understanding of disease. It was supported by an intuitive sense that in order to conquer disease more should be known, and that if hygiene in the public realm was of paramount importance, public policies supporting it had to be formulated. By the early nineteenth century public health was slowly coming into its own, culminating in the work of Edwin Chadwick, William Farr, and their colleagues in the 1830s and 1840s, who carefully documented the incidence of diseases and tried to unearth their correlates as long as they were unsure about their causes. It may seem to us that public health would be difficult to achieve in an age that still had not yet grasped that most infectious diseases were caused by microbes. Yet the age of Enlightenment developed another tool that allowed its experts to draw conclusions about what made people ill and how to avoid it. That tool was statistics. Probability theory had emerged in the eighteenth century as part of an attempt by philosophers and mathematicians to understand what reasonable individuals would do under uncertainty. They focused on the study of individuals rather than societies as a whole. This tendency changed in the early nineteenth century, when the study of large groups became respectable. In Daston's formulation, the *homme moyen* replaced the *homme éclairé* (Daston, 1988, p. 298). Although continental thinkers were at the forefront of this movement, it soon spilled over to Britain.

Early Victorian Britain witnessed the transformation of eighteenth-century political arithmetic into a body of knowledge which combined a quantitative approach with public policy. The 1830s witnessed the founding of many statistical societies, which soon developed an inordinate interest in medical and sanitary issues. Combining data collection with a zeal for social reform, men such as William Farr, James Kay-Shuttleworth, Neil Arnott, Southwood Smith, and above all Edwin Chadwick played an essential role in the diffusion of life-extending knowledge in the earliest stages of this movement in the 1820s and 1830s. The rhetorical power of statistics was tremendous. Chadwick's famous 1842 report, "a masterpiece of persuasion, subtly blending fact and fiction," is only one example of this power (Cullen, 1975, p. 56). It preached, above all, public reforms in the area of water supply, waste removal, cleaner air, less congestion, and similar measures aimed at improvement in sanitary conditions. Informed by a growing statistical sense, medical practices and household technology began to re-examine age-old beliefs and practices, including child care, drinking water purity, hygiene, and nutrition on the basis of large samples. Chadwick was clearly aware that "domestic mismanagement" as he called it was a "predisposing cause of disease." He cited with approval a set of reports that maintained that workers' wages would have been sufficient to supply the domestic comforts that would keep them in good health, but that these funds were spent "viciously or improvidently" and that "thoughtless extravagance" prevailed in their consumption habits (Chadwick [1843], 1965, pp. 204–05). Although Chadwick's work may have been theoretically flawed, his use of statistics lent his report the kind of persuasive power that social reformers needed. By mid-century, the sanitary movement had gathered enormous momentum.

The statistical methods allowed the sanitary movement to discern empirical regularities in epidemiology and public health even without much underlying knowledge or supporting theory. Chadwick and his colleagues used statistics to confirm the "miasmatic" or "environmentalist" theories of disease which—in the Hippocratic tradition—viewed foul air as the main source of infection, an approach consistent with the dominant medical paradigm of the time. The "miasmatic" theory (which held that infectious disease was spread by bad air), not unlike phlogiston theory in chemistry, was quite successful in explaining many of the observations known at the time, and by the time of the Industrial Revolution its implication that dirt was a source of disease was gaining ground. Its adherents gradually persuaded society that a strong correlation existed between disease and living conditions. Such statistical relations were often regarded as a sufficient basis for inferring causal connections and making direct life-extending recommendations. Miasma theorists correctly noted for example the connection between standing water and diarrhea and between excess heat and cold and the resistance to disease. It had an "unwitting effect ... by cleansing the habitat of breeding and feeding sites [their proposed measures] must have substantially reduced the pest population" (Riley, 1987, pp. 152–53). At least as far as airborne diseases are concerned, miasma theory was quite useful, especially because it recognized that traces of contagious miasmas could linger for extended periods and cause diseases with long time lags (Frank, [1786], 1976, p. 442).

Despite—and in some part because of—these ideas, life expectancy in the eighteenth century stayed more or less constant, and rose only in the early nineteenth century before stabilizing again. For one thing, improvement was slow because at the outset Britain was already a clean and healthy society compared to the Continent. Contemporary travelers, such as François de la Rochefoucauld, who visited Britain in 1784, noted the marked difference in cleanliness between the common people of England and the poor peasants of France, though he suspected that some of it was more for show than genuine ([1784], 1988, p. 33). Lord Kames, who noted the same thing, explicitly related cleanliness to industriousness and higher income (1788, Vol. 1, pp. 327–29). Such impressions are of course anecdotal, and do not adjust for differences in income. But the infant mortality statistics, such as they are, for the eighteenth century, show the same thing: they were substantially lower in Britain than anywhere on the Continent: in the second half of the eighteenth century they averaged about 165 per 1,000, compared to as high as 200 in Sweden and 273 in France. The most plausible explanation of low infant mortality was the prevalence of breast-feeding, mentioned above, as breast-fed children had a much lower mortality rate in their first year of life. Reducing infant mortality rates below the British levels of around 165 would prove to be difficult in a society that was already fairly highly urbanized and was rapidly becoming more so.

Moreover, the daily living environment in eighteenth- and early nineteenth-century Britain was unhealthy by our standards. Like most European societies, Britain was full of animals: pigs, chickens, and dogs ran freely around human dwellings, and the countryside (as well as many small towns) was full of cows and sheep, to say nothing of omnipresent horses. Animals produced energy, productivity, and wealth; but they also spread infectious diseases, attracted insects, and were a source of filth widely bemoaned by contemporaries. The unwholesome effects of animals were compounded by air pollution. Thanks to their superior transportation system and their wealth, Britons did not have to shiver in the cold damp winters—but they accomplished this by burning large amounts of coal. The great seventeenth-century diarist John Evelyn in his famous *Fumifugium* ([1661], 1772) spoke of a "hellish and dismal cloud of Sea-coale" hanging over London, "causing her inhabitants to breathe an impure and thick mist, accompanied with a fuliginous and filthy vapour which renders them obnoxious to a thousand inconveniences, corrupting the Lungs, and disordering the entire habit of their Bodies; so that Catharrs, Phthisicks, Coughs, and Consumptions, rage more in this one City, than in the whole Earth besides." Whether this pollution was more harmful to health than shivering in cold homes is of course an open question.

Public health was constrained by institutions. The idea of public health was taking shape in the eighteenth century, but measures to improve it required coordination: there is no point in me clearing my yard of unhealthy refuse unless my neighbors do so as well. Such coordination can come from a variety of institutions (shame, fear of punishment), but the most likely outcome is what economists would call a coordination failure, in which nobody cleans because they expect nobody else to do so. On the Continent, the solution to this problem was embodied in the idea of establishing a "medical police" (proposed by the eighteenth-century German doctor and hygienist Johann Peter Frank), a government agency in charge of public health. Britain, individualistic and increasingly suspicious of government intervention, did relatively little in this area, precisely when its rapid urbanization rate suggested that it should have done more. Institutional failure got in the way even when the little knowledge available suggested certain public policies. As one historian of medicine sighed, "Parliament left London's Salubrity to the city; and the City passed the buck to the parishes, which were mesmerized by the Poor Law philosophy of individual entitlement to relief" (Porter, 1991, p. 63). In the absence of much decisive action by the state, in Britain private order organizations, emerging spontaneously in fairly tightly networked local communities, at times overcame these collective action problems and contributed materially to bring about local solutions.

Comparing what people at the time knew with what we do, while satisfying to our predilection for modernist smugness, is not very helpful in understanding what factors drove the mortality rate of the age. Yet knowledge mattered. It would be easy to make a list of all the things medical science did *not* know about infectious disease and that were discovered only later in the nineteenth century. Among those was the danger that drinking water posed even when it looked and tasted clean—discovered in about 1850 by doctors examining the incidence of cholera and typhoid fever in British towns. It was realized that diseases were airborne—though the *modus operandi* of airborne substances, or "miasmas," was never made precise. It was as yet unsuspected that insects could also transmit disease, that surgical instruments and the unwashed hands of surgeons could be responsible for post-surgical fevers, that tuberculosis could be passed on by contaminated milk. As damaging as ignorance was were things that people —including best-practice medicine—knew that weren't so, to paraphrase Josh Billings's famous dictum. Bloodletting was still a widely used practice, and only in the 1840s did careful numerical studies establish what seems so commonplace to us, that the practice has no discernible curative power on infectious disease beyond placebo effects. The indiscriminate use of laxatives, emetics, and opiates aggravated conditions more than it relieved them. Children with food poisoning often succumbed to dehydration because their mothers were urged to withhold liquids. The obsession of the age with ventilation, inspired by the fear of "bad airs," probably did more harm than good.

The long-term stability of mortality rates should not be interpreted as evidence that few things were changing, but was largely the result of counteracting forces that to an extent offset one another. The favorable influence of advances in knowledge and the rise in income on mortality and the health of the population was offset until deep into the nineteenth century by urbanization. Cities had always been very unhealthy places to live in. Before 1700, most European cities experienced higher death rates than birth rates, and thus depended on a constant influx of immigrants from the countryside. With the rapid increase in urban population after 1750, the situation became rapidly worse: congestion, crowding, inadequate water supply, appalling sewerage facilities, and bad food all led to very high mortality and morbidity rates in the new urban centers. Perhaps the worst pressure was on water supply, with industrialization and growing population creating increasing pressure on available supplies. Slaughterhouses, tanneries, and bleachworks appeared on river banks, and springs and ponds were obliterated by building activity (Hassan, 1985, p. 532). Demographers speak of an "urban penalty"—the cost in terms of health and life expectancy of urbanization (Williamson, 1990). The new towns and neighborhoods built as a result of industrialization were famously ugly, unhealthy and depressing. Indeed, in many urban areas there was a marked deterioration in public health and urban life expectancy may have declined in some periods in the nineteenth century (Szreter and Mooney, 1998). Residential segregation of classes was common, and housing for working classes was supplied by overcrowded and shoddily constructed buildings in neighborhoods near dockside areas, mills, and warehouses in industrial zones, or in undesirable parts of commercial suburbs.

Computations based on mid-nineteenth-century data confirm these gaps even if by that time the worst was over. The crude death rate for rural England and Wales in 1841 was 20.4 per thousand; in urban areas it was 26 per thousand, and in the four largest cities it was 27.3. These numbers are only rough indicators. Birth rates in cities were somewhat higher than in the countryside, which would tend to push death rates there up further because of high infant mortality —especially in towns. On the other hand, cities tended to attract migrants from the countryside who were disproportionately in the 15–30 age bracket and had relatively low mortality rates in the country. Unlike the towns of the sixteenth and seventeenth century, however, England's towns in this period were not suffering from natural population deficits. Williamson has calculated that the urban population growth, which was about 2.2 percent per annum between 1776 and 1851, was jointly fed by natural growth and immigration, with immigration accounting for about 60 percent and natural growth about 40 percent in the 1770s; these ratios reversed in the 1840s (Williamson, 1990, pp. 26–27). There were, however, clearly different types of cities. The industrial towns of Liverpool and Manchester were by far the worst, and in a way atypical: life expectancy in them in the 1850s was estimated at 31 and 32 years respectively, whereas in Sheffield and Birmingham it was 36 and 37 years and in London 38 years—all of them well below the national average of 41 years (Szreter and Mooney, 1998, p. 87). Older market and cathedral towns grew at a slower pace and suffered fewer public health problems, and hence had better life expectancies, yet even they were less healthy than the countryside.

Cities were thus still death traps in the early nineteenth century and the view that they were becoming less so over time before 1870 seems inconsistent with the evidence (Szreter and Mooney, 1998, p. 102). Infant mortality was a high price for urbanization. From the point of view of society as a whole (to say nothing of the emotions of mothers), infant mortality is wasteful because society has to pay the costs of the mother's foregone earnings during pregnancy, delivery and post-partum, yet if the child dies in infancy there is no payback (which in an inter-generational context occurs when the child grows up and pays for its own children). The trend in infant mortality has been fairly well established on the basis of the parish records. British rates fell in the second half of the eighteenth century, but rather than a trend of improvement, the computations show that this decline was largely a recovery, after a sharp increase in infant mortality in the 1710–50 period compared to the earlier half-century. By the end of the eighteenth century, infant mortality had declined back to about 160–165 per thousand, about where it had been in the mid-seventeenth century. In the following decades, however, infant mortality fell below that level to around 140, until about 1825, after which it rose slightly, hovering around 150. After 1838, when the Registrar General began to collect this information, the rates remained around 150–160 per thousand—a level that changed little for the rest of the nineteenth century.

The regional data show substantial differences, however: London rates in the eighteenth century were as high as 350–400 per thousand. In the mid-nineteenth century, in the rural southern counties rates were often under 100 per thousand births, whereas in the industrial cities of the north, infant mortality rates could be considerably higher. Poor urban areas were especially tough on infants, and infant mortality rates in those regions were substantially higher than elsewhere (Huck, 1994), the gap between the low and high infant mortality regions exceeding the ratio 1:2 (Wrigley and Schofield, 1997, pp. 270–71). Childhood mortality shows similar gaps: in the 1840s it was 252 for rural England, but 341 in "large" (mostly industrial) towns (Woods, 2000, p. 369). Doubts about registration of both the numerator and the denominator in these computations and the problem of aggre-gating the unhealthy inner cities with the better environment of suburbs suggest caution in using these figures, but the basic conclusion, that by 1840 this variable had fallen as far as it was going to fall in the nineteenth century, and that urban areas were considerably less healthy for small children than rural areas, will survive any corrections.

In addition to the standard explanations of environment and nutrition, histo-rical demographers have found that a pivotal variable determining infant mortality was lactation habits: children were especially at risk of disease and death during and right after weaning. Contemporaries were aware of the advantages of breast-feeding even if they were unsure why and how these arose. The English physician and follower of Sydenham, Hans Sloan (1661–1753), noted that the ratio of mor-tality of dry-nursed to wet-nursed children was 3:1. When the London lying-in hospital made breast-feeding compulsory in the late eighteenth century, infant mortality fell by 60 percent (Garrison, 1929, p. 402). From the middle of the eighteenth century physicians strongly advised against artificial feeding if maternal milk was available. It stands to reason that a greater reliance on breast-feeding and somewhat better hygienic knowledge helped offset the greater risks to babies in an urban environment.

All in all, the country-wide mortality rate was subject to two different sets of influences. On the one hand, slowly increasing medical knowledge, improved public health, better transportation and food-processing technology, and slowly changing breast-feeding customs were working to bring down mortality rates. But because urban death rates were intrinsically higher than rural ones, and because the proportion of the population living in cities was increasing and expanding much faster than cities could expand the infrastructure that would maintain their health, the overall mortality rate (and its close relative, life expectancy at birth) showed relatively little improvement (Williamson, 1990). What needs to be considered, then, is what happened to the distribution of population between rural and urban centers, and across different regions.

*   *   *

Internal migration of population did not start with the Industrial Revolution. People in pre-1750 Britain did move around, despite the widespread complaints, discussed above, about the effects of the Settlement Acts. When all is said and done, the British Poor Law was a better coordinated system than the purely local systems on the European Continent, and thus by comparison encouraged migration, offering new immigrants more assurance that they would be supported if they needed it, provided they were not evicted and sent back. By comparison with much of the European Continent, the citizens of Britain were free to move around in their country without asking for permission from the police or the local landowner, without the hassles of border controls, enjoying as we have seen increasingly convenient and reliable means of transportation.

In any case, changes in population distribution over the entire period were remarkable, and although we cannot disentangle with great precision the differences in natural growth from the effects of migration, the latter clearly played a dominant role. Table 13.2 shows that the east and the south-west consistently lost population and that the north, south-east (including London), and to a lesser extent the Midlands were the gainers in the process. The counties that were already commercial and industrial in 1701 increased their share from around a third at the beginning of the eighteenth century to over 40 percent in 1801, to almost half in 1851. In those eight counties in the north and Midlands in which industrial growth was the fastest, population increased from 21.7 percent in 1700 to 29.3 percent in 1801 to 34.6 percent in 1851. For a region to increase its *share* of population required it to have high birth rates and immigration rates. On a smaller scale, such immigration also took place in Scotland, where the industrializing Lowland counties absorbed a continuous flow of migrants from the Highlands.

Paradoxically, most labor mobility was short-distance. This does not mean that no long-distance migration occurred, since people moved and then moved again, and in any case, even short-distance migration can in the long run lead to cumulative changes in the distribution of the population of the country as a whole. The Industrial Revolution was a highly regional affair; most of the mills were located in a small number of fairly small regions: cotton in Lancashire and Lanarkshire, wool in the West Riding of Yorkshire, pottery in Staffordshire, silk in Cheshire, hardware and the metal trade in the Birmingham region and the adjacent Black Country, steel in Sheffield. These regions relied primarily on labor from the surrounding areas, not from the agricultural south. What is also striking about the economic development of Britain is the relative unimportance of London in the industrialization process. London was huge: in 1750, it was still more than ten times as large as the next largest town in England (Bristol). London also absorbed many immigrants: it has been estimated that between 1701 and 1831, no fewer than 1.3 million people migrated to London, but the high mortality rates in the city meant that natural increase was negative (in the eighteenth century) or low (in the nineteenth), so that the relative size of London in the British economy changed but little.

Some historians (Wrigley, 1967) have ascribed to London a major role in creating the conditions leading to the Industrial Revolution. The size of London relative to England's population and its enormous needs in terms of food, fuel, and other products seem to support his claim. Sheer size, however, is not necessarily an advantage. A top-heavy capital might just as well be viewed as imposing a major cost on the country. The argument seems better suited to explain commercial development before 1750 than industrial development thereafter. During the Industrial Revolution, indeed, the demographic predominance of London declined somewhat. Between 1650 and 1750, London's share of the English population rose from about 7 percent to 11.8 percent. By 1800 this had declined to 10.5 percent. London was growing, but the rest of the country was growing faster. Some of the industrial towns were growing at rates that were nothing short of astounding, above all Manchester which turned from a sleepy little town of under 10,000 people in 1700 to a hefty 75,000 in 1801 and an astounding 303,000 in 1851. Glasgow went from 13,000 in 1700 to 77,000 in 1801, to 345,000 in 1851. Birmingham, the center of the hardware enterprise, similarly attracted migrants, growing from 7,000 people in 1700 to 69,000 in 1800 and 233,000 in 1851. London's growth could not match these rates in large part because it was already so disproportionately large in 1700, with 575,000 inhabitants.

It would be wrong to underestimate the importance of London in the economic development of Britain; it was by far the largest town in Britain through our entire period, with the largest concentration of consumers. It was also a major industrial town in which much of Britain's beer was brewed, its silk thrown and woven, its books printed, and many of the sophisticated machine tools made by Bramah, Maudslay, and their colleagues were first conceived and built there. Yet it is striking how European industrialization in the nineteenth century seems to have

Table 13.2: Regional distribution of population, England and Wales, 1700–1850 (per cent)

	1701	1751	1781	1801	1831	1851
By region:						
South-west	15.6	14.8	13.1	12.5	11.7	10.1
South-east	23.9	23.8	23.9	24.9	25.8	26.0
East	16.1	14.4	13.9	12.6	9.9	10.9
Midlands	20.2	20.8	21.7	21.3	21.6	21.1
North	17.7	19.2	20.7	22.6	25.0	26.8
Wales	6.6	6.8	6.6	6.1	6.0	5.1
Total	100	100	100	100	100	100
By main occup.[a]						
Primarily agricultural	33.4	31.9	31.0	28.5	26.3	24.3
Primarily manufact.-commercial	33.5	36.7	38.1	41.1	45.0	48.8
Mixed	33.0	31.4	30.9	30.4	28.8	27.0
Total	100	100	100	100	100	100

[a] As determined by Deane and Cole (1969).

Sources: Deane and Cole (1969, p. 103); Mitchell (1988, pp. 30–31).

skirted around the great capitals of Europe: neither Paris, nor Vienna, nor Madrid, nor Berlin, nor St Petersburg became a large industrial town; instead, new industrial regions developed in the north of France, Flanders, Bohemia, Saxony, and the Rhineland, in provincial towns such as Mulhouse and Liège, former powerhouses that had long ago fallen on hard times like Ghent, or entirely new urban centers such as Tilburg and Essen. In Britain, the rise of previously minor towns like Manchester and Birmingham was nothing less than spectacular. These cities provided a unique economic environment. They were relatively open to new ideas, free of regulatory shackles, politically heterodox, competitive, and acquisitive: the very embodiment of Enlightenment ideals. Manchester's modest origins may have been a substantial advantage, as the city was encumbered by few of the fetters and traditions of older towns with more established institutions. The weakness of trading associations and vested interests meant that the environment was more innovation-friendly and that its labor force lacked an organizational focus for effective resistance to innovation. Yet Manchester notwithstanding, southern Lancashire in 1770 was not yet the urban area it was to become shortly. Comparing it with Bristol and the west counties is revealing here: in 1750, Manchester's population was only 40 percent of Bristol's; in 1841, Manchester was twice as large. Bristol seems, on the surface, to be admirably located, close to mining areas of South Wales and the textile areas of the West Country and awash in profits from the Atlantic trade that could have been invested in modern manufacturing. And yet, although Bristol retained some importance as a banking and commercial center, it did not establish itself as a center of new industrial technology and its relative decline was partially due to the decline of its hinterland.

The rise of cities was, for better or for worse, ultimately one of the indirect and unintended outcomes of the Industrial Enlightenment, which set in motion a chain of technological events that in the end began to affect not only how and how long but also where people lived. There is some historical irony in that, since the Enlightenment was itself primarily an urban phenomenon. Yet the commercial and administrative towns in which the ideas of the Enlightenment first emerged were quite different from the manufacturing towns spawned by the Industrial Revolution. In these pre-industrial centers pollution and unhealthy environments were caused by home heating and human and animal refuse, not the by-products of manufacturing.

The exact connections between urbanization and the economic changes of this age are quite subtle. It might be thought that large factories would be concentrated in urban areas, but in fact it was more often the medium and small firms that required an urban location, since they depended on economies of agglomeration more than large businesses. Ancillary services such as banking, insurance, and large commercial enterprises also preferred to be located in towns because communications and transportation were better there. Other agglomeration economies that cities provided were, above all, lower access costs. If firms needed technical advice or support, they could draw on larger pools of knowledge. Sophisticated and highly educated workers often seek the proximity of others like themselves whose skills may complement their own. As Hohenberg and Lees (1985, p. 201) put it, "in every city, cafes served as the real place of business for journalists, stock jobbers, *littérateurs*, impresarios, and politicians." In that sense, the kind of agglomeration economies we see today in Silicon Valley could already be seen in embryonic form in London and some of the other industrial towns of the nineteenth century.

Internal migration was already quite substantial by 1850, in part because by that time railroads were in place and the Settlement Acts had been repealed. By 1851, of the close to 1.4 million adults (aged 20 and over) in London, only 645,000 were born in London proper, whereas tens of thousands had come to London from areas as far apart as Scotland (26,000) and Devon (32,000). Of the 1.12 million people over age 20 enumerated in Lancashire in the 1851 census, no fewer than 413,000 had come from other counties. Of those, 139,000 were from Ireland, 61,000 from neighboring Yorkshire, and 51,000 from Cheshire. In Scotland, of the 1.56 million people over age 20, 187,000 were born elsewhere, mostly in Ireland (147,000). In the less industrialized counties, the proportion of immigrants was of course smaller: in Devon, of the population of 319,000 people over age 20, 82 percent were born in the county and another 8 percent came from the neighboring counties of Cornwall and Somerset.

Overseas emigration from Britain before 1850 was of secondary demographic importance. During the eighteenth century Britons migrated to Australia or America, some of them as convicts, others as indentured servants who paid their fares by contracting themselves to work in America. There is no doubt that Britain lost some enterprising and able lads that way, but compared with the mass migrations of the second half of the nineteenth century, or the human hemorrhage suffered after 1840 by Ireland, these numbers were as yet not very significant. A rough estimate of the total number of English emigrants leaving Britain for the United States between 1700 and 1820 is about 1,125,000 or slightly over 9,300 a year, which comes to about 0.1 percent per year, which is a small proportion from a demographic point of view. In the three decades after 1820, the number of emigrants to the United States was about 370,000, but most of those left in the 1840s, when emigration from Britain rises sharply. Because the population was growing as well, the proportional rate of emigration grew much less. Even during the large outflows of the late 1840s, emigration from Great Britain came to about 50,000 per year, or about 0.3 percent by 1851.

By that time, however, the emigration of Britons to North America and other overseas possessions was more than offset by the influx of Irish immigrants into Britain. The collapse of domestic industries in Ireland in the 1830s was swift and brutal, and migration of workers to England and Scotland was widespread. After 1845, of course, this flow was increased by the exodus of Famine refugees. Were Irish immigrants an important supplement to the British labor force during the Industrial Revolution? One economic historian, Sidney Pollard, referred to these emigrants as "the mobile shock troops of the Industrial Revolution" (Pollard 1978, p. 113), but more sophisticated computations have questioned the importance of the Irish workers to British industrialization. Williamson's (1990) calculations have concluded that the main impact of Irish immigration was on agricultural output, as it slowed down the migration of British rural workers from the countryside to the cities. It should be kept in mind, however, that the Irish tended to concentrate in certain sectors and industries, such as mining, construction, and transportation, and in these industries their labor made substantial contributions. Indeed, by carrying out low-skilled, menial, and unpleasant work, the Irish probably were of considerable significance, comparable in some ways to the guest workers in Western Europe in the second half of the twentieth century. On the aggregate level, however, there is little reason to attribute a great deal of quantitative importance to immigration, simply because the number of Irish in Britain, though considerable, was just not large enough to make a decisive impact on Britain's economy. It is estimated that in 1841 there were 830,000 "effective Irish" in Britain, of whom 415,000 were Irish born and the rest descendants of Irish emigrants. If we assume that all the emigrants and half of the descendants were in the labor force, the Irish would have added 620,000 workers, which out of a total occupied labor force of about 6.8 million would have amounted to about 9 percent; this figure should be augmented by the tens of thousands of seasonal migrants who crossed the Irish Sea for a few months each year. The Irish workers were thus not a trivial addition, but not large enough to change the economic parameters dramatically.

*   *   *

Was there a relation between population growth and eighteenth-century economic development? The fact that population began to grow rapidly in the 1750s at the very time that technological progress began to accelerate in a few key sectors seems too close to be dismissed as a coincidence. But which way did the causality run? The argument that the causality ran from technological innovation to population growth seems untenable. The timing is simply wrong. As already noted, before 1830 the sectors affected by mechanization accounted for only a modest part of the economy. Moreover, it is hard to see how industrialization in Derbyshire or Yorkshire would influence population growth in, say, the rural south of England. Furthermore, the very fact that the one country in Europe that matched British population growth in the period 1750–1845 was Ireland, where the Industrial Revolution made few inroads, is enough to dispel the notion that population growth was affected by technological progress. That observation, however, is not enough to disconnect demographic change from economic growth altogether. Yet how precisely the connection worked remains the subject of a large literature, which is as fascinating as it is inconclusive.

What about the reverse direction? Much recent research seems to conclude that population growth somehow stimulated and enhanced technological progress (Galor, 2005). One mechanism that would imply such a connection is proposed by Kremer (1993), who argues that a larger population implied the emergence of more new ideas. By that logic, the Industrial Revolution should have occurred in eighteenth-century China. Other models are more sophisticated and propose a variety of scale effects that may explain faster economic development. Thus Galor and Weil (2000) suggest that population growth made human capital more valuable, leading to an improvement in the quality and not just the quantity of workers. Other models suggest that there were fixed costs in technological progress that can only be covered if the market is large enough, or risks that can be diversified only in a large-scale economy. While some of those notions seem apt for post-1870 growth, they do not fit the environment of eighteenth-century Britain. The economic and technological changes were propelled by a relatively small minority, a technological elite of dexterous and clever men. The size of the overall pool from which they were drawn may have been important to some extent, but it is hard to see it as a first-order effect. The Enlightenment, after all, did not reach all the way down to the laboring classes either. It did not have to. That is what "leadership" was all about. Quantity counted for little unless it was accompanied by quality.

Yet more can be said. In an innovative paper Lin (1995) has proposed that technological change could be related to population size if the sources of innovation were predominantly experience-based, that is to say, new technology emerged as a by-product of the production of goods and were thus first and foremost a function of numbers and size. In such a learning-by-doing world, population size (not its *rate of growth*) could be an asset, assuming that the information gathered by experience, or its fruits, disseminated through the entire economy, and that the economies were closed so that each economy was on its own as far as learning was concerned—both rather unrealistic assumptions. In open economies size matters little. Britain's unique strength was to learn, copy, imitate, and improve ideas made by others. Eighteenth-century Britain fell somewhere between the Netherlands and China in terms of openness and size, but its population *size* (much less its rate of growth) was at best a distinctly second-order cause of economic development. In any event, whatever scale effects may have existed in such pre-industrial societies disappeared when the process of invention started to depend less on experience and more on useful knowledge gathered through observation, experimentation, and theory, whether "scientific" or not, by a small minority of specialists. By the eighteenth century this transition was well on its way, and by the middle of the nineteenth century sheer population size of each economy began to matter less and less at exactly the time when technological change was accelerating. The fact that von Liebig was German and Lord Kelvin British actually mattered very little; what mattered was that both countries were able to take advantage of the totality of useful knowledge generated in the Western world.

While the almost simultaneity of the collapse of the Malthusian world and the beginning of the Industrial Revolution seems too close to be sheer coincidence, a convincing mechanism linking the two causally remains to be found. Perhaps they were linked to a third factor that explains both. As we have seen, the Enlightenment did affect death rates to some extent through some medical advances and improvements in public health and personal hygiene, but were these effects by themselves large enough as a full explanation of the sudden take-off in population? We are on safer ground, however, with the weak counterfactual that *without* the Industrial Revolution and changes in technology, population growth would have collided with a Malthusian wall at some point in the nineteenth century and Britain would have had to channel more and more resources toward food production. While that does not "explain" the population growth, it tells us why demographic change could be sustained.

CHAPTER 14

Gender and Family in an Enlightened Economy

Enlightenment thought was much concerned with women, children, and the family, but on this matter it did not reach many definite conclusions that would strike us as very "enlightened." The issues of women's position in the family and their political and intellectual rights were widely discussed, but it is unclear whether by the end of the period the overall position of women in society and the economy had greatly improved relative to 1700. Indeed, one of the great paradoxes of the time is that the age of Enlightenment gave birth to a perplexing phenomenon that emerged in the nineteenth century, namely that of "separate spheres." The ideological transformations associated with the Enlightenment created, among many things, an ideology of domesticity. Is this an accurate depiction of what happened and if so, how did it come about? What were the economic roots and consequences of the changing perceptions and realities of women and children?

The one fundamental assumption of the time, unchanged by the revolutions of Enlightenment thought, was that the household was the basic building block of society. The household was largely the nuclear family and its economic nature was, as might be expected, deeply affected by economic and technological change. Differentiation between households, firms, and plants was still rather rare in 1700. The vast majority of farmers, artisans, shopkeepers, and many of the professions worked in large numbers within their family, usually at their place of residence. The eighteenth and the first half of the nineteenth century witnessed a rapid expansion of what would eventually be known as a proletariat or a wage labor force. Unlike some historians and social scientists, economists do not tend to view proletarianization as a necessary worsening of people's economic status or quality of life. Much of the assessment of the effects of proletarianization depends on what the conditions of work in the traditional economy were, including wages or earnings, hours worked, the physical conditions at work, the mode of compensation, the social environment at the place of work, and whether other members of the household were involved in the same work. Wage labor, whether in a factory or workshop setting or not, is not necessarily alienating as some would have it. Yet there can be little doubt that economic development changed the way households operated and how they functioned as economic units.

One thing did not change during the prolonged period of economic change: the typical British household remained fairly small. It has been speculated (e.g. by Peter Laslett) that England's Industrial Revolution may have had something to do with the small size of the British household before industrialization began (cited by Humphries, 2004, p. 243). That might well be the case, but the mechanisms that would connect the two need to be specified. In a recent paper, Greif and Sasson (2009) suggest such a mechanism. They propose that small family size, coupled with an economic safety net (the Poor Law), allowed entrepreneurial and risk-loving individuals to take chances on innovation that might have been thwarted in an extended family system (such as larger clans) where highly risk-averse individuals might have vetoed innovative but risky projects.

It might be thought that as the economy changed and population growth suddenly attained a speed never experienced before, household size would change. But on the eve of the Industrial Revolution Britain was already a society of nuclear families, and it stayed this way. An average size of slightly under 4.75 members seems to have held in Britain for most of the period under discussion here. Marriage remained a pivotal mechanism for organizing society. Cohabitation of unmarried couples remained quite rare, and the vast bulk of all women and men did get married (including, to be sure, common-law marriages): the proportion never married rarely rose above 10 percent. For people born between 1701 and 1751, 92 percent eventually got married, and for people born between 1751 and 1801, 93. 2 percent took the vow, while for those born between 1801 and 1821 it was slightly lower, about 89.5 percent. About three out of every four households in Britain around the year 1800 were "simple" households, i.e. households that contained parents and children only. Better-off households often had a few live-in servants.

Household size was of course not a hard constant over the life cycle. Many households would, as part of natural processes, have older parents or unmarried siblings living with them. While the function and internal structure of households changed considerably in that century and a half, size and composition changed less than one would have imagined. It is also quite clear that whatever changes occurred were quite varied—different regions and members of different economic classes had very different experiences. In agricultural areas and market towns, the social evolution of households and families differed from that of manufacturing regions. The urbanizing and industrializing areas were facing a different economic and social environment for household formation.

Some of the apparent constancy of the British household size conceals deeper changes. Consider for instance the question of non-family residents within a household. Many pre-industrial households had live-in servants and apprentices, whereas nineteenth-century urban families often took in boarders and co-resided with relatives as a consequence of high rents in urban areas (some boarders were relatives of the household head). These seemingly similar arrangements mask a very different economic and social reality. In some areas such as Preston, a cotton center in Lancashire about which a lot is known (but which also seems to have been atypical), households were in fact larger than in a typical pre-industrial setting, on account of kin and boarders living with the nuclear families (e.g., Anderson, 1972). The number of people "in the household" may have been the same, but their relation to the household and the costs and benefits had changed.

The exact meaning of the term "household" changed over time. The eighteenth-century households had close ties with surrounding families, related or not, and concepts such as "family" and "kin" had wider significance than in our own time. Households may also have had flexible boundaries. The custom of sending one's own children as servants to other households while simul-taneously employing other servants created informal networks. Serving in another household or being apprenticed in one may have been less of a formal market transaction than appears because "other" families may not have been strangers. It is possible to take this analysis too far: the eighteenth-century British village was far from being a single happy family or a kibbutz. The household was the fundamental unit of economic organization, and its members supported one an-other; inter-household support and implicit mutual systems became weaker as the formal poor relief system increasingly became the safety net of the unlucky.

Industrialization, technological change, and the rise of the factory system meant above all that in many sectors the household came under pressure as the basic unit of production. With the decline of the domestic economy, more and more activity moved outside the family home: work, eating, entertainment, and social interaction increasingly took place away from home, while at the same time some houses may have had more strangers in them, such as servants, boarders, and child caretakers. All the same, the net impact of economic change over the period 1700–1850 on the overall functionality and cohesiveness of the family as the basic unit of society is far from clear. The household in Britain was subjected to considerable shocks. The most dramatic was its transformation from a producing unit to a primarily consuming entity. Enclosures, the loss of the commons, dramatic changes in the demand for labor in different sectors, the changing status of women, urbanization, changes in the Poor Law, and growing mobility, all were major shocks inflicted on the family. Yet at the end of the day, the mid-Victorian family, whether working or middle class, cannot be shown to be in any sense less stable or less functional than the British family around 1700.

Households make economic decisions, in miniature, that are similar to the problems that a market economy solves: how to allocate resources, which tech-niques to choose, how income and consumption are distributed among its members, and how much to save and invest and in what assets. Yet at the micro-level of the household these decisions are not normally made by market mecha-nisms, and there are no explicit prices and formal exchange mechanisms. None the less, these decisions are still "economic" in that the households have to allocate scarce resources, and they are constrained by budgets and knowledge. Matters were no different in the eighteenth and nineteenth centuries. Economists have pointed to "rational" elements in household economics, especially the gains that accrue to all members as a result of specialization and a division of labor, mutual insurance, and economies of scale. Some economic historians believe that one of the advantages of larger households was the "networking" aspect—the sharing of information and the mutual support in case of a negative shock to household resources. But rationality, while always a factor, had of course to share the stage with such emotive forces as love, sex drive, sibling rivalry, and tradition. Between the economic fundamentalists who think that relative prices, technology, and income alone determine household behavior and structure, and those who feel with Steven Ruggles (1987, p. 16) that the economists' reduction of emotional attachments to "particular non-marketable household commodities" seemed "unsubtle," there must be a middle ground that tries to combine human nature with the need to make ends meet and have some time for fun as well. More to the point, perhaps, is the fundamental point that whereas rationality may (or may not) be a good approximation to most individual decisions, households were by construction collective units in which members bargained, negotiated, log-rolled, and persuaded one another. Decisions on consumption, reproduction, location, and labor-force participation (often closely interrelated) were collective household decisions, not personal decisions (De Vries, 2008). Although the units were small in the nuclear families of Europe, they still differed from the unitary decision-maker that economists often presume in consumer behavior. The equilibria that such processes created are not necessarily identical to what a single consumer would have done, and may seem therefore incompatible with individual rationality.

Pre-modern households were clearly more vulnerable than households in our time. Health and life itself were more precarious. In part this was because people had fewer technological means to cope with inordinately cold winters, hot or rainy summers, unusually high (or low) prices, epizootics, and so on. Safety nets such as the welfare state and an insurance industry simply did not exist anywhere in eighteenth-century Europe. In emergencies, most people in pre-industrial Europe depended on their families and charity. It has often been maintained that Britain was an exception in this regard and that social insurance was carried out at the level of the community, through the poor relief provided by the parish. This made sense, since within nuclear families, the likelihood that bad luck would strike all members together was high (if they worked together in complementary fashion), whereas within the local community the covariation of random luck was sufficiently low that members could help one another. The standard free rider problems were overcome by making supporting the poor compulsory (that is, financed by ratepayers), and the incentive problems that normally bedevil such insurance schemes were alleviated by keeping them confined to the local level. In other words, the function of the family as a mutual insurance device was in part taken over by the public sector. Yet as industrialization proceeded and the center of gravity shifted to urban areas in the north and west, where the Poor Law was inadequate, the role of the family may actually have increased after 1815, especially after the Poor Law reform of 1834. Over the first half of the nineteenth century, then, as the uncertainty of employment and income apparently increased, this role of the family network if anything increased.

Yet the role of the family as a mutually supporting unit of individuals was disturbed after 1780 by the negative impact inflicted by economic changes on the ability of women and children to produce income. There is no neat or monotonic picture here. In some areas and sectors the opportunities increased, elsewhere they declined. What the factories and mines gave in terms of employment for workers other than adult males, they took away by weakening domestic industries. The standard story about the transformation of the family in the late eighteenth and nineteenth centuries is that the cash-earning capacity of household members other than the male breadwinner was weakened. The story is more complicated than that, and many factors contributed, but on the whole the rough picture that emerges in the long run is a decline in the contribution of women and children in farming and "outwork" after 1815 or 1820 and a rise in factory employment that made up for those losses until about the middle of the nineteenth century (Horrell and Humphries, 1992; Humphries, 2004, p. 259). Regional differences and variations in sector-specific demand for labor further complicate this messy picture. Can one still tell a coherent story despite such conflicting trends?

*   *   *

An enlightened economy is a relative thing. Our concepts of "Enlightenment" differ significantly from those of the time. This is especially true of our views of gender differences. The modern notion that women are in every way equal to men except for a few relatively minor biological differences and should be given equal employment opportunity, equal education, and equal pay (to say nothing of legal and political rights) would have been by and large alien to this age, although the dissenting voices of a few maverick feminists such as Mary Wollstonecraft —miles ahead of her time—could be heard in the late eighteenth century. The perplexing fact is that the British Enlightenment created a few radical writers calling for the emancipation of women, yet also had room for pious moralists such as Hannah More, whose influence before 1850 surely eclipsed that of all progressive writers taken together (Hilton, 2006, pp. 359, 368–69). As Colley (1992, pp. 274–76) has noted, More's thought was straight out of Rousseau, and while women were destined for a domestic role as mothers and wives, they could have indirect political influence through the men in their lives.

The Victorian reality of separate spheres was created in part by the ideological and institutional underpinning of eighteenth-century thought, and especially by the peculiar blend of Enlightenment ideas and the deeply religious sentiments that were the hallmark of English social thought in the first half of the nineteenth century. Politically, ambitious women were powerless except for what they could achieve by influencing their husbands and relatives; the Reform Act of 1832 explicitly gave the vote only to male voters (though customarily women had not been voting before that). Women who directly entered the political fray, such as the Duchess of Devonshire who campaigned on Charles James Fox's behalf in the 1790s, jeopardized their reputations. Another example was Harriet Arbuthnot, an informed and smart conservative diarist who was friendly with both Castlereagh and Wellington, as well as married to a parliamentarian, yet whose diary "reflects the frustrations felt by a politically-minded woman in a system that had no room for her" (Hilton, 2006, p. 356). Whatever political and ideological influence women had came through their moral suasion of males who actually made the decisions. What impact did these developments have on the economic facts on the ground?

Pre-Industrial Revolution Britain has sometimes been characterized as a "golden age" for female work. Many historians have depicted the period 1700–1850 as an era in which the position of women declined from a glorious past to one of subordination and marginalization. It was in this period, by this account, that the emergence of a class society was accompanied by the growth of separate spheres in which middle-class men and women were increasingly segmented (Davidoff and Hall, 1987) and by the end of the period, this separation was extending to working-class families (Clark, 1995, ch. 14). Capitalism, industrialization, and economic change have all been implicated in this process. Yet this stylized view of social change between 1700 and 1850 is based on an idealized characterization of the status of women in the pre-industrialized economy, and has been effectively demolished (Vickery, 1993; Shoemaker, 1998). How much of this image is consistent with the evidence?

In the first half of the eighteenth century, British women participated in cash-generating activities as never before. In part this was supply-related: more women wanted to work to generate cash in order to purchase more consumer goods as part of De Vries' (2008) industrious revolution. But some came from labor demand: the cottage industries that spread through much of rural Britain were miniature workshops, in which couples worked together to produce industrial goods. With the advent of the Industrial Revolution, as cottage industries had increasingly to compete with mechanized production, the incomes they generated declined and women and children had to pitch in to maintain living standards (Humphries, 2004, p. 256). On farms, similarly, women were partners to their men and found considerable employment in the livestock-rearing sector that increased steadily in the eighteenth century. In urban areas, many women tended to be employed outside the household away from their husbands. Whether such partnerships involved equal bargaining power is doubtful, but it is difficult to conclude that women in the new factory towns and the London metropolis were necessarily worse off. After all, we may well ask whether married women in the proto-industrial economy, pregnant and burdened with small children much of the time, who were also toiling at the spinning wheel or the chicken coop, would not perhaps have felt some envy toward their Victorian descendants a century and a half later, many of whom found themselves "confined" to the domestic sphere. As Vickery has perceptively noted, "it is not clear that a woman's industrial work was any more agreeable when directed by a husband, rather than a formal employer" (1993, p. 404).

What happened to the economic role and position of women in the years before and during the Industrial Revolution? The household was, as noted, a unit in which consumption decisions were made. It stands to reason that individual consumption (as distinct from the shared goods such as home heating) would bear some relationship to the bargaining power of the individuals. To judge by that criterion, the eighteenth century seems to indicate that women's position was anything but weakened. Women's clothing as a share of probate inventories increased quite dramatically throughout the eighteenth century, which indicates that they were the ones making the bulk of the purchases (De Vries, 2008, pp. 142–43). The decline in the consumption per capita of traditional alcoholic beverages such as beer during the Industrial Revolution seems equally suggestive.

Within the household and at the workplace (when the two were not identical), men and women practiced a division of labor. The causes of such a division of labor are not always clear, but it was a fact of life throughout this age. This is not to say that the two could never be substituted for one another, but the evidence shows that this was quite rare, and the spheres of activity of the genders remained fairly distinct. Before the Industrial Revolution, in the domestic industrial sector, women spun and men wove. Women, naturally, had to spend more time with the children during nursing time, but subsequently too were in charge of looking after children, as well as all other traditional household chores. It would have been satisfying to find signs of men participating actively in household work, but there is little evidence supporting such involvement. The "golden age" view—that the eighteenth century, before the onset of the Industrial Revolution was a time of approximate parity of women with men in terms of employment opportunities—runs into the objection that as long as there was no parity in household work, greater market opportunities for women meant more female activity in formal markets, work that came largely in addition to their domestic chores and thus at the expense of leisure. In other words, it may have meant more backbreaking toil for the poorest women. For better-off women, it meant the hiring of domestic servants, usually teenage girls, to help out with the hardest housework, while some of the labor time thus vacated could be allocated to market activity.

Women, on the whole, seem to have been less specialized than men even in the eighteenth century, presumably because less was invested in their training. Skilled artisans in pre-Industrial Revolution Britain, including those in the apparel industries (which, in the nineteenth century, became increasingly a haven for women workers), were predominantly men. Those women who worked outside their homes were often employed in casual and seasonal occupations or in domestic service and the "making and mending of clothes." A study by Peter Earle (1989) looking at London in 1700 and 1850, found that in the first quarter of the eighteenth century, women were more likely to work if they were married to low-skill, poorly paid laborers. Presumably these working women were low-skilled and poorly paid themselves. The occupational structure of Earle's London women in 1700 was not all that different, indeed, from the structure of female occupations in the 1851 census. Yet this similarity is misleading: London was quite different from the rest of Britain in the early eighteenth century (as well as in 1850), and the 1851 census tended to undercount women who were working hard but did not have a distinct "occupation."

For the entire period under discussion here, moreover, women were kept away from many occupations that involved a great deal of skill or a long apprenticeship. Law, medicine, pharmacy, the universities, the ministry, to say nothing of politics and the military, were wholly dominated by males, with the significant exception of midwives, of whom there were 2,024 in 1851, probably an undercount. Even in obstetrics, however, male midwives had become dominant. Feminist historians have noted that this difference reflects power asymmetries in society and the gender biases of male-dominated institutions such as guilds and professional associations. This kind of discrimination was common especially in industries that "were not disciplined by competition" (Burnette, 1997, p. 261).

A hard-nosed economist might reflect that from a social point of view, it made perhaps less sense to invest in the human capital of women if their active adult life would be punctuated by many pregnancies, nursing, and the heavy demands of child care. In an age in which women had many more pregnancies than today, and in which household work was unmechanized so that work such as laundry and cooking was highly labor-intensive, the amount of housework that mothers not rich enough to hire servants had to perform severely limited their ability to participate in the labor force. The apprenticeship system in principle applied to men and women. Snell (1985, ch. 6) has shown that in the eighteenth century women were in fact apprenticed to skilled crafts and has argued that many women who had not been formally apprenticed participated in their husband's trade. However, for whatever reason, in the later eighteenth century young girls were apprenticed increasingly into domestic service, preparing them for domesticity and housework and less for skilled occupations. Women were more likely to be apprenticed in the system of parish apprenticeships, which was often little more than exploitative labor, while males were more likely to be trained as private apprentices, which often led to a skilled craft. Labor market discrimination thus took place at the human-capital formation stage. It is hard to test whether men and women were paid the same for the same work, simply because they rarely performed the same work.

Some industries were dominated by female labor. Lace-making, for instance, was almost exclusively female, and women were heavily represented in industries such as millinery, upholstery, and above all manual spinning. In the domestic industries that spread through the countryside in the seventeenth and eighteenth centuries, women played a central role, with a division of labor practiced between the household members. But whether in cottage industries, farming, or urban households the majority of married women in eighteenth-century Britain were part of an "economic partnership" in which the wife did not expect to be kept by her husband but contributed to the surplus which allowed them to purchase ever more appealing goods and services in the market (Snell, 1985, p. 303). As long as the vast bulk of workers still labored at their homes or in workshops adjacent to them, such a partnership was no more than natural. It was disrupted not by some giant conspiracy of males to keep women in their place but by deeper forces over which individuals had little control.

A sharp decline in the demand for female labor occurred in late eighteenth- and early nineteenth-century agriculture. The enclosure movement curtailed job opportunities for women more than for men (Burnette, 1999). Allen (1992) has pointed out that female employment (primarily live-in servants) declined with farm size, and as farms grew larger over the eighteenth century, the employment per acre and thus opportunities for women fell, though it is not clear that women suffered relatively more than men (Burnette, 2004, pp. 681–82). Humphries (1990) has pointed to the loss of access to common lands as a source of the decline in women's employment opportunities in farming, since women and children were the main beneficiaries of these common rights (p. 21). Other scholars (e.g. Snell, 1985), using a very different methodology, have found the same, attributing the female labor shedding to enclosures. For many generations, women had been in a position to take advantage of the common lands that now were disappearing in those areas in which enclosures took place. The grazing and gleaning rights on common fields were exploited primarily by women, and the disappearance of these rights was a major blow to poor rural women. The replacement of the sickle by the much heavier scythe worked against female employment in agriculture, although the exact timing of this technological change is in dispute and differed from region to region, depending on local labor supply conditions (Collins, 1969). Davidoff (1995) argues that in the second quarter of the nineteenth century women were systematically excluded from farm work, including activities they had previously dominated, such as dairying. This is overstated: cheese-making remained in large part a female occupation, even if official statistics seem to have largely missed it (McMurry, 1992).

It remains an open question whether the decline in female rural employment was wholly demand-propelled. By the mid-nineteenth century supply might have have played a role as well. Collins (1969, p. 470) notes that it was becoming increasingly difficult to recruit married women for outdoor farm work and "unmarried girls preferred the superior status and more genteel environment of domestic service to the bucolic atmosphere of the harvest field." The 1843 *Report on the Employment of Women and Children in Agriculture* (Great Britain, 1843) is clearly consistent with this interpretation. All the same, areas that were subject to agricultural change, both organizational and technological, tended to replace live-in servants with day laborers, thus reducing employment opportunities for teenage girls for whom farm service had been a large employer. Farm service and domestic service in the homes of well-to-do farmers had become indistinguishable, and provided rural girls between the ages of 12 and 14 with an opportunity to leave home and be employed until they married. As population growth surged after 1750 and other forms of employment declined, there just were not enough of these positions. For many of these women the only option was to search for domestic service opportunities in large towns. The magnitude of this migration is confirmed by urban gender ratios: for England and Wales, the ratio of women to men aged 15–24 as enumerated by the 1851 census reports was about 1.06 women per man, but in London the ratio (all ages) in 1841 and 1851was about 1.13 women per man and 1.2 women per men for ages 15–24 (Great Britain, 1852–53b, p. cxcii).

The story of women's work in the Industrial Revolution has been often told. The early factory system, say between 1770 and 1820, relied heavily on the labor of women and children. In the early stages of mechanization, many machines were specifically adapted to them (Berg, 1993). The advantages of women and children in factories were that they were less costly than men, and that they were widely regarded as more amenable to the discipline and punctuality that the factories demanded. Evidently, women and children had been subject to discipline in their homes, and found it less difficult than adult men to adjust to the factory regime. Women were less likely to be committed to artisanal practices (which many of the factories bypassed) and at times the new technology was specifically adapted to the bodies of teenage girls (Berg, 1993, p. 35). Moreover, the growth in the labor supply of young women between puberty and marriage, who could be hired at low wages, created an important source of cheap labor to the rapidly growing textile sector (Goldstone, 1996). After 1830, the trend changed: factories and factory-like settings gradually were dominated by men. The "new economy" that emerged in the twilight years of the Industrial Revolution was heavily biased toward males. Few women found jobs in the railroads, the telegraph, blast furnaces, or the large engineering firms that were at the core of the "new economy" by the middle of the nineteenth century.

This general trend became more pronounced in the first half of the nineteenth century. There seems to have been a gradual net contraction of employment opportunities for married women and a rise in the central role of the father as the main breadwinner, a trend obscured by the well-documented and undeniable central role that female and child labor played in the early decades of the Industrial Revolution. The contribution of the earnings of women and children to family budgets has been found by the pioneering work of Horrell and Humphries (1992, 1995a, 1995b) to have declined in the first half of the nineteenth century. The direction of this trend is, however, ambiguous in some subperiods and scholars differ on when it started. The hard question is, however, whether this was a demand- or a supply-driven phenomenon. It may well be that the industrious revolution had run its course and that families began to withdraw non-male labor from the market. Possibly they preferred to keep members of the family at home and produce household goods that were, for one reason or another, harder to purchase on the open market such as education for the young or cleanliness. On the other hand, there is evidence to suggest that the employment demand for women and children was on balance declining after 1825, the factories notwithstanding.

The most dramatic changes occurred in manufacturing. After all, the sharp decline in the cottage industries with the mechanization of many domestic industrial activities that reduced demand for domestic work and the concomitant decline in employment opportunities may have been so big a phenomenon that the demand for female labor exerted by factories was inadequate to offset it (Berg, 1993, p. 23). The employment opportunities for women in factories should not be overstated: Richards (1974, p. 346) has estimated that only about 65,000 women were actually employed by cotton mills. Adding another 50 percent for the employment of women in their homes in jobs farmed out by factories, we arrive at about 100,000 women whose jobs were created by the cotton industry, perhaps 3 percent of the entire female labor force over age 15 in 1841. While women were thus quite central to the growth of the factory system, the reverse is much more questionable. The mechanized sector created far fewer jobs than were eliminated in the domestic system. These contradictory trends reflect different geographical experiences: in the regions where large textile mills or coal mines were prevalent, women and children remained important earners; in the south and the west counties in which rural industry all but vanished their economic role declined. In some regions domestic industries first declined and then were revived in a different form. At the bottom of this often tragic tale lies the complex history of domestic industry and its relation with modernized industry.

The rise and fall of cottage industry in the eighteenth century affected working women to a great extent. Domestic industry had provided them with an opportunity to participate in cash-generating market activity while engaging in what we would call today multi-tasking, that is, earning cash and simultaneously looking after the children and household chores. In textiles, by far the biggest sector, women suffered a double blow. First, after 1790 domestic spinning disappeared quite rapidly as mechanization in cotton and worsted spinning took place. Many of the women thus rendered unemployed joined their husbands in domestic weaving, since for a few decades handloom weaving enjoyed a boom (as the spinning industry produced large quantities of yarn and weaving had not yet been successfully mechanized). After 1820 or so, domestic weaving declined almost everywhere. The *Rural Queries* appended to the 1834 Poor Law Report (Great Britain, 1834b, App. B1; see also Blaug, 1964) asked specifically (question 11): "have you any and what employment for women and children?" The answers show that outside lace-knitting and straw-plaiting, there were precious few opportunities for women to earn cash in their homes. Increasingly sons and daughters of rural families were forced to look for work in factories. When this was unavailable, the next best strategy was to look for jobs in the service industries, especially domestic service, or to emigrate.

We should not underestimate the opportunities of married women to earn money by informal market production even after the demise of rural industries: taking care of livestock and chickens, casual cleaning, selling food, taking in lodgers, boarders, and laundry, gleaning (the collection of post-harvest crop residues), and the cultivation and sale of kitchen crops in small gardens were all options. Farmers' wives kept accounts and preserved foods, shopkeepers' wives served customers, and innkeepers' wives surely were expected to share equally in the work. In cities, working-class women were part of informal urban networks that minded children and mended clothes, painted toy soldiers, and often engaged in minor illegal activities such as selling stolen goods and filing false claims for poor relief. Middle-class women were often active behind the scenes in their families' businesses, by keeping accounts and correspondence, managing and monitoring servants and apprentices. Elizabeth Strutt (1729–74), wife to Jedediah, became a critical player in the establishment of one of the most successful businesses in Britain. In one way or another, many women contributed to household income, although the avenues through which they did so became narrower over time. The separate spheres concept, popularized by historians, should be modified by these informal arrangements. It may be added that middle-class males, too, dropped out of the labor force if they could afford to, though normally not before their wives did (Shoemaker, 1998, pp. 114–16).

Nonetheless, the demand for formal female labor—constrained by the limited choices that society allowed women to make—declined rather sharply in the decades after 1820, as the statistics collected by Horrell and Humphries (1995a) demonstrate. There were domestic industries that managed to survive into the era of the factory such as lace-making, millinery, embroidery, straw-plaiting, and hand-knitting. Many of these "tacit workers" (predominantly female) were associated with factories as subcontractors or outworkers. Some of these artisanal activities were eventually moved to so-called sweated trades or unregulated urban sweatshops, in which women and men were employed in large numbers in "degrading and unhealthy surroundings ... acquiring a reputation for squalid misery" (Schmiechen, 1984, p. 3). By the 1830s and 1840s, much of the finishing end of the textile industry (i.e., garment-making) in London was in the process of converting to this system (ibid., p. 18).

A considerable literature has maintained that, even if the economic position in the pre-industrial era is easily overidealized as a "golden age" that never was, the Industrial Revolution was responsible for a marginalization of female labor and the gradual relegation of women to the position of homemaker. Men monopolized the more remunerative and desirable jobs outside the home and also had the power to make decisions inside (Davidoff and Hall, 1987). By the time systematic nation-wide data become available, whatever their biases, it is clear that in early Victorian times women were kept out of skilled occupations by the gendered nature of the apprenticeship system, the sciences, and the liberal professions. There is truth in the argument that skill became associated with males, and women were viewed as largely unskilled (Honeyman, 2000, p. 64). The 1841 census provides us with one glimpse of this gap: it reported for instance that in the legal profession there were 16,291 "Barristers, advocates, and attorneys" in Britain, *none* of them female. There were 1,920 male bankers or bank agents and eight female ones. There were 18,482 male physicians, surgeons, and apothecaries and no female ones. Of the 505 newspaper editors, four were women. Even a somewhat less attractive profession such as "commercial clerk" counted 46,368 men and 152 women. Only in teaching did women outnumber men, 30,688 as opposed to 21,482 (all figures pertain to individuals over 20 years of age). The 1851 census, which counted and classified occupations in a very different way from the 1841 one, nonetheless presents a very similar picture. It counted 16,367 male attorneys and barrister, and no females, 1,793 male bankers and two females. In the newspaper business (editors, reporters) there were 1,220 males and 20 females. As noted, it is likely that these numbers exaggerated the reality of the occupational gender gap and that many married women assisted their husbands' commercial endeavors and in law and medical practices without formally designating themselves as professionals. All the same, the impression that the readers of Victorian novels have of the sharp asymmetries between the role of males and females in society is not contradicted by national statistics or by local studies.

Why was there such a gap? Between the two theoretical extremes of "the market did what was rational and efficient" and mindless conspiracy theories, there was a complex and regionally and sectorally heterogeneous world, in which women were formally regarded as less than men, but were in many areas able to find informal niches for themselves. While excluded from the Royal Society, they were often tolerated at provincial scientific societies, sometimes on the basis that the societies needed more members. By the 1830s, women were active in libraries, museums, botanical gardens, even Mechanics' Institutes (Elliott, 2003, p. 385). The eighteenth-century *Ladies' Diary* was actually full of rather sophisticated mathematical essays, suggesting that even if they were often excluded from many avenues of formal education, it was never possible (and probably never intended) to keep women altogether away from advanced learning. The eighteenth-century scientific lecturer Adam Walker charged a guinea entry for gentlemen and half a guinea for ladies (Musson and Robinson, 1969, p. 105). The price difference suggests, perhaps, that demand for such events was not the same across genders. The wives and daughters of the members of the Lunar Society were allowed to be exposed to the kind of knowledge their husbands and brothers were obsessed by, as long as it remained obvious that for them such activity would remain a hobby. But at least in this respect a century of enlightened thought brought little progress for most women, even educated ones. Hilton (2006, pp. 367–68) has maintained that women played a central role in science and political economy but this is unpersuasive. Apart from the horticultural and botanical societies, women were systematically excluded from membership in scientific societies, including the new British Association for the Advancement of Science. After some debate, it was decided that they would not be allowed to attend the reading of papers and could not be admitted as members, but could attend the gala. Over time, however, their presence was allowed and in 1853 the first female member was admitted to the BAAS (Morrell and Thackray, 1981, pp. 148–57). Shoemaker (1998, p. 201) has suggested that Enlightenment ideology placed an increasing value on rationality and a scientific approach to production. Because these characteristics were associated with maleness, women were pushed out of positions of management and responsibility. Hence their value to the informal networks they joined was reduced, and women may have been as reluctant to join as men were reluctant to accept them (Sunderland, 2007, p. 64). As medical professions came to be increasingly associated with scientific knowledge after 1800, women were increasingly excluded, and hence their gradual expulsion from midwifery.

Even when employed in seemingly similar positions, women often appear to have been treated differently from men: they seem to have been more often paid by the piece rather than by time, they were more often fined for errors, and their employment was more sensitive to business fluctuations. During a slump employers may have been less inclined to dismiss the primary breadwinner of a household than a woman whose income was regarded as supplementary. Above all, however, women were paid less than men. Some writers have viewed this wage gap as the result of "custom" (e.g., Berg, 1993) whereas others tend to blame monopolistic and collusive actions by males (Honeyman, 2000, pp. 61–62) —though these two explanations are inconsistent. The evidence on which either argument rests, to say nothing of the theory, is slender. If the wage gap was based on custom, it should not have fluctuated with changing market conditions, yet recent careful research shows that it did exactly that, and fluctuated in a direction that reflected the changing relative demand for labor (Burnette, 2004).

Wage comparisons between the genders are to some extent hazardous: discrimination predominantly took place through job segregation in that women and men did not do the same kind of work. Even when they did, one has to take into account more obvious economic explanations such as the greater upper-body strength of men and the reluctance of employers to invest in workers whose expected tenure might be limited (Burnette, 1997). Such "neo-classical" explanations are usually rejected out of hand by feminist historians (e.g., Honeyman, 2000, p. 55), but they are often no more than common sense. Even when piece wages were identical, male workers earned more than female ones simply because they could work longer hours and had more upper-body strength to carry out the often strenuous physical tasks involved in nineteenth-century production. Even though the difference in strength was more pronounced for adults than for teenagers, such differences account for the fact that of the persons aged 15–19 in 1851, there were over 15,000 males defined as "blacksmiths" (presumably most of them apprentices), but only 14 women. In the Lancashire cotton mills it can readily be seen how and why gender differences arose. Men and women earned about the same until age 18, at which time men's earnings continued to increase until it peaked in their early thirties, and then began to level off slowly. Women's earnings profiles remained essentially flat for the rest of their subsequent working life (Boot, 1995, p. 285). This seems consistent with a human capital explanation: employers invested in the skills (widely defined to include supervisory tasks) of men, not of women. The difference was more pronounced in the industrialized north and Scotland than in the south and east, suggesting that this was a decision made by industrialists (ibid., p. 297). Why they chose to do so, of course, is not fully understood. Prejudice and workers' pressure surely played a role, but it must be kept in mind that women between age 20 and 40 lost on average eight years of their adult employment span to pregnancies and child-rearing activities and retired on average four years before men, so the returns on the investment to both employer and worker were simply lower.

At the same time, standard economic arguments do not explain everything, since the same census records as "tailors" 14,440 men and 3,148 women. Was this outright discrimination? The problem with discrimination theories of the wage gap is, of course, that employers competed with one another, and if there was a significant difference between the ratio of the value of the marginal product to wage of women and that of men, employers would switch to the cheaper source of labor and eventually bid up its wage. There is evidence that precisely this kind of thing happened in handloom weaving in the south of England (Burnette, 1997, p. 267). There could well have been severe cases of gender discrimination based on prejudice and ignorance, but such an explanation should only be resorted to after all others have been exhausted, not before. We cannot preclude social norms and even informal "conspiracies" by organized skilled males and self-righteous moralists intent on keeping women "in their place," but the assumptions that have to be made for such a collusion to be successful should be made clear.

The real source of the inequality of women was not the discrimination of employers or the actions of unions but their lack of outside options. By our standards, the era after 1750 was an exceptionally lopsided age as far as the formal treatment of women was concerned. From the point of view of legal rights, married women barely existed as separate entities. Divorce was not an option, because until 1857 it required a private Act of Parliament. Any attempt to abandon or dissolve a formal relationship, no matter how abusive or unfair, would be extremely hazardous for the woman. The great legal authority, William Blackstone, explained in 1776 that "in marriage husband and wife are the same person, and that person is the husband." The law made some clear and unambiguous distinctions between men and women that put women at a disadvantage. Above all, under the legal doctrine known as coverture married women were not allowed to own property, which was legally their husband's. Married women could not sign bills of exchange, sue or be sued, and, in the words of Davidoff and Hall (1987, p. 200), "upon marriage a woman died a kind of civil death." Women who had inherited property prior to their marriage turned over formal ownership and control to their husbands upon marriage unless they wrote special contracts. Passive forms of property owned by women such as annuities, settlements, and trusts were still often controlled primarily by males. While the informal intra-household bargaining between husbands and wives in this age was no less complex than at any other time in history and could produce different actual allocations of work and consumption, and while coverture could be broken if expressly so stated in a will, in the final analysis the law and the almost universal consent to it placed women at a severe disadvantage.

Yet like so many other restrictive forms of legislation in this age, the letter of the law and actual practice on the ground were not always in tandem. For one thing, while married women in England were devoid of rights of control over property, unmarried women or widows in Britain were, at least *de jure*, the equals of men (unlike in the rest of Europe). That covered a large number of all adult women, especially in cities (Green and Owens, 2003, p. 513). Many households (around one-quarter in the big cities) were headed by women, and it seems reasonable to conclude that "the social position of these women was at odds with the ... ideology of separate spheres" (ibid., p. 512). Women who owned and managed businesses or controlled considerable assets were often widows or unmarried daughters of businessmen. Yet we should keep in mind that women tended to outlive men, and thus the country always had a large supply of widows. By the middle of the nineteenth century, widows outnumbered widowers by more that two to one (Great Britain, 1852–53b, part I, p. 179). A widow would assume the full legal rights of property after her husband's death and many businesses were run successfully by competent widows.

Moreover, even if it was not always formally acknowledged, married women could find spaces in which they transacted their business and indeed coverture could be used as a convenient shelter from creditors and bankruptcies. The common law recognized many exceptions to and ways around the strict interpretation of coverture. Private contracts and explicit exceptions were recognized by the common law courts. Within the law of coverture there was a delegation clause that allowed married women to use their husbands' credit to buy "necessary" goods, and such contracts were regarded as binding. While married women never had rights equal to those of their husbands or those of single women, then, they still could find some space in the law to engage in commerce if they so wished (Phillips, 2006, pp. 41–47). Indeed, the ability of British institutions to adapt to the changing needs of the times is manifest in this area as well. Erickson (2005, pp. 6–7) has argued that the complex needs of the marriage contract led to the development of legal precision and unintentionally resulted in the development of legal and financial instruments such as bonds, trusts, and settlements that circumvented the constraints of coverture. All the same, while there was far more female entrepreneurship than early feminist writers indicated, there can be no question that in 1850 women and men occupied very different roles in the economy. The revisionist literature is surely correct in pointing out that such a gender specialization was already firmly in place in 1700, but the balance of the evidence points to a strengthening of this phenomenon by 1850.

It is often maintained that gender inequality was the result of male political dominance in society and the ability of men to exclude women from positions that required skill or decision-making. Some writers employ the term "gender struggle"—a neat adaptation of Marxist terminology in a post-Marxist world, to depict the collective action by organized males to limit the economic options of women. The degree of gender-wide coordination that such collusion between males would require seems substantial, and its exact motivation a bit murky—after all, a woman's earnings accrued to her household, of which her husband was a member. The view that implicitly regards society as a gender struggle in which one gender successfully excludes the other to enhance its own earnings ignores the simple fact that wives and daughters were usually part of male-dominated households who could dispose of their earnings. Why would a man resist higher earnings for his wife or daughter if that income benefited him as well? One answer is that higher incomes by women in the household might have endangered the man's dominant bargaining position within the home. A man thus faced a trade-off between the economic costs of lower household income and his own power within that household to dispose of the income. The dominant position of men appears to have been sufficiently secure until the twentieth century, but it came at a price.

The actual historical record on the "gender struggle" is decidedly mixed. Some male-dominated labor unions such as hatters and calico printers made concerted efforts to keep women out. In the first half of the nineteenth century, a number of skilled workers' unions engaged in strikes aimed at protecting male domination. At times such struggles were successful, but there are enough cases in which they were not to raise serious questions about their role in bringing about the new gender division of the factory economy. Above all, some men struggled in vain against a repeal of the Statute of Artificers and Apprentices (1814), which for centuries had barred women from many occupations. Two years before, women had been admitted formally as silk weavers in Spitalfields (Clark, 1995, pp. 127–28). Weavers realized that women were as capable as men in weaving and that they stood to gain by including them. John Honeyford, a Bolton cotton weaver, testified to a parliamentary committee in 1808 that "women's talent is equal to men's when the work is not too heavy; we have some women whose talent is equal to any man's in the middle kind of work" (Great Britain, 1808, p. 27). The industry illustrates finely Burnette's (1997, 2008) description of how gender differences worked in rural Britain: women were paid at piece rates similar to men, but their earnings were much lower because married women, burdened with domestic responsibilities and often with pregnancies, worked on average fewer hours. This points to the household as the locus of inequality, not the labor market.

An illustrative example is that of cotton-spinning: the early mules required a highly skilled worker, invariably male, who was well-paid. Whether it was due to the skill or the physical requirement of this job, women were excluded from this position. Instead, women and children in the early stages of the Industrial Revolution were often members of the spinner's "team" as piecers. These male spinners employed their own family members on their team, thus recreating the family economy on the shop floor. However, the mule spinners' position as a labor aristocracy was sufficiently powerful that employers were increasingly threatened by them and sought technological ways to reduce their power. Richard Roberts' self-acting mule (first developed in 1825 as a result of a direct request by manufacturers threatened by a strike) became operational in the early 1830s. Yet despite the weakening of their bargaining power resulting from the simplification of the spinning process, there was no large influx of women into spinning. At the same time, however, mechanical weaving mills became a haven for female labor. In 1841, 33,000 women of all ages defined themselves as weavers (branch not specified), as opposed to 77,000 males. In "cotton manufactures" (spinning and weaving) there were 144,000 females as opposed to about 136,000 males. In other industries, too, such as the Kidderminster carpet industry, women were able to find niches despite male resistance.

As the trade union movement slowly evolved in the first half of the nineteenth century, it strove simultaneously to protect working families by providing a decent wage for the husband and to guarantee "domesticity" for the wife. The question, however, that needs to be raised is why this movement succeeded as well as it did in securing male dominance in the workplace. The real answer must go beyond a fanciful male conspiracy to subjugate women and confine them to the home. We should keep in mind that eighteenth-century and later Victorian Britain was a society that was quite different from our own in its dominant values and beliefs, and that little historical insight is gained by judgment and indignation. Even the most enlightened circles respected what they felt both society and biology decreed. Women were relegated to their "natural" role of mothers and wives, but there can be little doubt that the majority of them regarded this as acceptable and comfortable. John Stuart Mill, one of the most enlightened thinkers of his age, still thought that "the most suitable division of labor" between husband and wife was one in which the man worked outside the home and the woman "superintends the domestic expenditure" (Mill, [1869], 1970, p. 178). He added, however, that in an imperfect world it would be desirable for women to work to improve their bargaining power in the household. Even the most progressive elements of British society believed in separate spheres and disjoint roles. Thus the Owenite Grand National Consolidated Trade Union was quite segregated. The Chartist movement, the largest and most powerful protest movement of the 1840s, declared that it demanded the vote for all men so they could protect their women from factories, and it did not advocate anything like political equality for women and supported their confinement to domestic activities (Taylor, 1983, pp. 93, 268). The values and beliefs of segregation that implied separate spheres for men and women and that relegated working women to a number of well-enclosed niches in the economy—teaching, apparel, and domestic service—resonated with large segments of the population, female as well as male.

Some exclusionary statutes that may appear discriminatory to us were meant to protect human beings regarded as vulnerable. Legislation that excluded women and children from underground labor in mines cannot be interpreted as just another crass attempt to favor the employment opportunities of men over those of women. The Mines and Collieries Act of 1842 limited the employment of women in mines and specifically prohibited their employment in underground pits. The reasoning was "moral," a concern for the morality of women, reflecting the revulsion that an increasingly prudish society felt when unrelated men and women worked in close proximity in cramped, dark quarters. Contemporary wisdom had it that in the crowded environments of factories and similar workplaces, women matured earlier, and this led to sexual precocity and promiscuity. It was, after all, an age in which "respectability" counted for a lot. These, as well as the dangerous and noisome nature of the work, were the underlying motives of the legislation. Moreover, in many of these sectors the work of women was complementary to that of men, and thus males gained little or nothing by excluding women in addition to foregoing the earnings of female family members. To be sure, there are cases that support the hypothesis that organized male workers were concerned by female competition, and it is likely that some of the motivations behind political and social movements that led to segregation and the exclusion of married women from some industrial activities were in this spirit. But that is not how most contemporaries saw it: they regarded these as sincere attempts to protect a vulnerable group of people who were being exploited by naked greed. Whether the dominant (male) opinion of the time regarded women as competitors or as victims is hard to know. It is telling, however, that many of the Acts passed by Parliament limiting working hours pertained to *both* women and children—the two groups whose vulnerability had become quite apparent. It is possible to interpret "the ideology of respectability" and notions such as female domesticity among working-class men and women as a power play to make gender differences more pronounced. However, rather than view this primarily as the way by which one group took advantage of another, we could see this legislation as a sincere attempt by well-meaning groups to protect certain values that seemed sacrosanct to them.

In the reality of daily household life, the bargaining position of women was of course more complex, and wives always had means of persuading or cajoling their husbands. But the formal rules of the household game favored males. With a legal system thus stacked against women, divorce almost impossible, husbands controlling the household's property, the fate of children, and in the end every other major decision in the family, wives would be confined to the home if this was what their husbands desired. But were these decisions made over the objections of the women? There is little evidence that middle-class married women were in large numbers opposed to their confinement to the home. A modern historian has even argued that "to be an angel in the home was no bad bargain," given the growth in the importance of family and domestic life (Hilton, 2006, p. 363). The industrious revolution discussed above, in which women and children were increasingly engaged in market activities producing cash, was feasible in large part because much of this activity could take place within the household and did not require long absences.

A number of caveats should be introduced here. One is that after 1750, and especially after 1800, there was a considerable difference between married and unmarried women. Unmarried women almost invariably worked: teenagers in factories and in domestic service, older unmarried women in the textile industry and teaching (including nannies and governesses). The same is true for daughters who took over the businesses of their deceased fathers. Apart from that, for never-married women there were few options. Of course, women could "fall"—that is, sell their body. Most prostitutes lived wretched, disease-ridden lives of poverty and abuse, though here and there we can observe the odd *demi-mondaine* who made it into high society and wealth. As Roy Porter has noted memorably, "it was certainly easier for a woman to achieve notoriety than power" (1990a, p. 33).

The labor force status of married women is more difficult to analyze, and modern historians have pointed out that their classification as "unoccupied" by the mid-nineteenth-century censuses *itself* reflects an attitude to gender. From the late eighteenth century on, it became increasingly rare for married women to work outside the home, except in factories, which were located in only a few areas. All the same, the majority of these women were, in fact, working even if they stayed in their house. Large numbers were engaged in seasonal or casual work, which the censuses did not record. Especially in agriculture, the exact definition of what it means to be employed is subject to a certain arbitrariness. All in all, the role of women in the economy is surely understated by sources that disregarded that kind of work. And yet it can hardly be denied that if we define the "formal" economy as market activity that generated money income, on balance their position retreated in the late eighteenth and nineteenth centuries.

The growing separation between the productive units and the places where people lived and consumed was one of the most momentous developments of this era. The declining participation of married women in the formal labor force and the fall in their earnings as a proportion of household income were primarily the result of the fact that the home's role as a productive economic unit shrank during the second half of the period 1700–1850. Men thus faced a choice between the earnings that their wives could bring in if they worked outside the home, and enjoying the services that women generated inside the home. A growing number chose the latter. Many families made an attempt to make up the cash thus foregone, by trying to find other ways for married women to earn cash while staying at home. But on the whole, households decided that it was more effective to keep the wives at home and engage in household activities than to send them out to work. In that fashion, the rise of the factory system and the decline of the home as a productive unit were at the center of the changing position of women.

This process was gradual and uneven. In regions in which some form of domestic industry survived, women maintained an active economic role, although their earnings came under pressure whenever domestic production had to compete with more efficient factory methods. The erosion of the option to engage in domestic industry continued throughout the nineteenth century, culminating in the years around 1900 when formally employed married women became an almost negligible part of the economy. In the course of the nineteenth century, the aversion to married women working outside the household was strengthened by the growing realization that there was a strong connection between the health of household members and the amount of work that homemakers invested in cooking, cleanliness, and child care (Mokyr, 2002). The sanitary movement, based on the emerging understanding of the connection between dirt and disease after 1830 or so, appointed female homemakers as the guardians of health and well-being. This attitude reinforced the sense that by engaging in work away from home, women were not carrying out their main function in society, which was to look after the other members of their household. Such a responsibility required continuous presence, and precluded employment away from home. Around 1850 this notion was still confined primarily to middle- and upper-class families, but even then there were many families that belonged to the labor aristocracy and tried to follow a "respectable" lifestyle. For these families, increasingly, the outside employment of married women was not an option.

*   *   *

The question of child labor has been one of the more controversial issues among economic historians in large part because of its strong political overtones. Historians critical of industrial capitalism have almost without exception felt with E.P. Thompson (1963, p. 367) that the exploitation of little children by factory owners was "one of the most shameful events of our history." Historians defending the Industrial Revolution have pointed to the fairly limited dimensions of the phenomenon and argued that child labor was nothing new in the late eighteenth century and that only its enhanced visibility and the moral righteousness of well-meaning social critics made it seem more egregious in the early nineteenth century than before. As the ideological edges of the historiography of the Industrial Revolution have become blunter in recent decades, scholars have made an effort to distill a clearer and less politically charged picture from very partial records.

What did children do before the Industrial Revolution? The records of the eighteenth century show a considerable variation in practices, but we simply do not have access to the kind of information that would allow us to make any quantitative assessments. Needless to say, the children of the laboring poor, the small artisans and shopkeepers, and the smallholding tenant farmers were supposed to be working. John Locke felt in 1697 that "the children of the labouring people are an ordinary burthen to the parish and are usually maintained in idleness so that their labour also is generally lost to the public, until they are twelve or fourteen years old" (cited by Bouyer, 1789, p. 112). Apprentices, by all evidence, did not start their training before age 13 or 14. Given that physically a 13 year-old in the eighteenth century was probably equivalent to an 11-year old in our time, it should come as no real surprise that "employment" in the sense of regular hours of work in an organized setting was not a very common phenomenon. The value of what children could produce was not commensurate with what they cost their employers in terms of tools and materials. Labor, in those days, was mostly physical and the stunted and often malnourished children of the eighteenth-century poor simply could not pay for themselves. Locke himself felt that "computing all the earnings of a child from three to fourteen years of age, the nourishment and teaching of such a child, during that whole time, will cost the parish nothing." Yet, as Hugh Cunningham (1990, pp. 129–30) has pointed out, in Locke's calculations the nourishment was to consist merely of a "bellyful of bread daily" with, in cold weather, "if it be thought needful, a little warm water-gruel." Workhouses set up for children could not be made to pay for themselves, and either depended on charity or folded. Of course, the children who ended up in these institutions were the poorest of the poor and the weakest of the weak; few survived, and it may well be the case that rather than a humane and charitable set of organizations, they were simply meant to remove an eyesore. In sum, in the traditional agricultural, artisanal, and proto-industrial economy, society had few qualms about putting children to work, but it paid off only in a few cases. Eighteenth-century child labor was thus limited primarily by demand: work in this economy predominantly required physical strength or experience, with which very young children were poorly endowed. Cunningham (1990) has made a powerful argument that for most of the period under discussion here, children were seriously underemployed simply because there was no demand for their labor, describing the economic system as one in which child labor was "both desirable and hard to attain" (p. 131).

Once they reached their mid-teens, however, they were put to work. As a description of Britain in 1834, Cunningham's interpretation of the evidence as consistent with low opportunities for child and teenage labor is not sustainable (Tuttle, 1999, pp. 12–13). Kirby (2005a) has also criticized the statistical basis for Cunningham's paper, and shown that at least by the middle of the nineteenth century, his argument is not persuasive. But for much of the eighteenth century, idleness may have been a threat and a scourge. The demand for child labor was, like all labor demand, highly seasonal, irregular, and geographically uneven. To be sure, many of the anecdotal sources cited by Cunningham were sanctimonious railings by priests concerned with idle children developing patterns of dissoluteness and immorality (1990, p. 127). As the economy changed, the demand for child labor was transformed. The decline of cottage industries and the changes in agricultural structure reduced the opportunities for child labor within the household, but factories and mines created new ones. The latter jobs were, however, more visible and became socially unacceptable.

Indeed, the rise and fall of child labor is often associated in the popular literature with the factories and the mines in the early decades of the Industrial Revolution. Modern scholarship has been fascinated by the causes and consequences of the phenomenon. Factory work placed, as noted, a premium on docility and good behavior, and employers found that children could be easily manipulated and controlled, to be made part of a more complex production system. The division of labor on the factory floor made it possible to break the work into repetitive tasks simple enough to be learned in a short time. The premium on physical strength declined as heavy mechanical work was taken over by machines. Moreover, children were found to be more trainable and malleable than adults. In 1835 the theorist of the early factory, Andrew Ure, wrote with some exaggeration that "even in the present day ... it is found to be nearly impossible to convert persons past the age of puberty, whether drawn from rural or handicraft occupations, into useful factory hands" (1835, p. 20). Beyond that, however, the new technology created employment opportunities that were best filled by children, such as the coal mine cart "drawers" and "trappers" (horse drivers), and cotton mill "piecers" who tied the broken threads. Children were often employed as "doffers" who removed full bobbins of spun yarn and dressers who prepared the cloth for the weavers on looms. A particularly nasty occupation for youngsters was "climbing boys," essentially human chimney brushes. Here, clearly, a small youngster was essential to carry out the job (Tuttle, 1999, p. 24).

Children were cheap. In part, this was because of supply: with rising birth rates in Britain, the market was awash with youngsters. To illustrate: demographers' computations have estimated the proportion of persons aged 5–14 in the overall population at 20.6 percent in 1771 and at 24.4 percent in 1831, a huge increase. One reason is that their opportunity costs were low. Working-class children rarely went to school for extended periods, and although they did help in the domestic economy, the same economic changes that reduced the demand for female labor in cottage industries also affected the demand for child labor outside the factories. As a result, factory owners were quite keen on children as a source of labor. Especially employers in rural areas where cheap labor might be harder to find tended to "bind" pauper and orphan children as parish apprentices, a practice thought to be little better than slavery. Recruiting agents were often sent to scour the surrounding countryside in search of workhouse labor, and some of these children were brought in from the other end of the country. Robert Peel, father of the later prime minister, employed up to 1,000 of them in his mill and David Dale had close to 500 in New Lanark in Scotland. When asked by a parliamentary committee in 1816 whether he employed "parish apprentices," Peel responded "there were no others I could get"—presumably at that price. Pauper apprentices were indeed a cheap and satisfactory form of labor and gladly sold by parish authorities to manufacturers who needed them (Ward, 1962, p. 15). Recent research has taken a somewhat more charitable view of parish apprenticeship, pointing out that at least in some cases it saved youngsters from a life of begging or vagrancy and provided them with gainful employment in respectable work environments. By 1830, in any case, the practice had begun to fall into disuse and it disappeared with the Poor Law reform.

The economics of child labor in this period is anything but simple. Poor families needed children to generate cash to supplement the low or irregular income of parents, and so there can be little doubt that child labor was most prevalent among the laboring classes. Yet child labor competed with unskilled adult labor, and so the more laborers sent their children to work, the more they depressed adult wages. Moreover, in the longer run the number of children was itself affected by the opportunities for child labor or other ways in which children could be used to generate cash for their parents, especially through poor relief. Economic opportunities for non-male adults clearly helped people decide at what age to marry and influenced marital fertility. The presence of large numbers of children among the laboring poor, as Kirby (2003, p. 42) has noted, was at the same time a cause of poverty and the means for its alleviation. Within the life cycle of a typical worker there were difficult trade-offs. Even if children could be exploited, there was a long time lag between birth and the age at which they could start bringing in cash. Meanwhile, the wife's earning and productivity were affected. An 1841 document on handloom weavers points out that the first ten years of marriage of a typical worker are the hardest, because by the end of these years he has "a family of four, five, or six children too young to labour; the care of his family occupies the whole of his wife's attention, she cannot possibly contribute a shilling to the income of the family so that the whole must be fed by his hand alone" (cited by Kirby, 2003, p. 30). Changes in the economic structure due to technological change and changes in the geographical distribution of economic activity often caused young couples to miscalculate. To make things worse, the Poor Law was changed in 1834, and child allowances became more difficult to obtain.

The historical reality displays a profound asymmetry: the labor supply of youngsters was quite important for the modern factory sector in its early stages, but that sector remained a fairly marginal employer of children economy-wide. The 1834 Parliamentary Commission (Great Britain, 1834a, pp. 21–37) reported, by its admission on the basis of very partial reports, that in the cotton industry in Lancashire, 24 percent of all male and 21 of all female employees were aged 13 and under, and another 27 and 32 percent respectively were aged 14–18. In the Leeds wool industry, 23 percent of all male and 26 percent of all female workers were 13 and under, and another 22 percent and 33 percent respectively aged 14–18. All in all, half the workers were 18 and under. In the more traditional wool industries in the West Country, however, things were not very different: in Wiltshire, for example, 49 percent of all male workers were 18 and under, and 31 percent of all females. The 1842 Commission (Great Britain, 1842, p. 38) looked at child labor in coal mines, and reported that 38–40 percent of their labor force in Lancashire and Yorkshire were under 18, with similar proportions in East and West Lothian in Scotland (in Northumberland and Wales the numbers were around a third). Tuttle concludes (1999, p. 30) that between one-third and two-thirds of the labor force in the textile industries and coal mines of Britain consisted of children and youths. It should be stressed that in terms of their biological development, working-class teenagers in Victorian Britain were 2–3 years behind the adolescents of our time.

Child labor in factories and mines, on the other hand, never occupied more than a minority of British children. In 1851, about a third of all males aged 10–14 and 20 percent of all females of that age were "economically active"—about the same as in 1861. Moreover, as far as we can tell from the censuses, from a purely quantitative point of view factories and mines were a relatively small source of work for youngsters. In the middle of the century, the biggest employers of children were still traditional non-factory occupations: farms, artisans, and service industries. For boys aged 10–14, "agricultural labour" and "messenger" between the two of them occupied more than all textile industries plus coal mining. In addition, the number of children reported in agriculture is seriously biased downward, because the 1851 census did not count the farmer's own children as "employed" by him. Whether such children should be counted as "occupied" or "employed" may be a bit of an anachronistic way of formulating the question. In the mid-nineteenth century it was often rather arbitrary to decide whether a person participated in the labor force or not. Boys would be expected to work on the farm when there was work to be done, which was highly seasonal and irregular. For girls of the same age, "domestic" and "farm servants" between the two of them employed about as many as cotton, wool, silk, and lace together (each group accounting for about 60,000 girls, out of about 950,000 in the demographic cohort). The *actual* contribution of children under, say, the age of 15 to total national income was, of course, higher than these numbers suggest. Even by 1851, cottage industries had not wholly disappeared, and many children were still occupied in their parents' shop or craft, helping out on easy tasks, looking after younger siblings, or carrying out other domestic chores that freed up adult time for cash-generating activity.

Child labor, too, should be seen in the context of a household in which individuals bargained with one another. Tuttle's discussion of this issue (1999, pp. 51–56) shows how much insight can be gained by abandoning the extreme assumptions of the household as a single ("unitary") decision-making unit or one in which individuals maximize their own utility. Instead, she points out that children in the domestic system had at first little bargaining power within the household, as their threat points were extremely limited. As outside employment opportunities increased, youths began to realize that their bargaining power in the household had increased and they could exercise their clout. A Manchester merchant noted in 1816 that "children that frequent factories make almost the purse of the family ... and they share in the ruling of and are in a great state of insubordination to their parents" (cited by Tuttle, 1999, p. 53).

As the phenomenon of very young children hard at work expanded, public reaction ensued and child labor became a major public policy issue. What explains the political agitation against a minority phenomenon? In part, there was moral outrage at the abuse of defenseless innocents, led by such anti-child labor fire-brands as Richard Oastler and Michael Sadler. It became clear to a growing segment of society that in the case of children, the liberal notion that the free market worked properly and should be interfered with as little as possible, was simply not sustainable. The fundamental problem with child labor is that, unlike adult male labor markets, the decisions about work and leisure are made not by the economic agent him or herself, but by the parents. It is far from obvious that the child's interests and those of the parents always coincided. It is equally questionable whether those of the parents and those of society at large coincided. The Enlightenment view was that a rational solution had to be found for this contradiction. "The state," said Macaulay in the mid-nineteenth century about child labor, was "the legitimate protector of those who cannot protect themselves" (1864, p. 199). Parents heartlessly exploiting their children by sending them to dangerous and backbreaking work were only part of the problem. Equally serious was that education and learning would be undersupplied in areas in which they had substantial opportunity costs because of foregone earnings of children, either in the form of formal child labor or because children could be put to good economic use at home or on the farm. The net result, it was felt, was that by some social welfare criterion too few children went to school, and those who went to school attended too little and for too short a period. There were also physical and medical consequences of child labor that parents did not fully internalize, some out of callousness, some more probably simply due to ignorance. The horrid tales of children whose health was permanently ruined and whose lives were shortened by coal and cotton dust, accidents with machines, and skeletal damage caused by repeated mechanical operations were real enough to raise the level of righteous indignation of the Victorian middle classes, even if the actual percentage of children thus affected was never all that large. It may have helped the anti-child labor movement that the need for children in the factories declined in the decades after 1830. Some scholars, such as Nardinelli (1980), have argued that the demand for child labor declined in the second third of the nineteenth century as machines could increasingly substitute for the unskilled and routine labor children supplied, so that employers could afford to reduce the employment of small children and conveniently be seen to be on the politically correct side of a social issue with deep moral overtones.

For a combination of those reasons, Parliament passed repeated laws that limited the employment of children. The first Factory Act was passed in 1802, setting the maximum for children (meaning parish apprentices) at twelve hours day, followed by Peel's Act of 1819, which set the minimum age of employment at nine years in the textile industry. These early Acts were widely evaded and seem to have had little impact. The Regulation of Child Labor Act of 1833, the Mining Act of 1842, and the Ten Hours Bill of 1847, however, were, in the words of Carolyn Tuttle, "turning points in the history of government regulation of the employer/employee relationship" (Tuttle, 1999, p. 67). To be sure, the enforcement of the restrictions on child labor before 1850 has often been denigrated, and rightly so. Enforcement of well-meant legislation was difficult, and employers, then as now, computed the expected costs of being caught, convicted, and fined against the advantages of using cheap and easy labor. It has been calculated that the 1833 Act only delayed the entrance of children into the labor force by a year, and the Mining Act pertained to only a minuscule proportion (less than 1 percent) of the population under age 10.

Yet this does not mean that the Child Labor Acts were wholly insignificant, and not only as harbingers of a future in which child labor would become a fringe phenomenon in Britain and the industrialized West. Anonymous letters and newspaper articles informed the inspectors that laws were violated and Nardinelli (1980) feels that the 1833 law was "generally obeyed." Between 1835 and 1855, 7,378 cases were brought in Lancashire and the West Riding alone, and the conviction rate, including cases withdrawn upon fine payment, was over 90 percent (Peacock, 1984, p. 198). Fines and political pressure forced magistrates (many of them textile manufacturers themselves) to enforce the law; the cost of compliance to the large mill owners in the textile industry was not prohibitive (Nardinelli, 1985), and voluntary compliance was widespread (Kirby, 2003, pp. 105–10). The inquiries that preceded the legislation acted as exposés that alerted the public to the conditions of the factories and mobilized the informed and enlightened middle-class public against what were regarded as intolerable conditions of moral degeneracy. The laws signaled to employers what was socially acceptable, and that too blatant a violation would not be tolerated. Even political economists, committed as they were to unfettered markets, joined in and played a crucial role in framing the early factory laws. At least in textile mills, the proportion of children under 12 fell from 16 percent in 1835 to somewhere between 7 and 8 percent by mid-century. In any case, the widespread use of children in mills that peaked at some point in the first half of the nineteenth century started to decline fairly soon after the Factory Acts, even if mandatory schooling was not introduced until 1870. In mines, the proportion of children hovered around 12 percent in the 1840s. Clearly child labor was important, but the image conveyed by some social historians that the labor of small children was the backbone of the industrial labor force and therefore essential to the process of economic growth was no longer true by the 1840s, if it ever was.

When all is said and done, the employment of child labor in factories and mines on a large scale was a temporary phenomenon in Britain. Moral outrage was a major factor in creating a backlash against it, although economics contributed. Perhaps less than technological change that reduced the demand for children, what in the end mattered was what happened on the labor supply side. The first generation of adult males was stubbornly resistant to factory work; by 1840, however, Britain was awash with young men who had never known anything else and who became a willing factory labor force. Supplemented by Irish migrants, who arrived in large numbers in Britain in the 1840s, these people turned out in the end to be more effective workers. Legislation, too, mattered. The paperwork involved in employing children (certifying that they conformed to the limits set by legislation), the limitation on hours, and the requirement to set up factory schools, all raised the costs to employers and made them look for other sources of labor. On the supply side, rising incomes on the part of parents made them less dependent on the supplemental income earned by children, and it seems plausible that many parents gradually began to realize that if they wanted their children to have happier and better lives, they should keep them away from repetitious and dangerous work and send them to schools or apprenticeships where their human capital would be increased. As economists have pointed out (Galor and Moav, 2006), in this respect the interests of employers and of parents coincided. If skilled labor and capital were strongly complementary in the production process, but unskilled labor and capital were not, it would be in the interests of both the employer and the parent to minimize child labor, and instead invest in the child's education.

In summary, the century and a half before 1850 witnessed enormous changes in the nature of the family economy and the work of women and children. The changes in agriculture and the demise of cottage industry changed the economic function and nature of the household. By the middle of the nineteenth century, it was well on the way to losing its central function as a unit of production and was concentrating on consumption and increasingly on the formation of human capital. Married women and small children were gradually withdrawn from the labor market, women specializing increasingly in their function as homemakers, and children beginning a transition to a modern world in which their role would be radically redefined. These changes were driven by a number of factors. Technology clearly played a role through the growth of central locations for work, a topic I shall turn to in the next chapter. Demography and demographic behavior were also of considerable importance. We should not, however, underrate the importance of changing institutions, whether through changes in the politics, the ideology, or the cultural beliefs of the people who mattered. In the end, institutions are the constraints that society imposes on its actors, whether through formal legislation such as Factory Acts, or through informal customs and mores such as "proper behavioral codes" as they emerged in mid-Victorian Britain. The Victorian family was the final product of these intertwined historical forces.

CHAPTER 15

Factories and Firms in an Age
of Technological Progress

There were two major changes in the organization of production in Britain between 1700 and 1850. The rise of the factory system, one of the most dramatic sea changes in economic history, has been the subject of a large number of studies, going back to the early nineteenth century. The lesser emphasized change is the gradual replacement of the independent domestic worker by a system of merchant-manufacturers, sometimes known as the transition from the *Kaufsystem* to the *Verlagssystem*. Most of the work still took place in the laborer's cottage, but the coordination, marketing, and the supply of materials and capital all were in the hands of an entrepreneur. How this transition, regarded by some as the triumph of a superior market-based system, and by others as the emergence of an exploited and oppressed proletariat, should be assessed remains to be seen. There were economies of scale that an entrepreneur operating a large firm could exploit, and it is not obvious that such changes made his workers necessarily worse off. The transition to a factory system was especially marked in textiles, but can be seen throughout the manufacturing sector.

The Industrial Revolution is often not just associated with but actually *defined as* the rise of the factory, a large building in which workers congregated every day to do their work, in fixed (and long) hours, usually in unpleasant, noisy, dirty, and often dangerous conditions. The term "dark, Satanic mills," originates in a poem by William Blake about the poet John Milton and its original meaning is ambiguous. No matter; the term has come to signify the horrors of the industrial age. How bad things really were during this period for most people remains to be seen, but the long-term impact of the factory system on every aspect of the British economy and British society was undeniable. In traditional Britain, the spheres of consumption and production had been largely one and the same; the Industrial Revolution separated them. The idea of the factory system was larger than just the industrial mills. It eventually included non-manufacturing firms such as transportation, offices, and retail premises. They all shared an important characteristic, namely the precise circumscription of work in time and space, and its physical separation from homes.

The rise of the factory, however, was not entirely synonymous with the Industrial Revolution. For one thing, even before the Industrial Revolution, there were a number of establishments that would qualify as factories in Britain, foreshadowing what was to come. Ambrose Crowley's ironworks in county Durham and the Lombe brothers' silk throwing mills in Derby employed hundreds of workers in the decades before 1750. A brassmaker in Warmley in 1767 employed 800 at one site (plus 2,000 outworkers) and John Taylor's large plant in Birmingham employed 500 workers in 1755 (Hopkins, 1989, p. 10; Berg, 1994, p. 267). But these were, in the words of Michael Flinn (1962, p. 252), giants in an age of pygmies. Before the Industrial Revolution, Britain had industry but few industrialists, industrial firms but few industrial plants. The typical manufacturing firm was a local workshop, often in or near a home, employing family members, apprentices, and servants who often lived with the family. In the century and a half after 1750, this form of organization was slowly but relentlessly replaced by a factory setting. Observers from Marx on have felt that this change was the most dramatic and deep of all the changes that the Industrial Revolution wrought. Max Weber, reflecting on the Industrial Revolution and what it did, felt that the consequences of the rise of the factory were "extraordinarily far-reaching" (Weber, [1923], 1961, p. 136) and the French historian Paul Mantoux, who wrote the first full-blown account of it, remarked that the word "revolution" was indeed apt to describe it and that few political revolutions had such far-reaching consequences ([1905], 1961, p. 25).

The rise of the factory system was uneven, although in the end most industries and activities completed the transformation. In textiles, it happened in spinning before weaving, in iron it happened in forging before finishing. Pottery, glass, paper, and some food processing (e.g., breweries) established large works relatively early, but the manufacture of many consumer goods, especially durables such as shoes, guns, stockings, hats, and toys remained a small workshop industry until well into the nineteenth century. Even within industries that moved to the factory system, the old forms of industrial organization often coexisted for decades with the new ones, sometimes with the same firm subcontracting out some stage of the production process to workers' cottages. The rather poor statistics available indicate that by 1841 more than two-thirds of the cotton industry was concentrated in factories, perhaps half of the woolen and worsted industries, and a third of the metal trades. Moreover, it was geographically uneven. Much of England barely saw any factories by 1850: the south and parts of the east remained largely rural areas, in which change was barely visible. But by the middle of the nineteenth century the process had acquired a great deal of momentum, and the advance of the factory became inexorable. By 1900 the triumph of the factory system was complete: less than a third of industrial workers still worked at home.

This development is less self-explanatory than it may seem at first glance. The advantages of the old domestic system were quite substantial. A firm that used workers' homes as its main location could save itself the large capital expenditure of having to buy or rent a large structure and be concerned with maintenance, security, insurance, heating, and lighting. It did not need to pay for foremen, night guards, or worry about workers misbehaving, getting into fights with other workers, or being absentee. For the workers, domestic work meant the freedom and flexibility to work when and how much they felt like, the ability to carry out domestic tasks such as baby sitting while at the same time being gainfully occupied ("multitasking" in modern parlance), and saving themselves the time cost of walking to the factory and back. The factory system demanded new rules of behavior. Workers had to submit to discipline and obey strangers and that most tyrannical of all masters: the clock. The independent skilled artisan and even the lowly rural cottage worker had to deal with their suppliers and their markets, but one could not call this "discipline." In cottage industries, domestic workers often had to deal with the capitalist merchant-manufacturer, and to fill his orders. But while conflicts did occur between them, and there were some attempts by capitalists to exercise control over what workers did at home, such control was episodic and was not exercised on a daily basis. Factories changed all that, and discipline and economic hierarchy became increasingly common. Finding workers willing to submit to factory discipline and the harsh conditions of factory work was far from easy. Such behavior did not come naturally, especially to proudly independent adult males, who had always been large fish in the very small ponds of domestic industry. In the early stages of the growth of the factory, mill owners had great difficulty recruiting suitable laborers, and preferred women and children, who in a traditional society could be expected to be more docile. Those, like Boulton and Watt, who depended on skills that were monopolized by males, often found themselves at the mercy of men like James Taylor, who, Watt complained in a letter to Boulton, "had taken to dram-drinking at a most violent rate ... obstinate, self-willed and dissatisfied." Alcoholism was a problem even with skilled workers, and John Smeaton once gave an engine-man at Watt's firm some money, whereupon the man "drank so much the next day that he let the engine run wild, and it was thrown completely out of order" (cited by Smiles, 1865, pp. 227, 311).

Early industrialists discovered that in order to create a labor force, one had to influence the way workers behaved, through social control and conditioning. Complicated incentive systems were set up. A few managers, like Robert Owen, felt that if they treated workers rationally and humanely, these values would emerge naturally. Others often preferred the stick to the carrot: fines, instant dismissal and, in many cases, physical punishment. Economics decrees that people respond to incentives, but culture and institutions determine whether the incentives take the form of carrots or sticks. Factory schools were set up not just to train the young to read and write, but to imbue them with thrift, industriousness, respect for their superiors, temperance, the fear of God, and other good bourgeois values that would help the managers to run the factories smoothly. It is hard to know how much exactly of the Victorian ethic, with its emphasis on decency, family life, financial prudence, and similar virtues, was due to the needs imposed by the new system. Moral codes and informal rules of conduct have a life of their own and rarely emerge solely because they satisfy an economic need. At the same time, when informal institutions and economic success reinforced one another, as they increasingly did in the Victorian age, they could be hugely successful. Families were often employed as units, as Neil Smelser (1959, pp. 188–91) has shown. The advantages were that the firm's hierarchical structure took advantage of parental authority, as well as intra-family loyalty and solidarity. It minimized the friction between non-family members working at the same site and helped smooth the transition from domestic to factory work. Humphries (1981, p. 13) noted that "The need to control helpers explains the recourse to girls' labour, not necessarily because they were more docile, but because miners preferred to employ daughters over whom they had parental authority, rather than boys from another family." In coal mines family labor increased discipline and therefore relieved the hewer of the need constantly to supervise the ancillary labor process.

Nothing in economic history is simple, clean, and linear. The correspondence of centralized workplaces with the emergence of close supervision or "discipline" was far from perfect. For one thing, some employers in the putting-out system acquired the right to enter the premises of domestic workers and to inspect their work and the way they used the raw materials and the equipment that often belonged to the putting-out entrepreneur, thus inserting some of the elements of factory discipline into the workers' homes. At the same time, there were factory-like structures that simply rented out space to self-employed workers, who came and left as they pleased and the owner cared but little how hard they worked. Factories were not invariably associated with expensive machinery and the outlay of large amounts of fixed capital. Richard Arkwright's famous Cromford Mill in Derbyshire was equipped with expensive power and spinning equipment, but many early factories appear to have been little more than the concentration of domestic workers under one roof, doing things that were technologically not much different from what they had been used to at home. Other "mills," rather than being dark and forbidding castle-like structures, were haphazard assemblages of separate buildings and small cottages, such as Robert Peel's cotton-printing works in Bury.

What were the economic origins of the factory system? Clearly, it was a complex phenomenon, and no single one-line economic argument will fully explain its rise. The most obvious and least controversial explanation is that a great deal of the mechanization of the Industrial Revolution led to physical economies of scale at the level of the plant. Steam engines, large textile machinery, chemical plant, and puddling furnaces were all large, fixed-cost components and none of them could operate efficiently at the level of the small, domestic workshop. To that we can add certain other sources of economies of scale at the level of the plant, such as lighting, heating, security, inventory control, and so on. A finer division of labor, too, seems to be more economical if the different stages are concentrated in one building, although the domestic system was capable of considerable division of labor. Yet some scholars (e.g., Marglin, 1974–75) have argued that logically and historically there was reverse causation here: first, workers were concentrated in large premises, then entrepreneurs saw the opportunities to introduce more sophisticated and heavier equipment. Such a reverse causality stretches credibility in some cases, but there may have been enough of it to make simple technological stories pointing to the superiority of large-scale plants less than wholly satisfactory.

The other explanations that economists have proposed to explain the rise of the factory concern incentives and information costs (Williamson, 1980; Szostak, 1989). A domestic worker in the putting-out system, working for a merchant-entrepreneur or *Verleger*, would be paid by the piece. The harder the laborer worked, the more he or she earned. In a system in which the equipment was relatively cheap, and in which output quality was simple to observe, such a system worked well. Piece wages, of course, were not confined to domestic industry. Even in factories and mines, when and wherever possible, employers preferred to pay workers a piece rate. When the machinery became more sophisticated and expensive, however, the owner (that is, the capitalist) began to be concerned with how heavily it was utilized, and the care with which the worker maintained and ran it. Even if the equipment was small enough to fit into a worker's home and required just one person to operate it, it would make sense for the employer to try to monitor the production *process* itself (that is, the inputs), rather than just to count the output and pay the worker accordingly. A worker paid by the piece who was operating an expensive piece of machinery or using costly materials that belonged to his or her employer had an incentive to waste raw materials, run the equipment faster than optimal, and skimp on maintenance. This can be viewed as a problem of joint production, because each worker is simultaneously doing two things: producing output and performing equipment maintenance. If the employer observed one better than the other, inefficiencies would result because workers would over-allocate efforts to the more readily observable activity. Moreover, information was asymmetrical: for the employer it was difficult to determine if a machine broke down because of *force majeure*, normal wear-and-tear, or because of worker neglect, unless he could directly monitor the production process itself by placing the worker in a factory setting. A similar story holds true for the raw materials and semi-finished products that the putting-out merchant moved from cottage to cottage. In the eighteenth century, complaints proliferated about workers wasting or embezzling valuable materials that the employer owned. By monitoring what the worker did, the employer could reduce this damage, but to achieve that he had to locate work in a factory setting and hire foremen.

The other way in which information could help explain the rise of the factory system had to do with product quality. An employer who paid the worker by quantity alone of course ran the risk of being cheated by the worker who cut corners to maximize quantity and delivered a shoddy product. In many activities, such a dilution of quality would have been difficult to detect and when the work was finely subdivided, it was often hard to attribute bad workmanship to a specific worker and penalize him or her. Quality, moreover, had many dimensions. Workmanship and materials could be compromised in many ways, but in the eighteenth century the issue of standardization became increasingly important, as markets expanded and consumers demanded products with easily verifiable attributes. A well-made bolt that does not conform to a well-made nut makes for a poor product, as is a well-made and durable shoe that does not quite fit. Standardization of both output and input may well be the most underrated technological development of the Industrial Revolution. It required both technological and institutional breakthroughs: the sophisticated machine tools that created parts and products that were homogeneous, and the coordination on exact standards by different producers. But the payoff was substantial. Britain was gradually becoming a unified market, and consumers could choose from many suppliers if they did not get what they wanted, or were unsure. It became imperative for manufacturers to standardize their products, to make sure that once a customer knew the name of the manufacturer he or she did not have to spend valuable resources to verify product quality. Printing and stamping were of course the known and trusted methods of manufacturing more or less identical products, as was the printing technique of calicoes using cylinders (invented by Thomas Bell in 1783 and used with great success by, among others, the Peels). Factories, in which the industrial capitalists could impose standards on their workers and supervise the production process itself helped solve the problem. The meticulous quality control exercised by Josiah Wedgwood at his famous Burslem pottery in Staffordshire or Benjamin Gott at his progressive Park Mills (near Leeds) wool factory would have been unthinkable in a domestic setting. It is precisely here that the advances in machine-tool making paid their largest dividends. The screw-cutting lathes built by Henry Maudslay and his student Joseph Whitworth produced gears, screws, and bolts, of unprecedented accuracy and tolerance.

The factory, moreover, had another big advantage: it gave employers the option to pay workers a time wage, because they could monitor the time worked. Domestic workers, by their vary nature, could only be paid piece wages. The economics literature has thought long and hard about the issue of why one would want to pay workers a pure time wage, a pure piece wage, or some combination of the two. Piece wages have the advantage that they are, in the lingo of economists, *high-powered incentives.* They establish a proportionality between output and effort, and thus encourage the worker to exert herself even when the employer is not looking. Apart from the matters of product quality and joint production, piece wages are difficult to sustain when production is carried out by a *team* rather than an individual (Alchian and Demsetz, 1972). When two or more workers work together on a given task, it is hard to determine who does what, and thus to pay them a piece wage. Each worker, knowing that, would have an incentive to shirk. One could pay the entire team (as was often done), but this leaves the internal distribution within the team open. In the early factory days, owners solved this problem by hiring entire families as teams. Even factories that paid their "operatives" a piece wage, as many did, would end up paying overseers and maintenance personnel a time-wage. A finer division of labor would make the payment of piece wages difficult, although standardization of the output actually worked in the opposite direction and even Boulton and Watt were able to pay increasing numbers of their employees a piece wage (Roll, [1930], 1968, pp. 191–94). The teamwork issue became acute when factories adopted "continuous flow" processes in which the speed of production was no longer left to the individual worker but was controlled by the machines and their operators. Cotton-spinning was the harbinger of this technique, but other early examples of such systems can be found.

The famous Portsmouth block-making machines, devised by Henry Maudslay and Marc Brunel around 1801 to produce wooden gears and pulleys for the British navy, are an example of the penetration of the spirit of improvement into areas rarely covered by most scholars. The moving spirit behind it was Samuel Bentham, the brother of the philosopher, who had been appointed Inspector-General of Naval Works in 1796. Bentham introduced improvements wherever he could, including the commissioning of the navy's first steam engine in 1799, which was designed to power the woodworking machines by day and to pump out the dry-dock reservoir during the night. The proposal made by Brunel to use steam power for block-making machinery was carried out by Maudslay. The block-making machines were in many ways a sign of the industrial future. In their close coordination and fine division of labor they resembled a modern mass-production process, in which a strongly interdependent labor force of ten workers produced a larger and far more homogeneous output than the traditional technique that had employed more than ten times as many. In their rationality and innovativeness, the Portsmouth works were exactly the kind of advance the Baconian program dreamed about, designed by a Frenchman but requiring the the dexterity of a craftsman like Maudslay and the organizational skills of an entrepreneur like Bentham to become reality.

A complementary approach to understanding the rise of factories has to do with knowledge and expertise (Mokyr, 2001, 2002). With the advent of more sophisticated machinery and procedures, the production process became more complex and the skills and knowledge needed to implement all the procedures in production and deal with contingencies became so voluminous that a single person could not master them easily. Machinery of different kinds, involving the generation of motion and complex transmission mechanisms or chemical processes needed to be operated, monitored, maintained, and repaired. Production increasingly had to follow precisely complex "recipes" for making paper, glass, dyes, guns, soap, and metal objects, often requiring snap decisions by an expert. As a consequence, the advanced modern industries required the expertise of specialists such as machinists, chemists, engineers, blacksmiths, highly skilled carpenters, and so on. The specialized knowledge these people supplied was often needed on the spot, and had to come from someone who could be trusted and with whom the firm had repeated interactions , so firms had to keep these experts on the premises.

Recent research by Thomas Geraghty (2007) has shed new light on the causes of the rise of the factory. Geraghty reasons that rather than there being a single factor that explains the phenomenon, a number of independent factors complemented and reinforced one another. Technology, business organization, and product quality went hand in hand in bringing about the factory system. Hence an approach that tries to separate them in some way may not be the best way to understand the phenomenon. The factory system owed its existence to the growing sophistication of the economy, the emergence of new equipment, and the need of factory owners to introduce incentives and modes of organization that coped with the new reality. Geraghty's data show that empirically there were strong pairwise complementary relations between factory organization (in terms of the way shop rules and incentives were set up) and machinery, and factory organization and quality control. The nature of the profit-maximizing decision had become more complex, and employers needed to simultaneously determine the choice of technique, the level of worker effort, and the way incentives were set up and communications and decisions flowed through the firm hierarchy.

Despite the need for highly skilled experts, the belief that manufacturing required a high level of human capital on the part of the majority of workers is no more accurate for 1850 than for 1700. Most workers on the shop floor had little use for finely honed skills, let alone literacy. It is often thought that most laborers during the Industrial Revolution became "de-skilled" and that the division of labor led to the creation of mind-numbingly monotonous work, described by Marx in scathing terms. The hazards of the division of labor were recognized as much as the advantages. Even before Adam Smith famously qualified his rosy view of the division of labor by pointing to its ability to induce "a torpor of mind" ([1776], 1976, p. 782), Adam Ferguson (1767, p. 325) warned that "The separation of possessions [i.e., the division of labor], while it seems to promise improvement of skill, and is actually the cause why the productions of every art become more perfect as commerce advances; yet in its termination, and ultimate effects, serves, in some measure, to break the bands of society, to substitute form in place of ingenuity, and to withdraw individuals from the common scene of occupation, on which the sentiments of the heart, and the mind, are most happily employed."

To operate the new techniques, firms needed to employ supervisors, technical experts, and other specialists. Many firms ended up maintaining small machine workshops beside the main mill, where this work was carried out. Much of this work by "experts" consisted of advising, supervising, and instructing unskilled workers, as well as the owner and one another. In an age in which such information could only be transmitted by personal contact, there was a growing need to concentrate such workers in one place. As early as 1806, in a report to Parliament on the woolen industry, the commissioners noted that "it is obvious, that the little Master Manufacturers cannot afford, like the man who possesses considerable capital, to try the experiments which are requisite, and incur the risks, and even losses, which always occur, in inventing and perfecting new articles of manufacture, or in carrying to a state of greater perfection articles already established. He cannot learn by personal inspection the arts, manufactures, and improvements of foreign countries ... The Owner of a Factory, on the contrary, being commonly possessed of a large capital and having all his workmen employed under his own immediate superintendance may make experiments, hazard speculation ... may introduce new articles and improve and perfect old ones" (Great Britain, 1806, p. 12). Skilled workers and trained mechanics were still regarded as scarce and obviously commanded a premium during the early stages of the Industrial Revolution, yet Britain was better supplied with them than any other European economy. Boulton and Watt were constantly concerned about their best workmen being tempted by better-paying jobs overseas, not only in Russia but also in France and Germany (Smiles, 1865, p. 227).

Factories were the repositories of useful knowledge, the sites where techniques were executed through a growing process of specialization. But they were also places in which experimentation, in the best traditions of the Enlightenment, took place. Of course, only a minority of the great mills carried out such experimentation, but the members of this technological elite were the ones who counted. Stewart (2007) has pointed to some of the more famous early mill owners as deeply involved in such experimentation. Watt and Wedgwood, as in so many things, led the pack, but others such as textile manufacturers Benjamin Gott, John Marshall, and George A. Lee followed a similar course. Matthew Boulton was an "inveterate experimentalist" who in one view was just as deserving of being called a *savant* as a *fabricant* (Jones, 2008, p. 117). Enlightened industrialists were often in touch with the best scientific minds of their day, but there were constraints on what could be learned. The point was, of course, that the best-practice propositional knowledge of the time was usually inadequate to guide the industrialists in their technical choices. When the precise natural processes underlying a technique are poorly understood, the best way to advance is through systematic trial and error. James Watt wrote in 1794 that even in mechanics theory was inadequate and thus experiment was the only answer: "When one thing does not do, let us try another" (cited by Jones, 2008, p. 172). Experiments, once the realm of gentlemen-scientists, had by the late eighteenth century become a shop-floor activity. But they could only be carried out in outfits that were large enough and rich enough to afford failures. The railways reinforced this trend: by the mid-1840s, when large bridges were constructed out of wrought iron whose properties in that use were little known, engineers carried out careful experiments to ensure sound designs (Rolt, 1970, pp. 12–15).

It cannot be repeated often enough that the "factory," in our minds associated with a large and usually ugly and user-hostile mill employing many workers under conditions of strict discipline and control, was still not the typical employer in the British economy by the mid-nineteenth century. The large mill, associated with the Industrial Revolution, has caught the imagination of historians because it was so new and dramatic, it was growing, and eventually it was to become a much larger segment of the economy (although it never became totally dominant). Small flexible firms, even when they were quite "modern" in their technology, remained far more common, in part because they had the agility to adapt, to transform their techniques and products as demand patterns or other economic parameters changed. These features often more than offset the economies of scale that drove the emergence of larger plants. Such high-skill workshops served as sub-contractors for larger firms, served specialized markets and customized needs, and could be closed or opened with relatively little pain. Whether the metal-working firms in Birmingham and Sheffield, the milliners and tailors of London, or the producers of a huge array of consumer goods, from bread to picture frames to shoes, small workshops employing from one to ten workers were easily not only the modal firm but also accounted for the lion's share of employment and industrial output until well into the nineteenth century. Much of the cotton industry consisted of perhaps 900 establishments, many of which were still little more than workshops, employing fewer than twenty hands—hardly the captains of industry whom Schumpeter so admired. Similarly, in engineering, of the 677 firms in 1851, no fewer than two-thirds employed fewer than 10 employees. In much of the British economy, then, smallish workshops remained the rule.

To describe the new technology, whether in large mills or small workshops, as de-skilling, so popular in some circles, is to oversimplify the complex new reality that emerged in the age of the early factory. Many of the old artisanal skills became obsolete as mechanization and a more refined division of labor were introduced. It may well be that some of the more automated processes were easy to learn and that technological progress affected low-skilled activities more (O'Rourke, Rahman, and Taylor, 2007). Most of the new mill and mine workers were probably low-skilled, though if we count the willingness and ability to adapt to a factory setting as a "skill," this conclusion becomes murkier. Yet the changes in the British economy went far deeper than just the transformation of industrial artisans into low-skill factory workers. Large new sectors and occupations were created, such as the railways and machine-making, which required different and new skills. The new factories needed managers, engineers, machinists, accountants, foremen, mechanics, carpenters, boilermakers, blacksmiths, clerks, salespeople, and so on. In cotton-spinning, the new mules had to be operated by highly skilled operatives, whose experience and dexterity prevented the yarns from either becoming so taut that they could snap or so slack that they would not wind properly. Puddling, too, created a new and highly skilled occupation of workers who had to learn a skill the hard way "uneducated but not ignorant ... when he had learnt his trade a man was truly a craftsman" (Gale, 1961–62, p. 9). Berg (1994, pp. 255–79) has stressed the importance of skills in the metal trades, and shown how the need for *different* as opposed to *fewer* skills characterized the Industrial Revolution. Even within the mills themselves, a greater spread and variety of skills was required. The eighteenth-century domestic handloom weavers, roughly speaking, all had similar skills. In the factories, largely because the total amount of knowledge needed for mechanized looms was beyond what a single individual could control, a division of knowledge was practiced. The overall level of skills was not so much lower or higher, but their distribution was becoming more skewed. In Lancashire and Glasgow male cotton factory workers in 1834 experienced earnings-age profiles that were consistent with investment in human capital at a younger age, enjoying significantly higher earning in their late twenties and thirties than in their later teens, suggesting that experience and on-the-job training were required in the manufacturing sector as well (Boot, 1995). At the same time, however, because the new techniques kept on changing, skills and expertise kept becoming obsolete at an ever faster rate. As the labor force became specialized, it had to become more agile and adaptable to a protean technological environment.

*   *   *

The typical business firm of the Industrial Revolution was managed by its owner or the principal partner. Schumpeter (1934, p. 77) noted that the entrepreneur of the time, in addition to being a capitalist, was also often his own technical expert, his buying and selling agent, personnel manager, and legal advisor. Many of the early industrialists were technically able and original, resourceful persons, but that did not necessarily make them good business managers. There were some exceptions, of course, such as Wedgwood, who comes as close as can be hoped for to the model of an ideal entrepreneur, being technically able, a master of marketing, but equally adroit as a politician. Matthew Boulton, similarly, was a gifted manager with broad technical competence. There were lesser-known figures who shared this combination of business and technical ability, such as John Taylor, a Birmingham buttonmaker and enamel snuff box manufacturer, who died in 1769 worth £200,000 and was deemed by one local writer as the "Shakespeare or Newton" of his business (Hutton, 1795, p. 102). Some entrepreneurs knew enough to sense that a technique could be profitable, but not enough to make it work, so they relied on outside experts. In other cases, technological leaders were able to team up with good business managers, as the famous partnership of Boulton and Watt attests, or John Marshall, the Leeds flax spinner who could rely on his technical manager Matthew Murray. The great engineer Richard Roberts, notorious for having poor business management skills, had able partners such as Thomas Sharpe and Benjamin Fothergill. Other famous teams were that of Cooke and Wheatstone, one the businessman, the other the scientist, as were John Kay and Richard Arkwright, the railroad engineer George Stephenson and his partner and promoter Henry Booth, and the rubber pioneers Thomas Hancock and Charles Macintosh. Less famous but just as effective were partnerships such as that of William Woollat and his brother-in-law Jedediah Strutt, the inventors of the improved knitting frame that could produce ribbed stockings (1758), and that of James Hargreaves (inventor of the spinning jenny) and his employer Robert Peel. Others were not so fortunate: Richard Trevithick, an engineer of astonishing creativity and ingenuity, repeatedly failed because of bad business management. The inventor William Cookworthy, described as "more scholar than gentleman," sold his invention of hard-paste porcelain to his fellow Quaker Richard Champion in Bristol in 1773. Champion for a while was a successful manufacturer of now-famous Bristol porcelain, but eventually failed to secure an extension of the patent and had to close in 1781. The majority of business firms needed professional help, however, simply because few individuals were talented and energetic enough to run both the managerial and the technical sides of a firm, and because after the death of the founder, his heirs were not always a match for his abilities. Such professional help, however, was not easy to find. Managers were often relatives of the entrepreneurs; others emerged from the practical, day-to-day work, and through the promotion into managerial ranks of the more able workmen, or at times, clerical personnel. By 1830 or so, the gap (social and economic) between managing partners and salaried managers had become rather small and the two groups increasingly overlapped.

Industrial firms were privately owned, either as partnerships or by a single individual. The typical industrialists owned one firm which contained one plant that produced only a few lines; that mill was the life of the owner. As the modern sector expanded and management tasks became more complex, industrialists needed deputies and assistants they could trust. They often chose relatives or partners, to make sure that the deputy would have a stake in the success of the firm. The reliance on family indicates that issues of trustworthiness and loyalty were at least as important as technical and managerial ability. Peter Mathias has noted "that kinship must be regarded as one of the most fundamental considerations in the study of entrepreneurship in industry in the eighteenth century" (1959, p. 271). Dynasties also emerged in industries in which skilled fathers trained their sons and endowed them with a proclivity for mechanical matters and an aptitude to solve technical problems. But, as we shall see, the question of trust was deeper than that, and kinship alone could not solve the problem. As a class of professional managers slowly emerged in the first half of the nineteenth century, the dependence on immediate relatives weakened. In fact, in some of the partnerships of the era, capable managers often played a critical role. Some of them, such as William Murdoch and John Southern at Boulton and Watt, were indeed promoted to partners. Robert Sherbourne, who was appointed manager of the Ravenhead plate glass factory in St Helens in 1792 and rescued it from pending failure, saw his salary increase from £500 to £1,000 as profits increased (Barker and Harris, 1954, p. 116). A few did even better: Robert Owen, one of the most famous industrialists of his age, started off as a manager at the New Lanark cotton mill, as did John Guest, who became manager, then partner, then owner of the Dowlais ironworks in Wales, the largest ironworks in the world in the 1830s and 1840s. The early nineteenth-century industrialist had to worry about equipment, fuel, building and machine maintenance, housing for his workers, security, and discipline. As a manager he was a tactician, as an entrepreneur he had to think strategically. Usually, but not always, industrialists lived near their plants and often did not delegate more than they absolutely had to. Ambrose Crowley, the great early eighteenth-century ironmonger, lived in London and spent much of his working time writing and dictating correspondence. Stourbridge ironmonger James Foster in the 1830s still read 5,000 business letters a year.

Factories created new problems that demanded solutions. Some of these were problems of labor control and management, which were by and large new to the manufacturing sector. In addition to the problems of recruiting a docile and malleable labor force which we saw above, the early factory masters struggled with the question of how they could best motivate the workers they hired. How hard could workers be driven? As Sidney Pollard ([1965], 1968) has pointed out in his classic work, "management" was not a concept that was known or understood before the Industrial Revolution. Military and maritime organizations, the royal court, and a few unusual set-ups aside, the need for organizations in charge of controlling and coordinating large numbers of workers and expensive equipment was rare anywhere before 1750. British managers fumbled and stumbled into solutions, some of which worked and some did not. What we would call today "human resources" issues were confronted by people who were inexperienced and had nobody to ask. To what extent should factory owners supply workers with housing, education, insurance, and other "public" goods? Should they hire on the spot market or provide workers with some modicum of job and wage security? Should they pay the lowest possible wages, or provide workers with a "fair wage," or what economists would call an efficiency wage, that is, a wage higher than what the worker can earn elsewhere, so as to incentivize the worker to be loyal to the firm? Huberman (1996) has shown how industrialists answered many of these questions, and shown how large Lancashire cotton mills differed from smaller ones in that they paid higher wages and made an effort to protect their workers during a decline in demand in order to foster worker loyalty. They also needed to make personnel decisions. What kinds of penalties should be levied against workers who violated some rule? Should they choose foremen and supervisory workers from within or bring in outsiders? At times factory masters hit upon solutions that worked; but management knowledge lagged behind technological progress, and the notion that competition among rational economic agents drives firms toward optimal personnel practices is not even true today. Pollard ([1965], 1968) has remarked that one of the hallmarks of an industrializing society is that it does not realize how under-managed it is.

One of the more interesting issues in the history of the firm is the evolution of accounting practices. Double-entry bookkeeping had been practiced by merchants since medieval times. The accounting practices in use on the eve of the Industrial Revolution had evolved in estate management, as well as in overseas trade and the associated credit transactions, and in the putting-out system. Most accounting procedures were commercial record-keeping devices and did not lend themselves readily to assessments of the overall profitability of an industrial enterprise, let alone its constituent parts. In the type of business typical in Britain around 1760, the bulk of economic activity was still carried out in businesses run by their owner, whose living standards were regulated more by cash flow than by profits per se. Partnerships, the most popular form of larger businesses, often had simple formulas for the withdrawal of cash and goods, although when the partnership was dissolved or expanded, more information had to be extracted from the books.

The manufacturing plants of the Industrial Revolution, however, introduced many new accounting problems of which nobody had much experience. Plants needed to worry about overhead capital, depreciation of equipment, inventory control, and the revenues and costs of different divisions. Capital accounting was especially deficient, and the wide range of practices indicates the uncertainty of the time about the correct procedures. Moreover, and perhaps most damaging, the accounting methods of the time made it almost impossible for an entrepreneur or manager to assess the net profitability of an innovation. In the otherwise well-run firm of Boulton and Watt nobody had a clue as to which departments were earning or losing money, and in the Scottish Carron iron company one manager estimated a profit of £10,500 when in fact £10,000 had been lost. In the 1770s, Josiah Wedgwood overhauled the accounting procedures of his firm, applying costing techniques computing "every expence of vase making as near as possible from the Crude materials"—though it is unlikely that his cost-accounting technique spread quickly throughout the manufacturing sector. Overproduction and other errors of judgment occurred so often that one thoughtful economic historian sighs that they "can hardly fail to diminish any estimates of the commercial acumen of the cotton entrepreneurs" (Payne, 1978, p. 189). In some sense this judgment seems a bit harsh: the managerial problems of the new mills were a by-product of the rise of the factory system, designed mostly to deal with technological and informational problems. For the engineering side, the early managers could rely on technical experts; for the management issues, they were usually on their own. Neighboring firms in the same industry, which would closely watch one another for technical advances, might be decades apart in accounting practices. The vast bulk of firms expected their clerks and accountants to pay their workers and suppliers and to collect from their customers, to prevent embezzlement, and maintain stock control. It was not expected, however, that they would provide a complete picture of the profitability of the various activities of the firm, nor would they have been able to do so had they been asked.

Equally problematic were the confused and inconsistent notions held at the time of "capital" and its rate of return, whether it should earn interest or profits. Factory masters confused fixed investment with current expenditures, and additions to equipment were entered on current account. Such practices were still the rule even in very large firms like the Dowlais Iron Company in Merthyr Tydfil, Wales, where virtually all new equipment was written off against current revenue. Depreciation of fixed capital, which became essential once costly equipment became essential to the technology, was rarely computed. The idea was hardly revolutionary: it was mentioned by Vitruvius in Roman times and an eighteenth-century writer about accounting, John Mair (1786, p. 71), described a method of re-evaluating fixed assets such as "ships, houses and other possessions" in detail in a widely used eighteenth-century textbook on accounting. John Smeaton included a twenty-year depreciation on the gates of the locks of the Forth and Clyde Canal (Mason, 1933). Of course, some industrialists realized the same, though their practices rarely reflected it. Joshua Milne, a cotton spinner from Crompton, near Oldham, explained to a parliamentary committee in 1833 that every prudent manufacturer should debit himself with a certain percentage for the depreciation of machinery, since otherwise his capital would have a fictitious value, but admitted that he himself did not do so regularly, beyond the expenses to keep the machinery in repair (Great Britain, 1833, pp. 652–53). Often industrialists mixed up wear and tear (that is, cash outlays for repair) and depreciation, and altogether failed to understand technological depreciation. Pollard ([1965], 1968, p. 285) assesses that "as long as there was no purposeful capital accounting, there could be no rational use of accounts for managerial guidance." If the age of Industrial Enlightenment was the age of rational production practices, these did not yet extend to accounting procedures. Many of the accounting and management techniques were developed slowly as the need for them was more strongly felt, but it was not until the large railroads came along that many of the managerial techniques we associate with modern corporate entities were developed.

To some extent, the way that factory masters coped with management problems was through subcontracting. With the emergence of the early factories, outsourcing remained very much part of the organization of much manufacturing, despite some inevitable vertical integration. Pollard ([1965], 1968) points out that subcontracting, a remnant of the domestic system, survived into the factory age "if not as a method of management, at least as a method of evading management." By outsourcing some tasks, entrepreneurs, especially in the early engineering industry, could shift the risk around, make people responsible for their mistakes, and reduce overhead costs, while still attaining the precision and standards that many components required.

At least until the 1820s, the model of what Cookson (1997, p. 4) has aptly called the dispersed factory system was widely used. Master mechanics and builders came to the factories to install, maintain, and repair equipment in their own time, with their own tools, accompanied by their own paid assistants, and carried out the job according to their own judgment and taste. Coal, cloth, and cotton yarn were produced using this system. Technologically complex tasks were farmed out to mechanical or "consulting engineers." Many of the functions that eventually were to be carried out by management through a hierarchical structure of foremen and supervisors were still carried out in the first half of the nineteenth century by a "labor aristocracy" of skilled, well-organized operatives and foremen. These operatives exerted a fair amount of independent discretion over both the laborers and the equipment under their control even if formally the entrepreneur owned the capital and employed the workers. Subcontracting or "outsourcing" as it is called today is neither inefficient nor a sign of "incomplete development," but a rational result of specialization. In a world of costly and asymmetric information it can make sense for a firm to hire an outsider to carry out a certain activity rather than do the job itself. All the same, there may have been cases in which subcontracting occurred largely because supervising a large number of people and activities was beyond the powers of the factory master in an age before modern management. Subcontracting also relieved the firm of the need to compute complicated payrolls and by definition farmed out much of the labor supervision to lower levels.

As already noted, some of the teething problems in the factory system were on the part of workers: they had to learn to cope with the harsh and sometimes dangerous conditions on the shop floor, to learn to get on with other workers, and to combine with them for collective action in an age when labor unions were still largely prohibited. Workers had to bear the time-cost involved in walking to and from the factory, and arrive on time. Women needed to find child care arrangements. Some of the problems were society's problems: as we have seen, the early factory masters' predilection to hire women and children was held to be morally reprehensible and possibly socially costly. The rapid growth of cities led to serious costs and hazards in terms of housing, sanitation, and public health. Mills polluted the air and the water, and they were often unsightly and noisome. The factory system was one of the first recognized instances of an economic change in which the free market demonstrably produced an outcome that was deemed to have socially undesirable consequences and demanded regulatory intervention. The seeds of the regulatory state had been planted even if it was to be many decades till the sprouts became visible. That, too, was the inevitable consequence of the Enlightenment.

To what extent did factory owners have to deal with organized labor? British labor unions were not a product of the Industrial Revolution and did not arise de novo out of mechanization and factories. Unions in Britain were an old tradition, and many of them emerged from the old craft guilds. In the eighteenth century many skilled workers were organized, such as London tailors, silk workers, hatters, and shipyard workers. These workers often struck in attempts to secure higher wages and better working conditions, and their strikes displayed many of the hallmarks of modern unions such as strike funds and "rolling strikes" (in which some of the workers remained on the job so that their earnings could help support the strikers). Such activities became especially pronounced in the 1780s and 1790s, when mechanization accelerated. In the countryside, where much of the labor force consisted of domestic workers, organized labor was especially assertive in the woolen industries in the West Country, where workers aggressively opposed the introduction of new techniques, which they feared would increase unemployment. In this region, the new machines were met by violent crowds protesting against such machinery as jennies, flying shuttles, shearing frames, gig mills, and scribbling machines. Moreover, in these areas magistrates were persuaded by fear or by propaganda to support the machine breakers. The tradition of violence in this region deterred all but the most determined innovators. Worker resistance was responsible for the slow growth and depression of the industry rather than the reverse (Randall, 1989). The West Country, as a result, lost its supremacy to Yorkshire. Resistance in Yorkshire was not negligible either, but it was overcome. All in all, however, only a small fraction of British labor was organized: it has been estimated that even in the most successful years no more than 5 to 10 percent of all workers belonged to a union (Reid, 2004, p. 14).

The history of labor unions in the eighteenth century reflects one of the deep contradictions in the Enlightenment movement. Traditional pre-industrial institutions had imposed some order and security on the economy through local regulations and guilds. Yet workers' associations had become distributional coalitions that protected the special interests and state-enforced regulations that Enlightenment thinkers criticized. They were increasingly regarded by Enlightenment liberals as impediments to free markets, and many of them were outlawed or weakened after 1750; between 1750 and the Combination Act of 1799 which pertained to "workmen" in general, no fewer than fourteen Acts were passed outlawing a variety of specific workmen's combinations (Moher, 1988, p. 76). Workers did not lose out invariably: the Spitalfields Act of 1773 protected the wages of London silk workers, an especially unruly group. Union strikes were often in defense of exclusionary practices that limited female and child labor and traditional techniques, and thus protected the earnings of incumbent workers at the expense of economic progress. As the liberal views of Enlightenment-inspired thinkers prevailed, these practices were curbed. Such changes helped create free labor markets, as the liberal political economists advocated, but they also left the workers with few safety nets short of the Poor Law, especially in urban regions. Workers' associations served the dual purpose of mutual support and collective bargaining. In their function as friendly societies, they were organizations in which workers provided one another with some level of mutual insurance against old age, disease, and the costs of burial, as a substitute for the Poor Law. Eden estimated in 1801 that there were 7,200 such societies in England and Wales, and that they had 648,000 members, which, together with their families, meant that "nearly a fourth of the population received occasional relief from these useful establishments" (Eden, 1801, p. 8). The freedom to organize spontaneously and cooperate with others, a basic Enlightenment principle, clashed with the anti-guild and anti-monopolist sentiments that increasingly became part of the conventional wisdom in the eighteenth century. More ominously, it clashed with the post-1793 British reaction to the French Revolution.

During the French Wars, national security concerns about Jacobine and radical sentiments prevailed and inspired the harsh Combination Acts of 1799 and 1800 that prohibited the combination of both workers and employers. The London Corresponding Society, an organization of workmen led by Thomas Hardy, a shoemaker, was disbanded. Laws against the association of workers were not easy to enforce, and this was true a fortiori for the organization and collusion of employers. Workers, especially in highly specialized industries such as printing and shipbuilding, continued to organize, although the anti-union legislation weakened their bargaining power with employers. All the same, real wages did not show a decline in the period of the Combination Acts, the war-induced inflation notwithstanding. Demand for labor was increasing despite a few periods of slump, and with rising prices workers were strongly motivated to make sure their real wages did not find themselves behind the prices of necessities. It was at this time that the government gradually switched its strategy from regulating wages outright to trying to arbitrate disputes between workers and employers. After peace returned in 1815, a growing organization of workers took place in the new industrial areas, and in August 1819 a huge rally of working-class people in Manchester ended up being violently dispersed by soldiers, an event known as the "Peterloo Massacre." This event galvanized the radical movement, which demanded the repeal of the Combination Acts and extension of the franchise. Radical leaders such as the Lancashire weaver Samuel Bamford and the leather-worker turned politician Francis Place (1771–1854) played significant roles in bringing about a set of reforms in the 1820s that made labor unions more legiti-mate. In 1825, another Combination Act of Parliament guaranteed that the legal freedom of trade unionism would be fully secured.

How much power organized labor had in the first half of the nineteenth century is hard to tell. The trade unions that evolved were confined mostly to skilled workers. Less skilled and easily replaced factory workers often tried to organize at the plant level but were no match for the employers. The movement remained decentralized and uncoordinated. That something of a post-Enlightenment class consciousness emerged in those years is hard to deny, though liberal sentiments remained hostile to workers' associations. This conflict reached a climax in the notorious Tolpuddle affair of 1834: six agricultural wor-kers, who had formed an association which by that time should have been perfectly legal, were convicted on the basis of an obscure law and transported to Australia. The subsequent public outcry forced the government to do a *volte-face* and the men were released and allowed to return.

The trade union movement thus grew in numbers in the post-repeal years, but fell short of becoming a major factor in the political economy of Britain. There seems to be little evidence, then, that the movement was either extensive or coor-dinated enough to make much impact on the distribution of income in Britain before 1850. It had, as yet, neither a powerful workers' ideology nor the will to reach out to the majority of unskilled workers. Owenism and Chartism, the most significant ideologies before 1850, failed to galvanize an effective national labor movement. During trade slumps the demand for labor was reduced, and the power of unions usually weakened, especially so in the years after 1836. All the same, the sense that unions of same-skilled workers in different locations should coordinate their actions was becoming well established. Setting up national orga-nizations was a difficult proposition, and although "national unions" combining anywhere between twenty and eighty local organizations start to appear in the 1830s and 1840s, such "amalgamated" umbrella organizations had, as yet, little power; attempts to create a national organization, such as the Grand National Consolidated Trades Union of 1834 and the National Association of United Trades (1845), were short-lived.

*   *   *

Business organization, as noted, largely retained a simple structure in which management and ownership were more often than not in the same hands, and in which unlimited liability was the rule. Partnerships were common, and appear an inflexible and rigid form of business organization, in which the financial trouble of one partner or a conflict between them could bring down the firm. Yet oddly enough, there seems to have been little demand for corporate structures during the Industrial Revolution. Before 1825, it was not possible to set up a business with a corporate structure without a private Act of Parliament or a royal charter. The same Act, the Royal Exchange and London Assurance Corporation Act (1719), known to posterity as the "Bubble Act," also prohibited the formation of partnerships with more than six partners. The hostility to joint-stock companies with limited liability derived, in part, from the excesses of the South Sea Bubble of 1719, which fueled beliefs in the fraudulent intent of the joint-stock company promoters as well as the gullibility of the potential investors. But there was also fear that limited liability would provide a company with an unfair advantage over its competitors. Limited liability could be secured, when necessary, through parliament, as was the case with the Ravenwood plate glass factory in 1773, which needed to raise £50,000 to start producing. Lack of transparency due to inadequate accounting procedures compounded these suspicions. Yet the Bubble Act as such probably did not constitute a serious impediment to economic development. Only one criminal prosecution was based on it in the entire eighteenth century, and the leading expert on the topic has concluded that it was "practically a dead letter" (Harris, 2000, p. 79). For one thing, ad hoc statutory companies were created in impressive numbers to accommodate a particular need: canals, turnpike companies, gas lighting, and eventually railroads. For another, British lawyers found ways around the rigid constrictions of the Bubble Act, for example by vesting property in trustees who could then act for the company. Joint company mills, in which clothiers got together under a trust deed, became quite common in Yorkshire. This organizational form was not perfect. It was constrained by its inability to sue or be sued, and partners had no power over one another. It depended on gentlemanly behavior, on trust, on a set of moral codes. Its success demonstrates the power of these moral codes, which played a much under-rated role in the British Industrial Revolution. Trading in their shares, prohibited by the Bubble Act, did take place and was rarely if ever prosecuted. Ingenious solicitors even designed a substitute for limited liability by writing in the statutes of a company that the creditors could not claim anything beyond the assets of the company. By 1825, many of these legal strictures disappeared with the repeal of the Bubble Act. The odd thing is that it was not clear what was to fill the vacuum, since the repeal only restored the common-law status quo on joint-stock companies, but common law did not yet have a firm position on their nature. Only with the Joint Stock Companies Act of 1844 was the registration of joint-stock companies set up, and limited liability was formalized with the Limited Liability Act of 1855.

Economic change in the eighteenth and early nineteenth centuries was carried out by individuals whom we would call today entrepreneurs, men who recognized economic opportunities, were willing to take risks, worked hard, were able to organize and control others, were willing to delay gratification, and did not shy away from novelty. Yet prominent personalities by themselves could make a difference on an economy-wide level only if they were supported by a horde of lesser-known but technically capable men, who could assist them in turning their plans into reality. Economic historians have long argued about whether the supply of entrepreneurs in a society actually made a difference to its long-term development. The argument made by those who object to "entrepreneurial explanations" is largely that in each society there are always enough people to take advantage of economic opportunities, so that economic development can be explained by looking at the factors that *created* those opportunities. The counterargument is that entrepreneurs are precisely those who create the opportunities. What counted in this case was an institutional environment, which shaped the incentives that directed ambitious and resourceful individuals toward activities that benefited society as a whole. Yet for entrepreneurs to be effective, they depended on the presence of a complementary factor, technical competence. The great entrepreneurs may have been crucial to the industrial transformation of Britain, but the "vital few" remained a relatively small and selective group. Needless to say, the historical record has preserved those who were successful enough to be remembered. It stands to reason that the group of those who tried to become entrepreneurs but failed and disappeared without a trace is much larger, and that the ex ante expected value of becoming an entrepreneur was quite low (Nye, 1991).

Where did these vital few come from? Thanks to the pioneering work of François Crouzet (1985), we know a great deal about the backgrounds of the pioneers of the Industrial Revolution, even if that knowledge is not enough to quite decide whether the supply of such men was a binding constraint. There can be no question that the new technology required somewhat different entrepreneurial characteristics. The merchant-manufacturer of the mid eighteenth century, who managed a putting-out system, was above all a commercial entrepreneur and a financier. While some of them, especially in the Yorkshire worsted industry in which the *Verlagssytem* was predominant, transformed themselves into real industrialists, this was by no means true everywhere. The great entrepreneurs of the Industrial Revolution had to be far more involved in plant management, personnel issues, and above all technology. As a result, the firms remained small and specialized. A few industrial empires were built up, including that of Robert Peel whose family owned fourteen cotton mills as well as printing plants, but these remained the exception.

Who, then, were the businessmen and managers who helped create the modern economy? The old myth of self-made men, who rose from poverty and clawed themselves to economic success, was launched in Victorian times and has never quite refused to die, despite the preponderance of evidence against it. This is not to say that there were no Horatio Alger stories of poor young men, who through hard work, ingenuity, and luck found their way to success. Richard Arkwright was the thirteenth son of a poor village barber. Jedediah Strutt, who started off as a farmer and became an inventor, an entrepreneur, and Arkwright's partner, wrote his own epitaph: "Here lies J.S.—who, without Fortune, Family or Friends raised to himself a fortune, family, and Name in the World." Josiah Mason and Joseph Gillott, two Birmingham ironmongers who made a fortune selling machine-made steel pens, came from working-class backgrounds (Hopkins, 1989, p. 93). Samuel Smiles, whose books are often described as the epitome of Victorian values, wrote in his *Industrial Biography* that the early Lancashire cotton manufacturers were "men originally of the smallest means" ([1889], 1901, p. 317).

But the function of the scholar, when confronted with such a tale, is always to insist on the question: how typical? how representative? Here the research of modern scholars is quite unambiguous: while a few of the great industrialists came from the working class and a few came from the nobility, the vast bulk of the successful entrepreneurs of the Industrial Revolution came from the commercial and industrial middle classes. The "self-made man" was, statistically speaking, a myth. Crouzet's definitive compilation of 226 founders of large industrial undertakings whose fathers' occupations were known found that only 16 of them actually came from the working class and 20 from the "upper class" (mostly gentry). Of the 185 individuals who set up large industrial firms and whose first occupation was known (excluding engineers and ceramics) only 20 came from the working class (though almost half of the engineering entrepreneurs started off as "skilled workmen"). Over 70 percent of the 226 "founders" were the sons of middle-class fathers: merchants, traders, manufacturers, craftsmen, and yeoman farmers. What is interesting is that while "commerce and trade" were reasonably common, accounting for about a quarter of all industrialist origins, the bulk of them were inland, not foreign merchants. Despite the attempts of some scholars to place the foreign trade sector at the center stage of British economic transformation, the evidence here, too, does not support this. Instead, most industrialists and successful entrepreneurs came from a class of people who were already in some fashion involved with some industrial pursuit. About half of all "founders" were either merchant-manufacturers or involved in manufacturing as craftsmen, skilled workers, or managers. Entrepreneurship, much like the accumulation of capital, pulled itself up by the bootstraps; it was bred from within the individuals who were to transform it. An index of endogenesis, measuring the extent to which a modern firm was founded by people already active in that industry, shows that it is over 50 percent if the criterion is the previous occupation of the founder and around 40 percent if the criterion is the father's occupation. Of course, this glass is only half full: outsiders were entering every branch of the manufacturing sector and their impact was probably higher than their numbers would suggest, because the possibility of the entry of *homines novi* must have spurred incumbents to modernize and adopt more productive techniques. Every branch of manufacturing was contestable.

Often such contestability occurred through the entrance of people who were in an activity that either supplied or was a customer of the industry in question, that is, through vertical integration. Forward integration was important. Copper mine owners found opportunities in smelting and small-change coinage, spinners established powerloom sheds, and bleachers became dyers and printers. A good example is that of one Harvey Christian Combe, a London maltster, who purchased a large porter brewery in 1787 (Mathias, 1959, p. 256). Backward integration, equally, was a way of competing with existing firms: ironmongers and cutlers often decided to establish their own blast furnaces and foundries. Cloth manufacturers and hosiers often established spinning mills to procure the yarn they needed. Such integration moves usually had the purpose of making markets or the supplies of raw materials more secure and of saving on the costs of transacting in the market. At times these attempts turned out to be less than successful, as entrepreneurs ventured outside their fields of expertise. But the net result was a tightening of the competitive atmosphere. By the end of the eighteenth century, it could be said that British industry was, relative to what it used to be, a free-for-all. Progress was the progeny of contestability, easy entry and hard-fought competitive markets.

It is this institutional environment which was one of the keys to British economic success. A century of slowly growing belief in the salutary effects of free markets and competition made the British economic environment attractive to those who wanted to do something new and get rich in the process. Not all of those were home-grown. Many foreign entrepreneurs came to Britain when they felt frustrated by the unenlightened conditions in their home countries. Friedrich Koenig, a German printer, arrived in London in 1804 and set up the first high-speed printing press. In Smiles' predictable account, Koenig tried to bring his idea for an improved printing press to German printers, going "from town to town, but could obtain no encouragement whatever." In Koenig's own words, "There is on the Continent no sort of encouragement for an enterprise of this description ... after having lost in Germany and Russia upwards of two years in fruitless applications, I at last resorted to England" (cited by Smiles, 1884, p. 89). Smiles added, "besides, industrial enterprise in Germany was then in a measure paralysed by the impending war with France, and men of capital were naturally averse to risk their money on what seemed a merely speculative undertaking." Naturally,

Smiles added, he then turned to England which "was then, as now, the refuge of inventors who could not find the means of bringing out their schemes elsewhere" (ibid., p. 89). Koenig's steam-driven printing press was the first to use cylindrical impression and inking, and the first edition of *The Times* printed on a steam-driven press came out in 1814. Frederic Winsor (né Winzer) was a German-born entrepreneur who played an important role in the exploitation and commercialization of gas lighting in Britain. A London firm founded by a Swiss emigrant named Johann Jacob Schweppe (1740–1821), who had arrived in England in 1792, successfully exploited Joseph Priestley's invention of carbonated water, and no less an authority than Erasmus Darwin in his gigantic work recommended his product as a remedy for kidney stones (Darwin, 1794–96, Vol. 2, p. 45).

But most British entrepreneurs were locally grown. Their success stands as a testimony of the beneficial effect that improving institutions had on the economy and of how they could be instrumental in economic growth. Economists have long pointed out how important it is to have set up the correct incentives system. In an economy in which redistribution of wealth rather than its generation is acceptable, the most resourceful individuals will channel their resources and energy toward trying to exclude others from their occupations and lobby government to enforce such exclusionary arrangements to protect their rents. Such a "Grabbing Hand" economy, as Shleifer and Vishny (1998) have called it, need not necessarily be corrupt by modern standards, but it distorts incentives and increases the attractiveness of activities that are beneficial to the individual but costly to society at large (Baumol, 2002). The belief that Britain had a more favorable supply of entrepreneurs does not imply that Britons were in some sense superior (as many contemporaries believed), or that their economy was inherently stronger, but only that its institutions made it attractive for the most talented and those with a taste for risk to devote themselves to business rather than to military or bureaucratic careers, or a livelihood based on the redistribution of rents rather than their creation.

Much as in other societies, successful businessmen and entrepreneurs came disproportionately from the ranks of social classes who were, in one sense or another, outsiders. The most significant religious minorities in Britain were so-called nonconformists, Protestants who had remained outside the Church of England. Although a relatively small fraction (7 percent) of the population, these dissenters played a very large role in the Industrial Revolution and supplied a large proportion of the entrepreneurs in manufacturing, by some estimates around 50 percent. This was not unusual (in France, the small Protestant and Jewish minorities in the north-east played a similar role), but it remains all the same remarkable. Nonconformists, of course, could not serve in Parliament, the military, or the civil service before 1829, which left them few other career paths. Landowners were predominantly Anglicans, and dissenters were mostly artisans and merchants. Yet they differed in other ways, which may have given dissenters an advantage: being excluded from Oxford and Cambridge, they were educated in Scotland or in their own academies, which, as we have seen, provided in general a useful background in business and applied science. As a minority group, dissenters felt that they could trust co-religionists more than others, which gave them an advantage in networked occupations in which trust was important.

As Margaret Jacob has noted, Unitarians were a religious group uniquely well-situated to play a major role in economic progress. In the eighteenth century they included many of the major figures of the Industrial Enlightenment such as Watt, Wedgwood, the prominent physician Thomas Beddoes, and James M'Connel, one of Manchester's leading cotton masters. In Birmingham the Unitarian community was led by Priestley, who assured his congregation that the pursuit of money was virtuous and that business success and godliness were compatible (Jacob, 2000). In the nineteenth century, the Stephensons, the railway promoter and manager Henry Booth, and the engineer William Fairbairn were all members of the Unitarian Church. Booth's position in his Liverpool church made him a central figure in a "tightly knit and very wealthy community" (Marsden and Smith, 2005, p. 141). Unitarianism was the Enlightenment religion par excellence. It was optimistic, with a faith in progress and in the benefits of useful knowledge. Jacob has argued that it provided the belief of a rational and enlightened God, "not Calvin's inscrutable and judgmental one" (Jacob, 2000, p. 277). Many dissenters came from Scotland, which supplied the British economy with a disproportionate number of key persons in every aspect of the Industrial Revolution. Another source of successful businessmen were the Quakers, who numbered no more than 25,000 but whose reputation for fairness and probity, as well as their active philanthropic projects signaling their lack of greed, were a key to their disproportionate economic success (Isichei, 1970, p. 182). One micro-study of Birmingham suggests that in the late eighteenth century in that town Quakers made up 1 percent of the town's population but one-third of its ironmasters and tanners (Jones, 2008, p. 177). Among successful Quaker industrialists, the Darbys are the first to come to mind, but there were many others: the eighteenth-century banker David Barclay, the cocoa and chocolate pioneer John Cadbury, the biscuit manufacturer Jonathan Carr, railroad entrepreneur George Pease, the Welsh iron and tinplate tycoon James Harford, and the Welsh bankers Joseph Gibbins Sr. and Jr. Peter Mathias, while discussing the success of Quaker brewers, remarks that it was due to "the world of religious-cum-kinship group [that] provided an environment of mutual trust and confidence" (1959, p. 289).

The supply of entrepreneurial talent thus came primarily from the middle classes. If the argument that Britain occupied a leading position in the European Industrial Revolution thanks to its enterprising classes is to be maintained, we should look at the pre-existence of a substantial middle class in Britain by 1750. Roy Porter (1990a, p. 70) felt that the "middling men of Georgian England" had been in a historical limbo between the elusive search for a rising bourgeoisie in

Tudor or Stuart England and the triumphs of manufacturing wealth in the middle of the nineteenth century. Such a middle class existed in 1700 in an economy that was already relatively wealthy to start with. Its importance has been missed in part because the concept by definition is bounded both from above and from below by large gray areas. Was it exclusively urban? Did skilled artisans and yeomen belong to the "middling sort"? One estimate of the size of the middle class can be obtained from the work of the mid-eighteenth-century economist Joseph Massie as revised by Lindert and Williamson (1982). If we set the annual income of middle-class people at between £60 and £600, we obtain a total of 220,852 families in the 1750s, or about one in seven families, which seems perhaps low today, but which was quite respectable for the time. Moreover, these people, despite their numbers and their critical role in the growth of the economy, have tended to be offstage in Marxist accounts that picture social history as the struggle between plebeian workers and patrician landlords. Middle-class people, however, can be distinguished from others in that they deployed either physical or human capital in earning their living, that they lived above the minimum of subsistence, and that they were not normally candidates for poor relief. They differed in dress, speech, customs, and dwelling location from the working class, and while they would not be confused with the gentry or the landed classes, the ambition to become one of the gentry and imitate their putative habits and culture remained strong. Deirdre McCloskey (2006) has argued that the bourgeois mentality of thrift, honesty, and diligence became the ruling mindset of this class. Adam Smith ([1776], 1976, p. 432) noted that "merchants are commonly ambitious of becoming country gentlemen" and when they purchased land they became the best improvers. There can be little question that the middle classes in eighteenth-century Britain were full of practical men of enterprise, attuned to the markets, networked and connected, joined in a common ambition to make money and willing to work for it.

The growth of the middle class in Britain has been explained recently by the reliance on evolutionary dynamics, both theoretical (Galor and Moav, 2002) and historical (Clark and Hamilton, 2006; Clark, 2007). The way these models work is by differential reproduction of classes within society: middle-class people, it is argued, who embodied entrepreneurial values such as thriftiness, industriousness, and a willingness to invest in the human capital of their children, also experienced higher survival rates, and thus eventually multiplied and filled the kingdom, bringing better economic performance for the country as a whole. These Darwinian dynamics, however innovative and stimulating, have limited power, since a human generation is 25–30 years and it would take many generations for the transition to have a major effect. These models need to be complemented by models that allow for *cultural evolution* to occur through learning, both from parents (vertical transmission of culture) and horizontal (learning from and imitating non-parents). Much of the intergenerational transmission of culture occurs through channels other than genes (e.g., Boyd and Richerson, 1985, 2005; Jablonka and Lamb, 2005).

It is unknown to what extent "pure" Darwinian factors (that is, natural selection) played a role in this development relative to imitation and learning. The best we can say is that certain middle-class values and beliefs, such as an ethic of hard work, willingness to take risks, and an inclination to delay gratification, expanded in the period before the Industrial Revolution (Doepke and Zilibotti, 2008), thus accelerating the formation of the middle class. But in a highly stratified yet mobile society such as Britain, the incentives to imitate the behavior of others viewed as higher up in the hierarchy were strong. Boyd and Richerson (2005) distinguish between a number of "biases" in cultural evolution (by which they mean that offspring may adopt a culture different from that of their parents). One is content-biased cultural evolution, in which people persuade themselves (or are persuaded by others) that a certain set of propositions is more correct than the ones they previously held (the powerful logic of Enlightenment thought may well have played a role in this). Another is model-based cultural evolution, in which individuals observe certain other persons who have an attribute they regard as desirable (e.g., social status or wealth) and thus choose this other person as their role model. A third is conformist bias: people observe what the majority of their peers do, and change their behavior to conform to the majority (or perhaps to deviate in a contrary way). Many of these biases seem to fit British social history in this period quite well (Perkin, 1969, pp. 56–62, 94, 143; Langford, 1989, pp. 61–121). There was a dividing membrane between "polite society" and the unwashed poor, but it was permeable and worth the hard work and effort required to cross it. All in all, it seems that the growth of middle-class values can be well explained by these models, and we do not have to rely on genetics to explain economic history.

Other cultural explanations of entrepreneurship have argued (less plausibly) that this cultural change occurred through changes in religious beliefs in the Weberian tradition. Yet Protestantism as such, much discussed, has not been persuasively shown to "cause" entrepreneurial behavior, much less economic change. The fact that a correlation existed between certain religious beliefs and cultural traits proves little about the direction of causation. For instance, the disproportionate effect of cultural and religious minorities on economic success has been an empirical regularity, but the causation is far from obvious. Did religion lead people to behave in a certain way, or did certain cultural features or economic attainments help make people choose certain religious beliefs? The British Enlightenment, more than that of France, was able to coexist comfortably with Protestantism, even evangelism—but was it economically significant because of this link or in spite of it?

Making inferences about causality thus requires caution: the Dutch United Provinces had a substantial middle class, as did Venice and parts of west Germany.

The contestability of markets and the high degree of competitiveness of the British economy also contributed. Moreover, the British entrepreneurial class had the right kinds of values and beliefs. Through much of European history being middle class or "bourgeois" meant that one aspired to rise to a landowning leisure class and the lifestyle that came with it. Bourgeois values have been derided and dismissed for generations, yet a case could be made that they are the ones that in the end built the modern economy, as Deirdre McCloskey (2006) has argued in considerable detail. The critics observed that for many middle-class entrepreneurs economic success was a road to a higher social status that was less productive. This was the case in Britain as well. Many nineteenth-century peers and aristocrats living well in country estates were the heirs of successful industrialists. Brewers, paper-makers, potters, and ironmasters became barons, earls, MPs, and castle dwellers. Men of business could, through money, "advance in rank and contend with the landlords in the enjoyments of leisure, as well as luxuries," as Malthus (1820, p. 470) put it. Men with the humblest occupations and origins might call themselves "gentlemen" if their wealth permitted it. This was not a new phenomenon in the nineteenth century: in 1703, Defoe wrote the widely cited doggerel that "Wealth, however got, in England makes lords of mechanics, gentlemen of rakes; Antiquity and birth are needless here; 'Tis impudence and money makes a peer." Urbanization and the growth of the market eroded old social distinctions, and created new realities. As the titles and social conventions associated with gentility were usurped by the "professional, commercial and middling classes," a 1713 essay noted, no one knew what was meant by "a gentleman" (Clark, 2000, pp. 155–56). Yet, as we shall see, this classic example of cultural evolution through imitation had important economic consequences.

The flip side of the increased efficiency and the higher rate of technological progress that a stringent competitive environment implied, was that the failure rate of early industrialists was high. The eternal dilemma of the economic historian is that the majority of such failures are not the have-beens (who may have left some record) but the never-weres or the never-could-have-beens. Bankruptcies were highly cyclical: they tended to be particularly high during the so-called panics or crashes which occurred more or less regularly every ten or eleven years. The vulnerability of businesses to credit contractions was the result of the short-term loans, which could be called or not be rolled over during a crisis, and to the prevalence of partnerships of unlimited liability, which often meant that a partner, in trouble in an unrelated business, had to pull out his capital thus leaving a business in a capital crunch precisely when it was unable or could not afford to borrow. The years 1825–26 were among the worst crisis years of the nineteenth century: the number of bankruptcies, which had averaged about 1,400 in the early 1820, jumped to 3,300 in 1826; 1837, similarly had almost double the number of bankruptcies of the previous years. Bankruptcy did not necessarily mean that one's career was over, but it often did. William Hirst, a Leeds woolen manufacturer, was a classic self-made man, but the 1825 panic ruined him, and his business never recovered, leaving him embittered and poor. William Radcliffe, a Derbyshire cotton weaver and machinist, whose business was quite prosperous in the early 1800s, died bankrupt and penniless in 1848. There were surely many like them.

All the same, we may well ask whether the typical entrepreneur during the Industrial Revolution was unsuccessful to the point where he ended up worse than he would have been had he never tried. True, the history books inevitably select the winners and successful cases while ignoring the many who tried their hand at business and failed. It has been suggested that, if measured over the *entire* population of entrepreneurs, the rate of return to attempted entrepreneurship may well have been negative; but because the failures normally leave little trace, we focus on the successful cases (Nye, 1991). This is not quite as irrational as it seems. Just as the historian's perspective is distorted by selection bias emphasizing the winners, so contemporaries must have looked with admiration at the great fortunes made by self-made men like Arkwright and Owen, hoping to mimic them. Moreover, would-be entrepreneurs tended to be overly optimistic about their chances of success. Perhaps that is what made them entrepreneurs in the first place. Adam Smith felt that "the chance of gain is by every man more or less over-valued, and the chance of loss ... undervalued" (Smith [1776], 1996, p. 120). Modern economic theory, when informed by psychology, has shown that it is quite plausible for economic agents to be systematically over-optimistic about the future payoff of uncertain activities and that such over-optimism might system-atically distort the allocation of resources and efforts (Brunnermeier and Parker, 2005). It could be surmised, then, that entrepreneurs and inventors were fooling themselves into believing that their chances of success were better than they really were. Ironically, because most of the benefits of successful innovation spilled over to consumers, these distortions were socially beneficial.

And yet, despite many failures, some recorded, most not, the entrepreneur during the Industrial Revolution was probably on average doing better than this scenario suggests. In part, this was so because some failed entrepreneurs who went bankrupt after initial success continued afterward to have successful careers as managers or consultants, earning their opportunity costs perhaps rather than a huge rent, but still living respectably and comfortably. Thus Samuel Oldknow, the weaver of muslins, became insolvent after his business empire collapsed in 1792, owing Arkwright over £200,000. But would that have made him a "failed entrepreneur"? After his bankruptcy in 1792, he became a successful farmer in Derbyshire during the Napoleonic Wars, High Sheriff of his county, and chairman of its Agricultural Society, living the life of a highly respected rural gentleman till his death in 1828. The Scottish chemist and inventor John Roebuck failed in 1773 in a classic case of failed backward integration: in trying to supply his ironworks in Carron, Scotland, with coal, he bought a coal mine, which turned out to be beyond his technical capacities and he had to declare bankruptcy. Yet he remained manager of his works and a Scottish gentleman (though born in Sheffield) of considerable means. Roebuck's partner in the Carron works, Samuel Garbett, originally an uneducated brass-worker, was a highly successful businessman before failing in 1772 due to the incompetence of his son-in-law and partner. Yet he lived another thirty years as a successful lobbyist and highly respected leader in Birmingham. Samuel Clegg, one of the pioneers of gas lighting in the early nineteenth century, joined an ill-fated Liverpool engineering firm and "lost everything he possessed," yet had a good career as a consulting engineer afterward and served, among others, as a consultant to the Portuguese government, and as one of the surveying officers for conducting preliminary inquiries on applications for new gas bills. Another example of such "failure" is the career of the ironmaster and civil engineer Benjamin Outram, who died aged 41 at the peak of a feverishly active career in 1805 after building the largest iron and engineering business in the east Midlands, leaving a chaotic financial legacy which left his family with very little after his death. Was he a "failure" just because he did not die rich?

After all, unlike an unsuccessful professional athlete, the experience and connections an entrepreneur made in managing a business, even if it failed, were valuable assets that were not nearly so specific as to have no alternative uses. Furthermore, many would-be entrepreneurs were actually less interested in financial gain than in technical success and the challenges posed in an age of increasing technological dynamism. Some of the best engineers of the era, including such technological superstars as Richard Trevithick, Marc I. Brunel, and Richard Roberts, did not become rich primarily because they were not much good at business management. Others, like John Roebuck, were fascinated by technical matters and seemed little interested in financial gains in the first place once they had assured an acceptable level of comfort and respectability. Those who were more careful, like Joseph Bramah or Henry Maudslay, or those who found the right niche, like James Keir, died quite wealthy.

CHAPTER 16

Social Norms and a Civil Economy

The idea that institutions play a central role in determining economic outcomes and performance, long reviled by economists, has been revived in the past decades and become something of a mantra among economists interested in long-term development. The literature has not quite agreed what is precisely meant by "institutions," but clearly the definition includes the rules by which the economic game is played, and how they are enforced and obeyed. It has been realized that a central issue in economic performance is what protected property and enforced contracts, and that any agent who was placed in charge of justice and law enforcement needed to be constrained in critical ways to avoid a situation in which the state would be taken over by rent-seekers. Another insight of this literature is that some apparently inefficient past institutions that limited entry or protected privileges in one form or another, and which would have been detrimental in a world of well-functioning markets and perfect competition, may actually have been well suited to the highly imperfect world of pre-modern economies, where first-best arrangements were simply impossible. The interest in institutions has kindled a great deal of research into political power and arrangements, and how they affected the way resources were allocated and income was distributed. Especially the age-old matter of "who shall guard us from the guardians"—referred to as constraints on the executive—has captured the interest of economists. In addition, however, there has been a recognition that *informal* institutions, which have the nature of conventions, traditions, and habits and thus are as much in the realm of "culture" as in that of institutions, were of considerable significance in enabling economic exchange and making markets work, encouraging investment and innovation, and determining economic success. Institutional analysis has not confined itself to the state, governance, and power relations, although these are central components of the story; it has also examined so-called private-order institutions (Greif, 2005), in which arrangements emerged "from the bottom up." Oddly enough, not much of this new literature has turned to the details of British economic development in the era before and during the Industrial Revolution, though a start has been made (Mokyr, 2008).

Indeed, the entire issue of whether Britain's advantage in leading the Industrial Revolution was in its more efficient enforcement of property rights by the state needs to be revisited. What mattered for economic performance was a level of confidence that made it possible to transact with non-kin, and increasingly with people who were almost strangers. Market activity, and especially transactions at arm's length, increased throughout the period of the Industrial Revolution at ever accelerating rates. This happened, oddly enough, in an age during which the costs of legal action went up, its availability and efficiency were declining, and as a result fewer and fewer people took recourse to the law. We might have expected the reverse: the growing integration of goods and factor markets in the British Isles would seem to make a formal, nation-wide system of law enforcement more necessary. What kept this system operating is one of the more perplexing questions in British economic history.

Adam Smith, in his *Lectures on Jurisprudence*, thought he had the answer: "Whenever commerce is introduced into any country, probity and punctuality always accompany it. These virtues in a rude and barbarous country are almost unknown. Of all the nations in Europe, the Dutch, the most commercial, are the most faithfull to their word ... There is no natural reason why an Englishman or a Scotchman should not be as punctual in performing agreements as a Dutchman. It is far more reduceable to self interest, that general principle which regulates the actions of every man, and which leads men to act in a certain manner from views of advantage, and is as deeply implanted in an Englishman as a Dutchman. A dealer is afraid of losing his character, and is scrupulous in observing every engagement ... Where people seldom deal with one another, we find that they are somewhat disposed to cheat, because they can gain more by a smart trick than they can lose by the injury which it does their character" ([1757], 1978, p. 327). In other words, the correlation between people cooperating and behaving honestly was driven by a causal mechanism running from prior commercialization to behavior, much like Montesquieu's notion of *doux commerce*. Modern economists have restated this idea in considerable detail and taken it a step further by arguing that economic growth and not just commercialization led to moral improvement (Friedman, 2005, esp. ch. 2). McCloskey maintains that "modern economic growth has led to more, not less refinement for hundreds of millions who would otherwise have been poor and ignorant ... participation in capitalist markets and bourgeois virtues have civilized the world" (2006, pp. 25–26). But it seems plausible that the causal arrow went equally in the other direction, that is, the pre-existence of certain social norms led to cooperative behavior and a voluntary willingness to forego opportunistic behavior that made transactions, even at arm's length, possible. How did these norms affect economic outcomes? By supporting markets, they led to commercialization which brought about economic growth through gains from trade. Moreover, social norms were crucial in bringing about the Industrial Revolution. Cooperation through private-order institutions supported the progress of useful knowledge and advances of technology.

If formal law was a last resort in the enforcement of contracts and the protection of property rights, how did commerce function and what prevented transactions costs and opportunistic behavior from mushrooming to the point where attaining the levels of exchange and division of labor required for a sophisticated and productive economy became impossible? A different way of posing this question was expressed by the young French economist Jérôme-Adolphe Blanqui (1824, p. 326) who wondered when visiting London how a town twice the size of Paris (nearly a million people) could maintain order with just a handful of watchmen and constables. He seemed less than satisfied by the answer that the English go to bed and lock up their shops early, and was more inclined to believe that they were working harder and were more enlightened. The idea rather than the reality of the gentleman was central to the informal social norms that governed British society in this era. The French historian Hippolyte Taine, who stayed in London in 1858, summarized the concept of a gentleman as "the three syllables that summarize the history of English society" (Taine, [1872], 1958, p. 144). Asa Briggs (1959, p. 411) noted that a gentleman was someone who accepted the notion of progress but was always suspicious of the religion of gold.

Economists have come to the conclusion that social norms of cooperation and decency can prevail even in societies in which there is little or ineffective formal law enforcement. The prevalence of a social convention that defined "honorable" or "polite" behavior as a norm of respectability, and penalized serious deviations from it through irreparable damage to one's reputation, could substitute for formal, third-party law enforcement. The great jurist William Blackstone famously referred to Britain as a "Polite and Commercial People." Politeness was widely equated with law-abiding behavior, and it was intuitively sensed that commercial success depended a great deal on politeness. One way of seeing this is to stress that what made commerce and credit possible was that most people had absorbed and internalized a set of values that made them eschew opportunistic behavior that might have been personally advantageous but socially destructive. In other words, economic agents did not play necessarily "defect" in the famous prisoners' dilemma game (even if that might have been in their immediate interest) and they expected others to do the same. People needed to send out costly signals that indicated to others that they were reliable and trustworthy because they belonged to a class of reliable and trustworthy agents (see, e.g., Posner, 2000). It was important that they be costly, so that they could be credible. Such signals were the good manners in dress and language, residential location ("a good address"), rules on home furnishing and transportation, and the etiquette and manners observed by the British upper classes, and their adoption by the commercial classes created a stylized ideal of gentlemanly capitalism that resulted in an environment in which bourgeois entrepreneurs could deal with one another and with their subordinates in a cooperative fashion that made commerce work (Sunderland, 2007, pp. 15–32). During the Industrial Revolution these norms spread to the manufacturing sector, such as engineering, the backbone of British technology. Early engineers insisted on "gentlemanly conduct" as a hallmark of trustworthiness, and the signals they sent out were costly indeed, including grand country homes (Marsden and Smith, 2005, p. 256).

This kind of behavior was observed and blessed by Enlightenment thinkers. John Locke, for instance, wrote in 1693 that a gentleman's upbringing should instill in him a love of virtue and reputation, make him from within "a good, a vertuous, and able man" and endow him with "Habits woven into the very Principles of his Nature," not because he feared retribution but because this defined his very character (Locke, [1693], 1732, pp. 46–47). The essence of the gentleman as Locke and his successors saw him "was to be his integrity" (Carter, 2002, p. 335). The ideal of gentleman was not static and changed over the course of the centuries. In the seventeenth century, Steven Shapin (1994) has stressed, the concept of a gentleman became associated with integrity and reliability. By the middle of the nineteenth century, the importance of honesty and cooperative behavior had become paramount. Samuel Smiles (1859) described what really mattered for the gentleman: "The true gentleman has a keen sense of honour, scrupulously avoiding mean actions. His standard of probity in word and action is high. He does not shuffle or prevaricate, dodge or skulk; but is honest, upright, and straightforward. His law is rectitude—action in right lines. When he says YES, it is a law ... Above all, the gentleman is truthful. He feels that truth is the 'summit of being,' and the soul of rectitude in human affairs." Paul Langford (2000, p. 126) observes that one of the British aristocracy's prime characteristics was the belief in fair play and that a cheating lord was a traitor to his class. Coleman (1973, p. 98) adds that the concept of the English gentleman merged into a code of honor providing "a luxuriant undergrowth of unwritten and unspoken rules of behaviour." In his view, justice, magnanimity, and generosity were hardly compatible with industrial capitalism. But the point is that if a person was perceived to be generous and honest, others would be more willing to deal with him or her, and this created the institutional soil in which economic progress could thrive. The relation between ideal and norm on the one hand and reality on the other was always problematic. The question is not whether the preponderance of British economic agents behaved like this, as much as whether such ideals affected their behavior (and the way others expected them to behave) *enough* to make a market economy feasible without the heavy hand of law enforcement.

Economic analysis has shed considerable light on the question of how economic agents can be made to behave in ways that allow commerce to exist despite the selfishness of individuals. What is necessary is that there is a general expectation that opportunistic behavior will be credibly penalized, and that this knowledge is shared and known to be so. That kind of set-up will produce a self-enforcing equilibrium within which more sophisticated economic organization is feasible. Punishment by a central law enforcer seems to be an obvious answer, but this yields hard questions on how commercial systems emerge in societies in which law enforcement is weak or non-existent. Britain in the age of

Enlightenment was in an intermediate position, since it had a formal legal system, but one that would not have been up to the task if informal institutions had not been structured to encourage voluntary cooperative behavior. Because their social reputation was linked to business behavior, economic agents faced strong incentives to behave cooperatively and make a relatively smooth functioning of an exchange economy possible even in the absence (or at least high cost) of formal legal action. Linking market relations with non-exchange social interactions meant that individuals knew that opportunistic and non-gentlemanly actions would have severe social consequences. This awareness underpinned the market economy (Spagnolo, 1999). A striking example of such a linkage can again be found among Quakers, where a member of the Society of Friends (co-religionists) could be expelled from the Society if bankruptcy resulted from demonstrable misconduct (Hoppit, 1987, p. 31).

Politeness and manners were an important part of the mechanism through which the culture of gentility filtered down to the mercantile and artisanal classes as the upper middle class tried to imitate gentlemen. This permitted "people who lacked the traditional components of social class" to achieve it by adopting different behavioral codes (Langford, 2002, p. 312). It would be a gross simplification to link this kind of cultural change directly to economic development, but without understanding how property rights were increasingly respected and contracts honored (rather than enforced), we will miss something about the institutional roots of subsequent economic growth. The findings that the eighteenth century witnessed a sharp decline in civil litigation, that formally sealed documents were increasingly replaced by verbal informal contracts, and that violent crime fell (as far as we can establish) seem suggestive at least. It is hard to measure changes in "trust" in any direct way for the past, but it is significant that sealed and formal agreements, which were in widespread use in the seventeenth century, gave way by 1750 to verbal agreements and gentlemanly handshakes (Brooks, 1989, p. 393). The polite and honest conduct of business was a critical component of the way this economy worked. Merchants and manufacturers needed to signal to all other agents with whom they transacted that they observed certain cultural codes and respected values, so that their customers, suppliers, and employees could expect to be paid. If enough people behaved this way, a society could expect to have a successful exchange economy (Brewer, 1982, pp. 214–15). As the economy expanded after 1800, the efficiency of trust in preventing opportunistic behavior declined (Sunderland, 2007, p. 159).

While evidence for this view is inevitably anecdotal and even impressionistic, foreign commentators at the time felt that the English were different in this regard than other societies. The French traveler Pierre-Jean Grosley noted the "politeness, civility and officiousness" of citizens and shopkeepers "whether great or little" (Grosley, 1772, Vol. 1, pp. 89, 92). The eighteenth-century Italian writer and philosopher Alessandro Verri felt that London merchants were far more

trustworthy than Paris ones (cited by Langford, 2000, p. 124). One French visitor
to early nineteenth-century London noted the *probité* and good faith of British
shopkeepers, and that a child could shop as confidently as the most street-wise
market shopper. He thought that these habits had been copied by the merchant
class from the Quakers (Nougaret, 1816, p. 12). Charles Dupin (1825, pp. xi–xii)
went as far as to attribute Britain's economic successes to the "wisdom, the economy and above all the probity" of its citizens. Reputation was critical. Prosper
Mérimée, commenting on the open access policies in the British Museum Library
in 1857, observed that "The English have the habit of showing the greatest
confidence in everyone possessing *character*, that is, recommended by a gentleman
... whoever obtains one is careful not to lose it, for he cannot regain it once lost"
(1930, pp. 153–54). This reliance on informal rules and reputation was especially
marked in the securities trade. In 1734 Barnard's Act outlawed time bargains in
securities (i.e., options) on the London Stock Exchange, and this segment of the
securities market had to rely on an internally enforced code of conduct, based on
reputation and the fear of being excluded from trade if violations occurred
(Michie, 2001, p. 31). As a result, Barnard's Act and similar legislation were not
effective in curbing trade in these securities despite the difficulty in enforcing
contracts in an activity that was extra-legal (Harrison, 2003).

Perhaps the most palpable effect of the presence of trust between members of
the commercial class in Britain was the importance of credit. Early modern
Britain, as Muldrew (1998) has stressed, like all commercial societies in which
credit played a central role depended on trust and "credit became synonymous
with reputation" (p. 149). Even if we have no really good quantitative measure of
it, credit was omnipresent in eighteenth-century Britain. A writer in the 1750s
noted that "without credit neither domestic nor foreign trade could be carried out
... it so far superior to money that it enables a small dealer to have more concerns
... than a worthless wretch who owns thousands... of the Trade of this Nation you
may reckon at least two thirds is carried upon credit." What made that credit
possible, beyond any question, was "that *credit* or *reputation* that the Tradesman has
acquired by his industry, integrity and other virtues and good qualities" (*The
Tradesman's Director*, 1756, p. 10). Local tradesmen and shopkeepers gave customers personal credit ("paying on tick"), farmers signed short-term bonds, landlords mortgaged property, and long-distance merchants signed bills of exchange
(Hoppit, 1986a). Small debts could be settled through arbitration in small-claims
courts known as Courts of Conscience (also known as Courts of Requests), which
became increasingly popular after 1750 in settling debts without the burden of an
expensive court case.

Credit depended on the majority of people behaving honorably and on this
behavior being common knowledge. The Church, voluntary organizations and
societies, and schools, all played an important role in making the bulk of middle-
class society play by the rules and internalize the rules that made it possible to

engage in cooperative behavior and thus supported markets. More than any third-party enforcement of contracts, the prevalence of gentlemanly behavioral codes as a social lubricant and a facilitator of trust and market exchange is remarkable in this age, as evidenced by the expansion of personal credit. If too many people had behaved opportunistically and defaulted or absconded, the institutions supporting the British economy would have collapsed. It is inconceivable that the formal law enforcement system in eighteenth-century Britain could have dealt with massive fraud. A hard question is whether this trust was based on reputation mechanisms, or whether the system of values had mostly internalized these value, so that people saw cooperative behavior as a norm and reputation mechanisms became secondary. Reputations, it seems, remained a significant motive. Defoe, as always an astute observer, noted that a shopkeeper may borrow at better terms than a prince "if he has the reputation of an honest man" (1738, Vol. 1, p. 361). For him, reputation was the key to economic success and he strongly recommended that tradesmen sell at reasonable prices, advertise, and even be careful with the reputation of one's debtor, presumably because harming a reputation inflicted irreparable damage (Defoe, 1727, Vol. 2, p. 298). Adam Smith, in his analysis of markets that were formally weakly enforced or even outside the law, such as options trading and gambling, pointed out that even when there was no formal redress "yet all the great sums that are lost are punctually paid. Persons who game must keep their credit, else nobody will deal with them. It is quite the same in stockjobbing" ([1757], 1978, p. 458).

In many other ways informal moral codes determined the institutional environment of the British economy as much as formal legislation and created a set of private-order contract-enforcement institutions. Historians such as Lawrence Stone (1985) have argued that the social tensions and violence of the English world before 1650 gradually transformed into a kinder and gentler environment in which contentiousness declined. Other contemporary commentators felt that the changes came later. Francis Place, the radical politician and reformer, for instance, noted that "the progress made in refinement of manners and morals seems to have gone on simultaneously with the improvement in arts, manufactures and commerce ... we are a much better people than we were [half a century ago], better instructed, more sincere and kind-hearted, less gross and brutal" (cited by George, 1966, p. 18). Such impressionistic evidence indicates perhaps little more than a growing gap between the middle class and the "dangerous classes," the lumpenproletariat of menial workers, day-laborers, pedlars, beggars, and vagrants that remained a substantial part of the British population. The entire concept of cultural norms here was highly class-specific. Yet for those members of the middle-class whose activities propelled the economy forward, a sense of shared manners and codes was a substitute for formal laws.

These shared codes of behavior allowed the British middle and upper classes to overcome free rider problems that otherwise would have derailed many forms of collective action. The most palpable and easily observed forms of social capital in eighteenth-century Britain were clubs, societies, and lodges to which the members of these classes belonged. The late seventeenth century had witnessed the expansion of the coffee- and chocolate-houses, in which members of a new commercial and intellectual urban elite congregated (Cowan, 2005). The "associational society," while not entirely new in the eighteenth century, expanded enormously after 1750. It was felt, especially in the closing decades of the century, that the state was failing to create order and stability in an increasingly volatile society and that citizens had to create their own public goods through collective action (Clark, 2000, pp. 94–96; see also Sunderland, 2007, pp. 50–84). Eighteenth-century middle-class Britons did not bowl alone. They participated voluntarily in a bewildering variety of voluntary organizations, forming networks that provided support for credit markets, mutual insurance, and the pooling of artisanal knowledge. Some of these societies were artistic and scientific in nature, some were musical or sporting clubs, or professional associations. Some of them were patriotic, such as the anti-French associations that sprung up in the 1740s. Philanthropy was a major focus of voluntary action for the public good. Activity in charities was a good opportunity to network and signal good citizenship (Sunderland, 2007, p. 70). Another important component of the associational society were the old urban guilds such as the London livery companies, which in the mid-century had lost most of their regulatory functions but more and more reinvented themselves as social clubs and political associations, often involved in radical reform movements (Berlin, 2008, p. 339). The religious revival of these decades also contributed to the growth of "social capital," but so did concerns about education, leading for instance to the establishment (in 1785) of the National Sunday School Society, which promoted local schools and distributed textbooks. Many others were little more than eating and drinking clubs. But even those fulfilled an important function through gossip and networking, by spreading information about individuals and thus buttressing reputation mechanisms.

Social networks of this kind were essential if markets were to exist and contracts to be honored. They reflected and reinforced the underlying culture of respectable and "polite" conduct. British Masonic lodges and friendly societies provided mutual insurance and widows' pensions, but they also cemented commercial relations. Many societies that brought together artisans from different trades introduced the rule that only one person per occupation could be a member with the understanding that fellow members would have priority in any commercial transaction, thus mixing commercial business-to-business relations with social connections (Brewer, 1982, p. 222). The societies performed the linkage that Spagnolo's model points to: opportunistic and un-gentlemanlike behavior was penalized by the loss of both economic relationships and social connections. Of course, the associational society included far more than those organizations. Membership of friendly societies alone in 1800 was estimated at 704,000, with no fewer than 9,672 societies (Clark, 2000, p. 350). These societies included mostly skilled workers and some working-class members, provided death benefits to widows, paid for funerals, and provided relief to sick and aged members.

To be sure, for the economy to function properly, some level of *formal* law and order was essential. Formal institutions supported the informal rules by imposing penalties on hard-core "deviants" who would jeopardize the system through opportunistic behavior. The penalties for reneging on contracts were severe. As Brooks has pointed out, behind every credit transaction stood the threat of potential debtors' prison, which must have filled the hearts of potential defaulters with fear (Brooks, 1989, p. 395). The harshness with which losers were dealt with and the costs of litigation made disputes likely to be settled out of court. Daniel Defoe (1727, Vol. 2, p. 297) summarized his advice to "tradesmen" as follows: "go to law with no body tho for your just due if it may be obtained without it ... try all the methods of Gentleness and Patience before you proceed to Rigour and Prosecution." The (small claims) Courts of Conscience, significantly, were highly unpopular among working people who objected to the way they dealt with tallies run up in alehouses—a tell-tale sign that they were effective. During the eighteenth century the local powers of the Justices of the Peace increased significantly, by such legislation as the County Rates Act (1738) which gave JPs extensive powers of local taxation. The quarter sessions (courts located between the magistrate's and the assize courts) became increasingly concerned with roads, prisons, and minor infringements of the law such as public drunkenness and poaching in addition to indictable but not capital offenses.

The exact nature of the institutional foundations of law and order in eighteenth-century Britain is a topic on which there is still quite a lot of controversy (Hay et al., 1976; Langbein, 1983a). Large parts of Britain were "virtual lawless zones," whereas in others the actual practice deviated considerably from the letter of the law, as it was executed by amateurs and often people with a very different concept of what was legal and just (Brewer and Styles, 1980, p. 13). What counted, however, was an ideology—idealized if not fictional—that at least in principle this was a society of laws that constrained everyone at some level, and in which people of authority were held accountable. As Brewer and Styles point out, authority derived its legitimacy from the rule of law, and hence "authorities chose to limit themselves in order to acquire greater effectiveness; they traded unmediated power for legitimacy" (ibid., p. 14). This view of British governance has also found wide acceptance among economists (Acemoglu, Johnson, and Robinson, 2005a). An increasing number of people were bargaining "in the shadow of the law," that is, the parties in disputes knew what the stakes were and the (substantial) loss they would incur if the case went to trial. Yet the law itself set guidelines for dividing up the resources in dispute, and thus made the bargaining process more likely to result in cooperation, since knowledge of the law, as well as the costs of going to trial, was common to both sides. The cost and uncertainty of litigation discouraged people from going to trial and encouraged them to compromise or seek arbitration.

It is clear, all the same, that this system could not have functioned without a culture in which the crucial economic actors—merchants, craftsmen, bankers, farmers, professionals—were bound by moral codes or concerns about their reputation. The legal foundations for third-party enforcement were in place, but the administrative tools were not. JPs were unpaid, and were selected from persons of means (from 1732 they had to have an estate paying £100 a year). Many of these JPs were accused of being corrupt and incompetent, as Smollett's fictional Justice Gobble (in *Launcelot Greaves*, published in 1762) attests. Above all, what they did, when they were not feathering their own or their cronies' nests, was to protect the interests of the propertied class. Moreover, there were not enough of them. One of the more troublesome aspects of the enforcement of laws on a daily basis in eighteenth-century Britain was the shortage of JPs willing or able to carry out their functions. There were too many rules, regulations, and restrictions on the books, far more than local government run by overworked or incapable local authorities could or wanted to enforce. As early as 1699, Davenant, in a variation on a statement cited earlier, noted that "laws relating to the poor, the highways, assizes, and other civil economy and good order in the State, those are but slenderly regarded" ([1699], 1771, Vol. 2, p. 206). In 1754, the Lord Chief Justice was induced to resurrect an antiquated practice of indicting JPs who did not carry out their function; in urban areas, especially the rapidly industrializing ones, things were worse (Langford, 1991, pp. 391, 438). The entire system depended on the willingness of members of the local landed gentry to serve without pay, out of civic duty. In the rapidly growing industrial areas after the 1780s, such men were getting scarce. In 1792, the first stipendiary magistrates were set up in London, with a few professional constables under their authority. It was the beginning of a new age of justice administration, but outside London it was slow in coming. As in so many other areas, Britain in this age showed the institutional agility to change in response to changes in the economic and social environment, but it did so slowly and deliberately.

Secure property rights are central to the proper functioning of a sophisticated economy, but in eighteenth-century Britain the prosecution of crime was largely farmed out to the private sector. It has been estimated that over 80 percent of all prosecutions were carried out by the victims of the crime (Emsley, 2005, p. 183). There was no professional police force or constabulary. Instead, daily law enforcement was in the hands of gentleman-amateurs and part-time local parish constables. For the rest, justice had to rely on volunteers, local informers, vigilante groups, and private associations specializing in prosecutions of felons. Some 450 such organizations were established in England between 1744 and 1856. London developed its constables after John Fielding was appointed magistrate at Bow Street in 1748, and his professional assistants or thieftakers became known as "Bow Street Runners." London, precisely because it was large and complex, was in need of third-party enforcement. Colquhoun (1797) criticized law enforcement in London, and in addition to warning against assorted street hustlers and "idle and dissolute characters," pointed to the real dangers of white collar crime. "In a commercial country and a great metropolis," he opined, "from the vast extent of its trade and manufactures ... the danger is not to be conceived from the allurements which are thus held out to young men in business, having the command of money" (p. xxi). It was not until after 1830 that anything remotely resembling a professional police force started to emerge in Britain's large cities, and as late as 1853 half the counties in Britain were still without police.

The argument that economic development in Britain in the age of the Industrial Revolution was the result of "the rule of law," that is, well-defined and well-enforced property rights through third party (i.e. the state) enforcement, is a gross oversimplification. It was more important, as Rodrik et al. (2004, p. 157) note, to signal credibly that property rights would be protected than to enact them into formal law. Such signals did not have to go through the state. Law enforcement at this time was still in large part a private enterprise with the courts at best serving as an enforcer of the very last resort. The Hobbesian view that insisted that order can only be achieved through firm third-party enforcement may well be true for many societies, but it appears that for Britain in the century following Hobbes' death (1679) it was becoming an increasingly less apt description of social reality. What this means is that we cannot really place the efficiency of the state at the center of the stage of institutional explanations of the British economic miracle.

In the decades after Waterloo, however, much law enforcement was transferred back from the private to the public sector. The institutions that were suitable for the economy of 1750 were no longer appropriate in 1830. With the growth of the economy, urbanization, the rise in mobility, and the expansion of markets, the institutions that had supported the eighteenth-century economy were self-undermining and needed to be supplemented and eventually replaced. As Philips (1993, p. 159) has noted, in 1780 Britain was still policed by parish constables and uncoordinated local ad hoc agencies, whereas by 1856 the County and Borough Police Act made a professional police force mandatory for all of England and Wales (earlier laws had established the same for Scotland). It is clearly *not* the case that property rights enforcement cannot be left altogether to the private sector in any economy if a culture of trust and cooperation is strong. But the responsibility for law enforcement shifted between 1780 and 1850 from the private to the public sector. As the economy became larger, more urbanized, and more anonymous, reputation mechanisms were losing their effectiveness.

One original way to think about the problem proposed recently is to realize that property can be protected in two alternative ways. One is for the class of property owners to build a metaphorical wall around themselves (by purchasing guns and locks, hiring private security guards and so on). The other is to build a wall around the criminals by hiring police to arrest them, courts to judge them, and ships to sail them to penal colonies, or prison guards to lock them up. In the latter system, externalities are more prominent, because once a thief is removed from society all his potential victims have less to fear. Even when the wall-in-the-perp system is more efficient economically, to achieve it voluntarily through the private sector is difficult because of these externalities and the free rider problem. While every society adopts a combination of the two systems, the weights of the components differ over time and across countries. Britain in the period under discussion here shifted from a predominantly wall-in-the-property system to one of primarily wall-in-the-thief (Allen and Barzel, 2007, p. 15). The view that this happened because the latter system was more suitable to a more sophisticated and urbanized economy seems plausible, but is hard to demonstrate. What is clear is that a society that wants to make this transition must "nationalize" the criminal justice system so that the positive externalities accruing to property-owners from imprisoning thiefs are internalized. This is, in rough form, what happened. Yet any suggestion that this change was some kind of orderly march toward a more "modern" form of law enforcement would be far off the mark. Private law enforcement remained of substantial importance until well into the nineteenth century, as in the establishment of many local Associations for the Prosecution of Felons, in which property owners paid a fee to establish private security forces (Philips, 1993, p. 161).

The criminal justice system was on the whole a measure of last resort. In the British economy of the age of Enlightenment informal institutions and social norms favoring cooperative behavior worked, and worked well enough. Had moral codes been less widely respected and cultural beliefs been less cooperative, the worlds of credit and commerce would have disintegrated rapidly. Informal codes of behavior and formal third-party enforcement through the courts should not be regarded as substitutes but as complements. The self-enforcing nature of contracts and the maintenance of the economic order was reflected in the concepts of bankruptcy and insolvency. *In extremis* creditors were protected by the option to jail insolvent debtors, but obviously that draconian measure was effective primarily through deterrence rather than actual punishment. Debtors' jail was used only for flagrant cases. Recalcitrant insolvent debtors (defined as those who owed more than 40s., and who could not or would not be declared bankrupt) who refused to pay their debt could be confined to debtors' jail under the assumption that they were able to pay but refused. While languishing in prison, however, the likelihood that the insolvent debtor would make payments was not high. Bankruptcy proceedings became an attractive alternative. Under the

Lord's Act of 1759, Parliament allowed creditors to demand that bankrupt debtors prepare a list of their assets under oath, and they would be released when they did. The bankruptcy laws thus increasingly protected debtors from debtors' jail. Parliament repeatedly passed legislation clearing the crowded jails. The panic of 1825 was followed by the issuance of 101,000 writs for the arrest of debtors, but by the end of 1829 there were only 1,545 prisoners for debt in London (Ford, 1926, p. 28). Clearly, Parliament had realized that insolvent debtors could not be made to pay their debts by being put in jail (Cohen, 1982, p. 159). Debtors' prison was necessary to restrain the small minority of economic agents who played "defect", that is, behaved opportunistically and unscrupulously in a world that was based on trust and reputations for fair dealings. The system made opportunistic behavior more costly and unattractive. Of course, at times it misfired, but on the whole British commerce, credit, and industry operated in a favorable institutional environment.

Some contracts were abrogated because of an unexpected event beyond either one of the parties' control. Others reflected bad faith or default by one of the parties. The difficulty was to tell one from the other. On the whole, Britain's bankruptcy laws, originating in 1542 but reformulated in the 1706 Bankruptcy Act, recognized that some debtors could not pay because of events beyond their control, and that punishing such people would have neither a deterrence nor a signaling value. Originally, the intent had to be the reverse: the preamble to the 1706 Bankruptcy Act states that bankruptcy was caused not so much by unavoidable misfortunes as by an "intent to defraud and hinder creditors of their just debts" (4 & 5 Anne, c. 17, cited by Cohen, 1982, p. 157). The creditors had the option to initiate the bankruptcy proceedings or have the debtor declared insolvent and then initiate steps to have him confined to debtors' prison. Yet regardless of the intention, the eighteenth-century evolution of bankruptcy law increasingly benefited debtors. Bankruptcy discharged existing liabilities and thus gave the agent another fresh start—implicitly conceding that it was indeed misfortune and not intention that caused the insolvency. The obvious support for this position is that the law explicitly allowed the bankruptcy option only for "traders," though legal scholars differed on the exact definition of a trader. Yet Blackstone and other jurists felt that insolvent traders were far more likely to be so for reasons of bad luck than for fraudulence. Blackstone noted that the law of bankrupts took into consideration "the sudden and unavoidable accidents to which men in trade are liable" and gave them back their liberty upon condition that they give up their whole estate to be divided among their creditors. At the same time, bankruptcy was a powerful signal, as a writer in 1780 noted, a stigma that was "fixed perhaps forever, a stain or tarnish that may never be wiped off" (cited by Hoppit, 1987, p. 27). In this sense, the eighteenth-century British economy was still "traditional" in that such signals were personal. Society was sufficiently networked that bankrupt businessmen would be handicapped for the rest of their career. Such a penalty alone would be a powerful incentive for most people to meet their contractual obligations and refrain from opportunistic behavior. In that sense the formal institutions of this economy (bankruptcy proceedings) supported the social norms that created a self-enforcing equilibrium in which reliance on legal mechanisms was a last resort. Bankruptcies remained unusual events. Even in the turbulent decade of the 1790s, the annual rate of bankruptcy was one in 203 firms; in the more quiet decade of 1756–65, the rate was one in 605 businesses (Hoppit, 1987, p. 51).

The harshness of the penalty meted out to those who were regarded as *fraudulent* reflects the assumption that the vast majority of economic agents involved in market transactions were honest, and hence they were increasingly given the option to declare bankruptcy and have their debts eliminated. From that point of view, at least, large sections of the British economy had limited liability even if they were not joint-stock entities. The formal institutional structure and cultural norms thus reinforced one another in creating an environment in which economic activity could take place with a minimum reliance on formal legal means.

The enforcement of property rights through private-order institutions reflects something deep and supremely important about British institutions in the eighteenth century. The culture of respectability and gentility helped solve the standard collective action problems that bedevil the production of public goods. The emergence of a plethora of networks, clubs, friendly societies, academies, and associations created a civil society, in which the private provision of public goods became a reality and created what might be called a *civil economy*. What was true for property right enforcement was true for other projects, for which elsewhere in Europe the state had to play a major role. Roads, harbors, bridges, lighthouses, river navigation improvements, drainage works, and canals were initiated through private subscriptions. In some cases, of course, there was the hope of making a profit, but commonly the entrepreneurs were motivated by the desire to improve local trade and employment. Voluntary associations founded hospitals, schools, orphanages, prosecution societies, and charitable relief committees, as well as turnpike and canal trusts. Amateurs provided local administration and justice. In Scotland, rich landowners sponsored a Board of Trustees for Improving Fisheries and Manufactures (established in 1727) as well as the British Linen Company, which was a pioneering investment bank (Whatley, 1997, p. 54). The infirmaries (hospitals) represented an amalgam of philanthropic elements and more formal institutions such as the Poor Law system. Charitable organizations were of course popular, in part because the Poor Law was inadequate in many areas. The example of Thomas Coram, described eloquently by Colley (1992, pp. 56–60), is illustrative: a successful merchant, he became a leading philanthropist particularly concerned with foundlings and orphans, and established a famous foundling hospital in London in 1741. The Marine Society, established by Jonas Hanway in 1756, similarly was a project run by merchants. The belief that an improvement in the condition of the poor required knowledge of social conditions necessitated the collection of information and data about social conditions, and this knowledge, too, became a central tenet of the later Enlightenment. A typical institution was the Society for Bettering the Condition of the Poor, founded in 1797. Its founder wrote, "let us make the inquiry into all that concerns the poor and the promotion of their happiness into a science" (cited by George, 1966, p. 25). These philanthropic projects were voluntary and patterned after a commercial organizations, replete with a board of directors. Elsewhere they were usually carried out by formal bodies such as the state or the Catholic Church; in Britain they were usually private. Middle-class people participated in and subscribed to these projects to make sure they signaled to others that they were good citizens and thus trustworthy.

The way British society overcame the paradoxes of collective action in the eighteenth century, then, was first and foremost through reputation mechanisms. People wanted to do good, because they wanted to be seen as good, and that was to their advantage. This was particularly true in the new industrial urban areas, where the old Poor Law was less effective. Collective action to palliate the effects of economic crises were especially necessary and effective in the new industrial cities. Middle-class people wanted to take part in a community of socially minded individuals (Lewis, 2001, pp. 250–55). Many of these organizations were subsequently confirmed by statutory authority acts, but they were initiated and managed by the spontaneous organization of private individuals, who banded together voluntarily to accomplish a common goal. These organizations formed a substitute for a more powerful and aggressive central government and they go some way toward explaining how an economy with a weak state was so successful in transforming its economy faster and more smoothly than its rivals in Europe. Voluntary organizations also provided some measure of quality control in those products and services where consumers might be most at the mercy of sellers because of differences in information. An example was the "Law Society" (founded in 1740), which monitored the quality of practicing attorneys and maintained standards of honesty and transparency. Most of the professions followed a path of self-organization and self-regulation through private-order institutions, eventually sanctioned by official imprimatur. Such associations could have degenerated into rent-seeking organizations through exclusion mechanisms, but before 1850 they rarely used their influence to generate barriers to entry.

The impact of voluntary collective action should perhaps not be overstated. A large number of these organizations did not get close to achieving their stated goals. They competed fiercely with one another for membership, and often were riven by internal struggles. Their impact was "muffled and limited ... as a rule associational action was not effective action" (Clark, 2000, pp. 467–68). As urbanization, industrialization, and mobility increased after 1825, it became more and more difficult to overcome free rider problems, adverse selection, and other difficulties that bedevil associational activities. While they had some undeniable achievements early on, nineteenth-century Britain had increasingly to cope with the fact that for many public goods there simply was no substitute for a coercive coordinating agent, i.e., government. Judges and law enforcement agencies eventually had to be placed on a professional basis. What is certain, however, is that these associations increased the overall level of social networking, thus reducing access costs not only to useful knowledge, but also to information about other agents, and thus enforcing reputation mechanisms that supported social norms of respectable behavior in the economic sphere.

Entrepreneurship depended on the structure of institutions. Modern economists stress that for economic dynamism to have salutary effects on the economy, there has to be a system that creates order, that prevents opportunism from becoming so widespread and so deep that it deadens commerce and credit and extinguishes incentives. Yet Britain's law enforcement system was hardly responsible for creating the secure environment in which merchants, financiers and innovators could interact to produce economic progress. Instead, informal norms and codes of behavior, to which the middle class adhered, must be seen as crucial in this regard. The British entrepreneur thought of himself, in an ethical sense, as what we would call a gentleman. Ironically, this notion of a gentleman is closer to what McCloskey (2006) calls "bourgeois virtues" than the original leisurely landed squire. The idea of gentlemanly capitalism was emphasized by Cain and Hopkins: "gentlemanly ideals ... provided a shared code, based on honor and obligation, which acted as a blueprint for conduct in occupations whose primary function was to manage men rather than machines" (1993, p. 26). That definition, however, neglects the point that the typical entrepreneur during the Industrial Revolution had to be concerned with both men and machines, managing the men who ran the machines.

For a long time it used to be believed that the mixture of gentility and capitalism was an obstacle to economic growth. An artificial dualism was dreamed up between "commercial capitalism" and "industrial capitalism," the former acceptable and sufficiently similar in lifestyle and attitudes to the landowners to be entirely separable from the grim and grimy environment of the factories and the mines associated with the latter. As Daunton summarized the traditional argument, "the more an occupation or a source of income allowed for a life style which was similar to that of the landed classes, the higher the prestige it carried and the greater the power it conferred. The gentleman-capitalist supposedly did not despise the market economy, but he did hold production in low regard and avoided full-time work" (1989, p. 128). Coleman (1973) stressed the deep divide between gentlemen and "players" (that is, practical men). That businessmen who had made money desired to be regarded as members of the leisured landed class and that there was snobbism against the newcomers does not weaken the argument that the captains of industry and commerce copied some of their social codes from the elite, and in so doing shaped the face of British industrial capitalism as a basically honorable occupation, in which men kept their word, paid their debts, and kept up a pretense of mutual respect.

The contradiction is resolved once we keep in mind that the actual gentlemen of the time, many of whom may indeed have been idle and useless drones, were as different from the social ideal of an honest and reliable person as medieval sword-wielding thugs were from the ideal of chivalry. The norms and codes for gentlemanly behavior were a matter of education, of course, and they correlated with certain forms of etiquette such as clothing, accent, and more generally politeness. What mattered for the development of the economy was that people behaved honorably, kept their word, and did not renege on promises. The code of honor of gentility and respectability involved certain family and social obligations (the ability to support one's dependants and to keep one's promises). In other words, gentlemanly capitalism can be seen as a way in which opportunistic behavior was made so taboo that in only a few cases was it necessary to use the formal institutions to punish deviants. This made it possible to trade with strangers, deal with people with whom there might not be repeated transactions at arm's length, without trying to take short-term advantage of the situation. Gentlemanly enterprise, argue Cain and Hopkins, was strongly personal and held together by a social network (1993, p. 36). It was a set of relations that involved horizontal connections, with one's peers, suppliers, partners, customers, and creditors. It was not extended to persons who were demonstrably of a lower class, such as one's servants or employees. It was, as Davidoff (1995) has noted, heavily gendered—much like chivalry.

What mattered for the success of entrepreneurship in Britain was that if everyone could think of themselves as *noblesse*, everyone was, at least pro forma, *obligé* by a gentlemanly code of behavior. The typical entrepreneur in the Industrial Revolution was hardly the ferocious, unscrupulous, merciless money-grabber that some of the more sentimental accounts make him out to be. It was far more important "to be known and trusted in the locality" and to have "standing in the community" in addition to some form of property (Hudson, 1986, p. 262). Coleman's (1973) failure to find any common ground between gentlemanly ideals and the "ruthless, driving, dynamic tycoon" he associated with Schumpeter, is due to the fact that he employs a caricature of what successful entrepreneurs did. A measure of cooperation and trust was more of a key to the success of an entrepreneurial class than pure individual selfish maximization. The importance of trust to economic growth is now generally acknowledged. Knack and Keefer (1997), for instance, argue that "low trust can also discourage innovation. If entrepreneurs must devote more time to monitoring possible malfeasance by partners, employees, and suppliers, they have less time to devote to innovation in new products or processes" (pp. 1252–53). They find that high levels of trust are indeed associated with better economic performance. While it is of course impossible to find retroactive measures of trust like the modern data from the world value surveys, indirect measures seem to suggest that members of the class of "gentleman-capitalists" could, indeed, trust each other more than people who did not belong to this class.

As noted, trust required focal points and costly signaling. Dress, housing location, the inside of the home, modes of transportation, membership in societies and clubs, and the labor force status of women were crucial to the middle-class existence because they indicated their social position. Accent and mode of speech were more problematic, and hence the proper education of children to make sure no doubts could exist about their social position was imperative (Lewis, 2001, ch. 11). The ideas associated with gentility served this purpose. It is hard to know with any precision when the transformation of the idea of a gentleman of leisure, whose integrity was at best supported by his disinterestedness, to a person of integrity who could be trusted in business dealings took place. McCloskey (2006, pp. 294–96) traces the transformation of the word "honor" from its aristocratic sense ("reputation") to its more capitalist sense of "honesty" (reliability, truth-telling) and "politeness" ("doing the right thing") to a time when the importance of these concepts began to increase in the early eighteenth century, and discovers that the same change occurred in the Dutch language. A very similar point is made by Norbert Elias (1978, pp. 102–04) in relation to the terms "civilized" and "courteous." From terms associated with courts, they became terms denoting socially acceptable behavior and by 1694 *courtoisie* had become a "bourgeois concept." In short, gentlemanly enterprise was an informal institution, part of Elias' "civilizing process" but one that had important economic ramifications. It supported the increasingly integrated and soon-to-be national market in Britain. That market did not create the Industrial Revolution by itself, but it was an essential complement to it.

The typical entrepreneur in the eighteenth and early nineteenth centuries was thus far from being the solitary single-minded do-it-all genius who knew markets, technology, accounting, and labor management. A few such entrepreneurs may have existed, but they were far from the rule. The entrepreneur normally represented one side of the business (either technical or managerial) and had the ability to cooperate with others who represented a different comparative advantage. The most striking manifestation of the growth of social norms in which businessmen found people they could trust is the growth of partnerships; although partnerships had existed before 1700, they became more common after the middle of the eighteenth century (Smail, 1994, p. 75). Such cooperation often took the form of partnerships or even market transactions at arm's length even if a personal element was rarely missing altogether. In other cases it involved hiring a technical expert, a manager, an overseeing engineer, who could be trusted. Pollard (1965) has shown that the finding of such personnel was an important skill in itself and often a test of successful entrepreneurship. Some such employees eventually became successful entrepreneurs, Robert Owen being the best-known example. Entrepreneurship and hardware were complementary inputs, and a country such as Britain that was good at producing hardware (and the people who could use it) also provided unique opportunities to those who could take advantage of them. The partnering of individuals with technical skill with those with commercial acumen illustrates the great advantage that Britain enjoyed in this dimension: the complementarity of human capital and favorable institutions. Boulton found his Watt, Clegg his Murdoch, Marshall his Murray, Muspratt his Gamble, and Cooke his Wheatstone. Entrepreneurial success was based less on multi-talented geniuses than on successful cooperation between individuals who had good reason to think they could trust one another. Even at that level, the classical principles of division of labor and comparative advantage held.

Pearson and Richardson (2001) and Sunderland (2007, pp. 176–78) have argued that the entrepreneur in the Industrial Revolution was heavily diversified. Rather than a sharply focused owner-manager who spent his entire life on the one business he built, the typical entrepreneur of the age of the Industrial Revolution diversified into non-core ventures. Cotton masters and other textile producers in Manchester, Leeds, and Liverpool could be found as directors of insurance companies, canal and turnpike companies, gas companies, banks, and other sectors. Country banks were the diversifying instrument par excellence: many bankers were diversified in a variety of business, and so were their partners. Profits made in shipbuilding and banking were invested in breweries (Mathias, 1979, p. 240). Abraham Darby III invested not only in turnpike trusts but also in the large hotel built to face his great iron bridge in Coalbrookdale. The woolen manufacturer Edward Pease became George Stephenson's partner and a major entrepreneurial force in the early railroad enterprises. Innkeepers and victuallers in the west Midlands were often joint owners in metal working enterprises (Berg and Hudson, 1992, p. 32). Such diversifying behavior made sense in the highly risky environment of British business, but it is indicative of the capability of the shared codes of conduct to bring together people who might come from very different backgrounds. One could invest in a branch of business one knew little about, because the people one dealt with were expected to behave like gentlemen and therefore could be trusted. The entrepreneur-gentleman networked with people who trusted him on the basis of these social norms, helped develop local infrastructures, and signaled his trustworthiness by seemingly eschewing greed, by contributing to charitable works, by cultural patronage, and voluntary subscriptions (Pearson and Richardson, 2001, p. 672). Many of them displayed generosity that reveals long-term planning and willingness to cooperate. The Leeds flax spinner John Marshall repeatedly bailed out and supported the engineering firms which made and maintained his machinery (Cookson, 1997, p. 7). Even hard-nosed businessmen like Boulton and Watt felt the need to be reconstructed as generous gentlemen and public-spirited philosophers, and persuaded Watt's friend, the scientist John Robison, to present them as gentlemen who exhibited openness and generosity of spirit (Miller, 1999, p. 197). Watt's qualities were not supposed to be those of the avaricious entrepreneur, looking only to how he might profit. Trust and cooperation made diversification possible. It was particularly pronounced among Quakers, whose religion was a strong signal of trustworthiness. The Gibbins bank, for example, was a Quaker enterprise started by Welsh copper manufacturers. By not appearing too greedy, these businessmen signaled their membership in a community of cooperators who could be trusted.

What made this trust possible were social networks such as permanent members of taverns, coffee-houses, and inns, friendly societies, religious communities, Masonic lodges, and similar organizations in which businessmen and craftsmen got together and exchanged information and gossip. In eighteenth-century Britain, to be a gentleman one had to be sociable, to be part of a community. Urban society created special organizations that made polite society function, such as coffee-houses, philanthropic organizations, and intellectual societies. The social interaction that took place in these organizations was the core of civil society and its rules guided the actions of those who could claim to be "gentlemen" (Cowan, 2005, p. 101). Enlightenment writers urged sociability because this was their hope of creating a lasting moral order (Porter, 1981, p.15). What has not been fully realized is that such a moral order involved a culture of cooperation and responsibility. Any member of this *Gemeinschaft* who contemplated opportunistic behavior would know that such behavior, if revealed, would become public knowledge and that his reputation would be irreparably harmed. The point is that well-functioning institutions do not require people to be "moral" or altruistic; instead self-interested individuals behave cooperatively because they have adequate reason to believe that most others with whom they will come in contact will do the same.

Informal institutions, in other words, allowed society to operate far more efficiently than it would if every player had played pure Nash strategies, that is to say, displayed selfish and uncooperative behavior. That the country was not altogether devoid of Uriah Heep types is of course quite obvious, but as long as opportunistic behavior remained a minority phenomenon and was dealt with mercilessly, the cultural norms of cooperation could prevail. The British entrepreneur, far from being a ruthless egotist, was very much part of a shared value system that economists have only recently come to appreciate. The typical entrepreneur did his best to come across as trustworthy. Gentlemen, ideally, were men without occupation and presumably generous and not driven by greed. A new concept of "gentleman" arose, someone who did not behave opportunistically and could be trusted. The importance of these norms has not been fully appreciated in the history of development of the British economy.

It needs to be stressed, however, that what emerged in this economy in the eighteenth century was a mixed system in which competition and cooperation worked together, odd as it may sound. While entrepreneurs were operating in markets that were highly competitive, they still observed certain constraints in their competitive behavior. Driven by a mixture of concerns about their reputation and internalized values, they displayed a high level of "honor" and class solidarity, defined as sufficient trust in one another for pairwise cooperative behavior to be expected and maintained, and an external collective good (commercial prosperity) to be produced (Posner, 2000, p. 34).

Furthermore, the culture of gentlemen-entrepreneurs depended to a large degree on the desire for social acceptability. Apart from material advance, the hope for social promotion in itself contributed to economic success by providing the right kinds of incentive to would-be entrepreneurs. These incentives included more than just material goods. Harold Perkin (1969) pointed out that from the Restoration on, the principle upon which society was established was the link between wealth and status. Here status meant not only political influence and indirect control over the lives of one's neighbors, but also the houses to which one was invited, the partners eligible for one's children to marry, the rank one could attain (that is, purchase) in the army, where one lived, and how one's children were educated. In Perkin's view, the quality of life was determined not just by "consumption," as usually defined by economists, but by the relative standing of the individual in the social hierarchy. Whether this social relativity hypothesis is still a good description of today's society is an open question, but a case can be made, as Perkin does, that it is an apt description of Britain in the eighteenth century. The successful pursuit of riches, thus, meant not only enhanced material comforts, but elevated social status. Such hopes were essential to the sustained supply of talented, industrious, gutsy young men who would take up pursuits that enriched the nation, if not all entrepreneurs. It also helped determine the social norms of business. If the purpose of financial success was to eventually become a gentleman, one should start by behaving like one.

*   *   *

Culture has been identified by economists primarily as social relations: can people trust one another and thus behave in a cooperative fashion? Yet technology and useful knowledge relate in large part to beliefs about nature and the willingness to manipulate it. Max Weber and more recently Lynn White and David Landes have given equal weight to cultural attitudes that help determine the ability of society to generate the kinds of innovation that spur economic growth. Religion was of course central in an age in which almost everyone was still quite pious in one form or another, and the British Enlightenment more than anywhere else was comfortable with its approach to religion and found no difficulty reconciling it with the principles of the Industrial Enlightenment. In Britain, the question whether advances in science and technology constitute an irreverent encroachment upon realms previously reserved for a deity or whether they illustrate the wisdom of the creator and thus please him was answered resoundingly in favor of the latter. Eighteenth-century Christianity in Britain clearly had abandoned most qualms about perturbing nature and thereby incurring divine wrath. Between Bacon and Newton, the message was clear. Nature made sense, it could be understood, so it could be mastered for the material benefit of mankind. Moreover, it was realized that religion was itself an important contributor to the culture of cooperation and gentlemanly behavior. David Hume's character Cleanthes may have spoken for the spirit of this culture when he suggested that "the proper office of religion is to regulate the heart of men, humanize their conduct, infuse the spirit of temperance, order, and obedience" (Hume, 1773, p. 244).

Culture may have affected technological progress in other ways. I have suggested two examples of such attitudes that have little to do with religion and that may help explain the economic successes of the Western world (Mokyr, 1990a). One example is the willingness to borrow ideas from other societies. As already noted, the British (and most Western Europeans) had few compunctions about adopting and adapting useful knowledge generated in societies they may otherwise have detested. The slogan "Not invented here" was replaced by the ironic "Stolen with pride." The other example is the willingness to criticize and deviate from the accepted wisdom of previous generations. The degree to which society revered the wisdom of the past was an important element in its ability and desire to innovate. If intellectuals regarded the "canon" as sacrosanct, or if artisans were discouraged from altering technological practices passed from father to son and from master to student, innovation would be squashed. In Europe, heresy and rebelliousness became ingrained during the late Middle Ages and the Renaissance. These sentiments were not new in 1500, much less in 1700, but the Enlightenment constituted their apotheosis.

But culture also involved something more: the picking of a ranking of social priorities and through them one of social prestige and respect. These priorities are critical to the allocation of talent, and decide whether the most ambitious and brightest young people will choose to become rabbis or generals. One of the most interesting and potentially significant transformations in the eighteenth century was the rise in the social prestige of inventors and engineers. It is precisely in this area that the age of Enlightenment made a large difference. In Bacon's imaginary utopia *New Atlantis* inventors were treated with great respect: three of the fellows of the House of Salomon were collecting the "experiments of all mechanical arts" and three others were in charge of "how to draw out of them things of use and practice for man's life ... these were called Dowry men [sources of wealth] or benefactors" (Bacon, 1996, pp. 486–87). But the seventeenth-century reality was rather different. MacLeod (2007, p. 8) has argued that in the seventeenth century the patentee was regarded in society as little more than "the pickpocket and the fraudster." This characterization is of course exaggerated, but there was a lot of room for improvement. In 1679, William Petty sighed that "although the inventor often times drunk with the opinion of his own merit, thinks all the world will invade and incroach upon him ... for as when a new invention is first propounded, in the beginning every man objects, and the poor inventor runs the gantloop of all petulent wits ... not one [inventor] of a hundred outlives this torture" (Petty, 1679, p. 53).

It is precisely in explaining the changes in these attitudes that models of cultural evolution may provide some insights. One bias in the evolutionary transmission of beliefs and attitudes is model-based bias: an individual so admired that others want to emulate him. The work of Isaac Newton affected the eighteenth century much as Einstein's did in the twentieth century: although the majority of people were incapable of understanding the details, these breakthroughs became symbols of human ability to understand and tame nature. Newton was the thinking person's ideal, a role model whose work others wanted to emulate. In more applied fields, highly successful inventors occupied a similar position. A few of the Industrial Revolution's most celebrated inventors and entrepreneurs whose technological and entrepreneurial success became so commonplace as to turn them into "superstars," such as Watt, Wedgwood, and Arkwright, helped improve the standing of inventors in society.

Another cultural "bias" in the Boyd and Richerson mode discussed in the previous chapter is the "salient events" bias. People may change their beliefs and attitudes systematically as the result of some traumatic or memorable event that leaves a deep impression on a large number of individuals. If the event is "global," it can have deep cultural consequences. In our own generation, surely the attack of 9/11 qualifies, while in an earlier generation the events of 1940–45 played a similar role. The period of the Industrial Revolution witnessed no traumatic events, but some technological developments clearly must have impressed contemporaries and made them change their views of technology. Technology was working, and it was improving the lot of many Britons. Many of these improvements, however, were hardly conspicuous: they took the form of cheaper underwear and better nails and screws, hardly the stuff that would propel cultural evolution. But some events were dramatic and seen as such. Ballooning was one such event. The invention was of little intrinsic economic value, but greatly enhanced belief in the capability of technology to do truly remarkable things that mankind had dreamed about for endless generations (Mokyr, 1990b). The defeat of gravity by humans, which seems to us so commonplace, had never been accomplished until 1783, and ballooning became a highly popular form of entertainment, but one that carried a loud and clear cultural message. Some of the more spectacular engineering feats of the age, such as the monumental Pontcysyllte aqueduct built by canal giants Telford and Jessop and completed in 1805, and the astonishing Ouse railway viaduct completed in 1841 by John Rastrick (1,475 feet long and using 11 million bricks), also fired up the confidence of contemporaries in the ability of engineering to achieve ever higher goals. In a different area, Edward Jenner added to the respectability of innovation: human ingenuity that had defeated gravity could also defeat smallpox. Jenner became highly respected in his own time: a simple country doctor, he received honorary doctorates from Oxford and Harvard and an appointment as physician-extraordinary to George IV (Baxby, 2004).

Steam power played a similar role. The first steam engines were "salient" things—large, noisy, alien. They must have impressed contemporaries for reasons other than just their revolution in energy generation, but the cultural impression they made was one of power over nature. James Watt became, in the eyes of the general public, the true embodiment of the Industrial Revolution. Much of this respect grew after his death, in the 1820s and beyond. One could argue about whether such a view is historically justified—after all, he did not "invent" the engine and inventions by others in the area of steam may be considered equally ingenious—but it is clear that he had by the early nineteenth century become more than a cultural icon: he had become a symbol of the Industrial Enlightenment and everything that was progressive and innovative in Britain. Steam acquired a great deal of social prestige with the growth of railways and steamships, which were widespread and spectacular enough to qualify as "salient events." It was exactly in those years that the technological results of the Industrial Enlightenment were becoming visible to more and more people. Watt was turned into a role model even if he had no responsibility for those innovations (MacLeod, 2007). His role was puffed up, perhaps deliberately, by Whig writers, but the need to find such a person had existed all along. Cultural evolution, much like technological progress, needed focusing devices.

As a result, the social respectability of inventors and innovators kept rising in Victorian Britain. The changes in culture gave the successful inventors fame and the respect of a large group of peers. There is no easy way to measure the effects of such cultural changes. But the observed glory of Jenner, Watt, and others sent a powerful signal to other would-be inventors. Neither during the Industrial Revolution nor in any other period were inventors *solely* motivated by money, even if money was important. Fame, unlike today, did not equal wealth almost automatically, but there was a correlation all the same, and many ambitious innovators could see for themselves the changes in attitudes that constituted the Industrial Enlightenment, and which formed the cultural origins of the Industrial Revolution.

CHAPTER 17

Formal Institutions: The State and the Economy

The relations between the state and its citizens were at the heart of the Enlightenment discourse, embodied in ideas reflected in famous book titles such as *The Social Contract* and *The Civil Society*. Economists have a rather more sober and technical theory of the state, and for the present purpose, it seems logical to follow the latter. Most economists recognize that the state's activities in the economy can be reduced to two basic types. One is to do for the economy things that the free market cannot do on its own or cannot do well. Among those, the state needs to impose and monitor obedience to the "rules" of the economic game, such as property rights and contract enforcement, as well as to maintain peace and the rule of law. It solves coordination problems such as the provision of a credible means of exchange and thus lubricates the wheels of commerce and production, it tries to prevent the market economy from becoming unstable due to self-fulfilling fears and panics, and sets such useful conventions and standards as "drive on the left" or "a meter is a fixed fraction of the circumference of the earth." It also provides "public goods" such as infrastructural investments and national defense where problems of excludability and non-rivalrousness make private provision ineffective (though rarely altogether impossible). There is, perhaps, a certain naïveté about this approach in relation to eighteenth-century Britain. The state did primarily one thing: it waged war against other states, and raised revenues to pay for this activity. Whether such wars actually enhanced social welfare remains very much in doubt. Some citizens gained, but for the average taxpayer these wars constituted a net loss, and for the world as a whole a waste of human lives and resources. Government activities that enhanced social welfare were not altogether absent in the eighteenth century, but almost an afterthought. It is the changing balance between wars and the provision of public goods that is at the heart of the economics of the public sector in Britain between 1700 and 1850.

The other type of activity the state was engaged in was the redistribution of wealth and income. The British state in the eighteenth century was a mechanism of rent-seeking in which powerful groups and members of the political elite used the power of the state in their own interest to gain certain privileges and exclusionary rights, such as monopolies, import prohibitions, and other regulations whose purpose it was to generate income for a few at the expense of the many. In most cases these groups were part of the ruling elite itself. Rent-seeking and corruption can degenerate into a purely predatory "kleptocracy" in which the economy is condemned to poverty when its institutions become dysfunctional. But at all times the rulers need allies and supporters, and are in danger of being "captured" by redistributive coalitions and well-organized lobbies. Eighteenth-century Britain was dominated by fluid and changing coalitions, in which both the interests of the dominant landed elites and those of the merchants and financial classes needed to be accommodated.

In reality in all states, including the British state in the eighteenth century, these two types of activity were mixed up and intertwined. The *relative* importance of the two "types" was, however, neither homogeneous across nations nor invariant over time. One issue that has loomed large in the literature is that of credible commitment. What is meant by this is that the British government was given certain powers and resources by the taxpayers, in return for a believable promise that it would respect their property rights (including claims on future taxes). North and Weingast (1989), in an influential paper, argued that this credible commitment was attained only after the Glorious Revolution and the Bill of Rights, and date the successful relationship between the British state and the citizenry from that time. Others have argued that the relationship goes back to the Civil War and the Stuarts. Whatever the case may be, the credible commitment the government made around 1700 was most often to specific groups that had pressured or bribed the state to award it certain privileges.

The British state at that time, then, was wedded to mercantilist principles which were in large part rent-seeking in nature (Ekelund and Tollison, 1981, 1997). One way of thinking about the mercantilist state is to realize that it was a mutually beneficial alliance of the fiscal needs of the state and special interests seeking special considerations and advantages at the expense of their competitors or the consuming public at large. These interests deployed state power to secure benefits, many of which were exclusionary rents, in exchange for revenues needed by the government, largely for military purposes. Monopoly profits were easier to tax, and thus both sides gained, but at the expense of the economy at large. If mercantilism was not a systematic set of measures to transfer income from one single group to another, it was mainly because different groups of landowners, merchants, and manufacturers had conflicting interests. Indeed, as O'Brien, Griffiths, and Hunt (1991, p. 416), argue, much of what passes as mercantilist policy does not qualify as an "industrial policy," but should be regarded as a set of improvisations and ad hoc measures to pacify some especially troublesome pressure group or constituency and maintain peace and order. It was an adaptive and protean system, with few predetermined effects because the outcomes of the arcane struggles between coalitions were hard to predict and often abruptly reversed. Mercantilist doctrine postulated that British goods and interests should always be preferred to foreign ones, and that the military apparatus of the state should be deployed in the service of these interests.

Yet even in a mercantilist world, the importance of the interests of the nation as a whole and the need to provide for the common good cannot be dismissed altogether as a motive for public policy. Mercantilism was as much a doctrine of dynastic interests as a doctrine of national defense. It advocated a positive balance of trade because it was believed that a flow of gold into a country would enable its rulers to hire mercenaries and build ships to defend the realm. Moreover, mercantilist writers were, as we have seen, deeply concerned about unemployment and advocated what would be called in the twentieth century a "beggar thy neighbour" policy, supporting exports and curtailing imports in the hope of creating jobs. Most economists would regard these policies as questionable, but not all mercantilist policy measures can be dismissed as narrow-minded special interest. Yet these measures were invariably based on a mercantilist zero-sum view of the world, in which nations fought over fixed resources and tried to out-compete each other in what were believed to be fixed-sized markets. Mercantilist policies were neither irrational nor stupid; they may well have been a best response in a world in which all other nations may have been expected to play similar strategies (Findlay and O'Rourke, 2007, pp. 229, 351). Yet, while such Nash equilibria are not irrational, they are inefficient compared to a world in which all nations can commit to free-trade policies. This was the implicit objective of Enlightenment thinking.

At the risk of oversimplification, it seems a fair generalization that the century and a half after 1700 saw the slow decline and then dismantlement of the odd combination of beliefs and policies that we dub mercantilism. One symptom of the changing beliefs can be culled from the patent records, from what the patentees themselves declared to be the "aim" of their invention. In 1660–1719, 12.6 percent of all declared aims (up to two per patent) declared import substitution as their aim, and in 1740–49, this percentage was still 12.5. By 1790–99, this proportion had declined to a negligible 0.3 percent (MacLeod, 1988, p. 160). Crediting exclusively the growth of Enlightenment thought and an evolving new economic and social ideology for that transformation would be quite misleading, but so would be an interpretation that attributes the change *solely* to material forces of technology, demography, relative prices, and markets. Adam Smith's singularly effective and influential attack on the "mercantile system" as he called it could not by itself have dismantled it. Smith came at the end of a long stream of intellectuals and philosophers, both British and continental, who attacked the basic assumptions of the mercantile system and its rent-seeking rationale. In pointing out that "monopoly of one kind or another seems to be the sole engine of the mercantile system," Smith obviously realized that free-entry markets were the wave of the future. But the changes in the economy, however profound, would not in themselves inevitably have reformed British institutions. The movement toward economic growth could just as easily have been reversed, with the technological dynamism and entrepreneurial energies of the Industrial Revolution gradually running out of steam and in the end fizzling out, the victims of special interests and corruption.

Industrialization and the beginnings of mechanization did not terminate special interest politics, the economic extraction of resources through political power, lobbying for rents and extra-market advantages, and the activities of pressure groups vying for redistribution of income and wealth through the preservation of market power and exclusions. These characteristics are common to all societies, and our own time is far from immune (Olson, 1982). However, the Enlightenment meant that, at least for a while, rent-seeking and special interests were placed on the defensive. Many of the institutions of the British economy that had supported rent-seeking and redistribution were reformed or were weakened to make such activities relatively unattractive, and thus the efforts of Britain's most ingenious and resourceful people were channeled into more productive directions. By 1850, the elite that ran British government no longer saw political power as a means to acquire more privileges and to redistribute resources from others to itself. Instead, it made sure that no other political group would be able to do the same so that it could keep what it already had. Redistribution by and large vanished as an objective of policy.

The changes in the formal institutions of Britain after 1700 were the result of ideological change but also of the tensions and interactions between three elites. In eighteenth-century Britain the political elite consisted, with a few exceptions, of well-to-do landowners. When it is said that the British state at the time of the Glorious Revolution was a government by, of, and for private property, what is meant thereby primarily is "real property"—that is, land. After the Glorious Revolution of 1688, however, the concept of property was expanded to include government-issued debt and other financial and commercial assets. The identity of the political elite with the economic elite thus came under pressure. Wealth was increasingly based on profits made in commerce, finance, transport, and manufacturing, and government securities became a second form in which the wealth of the rich was held. As the *nouveaux riches* accumulated more economic power, they obviously demanded more influence in the political process, and they found channels through which their money could talk to politicians and change institutions to suit their needs. Yet there was a third elite that began to make its presence felt, namely the intellectual elite of philosophers who proposed new theories about what the state was supposed to do and not to do. Their power came from their prestige and rhetorical skills, and through those their ability to persuade members of the other elites about what a good society should look like. Their views were of course not homogeneous and did not coincide precisely with those of the other elites, and changes in British institutions should be viewed as the result of the discourses and alliances between these three groups.

Dating the transformation to a more liberal and enlightened state with precision is hazardous. For one thing, many archaic laws, regulations, and exclusionary arrangements remained on the books but were enforced with decreasing zeal and evaded with growing audacity and efficacy. For another, the mercantile system affected many areas and aspects of the British economy, both domestic and foreign, and its retreat was highly uneven. The entrenched interests fought back, and progress toward a more enlightened economy was subject to many temporary reversals. All the same, by 1850 the mercantile system as it had existed in the eighteenth century and before had been dismantled. Rent-seeking, of course, did not disappear altogether, though perhaps it was held at bay for the entire Victorian age. Nor is it easy to say what, precisely, would have happened if Enlightenment-inspired institutional changes had not taken place, or (as seems possible) if the direction of institutional change had become increasingly unenlightened, more stringently nationalistic, and the political institutions of the country increasingly corrupt and redistributive. We have examples of European nations such as Spain and Russia, in which the Enlightenment was successfully resisted and severely delayed. Their economic performance in the nineteenth century was disappointing. In other Western nations where the Enlightenment caught on in one form or another, an effective state, relatively free of corruption and not excessively controlled by special interests, emerged, and thus the Scandinavian countries, the Low Countries, and in their own ways France and Germany could eventually follow the British example, even if variations in tradition and temperament meant that institutions differed in detail.

The role of government in the economic transformation of Britain between 1700 and 1850 is controversial in more than one dimension. First, scholars disagree deeply in principle on the role of government in the development process, both what it has been and what it should have been. Second, they disagree as to the actual characteristics of government in eighteenth-century Britain. What is not in dispute is that eighteenth-century Britain was, on the surface, no laissez-faire economy. It was heavily taxed and regulated, with strong protection for many imports and "bounties" (subsidies) for some exports. It imposed encumbrances on businesses, first and foremost the various restrictions on the formation of joint-stock companies, and the usury laws which limited interest rates charged to a legal maximum. Parliament needed to give its consent to the formation of any kind of business organization such as canals that required a large outlay of capital. Labor markets were still subject to the ancient Statute of Apprentices and Artificers dating back to 1562, which constrainined workers in many occupations to a formal apprenticeship before they could be employed in their trade. Adam Smith ([1776], 1976, Vol. I, pp. 137–38) heaped scorn on this law, and dubbed some of its outdated provisions "as foolish as can well be imagined" and thought it "a manifest encroachment upon the just liberty both of the workman and those who might be disposed to employ him."

There is good reason to believe, however, that the regulations and rules, many of them relics from Tudor and Stuart times, were far from being enforced consistently. As the economy became more sophisticated and markets more complex, the ability of the government to regulate and control such matters as the quality of bread or the length of apprentice contracts without an expanding bureaucracy effectively vanished (Ashton, 1948, p. 95). The Statute of Apprentices and Artificers exempted many trades, and even where it was ostensibly in force it seems to have made little impact. In 1777 the calico printers admitted that fewer than 10 percent of their workers had served because "the trade does not require that the men they employ should be brought up to it; common labourers are sufficient" (Mantoux, ([1905], 1961, p. 453). London's carpenters and tailors did not enforce the Statute of Apprentices: the corporation of the City of London passed regulations releasing masters from the need to insist on formally trained apprentices, since "the City masters could not permit the enforcement of regulations that might damage their trade" (Schwarz, 1992, p. 219). Even the Bubble Act, as already noted, could be bent if not evaded altogether by extended proprietorship forms of organization, as was the case in the fire insurance industry (Pearson, 1997, p. 243). Trustees for large groups of people operated fairly well and reproduced a level of liquidity that was not all that different from what incorporation could provide (Dubois, 1938, p. 38). Barnard's Act of 1734, which tried to prevent "speculation" by prohibiting options as financial instruments, was passed again four times between 1745 and 1773, a tell-tale sign that its enforcement left something to be desired (Neal, 1982, p. 88). The central government controlled foreign trade, the military, and financial matters, but most other internal administration was left to local authorities. Internal trade, the regulation of markets in labor and land, justice, police, county road maintenance, and poor relief were all administered by local magistrates. Although in principle these authorities *could* exercise considerable power over daily life, they usually elected not to. This de facto laissez-faire policy derived not so much from any libertarian principles as from the pure self-interest of people who already had wealth and were making more and the reality that local administration was carried out by amateur officials who could exercise a great deal of discretion in the extent to which they implemented the laws of the land. By ignoring and evading rather than altogether abolishing obsolete rules and regulations, eighteenth-century Britain moved slowly toward a free market society. In the view of some scholars, *The Wealth of Nations* was already out of date when it was published: what it advocated had largely been accomplished (Perkin, 1969, p. 65).

Often the exact interpretation of exclusionary legislation such as the Bubble Act was left to the judiciary (Harris, 2000). Other restrictive legislation, such as usury laws, were widely evaded through a variety of bookkeeping mechanisms, though that does not mean they did not make business more difficult to conduct. A recent paper (Temin and Voth, 2008a) shows how one private London bank changed its lending practices when the usury ceiling was lowered from 6 to 5 percent in 1714, though it is far from clear how these laws affected the country banks that emerged half a century later. By treating loans as overdrafts and over-charging for such payments as postal fees, banks could tack on commissions to customers who otherwise might have been rationed out of the market, stretching formal rates of 5 percent to 6.5 or 7 percent (Cottrell, 1980, p. 8). By 1818, a Parliamentary Committee's verdict on the usury laws was that "the Laws regulating or restraining the rate of Interest have been extensively evaded, and have failed of the effect of imposing a maximum on such rate; and that of late years, from the constant excess of the market rate of interest above the rate limited by law, they have added to the expense incurred by borrowers on real security" (Great Britain, 1818, p. 4). The Navigation Laws, similarly, were by wide consent widely evaded not just through smuggling but through deliberately lax enforcement by British officials who recognized their folly, as was the case with the 1733 Molasses Act, widely evaded in the North American colonies (though quite harmful to British consumers). Many items in the Elizabethan Statute of Apprentices, such as the foolish requirement that parents of a lad wishing to be apprenticed to a handloom weaver have an estate worth at least £3, were already a dead letter in 1700. The 1721 Calico Act could not banish all Indian calicoes from England, and competitive printed textiles continued to threaten the silk and woolen producers (Lemire, 1991, p. 42). The laws to prevent the emigration of artisans and the exportation of machinery, which were essentially mercantilist laws, were widely evaded, despite draconian penalties (Henderson, 1954; Jeremy, 1977). Samuel Garbett was one of the most energetic supporters of these laws, but it is significant that he could not even prevent his own son-in-law from helping skilled iron-workers from being recruited to Russia (Ashton, 1924, p. 204). Adam Smith ([1776], 1976, p. 50) spoke of "a hundred impertinent obstructions with which the folly of human laws often incumbers the operations" [of an individual's effort]. He did not allow for the possibility that some of those "human laws" were simply not rigorously enforced by those who recognized their futility. Furthermore, when it needed to actually formally change the law to adapt to changing economic circumstances or to reflect new thinking about the way the economy functioned, Britain, more than any other polity on earth, had the wherewithal to do so. Its institutional adaptiveness, formal or informal, served Britain well. As Richardson and Bogart (2008) have recently pointed out, the ability of Parliament to establish statutory authorities and alter property rights that had become an obstacle derived from the strengthened position of Parliament after 1689.

What, then, was the role of the government in affecting economic change in Britain between 1700 and 1850? The difficulty in answering this question is illustrated by the unresolved issue among scholars of whether a "weak" or a "strong" government is better for economic development. Even for modern-day economies, this dispute is far from resolved. Depending on their predilections, some economists have viewed the market economy with a minimal government as superior, but the success of *étatisme* and *dirigisme* in bringing about economic growth in many of the nations of the European Continent (to say nothing of the East Asian "tigers") would suggest that one size does not fit all. The famed Gerschenkron thesis suggests that the role of the state in industrialization depends on the timing of industrialization, with the importance of government leadership and intervention rising with the lateness of industrialization. The later the industrialization process, argued Gerschenkron, the more infrastructural investments were necessary, and the less likely it was that private investors would be able to come up with these funds without some form of government support. By that logic the role of the British state in bringing about the Industrial Revolution should have been passive rather than active, because by comparison the investments in infrastructure in the eighteenth century were small and could be taken care of by the private sector. But this notion, too, as has been argued above, was seriously challenged by Patrick O'Brien (1994, 2006) and his followers, who have pointed to the aggressive application of so-called blue-water strategies by the mercantilist Hanoverian state (the use of naval power to secure control of the main oceanic trade routes) as the key to the rise in British world trade, and have maintained that the growth of global trade was the key component of economic development. For Britain to succeed, this theory goes, Britain's state had to be strong abroad and weak at home.

The argument I have made is that the Enlightenment changed the outlook of people in key positions on the way the economy (and society at large) functioned, and nowhere was this more remarkable than in the notions the *philosophes* had regarding the role of the state in the economy. Oversimplified views that the age of Enlightenment ushered in the triumph of liberal market economics will not do. What is, however, true is that people became increasingly aware of the dual role of the state. The role of government, it was felt, was to do for the citizens what they could not do for themselves, for whatever reason, but to eschew redistribution as much as possible. Exactly where to draw the line was disputed a great deal, but the principle was recognized. Modern institutionalist economists feel that the state's prime function was and is to enforce contracts and guarantee property rights. The historical implications of this approach are obvious. Douglass North (1981, pp. 147, 158–70) has argued that the British Industrial Revolution was facilitated by better-specified property rights, which led to more efficient economic organization in Britain. The link between property rights and economic growth consists of the greater efficiency in the allocation of resources that results from the equalization of private and social rates of return and costs. North pointed out that well-specified property rights are not the same as laissez-faire. The former were by far more important because they reduced transaction costs and thereby allowed more integrated markets, higher levels of specialization, and the realization of economies of scale. North's thesis attributes subsequent economic success to the nature of the regime that emerged in Britain after the Glorious Revolution.

Effective property rights are rightly considered crucial for economic development, but they were not the entire story. Arthur Young (1793, p. 89) noted that "the principle of our constitution is the representation of property ... imperfect in theory but efficiently in practice," and added "that the evils of such representation are trivial will appear from the ease ... and security of the lower classes." Such property rights should be contrasted, not with chaos and anarchy, but with traditional and customary rights, often disputed, undocumented, and hard to establish. In the eighteenth century the British government came down hard and persistently in favor of formal property and against customary rights. Adam Smith's candid wisdom in assessing his society was that "Civil government, so far as it is constituted for the security of property, is in reality constituted as a defence of the rich against the poor" (Smith, [1776], 1976, Vol. 2, p. 236). Yet this seemingly cynical remark hit the nail right on the head: property rights by definition defended those with property, so as to make it attractive to accumulate more. The trick was to induce people to do so by hard work, initiative, ingenuity, risk-taking, and saving rather than by manipulating state power so as to redistribute the property of others to themselves. It was the taproot of the free market ethic, and in no country was it as developed as in Britain in 1780. By the 1830s, Alexis de Tocqueville saw in much starker colors what Smith had seen sixty years earlier: the English, he noted, have left the poor the right of equality if they can obtain equal wealth. But, he noted, it is the rich who write the laws and use them to make ever more wealth for themselves (Tocqueville, 1958, p. 78).

These thoughts reflect a deep reality of the eighteenth and early nineteenth centuries. Those with the power to constrain the King, those who would permit the government to tax them in exchange for the protection of their property rights, had little incentive to protect the property of those who were not part of the political establishment. Colonials, smallholders, cottagers, beggars, vagrants, and women, to name but a few, often had their property rights denied, though even here there were rules and restraints. Although property rights remained one of the central mantras of eighteenth-century legislation, many of the activities of the British state "removed, reallocated, and in short, invaded property" (Langford, 1991, p. 146), although this was rarely arbitrary or predatory, and normally property owners would, at least in principle, be compensated. Creative destruction, however, required regulation of existing assets and at times it needed to be adapted because existing rights had become an obstacle. Some property rights, such as monopolies and other exclusionary "privileges," had to be extinguished if progress was to occur. The augmented power of Parliament in the eighteenth century provided Britain with the kind of flexibility missing in other countries, although it was used with discretion.

All the same, any story based on property rights must face up to the degree of day-to-day property security in Britain by 1700. Thomas Hobbes was obsessed by the question of how people could be made to keep promises. Early modern Britain, in many ways, had been a lawless and violent place. By the standards of contemporary British society, Britain in 1700 was in some views still a high-crime society. Highwaymen and vagabonds were the bane of travelers, while smugglers and excise officers often clashed violently. The Swiss tourist De Saussure ([1726], 1902, p. 127) found in 1726 that Britain had a "surprising quantity of robbers." Urban areas were notorious for street crime, some of it well organized. And yet, despite the many pitfalls of historical crime statistics, it seems increasingly clear that in the period 1700–1850 crime was subject to a sharp decline. By the mid-eighteenth century foreign travelers also commented widely on the low levels of murder and violent crime in Britain, and one scholar feels that the "remarkably low" murder rate in mid-eighteenth-century London would astonish a modern observer accustomed to modern American or even European cities (Langbein, 1983b). The admittedly somewhat tenuous evidence suggests that violent crime was declining over the eighteenth century and that crimes against property moved more or less pari passu with population growth (Beattie, 1974, 1986). Lawrence Stone (1983, 1985) came to the conclusion that crime, and especially violent crime, declined after 1650, and suggested that this was due to "the transformation of manners in the late seventeenth century, and then [facilitated] by the humanitarian ideology of the Enlightenment" (Stone, 1983, p. 29).

Not all crime was personal. Rioting, either for economic or political grievances, was common in eighteenth-century Britain. Machine-breaking, food riots, turnpike riots, or rioting against some unpopular group like Catholics, Irish immigrants, or dissenters was common. The Gordon riots of 1780, the Bristol Bridge riot of 1793, and the Luddite and Captain Swing riots in the nineteenth century, all sowed fear in the hearts of the property-owning classes. Yet actual daily crime seriously endangering the accumulation of capital and the proper conduct of commerce was on the whole rare. To be sure, eighteenth-century Britain passed a myriad of laws protecting property by imposing ferocious penalties on those who violated the sanctity of property. Blackstone complained that "Yet, though ... we may glory in the wisdom of the English law, we shall find it more difficult to justify the frequency of Capital Punishment to be found therein, inflicted ... by a multitude of successive independent statutes upon crimes very different in their natures." He added that the list was so dreadful that crime victims were reluctant to press charges and juries reluctant to convict (Blackstone, 1765–69, Vol. 4, p. 18). Food rioters, forgers, and those who used violence in resisting enclosures were all threatened with execution and transportation. The harshness of the penalties seems to suggest that violent crime and crimes against property were widely regarded as serious issues. Yet it also meant that the authorities were reluctant to spend resources on law enforcement, hoping that the harshness of the penalties would deter would-be criminals. It is hard to avoid the impression that they were a means devised by the law-abiding and property-respecting classes to control those who did not share their cultural attitudes.

To be sure, the actual number of people executed was not that large and the harsh penalties were applied in retribution less for crimes against property than for violent crimes. Of the 1,121 people sentenced to death at Old Bailey court in London between 1749 and 1771, 443 were reprieved. But the rate at which people were executed differed, as we should expect: 89 percent of murderers or attempted murderers were executed, but only 34 percent of pickpockets (still a frightful proportion, to be sure). Britain depended on the deterrent effect of draconian penalties embodied in the so-called Bloody Codes because in most of the country there was little or no professional police force. Prosecution was private and the crime prevention system was largely self-enforcing. Over 80 percent of all crimes were prosecuted by the victims themselves, but in view of the costs, the number of victims who were actually willing to proceed with the costly and burdensome tasks of prosecuting a crime was a small proportion (Emsley, 2005, pp. 183–86). Patrick Colquhoun noted that "[it is] not one in one hundred offences that is discovered or prosecuted" (1797, p. vii). The mere threat of terror against those who broke the codes of respectful and gentlemanly behavior and jeopardized the holiness of Britain's most revered institution may have worked better than the actual shedding of blood in deterring crime against property. Whatever the case, the constantly changing struggle between those who tried to protect their property and those who would take it from them never degenerated to the point where it seriously endangered the baseline security necessary for the orderly operation of an increasingly sophisticated commercial and industrial economy. Interestingly, the most frequent victims of crimes against property were not what we usually call "the propertied classes" (landowners and rentiers) but farmers, merchants, and artisans. As the needs for property protection changed after 1800, legal reforms ensued. The bloody codes of the eighteenth century fell into disuse, but minor trespasses and disorderly conduct could be adjudicated rapidly and efficiently thanks to the Vagrancy Act of 1824 and the Malicious Trespass Act of 1827, which gave the newly created police forces considerable powers to convict someone for being a "reputed thief."

On a closer look, day-to-day security depended more on social conventions and self-enforcing modes of behavior than on the administration of justice by an impartial judiciary. The decline in homicide rates after 1660 prompted one historian to conclude that "the court records suggest ... that men became more prepared to negotiate and talk out their differences" (Beattie, 1986, p. 112). Commercial disputes rarely came to court and were often settled through arbitration. Indeed, the number of civil cases that came to court in the eighteenth century declined precipitously relative to their mid-seventeenth-century levels: the number of cases heard at the King's Bench and Common Pleas in 1750 was only a sixth of what it was in 1670 (Brooks, 1989, p. 364; see also Muldrew, 1998, ch. 8). Most business was evidently conducted on the basis of informal codes of conduct, and relied on local reputation and religious moralizing to imbue honesty and responsibility.

In sum, voluntary compliance and respect for property and rank as social norms in middle-class society may have been as important as formal property rights in making the wheels of the British economy turn. Lawyers found their livelihood in intermediation and arbitration in an age less given to confrontation and litigation (Corfield, 1995, p. 73). "The bourgeoisie rarely came into contact with the law, except to implement it," notes Lewis (2001, p. 150). The poorer and criminal classes needed to be deterred, the middle class was, as a rule, law-abiding. Informal institutions, that is, customs, traditions, and conventions delineating acceptable behavior, were as important as formal law. Charles Davenant ([1699], 1771, p. 55) put it well: "Nowadays Laws are not much observed, which do not in a manner execute themselves" and felt that because the magistrates did not have a strong motive to perform their duty, private persons might be relied upon "to put the laws in execution." Defoe (1704–13, Vol. 1, p. 87) added caustically that "the English must be unaccountably blameable, whose Laws are the people's own Act and Deed, made at their Request ... yet no Nation in the World makes such a jest of their Laws as the English."

Intellectual property rights, in principle coordinated and enforced by the state, were viewed with mixed feelings by Enlightenment thinkers. Of those incentives, the patent system is considered most important by economists. Goethe may have been somewhat naive when he wrote that the British patent system's great merit was that it turned invention into a "real possession, and thereby avoids all annoying disputes concerning the honor due" (cited in Klemm, 1964, p. 173). Some modern economic historians have agreed with him, however (North and Thomas, 1973, p. 156). In his *Lectures on Jurisprudence* ([1757], 1978), pp. 11, 83, 472), Adam Smith argued that intellectual property rights were "actually real rights" and admitted that the patent system was the one monopoly (or "priviledge" as he called it) he could live with, because it left the decision on the merit of an invention to the market rather than to officials. Smith thought, somewhat unrealistically, that if an "invention was good and such as is profitable to mankind, [the inventor] will probably make a fortune by it." This argument re- mained the standard-bearer of the pro-patent forces, repeated almost verbatim by John Stuart Mill almost a century later ([1848], 1929, p. 933). A related approach regarded the patent as the quid pro quo that society paid for disclosure; otherwise the inventor would have the incentive to keep the invention secret, artificially raising the costs of access to knowledge (Dutton, 1984, p. 22). The reality was vastly more complicated. During the Industrial Revolution, not all inventors sought such rewards, and certainly not many attained them. Many inventors placed their inventions at the public's disposal, and others for one reason or another, failed to secure a patent or subsequently lost it. The effectiveness of secrecy in protecting the inventor's property depended on the ease of reverse engineering. For most mechanical inventions, secrecy was not an option. A lively debate on the desirability of patents continued between two parties, both of whom were inspired by Enlightenment thought. It was one issue for which no easy answers could be found.

Opponents of the patent system identified it as a rent-seeking device, often used to block new entry, conveniently ignoring the fact that those who resisted patents were sometimes similarly motivated by the desire to protect their own incumbency from unwelcome entrants. Among those, guilds were uppermost (MacLeod, 1988, p. 83). It was also noted in the late seventeenth century that patentees as monopolists often were not the best-qualified persons to exploit the inventions. Andrew Yarranton, a seventeenth-century tin-plater and navigation engineer, found his business harmed by a patentee incapable of exploiting it properly (ibid., p. 184). The problem remained, how should society reward those who gave their time and money to develop knowledge that was of great benefit to the rest of society? Such rewards, it was understood, needed to be established if society was to enjoy the fruits of sustained technological progress.

Britain was not the only Western nation to take this view. France and the Netherlands had patent systems in which innovations could yield considerable benefits to their propagators. In Britain, however, the state only recognized and enforced the inventor's right (Hilaire-Pérez, 2000). It did not normally take it upon itself to evaluate the invention's contribution to society. Britain's patent system was not exactly inviting: it charged a patentee £100 for the right to patent, not counting the costs of traveling to and staying in London (Khan and Sokoloff, 1998). That price would only cover England; if a patentee wanted to cover Scotland and Ireland as well, the cost could exceed £300.

The procedure for granting a patent dated from the Clerks Act of 1536, and the application process was mind-bogglingly cumbersome, and yet provided in the end little protection (Dutton, 1984, p. 35). The foremost legal nineteenth-century authority on the system, W.M. Hindmarch, referred to it as a "cumbrous machinery" (cited by Janis, 2002), and Charles Dickens' 1850 short story *A Poor Man's Tale of a Patent* illustrates the same, and tells with some literary license a tale in which the patentee "went through thirty-five stages ... began with the Queen upon the throne and ended with the Deputy Chaff-wax." The high cost of patenting meant that inventors tried to cover as much territory in their patent specification as they could, with the undesirable side-effect that the area blocked to others may have been excessive (Great Britain, 1851, p. 187). Many patents were infringed upon all the same, and British judges (especially before 1830) were often hostile to patentees, considering them monopolists. One justice expressed a standard eighteenth-century view of patents by noting that "on the whole there was a great deal of oppression of the lower orders of men from Patents, by those who were more opulent" (cited by Robinson, 1972, p. 137). This reflects the widespread belief that a patent was a sure way to become rich. In point of fact, precious few ever did, but the expectation may have been enough for many. A different critique, but equally telling, was made by J.T. Desaguliers (1763, Vol. 2, p. viii) who pointed out that (much as for modern venture capitalists), a patent was often interpreted by investors as an official imprimatur of the quality of an invention and thus "a great many persons were ready to subscribe considerable sums to the project," much of which would have been lost. In a similar vein, MacLeod (1988) points out that patents were used to signal, often falsely, product quality, especially in support of often dubious "patent medicine." Advertising used (and abused) the patent system mercilessly (Great Britain, 1864, pp. 28, 81).

Many patents were filed for absurd devices that were based on junk science or physically impossible. This was recently illustrated by MacLeod et al. (2003, p. 552), who showed that over the entire nineteenth century 18 percent of all 2,009 patents filed in steam engineering involved in one form or another a perpetual motion engine or similar devices judged to be technically unviable. Surprisingly, more than half of those were filed *after* 1860, when both the patentee and the Patent Office should have known that such machines were in violation of the laws of physics. Perhaps more pertinent to the significance of patents, however, is that a substantial number of important innovations were not patented. As we saw in chapter 5, this was especially the case for the great engineers and the inventions made by distinguished scientists. Of the 383 inventors born before 1850 extracted by MacLeod and Nuvolari (2006) from the *Dictionary of National Biography,* less than 40 percent ever took out a single patent, and another 18 percent took out just one patent, often not for the invention for which they were most famous (MacLeod and Nuvolari, 2006, p. 765).

A great deal of ambiguity remained unresolved by the patent system. Could an inventor patent a physical law (a "principle" as one unsuccessful patentee, Aimé Argand, called it)? Should drawings be submitted with the application? Should Lord Mansfield's principle of full revelation of details be such that laypersons could understand, or just other trained artisans? (Robinson, 1972). Given the unpredictable and often arbitrary decisions of courts, patentees felt that they were exposing their secrets with no real guarantee of protection. The complaints about the patent system came to a head in the 1820s, in the Report of the Select Committee appointed to investigate it in 1829, although not much happened as a result of this inquiry. Charles Babbage, never one to mince words, denounced the patent law as a "system of vicious and fraudulent legislation" which deprived the inventor of the fruits of his genius and put the most productive citizens of society in a position of "legalized banditti," and as "a fraudulent lottery which gives its blanks to genius and its prizes to knaves" (1830, pp. 333, 321). The objections were not so much against the system in general as against the way the law was written and implemented in Britain, especially the high cost of patenting and the sense that even the granting of a patent was "almost wholly illusory" till the patent had been sustained by a court of law, at an even higher cost (ibid., p. 334).

The precise impact of the patent system and other positive incentives for the technological creativity that eventually helped produce a more prosperous nation is still the subject of considerable controversy. Recently some economists have gone so far as to dismiss it altogether. Boldrin and Levine have argued that intellectual property rights have been unimportant in bringing about , and have specifically pointed to the Industrial Revolution as a period that provides "a mine of examples of patents hindering economic progress while seldom enriching their owners and of great riches and economic successes achieved without patents" (Boldrin and Levine, 2008, p. 51). Such an extreme position neglects the important qualification that the patent system was important *ex ante* by giving would-be inventors hope for success, in a fashion not dissimilar to the reason why people purchase lottery tickets. If no one ever won the lottery, people would stop buying tickets, but the number of winners need not be very large to keep hope alive. Yet unlike lottery tickets, inventors are not random; by definition they all differ from one another in systematic ways, and hence the belief that one could beat the odds because one was "different from the rest" was always based on some fact. It seems that the main effect of the patent system on innovation, then, was to goad potential inventors into believing that they, too, could make as much money as the Lombe brothers, Charles Tennant, or James Watt. But it exemplifies the complexity of the institution.

The type of encouragement given to inventors in Britain thus differed from the French *ancien régime* system, where government agents were put in charge of evaluating the contribution of certain inventions to the realm. The difference between the two systems can be overstated: at times the British authorities recognized the national interest and were willing to act to pursue it aggressively. An example was the Board of Longitude, established in 1714 by Parliament, which promised a large sum to the person who successfully cracked the age-old problem of measuring longitude at sea. Not only John Harrison was thus rewarded, but also the creators of the microinventions that made the marine chronometer economically feasible: in 1805 Thomas Earnshaw and John Arnold were awarded £2,500 and £1,672 respectively for their work on longitude-measuring clocks. Both Samuel Crompton, the inventor of the mule, and Edmund Cartwright, the inventor of the power loom, were rewarded by Parliament with considerable sums, though they captured but a minute fraction of the social surplus that their inventions eventually created. A petition for the estate of Henry Cort was denied by Parliament, but the fact that other iron-masters entered a subscription for the benefit of Cort's widow demonstrates that contemporaries were aware of the significant spillovers that his work had for theirs. The pioneers of the paper-making machines, Henry and Sealy Fourdrinier, too, were awarded a grant of £20,000 by a parliamentary committee (after many manufacturers testified that the continuous paper machines had been of huge benefit to their various branches), though this amount was later reduced to £7,000 and paid in 1840, when Henry was already in his seventies. Edward Jenner was voted a grant of £30,000 in 1815. The scientist William Sturgeon, one of the pioneers of electrical technology in the 1830s, fell on hard times toward the end of his life, and was awarded a one-off payment of £200 plus a small pension by Lord John Russell's government. In all these cases there was an explicit recognition that these people had added to the well-being of the realm; in other words, they had produced positive externalities. The awards reflect a recognition that invention was costly and risky, that its social benefits were hard to capture by the person who did the work, and that if society wanted a continuous stream of technical improvements, it had to make the activity that generated innovation financially attractive even to those who did not rely on patents. It is interesting that modern economics, unlike Smith and Mill, does not come down squarely for patents as a superior system for the encouragement of technological innovation. Alternative ways of compensating inventors, such as the advantages of the first firm to implement a new technique, might have been sufficient in many cases, especially because learning-by-doing reinforced the technological edge of the first firm to adopt a new technique (Boldrin and Levine, 2008, pp. 137–40). Under rather reasonable assumptions, moreover, it can be shown that a system of well-designed private contracts or optional government-determined rewards dominates a patent system in which a temporary monopoly generates quasi-rents to the successful inventor (Anton and Yao, 1994; Shavell and Van Ypersele, 2001) although the assumptions needed for these models to work were not likely to be satisfied for this period.

A few highly successful patents should not obscure the fact that many important inventions of the age either failed to be patented or, for one reason or another, did not pay off. We now have much improved information about the propensity to patent following the innovative research of Petra Moser (2005, 2007) who studied how many of the exhibitors at the Crystal Palace exhibition of 1851 had patented their inventions. Obviously, the exhibitors were hardly a representative sample of the population of inventors, but it seems plausible that theirs represented the best and most promising inventions, so that their propensity to patent would be an upper bound of the population. The 6,377 inventions that were selected for the exhibition were successful ideas, the best Britain felt it had to show the world. Of those, only 11.1 percent were patented. Of exhibited inventions that won awards, only 15.6 percent were patented. These figures mask a great deal of variation. On the whole, machinery tended to be patented more often than chemicals and food processing, presumably because machinery was easier to reverse-engineer while processes that involved biological or chemical reactions were easier to keep secret. These results confirm the observation that patenting was not all that important to the main thrust of innovation. Moreover, this was not wholly due to the special features of the British system: the more inventor-friendly US patent system generated only slightly more patenting: just 15.3 percent of all US exhibits were patented.

High filing and litigation costs together with hostile or uncertain judges made a patent a costly and insecure property right. The patent system in Britain before 1850 was considerably less user-friendly and accessible than its American counterpart yet Britain's technological leadership was never more paramount. Inventors relied on a more complex combination of secrecy, a first-mover's advantage, and keeping ahead of competitors to maintain their edge. Some of the best-known technological heroes of the Industrial Revolution, such as Richard Arkwright and Josiah Wedgwood, stayed away from patenting after frustrating attempts to deal with infringers. When successful, patents were at times used to block competitive or other research. The work on high-pressure engines was for many years blocked by James Watt who threatened with infringement litigation anyone working on this possibility, largely because he disapproved in principle of high-pressure engines. Similarly, Thomas Savery, the inventor of the first working steam-pump, the "miner's friend," which was patented in 1698 and extended till 1733, successfully forced competitors to pay him royalties or work with him. Savery's pump was not really an engine in the standard sense of the word, but Newcomen, whose invention was, was forced to come to terms with the company founded by Savery's estate and could not take out his own patent. It is not clear that blocking patents actually "promoted atrophy in mechanical engineering" as a recent work (Marsden and Smith, 2005, p. 63) suggests, or whether it stimulated others to somehow invent around the areas blocked. In later years, the patent system lent itself to even more strategic behavior due to the possibility of filing so-called caveats. This expression of the intent to file a particular patent later on could block other applications in the same area. Even Richard Roberts, a supporter of the patent system, complained to a parliamentary committee in 1851 that this institution was a way in which "unprincipled men" could take advantage of other inventors (Great Britain, 1851, pp. 182–83). Competitors could use caveats to delay the sealing of a patent as well as for industrial espionage. Others were of the view that the whole system was harmful. Some of the most prominent engineers of the time, such as Isambard K. Brunel, felt that patents were entirely unnecessary and positively harmful (ibid., pp. 246–57). Dutton has suggested that nineteenth-century preemptive patents were part of a competitive process (1984, pp. 182–83), and at least in some cases it may be more accurate to view patent struggles like other "races to the bottom" such as advertising campaigns, in which all participants end up in a socially less desirable equilibrium.

All the same, patents were widely perceived as an important incentive. James Watt, perhaps not the most objective of sources on this matter, wrote in 1785 that "we have for many years devoted our time and money to the bringing of the invention to perfection ... if our right to our patent should be taken away, we must drop any further pursuits of that scheme and apply ourselves to other businesses where our property can be more effectively guarded" (cited by Dutton, 1984, p. 109). Roberts told the 1851 committee that, were it not for the patent system, he would not have invented as much as he did, and the inventions he would have made would have lain on the shelves (Great Britain, 1851, p. 187). A patent made it possible for an independent inventor to find a manufacturer who would take up a proposed invention, giving him the security he required that profits would not be competed away right away. Otherwise, Henry Bessemer wrote in his *Autobiography*, "no manufacturer will go to the trouble and expense of trying to work out the proposed invention ... And so the invention is lost to the world in consequence of having been given away" (1905, ch. 8).

Equally important is the fact that patents provided an incentive to disclose the technical specifications of the new technique and that the alternative to patents would have been greater secrecy, which would have increased access costs and slowed down the diffusion of useful knowledge. While to some extent, of course, patents did block innovative activity in areas that they might have infringed, they inspired work in related areas that relied on similar principles simply because a successful patent indicated more general principles about what would work (Thomson, 2009, pp. 209–14). Some cases of collective invention, in which inventors, rather than excluding others through secrecy or patents, willingly shared and swapped knowledge can be documented (MacLeod, 1988, ch. 6; Nuvolari, 2004), but they tended to be rare. More common were cases such as the career of John Rennie who opened the revolutionary Albion Mills (using steam engines to grind flour) for anyone to see in 1786, to James Watt's horror. But Rennie was obviously signaling his capabilities rather than selling specific knowledge, soon securing consulting and special manufacturing jobs from all over Britain, as well as from the Continent. Similarly, ironmaster John Wilkinson saw his patent on cannon-boring (1774) voided by request of the navy (citing national security), but that did not stop him from continuing as a highly profitable manufacturer of ordnance.

The impact of patents, then, varied from industry to industry, and contemporaries were quite divided on it. One indicator that hints at the success of the pre-1852 system, despite its many shortcomings, is the important fact that there was a lively secondary market in patents, as Dutton (1984, ch. 7) has shown. While this market was thin, and certainly not representative of the population of patentees, it was growing impressively in the first half of the nineteenth century. Some patents were purchased lock, stock, and barrel. John Marshall, the flax spinner, purchased a combing machine from the French inventor Josué Heilman for £20,000. Licensing patents also became more common after 1800, though it was still fairly rare. Richards Roberts was convinced that it was the best and most commercial way to remunerate inventors (Great Britain, 1851, p. 195). One of the more dramatic technological breakthroughs of the post-1815 years, James Neilson's hot blast (1829), was licensed to about eighty producers throughout the United Kingdom. Finally, of course, we can think of partnerships between a patentee and an entrepreneur exploiting it as an implicit sale of a patent, much as Bessemer pointed out. Perhaps in some cases it was true that "partnership was a financial necessity forced upon reluctant inventors" (MacLeod, 1988, p. 90), but partnership also meant sharing the risks with and providing high-powered incentives to a person whose skills and abilities complemented those of the inventor.

Assessing the impact of the British patent system on its technological leadership should differentiate between the impact of the historical patent system as it existed in Britain, and the theoretical impact of a better-designed and enforced patent system. The British patent system was deeply flawed, as we have seen, and its thorough reform in 1852, including a steep reduction in filing fees and a streamlining of the application procedure, constituted a substantial improvement. However, it still did not provide for a full technical pre-granting examination. Intellectual property rights were viewed by North and his followers as the cornerstone of British technological creativity, but it now has become apparent that they cannot possibly bear the full explanatory burden of Britain's unprecedented technological creativity (MacLeod and Nuvolari, 2007). It stands to reason that the few spectacular success cases goaded many would-be inventors to try their luck, hoping to secure a patent like Watt's. Because by definition each invention is unique, the disappointments of past inventors may not have been sufficient to discourage new inventors from trying again. The vast bulk of them were disappointed, but the patent system, by cheating these aspiring patentees, benefited the larger economy immeasurably. Britain's patent laws represented, on balance, a positive institution, but they did not give Britain a significant advantage over its European competitors sufficient to explain its primacy. It was one way to stimulate technological innovation, but just one of many, and the relative importance of the various elements differed from industry to industry.

*   *   *

Well-enforced property rights, including "law and order," are surely crucial if investment is to be carried out, but in a realistic economic model not all property rights are created equal. Some "privileges" may have been secure and well-defined property rights, yet they still could have been obstacles to progress if they established a monopoly or created an exclusionary rent or a claim on a common resource that led to an inefficient allocation of resources. Property rights on highly specific assets could readily lead to a hold-up situation which reduced economic efficiency, and it is possible to imagine situations where, as in *ancien-régime* France, property rights were *too* well enforced (Rosenthal, 1992). Mercantilist states had set up certain institutions, such as monopolies, artificial barriers to entry, the control of prices, and trade encumbrances, (to name a few) that benefited a small elite but were detrimental to society as a whole. It was the realization of this cost that drove much of the Enlightenment critique of the old economic order. The British antipathy to monopolies pre-dated the eighteenth century, but in the seventeenth century it was largely based on the reluctance of Britons to have the King trade monopoly rights for cash and thus tax them without the permission of Parliament. During the eighteenth century, as Enlightenment writers persuaded others of the social costs of the effects of exclusionary arrangements, resentment of them grew and their survival became increasingly precarious. Lord Shelburne, an avowed disciple of Adam Smith, said in the House of Commons in 1783: "Monopolies, some way or other, are ever justly punished. They forbid rivalry, and rivalry is of the very essence of the well-being of trade ... I avow that monopoly is always unwise; but if there is any nation under heaven, who ought to be the first to reject monopoly, it is the English. Situated as we are between the old world and the new, and between the southern and northern Europe, all that we ought to covet upon earth is free trade, and fair equality" (Ross, 1998, p. 151).

The theory of the state is based on the idea that it can protect property rights because it awards itself a monopoly on violence. By maintaining a military force and not allowing anyone else to do so, it could force its will on its citizens when it had to. This of course created the main dilemma of the state: how can citizens trust the authorities not to abuse this monopoly by turning it into a source of excessive income for itself? Moreover, if individuals can reasonably foresee such an outcome, why should they ever agree to have a government at all? And if they are suspicious of such a monopolist, how can *any* government ever convince them that they are committed to stay within given boundaries of taxation and self-interested legislation? To do so, a government has to credibly commit to its citizens that it should be given the monopoly on power and the right to tax them, yet that it will not abuse these rights. In the seventeenth century the failure to resolve this commitment had led to two major conflagrations in Britain. One was the Civil War, the other the Glorious Revolution. As noted earlier, North and Weingast (1989) maintained that the system that emerged from these wars after the Glorious Revolution and the Bill of Rights in 1689 was one in which the British had made the government guarantee to its citizens that it would not tax them without Parliament's consent. In other words, it "pre-committed" to be constrained by Parliament. This created a solid basis for public finance and credit, established the trustworthiness of the British state and allowed the British government to borrow at relatively low interest rates. The historical irony is that precisely because the citizens of Britain represented in Parliament (a fairly narrow group, to be sure) agreed to be taxed, Britain could afford to impose higher taxes than any other nation.

The Glorious Revolution had other effects. It meant a century of Dutch influence on governance and fiscal policy in Britain. With William in 1688 came a large number of Dutch and Huguenot merchants and financiers whose experience and ideas influenced British commercial and financial practices. This elite of imported businessmen, bankers, and entrepreneurs were to play a central role in the British economy in the eighteenth century. In 1744, when 542 merchants signed a declaration of loyalty to King George II, at least a third of them were of non-British descent, many of them Huguenots and Dutch (Ormrod, 2003, pp. 92–93). The significance of the adoption of the Dutch model of public finance after 1688 is profound. The British state abandoned tax-farming and the venal sale of offices and peerages as a source of revenue and committed itself to collecting taxes to fund its debt. The fiscal revolution of the late seventeenth century was more than just a constraint on the power of the King. It was, as Carruthers (1996, p. 135) has noted, a whole set of institutional changes that streamlined the way the British state collected revenues, the growing reliance on direct collection, the growing assignability of public and private debts (which made impersonal financial markets work better), and the importance of joint-stock companies, which helped finance government debts. The importance of this fiscal revolution, as Stasavage (2003, p. 63) points out, is that it signaled that the British state not only was able to collect taxes, it was able to commit itself to do so in the future, thus reassuring potential creditors that it was creditworthy. The year 1688 was not only the year of the Glorious Revolution, it was also the beginning of a quarter of a century of almost uninterrupted war with France that was far more expensive than anything Britain had experienced before. Unless the way in which the Crown financed itself was altered dramatically, these expenditures would not have been sustainable. That reassurance in and of itself meant that running the state would be cheaper, because the state could borrow at more favorable terms. Non-specialists have taken this view as almost absolute (Dam, 2005, p. 85).

The North and Weingast view of British history has, however, come in for substantial criticism from experts and many issues remain open. The interest rates that the British government had to pay were not much lower than what the Dutch government had to pay (Quinn, 2001; Sussman and Yafeh, 2006). Moreover, the British system tied itself down less than the American Constitution would tie down its executive power a century later. Regardless of its legal commitments, Parliament retained the power to change any law it had previously passed by a simple majority. Britain had no written constitution and no law passed by Parliament could be invalidated or revoked by another body. The idea that government deliberately weakened itself to show commitment to the citizens whom it wanted to pay taxes without rebelling and purchase its consols was therefore far from absolute (Harris, 2004). Equally serious is the objection that even if Parliament controlled taxation, it failed to fully control spending. Indeed, Parliament often found it difficult to assess how much was spent by the various branches, whose accounts were organized in a chaotic compilation of various procurements and contractors serving government.

A theory of economic development that depends on the relationship between the state and individuals needs to confront the fact that in eighteenth-century Europe, the state did not have a monopoly on political power. It had to share it with non-state institutions that had many of the features we associate with "polities" (Greif, 2006). In Britain, this is illustrated by the many political powers exercised by the East India Company, which possessed some state-like features (Stern, 2008). But other autonomous "corporations" that exercised some degree of political independence such as universities, guilds, and municipalities existed everywhere in Europe in 1700 and Britain, too, was not immune. Over the century and a half after 1700, the autonomy of such independent polities was sharply curtailed and in 1857 the East India Company, by then little more than a branch of Her Majesty's government, was abolished. Guilds, too, had lost what little autonomy they had possessed in 1700, and local governments were increasingly controlled and regulated from London. Yet this process was slow and gradual, and focusing solely on the capabilities of the state as the sole "institution" of interest in 1700 can be seriously misleading.

And yet on all accounts formal institutions and politics mattered. Economists have recognized their central importance to economic change (North, 2005; Acemoglu, Robinson, and Johnson, 2005a; Rodrik et al., 2004). But their exact role during the British Industrial Revolution still needs much more detailed elaboration. It should be stressed that what matters is not just having the kinds of institution that are conducive to economic development, but also having the kind of agility that allows institutions to change when the environment changes. There are few features of institutions that are *invariably* suitable for growth; once we are beyond platitudes such as "law and order are better than chaos and crime," the institutional requirements for economic growth depend on the parameters of the economy and changes over time. It is hence important to judge not just whether an economy has inherited from the past appropriate institutions that allow it to grow, but also whether it has *flexible* institutions that can change and adapt at relatively low cost when the need arises.

In that regard, Britain's political structure set it apart. Its high capacity for endogenous institutional change was made possible by the existence of a *meta-institution* that could change and set the formal rules under which other institutions operated. This function was filled by Parliament. Blackstone

(1765–69, Book 1, ch. 2, section III) stated categorically that "It hath sovereign and uncontrollable authority in making, confirming, enlarging, restraining, abrogating, repealing, reviving, and expounding of laws, concerning matters of all possible denominations, ecclesiastical, or temporal, civil, military, maritime, or criminal." The existence of an organization like the British Parliament, rejuvenated during the Civil War, triumphant through the Glorious Revolution and the subsequent Bill of Rights in 1689, and further strengthened as a legislative body in the years of William and Mary and Queen Anne, was one key to the institutional component of British economic success. The Glorious Revolution was an important stage of this development even if it was perhaps not the discontinuity that North and Weingast have made it to be. Subsequent legislation eliminated the royal prerogative as a form of legislation, established parliamentary oversight on government spending and a "civil list" that specified what royal funds would be spent on. Parliament ensured that it met regularly and maintained control over the royal succession. The Act of Settlement of 1701 also established an independent judiciary, in which judges were appointed for life and could only be removed if convicted of a felony or impeached. Whether or not that really established a full "rule of law" on the ground remains controversial. The Glorious Revolution was a pivotal event, not just because it laid the foundation of the successful system of public finance, which was to play a central role in the growing political power of Britain. Equally important, it removed the contestability of rule-making from the British polity and established a body that was receptive to both the changing needs and the changing ideology of the elite, and could imbue the British polity with the most important institutional characteristic needed for economic change: agility and adaptability (Richardson and Bogart, 2008).

There is no question that in many ways Parliament was a highly imperfect institution, not only because it represented only the narrow top layer of British society, but also because its membership consisted of men who were often poorly educated, corrupt, and lazy. It was dominated by landed interests: as late as 1867, members of the landed elite occupied three-quarters of the House of Commons. All the same, the very fact that this was a deliberative body of men who had to get along, and who needed to face some kind of electoral responsibility to local constituencies as well as the Crown, provided Britain with the institutional agility and adaptiveness that set it apart from the rest of Europe. It was a place where different interest groups met, deliberated, bargained, and compromised within certain pre-specified rules that all sides had learned to respect. Provincial elites acquired access to the center, as Hoppit (1996) notes, and Acts were responses to local needs and ad hoc initiatives of an individual or small group. Such local changes, however, now depended more and more on the legitimacy of Parliament. In the eighteenth century Parliament experienced the proliferation and expansion of special interest lobbies that represented well-defined and focused groups in search of some economic advantage (usually local), and that tried to persuade MPs of the point of view of their group. Parliament was the target of innumerable petitions for some special legislation to be passed or rescinded, taxes and regulations to be lifted, and customs duty to be adjusted. These lobbies informed and persuaded through subtle contact with influential legislators, constrained by the often arcane rules of Parliament. The political process of lobbying legislators was in itself neither good nor bad. It all depended on what was successfully lobbied for. Insofar as legislation sought to redistribute resources in favor of vested interests that wanted protection or to maintain exclusionary rents, successful lobbying was costly and impeded economic growth. But when lobbies tried to abolish regulations, establish free markets, and encourage and reward innovation, their effects could be salutary.

Lobbies, in one form or another, had existed throughout most of the eighteenth century. For instance, a group of Edinburgh merchants hired a London attorney in the 1740s to lobby for such differing policies as standardizing weights and measures and changing the bankruptcy laws (Colley, 1992, p. 68). In the last third of the eighteenth century the new industrialists created more formal lobbies that reflected the manufacturing and commercial interests created by the Industrial Revolution. The most important of them, such as the General Chamber of Manufacturers founded by iron manufacturer Samuel Garbett and potter Josiah Wedgwood, had standing committees of the most influential members of the trade, employed solicitors and parliamentary officials, generated and circulated information pertinent to their case, and when they felt they did not get a sympathetic hearing from the Commons, they turned to the press and tried to influence public opinion. Garbett, a co-founder of the Carron ironworks in Scotland, may indeed be regarded as one of the earliest professional political lobbyists. The most successful lobbyists assiduously cultivated relationships with influential peers, and were on balance successful in persuading them to support the causes they favored (McCahill, 1976). Yet while interests played a major role, the role of ideology cannot be left out altogether. Thus, of the many patrons in the House of Lords who supported the Birmingham hardware manufacturers, the second Earl of Dartmouth was moved "by a strong sense of territorial responsibility ... and a deep religious fervour" (ibid., p. 97). Ideological commitment to economic development was of course often intertwined with material gain: the Staffordshire potteries' most ardent supporter, Earl Gower (Granville Leveson), was a personal friend of Wedgwood's, and his extensive Staffordshire estates benefited considerably from his political activities.

The ideological commitment of industrial lobbies to the principles of the Industrial Enlightenment is of course suspect. Their rhetoric, not surprisingly, consistently used the national interests as the justification for their demands, not the narrow interests of their trade (Norris, 1958). Given their superior knowledge of the details and their single-issue focus, however, their persuasive powers were substantial. They were neither consistently protectionist nor free-trade, but followed the narrow short-term interests of their industry. At the same time, of course, the interests of the various industries and regions diverged and conflicted, and uniting them into a single voice speaking for the new manufacturing sector was quite beyond the powers of anyone. The Chamber of Commerce fragmented in its debate on the Eden Treaty of 1786, and no single lobby spoke for its interests. The more technologically progressive industries tended to support free trade; traditional manufacturers wanted more protection. There was thus little in eighteenth-century British special-interest lobbies that looks inherently different from Washington's K-Street, except for the scale. It is striking that some of the most successful industrialists also turned out to be politically adroit. Nowhere was this as marked as in the Fire Engine Act (1775) in which the Boulton–Watt patent was extended by an unprecedented twenty-five years, during which Matthew Boulton showed his full colors as a brilliant manipulator of politicians (Robinson, 1964).

Parliament in the eighteenth century was by our standards a corrupt institution. Many MPs were endowed with sinecures or "places" in the terminology of the time, and expected to toe the party line in return. Under Robert Walpole, this system of patronage was extended considerably. Politicians and legal changes were often practically up for sale, through what was known as "private bills." These bills, however, demonstrate in some sense the growing ability of the eighteenth-century British economy to reinvent itself. One of the astonishing phenomena of this period is the rapid increase in the number of bills that Parliament passed after the Glorious Revolution. The total number of Acts passed during the rules of Charles II and James II was 564, or 20 per annum. In the twenty-five years between the Bill of Rights and the Hanoverian era (1689–1714), this increased to 1,752 or 70 per annum; by the period 1760–1800 it was 8,351 or 209 per annum (Hoppit, 1996, p. 117). The vast bulk of this legislation was a mechanism by which the richest and most powerful families of England manipulated the system to advance their interests. Legislation remained predominantly an affair tailored to specific individuals and localities. As the great legal historian F.W. Maitland described these actions, Parliament was "afraid to rise to the dignity of a general proposition; it will not say 'all commons may be enclosed' ... no, it deals with this commons and that marriage." He proceeded to call the eighteenth century "the century of *privilegia*" (Maitland, 1911, p. 383).

Parliament represented a small fraction of British male adults and was dominated by landed interests, though other interest groups did have to be reckoned with. It was anything but representative, with England's countryside, and especially the rural south, over-represented and elections determined by local custom rather than any kind of national uniform system. It established an equilibrium of power between the monarchy and Parliament, both of which were targeted by rent-seekers. Politicians who were so inclined could enrich themselves and their relatives. If this did not happen more, it was because many men in truly powerful positions either were already rich or were indifferent to money. All the same, Parliament played a unique role in the institutional development of the nation. Above all, in Britain Parliament could function as it did because after 1720 or so it had *legitimacy*. It was recognized by all players as the ultimate arbiter and the maker of credible rules (that is, rules that most people believed others would observe). By consensus, it was vested with the responsibility to create laws and institutions that benefited society at large and not just a few small interest groups, and to revise them when the need arose (Colley, 1992, pp. 50, 52). Even those who were not properly represented or stood to lose from its decisions would accept them as the final word. Needed changes and reforms may at times have taken longer to be brought to completion than they might have in a more authoritarian set-up than the awkward bicameral system in place in Britain, but when they were passed, they were rarely challenged. Parliament, moreover, combined local and central elements: it exercised power in and from the capital, but it represented local constituencies and thus ensured that its decisions resonated with provincial interests and sentiments.

Yet precisely for that reason it was crucial that British institutions turned out to be adaptable and flexible. There was no guarantee that establishing Parliament as "the place where absolute despotic power, which must in all governments reside somewhere, is entrusted," as Blackstone noted in 1765 (1765–69, Book 1, ch. 2, section III), was to be a key to economic progress. After all, the new-found power of Parliament could have been (and was to a considerable extent) abused by special-interest legislation that supported distributive coalitions. "Specific" legislation, directed at a particular place or institution, constituted between two-thirds and three-quarters of all Acts throughout the period 1688–1800 (Hoppit, 1996, p. 117). But changes occurred increasingly from the top down, even if the initiative came from below. By 1750 the ruling elite began to realize that the world was changing and that new interests had to be reckoned with. William Pitt the Elder shocked many of his peers by announcing in 1758 that he would be prouder to be a London alderman than a peer of the realm. An accommodation of sorts was found between some of the mightiest landowners and the industrial class. "Time and again the pioneers of the Industrial Revolution looked to Westminster to modify existing policies in directions more conducive to the needs of a growing economy, and time and again institutions dominated by landlords responded to those needs" (McCahill, 1976, p. 102). Opinions on what really served the nation changed over the eighteenth century. During the entire period under discussion, British Parliament changed British laws in accordance with what its members viewed as their local interests and Britain's needs. Their idea of the national interest, however, became increasingly liberal and critical of the old mercantilist order. Once the beliefs at the top began to change, this would affect the entire country, ruled as it was by a small elite.

Parliament made the enclosure of land in recalcitrant areas possible by simply passing a set of Bills of Enclosure. It solved the coordination problems inherent in having local interests collaborate in building canals and roads by passing Turnpike Acts. The process was, by the standard of the time, reasonably efficient in the sense that the money raised by turnpike trusts was spent mostly on actual road improvements rather than dissipated in great measure among greedy politicians, as happened in societies where rent-seeking and corruption were considered the normal way of doing business (Bogart, 2005b). It supported entrepreneurs and innovators against technologically conservative interests and those protecting their rents. It awarded pensions and prizes to inventors who solved a problem of national importance such as determining longitude at sea and spinning cotton mechanically. It slowly but irresistibly abandoned the protect- ionist-nationalist rules of commerce that mercantilism had imposed in the seventeenth century, in favor of freer markets. Parliament did so because the ruling elite became influenced by a new ideology, which transformed their view of the national interest. Melton (2001, p. 38) has argued that by the 1780s British political culture had undergone a fundamental transformation and that many in Parliament felt "beholden to public opinion" as never before.

Much as it is today, politics in eighteenth-century Britain was a mixture of narrow interests and ideological convictions. In the 1780s the influence of the new ideology became policy, as the liberal concepts of Charles Davenant, Shaftesbury, David Hume, Josiah Tucker, Adam Smith, and similar Enlighten- ment thinkers on political economy influenced Shelburne, William Pitt the Younger, William Eden (Lord Auckland), and their colleagues. These ideas led to more liberal trade policies towards Ireland and France and helped inspire the 1786 commercial treaty with France, a model of Enlightenment thought. In his speech to the House of Commons on February 12, 1787, Pitt explicitly referred to the non-zero-sum character of freer international trade: "We certainly ought not to give liberal conditions. We ought not hesitate, because this which must be so greatly advantageous to us must also have its benefit for them." Moreover, Pitt noted that "the treaty had the happy tendency to make the two nations enter into more intimate communion with one another ... and while they were mutually benefited by the connection ... it gave a better chance for the preservation of harmony between them" (cited in Ross, 1998, p. 155).

The parliamentary system, then, meant that British institutions could smoothly adapt to changing circumstances but, equally important, to changing ideas. The political system in Britain could be reformed without violence, without undue waste and destruction, and without tossing out Enlightenment babies with the *ancien régime* bathwater. It could even engage in local violations of property rights if this were considered necessary for the public good. When land needed to be confiscated for transport projects, or when certain property rights were deemed to be incompatible with Enlightenment notions, such as the slave trade (abolished in 1807) and slavery altogether (abolished in the British colonies in 1833), Parliament took the appropriate decision. When the informal institutions based on reputation and internalized norms became increasingly inappropriate for a rapidly growing, urban, and increasingly mobile economy, it expanded third-party enforcement of contracts through professional courts and law-enforcement officials. Its procedures were cumbersome and slow, and not always quite as efficient as they could have been, but the system worked better than elsewhere in Europe. The rule of Parliament meant that the existing system could be changed and reformed as needed with no bloodshed, often preserving many older forms while "reforming" them to make them more suitable to changing times.

The impact of beliefs and ideology on government policies varied with circumstances. The harsh years following the French Revolution hardened many positions into views which to the modern mind appear less than enlightened. The British government increasingly committed itself to siding with capitalists and ind-ustrialists in their battles with workers about conditions of work, and the right of workers to resist changes in work conditions and mechanization. Part of this was that the Enlightenment movement was morphing into liberal political economy, and the growing notion that free markets alone would provide the best arbiter of allocation decisions. As a result, the government took a more aggressive and un-ambiguous position against rioting workers and machine breakers. A parlia-mentary committee appointed in 1806 to report "on the State of the Woollen Manufactures of England" was charged to validate or repeal old statutes that prohibited machinery in these industries. The Report, written by none other than the enlightened anti-slavery crusader William Wilberforce, piously reiterated its conventional recognition of the "merits and value of the domestic system." The committee also felt that the "apprehensions about it being rooted out by the Factory System were at present at least wholly without foundation" (Great Britain, 1806, p. 10). Above all Wilberforce and his colleagues felt that "the right of every man to employ [his] Capital according to his own discretion ... is one of those privileges every Briton considers his birthright" (p. 12). At the same time, however, they noted that "we are at this day surrounded by powerful and civilized Nations, who are intent on cultivating their Manufactures and pushing their Commerce" and specifically mentioned the worrisome evidence of such an establishment being set up in Paris.

The Wilberforce Report was indicative of one of the hardest dilemmas of the Industrial Enlightenment, namely the debates about the economic and social effects of the adoption of new technology. Most societies do not welcome innovators and often treat them with hostility. Resistance to technological innovation derives from two different sources which often reinforce one another (Mokyr, 1998b). The first is strict selfish rational behavior protecting rents and vested interests. In most cases of technical advance, society gains in terms of cheaper or better products, but some equipment or skills become obsolete or redundant. The owners of those resources stand to lose more than they may gain as consumers, and have a strong interest in forming distributional coalitions to find some way to foil the market process and rely on political power to prohibit or severely limit the adoption of the new technique. Central to the phenomenon is the widespread fear that technological progress, by replacing labor with machines, will cause widespread unemployment, or at least a deterioration in the economic status of labor. Workers facing new technology worry about their way of life, social status, independence, and dignity in addition to a decline in their real income. A second source of resistance is an intuitive fear of novelty, the natural concern that people have about disrupting and manipulating nature, which somehow seems sinful and possibly dangerous. In our own age, the opposition to nuclear power, genetically modified organisms, and human cloning are examples of this concern.

Eighteenth-century Britain was not immune to such resistance, but in most cases fended it off. Time and again, groups and lobbies turned to Parliament requesting the enforcement of old regulations or the introduction of new legislation that would hinder the machinery. In 1776, workers petitioned the House of Commons to suppress the jennies that threatened the livelihood of the industrious poor, as they put it, but were rebuffed. In 1779, laborers in Lancashire and Nottinghamshire rioted and destroyed one of Arkwright's mills in a place called Birkacre in southern Lancashire. Parliament sent troops to quell the disturbance. The authorities sincerely believed that mechanization was in the national interest and essential to British supremacy in the world textile markets. To appease the workers, the penalties meted out to rioters were more lenient than they had to be, and Arkwright was denied compensation for the damage to his Birkacre mill. Parliament had to show who was in charge and in which direction it wanted the country to go, but it wisely avoided an all-out confrontation with the workers; industry needed them.

It is easy to see how a set of policies more protective of the status quo could have slowed down the Industrial Revolution. Most attempts by incumbents to prohibit the introduction of new machinery were unsuccessful. Some cases of mob action and machine-breaking against innovators occurred, but they rarely succeeded in arresting progress either. The widely recounted tale of the inventor of the flying shuttle, John Kay, who is supposed to have fled to France in 1747 to escape the violent wrath of other weavers, is apocryphal. In actuality, he got in trouble because of his patent and his unwillingness to share his knowledge with others (Wadsworth and Mann, 1931, p. 456). Kay may not have won a popularity contest, but the flying shuttle spread rapidly. In the wool preparation industry, where gig mills and scribbling machines were introduced, workers demanded that Parliament enforce ancient laws still on the books to prohibit them. The response was that the laws regulating employment were abolished (1809, 1814). Extralegal attempts to stop machines, especially in the West Country (Wiltshire,

Gloucestershire, Somerset), culminating in the Wiltshire riots of 1802, delayed the introduction of wool-shearing machinery in that region, but by so doing helped chase the industry out to Yorkshire and destroy the industrial base of the West Country (Randall, 1986, 1991). There can be little doubt that at a local level, artisans and domestic workers were able to delay mechanization, and that they earned some years of respite.

In other industries, too, resistance appeared, sometimes from unexpected corners. Gas lighting, for instance, was opposed by an odd coalition worried about light pollution. The steam engine was resisted in urban areas for fear of "smoky nuisances," and resistance to railroads was rampant in their early years. Sawmills were objected to and demolished by sawyers concerned about their employment (Cooney, 1991). Even in medical technology, where the social benefits were most widely diffused, the status quo tried to resist such obvious advances as smallpox vaccination, using scare tactics implying that introducing fluids from cows would somehow result in the patient developing bovine traits (Mokyr, 2002, p. 266). None of these efforts got anywhere with the British authorities. By the time Jenner made his discovery, the triumph of enlightened over benighted notions in this regard was indisputable. In similar fashion, anesthetics, another innovation that bestowed enormous and previously unimaginable benefits on mankind at disproportionately negligible cost, was also resisted. Motherhood, it was felt, was ordained by the scriptures to be accompanied by suffering, and if Providence had created it that way, contravening God's will was surely sinful. Again, none of those arguments, of course, won the day, because in Britain there was a sense of the feasibility and desirability of progress, and because it was felt that in an open economy any rejected innovation would just migrate to Britain's enemies and competitors. Such are the institutional underpinnings of economic progress.

The most dramatic insurrection against British machines occurred between 1811 and 1816 with a series of riots known as the "Luddite" riots whose name has become attached to anti-technological actions in any form. In truth, the Luddite riots were more complex than just a response to mechanization and while they were widespread, different areas had different grievances, and the movements were not coordinated. Not in all cases were the riots the result of a deep-seated animosity to machinery. Many of the attacks were as much against convenient targets for irate workers upset at deteriorating trade conditions. In Lancashire the attacks on machines were less against new techniques per se than against convenient targets in an unorthodox bargaining game between employees and employers. In any event, the riots failed: the British government took a resolute pro-innovation attitude, and did not hesitate to amass considerable military force to maintain law and order when necessary. Similarly, it deployed force against those resisting institutional change: when turnpike riots broke out around the middle of the eighteenth century, they were suppressed mercilessly.

The determined and sometimes harsh policy in support of innovation was not entirely due to enlightened beliefs in the salutary effects of technological progress. Nationalism (and especially the fear of France) played as important a role. Liberal political economy had assigned to government well-defined roles, and protecting incumbents' rents was not one of them.

But the government needed to do more than just protect innovators from their opponents. It needed to solve coordination problems that without some acceptable authority would lead to socially costly outcomes. An example is the system of weights and measures in use. During the age of Enlightenment this issue was the subject of a large literature, as its "irrationality" seemed paramount to writers at the time, who were keen on reforming the economy and reducing uncertainty and transactions costs. "It is a maxim in trade, no Kingdom can flourish by their commerce when Weight and Measure are not certain," stated one mid-eighteenth-century writer (cited by Hoppit, 1993, p. 91). While not as bewilderingly confusing as the one on the Continent, the British system (especially measures of volume) still left a lot to be desired, even after the Winchester bushel was made the national measure of volume in 1713, confusingly set to 8 gallons for grains and 8¼ gallons for coal, and the barrel was made the national measure of drinks, set to 34 gallons in 1688 but changed to 36 in 1803 (ibid.). While it seems that the majority of transactions were conducted using standardized measures and weights, there was enough use of local deviations to concern many contemporaries and to instigate some parliamentary inquiries. But adopting the radical (and "republican") French innovation of metric weights and measures was unacceptable in Britain, though it had some supporters. Instead, Britain considered its options in a deliberate fashion and in 1824 passed a standardization law that kept disruption to a minimum and was politically easy to accept. It allowed the use of local units and customary weights and measures provided their relation to the standard measures was generally known. It thus took a judicious middle road: it minimized transactions costs, while preserving familiar customs, unlike the more radical approach on the Continent, which completely replaced the old system by a new one, and thus generated far more resistance. The influence of Enlightenment ideology was unmistakable (many of the technical issues were resolved by a special committee of the Royal Society, and the scientific consultant and future President of the Royal Society, Davies Gilbert, was one of the MPs in charge of ensuring the passage of the Bill). Greenwich Mean Time was set in 1792 (Hoppit, 1993, p. 104), the measurement of time being an obvious area in which coordination was useful. Yet it was not until 1840 that railways ordered their stations to keep the same time throughout the kingdom. There was rarely anything very radical and revolutionary about the way institutional change in Britain paved the road for a more efficient economy, but in the long run it was more effective and less disruptive than the dramatic sequences of continental revolutionary reforms, which often lacked legitimacy.

By comparison, the attempts by Turgot to reform French institutions fifteen years before the revolution failed in the face of tenacious resistance. In the Netherlands, a French occupation, accompanied by profound immiseration and crisis, was needed before its institutions could be reformed. Prussia launched a set of reforms following military defeat at the hands of Napoleon in 1806. Elsewhere, as in Spain and Russia, reactionary forces eventually kept the upper hand and reforms were postponed or reversed, with devastating effects on these countries' long-term economic development. As the experience of the Continent shows, once violence is resorted to, the system can be catapulted into disequilibrium and unintended consequences may occur, including the Terror, a military dictatorship, and prolonged war. Many of the reforms introduced on the Continent during the French Revolution were repealed after 1815 and while in the long run the enlightenment genie could not be put back in the bottle, the spasmodic and disruptive processes of institutional change on the Continent—often accompanied by bloodshed—were less effective than the steady and deliberate path of Britain.

The tragedy of the European Enlightenment was that as a result of the French Revolution, the movement bifurcated into two hostile camps. After a few promising years, France turned from a set of moderate and enlightened politicians to increasingly radical and nationalist leaders and eventually degenerated into a military dictatorship (albeit with some distinctly enlightened characteristics). The reaction to French Jacobin radicalism and the two decades of war that followed set back many aspects of the Enlightenment program in Britain by decades. On both sides of the channel some form of proto-totalitarianism emerged. Some conservative thinkers even formulated a neomercantilist body of thought that harked back to an earlier age, while also vaguely pointing to a future in which unenlightened "infant industry" and "beggar thy neighbor" policies would be resurrected and self-sufficiency would be combined with the protection of landed interests. In terms of networking and communications, too, these years were difficult for those elements of the Enlightenment that were strategic for long-term economic development. The Seditious Meetings Act of 1795 curtailed the ability of small organizations to speak freely, and fear of informers and the persecution of those suspected of radical sympathies limited the free flow of ideas and knowledge. With the disappearance of the threats after Waterloo, these restrictions were lifted, but there can be little doubt that they slowed down the processes that the Industrial Enlightenment had started.

Reforms did not come easy, even to Britain. But the power of Enlightenment ideas became too strong to resist, and when the dust settled on the European battlefields after 1815, the dismantlement of old institutions of special interests and mercantilism by Parliament resumed. The discriminatory policies toward Ireland were abandoned from 1801, when Ireland was politically united with Britain, to become a full economic part of the kingdom in 1829. Discrimination against non-Anglicans was abolished in 1829, and an array of redistributive and exclusionary legislation, from the laws restricting the emigration of skilled artisans to the Bubble and Navigation Acts, were weakened, then abolished, as we saw in chapter 4 above. The Reform Act of 1832 expanded the electorate and made it more difficult for the rich and powerful to defend what was left of their sinecures. The Municipal Corporations Act (1835), another landmark of Whig reform, standardized city charters, and mandated that municipal councils actually be elected by ratepayers and that they publish their financial accounts. Monopolies and "privileges" were weakened and disappeared, and by 1850, arguably, Britain had come as close as any economy ever would to being a "liberal economy," in which the government intervened as little as it could to redistribute income. Within Britain, the notion that the state was a means to generate rents through redistribution came to be regarded as a relic of the past. The Poor Law Reform Act of 1834, in which a serious attempt was made to reduce redistribution through cash payments, was another example. Moreover, the new ideology helped Britain impose a European state of peace, in part by its own supposed military strength but in part because the leaders of most other European nations, too, had subscribed to the notion that internecine predatory wars over colonies and commercial advantages fought by mercantilist governments no longer suited the age. Coupled with Britain's undeniable technological creativity, the result was—at least for a while—the combination of the Pax Britannica and the great Victorian boom, in which Britain established economic and technological hegemony.

A revealing piece of evidence about the changing culture of government in Britain is the decline of corruption in government. Eighteenth-century Britain had been by our standards a corrupt society, in which rent-seeking took its most blatant and crass forms in direct pensions and grants paid by the government to well-placed individuals (known as "placemen"), well-remunerated sinecures in government that required no work, and the ability to award such transfers to relatives and retainers. These privileges were often regarded as freehold property, and were renumerated by negotiated fees for services rather than fixed salaries. Under the influence of Enlightenment ideas, these practices came under fire in the late eighteenth century. Radical critics raised questions of corruption and privilege at the expense of the well-being of the realm, and the ruling elite, whether under pressure from such critics (Harling, 1996), or because they themselves had been influenced by enlightened thought, reformed government.

The disastrous War of American Independence may have been a catalyst in this movement, but in any case a set of reforms were introduced in order to reduce what was known as "old corruption." Many of the reform proposals of the 1780s came from politicians and officials whose ideology, as we saw in chapter 4, had been influenced by Enlightenment thought, including Edmund Burke (the author of the 1783 India Reform Act), William Pitt the younger, and Shelburne, as well as Charles Middleton (later Baron Barham), who created the navy that won at Trafalgar, a profoundly religious evangelical man with deep anti-slavery sentiments. Pitt's policies of reducing patronage and preferment in the 1780s were quite remarkable (Hilton, 2006, pp. 113–17). He opened public contracts to competitive bidding, and reduced the number of excise officers significantly despite the growth in revenues, and most tellingly, raised the salaries of officers to discourage bribe-taking. His political success may seem surprising given the way public funds had been used before to secure a compliant Parliament. His own disinterest in the spoils of office and his desire to protect the incumbent elites from criticism were a cause of his success (Harling, 1996, pp. 38, 44). The transition from Walpole to Pitt marks a notable shift in political culture. The forms of government spending that constituted a possible source of corruption and waste (pensions, fees, and the salaries of corrupt officers) in the 1780s and 1790s accounted for at most 2 percent of annual spending, less than a quarter than that of France (Brewer, 1988, p. 73). These figures do not, of course, include further corruption and waste in military spending and the appointment of officers, but still indicate that the British government was turning away from *ancien régime* rent-seeking modes of government. Judges were no longer expected to accept gifts and in 1799 Parliament voted to pay them pensions.

During the French Wars of 1793–1815, the opportunities for corrupt practices increased as government procurement increased sharply, and it may well be that Pitt's zeal in carrying out his policies did not always match his rhetoric. In fact, one of the less noticed costs of war and of Britain's blue water policies was that war, by increasing government spending and procurement, created almost irresistible opportunities for graft, and thus slowed down and in some cases reversed the move toward the ideal of government as disinterested public service (Harling, 1996, pp. 56–88). Yet even in wartime, the movement toward reform continued. In 1812, for instance, the practice of "reversions" (which allowed the owners of sinecures to pass them on to others and essentially made them a tradeable asset) was discontinued. After the wars, radical writers such as William Cobbett and John Wade made it their calling to expose and denounce these practices, though in fact they had been on the decline for decades. Indeed, as Harling (1995, 1996) shows, taking this muckraking literature too literally can lead to overestimating the extent of corruption in Britain after 1815. An enlightened consensus had emerged that had no room in it for patronage, sweetheart deals, and other forms of rent-seeking. The abuses of "old corruption" and the patronage system were dismantled as the attitudes of the elites in power toward the profits of office were themselves reformed (Harling, 1996, pp. 138–39). The ruling class had become, in Linda Colley's terms, a service elite, who brought to government a new approach that consisted of professionalism, hard work, and uncompromising private virtue which proved remarkably effective (1992, p. 192). Moderate Tories such as Lord Liverpool and the Duke of Wellington who ran Britain in those years were "cultivating a governing style of disinterested public service" (ibid., p. 145). By 1830, Wellington said that as prime minister he commanded virtually no patronage (cited by Rubinstein, 1983, p. 57). There remained a few bad apples, but the post-1830 Whig reforms effectively disposed of those as well. By the mid-1830s, the cost of all unreformed sinecures was estimated at under £17,000, down from £200,000 two decades earlier (Harling, 1995, p. 136).

The fact of the matter, then, is that rent-seeking in all its manifestations had become socially and politically unacceptable in early nineteenth-century Britain. There is no good explanation for this decline except to attribute it to the impact of Enlightenment thought, filtering through many layers and channels to the minds of the members of the British political elite in both parties. The relative payoff of activities that involved redistribution had declined steeply, as the result of a radical change in the ideological mood of the nation. It illustrates the uniqueness of the English Enlightenment, which had deeper religious and moral-istic undertones than the French. Christian or evangelical beliefs of what was moral and fair were implausibly blended with radical Enlightenment notions of what was socially desirable, most effectively expressed by Jeremy Bentham and his notions of a central government as a tool of the interests of the majority. The net result was a realignment of economic incentives that was to have far-reaching consequences for economic growth, not only in Britain but also in other countries that sought to emulate her. As modern economists such as Baumol (1993) have pointed out, this is the crux of the significance of institutions for economic growth: shaping the incentives such that wealth creation becomes more attractive than wealth redistribution. Yet even here, ambiguities survived. British institutions until well into the nineteenth century reflected the recognition by some that in some cases redistribution was inevitable and possibly even desirable, and hence the continuous experimentation with schemes to relieve the poor. By the 1830s, however, a growing resistance to redistribution in any form except on the most niggardly terms led to the 1834 Poor Law Reform and a decade later to the miser-ly aid to Ireland during the Famine.

The distinction between "developmental" institutions that foster economic growth and "predatory" ones that hinder it is useful, but it is necessary to dig deeper into why one form wins out over the other. Ideological beliefs are a good place to start, although they are unlikely to be the place where the search ends. We need to learn more about the way in which people choose their views on what a good and efficient society consists of. Persuasion was a central ingredient here, although material interests and inertia were also important. It is in these areas that the evolution of cultural beliefs and norms must be studied in great detail.

Enlightenment in Britain did not mean laissez-faire. It meant recognizing where the boundaries between what was best left to the public sector and what was best left to the free market lay, and trying to have the government do only what it did best. Of course, the exact location of this boundary was a matter of dispute and changed over time, but outside a fairly limited area a majority opinion, if not a consensus, emerged about what the government should and should not do. One notion that made sense to most was that the public sector should be involved in the collection and organization of systematic and reliable information that could be of use to the public. The results were, for instance, the collection of data on population, trade, and other matters, and where there was a public interest in these data, making them available freely to the public. From 1801 a decennial census was taken; the Ordnance Survey was begun in 1791 and parliamentary inquiries, such as the massive Poor Law Commission *Report* (Great Britain, 1834b), provided enormous amounts of information on which quantitative historians have feasted.

The public sector was also seen as responsible for lubricating the wheels of foreign trade through diplomacy and, whenever necessary, gunboats. Nowhere is this better illustrated than by the famed Lord Macartney delegation sent to China (1792) in the hope of opening the Chinese market and learning what kind of opportunities existed there for British products. The expensive mission was financed by the East India Company but sponsored by the British government, which sought direct contact with the Chinese in order to enhance British commerce beyond the already substantial trade of the East India Company. Macartney carried a letter from King George III to the Qianlong Emperor (Berg, 2006). Decades later, the British government interfered more forcefully when the Chinese tried to interfere with the lucrative opium trade. Such actions were not considered at odds with free trade ideology, since the British persuaded themselves that they actually facilitated the natural flow of commerce.

It may seem odd at first glance that this combination of institutions should bring about such a successful outcome. Colley (1992, p. 62) has noted that in eighteenth-century Britain commercial energy and stable rule by an exclusive elite could be successfully combined. Yet British institutions also had to possess a built-in capability to adapt to radically changing circumstances, and every such adaptation led to further changes in the economic structure of Britain. It is this kind of dynamic that created the success that allowed the growth of useful knowledge and technological ingenuity to become the foundation of sustained economic development.

*   *   *

Despite the uniqueness of their political system or perhaps because of it, the British did not enjoy low taxes but rather the reverse: during the eighteenth century they were taxed at rates far higher than anyone else in the world save the Dutch. Yet the tax burden never led to really major political crises. The rub was that these taxes were largely indirect levies. For most of the eighteenth century, customs revenues and excise taxes accounted for about two-thirds of the state's revenues. Such taxes are highly regressive, so that the rich and powerful represented in Parliament paid a proportionally low amount whereas many of them were clearly beneficiaries of the expenditures. Yet, unlike the nobility in France and Spain, they were not exempt from these taxes; they just paid less than what seems to us their fair share. Government expenditure besides the costs of tax collection was primarily on two items: the military and debt-servicing. During war years, such as 1776–83 and 1793–1815, the normal spending pattern of the government was about 60 percent on military expenditure, 30 percent on debt service, and less than 10 percent on civil government. In the peace years in between, when military expenditures were much lower, the spending on civil government (including tax collection) never exceeded 20 percent and normally comprised somewhere around 15 percent of total government expenditures (O'Brien, 1988, p. 2). Because most of the debts serviced were incurred during wartime, it may seem that from an expenditure point of view, the British government ran a military state.

Such a conclusion would be quite misleading, however, since many of the functions of the government, including poor relief, local public goods, and administration, were carried out at the local level and relied on unpaid service and local taxes such as poor rates. Moreover, many of the coordinating and rule-setting functions of the government were fiscally inexpensive even if they were important to the economy. An example is the clause in the Statute of Apprentices, which stipulated that anyone fully completing a formal apprenticeship could practice his trade anywhere in the kingdom. While not enforced universally (and less and less in the eighteenth century), such a rule was nowhere to be found on the Continent, where the mastery of trades was still part of the jurisdiction of local guilds that did not formally extend beyond the limits of the city. The apparent impact of this coordinating rule of labor mobility should be obvious, since it would mean that a lad from one place could train in another without necessarily pre-committing to stay in the town of his master. Such legislation made sense, yet it was low-cost.

To link the tax system and military expenditures of the eighteenth century to subsequent economic development, as argued by O'Brien (2002, 2006), requires a two-stage argument. First, it has to be shown that these policies actually led to an increased volume of trade that raised economic welfare and performance, or at least to a change in the terms of trade that favored British merchants. Second, it has to be shown that these changes then fed back into further growth, through increased capital accumulation, for instance, or through some positive signal to would-be innovators. The argument that aggressive policies may have created a more secure and attractive environment for foreign trade (Ormrod, 2003) seems plausible. The seas in the eighteenth-century world were unsafe for merchant ships, and the big stick behind the Union Jack helped protect British property. Being prepared for war, British trade hoped for peace. Yet it actually got little of it, and during wartime, commerce and shipping were jeopardized by enemy ships and privateers. As argued in chapter 8 above, the case for a net favorable effect of aggressive British mercantilist policies on trade expansion, much less economic progress, is not persuasive.

If the argument is that government policy helped things along by creating a more favorable climate for merchants, surely this cannot hold for taxation. There is little dispute about the basic facts, even if the statistics lack accuracy. On the eve of the Glorious Revolution, the British government collected somewhere between 3 and 4 percent of national income in taxes (O'Brien, 1988, p. 3). By 1715 this figure had risen to about 10–11 percent, a range in which it stayed until the American War of Independence. By 1790 it had exceeded 12 percent and by 1810 it was over 18 percent. After 1815, this ratio settled down to a level of about 13 percent. Looked at differently, between the Glorious Revolution and 1815, the total nominal tax collected from British citizens rose by a factor of sixteen, or over six times if corrected for inflation. Once we factor in population growth and the rise of income per capita, this figure looks a lot less burdensome, yet high taxes in this period still stand out as one of the central phenomena of British economic history.

The dynamics of this path reveal a "ratchet effect"—during the eighteenth century each war raised taxes dramatically, and when peace returned, they fell back, but usually to a higher equilibrium value than before. This pattern reflected the habit of paying for most of the sudden increase of war-related expenses by borrowing, and the need to service a higher government debt after the war. Since in no economy is the tax system sufficiently elastic to fully pay for a sudden increase in government spending due to war, governments practice tax "smoothing," no doubt both a fiscally and politically wise strategy. Hanoverian Britain could do this precisely because it had a solid tax-raising mechanism that, lenders knew, would be capable of raising long-term revenues. During the wars of 1793–1815, Pitt and his successors raised 58 percent of the extra revenue from taxes and borrowed the rest. It was quite different in the eighteenth century, when governments had raised on average only 20 percent from taxes for wars, and relied on debt creation for the remainder. The ratchet effect consequently was mitigated in the nineteenth century. After 1815, in the absence of expensive wars and with an expanding economy, taxation rates declined, and by the middle decades of the century the proportion of GNP collected by taxes had fallen to around 10 percent. The pattern of public finance in the decades after 1815 reflects the paradigm of the new political economy: an enlightened world was one of peace, low government spending, and fiscal prudence. The Victorian state, by all accounts, had a smaller footprint on the economy than the Hanoverian state, and its impact as measured by the ratio of tax revenues to GDP was lighter than in Germany or France.

Britain's fiscal system was unique in that it raised most of its revenues from indirect taxes: throughout the eighteenth century between 70 and 75 percent of all tax revenues came from customs and excise taxes. By 1700 the British state had realized that it could tax goods consumed by a substantial middle class that was no longer on the verge of subsistence and consumed goods that were not essential to survival and therefore could be taxed, such as tobacco, sugar, alcoholic drinks, glass, and paper. As the eighteenth century proceeded, new taxes were imposed: on carriages, dice, playing cards, newspapers, and even commercial transactions in the form of a stamp tax. The taxes fell neither on the necessities of subsistence nor on the goods that were produced by the most technologically progressive sectors. The land tax, on the other hand, which was paid primarily by the rich, was reduced sharply by Walpole, whose constituency was primarily Whig landowners. Yet in the 1740s, during the expensive War of the Austrian Succession, land taxes were raised but excise remained the principal source of revenue. Tariffs, too, were an important source of state income, accounting for somewhere between 20 and 30 percent of revenues in the eighteenth century. Until 1785, the tariff on tea was so high that the bulk of imports was smuggled in, inducing Pitt to sharply reduce the rate of tariff and find the revenues virtually unchanged, a classic example of what became known in our time as "supply-side" fiscal effects. Although for the entire eighteenth century Britain was able to avoid the much-feared income tax, some taxes (such as window and house taxes) were in fact so general that they might as well have been an income tax.

Britain's custom of paying for wars through borrowing did not survive the national emergency of the French and Napoleonic Wars. In 1799 the exigencies of the Napoleonic Wars forced Pitt to introduce a highly unpopular income tax, but it was abolished soon after the war and its records burned—to the everlasting chagrin of quantitative economic historians, for whom these records would have been a unique source of information on income distribution in this era. Yet the detestation felt by the British for the income tax was not so much about its cost (only those making more than £150 per year paid the full 10 percent income tax) as about the invasion of privacy which was held to be incompatible with the personal liberties that eighteenth-century philosophers had taught them they were entitled to (MacDonald, 2006, p. 338). Other infringements of these rights, part of Pitt's anti-terror campaign, had been bad enough. It was not for the last time that the ideas of the Enlightenment clashed with the needs, real or putative, of national security.

And yet, unlike France and the United Provinces, British public finance never experienced a meltdown. How did Britain succeed in avoiding the fiscal disasters of its continental neighbors? In large part this could take place because the British compromise forged in the years after the Glorious Revolution (and consolidated in 1720) was that its public finances would be controlled by the mercantile class even if the rest of the decision-making in society remained largely in the hands of agrarian interests. By the middle of the eighteenth century, the national debt was owned by perhaps 50,000 individuals, many of them located in London, a powerful group that guarded its interests well. Taxes in Britain were paid disproportionately by the middle class—neither gentry nor paupers, which was already large in 1700, and kept growing throughout the eighteenth century. This class was large enough to pay for the extravagantly expensive wars that others decided to fight. It did so, not so much by being taxed to pay for the war as much as by being taxed to service the debt that paid for the war. The three major wars between 1715 and 1793 were mostly (70–80 percent) paid for by borrowing. But because of the soundness of Britain's credit, this fiscal smoothing was, comparatively speaking, inexpensive. Enlightenment thinkers observed this and saw it as support for their view, most eloquently expressed by Montesquieu, that a "natural law" decreed that personal liberty and financial soundness went hand in hand. While Adam Smith and David Hume were concerned about the long-term feasibility of a large public debt and the "waste and extravagance of government" (as Adam Smith put it), they realized that well-designed and flexible institutions added to the viability of a nation. When the cost of war exceeded the ability of the nation to borrow, it raised taxes. About half of the costs of the French Wars between 1793 and 1815 were paid for by taxes, and the Bank of England assumed a new role by providing the printing presses that *in extremis* produced liquidity that staved off financial crises.

Indirect taxes had general equilibrium effects on other products (spending more on beer left consumers with less money for cotton goods), but they left the real income of the richest people in society intact. Had these rich landowners and merchants invested larger amounts in the most dynamic sectors of the economy, it would have certainly aided development. Some of the funds that were available for canals, turnpikes, mines, harbors, and other expensive projects were indeed larger because their owners paid relatively low taxes. On the other hand, the high-tech manufacturing sector probably benefited little from this policy. The wealthy were likely to save more of their income, but many of these savings were invested in expensive Georgian country homes or Gainsborough paintings, which did little for the growth of the economy. Furthermore, a large proportion simply ended up in government securities, thus in essence offsetting budget deficits incurred through wars of dubious economic value. At the same time, the British fiscal system may have been central to the creation of the incentives that helped Britain transform its economy by acts of omission. Had the great cotton- and ironmasters been obliged to pay a large amount of their profits to the government, their efforts and successes might have been reduced.

There are good explanations of the British state's ability to tax its citizens so heavily without leading to a tax revolt or even to massive non-compliance. On the one hand, Parliament avoided taxing the basic necessity of life, namely bread. This policy prevented more food riots and upheavals and avoided worse distortions.

Charles Davenant, one of the more insightful writers on economic matters of his time, remarked in 1695 that "excises seem the most proper ways and means to support a government in a long war because they would lye equally upon the whole and produce great sums proportionable to the great needs of the publick ... this tax would fall easily upon the poor and not very heavily on the richer sort ... [it is] very easy, when everyone, in a manner, taxes himself, making consumption according to his will or ability" (Davenant, 1701, pp. 116–20). What is equally interesting is that the British tax collection system was efficient by the standards of the time, as taxes were collected by a professional administration and no longer farmed out to private entrepreneurs, a source of endless chagrin elsewhere in Europe. The high taxes that Britons paid have been identified with the rise of a professional tax administration, and in many ways are linked to the "rise of the national bureaucracy." John Brewer (1988, p. 139) has argued that after 1688 the House of Commons restrained malfeasance and secured public accountability of military spending. It did not prevent corruption and waste, but surely it kept them limited and at low levels relative to other nations. The tax collection apparatus did not have, as in France, to deal with quasi-autonomous jurisdictions, each of them with their own tax codes, exemptions, and judiciaries. The indirect tax system was unified and uniform, run tightly from London. Moreover, the system was public, and accounts and reports were presented to Parliament. Contemporaries felt that transparency and openness increased confidence and trust in the system. Foreigners such as Jacques Necker hoped to reform the finances of their own country following what they saw as the British example. The system worked, in Brewer's words, "with remarkable smoothness and very little friction" (Brewer, 1988, p. 131).

The success of the British state as a tax collection machine is consistent with the kind of economy it was in 1700. Britain was not a subsistence economy, both in the sense that Britons no longer lived on the edge of starvation, and in the sense that they were far from insulated from markets. It was a thriving, bustling market economy, in which individuals bought rather than made or grew the things they consumed. Moreover, people consumed goods they did not really need for physical survival, such as tobacco, cider, soap, sugar, paper, candles, wig powder, playing cards, racehorses, and silk gloves, and the networks selling them were dense. These "middle-class goods" were the prime objects of taxation. By the last quarter of the eighteenth century, the excise tax administration had jurisdiction over approximately 100,000 businesses and premises, which manufactured and/or sold goods to the public at large. Many of these shops must have been small and probably part-time affairs. It seems unlikely that Britain had 103,000 cider producers in the 1760s, as Brewer (1988, p. 263) reports. However, what made a sophisticated tax collection administration possible was the existence of a commercial market economy that had penetrated deeply and broadly into Britain, and in which the majority of British families participated on a daily basis.

The excise tax worked because there were enough middle-class consumers who could pay it and did so without rebelling. The fiscal revolution was made possible by the industrious revolution.

The need to collect taxes and manage the national debt did, of course, have unintended consequences and created institutions that in the end may well have had a salutary effect on the British economy. Among those, the Bank of England, founded in 1694 to manage the government's debt comes first to mind, but the entire tax bureaucracy created in the eighteenth century may be regarded as the harbinger of the modern state. As noted, by the standards of the time it was effective and fairly incorruptible. All the same, the high taxes in the eighteenth century in and of themselves contributed little to economic development. They tended to be costly because they distorted the relative prices that the economy needed to allocate resources. At least in the early stages, government debt was directly associated with rent-seeking arrangements. Under William and Mary, and even more markedly under Queen Anne, the government borrowed from large joint-stock trading companies at below market rates, in exchange for privileged trading positions. This form of government finance amounted to classic rent-seeking. But after 1720 such practices fell into disrepute. This decline cannot wholly be chalked up to Enlightenment ideology: the South Sea Company in 1719 proposed to purchase the government debt; before and after its collapse the government made a range of attempts to find other sources of income; among them a variety of lotteries, annuities, and other ways of raising funds.

In the end, however, orderly borrowing by the government became standard in eighteenth-century Britain. It was the biggest lesson the British learned from their Dutch cousins in 1688. What we call today sovereign debt was no longer just the debt of the sovereign; it was the debt of the state. Once this distinction was blurred, the door was open to the enlightened ideas about the responsibility of the Crown to the state. Equally important, the effective system of taxation by the state itself reduced the dependence of the sovereign on other agencies that it could have commissioned to collect its taxes for it. Elsewhere in Europe, such agencies exacted a high price from the economy for doing so. In France and elsewhere the guilds and tax farmers were fiscal tools that traded revenue collection for exclusionary rents—exactly the kind of phenomenon that the *philosophes* would rail against. As MacDonald (2006, p. 232) has put it, eighteenth-century Britain, despite being still an agrarian country run by a landed aristocracy, had developed a system of public finance suitable to a "mercantile republic." Yet its system was superior to that of the United Provinces, not only because Britain was larger but because the Bank of England was a flexible and powerful instrument and because credible decisions could be made at the national level by Parliament. Once again, it is apparent that what stood the British economy in good stead was not that its institutions were in some sense "superior" but that they were flexible and could be changed as circumstances demanded.

The emergence of a national debt in Britain over this period is of substantial interest to economists. The debt rose from £14 million in 1700 to £243 million in 1784 at the end of the American War to £745 million in 1815. From then on it stayed more or less constant at around £800 until 1850, but as a proportion of nominal income, it declined. The exact significance of these changes is less easy to assess. At one level it may seem that the growth of the national debt attracted savers who would otherwise have purchased more productive assets such as physical capital to buy unproductive government securities. Government debt was held as an asset in the portfolios of the rich. It is at least possible that to some extent it "crowded out" the accumulation of private assets that might have been beneficial to the economy. This argument is based on impeccable economic logic, but its exact historical significance is still a matter of debate. Had the savers not purchased government securities, what would they have done with their money? If the answer is that they would have spent it or gambled it away, then the crowding-out story is less compelling. More plausibly, government debt was a substitute for land, and was held in many portfolios as a secure and reliable form of wealth. It was not a close substitute for commercial paper and discounting bills, much less manufacturing equipment. Hence, it is far from clear that government debt competed with productive capital and that its expansion reduced capital formation. To the extent that the issuance of the national debt actually encouraged savings, or even crowded in investors (who saw government bonds as a secure investment ideally suited to balance portfolios that also contained more risky assets), the view that the growing national debt had a detrimental effect on economic growth is further weakened. Moreover, many securities attracted overseas investors, thus increasing the resources at Britain's disposal (Mokyr, 1987).

Above all, as David Hume ([1777], 1985, pp. 353–54) was the first to point out in his "Of Public Credit," public credit created liquid assets that served as a means of exchange, and created the secondary financial markets in which these securities were traded, thus helping the intermediation of other securities. Modern historians, on the whole, concur. As Carruthers (1996, p. 17) put it, the financial machinery for the state to borrow large amounts, once created, could be used for other purposes. By the second half of the eighteenth century there were over 20,000 registered sales of securities a year, a "bedrock on which a securities market could be built" (Michie, 2001, p. 19). The vast expansion of government debt during the French Wars implied a considerable expansion of the activities of the brokers and jobbers on the London Stock Exchange, and when the size of government finally started to decline after 1820, this market needed new outlets. By 1820, the London capital market was substantial enough to make it possible for some entrepreneurs in need of capital to issue and sell bonds. The newly constructed canals, turnpikes, and later railroads, which all relied heavily on capital markets, were the beneficiaries. It seems excessive to suggest, as does Neal (2004), that this was the idea underlying eighteenth-century British government finance all along. But the history of economic institutions is a sequence of unintended consequences, and this may be a case in point.

As a proportion of GDP, the national debt increased from about 35 percent to 250 percent between the early eighteenth century and 1815. This growth was regarded with alarm by contemporaries, who had no idea what the growth of this debt would do to the economy. In fact, however, management of the government debt can be seen as one of the triumphs of eighteenth-century British institutions. Modern economists rightly see it as a symptom of how Britain had solved the "commitment problem"—the owners of financial capital had reached the point at which they felt sufficiently secure to lend large amounts to the government without undue concern for default. Property rights, even on vulnerable liquid assets, were no longer contestable because the owners of assets had tamed the rulers and controlled the reins of power. It was also, however, the result of the professionalism of those in charge of the Bank of England, as well as those in the exchequer. The chaotic debt instruments issued during the wars against Louis XIV consisted in part of short-term debt, such as procurement bills due and exchequer bills. As these bills mushroomed during the long War of Spanish Succession, credit became increasingly hard to secure. The project that British politicians took on after 1714 was to convert short-term debts into long-term funded debts, that is, debts that imposed taxes earmarked to pay for them. The popular form of such securities was either for 99 years or for a "life," and after 1751 the increasingly popular 3 percent consol was introduced. Henry Pelham, the prime minister who ended the costly war of 1740–48, sought to consolidate the national debt by issuing an irredeemable security paying 3 percent that was liquid in that it could readily be sold in secondary markets. It was not wholly risk-free: because it was a perpetuity, the market price fluctuated inversely with the prevailing interest rate, but consols were liquid and default-risk was negligible. British investors liked it and it became the core of what in later years was referred to as "the funds." Britain's government was in debt, but it was solid and reliable. Its liabilities became the asset of choice (with land) of the classes that owned property. One contemporary wrote in 1748 that "the debts of the public are part of the constitution, interwoven with all kind of property and cannot be separated without subverting the constitution ... we are neither the richer nor the poorer for the debt to one another" (*An Essay upon Public Credit*, 1748).

The 3 percent coupon interest rates that consols paid thus became a fixture of the British economy; as Walter Bagehot was fond of pointing out, "John Bull can stand many things, but he cannot stand two percent." When peace returned in 1783, Britain had hopes to reduce the national debt, which turned out to be rather tricky, since redeeming the consols at par would have created a windfall for bondholders. William Pitt found a solution by creating a sinking fund (1786), inspired by Richard Price, the radical philosopher and enlightened social activist.

The idea of a sinking fund was to create a portfolio of assets to offset the liabilities of the national debt. It had already been tried earlier in the century by Robert Walpole, but Pitt allocated £1 million to a fund that was supposed to grow through compound interest to offset the national debt. The idea was widely criticized and ridiculed, but the fund was sound enough in peacetime. While fiscally it made little sense, MacDonald (2006, p. 343) feels that Pitt's fund gave markets a psychological boost. Be that as it may, the fiscal pressures of war after 1793 proved too much for Pitt's scheme and it was finally abandoned in 1827. Evidently, not all ideas proposed by Enlightenment thinkers were sensible or sound—it was in many respects still an age of experimentation.

To sum up: the surprising thing is how effective, on the whole, British taxation and public finances were. In 1788, it is estimated, the British tax burden amounted to about 12.4 percent of GNP compared to France's 6.8 percent. Yet the interest that Britain had to pay on its national debt was far lower than France's: the market appreciated a sound fiscal system when it saw one. Borrowing was an inevitable part of public finance: the government's debt, estimated at 5 percent of GNP in 1688, rose to 200 percent of GNP in 1815 (though it declined from then on, as Britain was spared further expensive wars until 1914). All the same, the overall damage caused by high debt and taxes to incentives and the dynamics of the economy, considering the political environment, was not as large as it could have been. Consumption was hit more than investment, bad perhaps for the people living at the time, but good for the long-term growth of the economy.

But there is more to the fiscal history of eighteenth-century Britain than the growth of the national debt. As John Nye (2007) has pointed out, the success of the Hanoverian state in raising more taxes depended in part on a bargain that the government struck with some powerful local interests, such as wealthy brewers. In return for strong protection against French wine, brewers agreed to be taxed (a tax that was shifted largely onto consumers in any case). Originally, the tariffs placed on French wines in the 1690s were part of a mercantilist policy to weaken France. Hence British consumers, except the very rich and some Oxford dons, were induced by relative prices to drink beer instead of wine, a habit that lasted until deep in the nineteenth century. But the matter goes further: because collecting taxes from a highly decentralized industry is costly, the government encouraged the concentration of the industry and set up barriers to entry, thus reducing competitiveness. Nye argues that in exchange for a high level of protection, Britain's brewers complied with the high taxes. Beer, hops, malt, and related products accounted for about 75 percent of all excises, so this implicit contract between the tax collector and the industry was central to the success of the British excise after 1714. Moreover, both the government and the industry were interested in a high level of market concentration and oligopoly. For the government this made collection easier, for the industry it made price-fixing and a low level of competitive pressure possible, so that the consumer got gouged twice.

Sympathizing with the plight of the British beer drinker appears perhaps a bit far-fetched, but given the health hazards of eighteenth-century water, beer may well have been a necessity. De Saussure noted in 1726 that "The lower classes, even the paupers, do not know what it is to quench their thirst with water. In this country nothing but beer is drunk, and it is made in several quantities" ([1726] 1902, p. 157). Yet per capita consumption of beer declined over the eighteenth century, and other, more potent drinks like gin, became popular. The famous gin mania of the 1720s and 1730s was a cause of great concern to the government, yet its worst excesses might have been avoided if beer had been cheaper. Moreover, the high price of beer encouraged home-brewed beer of low quality, and smuggling and fraud were rampant. In all practical situations, high taxes cannot but distort the way the market operates. Moreover, tax collection intruded upon the life and operation of small businesses. Candlemakers, to pick one example, were tightly regulated and supervised to make sure they paid the correct taxes. Candles could only be sold on designated premises, manufactured at designated hours, and shipped following carefully designated rules (Brewer, 1988, pp. 214–15). The 1733 Molasses Act, which imposed a high tariff on cheap sugar imported from the French Caribbean, raised the price of sugar in Britain substantially above the level on the Continent. It is questionable if these restrictions were obeyed to the letter, and smuggling was one of the eighteenth century's largest industries. However, the complexity of the tariffs and the threat of serious penalties, much like modern tax codes, were a serious impediment to business. Their dismantlement took a long time and became a prime target for enlightened reformers.

If the fiscal regime in Britain had any advantages, it was not that its net effect on the economy was on balance salutary, but that it could have been a lot worse, and was elsewhere. In France, where the two upper classes were largely exempt from taxes and where different localities had different rates and structures, the fiscal situation was considerably more wasteful and costly, and in the end could only be resolved by a political revolution that threw the entire Continent into disarray for a quarter of a century. The Dutch tax system was equally decentralized and uneven. The fiscal state created in Britain between 1688 and 1720 was sufficiently stable and well organized to avoid the kind of political instability that eventually wrought havoc upon France. The excise tax administration grew very rapidly after 1690, as excise became increasingly the tax of choice. In 1710 it became the largest source of revenue and from 1735 on it averaged about half of all central government tax receipts. Its success was undoubtedly attributable in large part to political factors, but also to its effective collection by a central government administration that employed competent professionals. Brewer (1988, p. 112) assesses that the excise administration was remarkable for the industry that it was able to elicit from its officers and the care with which administrative abuses were anticipated and pre-empted. And while the eighteenth-century evidence shows undeniably that many offices were still sinecures occupied by corrupt and incompetent beneficiaries of nepotism and patronage, by comparison to other nations, the British system was remarkably effective and the costs of corruption were not high enough to make much difference, and were declining to boot.

The historical question remains, however, whether a relatively effective fiscal bureaucracy can be linked in some way to the modernization of the British economy and perhaps even the Industrial Revolution. Had the funds that the state raised been spent on overhead capital, education, or the encouragement of industrial research, such a case would have been transparent. But the money was spent on wars, battleships, mercenaries, the subsidization of foreign armies, and the interest on funds borrowed to pay for them. These funds may have helped Britain to build a larger empire, but the British government provided little in the way of the state-supported infrastructure and public goods that helped along industrialization elsewhere. Empire has been argued to have created economic and technological development; but the reverse seems more plausible. The reverse causation is easier to demonstrate. As the British economy grew and its population increased, tax revenues could expand, and the government could fight more successful wars. As technology advanced, the British military had more effective weapons and tools at its disposal that could be used against non-Europeans with devastating effectiveness and low cost. This was not a government that was concerned with spending on public goods or investing in overhead capital. As late as 1829, close to nine in ten of all civilian employees in the British government were revenue officers; it employed no teachers, few postal workers or clerks, and was for all practical purposes a revenue-raising machine. As John Bowring, a liberal intellectual and politician and friend of Jeremy Bentham's, told Alexis de Tocqueville in 1833, "we have got a government, but we have not got a central administration. Each town, each county, each parish looks after its own interests ... decentralization is the chief cause of the progress we have made" (Tocqueville, 1958, pp. 61–62).

If the large expenditure on wars and the debt services they entailed had a deleterious effect on the economy (aside from the damage to commerce caused by the hostilities themselves), it may have been that they crowded out other public projects that the government could have undertaken that might have been more beneficial. Among these projects, investment in infrastructure such as roads and harbors, often left to private interests or cash-strapped local authorities, was certainly of primary importance. With rapid urbanization, there certainly was a need for investment in water supply, transport, sewerage, and construction, yet these projects were often taken on too little and too late (Williamson, 1990). The British law enforcement system was also managed on the cheap, with volunteers and amateurs running much of the day-to-day operations. There was very little money spent by the government on education: whereas continental governments began to recognize the social usefulness of such institutions as the *École Polytechnique* in France and the technical universities and mining schools in Germany and elsewhere, the British government did little in this regard. It is hard to know, of course, if it was constrained by funds or simply did not feel that many of these areas were the proper purview of the authorities. The high level of taxes in Britain left the government little room to maneuver before 1815. Arguably, after 1815 it could have readily afforded to spend more resources on public goods and social overhead, but it did little of that.

The British state, and the rule of Parliament as the supreme rule-writing institution of the nation, were above all a government of the well-to-do. Workers did not vote and when a conflict erupted between labor and capital, normally the government sided with the employers. The harsh union-busting policies of the late 1790s were only the culmination of a century of decisions favoring the wealthy and the powerful. Law and authority were invoked against perceived embezzlement by workers, and in disputes over pay, machinery, and other grievances. When workers or consumers rioted for one reason or another, the government did not hesitate to use violence. At times this could lead to ugly scenes, as during the Peterloo massacre and the Captain Swing riots of 1830, but on the whole such scenes were rare in Britain. It has often been noted that the two European capitals that were spared the violent upheavals of 1848 were London and St Petersburg, but obviously for very different reasons. In Britain it was not necessary to resort to violence to change the system; in Russia it was ineffective.

After 1815, this attitude began to change. The Combination Acts were repealed and workers could form unions again. Questions began to be asked about working conditions, first of children and women, then of others. It became increasingly obvious that in urban settings the efficiency of the free market was threatened by "externalities" and that free markets did not always guarantee sanitary and healthy living conditions. Free enterprise did not always supply the correct amount of education and public safety. Nor, it was increasingly realized, did it supply reliable drinking water and other aspects of public health. By 1840 the water supply was still predominantly in private hands, but both consumers and firms began to realize that the free market did not work well here, and that municipal control was preferable (Hassan, 1985). Faith in the wisdom of markets had to make room for the realization that in certain conditions the markets malfunctioned and required government intervention. By 1851, to be sure, this process was still only starting, but again, Britain's institutional suppleness stood it in good service and in the second half of the nineteenth century a combination of better management and superior technology resolved many of the worst crises. Urban areas and factories led this process, but over time it slowly but irresistibly spread to the rest of the economy.

If there was any striking and unique feature in the British eighteenth-century polity, it was the Poor Law. Contemporaries wrote extensively about it, and foreigners were either deeply impressed or repelled by it. Britain's Poor Law was far more inclusive and generous than that of any other country. Until 1834, there was considerable redistribution from the well-to-do and the powerful to the poorest citizens of the realm. It differed from other eighteenth-century European relief systems in that it was not financed by voluntary donations but by a local tax, the poor rate. The Poor Law was in part motivated by a genuine concern for the poor, especially those whose destitution was patently not their fault, such as orphans, invalids, and the aged. There were, of course, others who benefited from the system, such as farmers who used the Poor Laws to subsidize their workers in the off-season and thus secure a labor supply in the harvest months. At a higher level, the Poor Law was meant to keep the very poor from rioting or from starving to death in difficult years, which could be costly to the better-off classes.

The administration of the Poor Law was decentralized and to an extent un-coordinated, except that by the Settlement Act of 1660 any pauper in England had to be supported by the parish of his or her residence. Poor rates and relief were administered by local authorities, the so-called Poor Law overseers, usually unpaid local notables. Many decisions (including the amounts needed to sustain the destitute) were left to local discretion. The overall size of the program was not huge relative to the economy, accounting for perhaps 2 percent of GNP at its peak, but to the people covered by it, it made a large difference. In the early nineteenth-century peaks, perhaps as many as 14 percent of the population of England were covered although normally 9–10 percent received support. Scotland had a separate system and Ireland had none until 1838. The system affected the decisions and margins of those close to poverty even if they were not them-selves on the dole. Britain was by no means a welfare state, but certain aspects of what the Poor Law officials could do sound eerily modern. For instance, in the case of dysfunctional or broken families, they could operate *in loco parentis,* apprenticing out pauper children, removing them to foster families, and in one case paying for their smallpox vaccination (Snell, 1985). There were cases in which these arrangements were abused and in which pauper apprentices were sold to factory masters and treated little better than slaves, but such cases were not the rule.

Britain experimented with two alternative systems: transfers in cash and kind (known as "outdoor relief"), and indoor relief through the provision of work and housing, orphanages, hospitals and the like. Besides cash payments, the Poor Law often provided the needy with clothing, medical care, the costs of apprenticeships, and funerals. The pendulum swung back and forth repeatedly between the two systems. Both were imperfect, and there were no obvious criteria to decide which one was preferable. In the early eighteenth century the system mainly provides the poor with cash transfers, but from 1723 on Parliament permitted local parishes to establish workhouses in which the able-bodied poor ("sturdy beggars" in the odd parlance of the day) and others would be provided with free housing and guaranteed employment in lieu of cash. In 1776, 2,000 such establishments existed, most of them having a reputation for being loathsome places, in which inmates were abused and contracted diseases. By 1782, Gilbert's Act reversed course and once again reasserted the principle of outdoor relief by authorizing parishes to set up workhouses. In 1795, high prices and severe unemployment led to the establishment of the Speenhamland system in the south of England, which made relief a direct function of the price of bread and family size. Yet not all of Britain adopted this system, and even those counties that did relied heavily on the "allowance system" only in years of unusually high prices. After 1815, with falling food prices, the need for poor relief was less acutely felt, and the concern about "indolence" voiced by conservative political economists became paramount. They led to the great Poor Law Reform of 1834, in which outdoor relief for able-bodied indigents was abolished and a system of workhouses was instituted, in which the poor would be fed and housed, but the workhouses were made so unpleasant that nobody but the truly needy would resort to them. The reform of 1834 reduced poor relief spending from about 2 percent of national income to about 1 percent, but because the new system had higher administration costs, the net resources that accrued to the poor probably fell by more. By 1850, 123,000 or about 0.7 percent of the population of England were in a poorhouse on at least January 1 of that year and July 1 the preceding year, whereas 955,000 "deserving poor" (5 percent) were receiving some form of outdoor relief (Williams, 1981, p. 158). The reform of 1834 represented one of the uglier streams in Enlightenment thought, namely the belief that able-bodied poor had only themselves to blame and were lazy, licentious, and improvident. The liberal ideology recommended that the bread of charity should be made so bitter that only the most desperate would be tempted by it (Hughes, 1969, p. 533). The British establishment seemed as yet unaware that both the cyclicity of business and the ever more rapid structural changes in an industrial capitalist economy could produce serious episodes of unemployment and suffering for people whose only fault was to be born at the wrong time in the wrong place. But that was soon to change.

The classical British Poor Law system was to a large extent a rural and regional system, meant in part to support agricultural workers in the off-season. It provided support for regular clients as well as for occasional ones who had to deal with temporary hardships. It was highest in the counties of the south-east and Midlands where agricultural wages were relatively low and wage-support was paid out. Urban dwellers had access to occasional relief, but in cities beggars, vagabonds, and prostitutes were far more common, in the absence of regular poor relief. In the rapidly growing northern industrial towns, equally, the local authorities were incapable of dealing with the urban miseries of unemployment and disease. As industrialism and urbanism expanded after 1815, the "old" Poor

Law became increasingly controversial and authorities, local and central, were powerless to cope with the unfamiliar social problems that emerged as a result of the Industrial Revolution. The system was expensive, and many argued with Malthus that it should be done away with altogether. Yet reforming the Poor Law was something that policy-makers had a difficult time agreeing on. Enlightenment ideology gave little guidance here, and political economists disagreed with one another. The Malthusians and the utilitarians led by Bentham supported a radical reform of the old system, but the eminent economist J.R. McCulloch, for instance, argued that the old Poor Law might be quite consistent with continued economic development (Innis, 2002, p. 394). Increased outdoor relief may para-doxically have been the result of the growing unwillingness of the authorities to meddle with market prices in the late eighteenth century. Once the price controls on grain were abandoned, cash outdoor relief may have been inevitable to avoid food riots during years of dearth. When food prices declined sharply in the 1820s, outdoor relief became less necessary.

Observers were thus divided about the net effects of the British Poor Law. Enlightenment thought about society clearly was concerned with the issue of poverty. In line with the overall view of society, eighteenth-century thinkers refused to regard poverty as an inevitable evil and they proposed various prog-rams in the meliorist tradition. Despite very different suggestions, most shared the feeling that relief should be rationalized and that the causes of poverty should be better understood so that institutions could be redesigned to cope with them. Debates raged over whether poverty resulted from "indolence" and "improvidence," or whether most paupers were deserving of relief. It was also far from obvious where to draw the line to identify who could be defined as destitute. Gregory King's tables designated 400,000 families comprising 1.3 million people as "cottagers and paupers" in 1688, close to half the population (King [1688], 1936, p. 31). Surely not all of those were destitute to the point of being permanently supported by poor relief, but many of them might become likely candidates for relief if they were struck by bad fortune or survived to old age. In addition, King counted 30,000 peripatetic "vagrants" who were equally poor but did not qualify for relief. One approach, shared by many Enlightenment thinkers, was that a solution to the problems of mendicity and vagrancy was to supply the poor with work. The assumption was that the poor could and would work if only employment was available, and that relief by the authorities should be focused on providing the needy with this opportunity to work.

Above all, Enlightenment thinkers struggled with the ever-present poor relief dilemma, which is how to combine compassion for the unfortunate with what economists would call incentive-compatibility. No less eminent a thinker than the German philosopher Hegel felt that pervasive uncertainty made men idle and frivolous, whereas in England the poorest had rights and were more secure, and therefore more industrious (cited in Rothschild, 2002, p. 42). Others saw it differently, and were concerned with what would be called today moral hazard, that is, the tendency of insurance schemes to encourage the behavior that led to the need for aid in the first place. Some contemporaries suggested that the Poor Law led to a state in which half the population ended up supporting the other half, and that it encouraged the poor to have large families or to "improvidence" as the Reverend Malthus liked to say, and specifically encouraged high birth rates. Economic historians have found the British poor relief system more beneficial than some of its vocal contemporary opponents, yet its overall impact on the rate of development of the economy has remained controversial (Solar, 1995). To the extent that it reduced riskiness and mitigated social unrest, it may have contributed to an environment that was more friendly toward innovation (Greif and Sasson, 2009). Some have regarded it as a proto-welfare state, providing a rather effective form of insurance at least for those in the lower deciles of the income distribution. In any case, the Poor Law does epitomize the unique division of authority between the private and the public sphere that Britain developed, and the equally unique compromise between local and central government, with its very British system of constrained local autonomy. Designed for a pre-industrial society, the old Poor Law was felt to have become increasingly dysfunctional in the nineteenth century, as a growing problem of urban "mendicity" concerned contemporaries. Yet the new law of 1834 was another compromise, and by most accounts did not work much better.

The trenchant criticisms by contemporary political economists of the Old Poor Law have been carefully examined by economic historians in recent years. The effects of the Poor Laws on the Industrial Revolution were not nearly as negative as used to be thought. The research of Boyer (1990), on the other hand, has supported Malthus' demographic concerns. The use of multivariable regression shows that the introduction of child allowances after 1795 did have a significant effect on the birth rates. Boyer estimates (1990, p. 170) that in the absence of child allowances, the birth rate would actually have declined by 6.4–9.2 percent. He concludes that allowances in aid of wages did to some extent "create the poor which they maintain" (p. 142). The numbers he provides imply that in the absence of the Poor Laws, English population would still have been larger in 1826 than it was in 1781, but it would have grown at a much slower rate after 1795. A rough computation suggests that on Boyer's assumptions the population of England and Wales in 1826 without a Poor Law would have been 9.78 million instead of the 12.4 million actually there by the best estimates available. Whether the old Poor Law was somehow responsible for the creation of an army of able-bodied paupers is still unclear, and awaits further research. On the other hand, the alleged negative effects of the Poor Law on labor mobility have not stood the test of time.

As to the work-incentive effect stressed by Malthus and his followers, research carried out by Blaug (1964) was supported by the work of Pollard (1978, pp.

109–10) and Boyer (1990). It seems that the causality ran mostly the other way. Wage-support payments were made in areas that suffered from seasonal un-employment and the decline of cottage industry, which explains the association of Speenhamland with the agricultural areas of England. Boyer's regressions provide little support for the hypothesis that outdoor relief caused an increase in voluntary unemployment, although it was not possible to estimate the relation between the two directly (Boyer, 1990, pp. 142–43). The effect of Poor Law variables on male labor income was statistically insignificant, which it would not have been if poor relief had been treated as a substitute for labor income. There is little evidence that the abolition of the Old Poor Law increased rents, as might have been expected if it had seriously distorted the allocation of resources (Clark and Page, 2008).

It is unclear how much the poor relief system contributed to the economic security of British life in the eighteenth century. Prices of necessities still fluctuated greatly from year to year, and employment was always precarious, either because markets were unstable or because the supply of raw materials or power depended on weather conditions as well as on wars. In addition to the poor relief system, people could depend on personal networks (family, neighbors), or on local charity, though these solutions probably worked better in the short run and for palpable personal misfortunes than for more widespread problems such as depressions or harvest failure. In any event, the data suggest that in the eighteenth century such periodic crises no longer led to mass mortality. There were few years in which the crude death rate exceeded the death rate by a significant amount, the most notable being the mortality peaks during the very hard years of the late 1720s and early 1740s, when gross mortality rates leaped from about 31 per 1,000 in the early 1720s to 39.8 in 1728 and 44.7 in 1729, and again to 36.7 in 1742 (Wrigley and Schofield, 1981, p. 533). In the late eighteenth century, however, the Old Poor Law provided an adequate safety net for the laboring classes when food prices rose to the point where they seriously threatened health and life (Post, 1990, pp. 59–60), and the demographic effects of high food prices were minor.

In terms of living standards, then, the impressive achievement of modern (post-1750) Europe compared to earlier times was that the periodic famines that devastated the population became increasingly rare. Famines cease to play a role in British demography: the coefficient of variation of the death rate (which measures the annual fluctuations in deaths due to mortality peaks) in England is 0.049 in the period 1756–1870, as opposed to 0.229 in Prussia in the same period and 0.101 in England in the period 1675–1755 (Galloway, 1988, p. 281). Even in the grim years of 1801, 1811/12 and 1816/17, when food prices peaked, there is little evidence of a serious mortality crisis.

Modern research has emphasized the importance of poor relief in providing a safety net to the rural poor for more lasting changes as their livelihood became increasingly precarious after 1790. The serious shocks imposed on Britain by war and bad weather compounded the long-term decline in cottage industries. In 1801, it was estimated, one-third of the population received some occasional relief (K. Williams, 1981, p. 38). That year, surely, was an exception, but in the 1820s and 1830s around 15 percent of the population of two villages in Bedfordshire benefited from one form of relief or another (S. Williams, 2005). As a result, the first third of the nineteenth century witnessed a sharp increase in spending on the poor, an increase that seems to have been unaffected by the end of inflation in 1815. In one village, for which continuous records exist, the increase between 1767 and 1833 was eleven-fold (S. Williams, 2005, p. 492).

The burden that the Poor Law imposed on the ratepayers was, of course, minuscule compared with the large expenses on war that served the interests of far fewer people. But by the 1830s the liberal turn that the British Enlightenment had taken had made people increasingly suspicious of any kind of state intervention in the decisions and choices of individuals. The impact that free market ideology had on the institutions of the state was to make the government increasingly stingy and to bring down government spending. While on the whole less government intervention was a policy that may have favored economic development and growing efficiency, the built-in paradox of modern economic growth is that as the British economy became more sophisticated and richer, the men in power and the ideologues behind them were beginning to realize the limitations of the free market. Getting rid of income redistribution policies while maintaining compassion toward the deserving poor and domestic peace turned out to be a harder task than anyone had imagined.

*   *   *

Britain in this age was a monetized economy. As a unit of account and a store of value, its monetary system functioned well. Eighteenth-century Britain had more or less abandoned silver as part of its monetary system, largely because Isaac Newton, in his capacity as master of the mint, had failed to erase the overvaluation of silver relative to gold. As a result, silver largely disappeared into hoards and overseas, a classic example of Gresham's Law, although worn coins of a shilling or sixpence remained in circulation. Britain was thus on a de facto gold standard long before this standard became universal in Europe after 1870 even though the pound sterling, oddly enough, was formally a silver unit. In periods of extreme foreign crisis, when the government had to spend large amounts of money overseas, adherence to the gold standard jeopardized the entire money supply, and in 1797 the British government had to break that link and suspend gold convertibility. For the next twenty-four years, the country's currency was only backed by the Bank of England's security. This, of course, permitted the system to create more money, and the net result was an inflation the like of which Britain had not witnessed since the sixteenth century, especially as it allowed banks once again to issue relatively small denomination notes (under £5). As soon as the French and Napoleonic Wars were over, however, monetary contraction took place, and by 1821 gold conversion could be resumed. The liberal economics that had come out of the eighteenth-century Enlightenment and that by now was dominant in Britain strove for a system that was believed to be self-regulating and automatic, much like a steam engine to which William Huskisson likened it (Hilton, 2006, p. 324). The financial crises of 1825 and 1837, however, raised doubts about the unfailing wisdom of such simplified approaches. At a deeper level, the growing severity of financial crises in the nineteenth century raised serious concerns about the wisdom of a deregulated laissez-faire economy. A reader in the twenty-first century may sympathize.

As in every advanced commercial society, some of the medium of exchange was internally manufactured by the financial system. One form of circulation in the eighteenth century was the inland bill of exchange, which, following legislation in 1698 and 1705, became "assignable" that is, payable to bearer, and thus basically could circulate like money among people willing to accept it. It became an important form of exchange for denominations of £20 and above. Banks printed notes which circulated as currency. These notes, however, did not alleviate the "big problem of small change"—for many transactions gold coins and banknotes were too large, and the small-denomination (copper) coins were scarce. Silver, as noted, had lost much of its role as a medium of circulation because it was overvalued. Complaints about the scarcity of low-denomination coins in eighteenth-century Britain were rampant, and many firms solved the problem by issuing their own tokens. One historian, L.S. Pressnell (1956, p. 15), has sighed that "the currency was in an unsatisfactory, even lamentable condition throughout the Industrial Revolution."

It may seem rather odd that what was otherwise a sophisticated commercial economy could not come up with a satisfactory solution to the issue of small coinage for many decades. What happened was that in 1696 Parliament ordered a recoinage of all silver coins (which had been subject to serious clipping and adulteration) and then essentially withdrew from issuing small change. Although small numbers of copper coins were minted in the eighteenth century, most of the circulation consisted of counterfeit coins that barely tried to mask their lack of authenticity, bearing legends such as "British Girl" instead of "Britannia." After 1775, the mint ceased to issue copper coins. By 1787, only 8 percent of all copper coins in circulation "had some tolerable resemblance to the 'King's coin' and most were adulterated (Sargent and Velde, 2002, p. 271). The scarcity of small change became a serious threat to the development of a monetized market economy, and not a few employers resorted to paying their workers in kind. They forced them to buy in company-stores (known as "the truck system") or paid them in company-issued "Tommy notes" simply because acceptable small change was not available (Selgin, 2008, pp. 25–29).

By that time, however, technology and the flexibility of British institutions came to the rescue. A large number of copper coins were minted in the 1780s in Holywell (in northern Wales) by a private enterprise named the Parys company owned by the ruthless but effective Welsh copper tycoon Thomas Williams. As Selgin notes, the mint officials were more than happy to let private industry mint its own small coins as long as they were left alone "to enjoy their sinecures" (ibid., p. 44). Large employers such as the ironmaster John Wilkinson, fed up with the inability of the mint to supply him with the means of exchange to pay his workers, had his own copper coins minted and issued them to his workers. These "Willeys" (named after Wilkinson's company) became a widely accepted means of exchange for relatively small transactions, *faute de mieux*. Matthew Boulton and James Watt converted their steam engines to make high-quality copper coins at a fast rate, and Birmingham, the center of the hardware industry, found itself issuing private low-denomination currency. By the end of the century private issuers had minted close to 600 tons of copper coins, worth over 100,000 guineas (Selgin, 2008. p. 124). Sargent and Velde note that "this system of reliable convertible token coins was the market's way of supplying small change" (2002, p. 271). In 1797, after the suspension of specie payments, the government ordered a large amount of copper coins to be minted at Boulton's Soho works. At the end of the Napoleonic wars, the government finally took over, making private coinage illegal in 1817, and making *de facto* convertible copper coinage a government monopoly (ibid., p. 303). Britain's institutions, after much stumbling, in the end figured out the solution that worked. Before that, the economy managed to make do, somehow. It was far from the best possible course, but at the end of the day it was good enough.

In the London area, the Bank of England enjoyed a formal monopoly, but in the countryside, bank notes issued by country banks circulated as currency. In terms of overall monetary development, it is clear that inside money (that is, money manufactured by the banking system) remained fairly small throughout the eighteenth century and that assertions that bills made up the bulk of the money supply simply do not stand up. Forrest Capie (2004, p. 224) has estimated that by 1750 the monetary base consisted of about £23 million, of which £18 million were coins and £4 million were Bank of England notes. With an overall money supply of about £30 million, he estimates, the proportion of inside money was still small. By 1790, the money supply had increased to £76 million, of which £44 million consisted of coin and another £12 million of Bank of England and other notes. These numbers are quite approximate and based on indirect calculations, but they should serve as a warning against the rather easy conclusion that monetary development was an essential precondition of industrialization.

Only in the nineteenth century did inside money become the dominant element. In 1870, coins formed about 18 percent of the total money supply, and the monetary base had increased from £56 million to £141 million. But since the overall money supply had increased by that time to £540 million, inside money constituted the overwhelming bulk of the money supply. Capie also computes what has been called "contract-intensive money"—essentially the kind of money that was accepted at mutual trust—and shows that its proportion relative to total money changed little in the eighteenth century but had tripled between 1790 and 1870. Banks before 1826 were constrained in size to have no more than six partners, and their contribution to financial development was accordingly limited.

The problems of the means of circulation were not resolved by the return to gold in 1821, and in some ways got worse in the next decades. The Bank of England was not a central bank the way the institution is today. During "panics" and "runs" on banks it did not originally see itself as the guarantor of monetary stability by lending money to banks in trouble. Yet it slowly assumed that function, almost willy-nilly. The result was a number of monetary crises, such as those of 1825, 1836–37, and 1847–48, during which banks were often the first to land in serious trouble by having to suspend payments and consequently the money supply contracted exactly at times when it should have expanded. It was a lesson that was learned slowly, and not before the end of the nineteenth century could it be said that Britain's monetary system was sound and the institutions regulating it effective in their task. Hence the role of government policy in bringing about economic growth in this area, too, is questionable to say the least.

CHAPTER 18

Living Standards and Inequality

Did the changes in the British economy actually make people living at the time better off? Naturally, all depends on who "people" were. But if we confine ourselves to the majority of working Britons (including men and women in all sectors), the picture turns out to be remarkably confused and the subject of a complex and at times acrimonious debate. Part of the reason is implicit in what was happening to the economy as a whole. The sectors affected by progress and productivity growth comprised at first a fairly small slice of the economy, so that their effect on the aggregate was perforce limited in the early stages. The most important insight in this debate is to realize that the history of living standards at this time is not the history of the Industrial Revolution. While technological change and industrialization by their very nature affected living standards, it was not the only phenomenon, and not even the most important, that determined how well people lived before 1850.

One factor affecting living standards was war. There were severe disruptions of international trade during the period 1756–1815, which roughly coincided with the Industrial Revolution. In this period peace years were outnumbered by war years by a ratio of almost two to one. The net effect of war on economic growth is not as clear as it may seem at first glance. After all, the aggregative measures we use for economic performance include government spending on the military, even though this spending arguably does not contribute materially to economic welfare as traditionally defined. By increasing spending that was only partially matched by higher taxes, the government exerted inflationary pressures on the economy. Keynesian theory suggests that if the economy had any slack resources, higher government spending would yield economic growth much as it did, for example, in the United States after the 1930s. Although some scholars (e.g., Anderson, 1974) have taken such a position, evidence that the British economy in the early 1790s was suffering from the kind of unemployment that could be alleviated by massive government spending is absent. Instead, the economy was subjected to considerable inflation, which seems to contradict the Keynesian supposition of "slack" resources. In any case, the disruptions in international trade, the sharp increase in marine insurance (due to the increase in privateering), and the loss of foreign markets and suppliers due to blockades and embargoes, compounded the effects of the harvest failures and in a few years, especially in 1800–01 and 1811–12, seriously threatened Britain with disaster.

Despite the fact that for the entire period in question no military action took place on British soil (some fighting took place in Ireland), wars disrupted international trade and caused the prices of necessities to increase. At the same time export industries were suffering as British goods were barred from European markets, leading to unemployment during inflationary periods. Credit crunches, triggered by political concerns, and higher taxes contributed to misery. In particular, the years between 1795 and 1812 had a number of severe crises (Mokyr and Savin, 1976; Crouzet, 1987). In view of these events, it was an achievement of British society that sharp increases in mortality were averted in these years. That achievement must be chalked up in part to the poor relief system, which, especially in crisis years, prevented the most vulnerable parts of society from dropping below subsistence level and served as a mechanism by which the more fortunate in British society supported the poor, even if they did not always pay their poor rates with enthusiasm.

An alternative view has it that increased government spending crowded out investment during the years of the French wars, and that this lower investment was in part responsible for the slowdown in during a critical period of the Industrial Revolution and thus might have slowed down the rise of living standards (Williamson, 1984). But it turns out that the evidence for such crowding out is mixed. Table 12.3 above shows that despite the surge in government spending, fixed domestic capital formation did not fall by a lot in those years, and that the extra resources needed to fight the French came from a decline in consumption and negative foreign investment (that is, a balance of payment deficit). A large part of the extra resources spent by His Majesty's government between 1793 and 1815 was raised from the newly imposed income tax and indirect taxes (especially excises and duties on such products as malt, tea, sugar, spirits, and tobacco). The resources used to fight the French thus came from reduced consumption due to lower disposable incomes, an increase in the savings of upper middle-class and rich people, and a tendency of foreign savers, especially Dutch ones, to buy British consols. Indeed, the wars of 1793–1815 were the only wars in this era in which most (58 percent) of the extra revenue raised to finance the war came from taxes. In the eighteenth century this had been around 20 percent (O'Brien, 1988, p. 4). Recalculation of the debt issues in those years indicates that a number of accounting and economic adjustments (including the fact that some of the resources used by Britain were paid for by foreigners) cut the total amount of crowding out from £293.6 million (1850 prices) to a figure between £70 million and £100 million (Mokyr, 1987). This is still a substantial amount (around 3.1 percent of annual national income), but not one that could not have been covered jointly by a rise in saving and borrowing from foreign nationals. The other test of crowding out is whether government borrowing drove up the cost of capital for other users. Such a rise is not observed for the years when the deficit was in fact the worst (Clark, 2001). It is possible, however, that crowding out was still taking place through credit rationing. Private banks reduced lending during the Napoleonic Wars, but it is not clear to what extent that affected the overall national level of investment (Temin and Voth, 2005).

There are reasons to believe that the external environment became more hostile at the time of the Industrial Revolution. Weather conditions turning worse after 1750, with summers getting colder and wetter, crop failures became more common. Arthur Young noted in 1790 that "no wet year in England was ever a great wheat one ... and no summer has ever been too dry for this grain" (cited by Jones, 1964, pp. 65–66). Small differences may have made a large impact: even if the temperatures declined on average by only one degree or rainfall increased by 10–20 millimeters, such changes could have a serious impact. Between the years 1700–50 and 1750–1800 annual temperature averages fell from 9.26° C to 9.06° C and winter temperatures from 3.71° to 3.36°, but these averages mask considerable variation. The 1730s and 1780s were unusually cold decades, and some years stand out as particularly difficult. Rainfall data only go back to 1766, but in the long run, they show little change. Again, however, some medium-term fluctuations may have been important to the economy. The summers of the 1830s were substantially more rainy than those in the 1810s and 1840s. The average summer rainfall in 1830–39 was 256 millimeters compared to 230 millimeters for the entire period 1800–50 (Jones and Hulme, 1997). But it remains to be seen whether we can attribute a great deal of significance to this in explaining the failure of living standards to rise after 1815. Overall rainfall 1800–49 was not much different than for 1766–99, and summer rainfall was substantially lower in the later period. High prices of corn and bread could still cause serious misery, as happened in the disastrous year of 1816 when the effects of the explosion of a volcano on the Indonesian island of Tamboro were felt throughout Europe. After 1817, very expensive years were rare until the mid-1840s when, again, bad weather and a potato blight disrupted life and caused a cataclysm in Ireland. Whether the epidemiological environment worsened considerably in the early nineteenth century, as claimed by some (e.g. Voth and Leunig, 1996), is also still being debated, but urbanization by itself, plus some diseases associated with urban sanitation and air pollution (cholera being the main novelty on this front, though typhus and typhoid fever, too, assumed epidemic proportions in this period), may have been enough to affect biological measures negatively.

The weather thus remained a factor in the cost of living and thus material conditions. If we accept real wages as one proxy for living standards, it is striking how little movement there is in the numerator relative to the denominator. In other words, nominal wages changed little, and real wages were dominated by changes in the cost of living. Although harvest failures affected directly only that part of national income produced on the land, it is easy to see how high food prices would affect nominal wages, and thus reduce the profitability of manufacturing and services. Moreover, many agricultural products, from the barley used to brew beer to the oats fed to draft horses to the leather used in the shoe industry, were direct inputs in other sectors. Harvest failures, in short, affected the entire economy in a fashion comparable, say, to the way a sudden oil shortage affects a modern economy.

In view of the serious supply shocks to which war and weather exposed the British economy, it must be deemed remarkable that living standards did not decline during the critical years of the Industrial Revolution. It is hard to know to what extent this achievement can be attributed to the events we normally associate with the Industrial Revolution in its strict sense, as opposed to other phenomena such as the continued growth of internal trade and specialization. In any event, while the economy did go through a number of crises, by 1820 it had not lost much of its momentum, and during the next four decades growth picked up. Yet till the middle of the nineteenth century the rate of growth remained slow by our standards.

∗   ∗   ∗

The Enlightenment view of the economy was that it could be improved and that material life would get better if radical changes were made in the way institutions were set up and useful knowledge was utilized. The exact nature of these changes, of course, was in dispute, but there was remarkably little disagreement on the principles of progress itself. The great historical irony is that before 1850 living standards in Britain improved at a rate that can only be deemed disappointing by a historian writing in the twenty-first century. It would be too strong to state that the quality of material life in 1850 was still at the same level it had been in 1700. But the hopes that useful knowledge, investment, and hard work would raise the living standards of most people including the very poor did not materialize before 1850. A long and contentious debate has emerged in the second half of the twentieth century between so-called pessimists who maintained that the Industrial Revolution was a period in which living standards improved very little if at all, and the optimists who argued that before 1850 improvement was quite noticeable, especially after 1815. Others (e.g., Mokyr, 1988; Feinstein, 1998a) have argued that the rise in living standards before 1850 was modest and that improvements for most of the British working class were slow and late.

The long debate has been indecisive because the data are hard to interpret and because it is not even clear what the correct data should be. In the long run, economics teaches us, comparing living standards between different periods is difficult because there is no good way of measuring real income or spending when the composition of the basket of goods on which the income is spent is changing. Comparisons are even harder when the quality of goods is improving, especially when they can be made of a quality and variety previously unattainable. Moreover, many entirely new products appeared on the markets: the era of the Industrial Revolution witnessed the advent of steel pens (instead of quills), of smallpox vaccination, of canned foods (admittedly not of great culinary quality), gaslight, and the telegraph. Many of these novelties were relatively minor, but their cumulative impact on economic welfare was large. Consider, for instance, the discovery of carbonated water by the chemist Joseph Priestley in 1767. The new product was snapped up in large quantities not only because it tasted better, but because it was widely believed at the time that fizzy substances somehow counteracted putrefaction, thought to be a main cause of disease. The new invention was a huge success, even if it was a more acquisitive entrepreneur and not Priestley who got rich thanks to the new product. Other most dramatic examples of product innovation were in medicine, such as the introduction of anesthesia in surgery in the late 1840s. How much would people have been willing to pay for such novelties at an earlier time? New products that have no comparable earlier counterparts make the correct estimation of the growth of living standards very difficult indeed. Yet because the quality of goods was improving the bias was all in one direction, meaning that the rise in the standard of living was higher than real wage data or real consumption data indicate. The same was true for the seventeenth century with the introduction of tea, coffee, and tobacco into the baskets of Britons (Hersch and Voth, 2009). The growth in choice and variety were as much an improvement in economic welfare as falling prices and growing consumption.

There are also difficult issues of distribution: whose living standards are being compared? There were substantial shifts in the distribution of income. Geographically, some regions gained in terms of income, others were impoverished due to the decline in some traditional industries and the failure of potatoes in the late 1840s. By class and occupation, too, some groups gained, others did not. Adding everything up and looking at the overall experience is not easy, nor does it necessarily tell us what we want to know. There is an even harder problem of intertemporal distribution. Even if the pessimist case holds true on average for living standards before 1850, should we therefore assess the Industrial Revolution as a failure? After all, the rapid and undisputed improvement that characterized the British economy after the mid-nineteenth century would not have taken place had there been no Industrial Revolution. How do we compare the welfare of those who were born after 1840, say, with those born at an earlier date?

Subject to such warnings, there is a large and rich literature that is concerned with living standards during this period and has tried to measure them in a variety of ways. Of course, among economists conventional quantitative measures such as real GDP per capita, consumption per capita, and real wages have been popular, but all have their pitfalls. A rise in real national income or consumption per capita, as presented in tables 12.1 and 12.3 above, is subject to the standard measurement problems of this variable: how is it distributed, and how sensitive is it to the way income and consumption are measured? Looking at rises in real wages may seem to be a better approach to the living standards of the working class (that is, the vast majority of Britons), but there are statistical pitfalls here too: what to do about changes in hours, working conditions, participation rates, and unemployment, to name but four of the more obvious problem areas. Hence economists have looked at a second set of indicators, the changes in consumption of certain goods that seem somehow representative of what the majority might have wanted: housing, bread, other sources of food, sugar, tobacco, tea, beer, and so on. Presumably, even if we cannot quite measure income, but can verify that people were able to purchase more goods, this will indicate changes in living standards. Here, too, there are many pitfalls, not least of which are changing relative prices and product qualities, as well as the need to incorporate into any measure of economic welfare the physical conditions and changing disamenities at the workplace and residential areas. A third approach looks at the "output" of consumption. We cannot readily measure "utility" or "happiness" for this (or any) period, but certain physical features of the population such as mortality, morbidity, and height have been recognized as capturing at least some aspects of the standard of living. As research in recent years has increased our knowledge of these variables, economic historians have been able to enlarge their bag of tools to assess what happened to the material conditions of the majority of Britons.

It bears emphasizing that changes in technology, the main engine affecting living standards in the twentieth century, was as yet a second-order factor in the economic welfare of the masses. It was a promissory note, an inkling of what was possible, but the bulk of changes in daily life that technology wrought had to wait for the second half of the nineteenth century and beyond. Most of the advances in the first Industrial Revolution had been in the area of capital goods, not final outputs. There were important exceptions to this statement. Cotton goods had become widely available, at low prices and in many colors and fabrics. By 1850, even poor people could travel rapidly and cheaply by train. Streets and public places, if not the homes of the working classes, were lit by gas. Paper, glass, leather, pottery, and candles had become both cheaper and of better quality. Goods that used to be regarded as luxuries, to be enjoyed only by the rich and mighty, became available to larger numbers of consumers. Some altogether new consumer goods became available, although compared to the torrent of such innovations in our own age, they look marginal. Finally, population growth did not have much of a discernible downward effect on living standards, much to the relief of contemporaries. All in all, not a bad record, but perhaps not what the optimists had been hoping for.

Perhaps the most striking changes in the standard of living were associated with urbanization. In cities, to be sure, wages were higher, but the quality of life was in some measurable ways lower. Mortality rates were higher, as we saw in chapter 13. Life expectancy at birth could be around 25–27 in major industrial cities such as Manchester and Glasgow, which meant that life in these cities was no less than fifteen years shorter than the national average (and thus perhaps twenty years shorter than in the rural countryside). These data are confirmed by more recent research (Huck, 1995). In the cities goods that had been free in the countryside (such as clean water) had to be paid for. Housing in cities, as contemporaries pointed out, was poor and expensive for many decades as cities were unable to cope with rapid population growth. The same was true for food. This was the very steep price that hundreds of thousands paid in order to escape what Marx and Engels in their most condescending mood called "the idiocy of rural life." Yet were these infamous Dickensian conditions representative of urban life in Britain in this period?

The changes in manufacturing and the rise of the industrial factory or mill were to have an even deeper and more far-reaching economic consequence: the creation of a large class of urban wage-laborers sometimes known as the industrial proletariat. Wage labor was neither wholly new in 1750 nor confined to the manufacturing sector in Britain, but its growth, at the expense of self-employed domestic workers, remains one of the defining features of the age. The Industrial Revolution was responsible for the unprecedented growth of the new industrial towns, of which Manchester and Glasgow were the best examples. Even non-Marxist historians will agree that the creation of an industrial and urban wage-labor class, whether one uses the term "proletariat" or not, was a determining factor in the formation of Victorian society. The emergence of an urban working class was described with alarming detail in the writings of contemporaries. Of those, Friedrich Engels' famous book *The Condition of the Working Class in England in 1844* has received the most fame or notoriety, but his descriptions are consistent with (and to some extent derived from) those of other contemporary observers of life in the new industrial towns, such as Peter Gaskell, William Alison, and James Kay-Shuttleworth. The conditions described by these authors were no doubt horrendous, but the dimensions of the problem should be kept in perspective. The particular urban environments they described can hardly be regarded as representative of industrial Britain, much less of the British working class in general. For the urban sector as a whole, including not only the new urban centers but also port cities and less environmentally impacted towns, death rates show much more modest trends and may well have stabilized in the pre-1850 years (Williamson, 1990, p. 259).

All the same, the astonishing growth of the urban sector in the years of the Industrial Revolution resulted in social and economic problems not unlike the hardships imposed in our own time on the huge and rapidly growing urban conglomerates of third world countries such as Mexico City or Manila. The problem was that urban infrastructure, such as housing, water, and sanitation, were inflexible in the short run and expensive to expand. "Coping with City Growth" (Williamson, 1990) became one of the central problems of the Industrial Revolution. Once again, it began to dawn on most contemporary observers that some difficulties might not be solved by the free market and that direct intervention by the authorities, whether in London or local, would be necessary to avert disasters. Cities underinvested in their infrastructure and the "urban disamenities" in many of the new urban centers became more than a nuisance, they became serious social and public health problems. The onslaught of cholera in Britain in 1830 and 1831 accentuated the health problems that the new urban areas brought along. The public health consequences of the urbanization movement during the Industrial Revolution led to a growing sense that something was fundamentally rotten in the new society that the factories were building. No document laid this fact out more clearly than Edwin Chadwick's justly celebrated *Report on the Sanitary Condition of the Labouring Population of Great Britain*, published in 1842. In it, the plight of the newly created urban laborers was described in great detail. Chadwick, a loyal follower and friend of Jeremy Bentham, though no ideologue, described the conditions he saw in terms that would do Friedrich Engels proud: "The familiarity with the sickness and death constantly present in the crowded and unwholesome districts, appears to re-act as another concurrent cause in aggravation of the wretchedness and vice in which they are plunged. Seeing the apparent uncertainty of the morrow, the inhabitants really take no heed of it, and abandon themselves with the recklessness and avidity of common soldiers in a war to whatever gross enjoyment comes within their reach" ([1843], 1965, p. 198).

Yet despite the urban penalty, people went. Between 1700 and 1750, the proportion of people living in cities with over 5,000 inhabitants increased from 17 to 21 percent, then to 28 percent in 1800 and to 45 percent in 1850 (Wrigley, 1987, p. 162; Bairoch, 1988, p. 221). By 1850 Britain had surpassed the Netherlands as the most urbanized country in Europe. This creates a logical dilemma. If the living conditions of the working class in industrial centers were as execrable as all that, how do we explain the continued migration to towns? The answer has three components. The first is that cities lured those segments of the population who were attracted to the relatively high urban wages even if these were in large part compensation for the urban disamenities, because preferences were heterogeneous and some people were less concerned with these amenities, and more with income, than others who stayed behind. Second, migration to the cities had, as Michael Todaro and others have argued, a lottery component to it. Some of the new urban dwellers did land good factory jobs and ended up doing well, whereas others suffered bouts of unemployment or ended up as part of a semi-employed lumpenproletariat. Some people were willing to take that risk, either because they optimistically overestimated their own ability to beat the odds, or because they were not very risk-averse. Finally, it is possible that many immigrants were for-ward-looking. If in the short run life in the cities might be bad, the long-run prospects in the countryside (or in Ireland, whence many of the new urban dwellers came) were looking even bleaker. While urban employment may have been risky, rural prospects were perceived to be little better for the unskilled poor. Williamson has shown that migrants to cities—the Irish excepted—did not have a very different experience from non-migrants, and that, some slumps aside, "British cities absorbed the flood of immigrants with considerable ease" (1990, p. 123).

The Industrial Revolution and the rise of the factory did not simply mean an improvement in technology, which just made the same processes more pro-ductive. Most of the goods that were being made cheaper and better in factories had previously been made by people in their homes or in small workshops. On average, there is not much evidence that factories created technological unemployment and their effect on the demand for labor was not to create large "armies" of the unemployed, though this had been widely feared (Berg, 1980). But for the handloom weavers and the domestic straw plaiters, the spinners and small-time ironmongers, the competition of the factory meant that there was less and less need for them in the countryside, and they (or more often, their children) went to the cities simply because that is where the jobs were. They either worked in the factories or catered to those who did. The downfall of the domestic system was deeply traumatic for those whose skills and tools had been made obsolete by the machines, and who had to live in crowded urban tenements, and such trauma must become part of the welfare calculus of the Industrial Revolution.

Real wage statistics of the time must be treated with caution as proxies for living standards. There are two reasons for this caveat. The first one is quite obvious. Work in the "modern sector" was often unpleasant in many dimensions in ways that work at home had not been. Some occupations, such as those of collier and puddler, were physically downright dangerous and onerous. In others, the workplace was noisy, dusty, smelly, drafty, and filled with strangers, and the work was often monotonous and routine. The factory required workers who were willing to submit to discipline and in many cases workers had to commute (that is, walk) to and from the workplace, an effort for which they were not paid directly. Economic analysis suggests that for all those reasons these workers should be paid higher wages, known as compensating differentials or disamenities premiums, necessary to attract workers to employments regarded as unpleasant. Economic historians have estimated these premiums and found them to be on the whole between 15 and 30 percent of the wage (Brown, 1990; Williamson, 1990). The significance of this finding is two-fold. First, it means that the argu-ment of the so-called pessimist school that poorer working conditions were an important part of laboring life during the Industrial Revolution is correct, but that the optimists were right in noting that workers were compensated for these conditions in terms of higher wages. Second, however, this also means that the observed higher wages in factory towns cannot be taken as prima facie evidence for better living standards, since the "raise" that workers received only compensated them for disamenities and did not really improve their welfare.

The second reason why structural changes in the economy affect the interpretation of real wage data is slightly more subtle. In an economy in which such a transition occurs on a large scale, labor markets are out of equilibrium, and the economist's assumption, based on competitive market analysis, that when you have seen one wage you have seen them all may not hold true. Workers in the domestic sector, especially handloom weavers, rarely "earned" a wage; instead, they either were small-time independent operators, or they worked for a merchant-entrepreneur, who paid them by the piece. Either way, wage data from the domestic sector are rare and unreliable. Because the labor market was not in equilibrium, it is hazardous to infer what these people earned from what employees in factories or in the construction industry earned. While factory wages were rising after 1815, the real income of most domestic workers and independent artisans were falling (Allen, 1992, pp. 255–56; 296–97; Lyons, 1989). This discrepancy constituted the market "signal" that the death bell was sounding for much of the domestic sector. For our present purpose it means that using formal wages as a proxy for all "labor income" may be quite misleading. Real wage data were upward biased because they did not fully reflect the declining earnings of this sector. Huberman (1996, pp. 154–55) has argued similarly that the labor markets in much of industrialized Britain were "dual" and that wage determination in the "primary" large textile mills was quite different from that in smaller firms. Excess supply of labor in the "secondary" firms did not necessarily bring down wages in the large mills, and thus the assumption that even within the formal labor markets wages moved in tandem may need to be revised.

Furthermore, what mattered for material living standards was total earnings, not hourly or daily wage rates as such. Increasing dependence on male earnings in the 1830s and 1840s meant that family income may not have risen as fast as male wages, since the share of women and children in household earnings declined after 1815 or 1820, as can be inferred from the difference between household earnings and male earnings in table 18.1-b. The interpretation of this finding is not simple, since there is no easy way of disentangling supply from demand factors. It is possible that as male earnings rose, the income effect led to declining participation of other family workers in the labor force, thus reflecting rising living standards. But if it reflected declining demand for the labor of children and women, leading to involuntary unemployment (or falling wages), this would point in the opposite direction. Given the modest rise in male wages, the demand story seems the more plausible, at least before 1850. Finally, real wage data may be biased by the fact that eighteenth-century employers preferred to pay some of the wage in kind (in part because of the coinage shortage), whereas in the nineteenth century this custom declined. Thus part of the measured wage increases could be spurious.

Even so, real wages, as well as they can be measured, show a complicated trend. Table 18.1 (both parts) illustrates some of the dilemmas. Should we adjust for unemployment or not, should we measure wages for Britain or for the United Kingdom (inclusive of Ireland)? What the figures computed by Feinstein show is that nominal wages did keep up with inflation during the difficult years of the French and Napoleonic Wars. Even adjusting for unemployment, which reduces these wages somewhat, real wages keep pace. The striking fact is, however, that in the three decades after 1815, when the Industrial Revolution spread from a local phenomenon confined to a few industries to large segments of the production economy, real wages rose. Three facts stand out: first, all series presented in table 18.1 agree that there was little improvement before 1815 but *some* improvement between 1815 and 1850 but that there still is debate on the extent. Second, throughout this period, the real wage index was strongly affected by fluctuations in the cost of living. The year 1851, for instance, was an exceptionally abundant year, the cheapest year of the century. The high real wage attained in that year was not permanently achieved till the mid-1860s. Clark's cost of living index registers sharper falls in prices after 1815; adjusting for it means a faster rise in real wages. Third, accounting for the differences in male vs. family earnings, unemployment, and the fact that the economy formally included Ireland tends to temper optimism.

What about consumption? During much of the eighteenth century, there is strong if not very systematic evidence of rising levels of consumption, at least among the "middling sort," whose numbers were swelling (De Vries, 2008). By 1750 consumption of many luxury goods, such as chinaware, upholstered furniture, and mirrors was no longer confined to the rich, and it extended to greater and greater segments of the population. What was true for goods was equally the case for services. Local studies show an increase in the number of practicing lawyers, doctors, and teachers during the eighteenth century (e.g., Smail, 1994, pp. 93–113). This kind of consumption, in part, should be regarded as the kind of costly signaling device by which people who felt that they belonged to the "middling sort" indicated that they were entitled to the social esteem and trust of other members of this class, with whom they might want to deal economically and socially. In the eighteenth century, working class consumption seems to have increased, in part as a result of having more members of the household work, and having them work longer hours (De Vries) and in part because the composition of the labor force was shifting from low-wage agriculture into higher wage manufacturing and service jobs (Wrigley, 2009, p. 116). What is striking, however, is that the increase in consumption of the working classes seems to have slowed down and then come to a stop during the Industrial Revolution and the difficult

Table 18.1-a: Estimates of real wages and real earnings, 1770–1852, Great Britain and United Kingdom, 1778/82 = 100

Period	Wage rates (full employment real earnings, Great Britain)	Adjusted for unemployment (Great Britain)	Adjusted for unemployment (United Kingdom)
1770–72	95	96	97
1773–77	95	96	96
1778–82	100	100	100
1783–87	101	102	101
1788–92	106	106	105
1793–97	109	108	105
1798–1802	103	103	99
1803–07	115	114	109
1808–12	104	103	98
1813–17	105	102	97
1818–22	111	108	102
1823–27	113	111	104
1828–32	114	111	104
1833–37	124	121	113
1838–42	118	114	107
1842–47	126	124	118
1847–52	137	133	129

Table 18.1-b: Real wages and earnings, Great Britain, 1700–1850

Period	Clark: Crafts-men's real wages (1860s = 100)	Clark:: helper's real wages (1860s = 100)	Feinstein: real wages, Great Britain (1778/82 =100)	Horrell and Humphries: real earnings, males only, deflated by Feinstein's COL index (1790/99 = 100)	Horrell and Humphries: real earnings, males only, deflated by Clark's COL index (1790/99 = 100)	Horrell and Humphries: real earnings, households, deflated by Feinstein's COL index (1790/99 = 100)	Horrell and Humphries: real earnings, households, deflated by Clark's COL index (1790/99 = 100)
1700–09	54.2	51.8					
1710–19	54.1	50.8					
1720–29	55.8	52.8					
1730–39	61.1	57.7					
1740–49	61.4	57.4					
1750–59	57.8	56.4					
1760–69	56.8	56.8					
1770–79	54.1	56.1	96.2				
1780–89	55.2	55.2	101.5				
1790–99	55.0	56.0	108.9	100	100	100	100
1800–09	54.3	55.2	108.0	n.a.	n.a.	n.a.	n.a.
1810–19	60.1	62.5	103.7	79.2[a]	75.0[a]	84.5[a]	79.9[a]
1820–29	68.9	67.7	113.5	n.a.	n.a.	n.a.	n.a.
1830–39	78.4	78.5	119.5	110.0	105.6	128.3	123.0
1840–49	82.7	84.9	125.4	128.4	136.3	114.5	121.7

a 1816-20 only.

Sources: Feinstein (1998a, pp. 652–53); Clark (2005, pp. 1324–25); Horrell and Humphries (1992, pp. 868–69).

years during and following the French Wars, while the consumption of middle-class families experienced continuous and substantial improvements (Horrell, 1996).

Most other indicators, even though they may reflect different definitions of what we mean by standard of living and different methodologies, concur with this trend. It has become part of the consensus that the average amount of food consumed in Britain during the Industrial Revolution did not increase until the later 1840s (Helling, 1977; Clark, Huberman, and Lindert, 1995). The odd part is that the most recent research (Fogel, Floud, and Harris, n.d., forthcoming) has calculated that in the eighteenth century food supplies available to the average person in England and Wales increased by 12 percent from 2,445 cals./day to 2,740 cals/day (see also Fogel, 2004, p. 9 for similar numbers). Half of this was due to an increase in imports, and most of the rest due to an increase in the growing of potatoes (which remained, however, a small component of the diet, supplying fewer than 6 percent of daily calories). During the fifty years when the Industrial Revolution should have had an effect, 1800–1850, food supplies were totally flat (Fogel, Floud, and Harris, n.d., table 6, p. 35).

The so-called "food-puzzle," as Clark, Huberman, and Lindert (1995) call it, that is, the question of why the average food intake in Britain did not increase in the first half of the nineteenth century, is in reality no puzzle at all. In Feinstein's (1998a, p. 652) view, real wages did not increase much in the first half of the nineteenth century, and hence there was no increased purchasing power that the workers could have spent on food. Moreover, the relative price of food products rose through much of the period 1760–1815, and it seems therefore reasonable that food consumption did not increase in that period, although the failure of food consumption to rise significantly after 1815 does indicate that price elasticities were low. In the same period the consumption of some manufacturing products such as cotton textiles, whose prices declined sharply, rose. The lack of data on exactly how much food was consumed makes this conclusion inevitably tentative. The consumption of the few other items on which we have good year-to-year information such as sugar, tea, and tobacco, however, almost perfectly mirrors Feinstein's real wage data. The advantage of examining these products is precisely that they were mass-consumed, but for the vast bulk of the population had not reached the saturation point they must have reached for the very wealthy. Hence consumption was sensitive to income, and in the absence of income data, we can look at these consumption series and infer incomes (Mokyr, 1988). These "synthetic" income estimates show rather stationary behavior until the mid-1840s, after which they start rising. To be sure, some commodities fell in price and thus were made more available to members of the working class but the income effect from these supply shifts was not sufficient to affect the major items on which the quality of life depended. To phrase it differently: if real wages were rising for the working class as a whole, why were they not spending them on goods which they demonstrably desired?

Given the contentious nature of the standard of living debate, it is helpful to get as many independent sources of information as possible to corroborate the hypotheses. In recent decades, research has focused on an alternative approach to the standard-of-living problem, namely to look at biological indicators of economic welfare in addition to purely economic ones. It has long been recognized that indicators such as life expectancy and physical health are strongly correlated with economic living standards. Indeed, some economists (notably Sen, 1987) maintain that such physical measures are the standard of living. Thus in the absence of unambiguous economic measures of living standards, economic historians have increasingly turned to biological measures to try to test the hypothesis of rising economic welfare before 1850. On the whole, these measures are consistent with the finding that there was little improvement before the middle of the nineteenth century. The broadest such measure is the crude mortality rate. In about 1760, the crude death rate for England was still about 27.5 per thousand, declining steadily (with a few reversals) to about 22.5 per thousand by 1850. Gross mortality rates, however, are flawed indicators for many reasons, primarily because of their sensitivity to the age structure of the population. A better measure is life expectancy at birth. This variable, as we have seen in chapter 13, shows some improvement over the eighteenth century but its rise stops in 1820, and then remains essentially static at about 40 years until 1860 (Wrigley and Schofield, 1981, p. 529). Data on infant mortality tell very much the same story. In a sample of seven parishes, Huck (1994) finds rising infant mortality rates in the period between 1813 and 1836, with no appreciable decline until 1845. More recent data reported by the Cambridge Group, based on family reconstitution and thus more representative of England as a whole, show infant mortality rates that declined sharply in the last two decades of the eighteenth century, but then rose slightly until 1837 (Wrigley and Schofield, 1997, p. 215).

A biological indicator that has enjoyed considerable interest in recent years is human height. Anthropometric evidence has become accepted as a measure of living standards, because adult height is a function of net nutritional status during childhood and adolescence, that is, the amount of food taken in by young people net of demands made on their bodies by labor and diseases (Steckel, 2008). All other things equal, a child born in a family that enjoyed a higher standard of living would grow up to be taller. The idea that observed height data could therefore be used to approximate the elusive standard of living was proposed by Fogel (1983) and his associates, and has since then stimulated a large number of research projects. The research that is most pertinent to the standard-of-living debate in Britain is Floud, Wachter, and Gregory (1990) and Komlos (1997). Their finding is that net nutritional status, as measured by stature, increased between about 1760 and 1820 and then went into a secular decline for half a century, reflecting more or less what we know about food consumption. Indeed, the cohorts born in 1850–54 are shorter than any cohort born in the nineteenth century, and the levels attained in the first decades of the century are not attained again before the last decade (Floud, Wachter, and Gregory, 1990, ch. 4, *passim*). Although the temporal pattern measured by Floud et al. differs a bit from that measured by Komlos, both concur that by 1850 men were shorter than they had been in 1760. Based on this evidence, they maintain, the debate on living standards during the second and third quarters of the nineteenth century is still very much open, and "if there were significant gains in real incomes for the working class between the 1820s and the 1850s they were bought at a very high price" (ibid., p. 305). John Komlos, whose figures are even more pessimistic than those of Floud et al., has been led to regard the height data as a major "puzzle" in economic history. His computations were recently confirmed by Cinnirella (2008). In other words, if there were economic gains, why did they not lead to physical improvements in the lives of English men and women?

The use of demographic and anthropometric information to cast light on the standard-of-living controversy brings with it its own package of problems and doubts. An individual's potential height is determined in part by his or her genetic heritage (which we can assume did not change much, on average, over time), and the environment which determines how much of the body's potential for growth is realized. The majority of people in the past, it is now realized, did not grow to their full biological maximum potential height. This is in part because during childhood and adolescence bodies were ravaged by diseases that caused some measure of stunting. In part, inadequate or unbalanced nutrition and environmental conditions (such as poor home heating in winter) contributed to the stunting. Separating nutrition from disease is difficult, because the interaction of the two is quite strong.

The environment determining final height was influenced by economic well-being but not identical to it. Cultural and social changes not necessarily correlated with income variables played important roles as well. An example is breast-feeding: children who are breast-fed are consistently healthier and grow up to be taller than children who are not. Diseases tended to take their toll on children if they survived; a decline in child morbidity due to some autonomous change in the disease environment will affect health and height. Vaccination against smallpox was the most important change in the disease environment of the period, but other factors, such as the sudden appearance of cholera in European towns in the late 1820s, can also be mentioned here (Voth and Leunig, 1996). The disappearance of smallpox accounted for a significant gain in height. Should we therefore revise our estimates of the rise in living standards even further down? While not attributable to economic growth per se, the breakthrough in smallpox at the end of the eighteenth century was very much part of the Medical Enlightenment, and therefore part and parcel of knowledge-propagated social progress. In that sense, one might regard it as a key outcome of the age of progress, and not a random shock. Contradictions thus abound in using this measure. Irish lads were taller than British lads, even though Ireland by most measures was poorer than Britain (Mokyr and Ó Gráda, 1988, 1996). Urban lads were consistently shorter than rural ones, and thus the migration movement to the city by itself must have depressed this measure (Steckel, 1995; Mokyr and Ó Gráda, 1996). Better nutrition (in terms of health, not necessarily in terms of variety and pleasure) outweighed the other forms of lower living standards in Ireland or in the British countryside. The shorter men from London were on the whole not so much poorer but just consumed *different* baskets than their taller rural counterparts. This perverse correlation indicates that richer people were not necessarily healthier. If they spent the additional resources they controlled on health-reducing items such as tobacco and excessive alcohol consumption, higher incomes may have led to lower health. In the nineteenth-century British Isles, the poorest ate potatoes, the middling people ate coarse bread, while only the better-off ate fine white bread made from finely ground (and often bleached and adulterated) wheat flour. In terms of nutrients, the quality ordering may well have been reversed, with potatoes being a wholesome and nutritious food, whereas the white bread was often adulterated with toxic substances such as alum.

To confound the picture further, almost all of the data on heights come from recruits to the British military or the East India Company army, and it seems likely that these samples, however large, underrepresented the better-off classes. If the degree to which this was true was increasing over time, the observed decline in heights may well be spurious. Unlike infant mortality, which is another indicator of living standards, height was not desirable for its own sake; it is only useful as an indicator or correlate of other variables we would really like to observe. Yet it reflects living standards in a matter that is distorted, error-ridden, and subject to a time lag of unknown and variable length. All the same, had the heights data shown that British lads were getting considerably taller in this period, the inference could have been made that something had gotten substantially better in this economy—as happened throughout the Western world in the twentieth century. Yet quite unequivocally, this did not happen before 1850.

How, then, to reconcile the stagnant living standards with so much evidence of dynamism and progress in the British economy after 1750? Part of the answer is that the historiography of the Industrial Revolution, focusing on the dynamic aspects of the British economy, has tended to gloss over stagnant sectors in which little technological progress was taking place. The false impression thus created is of an entire economy in flux and rapid advance, producing an expectation for living standards to improve sooner than later. Coal mining and construction, to use just two examples, still accounted for significant segments of the economy, yet the techniques in use—with some exceptions—were not dramatically different in 1850 from those used in 1700. As late as 1850 most Britons were still working in sectors in which productivity advance had been slow or non-existent, and the economy-wide real wage could not but reflect that. Second, as we have seen, population had grown enormously between 1750 and 1850, and the number of mouths to be fed threatened to outstrip the capability of the economy to supply them with necessities. The rise in the dependency ratio compounded this effect. Rising relative food prices did not mean that people went hungry. As Komlos (1998, p. 785) notes, such price movements often induced consumers to switch from protein foods to cheaper starchy foods. In the long run, such switches may have affected their immune systems and health. It is perhaps an exaggeration to say that "the European diet became essentially vegetarian" (ibid.), but as Clark, Huberman, and Lindert (1995, p. 223) suggest, meat consumption per capita certainly did not increase. Urbanization complicated matters: dairy products and eggs, staples of the farm diet, were hard to transport and subject to spoilage, and hence considerably costlier in cities. Fruit and vegetables, too, cost more in cities than their farm-gate price. Yet at the same time the growing demand of cities for protein-rich foods made it costlier for farmers to consume them, and so for a while, diets deteriorated all around as a result of the combination of population growth and urbanization.

The biological variables, moreover, reflected other changes, above all urbanization. One of the notable arithmetical truths about the period of the Industrial Revolution is that it is quite possible (if not certain) that biological living standards in *both* urban and rural areas rose and yet average living standards declined. This can happen if urban living conditions are significantly worse than rural ones, and the proportion of people living in cities is rising because of migration from the countryside to the towns. It seems likely that the biological measures of living standards were especially sensitive to urbanization. While urban areas may have offered some positive amenities (such as entertainment and more choice in shopping), healthy living conditions were surely not among them. The most observant contemporaries knew this well. Chadwick, ([1843], 1965, p. 423) submitted that cities tended to breed a "younger population ... under noxious agencies, [that] is inferior in physical organization and general health ... [and] producing an adult population that was short-lived and ... intemperate." Indeed, contemporaries commented on how short urban lads tended to be (ibid., pp. 247, 251).

A plausible interpretation of the history of living standards in Britain before 1850 is that technological progress, income distribution, and population growth pulled in opposite directions. Before 1850 or so they more or less seem to have neutralized one another: living standards did not collapse under the weight of population growth as the pessimists had predicted, nor did they take off after 1815 with industrialization, as the meliorist school has suggested. In addition to these two long-term trends, the standard of living was affected by medium- and short-term factors such as wars and weather. Resolving the issue is further complicated by the finding that even in the United States these trends in height and consumption seem to have obtained, yet it is hard to think of the United States as an economy in which population pressure on the land would strongly affect living standards.

The economic history of the standard of living in Britain is thus full of contradictions. The biggest contradiction of all, without any question, was the contrast between what happened in Britain and what happened in Ireland. In a sophisticated and industrialized nation, which has considerable capital and reserves, and which can use them to purchase food on the world market during a major shortfall, harvest failures will normally not cause many actual additional deaths, even if they have other bad economic consequences such as unemployment. The Irish potato famine, which killed about 1.1 million people who would not have died otherwise and left the country in a state of devastation not witnessed in Western Europe since the seventeenth century, is therefore a sore and difficult point in the history of the British standard of living (Mokyr, 1985; Ó Gráda, 1999). If we count Ireland as part and parcel of the British economy—as legally and formally it was—our conclusions about ambiguity in living standards need to be revised, since the century before 1845 was punctuated by a colossal disaster in living standards. Even if the Great Famine lasted only five years, it was in many ways the defining moment in nineteenth-century Irish history. The historiography of the British economy of this age has declined to confront this matter, therefore implicitly admitting that Ireland was really a different society, a separate economy, where economic development and living standards followed very different patterns.

T.S. Ashton (1948, p. 111), in a famous paragraph, used the example of Ireland as a warning against what could happen without industrialization, but clearly there are no simple lessons to be learned from the Irish example. In fact, average living standards in pre-famine Ireland did not decline much, even if there was a sharpening in the distribution of income (Mokyr and Ó Gráda, 1988). The Great Famine might well have been much mitigated, if not averted, had Ireland developed more of a modern sector and diversified its economy. The example of Scotland, in which the industrialized south was able to prevent mass starvation in the famine-stricken Highlands, comes to mind. Had the potato blight not happened at all, however, our verdict on this example of a non-industrializing country that experienced population growth might have been less harsh. But industrialization and structural change in the British economy reduced its vulnerability to disasters, and that, too, should be counted as progress. In Ireland, Finland, and Russia, to name three examples, such vulnerability persisted well into the nineteenth century.

The other contradiction is that some of what was achieved in terms of income and security may have been purchased at the cost of reduced leisure. Economists' conventions measure the economy's success by national income, and traditionally do not include leisure in that measure. Such a procedure is in principle mistaken because leisure should be an important component in economic well-being. The rationalization for the omission is that work habits change relatively little for most of the uses of short-term national income comparisons. However, when we are comparing different societies, such as Western Europe and the United States today, or Britain in 1700 and Britain in 1850, it clearly must be taken into account that changes in the number of hours worked affect economic welfare. Modern research has pointed in the direction of longer hours during the Industrial Revolution, and as such, assessments of welfare based on income per capita or the consumption of commodities have to be tempered even further than I have tempered them. Work in the factory or the industrial workshop was not only unpleasant and physically exhausting, it was usually an all-or-nothing proposition, without the flexibility of hours and the opportunities for multi-tasking that the self-employed cottage industry workers had enjoyed in an earlier age. Again, the issue is full of ambiguities. Increased work hours per year may in part have reflected better opportunities, less involuntary seasonal unemployment, improved workplace technology (e.g., better lighting), changing attitudes to female work, and changing limitations on the participation of women. It thus did not necessarily replace voluntary leisure. As we have seen, the demand for child and female labor fluctuated a lot in the century and a half between 1700 and 1850. Yet economics does not have an unequivocal answer to the question of whether increased participation and longer hours were on balance a deterioration in economic welfare because it is simply hard to know to what extent the prolonged periods of idleness before the Industrial Revolution were voluntary.

Modern researchers have taken a more inclusive approach to the standard of living and tried to construct a so-called Human Development Index (HDI) which would sum up such purely economic measures as real wages and income per capita, biological indices such as life expectancy and anthropometric data, and political and social indicators such as literacy, political freedom, and civil rights. Crafts (1997), who first performed this exercise, and others who have tried to improve and adjust it (Voth, 2004), have found that by this token some version of the optimist account can be resurrected. Interestingly enough, the economic variables on the whole do poorly, but they are pulled up by the improvements in the political climate after 1820, which, as we have seen, were a consequence of the eighteenth-century Enlightenment. It is thus interesting to observe that the Enlightenment affected the political dimensions of living standards before it helped bring about economic improvement for the masses. Whether variables such as political freedom and access to information should be included at all in what economists think of as the standard of living remains a matter of taste. What should be clear, however, is that improved institutions, more sophisticated commerce and communications, and technological progress did not affect living standards in an additive way, but reinforced one another.

In an analysis of living standards in this period it makes sense to distinguish between two separate issues (Hartwell and Engerman, 1975; von Tunzelmann, 1985; Engerman, 1994). One is the factual debate: what actually happened to standards of living, however measured. The other is the *counterfactual* debate: what might have happened in Britain had economic change and technological progress not taken place? Would Britain have ended up following the economic trajectory of Denmark, Bulgaria, or Latin America? It can be shown with some simple calculations (Mokyr, 1998a, pp. 114–15) that while *actual* conditions may not have improved much before 1850, the achievement of the first two generations of the Industrial Revolution was to prevent the growing population and the external negative shocks from creating the kind of pressure that could have caused living standard to fall dramatically. That such a decline did *not* occur despite these shocks is an indication of the strength of this economy. Without the Industrial Revolution and all it entailed, it is inconceivable that Britain would have been able to sustain in the long run simultaneous population growth, a rise in the capital/labor ratio, a series of major and expensive wars before 1815, and stationary or slowly rising living standards for the bulk of the population before 1850.

Some of the political ideas of the age of Enlightenment were implemented in Britain in the late eighteenth century and again by the reform governments of the 1820s and 1830s. The Baconian program of expanding useful knowledge was at the heart of the Industrial Revolution. Yet the full results in terms of material improvement for the masses did not arrive before 1850. In his *Principles of Political Economy*, John Stuart Mill ([1848], 1929, p. 751) wrote that "hitherto [1848] it is questionable if all the mechanical inventions yet made have lightened the day's toil of any human being. They have enabled a greater population to live the same life of drudgery and imprisonment, and an increased number of manufacturers and others to make fortunes. They have increased the comforts of the middle classes. But they have not yet begun to effect those great changes in human destiny, which it is in their nature and in their futurity to accomplish." These were prophetic words. If there is anything that we may conclude from the history of the standard of living it is that the fruits of improvement and progress were a long time in the ripening.

*   *   *

Issues of income distribution have also been of great interest to economic historians and for good reason. Elementary economic logic is enough to demonstrate that the effects of economic growth will differ a great deal depending on whose slice of the pie grows the fastest. Estimates for the eighteenth century must be very tentative, but there is some cause to believe that the gap between the middling sort and the unskilled laborers and unwashed poor was growing after 1750. The proportion of people in Halifax, Yorkshire, who were sufficiently poor to be exempt from the land tax in 1782 was 83 percent, twice what it had been in 1664 (Smail, 1994, p. 102). Such comparisons are, of course, hard to make. But it seems that by the closing decades of the eighteenth century, the authorities were increasingly concerned with poverty and poor relief.

An alternative approach to reconcile a rising income per capita, such as it was, and the absence of notable improvements for the bulk of the population is an increase in income inequality, which implies that the lion's share of the gains in income accrued to a small proportion of the population, mostly merchants, landowners, professionals, and a few lucky groups of artisans and workers in high demand. How, then, did the Industrial Revolution affect income distribution? Simon Kuznets (1955), the founder of modern growth economics, once postulated that in the early stages of economic development income distribution became more and more unequal and that only after a few generations did the distribution become somewhat more equal. This phenomenon has been dubbed the Kuznets curve, and some quantitative historians (Williamson, 1985) have made heroic attempts to find it in Britain in this period. This has, however, turned out to be very difficult to do. The available data have been shown to be too dispersed and too fragmentary for anything that can be reliably interpreted as a measure of income inequality to be estimated (Feinstein, 1988). Part of the difficulty has been that inequality has been defined variously as *between wage earners* (specifically the so-called skill premium, that defined the wage gap between skilled workers and unskilled laborers) or *between labor and other factors*, such as capital and land. The latter is a better proxy for income inequality in general, but it is far from perfect, especially because of the difficulty in measuring the returns to capital.

There is some indirect and partial evidence to support the possibility that inequality did indeed increase between 1780 and 1850, even if the aggregative statistics are inadequate (Allen, 2006). Real per capita consumption, by all estimates, stagnated between 1770 and 1820, and given that some people in the high brackets, especially landlords, did quite well, it seems almost inescapable that inequality worsened in that half-century. Students of agriculture have found that the main beneficiaries of the changes in agricultural organization and rise in productivity were landlords. This is consistent with a recent finding that rents increased quite steeply during the Industrial Revolution, until 1815. Since the distribution of ownership of real estate was extremely skewed in Britain, and since rents were what the agrarian population paid the fortunate few who owned the land, a sharp increase in rents would be consistent with an increase in inequality. In a rapidly growing population this is what one should expect, and an increase in inequality may be related to demographic growth. But more was involved. After 1815, the increase in rents came to an abrupt halt, as agricultural prices declined relative to other products. Because any change in the terms of trade in favor of non-agricultural goods benefited workers (who consumed farm products) at the expense of landlords, most of the period after 1815 may not have experienced a growing gap between landlords and workers. But by that time non-land property was starting to increase sharply. The consensus of scholars is that some measure of income per capita started to increase in the years after 1825, but that real wages show little tendency to increase until the mid-century. Hence the share of non-wage-labor income may well have increased substantially after 1825 until the sharp increases in wages later in the nineteenth century.

This hypothesis is consistent with the rapid acceleration in capital formation in this period, including the construction of the railroad network in Britain and the financing of railroads overseas. If it is assumed that workers saved little or nothing of their income whereas those who lived off property income saved substantial amounts, the increase in income inequality seems to fit the facts (Allen, 2006). This macrointerpretation of the British economy, then, would imply that technological progress was strongly complementary with capital goods, and raised the marginal product of capital considerably, thus helping to raise the rate of profit in the economy. These profits accrued to a wealthy section of the population with high savings rates, and tended to be reinvested in industry and infrastructure, supplying it with the capital it needed to implement the new technologies.

Some careful studies of specific sectors also seem to suggest that economic change favored a few, but left the masses unaffected. Allen (1992, p. 285) concludes, for instance, that the landlords and not the workers were the ones to gain from whatever productivity improvements occurred in farming in the later eighteenth and nineteenth centuries. Sara Horrell's work (1996), based on household micro-data, lends indirect support to the Kuznets-curve notion that inequality sharpened before the middle of the nineteenth century. She finds steeply increasing consumption by middle-class families but practically none for the working class. Surely the Poor Law reform of 1834, by cutting the amount of support provided to the poor in half, reduced disposable real income of the poorest. The statistical complications are considerable: there is, for example, a difference between the inequality of the distribution of income among *households* and the distribution among *individuals*. Studies of wages and consumption, as we have seen, also seem to indicate that the poor and working masses of Britain may not have shared in the increasing prosperity.

There were complicating factors: after 1821 Britain absorbed a large number of Irish immigrants who arrived by and large penniless. Should immigrants be included in the computation of income inequality, or should we only consider people present in Britain at some early date? There are also difficult issues of the exact unit: do we care about the distribution of income over individuals or over households? In an age of high birth rates, as Britain was between 1780 and 1840, the number of young people who are not yet working or are working at low pay is relatively large, and will make income distribution seem skewed even if these youngsters can expect to do well later in life. Although the statistical evidence is too fragile to clinch the case, the possibility of a Kuznets-curve kind of phenomenon between 1780 and 1850 seems not unreasonable but remains unproven. The current state of the art is that we simply do not know for sure that income distribution for the population *as a whole* became more unequal between 1760 and 1850. But it seems likely. That kind of hedged and qualified statement may be the best we can do.

Income distribution was also affected by short-term fluctuations in the economy. We must keep in mind that, while the "old wealth" of the landowning squires was fairly stable in value, many of the fortunes made in commerce and industry were unusually risky and those who ended up in the wealthy part of the income distribution were the lucky survivors of economic crises and depressions. Booms and busts in the level of economic activity became a regular feature of economic life, and their effect on both workers and employers was felt strongly. It is hard to ascertain when the phenomenon of "business cycles" or macroeconomic fluctuations really began. In the eighteenth century, the British economy was subject to economic ups and downs, but they were by and large dominated by two types of phenomenon. One was recognizable supply shocks, such as wars and harvest failures. Some of these crises can be readily identified, such as the early 1740s, which were a period of very poor harvests, followed by the impact of the war with France after 1744 or the difficult years of 1799–1800. Such events led to higher prices, and often economic contraction and unemployment, but they did not normally last for very long.

The other source of volatility in the economy was the capital market. Precisely because so much credit was short term and provided by overlapping networks, and because business organization depended on partners with unlimited liability, individual failures often led to "domino effects," with reverberations in the credit community and the failure of innocent bystanders. During times of credit crunches and panics, short-term loans were called in; for those who had used these funds to invest in producer durables and equipment, this could mean bankruptcy. Indeed, such panics were accompanied by what may seem to us disastrous waves of bankruptcies. The increase in private credit through bills of exchange and the proliferation of country banks led to an increased volatility due to increases in bankruptcies after 1765, whereas before most disruptions had been caused by exogenous events such as wars or harvest failures. By the late eighteenth century the nature of the fluctuations had changed, although it is hard to agree with the statement that this was the inevitable consequence of economic growth (Hoppit, 1986b) for the simple reason that there was so little growth at that time. Yet before there was growth there was an expansion of credit markets, a growth in overhead investment in transport, and expansion of trade. These depended on private credit. The still small modern industrial sector was more likely to be a victim than a cause of these crises. In 1788, for example, a wave of bankruptcies hit the young

Manchester textile industry, with manufacturers and merchants dragging each other down. The average number of firms going bankrupt in England in the 1780s was 496 per year, but in the panic year of 1793 it was 1,256 (Ashton, 1955, p. 254). In the nineteenth century volatility heralding the modern business cycle emerges. These cycles were fueled by credit crunches, panics, and waves of bankruptcies and started to recur at roughly eleven-year intervals: 1825, 1837, 1847. During such crises, workers were laid off, output was sharply reduced for a while, credit was very scarce, banks and businesses failed in large numbers, and prices and wages fell. For the self-employed, the artisans, and farmers, it would mean a decline in demand and the virtual impossibility of getting credit for a while. For businessmen it meant high interest rates and rapid changes in ownership of assets through bankruptcy. Yet such downturns lasted for relatively short periods, and recovery was usually swift, and their macroeconomic effect was short-lived and limited.

The instability caused by these panics was compounded by price instability, though price movements were usually caused by other kinds of disturbance. The basic movement of prices, shown in table 18.2, indicates a great deal of short-term instability with a number of rather sharp peaks. The peaks and troughs clearly coincided with harvest fluctuations, because agricultural prices still constituted the lion's share of the consumers' price index. The volatility of prices does not seem to have declined much over time. The coefficient of variation for agricultural prices in the years 1750–70 was about 9.5 percent and that of 1830–50 8.9 percent. It is unmistakable, however, that between 1760 and 1815 there was a secular rise in prices and that after 1815 prices started a long period of decline until deep in the 1840s. Inflation as such was unlikely in an economy that was firmly committed to the gold standard, as Britain was in most of the period under discussion here. Sustained inflation can occur only in economies that have some kind of fiat money issued by the government or some other issuing institution, as was the case during the Napoleonic Wars. Most economies in the eighteenth and nineteenth centuries were on metallic standards, meaning roughly that the supply of gold and silver constrained the supply of money in the economy and that these precious metals were widely accepted as means of international payments. As David Hume pointed out in *Of the Balance of Trade*, published in 1752, these two functions of specie implied a fundamental stability in the price level: a country that for some reason had "too much" gold, say, would experience rapid increases in its prices (Hume, [1777], 1985). That would mean, however, that its goods would have become more expensive in international markets, exports would fall, imports would rise, and the country would have to pay for its worsening balance of trade by sending some of the gold overseas, and would continue to do so until prices had stabilized. This price-specie-flow mechanism became a lethal argument to undermine the mercantilist obsession with balance of payment surpluses, and convinced people that a liberal economy without direct government management of foreign trade was safe and desirable. That, too, was part of the Enlightenment program.

Table 18.2: Price movements, 1749–1850 (1701 = 100)

Year	CPI	Farm prices	Year	CPI	Farm prices	Year	CPI	Farm prices	Year	CPI	Farm prices
1749	96	102.3	1775	113	141.8	1801	228	291.6	1827	140.2	211.9
1750	95	101.0	1776	114	131.8	1802	174	213.0	1828	136.1	198.1
1751	90	104.2	1777	108	138.9	1803	156	205.6	1829	135.3	196.7
1752	93	110.9	1778	117	132.4	1804	161	206.9	1830	133.4	197.8
1753	90	109.4	1779	111	120.0	1805	187	244.3	1831	134.6	201.3
1754	90	109.6	1780	110	119.8	1806	184	226.2	1832	129.2	190.5
1755	92	101.6	1781	115	127.8	1807	186	234.5	1833	125.1	175.4
1756	92	107.9	1782	116	132.8	1808	204	247.1	1834	122.1	176.1
1757	109	129.9	1783	129	150.4	1809	212	264.9	1835	119.3	169.4
1758	106	122.9	1784	126	151.7	1810	207	281.2	1836	134.4	183.6
1759	100	106.2	1785	120	139.5	1811	206	273.9	1837	133.2	193.4
1760	98	104.3	1786	119	142.4	1812	237	314.4	1838	138.1	202.5
1761	94	98.4	1787	117	141.9	1813	243	301.4	1839	147.3	215.7
1762	94	106.3	1788	121	140.3	1814	209	253.1	1840	144.7	205.2
1763	100	117.3	1789	117	149.3	1815	191	227.8	1841	138.0	204.2
1764	102	119.0	1790	124	153.1	1816	172	227.0	1842	125.4	183.9
1765	106	126.0	1791	121	148.1	1817	189	251.3	1843	112.5	172.2
1766	107	129.0	1792	122	149.0	1818	194	268.7	1844	114.5	175.3
1767	109	133.7	1793	129	160.0	1819	182	257.2	1845	117.6	180.9
1768	108	127.8	1794	136	168.9	1820	162	215.7	1846	121.4	188.2
1769	99	116.6	1795	147	198.8	1821	139	186.6	1847	136.7	221.0
1770	100	119.0	1796	154	202.5	1822	125	165.4	1848	115.5	177.6
1771	107	134.1	1797	148	177.9	1823	128	186.6	1849	104.3	170.6
1772	117	144.6	1798	148	165.6	1824	144	215.2	1850	103.8	154.3
1773	119	149.8	1799	160	201.4	1825	160	231.8			
1774	116	146.6	1800	212	271.6	1826	141.2	211.0			

Sources: CPI: Schumpeter Gilboy Consumer Price Index (1701–1823), spliced to Gayer-Rostow-Schwartz domestic and imported commodities (1823–1850). Farm prices courtesy of Gregory Clark http://www.econ.ucdavis.edu/faculty/gclark/data.html

CHAPTER 19

The Results: The British Economy in 1851

By the middle of the nineteenth century, Britain was the premier industrial nation of Europe. It was the first economy to shake itself loose from the many constraints and obstacles that had prevented economies before 1750 from turning into permanent-growth economies. The mid-Victorians knew this all too well. The great Crystal Palace Exhibition of 1851 marks the crowning achievement of a century of technological progress and economic advance, but also of the growing integration and collaboration of the advanced economies. It was the embodiment of the Enlightenment program. The triumphalism of the Whigs was permeated by their sense of gratitude to Francis Bacon, whose vision they felt they had carried out. This was best expressed by the arch-Whig historian and essayist T.B. Macaulay in his long essay on Bacon published in 1837. For Macaulay, Bacon's significance consisted of two words, "Utility" and "Progress." The purpose of knowledge was the multiplying of human enjoyments and the mitigating of human suffering (Macaulay, [1837], 1880, pp. 409–10). He did not hesitate to credit the new philosophy with the technological miracles he saw around him, steamships, balloons, lightning rods, enhanced agricultural productivity, and the extinction of diseases, yet these were "but the first fruits ... this philosophy never rests, its law is progress" (ibid., p. 431). These words may sound almost absurdly naive to today's historians, and yet representing them purely as smug and self-congra-tulatory misses an important part of the story. They do represent a genuine if perhaps ingenuous sentiment that we should neither mock nor dismiss out of hand. Romantic critics of the Industrial Revolution, while strongly disapproving of it, conceded the same. Thomas Carlyle (1829) sighed that he was living in "the Mechanical Age ... It is the Age of Machinery, in every outward and inward sense of that word; the age which, with its whole undivided might, forwards, teaches and practises the great art of adapting means to ends ... how much better fed, clothed, lodged and, in all outward respects, accommodated men now are, or might be, by a given quantity of labour, is a grateful reflection which forces itself on every one." His complaint was, of course, that "Only the material, the immediately practical, not the divine and spiritual, is important to us. The infinite, absolute character of Virtue has passed into a finite, conditional one; it is no longer a worship of the Beautiful and Good; but a calculation of the Profitable." No less than Macaulay, he fully realized how much of the daily comforts he enjoyed were owed to the Enlightenment.

The commitment to an ideology that was at once pragmatic-materialist and theoretically committed to a utilitarian-individualist philosophy was the outcome of the Enlightenment. As Porter (1981, p. 17) expressed it, "in the long term the Enlightenment ideology had got deeply under the skin." Carlyle meant his tirade to be a critique; in the eyes of an eighteenth-century writer or a liberal Victorian his words would have been seen as praise. The Victorians must have felt so pleased with themselves because of their realization that the Enlightenment values that their liberal society embraced were at the same time morally virtuous and economically beneficial. Their ideology, it seemed to them, had solved simultaneously the questions of "How do we make a good society" and "How do we make a happy society." They were in for a rude awakening.

By 1850, according to most statistics, Britain was the most sophisticated economy in the world. The nineteenth-century British statistician Robert Mulhall compiled a treasury of retrospective comparative statistics, in which he illustrated the huge gap that had opened in key industries between Britain and the other nations of the Western world by the mid-nineteenth century. Total cotton consumption in Britain in the 1840s was estimated at 2.3 million tons, compared to 610,000 in France and 410,000 in Germany. Coal consumption in Britain in 1850 was estimated in 1850 at 49 million tons as opposed to 4.4 million in France and 6.7 million in Germany. Iron consumption in 1850 was respectively 1.97 million tons, 600,000 tons, and 420,000. Steam power in 1850 was estimated at 1.29 million hp in Britain, 370,000 hp in France and 260,000 in Germany (Mulhall, 1899, passim). The respective populations of the three countries in 1850 were 21 million in Great Britain, 35 million in France and 33 million in Germany. In per capita terms, hence, the gaps were even larger. Britain had 10,000 kilometers of railroad open as opposed to 6,600 in Germany and 3,200 in France (Mitchell, 1975, p. 582). Modern national-incomes accounting confirms the gap, though at an aggregate level it is smaller. Maddison (1995, pp. 194–96) has put UK per capita GDP at $2,362, almost 65 percent higher than Germany and 30 percent higher than the United States and the Netherlands at that time. By 1851, moreover, the share of agriculture in employment in Great Britain had been falling: from 35 percent of the labor force in 1801 to 22 percent in 1851, and from 32 percent of national income in 1801 to 20 percent in 1851 (Deane and Cole, 1969, pp. 143, 167). These numbers are hard to compare to other countries, because consistent definitions are hard to devise but in 1856 the French census still reported 53 percent of the labor force in agriculture and related activities, and 37 percent of GNP still originated in agriculture in 1850 (Lévy-Leboyer and Bourguignon, 1985, p. 319). The "indices of industrialization" calculated by Paul Bairoch (1982) give Britain a value of 64 (UK in 1900 = 100); its closest competitors are Belgium and Switzerland with 28 and 26 respectively, with France at 20 and Germany at 15. The orders of magnitude are a testimony to a century of technological leadership, that had translated itself into economic leadership.

The achievements of the British economy were celebrated in the Crystal Palace exhibition of 1851. The spectacular aspects of this event have been described in detail. The meaning of the Great Exhibition to human—and not just British —history was summarized recently by Benjamin Friedman: "the Great Exhibition ... [was] an exuberant celebration of the idea not just of scientific and therefore material progress but ... of progress in social, civic and moral affairs as well" (2005, p. 20). The exhibition displayed 100,000 items by 14,000 individuals or firms, containing everything from raw materials to finished handicraft products. The exhibition was such a gigantic event that it has meant different things to different scholars, who have commented on its social, technological, or colonial aspects. The construction mode of the Crystal Palace by itself symbolized the new age. It was designed by Joseph Paxton and built exclusively from prefabricated iron rods that supported a structure made largely out of glass. Glass itself had become far less expensive after the duties had been repealed, and the firm of Chance brothers in Smethwick (near Birmingham) was large and sophisticated enough to meet the huge and unexpected order of nearly a million square feet at short notice. After the exhibition closed, the structure was taken down piece by piece from its original site in Hyde Park, and reassembled (and augmented) at Sydenham Hill in the southern London suburbs. In this way it heralded the new age of cheap materials, interchangeable parts, and mass production that were embodied in many of the exhibits. Cantankerous critics such as John Ruskin (who likened the building to a cucumber frame) aside, the bulk of observers liked the modernity that the revolutionary design represented.

But above all, the Great Exhibition was a celebration of useful knowledge. Prince Albert, the main instigator of the exhibit, much like Francis Bacon a quarter of a millennium earlier, felt that knowledge needed to be organized and taxonomized in order to be accessed, and devised a (somewhat cumbersome) system in which the products were categorized. It was explicitly global and cosmopolitan in its reach, the sort of transnational culture that eighteenth-century *philosophes* had hoped for. It was to be a symbol of international peace. One contemporary, James Ward, concluded from the exhibition that "mankind seem tacitly agreed to rival each other in the manufacture of commodities essentially requisite for mutual advantage ... in lieu of fabricating weapons for mutual destruction" (cited by Auerbach, 1999, p. 162). The French liberal economist, Jérôme-Adolphe Blanqui (1798–1854), who published a number of letters commenting on the exhibition, saw it as an affirmation of the principle of comparative advantage and the international division of labor. The exhibition, he wrote, will teach many people that the growth of the mutual dependence of nations is the soundest guarantee of peace (Tallis, 1852, Vol. 2, p. 16). For a modern scholar of economic growth like Friedman, it means above all the culmination of the realization that the dissemination of useful knowledge was at the heart of sustainable economic development.

Yet nationalism had not died, and side by side with the internationalism the exhibition stood for, there were signs of British pride everywhere. Commentators on the exhibition used it to mock Russian serfdom, American slavery, German militarism, and French *dirigisme*, to say nothing of the contemptuous attitudes toward non-Europeans. While Britain was proud to display its own achievements, especially in machinery, it also displayed American goods with a tang of jealousy of the progress that US manufacturers had achieved in the area of modularity and interchangeability. The spirit of the Enlightenment lived in the centrality of the concept of improvement. The exposition placed a great emphasis on "new" and "improved"—the sense of past and future progress was everywhere. Despite the awarding of prizes, it placed the greatest emphasis on market outcomes, providing the public with an array of choices, from mass-produced cheap goods, to fine, custom-made products of artists and skilled artisans (Auerbach, 1999, pp. 122–27). Yet some observers criticized the tasteless commercialism that the free market could produce. The contradictions of the Industrial Enlightenment, then, were mirrored in the Crystal Palace exhibition. All the same, contemporaries above all saw it as a symbol of the superiority of the ideas on which the Victorian economy was built.

What could go wrong? To the Victorians, Britain's leadership seemed like a natural outcome, reflecting the superiority of their institutions and their social order. To the economic historian it has become increasingly clear that Britain's leadership in the Industrial Revolution was temporary and that eventually its European rivals and the United States would catch up. If the driving engine behind economic development was the changing set of beliefs we associate with the Enlightenment, it would only be a matter of time until other economies that had been affected by the Enlightenment would be on a par with Britain. British leadership had been achieved on borrowed time. Moreover, the informal institutions on which British progress had rested could carry it a long way, but by the middle of the nineteenth century they had reached their limit and needed to be supplemented by more formal ones. Above all, the informal system in which human capital and competence were acquired by self-teaching and personal contact with a master, which had produced such brilliant but poorly educated mechanics as George Stephenson, Henry Maudslay, and Richard Roberts, was no longer enough to keep up in the following decades. Technological progress in Britain during the Industrial Revolution had owed a lot to "unscientific tinkerers" and dexterous and clever mechanics, who had carried much of the pre-1830 progress in textiles and mechanical engineering. It seems clear that the informal institutions of trust and information exchange that produced these men would no longer suffice after 1850. During a lecture given at the Crystal Palace exhibition, the chemist Lyon Playfair, who had played an important role in organizing the event, warned that "a rapid transition is taking place in industry ... industry must in the future be supported, not by a competition of local advantage, but by competition of intellect. All European nations, except England, have recognized this fact"

(Tallis, 1852, Vol. 2, p. 194). This may seem unfair, since the ingenuity of a Maudslay or a Richard Roberts represented no less of an intellect than that of a Lord Kelvin. But it was a *different* kind of intellect. Late Victorian Britain did not "fail," but it needed to reinvent itself. Playfair thought he knew the answer. Everywhere but in England, he told his audience, governments have adopted the cultivation of science as a principle of state, and everywhere else there are towns in which schools teach the principles involved in manufacturing. Technical universities taught the "alphabet of science in reading manufactures aright." Other European nations had just raised themselves on the shoulders of science, "while we are merely hovering about its skirts." He called for a reform of Britain's educational system devoted to the study of "God's works" (i.e., science and technology) which were more likely to increase the resources of the nation than "the amours of Jupiter or Venus." He complained that science and industry in Britain had not received the respect they deserved despite the fact that the country owed her success to them, mirroring similar complaints voiced twenty years earlier by Charles Babbage (Tallis, Vol. 2, pp. 195–202). The issue of technical curricula and educational reform, increasingly indispensable if Britain was to stay a member of the advanced industrialized nations, was to dog the country for the rest of the century.

Moreover, in the mid-nineteenth century Britain started to discover the limits of liberal ideology: free trade, mobility, easy entry, and a reliance on the competitive market wherever possible ran into the hard reality of market failures and inequality. The horrors of the Irish Famine illustrated to contemporaries the hollowness of liberal political economy in the face of disasters. But even in Britain itself, its limitations became apparent. Two of the most important historical documents of the early Victorian era illustrate these twin contradictions. One of these, Edwin Chadwick's *Report on the Sanitary Condition* ([1843], 1965) has already been referred to. The other was Henry Mayhew's five-volume *London Labour and the London Poor* ([1861–62]; 1967), about which more below. What Chadwick was really cataloguing was a series of market failures or spillover effects. He and other concerned Victorians of his age were facing the dilemma that the free market would not solve the hard problems of congested urban areas, unhealthy work and living places, adulterated food, and above all issues of public health. By the time of the Great Exhibition, Britain had already twice been hit by cholera epidemics. The first one, in 1831–32, killed about 32,000 people, and the one in 1848–49 about 62,000. The impact of the fear that the disease caused may have been disproportionately larger than these numbers suggest, because it was quite shocking to the people who witnessed it, especially because it was new. Sanitation and public health had not kept pace with the remarkable progress the nation had experienced. Something was clearly wrong in the Victorian paradise.

Chadwick's document sold over 100,000 copies. It was a ringing indictment of conditions in Britain, and it proposed a clear-cut program for reform. As Flinn (1965) noted, it constitutes definitive proof that liberal political economy was never as doctrinaire in favor of laissez-faire as it has been made out to be. The political economists of the time (including Bentham himself), Flinn pointed out (ibid., p. 39), were too intelligent and too informed ever to advocate all-out non-intervention principles. Between his work on the Poor Law Report in 1834 and the Sanitary Report of 1842, Chadwick had undergone a learning process that was typical of the age, that is a constant probing and reassessing of where the correct boundaries between the private and the public ought to be. Public money could and should be spent on social projects, but it should be done sensibly. His argument was not so much emotional and moral as logical, based on cost-benefit analysis. The prevention of unsanitary and unhealthy conditions made economic sense. Thomas Southwood Smith, one of Chadwick's most dedicated lieutenants, wrote in 1838 that "setting aside all higher considerations ... the prevention of evil, rather than the mitigation of its circumstances, is not only the most beneficent but also the most economical course" (cited by Wohl, 1983, pp. 146–47). William Farr, who was a statistician as well as a physician, and had become part of the Registrar General's office in 1839 where he pursued an energetic program in support of public health, suggested that "it is possible to reduce the annual deaths in England and Wales by 30,000 and to increase the vigour (may I add the industry and wealth) of the population in an equal proportion. For diseases are the iron index of misery, which recedes before strength, health, and happiness as the mortality declines" (Great Britain, 1839, p. 65). Farr, Chadwick, and their colleagues realized, more clearly than most, that the principles of laissez-faire simply did not hold here. The removal of "public nuisance" was the responsibility of the government, because it endangered the public yet there was no way the market could supply this good. The Slaney Committee on the health of towns (Great Britain, 1840) reached the same conclusion: only regulations, both local and parliamentary, could remedy the situation. In the late 1840s, a series of laws was passed that began to carry out the program envisaged by Chadwick and his followers. Among these were the Nuisance Removal Act of 1846, the Town Improvements Clauses Act of 1847, the Metropolitan Commission of Sewers Act of 1848, and the Public Health Act of 1848. By that time local authorities could prosecute those responsible for the worst urban health hazards, the cities were authorized to provide water supplies and sewerage systems, and a general Board of Health had been established that under some circumstances could compel cities to establish local boards. The much-heralded Public Health Act remained largely a set of options rather than a mandate for local authorities, and in the first years not many localities took advantage of them. But the principle had been established.

Some wanted to go further, and argued that public health was the result of social conditions and inequality. An example is the work of William Alison (1790–1859), an Edinburgh physician and a typical product of the later Scottish Enlightenment, who was personally influenced by the teaching of Dugald Stewart, as were so many others of his cohort. Alison insisted that low wages could be a direct cause of disease, thus drawing a more direct link between poverty and public health than Chadwick and his close collaborator Dr. Neil Arnott were willing to make. For him, it was inevitable that a physician who had been applying remedies to diseases obviously afflicting the poorest of his fellow citizens and who had found these cures ineffectual, should "extend his inquiries to the grand evil of poverty itself" (Alison, 1840, p. vii). Destitution, poor nourishment, unemployment, and the concomitant mental depression, he argued, were not the sole cause of disease but led to their more rapid diffusion (ibid., p. 19). Alison understood, like others, the great Victorian dilemma. The political economists had persuaded the establishment that "the relief of poverty leads ultimately to its continual recurrence and increase" (ibid., p. 173), and that public health problems should be attacked by removing the nuisances, not by eliminating poverty. This conclusion seemed objectionable to him. As a medical doctor, he felt strongly that there was a nexus between living standards and public health, and that health would not be improved as long as there was widespread poverty. In that sense he was closer to his German colleague Rudolf Virchow than to Chadwick and his colleagues (Hamlin, 2006).

Chadwick disagreed. The *Report on the Sanitary Condition* was no radical document, and it differed in tone and objective from Engels' *Condition of the Working Class*. Whereas Engels' book was an indictment, Chadwick's was on the face of it a technical document about a set of bad conditions that needed to be remedied. Unlike the more radical thinkers, the Benthamites did not conclude that public health hazards and urban disamenities were by-products of inequality and poverty. Chadwick ([1843], 1965, p. 216) was curt about the connection between poverty and disease that Alison had made his mantra: "the false opinions as to destitution being the general cause of fever ... have had extensively the disastrous effect of preventing efforts being made for the removal of the circumstances which are proved to be followed by a diminution of the pestilence." For Chadwick and his circle, public health was not a social but an engineering problem. Drainage, street and house cleaning, urban design, garbage removal, and a clean drinking water supply were the solutions needed, and the free market could not supply them. Hence a role for the government, limited and circumscribed, of course, but unassailable. For many Victorians, this must have been more reassuring than disturbing. In other words, the poor got sick because they lived in noisome and unhealthy environments. Fix the environment, and you will have healthy poor, and many of the urban disamenities and other undesirable consequences of industrialization that increasingly came to the fore in the 1830s and 1840s would be resolved.

Much as has been the case with child labor and factory conditions, public health concerns thus drove home the recognition of the limits of the free market economy. An enlightened economy, it was clear, was not a laissez-faire one, but one in which the limitations of the free market were recognized as much as its blessings. That was the inevitable conclusion of enlightened thinking, which was not dogmatic in its free market liberalism, but pragmatic and utilitarian in its approach. The more difficult issue for Victorian Britain was that the free market, even when corrected for market failures, could not produce an income distribution that many felt comfortable with. In other words, the enlightened economy had not solved the problem of poverty, and in many ways had made it, if not worse, more visible, and more intolerable politically. In that regard, focusing on the years around the Great Exhibition is perhaps a poor choice, since they come at the end of a few years in which a series of unrelated disasters rained down on Britain's poor: the financial crisis that accompanied the end of the railway boom in 1847, followed by a few years of depression, the Irish Famine, and the cholera epidemic of 1847/48. In the midst of these events, Henry Mayhew compiled his enormous work describing London's poor, a harrowing picture of an urban lumpen-proletariat, the flip side of the society produced by the Industrial Enlightenment.

The contrast between Edwin Chadwick and Henry Mayhew seems large in many dimensions. Chadwick was a committed Benthamite and a man with deep instincts as a civil servant, which were mostly frustrated because of his temper and lack of tact. Mayhew was a social radical, with a Dickensian writing style and sense of indignation but a disorganized lifestyle, the "chap who couldn't finish his thesis and in the process produced an eccentric masterpiece" (Hughes, 1969, p. 536). Yet both realized that the Victorian economy in the middle of the nineteenth century was still a project in the making, that it had been a resounding success for some and a dismal failure for others, that it needed a great deal of work, but that this work was within reach of the institutions of Britain. They share, above all, the impact of the "urban condition," that is the realization that the cities that had sprung up as a result of the growth of the economy contained serious disamenities and that they made poverty more visible, more dramatic, more salient and therefore less acceptable.

The descriptions that Mayhew ([1861-62], 1967) provided are in many respects harrowing in their minute details of the horrors of the daily life of the urban underclass. His work may well, as E.P. Thompson thought, be "the most impressive survey of poverty at mid-century which exists" (1967, p. 46). But Mayhew was not in the business of describing the life of the representative consumer or even laborer. He was describing the poorest of the poor, the desperate refugees from the Irish Famine, and the urban misfits and rejects who refused or were denied the terrors of the Victorian workhouse and instead tried to make their life in the seams and on the fringes of the industrial economy (Hughes, 1969; Himmelfarb, 1971). By his own account (Mayhew, [1861-62], 1967, Vol. 1, p. 6), he was describing the bottom 2.5 percent ("one fortieth") of the distribution. As long as we do not confuse Mayhew's people with the British working poor, there is still a lot to be learned here. The people described by Mayhew were not just living among filth and offal as Chadwick had stressed, they were actually thriving on it. Examples were bone grubbers, rag gatherers, the finders of "pure" (dog excrement, in demand by tan-yards), the cigar-end finders, dredger-men who collected refuse from ships (ibid., Vol. 2, pp. 136–81). More significant numerically were the street orderlies and scavengers, whose jobs basically consisted of keeping the streets clean (ibid., pp. 253–73). Such occupations may not have been attractive or appetizing, but it is hard to see how sanitarian advocates might have achieved their hopes of clean streets without this labor.

While these people may have been quite visible and picturesque, they were not only a small minority within London but were only very indirectly a result of the economic transformations of the previous decades. Mayhew was a miniaturist, not a statistician, and his computation that perhaps up to one-seventh of England's population continued their existence either by pauperism, mendicancy, or crime (ibid., vol. 3, p. 429) is based on a misunderstanding of the Poor Law statistics, among other errors. Consider the problem of "vagrants" whom he describes as unemployable, people who "will not work" because of the "non-inculcation of a habit of industry" (ibid., p. 368). On the basis of mostly guesswork, he computed that there are about 150,000 "depredators of known bad character" in England (ibid., p. 377). Other vagrants were young lads aged 17 and younger, Irish immigrants, and the "temporary destitute in search of employment." These categories are essentially empty of meaning, as well as overlapping. His volumes are full of poor children, trying to eke out a living in London's streets. Yet the fact is that the 1851 census indicates that child and teenage labor in London was significantly less than in the rest of England: of those aged 10–14, only 23 percent in London were "occupied" as opposed to 41.6 in the rest of England and Wales (Kirby, 2005b). To be sure, the census data under- and miscounted many of the children that Mayhew describes because selling flowers on the street may not have counted as an occupation, but if child labor had been a deeper social problem in London than elsewhere, it would have shown up in the census. In Volume 4, Mayhew produced an odd classification of the population into those that will work, those that cannot work, those who will not work, and those that need not work. His London street folk contained many people who "will work" such as musicians, dancers, and various showmen, as well as myriads of street hawkers and pedlars, selling everything from fried fish to dog collars to religious tracts. Those "who will not work" represented a dark side of the economy, and all of Volume 4 was devoted to them. But it would be hard to find a society at that time that did not have its share of vagrants, beggars, cheats, thieves, and prostitutes. Mayhew had no qualms about including in the latter "ladies of intrigue," that is, married women who have connections with men other than their husbands and unmarried women who gratify their passion secretly, as well as women whose "paramours" could not marry them (Vol. 4, p. 258).

The really ugly underbelly of the Victorian economy, and the one that informed contemporaries worried about a great deal, consisted of the new industrial towns in Scotland, the northwest, and the Midlands. Urbanization inexorably shifted the boundary between the public and the private sphere of action. As early as 1833, Peter Gaskell, a Manchester surgeon, had published his description of the manufacturing population in the new urban Britain (1833), a book that was to inspire Engels in his more famous work (1845) and from which he copied liberally.

Gaskell was no revolutionary, but he could see what technological progress and rapid urbanization had done to the physical and moral conditions of the working population in the manufacturing districts, and compared their living conditions to that of pre-civilization savages, a ringing indictment for a nineteenth-century writer (1833, pp. 132–33). Gaskell, James Kay-Shuttleworth (one of Chadwick's associates), and many others wrote about the conditions of factory workers in the industrial districts in England and Scotland in the 1830s and early 1840s. Their indignation and eloquence, while not as detailed as that of Mayhew, were perhaps more telling. Gaskell described in detail the devastating effect of factory work on family life, physical appearance, and moral habits such as alcoholism and a decline in religion. Gaskell was, however, most appalled by the physical degeneration of these populations, and unlike Chadwick he blamed the factory, not only the urban infrastructure. "The population crowded in the large manufacturing towns," he thundered, "is exposed to many causes tending to very powerfully depressing its vital activity ... its improvidence, neglect of domestic comforts, general immorality, thin and innutritious diet, joined to the peculiarity of their labour, continued unremittingly for twelve or fourteen hours, cooped up in a heated atmosphere" (1833, pp. 226–27). Both he and Kay-Shuttleworth stressed the problem of chronic and debilitating diseases, linked directly to industrialization (ibid., p. 213; Kay-Shuttleworth, 1832, p. 43). As enlightened physicians, they saw symptoms, understood their causes, and suggested a specific cure. Unlike Engels, then, most of these British writers concerned about public health and morality realized that Britain's political structure was capable of reform, and while such a movement might take effort and time, they thought that it was the correct solution to the horrendous by-products of industrialization and economic progress. They demanded, and fully expected, the existing institutions to deal with the unacceptable by-products of technological change. The indignation about the undesirable outcomes of industrialization and the proposals to set them straight were as much inspired by the Enlightenment as the advances themselves.

What Chadwick and his physician followers did for urban sanitation, another physician, Arthur Hill Hassall, did for food adulteration. Serious complaints about the unobservable qualities of the goods sold to consumers had already been raised in 1820. By using improved microscopes and other advanced laboratory techniques, Hassall was able to show the extent of food adulteration in Britain. In a series of articles culminating in a book (Hassall, 1855), he mercilessly exposed the risks that the free market brought to the unwary consumers of food in Britain. In excruciating detail, Hassall described how product after product was adulterated and their flavor artificially enhanced with inferior and at times hazardous substances such as strychnine, cocculus indicus (a poisonous hallucinogen used to add flavor to beer), Prussian Blue (ferro-cyanide), lead, copper, arsenic, and mercury. His tireless ally in the war against product adulteration was Thomas Wakley, who as we have seen combined medical science with a deep social awareness. A few years later, these efforts led to a parliamentary investigation (Great

Britain, 1856). Again, it became abundantly clear that in a truly enlightened economy the government had a positive responsibility to protect consumers when the
age-old faith in *caveat emptor* was no longer justified. The Food Adulteration Act of
1860 was the beginning of a series of reforms that led to much strengthened
consumer protection by the end of the century.

Why was the implementation of these reforms so slow? The obstacle that men
like Hassall, Chadwick, and Alison ran into was that mid-nineteenth-century
Britain was still a nation committed to Whiggish principles. Some progressive
thinkers might have had acute spells of conscience pangs about their less fortunate
compatriots, but such events conflicted with the strong reluctance to spend public
money on anything and the general sense of self-satisfaction of having achieved
a successful society. Mayhew, wrote E.P. Thompson, did not discover Victorian
poverty, and for a brief period he "pierced this protective shell of Podsnappery"
(Thompson, 1967, p. 43). The two massive reports published by the Health of
Towns Commission (Great Britain, 1844a, 1845) produced a great deal of
information on sanitary conditions but never recommended an outright increase
in government spending. But the shell healed quickly, Thompson thought, and
within a few years Mayhew was already dismissed as quaint and an excuse for
those who wanted to take advantage of the generosity of others. Thompson's view
is too schematic, and the ills that Chadwick and his physician assistants, as well as
the many parliamentary reports, had pointed to, were too large and too disturbing
to ignore. The Victorian shell remained pierced and, while perhaps the zeal for
social and sanitary reform waxed and waned, remained very much part of the
agenda of the later Victorian era. The Public Health Act of 1848, the culmination
of many years of hard work by Chadwick, was watered down and although he was
appointed to the Central Board of Health it called for, it effectively ceased to
operate in 1854, and Chadwick's career as a reformer came to an end. All the
same, as Flinn (1965, p. 73) argues, the Act had "put a foot in the door which had
hitherto defied all attempts at opening, and the *principle* of state responsibility was
preserved." New Acts of Parliament in the second half of the nineteenth century
established public responsibility for a widening array of perceived market failures.
Pauperism, unemployment, unemployability, and a highly inequitable income
distribution were placed on the public policy agenda and remained there for many
decades before serious solutions were attempted.

*   *   *

How did Britain fare in the longer run? The formal institutions that had shown
themselves suitable to economic change in the century and a half before 1850

remained adaptive and agile after 1850, even if they had to overcome both political and ideological resistance. Many crucial reforms were introduced in the 1820s and 1830s and reform continued through the later Victorian era. After 1850, the patent system was reformed, free education was provided, the franchise was extended repeatedly. This was the advantage of having Parliament as a meta-institution. Informal institutions, however, were harder to change and more subject to crystallization. The Industrial Revolution had produced an entirely new set of problems, and the institutions that had been able to liberate Britain from mercantilism and rent-seeking now needed to concern themselves with the social issues, the negative externalities, and the technological bite-back of the industrial economy they had helped construct. This demanded a reexamination of their belief in the free market as the ultimate decision-maker in the economic game.

In the second half of the nineteenth century, moreover, Britain needed to set up an entirely new technical training structure in which a *different* kind of human capital would be generated, one that could absorb and compete with the closer dependence of technology on formal science and mathematics. It had too few people like Lord Kelvin and Charles Parsons, who combined mathematics and scientific insight with inventive ability, and William Rankine, who did all he could to make engineering science more exact and more useful at the same time, and to turn it into a formal part of the curriculum of universities. Once again, Britain needed to examine its institutions and adapt them to the changed environment, using the built-in mechanisms it had developed over many centuries. Yet no single set of institutions was uniquely suited to make economic progress. France, Germany, Japan, and the United States, each under very different sets of institutions, were able to join the club of industrialized nations.

Economic growth is all about creative destruction, the continuous obsolescence of techniques and practices, artefacts and designs, as Schumpeter described it. The idea of creative destruction can be extended to the realm of institutions. Economic growth requires the social and political capabilities of the economy to adapt. Institutional agility was thus necessary if growth was to be sustained. It still is. The same holds for informal institutions such as cultural beliefs and ideology. Ideology was an integral part of economic change, but just as there is no fixed set of "good" institutions, that are suitable for the economy under all circumstances, there is no "right" ideology that works in all circumstances toward economic progress. The Enlightenment in its different manifestations advocated a set of new institutions that cleared up centuries of mercantilist policies, regulations, and social controls, whose objective had been primarily to redistribute resources to politically connected groups and to enhance the interests of the Crown (the best connected group of all). The mercantilist world was unsuitable to a brave new world of continued technological progress driven by free markets, innovative entrepreneurship, and an internationally collaborative effort to advance technology. By the mid-nineteenth century, however, some of the enlightened ideas were themselves in the process of being revised.

The belief that has survived was that useful knowledge had the potential to become the greatest and most powerful agent for historical change even as the risks and social repercussions were increasingly recognized. Even that conviction has had to overcome resistance and opposition, from a variety of sources who felt that the dangers and costs of new technology surpassed the gains. In the second half of the nineteenth century, such voices as John Ruskin and William Morris, railing about the hazards of new technology as they saw them, were getting stronger in Britain. Industrialization was regarded as an evil force that oppressed and exploited workers, created ugly and unhealthy cities, and sold consumers shoddy and cheap goods they did not want or need. Commercial objectives and economically productive careers became unpopular among certain groups within the British elite. Yet the world that the Enlightenment had built was resistant to such voices. The simple reason was that the benefits of technological progress were too obvious to ignore and even economies that had turned their backs on the Enlightenment at first eventually had to climb on the bandwagon. The creation of a system of open economies that competed with one another through a peaceful market system meant that no single country could unilaterally turn its back on the economic progress that the Enlightenment had unleashed. Britain was no exception.

Was the Enlightenment as defined here a "cause" of the British Industrial Revolution? It surely was not *the* cause. Other factors, from a favorable location and mineral resources to the pre-existence of a middle class and the skills of artisans, played a role in the story. It was a remarkable confluence of circumstances that led to the events described here, and one of the irrepressible sentiments of the economic historian studying the Industrial Revolution is a sense of amazement that it occurred *at all*. Yet the Enlightenment is the 600-pound gorilla in the room of modern economic growth that nobody has mentioned so far. Never mind that it had its real effects in the nineteenth century, after the formal age of Enlightenment had ended. To turn Kant's famous dictum on its head, the century after Waterloo was not the age of Enlightenment but it was an enlightened age. And an enlightened age was what was necessary to create the modern age of industrialism and opulence. The people who lived during this age were no more "enlightened" in a moral sense than their ancestors, as they were perfectly capable of inflicting ghastly cruelty on non-Europeans (and at times on one another). What matters for economic history, however, is that the enlightened age differed from the age of mercantilism in the way it accumulated, disseminated, and employed useful knowledge, and in the way its economic institutions operated to *create* rather than *redistribute* wealth.

Beliefs and ideologies affected economic outcomes. They did not invariably do so with the same force. But there were historical episodes in which the economic effect of changes in beliefs is there for all to see. The impact of the Enlightenment on economic outcomes was perhaps more subtle and more gradual than the impact of the new ideas of Muhammad, Marx, or Keynes. But it was more long-lasting (Muhammad being an exception) and more beneficial. Without these ideas, it is impossible to imagine how the wave of technological innovations after 1760 could have been transformed into what we now recognize as modern economic growth, a sustained process in which economies become richer year after year. As had happened before, after an initial flourishing the process would have settled down in a new stationary state. The Enlightenment, then, was indispensable not in "causing" the Industrial Revolution but in turning it into the taproot of economic growth.

The predictable objection to this line of argument is that it replaces one unexplained event (the Industrial Revolution) by another (the Enlightenment) (e.g., Clark, 2007, p. 183). It just pushes the chain of causation one step higher, but it does not provide a complete and satisfactory theory. A persuasive argument why Europe had an Enlightenment and the rest of the world did not is outside the comparative advantage of the economic historian and certainly outside the scope of this book (but see Mokyr, 2006c; 2007). Prevalent beliefs are the outcome of a past flow of innovations that were "proposed" to the accessible population (meaning here mostly a literate and intellectually engaged elite). These innovations were the result of supply factors (why did they occur and not others?) and demand factors (why were some ideas accepted and others not?). Some of those outcomes must be attributed in part to historical contingency: the triumph of Islam in the seventh century or that of Marxism-Leninism in the twentieth, to pick just two examples, depended on historical luck and personalities as much as anything else. Nor can the Enlightenment be attributed to a single individual, but its success in parts of Europe owed a lot to contingent factors such as the military defeats of the reactionary Spanish Habsburgs and the Ottoman Turks, and above all the failures in coordination among those who would suppress new ideas (Mokyr, 2007). The supply side owed a great deal to prior intellectual movements such as Humanism and the Reformation, and Baconianism had deep medieval roots. Like all intellectual movements its success was a function of technological developments such as the printing press and better communications.

None of those prior developments made the Enlightenment inevitable. Neither did the Scientific Revolution of the seventeenth century. On the demand side, we may point to the prior rise of commercialism, the growth of global trading networks, the rise of urban middle classes in the north Atlantic ports, and the deeper penetration of markets, as well as rising literacy. But again, such developments had existed elsewhere at other times without leading to the crucial ideological developments of the eighteenth century. The widespread acceptance of certain ideas, much like other forms of mass behavior, depended on emulation, conformism, and what is known as "frequency-dependence," that is, people willing to accept ideas if their neighbors do. It also depended on the rhetorical skills of the leaders of the movement, and on the willingness of their audiences to be persuaded. In such models exact predictions of outcomes are hard to derive. Multiple equilibria may prevail, and it is the challenge of economic history to explain why one did rather than another.

What, then, was the role of Britain in creating modern growth? The critical changes associated with the eighteenth-century Enlightenment were not specific to Britain, although in Britain the fruits of the Enlightenment tree ripened earlier than elsewhere in the Western world. The Industrial Revolution was not a marginal phenomenon as some economic historians have made it out to be, an accidental flourishing of cotton and steam, but all the same the dimensions of the British Industrial Revolution have to be kept in perspective. Much of the economic history of Britain between 1700 and 1850 has little to do with the Industrial Revolution, and many of the attempted advances led to failure and frustration. By 1850 only a part, if a rapidly growing one, of the British economy had been affected by mechanization, and while per capita income growth and urbanization by that time were in full swing, Britain's economic leadership was already under threat.

*   *   *

Modern intellectuals, following Horkheimer and Adorno ([1947], 2002) have insisted that we judge the Enlightenment by what it produced, not by what it meant to do. Whether or not one accepts this methodology, it is clear that the legacy of the Enlightenment for Europe and the world was mixed and cannot be assessed as either wholly negative or benign. The same, mutatis mutandis, may be said about economic growth. What must be confronted, however, is that the Enlightenment was not neutral with respect to economic performance. As long as what people believe to be true affects the way they interact with one another and with their physical environment, changes in ideology and attitudes will affect economic performance. Any argument that takes the extreme historical materialist position that ideology and beliefs are entirely an outcome of economic conditions is as likely to be off the mark as one that leaves those factors out altogether. The Enlightenment was what set Europe on a different track toward economic modernity. Britain between 1700 and 1850 was the trailblazer in this achievement. As fate would have it, it turned out to be neither the richest nor the most enlightened nation in Europe, but in both dimensions it did more than respectably. Material life in Britain and in the industrialized world that followed it is far better today than could have been imagined by the most wild-eyed optimistic eighteenth-century *philosophe*—and whereas this outcome may have been an unforeseen consequence, most economists, at least, would regard it as an undivided blessing.

References

Acemoglu, Daron, Johnson, Simon, and Robinson James. 2005a. "Institutions as a Fundamental Cause of Economic Growth." In Philippe Aghion and Steven Durlauf, eds., *Handbook of Economic Growth*. Amsterdam: Elsevier, pp. 385–465.

————. 2005b. "The Rise of Europe: Atlantic Trade, Institutional Change, and Economic Growth." *American Economic Review*, Vol. 95, No. 3 (June), pp. 546–79.

Acemoglu, Daron and Robinson, James. 2006. *Economic Origins of Dictatorship and Democracy*. Cambridge: Cambridge University Press.

A'Hearn, Brian, Baten, Jörg, and Crayen, Dorothee. 2009. "Quantifying Quantitative Literacy: Age Heaping and the History of Human Capital." *Journal of Economic History*, Vol. 69, No. 3 (Sept.), pp. 783–808.

Alchian, Armen and Demsetz, Harold. 1972. "Production, Information Costs, and Economic Organization." *American Economic Review*, Vol. 62, No. 5 (Dec.), pp. 777–95.

Alison, William P. 1840. *Observations on the Management of the Poor in Scotland and its Effects on the Health of the Great Towns*. Edinburgh: W. Blackwood and Sons.

Allan, D.G.C. 1979. *William Shipley: Founder of the Royal Society of Arts*. Aldershot: Scolar Press.

Allen, Douglas W. and Barzel, Yoram. 2007. "Legal Institutions Supporting the Industrial Revolution." Unpublished ms., University of Washington.

Allen, Robert C. 1992. *Enclosure and the Yeoman: The Agricultural Development of the South Midlands, 1450–1850*. Oxford: Clarendon Press.

————. 1999. "Tracking the Agricultural Revolution in England." *Economic History Review*, Vol. 52, No. 2 (May), pp. 209–35.

————. 2001. "The Great Divergence in Wages and Prices from the Middle Ages to the First World War." *Explorations in Economic History*, Vol. 38, No. 4 (Oct.), pp. 411–47.

————. 2004. "Agriculture during the Industrial Revolution, 1700–1850." In Roderick C. Floud and Paul Johnson, eds., *The Cambridge Economic History of Britain, 1700–2000*, Vol. 1. Cambridge: Cambridge University Press, pp. 96–116.

————. 2006. "Capital Accumulation, Technological Change, and the Distribution of Income during the British Industrial Revolution." Unpublished ms., Nuffield College, Oxford University.

————. 2008. "The Nitrogen Hypothesis and the English Agricultural Revolution: A Biological Analysis." *Journal of Economic History*, Vol. 86, No. 1 (March), pp. 182–210.

————. 2009. *The British Industrial Revolution in Global Perspective*. Cambridge: Cambridge University Press.

Allen, Robert C. and Ó Gráda, Cormac. 1988. "On the Road Again with Arthur Young: English, Irish, and French Agriculture during the Industrial Revolution." *Journal of Economic History*, Vol. 38, No. 1 (March), pp. 93–116.

Anderson, B.L. 1982. "The Attorney and the Early Capital Market in Lancashire." In François Crouzet, ed., *Capital Formation in the Industrial Revolution*. London: Methuen, pp. 223–55.

Anderson, Gary M. and Tollison, Robert D. 1985. "Ideology, Interest Groups, and the Repeal of the Corn Laws." *Journal of Institutional and Theoretical Economics*, Vol. 141, No. 2 (June), pp. 197–212.

Anderson, J.L. 1974. "A Measure of the Effect of British Public Finance, 1793–1815." *Economic History Review*, New Series, Vol. 27, No. 4 (Nov.), pp. 610–19.

Anderson, James. 1777. *Observations on the Means of Exciting a Spirit of National Industry*. Edinburgh: Printed for T. Cadell.

————. 1782. *The Interest of Great Britain with Respect to the American Colonies*. London: Printed for T. Cadell.

Anderson, Michael. 1972. "Household Structure and the Industrial Revolution: Mid-Nineteenth-Century Preston in Comparative Perspective." In Peter Laslett and Richard Wall, eds., *Household and Family in Past Time*. Cambridge: Cambridge University Press, pp. 215–36.

Anton, James J. and Yao, Dennis A. 1994. "Expropriation and Inventions: Appropriable Rents in the Absence of Property Rights." *American Economic Review*, Vol. 84, No. 1 (March), pp. 190–209.

Antrás, Pol and Voth, Joachim. 2003. "Factor Prices and Productivity Growth during the British Industrial Revolution." *Explorations in Economic History*, Vol. 40, No. 1 (Jan.), pp. 52–77.

Armstrong, John. 1987. "The Role of Coastal Shipping in UK Transport: an Estimate of Comparative Traffic Movements in 1910." *Journal of Transport History*, Vol. 8, No. 2, pp. 164–78, repr. in Amstrong, 1996, pp. 148–62.

————.1996. "Introduction." In John Armstrong, ed., *Coastal and Short Sea Shipping*. Aldershot: Scolar Press, pp. ix–xxiv.

Ashton, T.S. 1924. *Iron and Steel in the Industrial Revolution*. Manchester: Manchester University Press.

————. 1948. *The Industrial Revolution, 1760–1830*. Oxford: Oxford University Press.

————. 1955. *An Economic History of England: The 18th Century*. London: Methuen.

Auerbach, Jeffrey A. 1999. *The Great Exhibition of 1851: A Nation on Display*. New Haven, CT and London: Yale University Press.

Austen, B. 1981. "The Impact of the Mail Coach on Public Coach Service in England and Wales, 1784–1840." *Journal of Transport History*, 3rd series, Vol. 2, No. 1, pp. 164–78, repr. in Gerhold, 1996b, pp. 207–19.

A.Z. 1754. *Some Thoughts relating to Trade in General and to the East India Trade in Particular*. London: printed for R. Baldwin.

Babbage, Charles. 1830. "Reflections on the Decline of Science in Britain and on Some of its Causes." *Quarterly Review* (London), Vol. 43 (May and Oct.), pp. 307–42, repr. New York: Augustus Kelley, 1970.

Bacon, Francis. 1850. *The Works of Francis Bacon*, ed. Basil Montagu. 3 vols. Philadelphia, PA: A. Hart.

————. 1996. *The Major Works*, ed. Brian Vickers. Oxford: Oxford University Press.

Bagwell, Philip S. 1974. *The Transport Revolution from 1770*. London: Batsford.

Baily, Francis. 1808. *The Doctrine of Interest and Annuities Analytically Investigated and Explained*. London: Sold by J. Richardson.

Baines, Edward. 1835. *History of the Cotton Manufacture in Great Britain*. London: H. Fisher.

Baines, Thomas. 1875. *Yorkshire Past & Present: A History and Description of the Three Ridings of the Great County of York*, London: William Mackenzie. http://freepages. genealogy. rootsweb.com/~wakefield/history/baines3.html

Bairoch, Paul. 1982. "International Industrialization Levels from 1750 to 1980." *Journal of European Economic History*, Vol. 11, No. 2 (Spring), pp. 269–333.

Bairoch, Paul. 1988. *Cities and Economic Development from the Dawn of History to the Present.* Chicago: University of Chicago Press.

————. 1989. "European Trade Policy, 1815–1914." In P. Mathias and S. Pollard, eds., *The Cambridge Economic History of Europe,* Vol. 8: *Industrial Economies: The Development of Economic and Social Policies.* Cambridge: Cambridge University Press, pp. 1–160.

Banta, James E. 1987. "Sir William Petty: Modern Epidemiologist." *Journal of Community Health,* Vol. 12, Nos. 2/3 (Summer/Fall), pp. 185–98.

Barbon, Nicholas [N.B., M.D.] 1690. *A Discourse of Trade.* London: Thomas Milbourn, for the author.

Barker, T.C. and Harris, John R. 1954. *A Merseyside Town in the Industrial Revolution: St. Helens, 1750–1900.* Liverpool: Liverpool University Press.

Baston, Thomas. 1728. *Thoughts on Trade, and a Publick Spirit, considered under the following heads, viz. I. Companies in trade. II. Stock-jobbers. III. Projectors ...* 2nd edn., with additions. London: Printed for the Author.

Baumol, William J. 1993. *Entrepreneurship, Management, and the Structure of Payoffs.* Cambridge, Mass.: MIT Press.

————. 2002. *The Free-Market Innovation Machine: Analyzing the Growth Miracle of Capitalism.* Princeton, NJ: Princeton University Press.

Baxby, Derrick. 2004. "Jenner, Edward (1749–1823)." *Oxford Dictionary of National Biography.* Oxford: Oxford University Press.

Beattie, J.M. 1974. "The Pattern of Crime in England, 1660–1800." *Past and Present,* No. 62 (Feb.), pp. 47–95.

————. 1986. *Crime and the Courts in England, 1660–1800.* Princeton, NJ: Princeton University Press.

Beckett, J.V. 1989. "Landownership and Estate Management." *The Agrarian History of England and Wales,* Vol. 6: *1750–1850,* ed. G.E. Mingay. Cambridge: Cambridge University Press, pp. 545–640.

Beckett, J.V. and Turner, Michael. 1990. "Taxation and Economic Growth in Eighteenth-century England." *Economic History Review,* Vol. 43, No. 3 (Aug.), pp. 377–403.

Beddoes, Thomas. 1793. *A Letter to Erasmus Darwin, M.D. on a New Method of Treating Pulmonary Consumption, and Some Other Diseases Hitherto found Incurable.* Bristol: Bulgin and Rosser.

Berg, Maxine. 1980. *The Machinery Question and the Making of Political Economy, 1815–1848.* Cambridge: Cambridge University Press.

————. 1993. "What Difference Did Women's Work Make to the Industrial Revolution?" *History Workshop Journal,* Vol. 35 (Spring), pp. 22–44.

————. 1994. *The Age of Manufactures.* London: Fontana Press. 2nd revised edition, London: Routledge.

————. 2005. *Luxury and Pleasure in Eighteenth-Century Britain.* Oxford: Oxford University Press.

————. 2006. "Britain, Industry and Perceptions of China: Matthew Boulton, 'Useful Knowledge' and the Macartney Embassy to China 1792–94." *Journal of Global History* Vol. 1, No. 2 (May), pp. 269–88

Berg, Maxine. 2007. "The Genesis of Useful Knowledge." *History of Science*, Vol. 45, pt. 2, No. 148 (June), pp. 123–34.

Berg, Maxine and Hudson, Pat. 1992. "Rehabilitating the Industrial Revolution." *Economic History Review*, Vol. 45, No. 1 (Feb), pp. 24–50.

Berlin, Michael. 2008. "Guilds in Decline? London Livery Companies and the Rise of a Liberal Economy." In S.R. Epstein and Maarten Prak, eds., *Guilds, Innovation, and the European Economy, 1400–1800*. Cambridge: Cambridge University Press, pp. 316–41.

Bessemer, Henry. 1905. *An Autobiography*. HTML version produced by Eric Hutton, available at http://www.history.rochester.edu/ehp–book/shb/start.ht

Birse, Ronald M. 1983. *Engineering at Edinburgh University: A Short History, 1673–1983*. Edinburgh: School of Engineering, University of Edinburgh.

Blackstone, William. 1765–69. *Commentaries on the Laws of England*. 1ˢᵗ edn. Oxford: Printed at the Clarendon Press. http://www.yale.edu/lawweb/avalon/blackstone/ blacksto. htm

Blanqui, Adolphe–Jérôme. 1824. *Voyage d'un jeune Français en Angleterre et en Ecosse, pendant l'automne de 1823*. Paris: Dondey–Dupré père et fils.

Blaug, Mark. 1964. "The Poor Law Report Reexamined," *The Journal of Economic History*, Vol. 24, No. 2. (June), pp. 229–45.

Bogart, Dan. 2005a. "Turnpike Trusts and the Transportation Revolution in 18ᵗʰ Century Britain." *Explorations in Economic History*, Vol. 42, No. 4 (Oct.), pp. 479–508.

———. 2005b. "Did Turnpike Trusts Increase Transportation Investment in Eighteenth-century England?" *Journal of Economic History*, Vol. 65, No. 2 (June), pp. 439–68.

Boldrin, Michele and Levine, David K. 2008. *Against Intellectual Monopoly*. Cambridge: Cambridge University Press.

Boot, H.M. 1995. "How Skilled Were Lancashire Cotton Factory Workers in 1833?" *Economic History Review*, Vol. 48, No. 2 (May), pp. 283–303.

Boswell, James. 1793. *The Life of Samuel Johnson, LL.D. Comprehending an Account of his Studies and Numerous Works*. London: Printed by Henry Baldwin.

Boussingault, J.B. 1821. "On the Presence of Silicia Platina and its Presence in Steel." *Repertory of Arts, Manufactures and Agriculture*, 2nd series, Vol. 39, pp. 366–73.

Bouyer, Reynold Gideon. 1789. *An account of the Origin, Proceedings, and Intentions of the Society for the Promotion of Industry*, 3ʳᵈ edn. *To this Edition is also added, a Report of the Board of Trade to the Lords Justices, by Mr. John Locke, with Notes by the Editor*. Louth: R. Sheardown.

Bowler, Peter J. and Morus, Iwan Rhys. 2005. *Making Modern Science*. Chicago: University of Chicago Press.

Boyd, Robert and Richerson, Peter J. 1985. *Culture and the Evolutionary Process*. Chicago: University of Chicago Press.

———. 2005. *Not by Genes Alone: How Culture Transformed Human Evolution*. Chicago: University of Chicago Press.

Boyer, George R. 1990. *An Economic History of the English Poor Law, 1750–1850*. Cambridge: Cambridge University Press.

Boyle, Robert. 1744. *The Works of the Honourable Robert Boyle*, 5 vols. London: Printed for A. Millar.

Braggion, Fabio. 2006. "Credit Market Constraints and Financial Networks in Late Victorian Britain." Unpublished working paper, Northwestern University, July.

Brenner, Robert. 1985. "Agrarian Class Structure and Economic Development in Pre-Industrial Europe." In T.H. Aston and C.H.E. Philpin, eds., *The Brenner Debate.* Cambridge: Cambridge University Press, pp. 10–63.

Brewer, John. 1982. "Commercialization and Politics." In Neil McKendrick et al., eds, *The Birth of a Consumer Society: The Commercialization of Eighteenth-century England.* Bloomington: Indiana University Press, pp. 197–262.

———. 1988. *The Sinews of Power: War, Money and the English State, 1688–1783.* New York: Alfred A. Knopf.

Brewer, John and Styles, John, eds. 1980. *An Ungovernable People: The English and their Law in the Seventeenth and Eighteenth Centuries.* New Brunswick: Rutgers University Press.

Briggs, Asa. 1959. *The Age of Improvement.* London: Longman.

Broadberry, Stephen and Bishnupriya Gupta. 2009. "Lancashire, India, and Shifting Competitive Advantage in Cotton Textiles, 1700–1850: The Neglected Role of Factor Prices." *Economic History Review*, Vol. 62, No. 2 (May), pp. 279–305.

Brooks, C.W. 1989. "Interpersonal Conflict and Social Tension: Civil Litigation in England, 1640–1830." In A.L. Beier et al., eds., *The First Modern Society: Essays in English History in Honor of Lawrence Stone.* Cambridge: Cambridge University Press. Repr. in Brooks (1998), pp. 27–62.

———. 1998. *Lawyers, Litigation and English Society since 1450.* London: Hambledon Press.

Brown, John C. 1990. "The Condition of England and the Standard of Living: Cotton Textiles in the Northwest, 1806–1850." *Journal of Economic History*, Vol. 50, No. 3 (Sept.), pp. 591–614.

Brown, Jonathan, and Beecham, H.A. 1989. "The Breeding of Horses." In G.E. Mingay, ed., *The Agrarian History of England and Wales:* Vol. 6: *1750–1850.* Cambridge: Cambridge University Press, pp. 351–53.

Broz, J. Lawrence and Grossman, Richard S. 2004. "Paying for Privilege: The Political Economy of Bank of England Charters, 1694–1844." *Explorations in Economic History*, Vol. 41, No. 1 (Jan.), pp. 48–72.

Brunnermeier, Markus K. and Parker, Jonathan A. 2005. "Optimal Expectations." *American Economic Review*, Vol. 95, No. 4 (Sept.), pp. 1092–118.

Brunt, Liam. 2003. "Mechanical Innovation in the Industrial Revolution: The Case of Plough Design." *Economic History Review,* Vol. 56 No. 3 (Aug.), pp. 444–77.

———. 2006a. "Why Was England First: Agricultural Productivity Growth in England and France, 1700–1850." Unpublished ms.

———. 2006b. "Rediscovering Risk: Country Banks as Venture Capital Firms in the First Industrial Revolution." *Journal of Economic History,* Vol. 66, No. 1 (March), pp. 74–102.

———. 2007. "Where There's Muck, There's Brass: The Market for Manure in the Industrial Revolution." *Economic History Review*, Vol. 60, No. 2 (May), pp. 333–72.

Buchan, William. 1772. *Domestic Medicine: or, a Treatise on the Prevention and Cure of Diseases by Regimen and Simple Medicines.* 2nd edition, with considerable additions. London: W. Strahan.

Buchinsky, Moshe, and Polak, Ben. 1993. "The Emergence of a National Capital Market in England, 1710–1880." *Journal of Economic History*, Vol. 53, No. 1 (March), pp. 1–24.

Burke, Peter. 2000. *A Social History of Knowledge.* Cambridge: Polity Press.

Burnette, Joyce. 1997. "An Investigation of the Female–Male Wage Gap During the Industrial Revolution in Britain." *Economic History Review*, New Series, Vol. 50, No. 2 (May), pp. 257–81.

———. 1999. "Laborers at the Oakes: Changes in the Demand for Female Day Laborers at a Farm near Sheffield during the Agricultural Revolution." *Journal of Economic History*, Vol. 39, No. 1 (March), pp. 41–67.

———. 2004. "The Wages and Employment of Female Day Labourers in English Agriculture, 1740–1850." *Economic History Review*, Vol. 57, No. 4, pp. 664–90.

———. 2008. *Gender, Work, and Wages in Industrial Revolution Britain.* New York: Cambridge University Press.

Burton, Anthony. 2000. *Richard Trevithick: Giant of Steam.* London: Aurum Press.

Bythell, Duncan. 1978. *The Sweated Trades.* New York: St Martin's Press.

Cain, P.J. 2006. "Bentham and the Development of the British Critique of Colonialism." Unpublished ms. University of Geneva.

Cain, P. J. and Hopkins, Anthony G. 1980. "The Political Economy of British Expansion Overseas, 1750–1914." *Economic History Review*, New Series, Vol. 33, No. 4 (Nov.), pp. 463–90.

———. 1993. *British Imperialism: Innovation and Expansion.* Harlow, Essex: Longman.

Caird, James. [1852], 1967. *English Agriculture in 1850–51*, ed. with a new introduction by G.E. Mingay. London: Frank Cass.

Campbell, Bruce. 1983. "Arable Productivity in Medieval England: Some Evidence from Norfolk." *Journal of Economic History*, Vol. 43, No. 2 (June, 1983), pp. 379–404.

Campbell, Bruce and Overton, Mark. 1993. "A New Perspective on Medieval and Early Modern Agriculture: Six Centuries of Norfolk Farming c.1250–c.1850." *Past and Present*, No. 141, pp. 38–105.

Campbell, R.H. 1982. "The Enlightenment and the Economy." In R.H. Campbell and Andrew Skinner, eds., *The Origins and Nature of the Scottish Enlightenment.* Edinburgh: John Donald, pp. 8–25.

Capie, Forrest. 2004. "Money and Economic Development in Eighteenth-century England." In Leandro Prados de la Escosura, *Exceptionalism and Industrialization: Britain and its European Rivals, 1688–1815.* Cambridge: Cambridge University Press, pp. 216–34.

Cardwell, Donald S. L. 1972. *Turning Points in Western Technology.* New York: Neale Watson, Science History Publications.

———. 1994. *The Fontana History of Technology.* London: Fontana Press.

Carlyle, Thomas. 1829. "Sign of the Times," *Edinburgh Review* Vol. 49, available at http://www.victorianweb.org/authors/carlyle/signs1.html

Carnot, Sadi. 1824. *Reflections on the Motive Power of Heat.* At http://www.history.rochester.edu/steam/carnot/1943/

Carruthers, Bruce G. 1996. *City of Gold: Politics and Markets in the English Financial Revolution.* Princeton, NJ: Princeton University Press.

Carter, Philip. 2002. "Polite Persons: Character, Biography, and the Gentleman." *Transactions of the Royal Historical Society.* Vol. 12, pp. 333–54.

Chadwick, Edwin. [1843], 1965. *Report on the Sanitary Condition of the Labouring Population of Great Britain.* London: Her Majesty's Stationery Office, ed. M.W. Flinn. Edinburgh: Edinburgh University Press.

Chaloner, W.H. 1963. *People and Industries.* London: Frank Cass.

Chambers, J.D. and Mingay, G.E. 1966. *The Agricultural Revolution, 1750–1880.* London: Batsford.

Chandler, J.A.C. 1934. "Jefferson and William and Mary." *The William and Mary Quarterly,* 2nd series, Vol. 14, No. 4 (Oct.), pp. 304–07.

Chapman, S.D. 1979. "Financial Restraints on the Growth of Firms in the Cotton Industry, 1790–1850." *Economic History Review,* Vol. 32, No. 1 (Feb.), pp. 50–69.

Chaptal, J.A. 1819. *De l'Industrie Française.* 2 vols. Paris: A.A. Renouard.

Chitnis, Anand. 1976. *The Scottish Enlightenment.* London: Croom Helm.

————. 1986. *The Scottish Enlightenment and Early Victorian English Society.* London: Croom Helm.

Chorley, G.P.H. 1981. "The Agricultural Revolution in Northern Europe, 1750–1880: Nitrogen, Legumes, and Crop Productivity." *Economic History Review,* New Series, Vol. 34, No. 1 (Feb.), pp. 71–93.

Church, Roy. 1984. *The History of the British Coal Industry, Vol. 3: 1830–1913: Victorian Pre-eminence.* Oxford: Clarendon Press.

Cinnirella, Francesco. 2008. "Optimists or Pessimists? A Reconsideration of Nutritional Status in Britain, 1740–1865." *European Review of Economic History,* Vol. 12, No. 3 (Dec.), pp. 325–54.

Clapham, John. 1916. "The Spitalfields Acts, 1773–1824." *Economic Journal,* Vol. 26, No. 104 (Dec.), p. 459–71.

Clark, Anna. 1995. *The Struggle for the Breeches: Gender and the Making of the British Working Class.* Berkeley: University of California Press.

Clark, Gregory. 2001. "Debt, Deficits, and Crowding Out: England, 1727–1840." *European Review of Economic History,* Vol. 5. No. 3 (Dec.), pp. 403–36.

————. 2005. "The Condition of the Working Class in England, 1209–2004." *Journal of Political Economy,* Vol. 113, No. 6 (Dec.), pp. 1307–340.

————. 2007. *A Farewell to Alms.* Princeton: Princeton University Press.

Clark, Gregory and Hamilton, Gillian, 2006. "Survival of the Richest: The Malthusian Mechanism in Pre-Industrial England." *Journal of Economic History,* Vol. 66, No. 3 (Sept.), pp. 707–36.

Clark, Gregory, Huberman, Michael, and Lindert , Peter. 1995. "A British Food Puzzle." *Economic History Review,* New Series, Vol. 48, No. 2 (May), pp. 215–37.

Clark, Gregory and Jacks, David. 2007. "Coal and the Industrial Revolution." *European Review of Economic History,* Vol. 11, No. 1 (April), pp. 39–72.

Clark, Gregory, O'Rourke, Kevin H., and Taylor, Alan M. 2008. "Made in America? The New World, the Old, and the Industrial Revolution." Presented to the session New Comparative Economic History, ASSA, New Orleans, January 5, 2008.

Clark, Gregory and Page, Marianne. 2008. "Welfare Reform, 1834." Unpublished ms., University of California, Davis.

Clark, Jonathan C.D. 1985. *English Society, 1688–1832.* Cambridge: Cambridge University Press.

Clark, Peter. 2000. *British Clubs and Societies, 1580–1800: The Origins of an Associational World.* Oxford: Clarendon Press.

Clark, William. 1991. "The Scientific Revolution in the German Nations." In Roy Porter and Mikuláš Teich, eds., *The Scientific Revolution in National Context*. Cambridge: Cambridge University Press, pp. 90–114.

Clarkson, Leslie A. 1985. *Proto-Industrialization: The First Phase of Industrialization?* London: Macmillan.

Clow, Archibald and Clow, Nan L. 1952. *The Chemical Revolution: A Contribution to Social Technology*. London: Batchworth, repr. New York: Gordon and Breach, 1992.

Cobbett, William. 1821. "Letter to Mr. Gooch." *Cobbett's Political Register*, Vol. 38, pp. 749ff.

Cockburn, Henry. 1856. *Memorials of His Time*. New York: D. Appleton.

Cohen, H. Floris. 2004. "Inside Newcomen's Fire Engine: The Scientific Revolution and the Rise of the Modern World." *History of Technology*, Vol. 25, pp. 111–32.

Cohen, Jay. 1982. "History of Imprisonment for Debt." *Journal of Legal History*, Vol. 3, No. 2 (Sept.), pp. 153–71.

Coleman, Donald C. 1958. *The British Paper Industry: A Study in Industrial Growth*. Oxford: Clarendon Press.

———. 1973. "Gentlemen and Players." *Economic History Review,* Vol. 26, No. 1 (Jan.), pp. 92–116.

———. 1983. "Proto–Industrialization: A Concept Too Many." *Economic History Review*, New Series, Vol. 36, No. 3 (Aug.), pp. 435–48.

Coleman, Donald C. and MacLeod, Christine. 1986. "Attitudes to New Techniques: British Businessmen, 1800–1950." *Economic History Review*, New Series, Vol. 39, No. 4 (Nov.), pp. 588–611.

Colley, Linda. 1992. *Britons: Forging the Nation, 1707–1837*. New Haven, CT: Yale University Press.

Collins, E.J.T. 1969. "Harvest Technology and Labour Supply in Britain, 1790–1870." *Economic History Review*, New Series, Vol. 22, No. 3 (Dec.), pp. 453–73.

Colquhoun, Patrick. 1797. *A Treatise on the Police of the Metropolis; Containing a Detail of the Various Crimes and Misdemeanors*. 5th edn. London: Printed by H. Fry, Finsbury-Place.

Cookson, Gillian. 1997. "Family Firms and Business Networks: Textile Engineering in Yorkshire, 1780–1830." *Business History*, Vol. 39, No. 1 (Jan.), pp. 1–20.

Cooney, E.W. 1991. "Eighteenth Century Britain's Missing Sawmills: A Blessing in Disguise?" *Construction History*, Vol. 7, pp. 29–46.

———. 1998. "Eighteenth-century Britain's Missing Sawmills: A Return Visit." *Construction History*, Vol. 14, pp. 83–88.

Corfield, Penelope. 1995. *Power and the Professions in Britain 1700–1850*. London and New York: Routledge.

Cottrell, P.L. 1980. *Industrial Finance, 1830–1914*. London: Methuen.

Cowan, Brian. 2005. *The Social Life of Coffee: The Emergence of the British Coffeehouse*. New Haven, CT. and London: Yale University Press.

Crafts, Nicholas. 1985. *British Economic Growth during the Industrial Revolution*. Oxford: Oxford University Press.

———. 1997. "Some Dimensions of the 'Quality of Life' during the British Industrial Revolution." *Economic History Review*, Vol. 50, No. 4 (Nov.), pp. 617–39.

———. 2004. "Steam as a General Purpose Technology: A Growth Accounting Perspective." *Economic Journal*, Vol. 114 (April), pp. 338–51.

Crafts, Nicholas and Harley, C. Knick. 1992. "Output Growth and the Industrial Revolution: A Restatement of the Crafts–Harley View." *Economic History Review*, New Series, Vol. 45, No. 4 (Nov.), pp. 703–30.

———. 2004. "Precocious British Industrialization: A General-Equilibrium Perspective." In Leandro Prados de la Escosura, ed., *Exceptionalism and Industrialization: Britain and its European Rivals, 1688–1815*. Cambridge: Cambridge University Press, pp. 86–107.

Crafts, Nicholas and Mills, Terence C. 1997. "Endogenous Innovation, Trend Growth, and the British Industrial Revolution." *Journal of Economic History*, Vol. 57, No. 4 (Dec.), pp. 950–56.

Croarken, Mary. 2002. "Providing Longitude for All: The Eighteenth-century Computers of the Nautical Almanac." *Journal for Maritime Research*, Sept., pp. 1–22.

Crouzet, François. 1965. "Capital Formation in Great Britain During the Industrial Revolution." In *The Proceedings of the Second International Conference of Economic History*. The Hague. Reprinted in Crouzet, ed. 1972, pp. 162–222.

———. ed. 1972. *Capital Formation in the Industrial Revolution*. London: Methuen.

———. 1985. *The First Industrialists: The Problems of Origins*. Cambridge: Cambridge University Press.

———. 1987. *L'Economie Britannique et le blocus continental*. 2nd edn. Paris: Economica.

Crowhurst, Patrick. 1977. *The Defence of British Trade: 1689–1815*. Folkestone: Dawson.

Crowley, John E. 1990. "Neo–mercantilism and the Wealth of Nations: British Commercial Policy after the American Revolution." *The Historical Journal*, Vol. 33, No. 2 (June), pp. 339–60.

Cuenca Esteban, Javier. 1994. "British Textile Prices, 1770–1831: Are British Growth Rates Worth Revising Again?" *Economic History Review*, New Series, Vol. 47, No. 1 (Feb.), pp. 66–105.

———. 1997. "The Rising Share of British Industrial Exports in Industrial Output, 1723–1851." *Journal of Economic History*, Vol. 57, No. 4 (Dec.), pp. 879–906.

———. 2004. "Comparative Patterns of Colonial Trade: Britain and its Rivals." In Leandro Prados de la Escosura, ed., *Exceptionalism and Industrialization: Britain and its European Rivals, 1688–1815*. Cambridge: Cambridge University Press, pp. 35–66.

Cullen, M.J. 1975. *The Statistical Movement in Early Victorian Britain*. New York: Barnes and Noble.

Cunningham, Hugh. 1990. "The Employment and Unemployment of Children in England, c. 1680–1851." *Past and Present*, No. 126 (Feb.), pp. 115–50.

Dam, Kenneth W. 2005. *The Law-Growth Nexus: The Rule of Law and Economic Development*. Washington: Brookings Institution Press.

Darwin, Erasmus. 1794–96. *Zoonomia; or, the Laws of Organic Life*. London: Printed for J. Johnson.

Daston, Lorraine. 1988. *Classical Probability in the Enlightenment*. Princeton, NJ: Princeton University Press.

Daunton, Martin J. 1989. "Gentlemanly Capitalism and British Industry 1820–1914." *Past and Present*, No. 122 (Feb.), pp. 119–58.

Davenant, Charles. [1698], 1771. "Discourses on the Public Revenues, and on the Trade of England." Repr. in Davenant, Charles, *The Political and Commercial Works of that Celebrated Writer Charles D'avenant, LL.D.*, collected and revised by Sir Charles Whitworth, Vol. 1, pp. 150–67. London: Printed for A. Horsfield.

Davenant, Charles.[1699], 1771. *Essay upon the Probable Methods of Making a People Gainers in the Balance of Trade*. London: Printed for J. Knapton. Repr. in Davenant, Charles, *The Political and Commercial Works of that Celebrated Writer Charles D'avenant*, collected and revised by Sir Charles Whitworth, Vol. 2, pp. 168–382. London: Printed for A. Horsfield.

―――. 1701. *An Essay upon Ways and Means of Supplying the War*, 3rd edn. London: Jacob Tonson.

David, Paul A. 1975a. "Labor Scarcity and the Problem of Technological Practice and Progress in Nineteenth-century America." In David, *Technical Choice, Innovation and Economic Growth*. Cambridge: Cambridge University Press, pp. 19–91.

―――. 1975b. "The Landscape and the Machine." In David, *Technical Choice, Innovation, and Economic Growth*. Cambridge: Cambridge University Press, pp. 233–75.

―――. 2004. "Patronage, Reputation, and Common Agency Contracting in the Scientific Revolution." unpub. ms., Stanford University, Aug.

Davidoff, Leonore. 1995. "The Role of Gender in the 'First Industrial Nation': Farming and the Countryside in England, 1780–1850." In Davidoff, *Worlds Between: Historical Perspectives on Gender and Class*. New York: Routledge, pp. 180–205.

Davidoff, Leonore and Hall, Catherine. 1987. *Family Fortunes: Men and Women of the English Middle Class, 1780–1850*. London: Routledge.

Davies, Glyn. 2002. *History of Money from Ancient Times to the Present Day*. Cardiff: University of Wales Press.

Davis, Ralph. 1979. *The Industrial Revolution and British Overseas Trade*. Leicester: Leicester University Press.

Davy, Humphry. [1802], 1840. "A Discourse, Introductory to a Course of Lectures on Chemistry." In *The Collected Works of Sir Humphry Davy*, ed. John Davy, Vol. 2. London: Smith, Elder & Co.

Day, Lance and McNeil, Ian. 1996. *Biographical Dictionary of the History of Technology*. London and New York: Routledge.

Deane, Phyllis and Cole, W.A. 1969. *British Economic Growth, 1688–1959*. 2nd edn. Cambridge: Cambridge University Press.

Defoe, Daniel. 1703. *A Collection of the Writings of the Author of The true-born English-man*. London [no publisher listed].

―――. 1704–1713. *Defoe's Review*. Reproduced from the original editions, with an introduction and bibliographical notes by Arthur Wellesley Secord. New York: Published for the Facsimile Text Society by Columbia University Press.

―――. 1710. *An Essay upon Publick Credit*. London: Printed and Sold by the Booksellers.

―――. [1726–27], 2001. *A General History of Discoveries and Improvement*. Repr. in W.R. Owens and P.N. Furbank, eds., *Writings on Travel, Discovery, and History by Daniel Defoe*. London: Pickering & Chatto.

―――. 1727. *The Compleat English Tradesman*. 1st edn. 2 vols. London: C. Rivington.

―――. 1728. *A Plan of the English Commerce*. London: Charles Rivington.

―――. 1738. *The Complete English Tradesman*. 4th edn. 2 vols. London: C. Rivington.

De Moivre, Abraham. 1725. *Annuities upon Lives: Or, the Valuation of Annuities upon any Number of Lives; as also, of Reversions*. London: Printed by Francis Fayram.

Deng, Kenneth. 2004. "Why the Chinese Failed to Develop a Steam Engine." *History of Technology*, Vol. 25, pp. 151–71.

Desaguliers, John T. 1734–44. *A Course of Experimental Philosophy*, 2 vols. London: printed for John Senex.

———. 1763. *A Course of Experimental Philosophy*, 3rd edn., 2 vols. London: Printed for A. Millar.

De Vries, Jan. 1984. *European Urbanization, 1500–1800*. London: Methuen.

———. 1993. "Between Purchasing Power and the World of Goods: Understanding the Household Economy in Early Modern Europe." In John Brewer and Roy Porter, eds., *Consumption and the World of Goods*. London: Routledge, pp. 85–132.

———. 1994. "The Industrial Revolution and the Industrious Revolution." *Journal of Economic History*, Vol. 54, No. 2 (June), pp. 249–70.

———. 2008. *The Industrious Revolution: Consumer Behavior and the Household Economy, 1650 to the Present*. Cambridge: Cambridge University Press.

d'Holbach, Paul Henri Thiry, Baron. 1786. *Le Bon-sens, ou idées naturelles opposées aux idées surnaturelles*. London: n.p.

Diamond, Jared. 1997. *Guns, Germs and Steel: The Fates of Human Societies*. New York: Norton.

Dickinson, G.C. 1959. "Stage-coach Services in the West Riding of Yorkshire between 1830 and 1840." *Journal of Transport History*, Vol. 4, No. 1, pp. 1–12.

Dickinson, H.W. and Jenkins, Rhys. [1927], 1969. *James Watt and the Steam Engine*. London: Encore Editions, repr. edn.

Doepke, Matthias and Zilibotti, Fabrizio. 2008. "Occupational Choice and the Spirit of Capitalism." *Quarterly Journal of Economics*, Vol. 123, No. 2 (May), pp. 747–93.

Donovan, Arthur L. 1982. "William Cullen and the Research Tradition of Eighteenth-Century Scottish Chemistry." In R.H. Campbell and Andrew Skinner, eds., *The Origins and Nature of the Scottish Enlightenment*. Edinburgh: John Donald, pp. 98–114.

Dubois, A.B. 1938. *The English Business Company after the Bubble Act 1720–1800*. New York and London: Oxford University Press.

Dupin, Charles. 1825. *The Commercial Power of Great Britain: Exhibiting a Complete View of the Public Works of this Country*. London: Printed for C. Knight, 2 vols.

Dutton, H.I. 1984. *The Patent System and Inventive Activity during the Industrial Revolution 1750–1852*. Manchester: Manchester University Press.

Earle, Peter. 1977. *The World of Defoe*. New York: Atheneum.

———. 1989. "The Female Labour Market in London in the Late Seventeenth and Early Eighteenth Centuries." *Economic History Review*, Vol. 42, No. 3 (Aug.), pp. 328–53.

Eastwood, David. 1994. *Governing Rural England: Tradition and Transformation in Local Government 1780–1840*. New York: Oxford University Press.

Eden, Frederick Morton. 1797. *The State of the Poor: or, an History of the Labouring Classes in England,* 3 vols. London: J. Davis.

———. 1801. *Observations on Friendly Societies, for the Maintenance of the Industrious Classes, during Sickness, Infirmity, Old Age, and other Exigencies*. London: Printed for J. White.

Ekelund, Robert B. Jr. and Tollison, Robert D. 1981. *Mercantilism as a Rent-Seeking Society*. College Station: Texas A&M University Press.

———. 1997. *Politicized Economies: Monarchy, Monopoly, and Mercantilism*. College Station: Texas A&M University Press.

Elias, Norbert. 1978. *The Civilizing Process, Vol. I: The History of Manners*. New York: Pantheon Books.

Elliott, Paul. 2000. "The Birth of Public Science in the English Provinces: Natural Philosophy in Derby, c. 1690–1760." *Annals of Science*, Vol. 57, No. 4 (Oct.), pp. 61–101.

————. 2003. "The Origins of the 'Creative Class': Provincial Urban Society, Scientific Culture, and Socio-political marginality in Britain in the Eighteenth and Nineteenth Centuries." *Social History*, Vol. 28, No. 3, pp. 361–87.

Ellis, William. 1750. *The Modern Husbandman*, 8 vols. London: Printed for D. Browne, C. Davis, J. Shuckburgh, J. Whiston, and L. Davis, and J. Ward.

Eltis, David and Engerman, Stanley L. 2000. "The Importance of Slavery and the Slave Trade to Industrializing Britain." *Journal of Economic History*, Vol. 60, No. 1 (March), pp. 123–44.

Emerson, Roger. 2003. "The Contexts of the Scottish Enlightenment." In Alexander Broadie, ed., *The Cambridge Companion to the Scottish Enlightenment*. Cambridge: Cambridge University Press, pp. 9–30.

Emsley, Clive. 2005. *Crime and Society in England, 1750–1900*. 3rd edn., Harlow, Essex: Pearson Longman.

Engels, Friedrich. [1845]. 1958. *The Condition of the Working Class in England*. Ed. and trans. by W.O. Henderson and W.H. Chaloner. Stanford, Calif.: Stanford University Press.

Engerman, Stanley L. 1994. "Reflections on the 'Standard of Living Debate': New Arguments and New Evidence." In John A. James and Mark Thomas, eds., *Capitalism in Context: Essays on Economic Development and Cultural Change in Honor of R.M. Hartwell*. Chicago: University of Chicago Press, pp. 50–79.

————. 2004. "Institutional Change and British Supremacy, 1650–1850: Some Reflections." In Leandro Prados de la Escosura, ed., *Exceptionalism and Industrialization: Britain and its European Rivals, 1688–1815*. Cambridge: Cambridge University Press, pp. 261–82.

Erickson, Amy Louise. 2005. "Coverture and Capitalism." *History Workshop Journal*, Vol. 59, No. 1, pp. 1–16.

An Essay upon Public Credit, in a Letter to a Friend. Occasioned by the Fall of Stocks, 3rd edn. London: H. Carpenter, 1748.

Evelyn, John. [1661], 1772. *Fumifugium: or, the Inconvenience of the Aer, and Smoake of London Dissipated. Together with some Remedies Humbly Proposed*. London: Printed by W. Godbid.

Falkus, M.E. 1967. "The British Gas Industry before 1850." *Economic History Review*, Vol. 20, No. 3 (Dec.), pp. 494–508.

————. 1982. "The Early Development of the British Gas Industry, 1790–1815." *Economic History Review*, Vol. 35, pp. 217–34.

Farey, John. 1827. *A Treatise on the Steam Engine, Historical, Practical and Descriptive, Vol. I*. London: Longman.

————. 1971. *A Treatise on the Steam Engine, Historical, Practical and Descriptive, Vol. II*. Newton Abbot: David and Charles.

Feinstein, Charles. 1978. "Capital Formation in Great Britain." In P. Mathias and M. M. Postan, eds., *The Cambridge Economic History of Europe*, Vol. 7. Cambridge: Cambridge University Press, pp. 28–96.

————. 1981. "Capital Accumulation and the Industrial Revolution." In Roderick C. Floud and D.N. McCloskey, eds., *The Economic History of Britain since 1700. Vol. 1*. Cambridge: Cambridge University Press, pp. 128–42.

Feinstein, Charles. 1988. "The Rise and Fall of the Williamson Curve." *Journal of Economic History*, Vol. 48, No. 3 (Sept.), pp. 699–729.

———. 1998a. "Pessimism Perpetuated: Real Wages and the Standard of Living in Britain During and After the Industrial Revolution." *Journal of Economic History*, Vol. 58, No. 3 (Sept.), pp. 625–58.

———. 1998b. "Wage-earnings in Great Britain during the Industrial Revolution." In Iain Begg and S.G.B. Henry, eds., *Applied Economics and Public Policy*. Cambridge: Cambridge University Press, pp. 181–208.

Ferguson, Adam. 1767. *An Essay on the History of Civil Society*. Dublin: Boulter Grierson.

Ferguson, Eugene S. 1971. "The Measurement of the 'Man-Day'." *Scientific American*, Vol. 225 (Oct.), pp. 96–103.

Fildes, Valerie A. 1986. *Breasts, Bottles and Babies: A History of Infant Feeding*. Edinburgh: Edinburgh University Press.

Findlay, Ron and O'Rourke, Kevin. 2007. *Power and Plenty: Trade, War, and the World Economy in the Second Millennium*. Princeton, NJ: Princeton University Press.

Finn, Margot. 2003. *The Character of Credit: Personal Debt in English Culture, 1740–1914*. Cambridge: Cambridge University Press.

Flinn, Michael W. 1959. "Timber and the Advance of Technology: A Reconsideration." *Annals of Science* Vol. 15, pp. 109–20.

———. 1962. *Men of Iron: The Crowleys in the Early Iron Industry*. Edinburgh: Edinburgh University Press.

———. 1965. "Introduction" to Chadwick [1843], 1965.

———. 1978. "Technical Change as an Escape from Resource Scarcity: England in the Seventeenth and Eighteenth Centuries." In William N. Parker and Antoni Maczak, eds., *Natural Resources in European History*. Washington, D.C.: Resources for the Future.

———. 1981. *The European Demographic System, 1500–1820*. Baltimore, MD.: Johns Hopkins University Press.

———. 1984. *The History of the British Coal Industry, Vol. 2: 1700–1830, The Industrial Revolution*. Oxford: Clarendon Press.

Floud, Roderick C., Wachter, Kenneth, and Gregory, Annabel. 1990. *Height, Health, and History: Nutritional Status in the United Kingdom, 1750–1980*. Cambridge: Cambridge University Press.

Fogel, Robert W. 1983. "Scientific History and Traditional History." In Robert W. Fogel and G.R. Elton, eds., *Which Road to the Past?* New Haven, CT and London: Yale University Press, pp. 5–70.

———. 2004. *The Escape from Hunger and Premature Death: Europe, America, and the Third World*. Cambridge: Cambridge University Press.

Fogel, Robert W., Floud, Roderick C., and Harris, B. forthcoming. "A Treatise on Technophysio Evolution and Consumption." In progress.

Ford, Richard. 1926. "Imprisonment for Debt." *Michigan Law Review*, Vol. 25, No. 1 (Nov.), pp. 24–49.

Foreman-Peck James. 1991. "Railways and Late Victorian Economic Growth." In James Foreman-Peck, ed. *New Perspectives on the Late Victorian Economy: Essays in Quantitative Economic History, 1860–1914*. Cambridge: Cambridge University Press, pp. 73–95.

Fouquet, Roger and Pearson, Peter J.G. 2006. "Seven Centuries of Energy Services: The Price and Use of Light in the United Kingdom, 1300–2000." *The Energy Journal*, Vol. 27, No. 1, pp. 139–77.

Frank, Johann Peter. [1786], 1976. *A System of Complete Medical Police*, selected and edited by Erna Lesky. Baltimore, MD.: Johns Hopkins University Press.

Franklin, Benjamin. 1760. *New Experiments and Observations on Electricity. Made at Philadelphia in America. By Benjamin Franklin, Esq; and Communicated in Several Letters to Peter Collinson, Esq; of London, F.R.S.* Part I. 3rd edn. London: D. Henry and R. Cave at St. John's Gate.

———. [1783], 1907. *The Writings of Benjamin Franklin*, edited by Albert Henry Smyth. New York: Macmillan.

———. 1887. *The Works of Benjamin Franklin* edited by John Bigelow. New York: Putnam's Sons.

Freeman, Michael. 1980. "Transporting Methods in the British Cotton Industry during the Industrial Revolution." *Journal of Transport History*, 3rd Series, No. 1, Col. 1 (Sept.), pp. 59–73.

Friedman, Benjamin M. 2005. *The Moral Consequences of Economic Growth*. New York: Alfred Knopf.

Gale, K.W.V. 1961–62. "Wrought Iron: A Valediction." *Transactions of the Newcomen Society*, Vol. 36, pp. 1–11.

Galloway, Patrick R. 1988. "Basic Patterns in Annual Variations in Fertility, Nuptiality, Mortality, and Prices in Pre-industrial Europe." *Population Studies*, Vol. 42, No. 2 (July), pp. 275–302.

Galor, Oded. 2005. "From Stagnation to Growth: Unified Growth Theory." In Philippe Aghion and Steven N. Durlauf, eds., *Handbook of Economic Growth*, Vol. 1A, pp. 171–293.

Galor, Oded and Moav, Omer. 2002. "Natural Selection and the Origins of Economic Growth." *Quarterly Journal of Economics*, Vol. 117, No. 4 (Nov.), pp. 1133–91.

———. 2006. "Das Human Kapital: A Theory of the Demise of the Class Structure." *Review of Economic Studies*, Vol. 73, No. 1 (Jan.), pp. 85–117.

Galor Oded and Weil, David N. 2000. "Population, Technology, and Growth: From Malthusian Stagnation to the Demographic Transition and Beyond." *American Economic Review*, Vol. 90, No. 4 (Sept.), pp. 806–28.

Garrison, Fielding H. 1929. *Introduction to the History of Medicine*. 4th edn., Philadelphia, PA: W. B. Saunders.

Gaskell, Peter. 1833. *The Manufacturing Population of England, its Moral, Social and Physical Conditions*. London: Baldwin and Cradock.

Gay, Peter. 1966. *The Enlightenment*. Vol 1: *The Rise of Modern Paganism*. New York: Norton.

———. 1969. *The Enlightenment*. Vol. 2: *The Science of Freedom*. New York: Norton.

George, M. Dorothy. 1966. *London Life in the Eighteenth Century*. 2nd edn., Harmondsworth: Penguin Books.

Geraghty, Thomas M. 2007. "The Factory System in the British Industrial Revolution: A Complementarity Thesis." *European Economic Review*, Vol. 51, No. 6 (Aug.), pp. 1329–50.

Gerhold, Dorian. 1996a. "Productivity Change in Road Transport before and after Turnpiking, 1690–1840." *Economic History Review*, Vol. 49, No. 3 (Aug.), pp. 491–515.

———. ed. 1996b. *Road Transport in the Horse-Drawn Era (Studies in Transport History)*. Aldershot: Scolar Press.

Gillispie, Charles C. 1960. *The Edge of Objectivity*. Princeton, NJ: Princeton University Press.

Gillispie, Charles C. 1980. *Science and Polity in France at the End of the Old Regime*. Princeton, NJ: Princeton University Press.

Godwin, William. 1798. *Enquiry Concerning Political Justice and its Influence on Morals and Happiness*. 3rd edn., corrected. London: Paternoster Row, printed for G.G. and J. Robinson.

Goldstone, Jack A. 1991. "The Cause of Long Waves in Early Modern Economic History." In Joel Mokyr, ed., *The Vital One: Essays in Honor of J.R.T. Hughes*. Greenwich, CT: JAI Press, pp. 51–92.

———. 1996. "Gender, Work, and Culture: Why the Industrial Revolution came Early to England but Late to China." *Sociological Perspectives*, Vol. 39, No. 1 (spring), pp. 1–21.

Golinski, Jan. 1992. *Science as Public Culture: Chemistry and Enlightenment in Britain, 1760–1820*. Cambridge: Cambridge University Press.

———. 2004. "Nicholson, William (1753–1815)." *Oxford Dictionary of National Biography*. Oxford: Oxford University Press.

Gourvish, T.R. 1980. *Railways and the British Economy*. London: Macmillan.

———. 1988. "Railways 1830–1870: The Formative Years." In Michael J. Freeman and Derek H. Aldcroft, eds., *Transport in Victorian Britain*. Manchester and New York: Manchester University Press, pp. 58–91.

Grabiner, Judith. 1998. "'Some Disputes of Consequence': MacLaurin among the Molasses Barrels." *Social Studies of Science*, Vol. 28, No. 1, pp. 139–68.

———. 2004. "Newton, Maclaurin, and the Authority of Mathematics." *American Mathematical Monthly*, Vol. 111, no. 10 (Dec.), pp. 841–52.

Grampp, William D. 1987a. "How Britain Turned to Free Trade." *Business History Review*, Vol. 61, No. 1 (spring), pp. 86–112.

———. 1987b. "Britain and Free Trade: In Whose Interest?" *Public Choice*, Vol. 55, No. 3, pp. 245–56.

Great Britain, B.P.P. 1806. Vol. III, No. 268 ("Select Committee on the State of the Woollen Manufacture of England").

———. B.P.P. 1808. Vol. II, No. 177 ("Select Committee on Petitions of Cotton Manufacturers and Journeymen Cotton Weavers").

———. B.P.P. 1818. Vol. VI, No. 376 ("Report from the Select Committee on the Usury Laws").

———. B.P.P. 1829. Vol. III, No. 332 ("Select Committee on State of Law and Practice relative to Granting of Patents for Inventions").

———. B.P.P. 1831–32. Vol. XXVI, No. 90 (" Return of Number of Friendly Societies filed by Clerks of Peace in Great Britain and Ireland, 1793–1831").

———. B.P.P. 1833. Vol. VI, No. 690 ("Select Committee on the State of Manufactures, Commerce and Shipping").

———. B.P.P. 1834a. Vol. XIX, No. 167 ("Royal Commission on Employment of Children in Factories, Supplementary Reports, Parts I and II").

———. B.P.P. 1834b. Vols. XXVII–XXXIX ("Report from His Majesty's Commissioners for Inquiry into the Administration and Practical Operation of the Poor Laws").

Great Britain. B.P.P. 1839. Vol. XVI, No. 187 ("First Annual Report of the Registrar General").

————. B.P.P. 1840. Vol. XI, No. 384 ("Report of the Select Committee on Health of Towns").

————. B.P.P. 1841. Vol. VII, No. 201 ("Select Committee on Operation of Laws Affecting the Exportation of Machinery, first report").

————. B.P.P. 1842. Vols. XV–XVII, Nos. 380–382 ("First Report of the Royal Commission on Children's Employment in Mines and Manufactories").

————. B.P.P. 1843. Vol. XII, No. 510 ("Reports of Special Assistant Poor Law Commissioners on Employment of Women and Children in Agriculture").

————. B.P.P. 1844a. Vol. XVII, No. 572 ("First Report of Royal Commission for inquiring into State of Large Towns and Populous Districts").

————. B.P.P. 1844b. Vol. XXVII, No. 587 ("Abstract of the Answers ... for Taking an Account of the Population of Great Britain," [1841 Census]).

————. B.P.P. 1845. Vol. XVIII, Nos. 602, 610. ("Second Report of Royal Commission for inquiring into State of Large Towns and Populous Districts").

————. B.P.P. 1851. Vol. XVIII, No. (486) ("Select Committee of House of Lords to consider Bills for Amendment of Law touching Letters Patent for Inventions").

————. B.P.P. 1852–53a. Vols. LXXXV–LXXXVIII, Nos. 163–66 ("Census of Great Britain: Population Tables").

————. B.P.P. 1852–53b. Vol. LXXXVIII, Pts 1–2, Nos. 1691–I–II ("Population Tables, 1851, Part II. Ages and Occupations").

————. B.P.P. 1856. Vol. VIII, No. 379 ("Select Committee to Inquire into Adulteration of Food, Drinks and Drugs").

————. B.P.P. 1864. Vol. XXIX, No. 3419 ("Royal Commision to Inquire into Working of Law Relating to Letters Patent for Inventions").

Green, David R. and Owens, Alastair. 2003. "Gentlewomanly Capitalism? Spinsters, Widows and Wealth Holding in England and Wales, c. 1800–1960." *Economic History Review*, Vol. 56, No. 3 (Aug.), pp. 510–36.

Greif, Avner. 2005. *Institutions and the Path to the Modern Economy: Lessons from Medieval Trade.* Cambridge: Cambridge University Press.

————. 2006. "Family Structure, Institutions, and Growth: The Origins and Implications of Western Corporations." *American Economic Review*, Vol. 96, No. 2 (May), pp. 308–12.

Greif, Avner and Sasson, Diego. 2009. "Risk, Institutions and Growth: Why England and Not China?" Unpublished ms., Stanford University.

Griffiths, John. 1992. *The Third Man: The Life and Times of William Murdoch.* London: André Deutsch.

Grosley, Pierre Jean. 1772. *A Tour to London; or, New Observations on England, and its Inhabitants,* translated from the French by Thomas Nugent. London: Printed for Lockyer Davis.

Grossman, Richard S. 2009. *The Evolution of Commercial Banking in the Industrialized World since 1800.* Unpublished ms., Wesleyan University.

Habakkuk, H.J. 1962. *American and British Technology in the Nineteenth Century: The Search for Labor-saving Inventions.* Cambridge: Cambridge University Press.

Habermas, Jürgen. 1991. *The Structural Transformation of the Public Sphere: An Inquiry into a Category of Bourgeois Society.* Cambridge, MA: MIT Press.

Halstead, P.E. 1961–62. "The Early History of Portland Cement." *Transactions of the Newcomen Society*, Vol. 34, pp. 37–54.

Hamlin, Christopher. 2006. "William Pulteney Alison, the Scottish Philosophy, and the Making of a Political Medicine." *Journal of the History of Medicine and Allied Sciences*, Vol. 61, No. 2, April 2006, pp. 144–86.

Hammersley, G. 1973. "The Charcoal Iron Industry and its Fuel, 1540–1750." *Economic History Review,* Vol. 24, pp. 593–613.

Hampson, Norman. 1968. *The Enlightenment: An Evaluation of its Assumptions, Attitudes and Values.* Harmondsworth: Penguin Books.

Harley, C. Knick. 1988. "Ocean Freight Rates and Productivity, 1740–1913: The Primacy of Mechanical Invention Reaffirmed." *Journal of Economic History*, Vol. 48, No. 4 (Dec.), pp. 851–76.

————. 1994. "Foreign Trade: Comparative Advantage and Performance." In Roderick C. Floud and D.N. McCloskey, eds., *The Economic History of Britain Since 1700*, Vol. 1. Cambridge: Cambridge University Press, pp. 300–31.

————. 1998. "Re-assessing the Industrial Revolution: A Macro View." In Joel Mokyr, ed., The British Industrial Revolution: An Economic Perspective. Boulder, CO: Westview Press, pp. 160–205.

————. 2004. "Trade: Discovery, Mercantilism and Technology." In Roderick C. Floud and Paul Johnson, eds., *The Cambridge Economic History of Britain, 1700–2000*, Vol. 1. Cambridge: Cambridge University Press, pp. 175–203.

Harling, Philip. 1995. "Rethinking 'Old Corruption'." *Past and Present*, No. 147 (May), pp. 127–58.

————. 1996. *The Waning of 'Old Corruption': The Politics of Economical Reform in Britain, 1779–1846*. Oxford: Clarendon Press.

Harris, John R. 1956. "Liverpool Canal Controversies." *Journal of Transport History*, Vol. 2, No. 3, pp. 158–74.

————. 1966. "Copper and Shipping in the Eighteenth Century." *Economic History Review*, New Series, Vol. 19, No. 3 (Aug.), pp. 550–68.

————. 1988. *The British Iron Industry, 1700–1850*. Houndsmill and London: Macmillan Education.

————. 1992. "Skills, Coal and British Industry in the Eighteenth Century." In J.R. Harris, *Essays in Industry and Technology in the Eighteenth Century*. Aldershot: Ashgate/Variorum.

————. 1998. *Industrial Espionage and Technology Transfer: Britain and France in the Eighteenth Century*. Aldershot: Ashgate.

————. 2004. "Williams, Thomas (1737–1802)", *Oxford Dictionary of National Biography*, Oxford: Oxford University Press.

Harris, Ron. 2000. *Industrializing English Law: Entrepreneurship and Business Organization, 1720–1844*. Cambridge: Cambridge University Press.

————. 2004. "Government and the Economy, 1688–1850." In Roderick C. Floud and Paul Johnson, eds., *The Cambridge Economic History of Modern Britain*, Vol. 1. Cambridge: Cambridge University Press, pp. 204–37.

Harrison, Paul. 2003. "The Economic Effects of Innovation, Regulation, and Reputation on Derivatives Trading: Some Historical Analysis of Early 18th Century Stock Markets." Unpublished, Federal Reserve Board, Washington, D.C.

Hart, Ivor Blashka. 1949. *James Watt and the History of Steam Power*. New York: Henry Schuman.

Hartwell, R.M. 1971. *The Industrial Revolution and Economic Growth*. London: Methuen.

Hartwell, R.M. and Engerman, S.L. 1975. "Models of Immiseration: The Theoretical Basis of Pessimism." In Arthur J. Taylor, ed., *The Standard of Living in Britain During the Industrial Revolution*. London: Methuen, pp. 189–213.

Hassall, Arthur Hill. 1855. *Food and its Adulterations*. London: Longman, Brown, Green and Longmans.

Hassan, J.A. 1985. "The Growth and Impact of the British Water Industry in the Nineteenth Century." *Economic History Review*, Vol. 38, No. 4 (Nov.), pp. 531–547.

Hawke, G.R. 1970. *Railways and Economic Growth in England and Wales, 1840–1870*. Oxford: Oxford University Press.

Hawke, Gary and Higgins, J.P.P. 1981. "Transport and Social Overhead Capital." In Roderick C. Floud and D.N. McCloskey, eds., *The Economic History of Britain Since 1700*, Vol. 1, 1st edn., pp. 227–52.

Hawkins, Francis Bisset. [1829], 1973. *Elements of Medical Statistics*. Repr. edition, Farnborough, Hants.: Gregg, International.

Hay, Douglas et al., eds. 1976. *Albion's Fatal Tree: Crime and Society in Eighteenth–Century England*. New York: Pantheon Books.

Headrick, Daniel. 2000. *When Information Came of Age: Technologies of Knowledge in the Age of Reason and Revolution, 1700–1850*. New York: Oxford University Press.

Heaton, Herbert. 1946. "A Merchant Adventurer in Brazil." *Journal of Economic History*, Vol. 6, No. 1 (May), pp. 1–23.

Heesom, A.J. 2004. "Buddle, John (1773–1843)." *Oxford Dictionary of National Biography*. Oxford: Oxford University Press.

Heilbron, J.L. 1990. "Introductory Essay." In *The Quantifying Spirit in the 18th Century*, ed. by Tore Frängsmyr, J.L. Heilbron, and Robin E. Rider. Berkeley: University of California Press, pp. 1–23.

Helling, Gertrud. 1977. *Nahrungsmittel-Produktion und Weltaussenhandel seit Anfang des 19. Jahrhunderts*. Berlin: Akademie Verlag.

Henderson, W.O. 1954. *Britain and Industrial Europe, 1750–1870; Studies in British Influence on the Industrial Revolution in Western Europe*. Liverpool: Liverpool University Press.

Herman, Arthur. 2001. *How the Scots Invented the Modern World*. New York: Crown.

Hersch, Jonathan and Voth, Joachim. 2009. "Sweet Diversity: Colonial Goods and the Rise of European Living Standards after 1492." Unpublished ms., University Pompeu Fabreu.

Hilaire–Pérez, Liliane. 2000. *L'Invention technique au siècle des lumières*. Paris: Albin Michel.

———. 2007. "Technology as Public Culture." *History of Science*, Vol. 45, pt. 2, No. 148 (June), pp. 135–53.

Hills, Richard L. 1970. *Power in the Industrial Revolution*. Manchester: Manchester University Press.

———. 1989. *Power from Steam: A History of the Stationary Steam Engine*. Cambridge: Cambridge University Press.

———. 1994. *Power from Wind*. Cambridge: Cambridge University Press.

Hilton, Boyd. 1977. *Corn, Cash, Commerce: The Economic Policies of the Tory Governments 1815–1830*. Oxford: Oxford University Press.

Hilton, Boyd. 1979. "Peel: A Reappraisal." *Historical Journal*, Vol. 22, No. 3 (Sept.), pp. 585–614.

————. 2006. *A Mad, Bad and Dangerous People? England, 1783–1846*. Oxford: Clarendon Press.

Himmelfarb, Gertrude. 1971. "Mayhew's Poor: A Problem of Identity." *Victorian Studies*, Vol. 14, No. 3 (March), pp. 307–20.

————. 2004. *The Roads to Modernity: The British, French, and American Enlightenments*. New York: Vintage Books.

Hirsch, Fred. 1976. *Social Limits to Growth*. Cambridge, Mass.: Harvard University Press.

Hirschman, Albert O. 1977. *The Passions and the Interests: Political Arguments for Capitalism before its Triumph*. Princeton, NJ: Princeton University Press.

Hobsbawm, Eric. 1968. *Industry and Empire*. Harmondsworth: Penguin Books.

————. 1997. "Barbarism: A User's Guide." In Hobsbawm, *On History*. New York: New Press, pp. 253–65.

Hobson, John M. 2004. *The Eastern Origins of Western Civilisation*. Cambridge: Cambridge University Press.

Hodgskin, Thomas. 1825. *Labour Defended against the Claims of Capital*. 2nd edn. London: Knight and Lacey.

Hodgson, R.A. 1976. "The Economics of English Country Banking." *The Banker*, Vol. 126, Part 1. London: Banker Division of the *Financial Times*.

Hohenberg, Paul M. and Lees, Lynne Hollen. 1985. *The Making of Urban Europe, 1000–1950*. Cambridge, Mass.: Harvard University Press.

Hollingsworth, T.H. 1977. "Mortality in the British Peerage Families Since 1600." *Population* (French edn.), Vol. 32, special issue (Sept.), pp. 323–52.

Home, Francis. 1756. *The Principles of Agriculture and Vegetation*. Edinburgh: Sands, Donaldson, Murray, and Cochran for A. Kincaid and A. Donaldson.

Home, R.W. 2003. "Electricity." In J.L. Heilbron, ed., *The Oxford Companion to the History of Modern Science*. Oxford: Oxford University Press, pp. 234–36.

Honeyman, Katrina. 2000. *Women, Gender and Industrialisation in England, 1780–1870*. New York: St Martin's Press.

Hont, Istvan. 2005. *Jealousy of Trade: International Competition and the Nation-State in Historical Perspective*. Cambridge, Mass.: Harvard University Press.

Hopkins, Donald R. 1983. *Princes and Peasants: Smallpox in History*. Chicago: University of Chicago Press.

Hopkins, Eric. 1989. *Birmingham: The First Manufacturing Town in the World, 1760–1840*. London: Weidenfeld and Nicolson.

Hoppit, Julian. 1986a. "The Use and Abuse of Credit in Eighteenth-century England." In Neil McKendrick and R.B. Outhwaite, eds., *Business Life and Public Policy: Essays in Honour of D.C. Coleman*. Cambridge: Cambridge University Press, pp. 64–78.

————. 1986b. "Financial Crises in Eighteenth-century England." *Economic History Review*, Vol. 39, No. 1 (Feb.), pp. 39–58.

————. 1987. *Risk and Failure in English Business, 1700–1800*. Cambridge: Cambridge University Press.

————. 1990. "Attitudes to Credit in Britain, 1680–1790." *Economic History Review*, Vol. 33, No. 2 (July), pp. 305–22.

————. 1993. "Reforming Britain's Weights and Measures, 1660–1824." *English Historical Review*, Vol. 108, No. 426 (Jan.), pp. 82–104.

Hoppit, Julian. 1996. "Patterns of Parliamentary Legislation, 1660–1800." *The Historical Journal*, Vol. 39, No. 1 (March), pp. 109–31.

———. 2000. *A Land of Liberty? England, 1689–1720*. Oxford: Oxford University Press.

Horkheimer, Max and Adorno, Theodor W. [1947], 2002. *Dialectic of Enlightenment*, ed. by Gunzelin Schmid Noerr. Stanford, Calif.: Stanford University Press.

Horrell, Sara. 1996. "Home Demand and British Industrialization." *Journal of Economic History*, Vol. 56, No. 3 (Sept.), pp. 561–604.

Horrell, Sara and Humphries, Jane. 1992. "Old Questions, New Data, and Alternative Perspectives: Families' Living Standards in the Industrial Revolution." *Journal of Economic History*, Vol. 52, No. 4 (Dec.), pp. 849–80.

———. 1995a. "Women's Labor Force Participation and the Transition to the Male-Breadwinner Family, 1790–1865." *Economic History Review*, New Series, Vol. 48, No. 1 (Feb.), pp. 89–117.

———. 1995b. "'The Exploitation of Little Children': Child Labor and the Family Economy in the Industrial Revolution." *Explorations in Economic History*, Vol. 32, No. 4 (Oct.), pp. 485–516.

Houghton, Walter E. Jr. 1941. "The History of Trades: Its Relation to Seventeenth-Century Thought As Seen in Bacon, Petty, Evelyn, and Boyle." *Journal of the History of Ideas*, Vol. 2, No. 1 (Jan.), pp. 33–60.

Howe, Anthony. 2002. "Restoring Free Trade: The British Experience, 1776–1873." In Donald Winch and Patrick O'Brien, eds., *The Political Economy of the British Historical Experience, 1688–1914*. Oxford: Oxford University Press, pp. 193–213.

Hubbard, Philippa. 2009. "The Art of Advertising: Trade Cards in Eighteenth-Century Consumer Cultures." PhD diss., University of Warwick.

Huberman, Michael. 1996. *Escape from the Market: Negotiating Work in Lancashire*. Cambridge: Cambridge University Press.

Huck, Paul F. 1994. "Infant Mortality in Nine Industrial Parishes in Northern England, 1813–1836." *Population Studies*, Vol. 43, No. 3 (Nov.), pp. 513–26.

———. 1995. "Infant Mortality and Living Standards of English Workers During the Industrial Revolution." *Journal of Economic History*, Vol. 55, No. 3 (Sept.), pp. 528–50.

Hudson, Pat. 1986. *The Genesis of Industrial Capital: A Study of West Riding Wool Textile Industry, c. 1750–1850*. Cambridge: Cambridge University Press.

Hughes, Jonathan R.T. 1969. "Henry Mayhew's London." *Journal of Economic History*, Vol. 29, No. 3 (Sept.), pp. 526–36.

———. 1970. *Industrialization and Economic History*. New York: McGraw-Hill.

Hume, David. 1758. *Essays and Treatises on Several Subjects*. London: Printed for A. Millar.

———. 1773. *Dialogues concerning Natural Religion*, 2nd edn. London: n.p.

———. [1777], 1985. *Essays: Moral, Political, and Literary*. Ed. by Eugene F. Miller. Indianapolis: Liberty Fund.

Humphries, Jane. 1981. "Protective Legislation, the Capitalist State, and Working Class Men: The Case of the 1842 Mines Regulation Act." *Feminist Review*, No. 7 (spring), pp. 1–33.

———. 1990. "Enclosures, Common Rights, and Women: The Proletarianization of Families in the Late Eighteenth and Early Nineteenth Centuries." *Journal of Economic History*, Vol. 50, No. 1 (March), pp. 17–42.

Humphries, Jane. 2003. "English Apprenticeships: A Neglected Factor in the first Industrial Revolution." In Paul A. David and Mark Thomas, eds., *The Economic Future in Historical Perspective*. Oxford: Oxford University Press, pp. 73–102.

———. 2004. "Household Economy," In Roderick C. Floud and Paul Johnson, eds., *The Cambridge Economic History of Modern Britain*, Vol. 1. Cambridge: Cambridge University Press, pp. 238–67.

———. 2009. *Through the Mill: Child Labour and the British Industrial Revolution*. Cambridge University Press, in press.

Hutchinson, Terence. 1988. *Before Adam Smith: The Emergence of Political Economy, 1662–1776*. Oxford: Blackwell.

Hutton, William. 1795. *An History of Birmingham* 3rd edn. Birmingham: Thomas Pearson.

Hyde, Charles. 1977. *Technological Change and the British Iron Industry*. Princeton, NJ: Princeton University Press.

Inikori, Joseph. 2002. *Africans and the Industrial Revolution in England: A Study in International Trade and Economic Development*. New York: Cambridge University Press.

Inkster, Ian. 1976. "Science and the Mechanics' Institutes, 1820–1850: The Case of Sheffield." *Annals of Science*, Vol. 32, pp. 451–74.

———. 1991. *Science and Technology in History: An Approach to Industrial Development*. New Brunswick, NJ: Rutgers University Press.

Innis, Joanna. 2002. "The Distinctiveness of the English Poor Laws, 1750–1850." In Donald Winch and Patrick O'Brien, eds., *The Political Economy of the British Historical Experience, 1688–1914*. Oxford: Oxford University Press, pp. 381–407.

Irwin, Douglas A. 1988. "Welfare Effects of British Free Trade: Debate and Evidence from the 1840s." *Journal of Political Economy*, Vol. 96, No. 6 (Dec.), pp. 1142–64.

———. 1989. "Political Economy and Peel's Repeal of the Corn Laws." *Economics and Politics*, Vol. 1, No. 1 (spring), pp. 41–59.

———. 1996. *Against the Tide: An Intellectual History of Free Trade*. Princeton, NJ: Princeton University Press.

Isichei, Elizabeth. 1970. *Victorian Quakers*. Oxford: Oxford University Press.

Jablonka, Eva and Lamb, Marion J. 2005. *Evolution in Four Dimensions*. Cambridge, Mass.: MIT Press.

Jackman, W.T. [1916], 1962. *The Development of Transportation in Modern England*, with a new introduction by W.H. Chaloner. London: Frank Cass.

Jacob, Margaret C. 1997. *Scientific Culture and the Making of the Industrial West*. 2nd edn., New York: Oxford University Press.

———. 2000. "Commerce, Industry, and the Laws of Newtonian Science: Weber Revisited and Revised." *Canadian Journal of History*, Vol. 35, No. 2 (Aug.), pp. 275–92.

———. 2007. "Mechanical Science of the Factory Floor." *History of Science*, Vol. 45, part 2, No. 148 (June), pp. 197–221.

———. forthcoming. *Scientific Culture and the Making of the Industrial West*, 3rd revised edn.

Jacob, Margaret C. and Reid, David. 2001. "Technical Knowledge and the Mental Universe of Manchester's Early Cotton Manufacturers." *Canadian Journal of History*, Vol. 36, No. 2 (Aug.), pp. 283–304.

Jacob, Margaret C. and Stewart, Larry. 2004. *Practical Matter: Newton's Science in the Service of Industry and Empire, 1687–1851*. Cambridge, Mass.: Harvard University Press.

James, Frank A.J.L. 2005. "How Big a Hole?: The Problems of the Practical Application of Science in the Invention of the Miners' Safety Lamp by Humphry Davy and George Stephenson in Late Regency England." *Transactions of the Newcomen Society*, Vol. 75, pp. 175–227.

Janis, Mark D. 2002. "Patent Abolitionism." *Berkeley Technology Law Journal*, Vol. 17, No. 2, pp. 899–952.

Jeremy, David I. 1977. "Damming the Flood: British Government Efforts to Check the Outflow of Technicians and Machinery, 1780–1843." *Business History Review*, Vol. 51, No. 1 (spring), pp. 1–34.

Jewkes, John, Sawers, David, and Stillerman, Richard. 1969. *The Sources of Invention*. 2nd edn. New York: Norton.

Johnson, Dr Samuel. [1759]. 1800. *The Idler. With Additional Essays*. Vol. 1. London: Printed for the proprietors, by J. Cathnach, Alnwick.

Jones, E.L. 1964. *Seasons and Prices: The Role of the Weather in English Agricultural History*. London: George Allen and Unwin.

Jones, Peter M. 2008. *Industrial Enlightenment: Science, Technology, and Culture in Birmingham and the West Midlands, 1760–1820*. Manchester and New York: Manchester University Press.

Jones, Phil and Hulme, Mike. 1997. "The Changing Temperature of 'Central England'." In Mike Hulme and Elaine Barrow, eds., *Climates of the British Isles: Present, Past and Future*. London: Routledge. pp. 173–96.

Jones, Phil et al. 1997. "Precipitation Variability and Drought." In Mike Hulme and Elaine Barrow, eds., *Climates of the British Isles: Present, Past and Future*. London: Routledge, pp. 197–219.

Kames, Henry Home, Lord. 1776. *The Gentleman Farmer. Being an Attempt to Improve Agriculture, by Subjecting it to the Test of Rational Principles*. Edinburgh: Printed for W. Creech.

―――――. 1788. *Sketches of the History of Man. Considerably Enlarged by the last Additions and Corrections of the Author*. 4 vols. Edinburgh: A. Strahan and T. Caddell.

Kant, Immanuel. 1784. "An Answer to the Question: 'What is Enlightenment?'" http://philosophy.eserver.org/kant/what–is–enlightenment.txt, last accessed 8/9/2008.

Karakacili, Eona. 2004. "English Agrarian Labor Productivity Rates Before the Black Death: A Case Study." *Journal of Economic History*, Vol. 64, No. 1 (March), pp. 24–60.

Kay-Shuttleworth, Sir James. 1832. *The Moral and Physical Condition of the Working Classes Employed in the Cotton Manufacture in Manchester*. London: J. Ridgway.

Keynes, John Maynard. [1936], 1964. *The General Theory of Employment, Interest, and Money*. New York: Harcourt Brace and World.

Keyser, Barbara Whitney. 1990. "Between Science and Craft: The Case of Berthollet and Dyeing." *Annals of Science*, Vol. 47, No. 3 (May), pp. 213–60.

Khan, B. Zorina. 2006. "The Evolution of Useful Knowledge: Great Inventors, Science and Technology in British Economic Development, 1750–1930." Unpublished paper, Bowdoin College.

Khan, B. Zorina and Sokoloff, K.L. 1998. "Patent Institutions, Industrial Organization, and Early Technological Change: Britain and the United States, 1790–1850." In Maxine

Berg and Kristin Bruland, eds., *Technological Revolutions in Europe*, pp. 292–313. Cheltenham: Edward Elgar.

——. 2005. "Of Patents and Prizes: Great Inventors and the Evolution of Useful Knowledge in Britain and the United States, 1750–1930." Unpublished paper, Bowdoin College.

King, Gregory. [1688], 1936. *Two Tracts*. Baltimore, MD.: Johns Hopkins University Press.

Kirby, Peter. 2003. *Child Labour in Britain, 1750–1870*. Houndmills, Basingstoke: Palgrave Macmillan.

——. 2005a. "How Many Children were 'Unemployed' in Eighteenth- and Nineteenth-century England? A Comment." *Past and Present,* No. 187 (May), pp. 187–202.

——. 2005b. "A Brief Statistical Sketch of the Child-labour Market in Mid-nineteenth Century London." *Continuity and Change*, Vol. 20, No. 2 (Aug.), pp. 229–45.

Klemm, Friedrich. 1964. *A History of Western Technology*. Cambridge, Mass.: MIT Press.

Knack, Stephen and Keefer, Philip. 1997. "Does Social Capital Have an Economic Payoff? A Cross-Country Investigation." *Quarterly Journal of Economics*, Vol. 112, No. 4 (Nov.), pp. 1251–88.

Komlos, John. 1997. "Modern Economic Growth and the Biological Standard of Living." Unpublished paper, University of Munich.

——. 1998. "Shrinking in a Growing Economy? The Mystery of Physical Stature during the Industrial Revolution." *Journal of Economic History*, Vol. 58, No. 3 (Sept.), pp. 779–802.

Kremer, Michael. 1993. "Population Growth and Technological Change: One Million B.C. to 1990." *Quarterly Journal of Economics*, Vol. 108, No. 3 (Aug.), pp. 681–716.

Kuhn, Thomas S. 1977. *The Essential Tension: Selected Studies in Scientific Tradition and Change*. Chicago: University of Chicago Press.

Kunitz, Stephen and Engerman, Stanley. 1992. "The Ranks of Death: Secular Trends in Income and Mortality." *Health Transition Review*, Vol. 2 (special issue), pp. 29–46.

Kuznets, Simon. 1955. "Economic Growth and Income Inequality." *American Economic Review*, Vol. 45, No. 1 (March), pp. 1–28.

Landau, Norma. 1990. "The Regulation of Immigration, Economic Structures and Definitions of the Poor in Eighteenth–Century England." *The Historical Journal*, Vol. 33, No. 3 (Sept.), pp. 541–71.

Landes, David S. 1969. *The Unbound Prometheus*. Cambridge: Cambridge University Press.

——. 1983. *Revolution in Time: Clocks and the Making of the Modern World*. Cambridge, Mass.: Harvard University Press.

Langbein John H. 1983a. "Albion's Fatal Flaws." *Past and Present*, No. 98 (Feb.), pp. 96–120.

——. 1983b. "Shaping the Eighteenth-Century Criminal Trial: A View from the Ryder Sources." *University of Chicago Law Review*, Vol. 50, No. 1 (winter), pp. 1–136.

Langford, Paul. 1989. *A Polite and Commercial People: England 1727–1783*. Oxford and New York: Oxford University Press.

——. 1991. *Public Life and the Propertied Englishman, 1689–1798*, Oxford: Clarendon Press.

——. 2000. *Englishness Identified: Manners and Character, 1650–1850*. Oxford: Oxford University Press.

Langford, Paul. 2002. "The Uses of Eighteenth-Century Politeness." *Transactions of the Royal Historical Society*, Vol. 12, pp. 311–31.

Langton, John. 1984. "The Industrial Revolution and the Regional Geography of England." *Transactions of the Institute of British Geographers*, New Series, Vol. 9, No. 2, pp. 145–67.

Laudan, Rachel. 1990. "The History of Geology, 1780–1840." In R.C. Olby et al., eds., *Companion to the History of Science*. London: Routledge, pp. 314–25.

Lauderdale, James Maitland, Earl of. 1804. *An Inquiry into the Nature and Origin of Public Wealth, and into the Means and Causes of its Increase*. Edinburgh: Printed for A. Constable and Co.

Lee, C.H. 1986. *The British Economy since 1700: A Macroeconomic Perspective*. Cambridge: Cambridge University Press.

Lemire, Beverly. 1991. *Fashion's Favourite: The Cotton Trade and the Consumer in Britain, 1660–1800*. Oxford: Oxford University Press.

————. 1997. *Dress, Culture, and Commerce: The English Clothing Trade before the Factory, 1660–1800*. Houndmills, Basingstoke: Macmillan.

Leunig, Timothy. 2006. "Time is Money: A Reassessment of the Passenger Social Savings from Victorian British Railways." *Journal of Economic History*, Vol. 66, No. 3 (Sept.), pp 635–73.

Leunig, Timothy and Voth, Hans-Joachim. 2003. "Height and the High Life: What Future for a Tall Story?" In Paul A. David and Mark Thomas, eds., *The Economic Future in Historical Perspective*. Oxford: Oxford University Press, pp. 419–38.

Levine, David. 1977. *Family Formation in an Age of Nascent Capitalism*. New York: Academic Press.

Lévy–Leboyer, Maurice and Bourguignon, François. 1985. *L'Économie française au XIXᵉ siècle*. Paris: Economica.

Lewis, Brian. 2001. *The Middlemost and the Milltowns: Bourgeois Culture and Politics in Early Industrial England*. Stanford, Calif.: Stanford University Press.

Lewis, William. 1763. *Commercium Philosophico-technicum, or the Philosophical Commerce of the Arts*. London: H. Baldwin.

Lin, Justin Yifu. 1995. "The Needham Puzzle: Why the Industrial Revolution Did Not Originate in China." *Economic Development and Cultural Change*, Vol. 43, No. 2 (Jan.), pp. 269–92.

Lindert, Peter H. 1980. "English Occupations, 1670–1811." *Journal of Economic History*. Vol. 40, No. 4 (Dec.), pp. 685–712.

————. 2004. *Growing Public: Social Spending and Economic Growth Since the Eighteenth Century*. Cambridge: Cambridge University Press.

Lindert, Peter H. and Williamson, Jeffrey G. 1982. "Revising England's Social Tables 1688–1812." *Explorations in Economic History*, Vol. 19, No. 4 (Oct.), pp. 385–408.

Lipkowitz, Elise. 2008. "Scientific Letters and Political Power: The Geography and Content of Cosmopolitan Scientific Correspondence during the French Revolution and the Napoleonic Wars." Unpublished paper, Northwestern University, Department of History.

Lipsey, Richard G., Carlaw, Kenneth I., and Bekar, Clifford T. 2005. *Economic Transformations: General Purpose Technologies and Long-term Economic Growth*. Oxford: Oxford University Press.

Locke, John. [1693], 1732. *Some Thoughts Concerning Education.* 9ᵗʰ edn., London: Printed for A. Bettesworth.

———. 1976. *The Correspondence of John Locke,* ed. E.S. De Beer. Oxford: Clarendon Press.

Long, Jason. 2006. "The Socioeconomic Return to Primary Schooling in Victorian England." *Journal of Economic History*, Vol. 66, No. 4 (Dec.), pp. 1026–53.

Long, Jason and Ferrie, Joseph P. 2010. "Intergenerational Occupational Mobility in Britain and the U.S. Since 1850." *American Economic Review,* in press.

Lucas, Robert E. 2002. *Lectures on Economic Growth.* Cambridge, Mass.: Harvard University Press.

Lyons, Henry George. 1944. *The Royal Society, 1660–1940, A History of its Administration under its Charters.* Cambridge: Cambridge University Press.

Lyons, John S. 1989. "Family Response to Economic Decline: Handloom Weavers in Early Nineteenth-Century Lancashire." *Research in Economic History*, Vol. 12, pp. 45–91.

Macaulay, Thomas Babington. 1864. *The History of England from the Accession of James II*, Vol. 1. London: Longman, Brown, Green, and Longmans.

———. [1837] 1880. "Lord Bacon." In Lady Trevelyan, ed., *Miscellaneous Works of Lord Macaulay*, Vol. 2. New York: Harper and Brothers, pp. 330–458.

Macdonald, Fiona. 2000. "The Infirmary of the Glasgow Town's Hospital Care: Patient Care, 1733–1800." In Paul Wood, ed., *The Scottish Enlightenment: A Reinterpretation.* Rochester, NY: University of Rochester Press, pp. 199–238.

MacDonald, James. 2006. *A Free Nation Deep in Debt: The Financial Roots of Democracy.* Princeton, NJ: Princeton University Press.

MacFarlane, Alan. 1997. *The Savage Wars of Peace.* Oxford: Blackwell.

Machlup, Fritz and Penrose, Edith. 1950. "The Patent Controversy in the Nineteenth Century." *Journal of Economic History*, Vol. 10, No. 1 (May), pp. 1–29.

MacLaurin, Colin. 1750. *An Account of Sir Isaac Newton's Philosophical Discoveries.* London: Printed for A. Millar.

MacLeod, Christine. 1988. *Inventing the Industrial Revolution: The English Patent System, 1660–1880.* Cambridge: Cambridge University Press.

———. 2007. *Heroes of Invention: Technology, Liberalism and British Identity.* Cambridge: Cambridge University Press.

MacLeod, Christine and Nuvolari, Alessandro. 2006. "The Pitfalls of Prosopography: Inventors in the *Dictionary of National Biography*." *Technology and Culture*, Vol 47, No. 4 (Oct.), pp. 757–76.

———. 2007. "Inventive Activities, Patents, and Early Industrialization: A Synthesis of Research Issues." Unpublished ms.

———. 2009. "Glorious Times: The Emergence of Mechanical Engineering in Early Industrial Britain, c. 1700–1850." *Brussels Economic Review*, forthcoming.

MacLeod, Christine et al. 2003. "Evaluating Inventive Activity: The Cost of Nineteenth-century UK patents and the Fallibility of Renewal Data." *Economic History Review*, Vol. 56, No. 3 (Aug.), pp. 537–62.

Maddison, Angus. 1995. *Monitoring the World Economy.* Paris: OECD.

———. 2002. *The World Economy: A Millennial Perspective.* Paris: OECD.

———. 2007. *Historical Statistics: World Population, GDP and Per Capita GDP, 1–2003 AD* (last update: August 2007), available at http://www.ggdc.net/maddison/

Mair, John. 1786. *Book-keeping Modernised: or, Merchant-accounts by Double Entry,* 4th edn. Edinburgh: Printed for John Bell and William Creech.

Maitland, F.W. 1911. *The Constitutional History of England.* Cambridge: Cambridge University Press.

Malanima, Paolo. 2003. "Energy Systems in Agrarian Societies: The European Deviation." In Simonetta Cavaciocchi, ed., *Economia e Energia secc. XIII–XVIII.* Florence: Le Monnier, pp. 61–99.

———. 2006. "Energy Crisis and Growth 1650–1850. The European Deviation in a Comparative Perspective." *The Journal of Global History,* Vol. I, No. 1 (March), pp. 101–21.

Malthus, Thomas Robert. [1798], 1914. *An Essay on the Principle of Population.* London: Dent Everyman's Library.

———. 1820. *Principles of Political Economy.* London: J. Murray.

Mandeville, Bernard de. [1724], 1755. *The Fable of the Bees; Or, Private Vices, Public Benefits, Part II.* Edinburgh: Printed for W. Gray and W. Peter.

Mantoux, Paul. [1905], 1961. *The Industrial Revolution in the Eighteenth Century.* New York: Harper Torchbooks.

Marglin, S.A. 1974–75. "What Do Bosses Do?" *Review of Radical Political Economy,* 6, (1974) and 7, (1975). Repr. in A. Gorz, ed. *The Division of Labour: The Labour Process and Class Struggle in Modern Capitalism.* Hassocks: Harvester Press. 1976, pp. 13–54.

Marsden, Ben and Smith, Crosbie. 2005. *Engineering Empires: A Cultural History of Technology in Nineteenth-century Britain.* Houndmills, Basingstoke: Palgrave Macmillan.

Marshall, William. 1785. *Planting and Ornamental Gardening: A Practical Treatise.* London: Printed for J. Dodsley.

Mason, Perry. 1933. "Illustrations of the Early Treatment of Depreciation." *Accounting Review,* Vol. 8, No. 3 (Sept.), pp. 209–18.

Massey, Edmund. 1722. *A Letter to Mr. Maitland, in Vindication of the Sermon against Inoculation.* Norwich: Repr. by order of S. Mascott.

Mathias, Peter. 1959. *The Brewing Industry in England, 1700–1830.* Cambridge: Cambridge University Press.

———. 1979. *The Transformation of England.* New York: Columbia University Press.

Matsuyama, Kiminori. 1992. "Agricultural Productivity, Comparative Advantage, and Economic Growth." *Journal of Economic Theory,* Vol. 58, pp. 317–34.

Mayhew, Henry. [1861–62]. 1967. *London Labour and the London Poor: A Cyclopaedia of the Condition and Earnings of Those that Will Work, Those that Cannot Work, and Those that Will not Work.* Repr. edn., London: Frank Cass.

McCahill, Michael W. 1976. "Peers, Patronage, and the Industrial Revolution, 1760–1800." *Journal of British Studies,* Vol. 16, No. 1 (autumn), pp. 84–107.

McCloskey, Deirdre N. 1972. "The Enclosure of Open Fields." *Journal of Economic History,* Vol. 32, No. 1 (March), pp. 15–35.

———. 1980. "Magnanimous Albion: Free Trade and British National Income, 1841–1881." *Explorations in Economic History,* Vol. 17, No. 3 (July), pp. 303–20.

———. 1981. "The Industrial Revolution: A Survey." In Roderick C. Floud and D.N. McCloskey, eds., *The Economic History of Britain Since 1700,* 1st edn., Vol. 1. Cambridge: Cambridge University Press, pp. 103–27.

McCloskey, Deirdre. 1994. "1780–1860: A Survey." In Roderick C. Floud and D.N. McCloskey, eds., *The Economic History of Britain Since 1700*, 2nd edn., Vol. 1. Cambridge: Cambridge University Press, pp. 242–70.

———. 2006. *The Bourgeois Virtues: Ethics for an Age of Commerce*. Chicago: University of Chicago Press.

McCulloch, J.R. 1864. *The Principles of Political Economy*. Edinburgh: Adam and Charles Black.

McCusker, John J. 2005. "The Demise of Distance: The Business Press and the Origins of the Information Revolution in the Early Modern Atlantic World." *American Historical Review*, Vol. 110, No. 2 (April), pp. 295–319.

McKendrick, Neil. 1982. "Commercialization and the Economy." In Neil McKendrick, John Brewer, and J.H. Plumb, eds., *The Birth of a Consumer Society*. Bloomington: Indiana University Press, pp. 9–194.

McKeown, Timothy J. 1989. "The Politics of Corn Law Repeal and Theories of Commercial Policy." *British Journal of Political Science*, Vol. 19 (July), pp. 353–80.

McLaren, Angus. 1990. *A History of Contraception from Antiquity to the Present*. Oxford: Blackwell.

McMurry, Sally. 1992. "Women's Work in Agriculture: Divergent Trends in England and America, 1800 to 1930." *Comparative Studies in Society and History*, Vol. 34, No. 2 (April), pp. 248–70.

McNeil, Maureen. 1987. *Under the Banner of Science: Erasmus Darwin and his Age*. Manchester: Manchester University Press, 1987.

Melton, James Van Horn. 2001. *The Rise of the Public in Enlightenment Europe*. Cambridge: Cambridge University Press.

Mendels, Franklin. 1972. "Proto-Industrialization: The First Phase of the Industrialization Process." *Journal of Economic History*, Vol. 32, No. 1 (March), pp. 241–61.

Mercer, Alex. 1990. *Disease, Mortality, and Population in Transition*. Leicester: Leicester University Press.

Mérimée, Prosper. 1930. "Études Anglo-Americaines." In *Oeuvres complètes*, eds. Pierre Trahard and Édouard Champion, Vol. 8. Paris: Librairie Ancienne Honoré Champion.

Michie, Ranald. 2001. *The London Stock Exchange: A History*. Oxford: Oxford University Press.

Miège, Guy. [1701], 1748. *The Present State of Great Britain, and Ireland,* 11th edn., completed, improved, and revised by S. Bolton. London: J. Brotherton and others.

Mill, John Stuart. [1848], 1929. *Principles of Political Economy* ed. W.J. Ashley. London: Longmans, Green and Co.

———. [1869]. 1970. "The Subjection of Women." In *Essays on Sex Equality*, ed. A.S. Rossi, Chicago: University of Chicago Press, pp. 123–250.

Miller, David Philip. 1999. "The Usefulness of Natural Philosophy: The Royal Society and the Culture of Practical Utility in the Later Eighteenth Century." *British Journal for the History of Science*, Vol. 32, No. 2 (June), pp. 185–201.

Mingay, G.E., ed. 1989. *The Agrarian History of England and Wales,* Vol. 6: *1750–1850*, Cambridge: Cambridge University Press.

Mitch, David. 1992. *The Rise of Popular Literacy in Victorian England*. Philadelphia, PA: University of Pennsylvania Press.

Mitch, David. 1999. "The Role of Education and Skill in the British Industrial Revolution." In Joel Mokyr, ed., *The British Industrial Revolution: An Economic Perspective*, 2nd edn. Boulder, CO: Westview Press, pp. 241–79.

————. 2004. "Education and the Skill of the British Labor Force." In Roderick C. Floud and Paul Johnson, eds., *The Cambridge Economic History of Britain, 1700–2000*, Vol. 1. Cambridge: Cambridge University Press, pp. 332–56.

Mitchell B. R. 1964. "The Coming of the Railway and United Kingdom Economic Growth." *Journal of Economic History*, Vol. 24, No. 3 (Sept.), pp. 315–36.

————. 1975. *European Historical Statistics, 1750–1970*. London: Macmillan.

————. 1988. *British Historical Statistics*. Cambridge: Cambridge University Press.

Moher, James. 1988. "From Suppression to Containment: Roots of Trade Union Law to 1825." In John Rule, ed., *British Trade Unionism, 1750–1850: The Formative Years*, London: Longman, pp. 74–97.

Mokyr, Joel. 1976. *Industrialization in the Low Countries, 1795–1850*. New Haven, CT: Yale University Press.

————. 1985. *Why Ireland Starved: An Analytical and Quantitative Study of Irish Poverty, 1800–1851*. Revised paperback edition, London and Boston: George Allen and Unwin.

————. 1987. "Has the Industrial Revolution Been Crowded Out? Some Reflections on Crafts and Williamson." *Explorations in Economic History*, Vol. 24, No. 3 (July), pp. 293–319.

————. 1988. "Is There Still Life in the Pessimist Case? Consumption During the Industrial Revolution, 1790–1850." *Journal of Economic History*, Vol. 48, No. 1 (March), pp. 69–92.

————. 1990a. *The Lever of Riches: Technological Creativity and Economic Progress*. Oxford and New York: Oxford University Press.

————. 1990b. "Was There a British Industrial Evolution?" In Joel Mokyr, ed., *The Vital One: Essays Presented to Jonathan R.T. Hughes*, Greenwich, CT: JAI Press, pp. 253-86.

————. 1998a. "Editor's Introduction: The New Economic History and the Industrial Revolution." In Joel Mokyr, ed., *The British Industrial Revolution: An Economic Perspective*. Boulder, CO: Westview Press, pp. 1-127.

————. 1998b. "The Political Economy of Technological Change: Resistance and Innovation in Economic History." In Maxine Berg and Kristin Bruland, eds., *Technological Revolutions in Europe*, Cheltenham: Edward Elgar, pp. 39–64.

————. 2001. "The Rise and Fall of the Factory System: Technology, Firms, and Households since the Industrial Revolution." *Carnegie–Rochester Conference Series on Public Policy*, Vol. 55 (December), pp. 1–45.

————. 2002. *The Gifts of Athena: Historical Origins of the Knowledge Economy*. Princeton, NJ: Princeton University Press.

————. 2004. "Accounting for the Industrial Revolution." In Roderick C. Floud and Paul Johnson, eds., *The Cambridge Economic History of Britain, 1700–2000*, Vol. 1. Cambridge: Cambridge University Press, pp. 1–27.

————. 2005a. "The Intellectual Origins of Modern Economic Growth." [Presidential address]. *Journal of Economic History*, Vol. 65, No. 2 (June), pp. 285–351.

Mokyr, Joel. 2005b. "Long–term Economic Growth and the History of Technology." In Philippe Aghion and Steven Durlauf eds., *Handbook of Economic Growth*. Amsterdam: Elsevier, pp. 1113–80.

————. 2006a. "Mercantilism, the Enlightenment, and the Industrial Revolution." In Ronald Findlay et al., eds., *Eli Heckscher, International Trade, and Economic History*. Cambridge, Mass.: MIT Press, pp. 269–303.

————. 2006b. "The Great Synergy: The European Enlightenment as a Factor in Modern Economic Growth." In Wilfred Dolfsma and Luc Soete, eds., *Understanding the Dynamics of a Knowledge Economy*. Cheltenham: Edward Elgar, pp. 7–41.

————. 2006c. "Mobility, Creativity, and Technological Development: David Hume, Immanuel Kant and the Economic Development of Europe." In G. Abel, ed., *Kolloquiumsband of the XX. Deutschen Kongresses für Philosophie*, Berlin, pp. 1131–61.

————. 2007. "The Market for Ideas and the Origins of Economic Growth in Eighteenth Century Europe." [Heineken Lecture]. *Tijdschrift voor Sociale en Economische Geschiedenis*, Vol. 4, No. 1, pp. 3–38.

————. 2008. "The Institutional Origins of the Industrial Revolution." In Elhanan Helpman, ed., *Institutions and Economic Performance*. Cambridge, Mass.: Harvard University Press, pp. 64–119.

Mokyr, Joel, and Ó Gráda, Cormac. 1988. "Poor and Getting Poorer? Living Standards in Ireland Before the Famine." *Economic History Review*, New Series, Vol. 41, No. 2 (May), pp. 209–35.

————. 1996. "Height and Health in the United Kingdom, 1815–1860: Evidence from the East India Company Army." *Explorations in Economic History*, Vol. 33, No. 2 (April), pp. 141–69.

Mokyr, Joel and Savin, N.E. 1976. "Stagflation in Historical Perspective: The Napoleonic Wars Revisited." In P. Uselding, ed., *Research in Economic History*, Vol. 1. Greenwich, CT: JAI Press, pp. 198–259.

Montesquieu, Charles de Secondat. 1768. *De l'esprit des lois*. New revised edn., 4 vols. London: n.p.

Morgan, Kenneth. 2002. "Mercantilism and the British Empire, 1688–1815." In Donald Winch and Patrick O'Brien, eds., *The Political Economy of the British Historical Experience, 1688–1914*. Oxford: Oxford University Press, pp. 165–92.

Morrell, Jack and Thackray, Arnold. 1981. *Gentlemen of Science: Early Years of the British Association for the Advancement of Science*. Oxford: Oxford University Press.

Moser, Petra. 2005. "How Do Patent Laws Influence Innovation?" *American Economic Review*, Vol. 94, No. 4 (Sept.), pp. 1214–36.

————. 2007. "Why Don't Inventors Patent?" *NBER* working paper 13294.

Mowery, David C. and Rosenberg, Nathan. 1998. *Paths of Innovation*. Cambridge: Cambridge University Press.

Moxon, Joseph. [1677], 1703. *Mechanick Exercises: or the Doctrine of Handy-works. Applied to the Arts of Smithing Joinery Carpentry Turning Bricklayery*, 3rd edn. London: Dan Midwinter and Thomas Leigh.

Muldrew, Craig. 1998. *The Economy of Obligation*. New York: St. Martin's Press.

Mulhall, Michael. 1899. *The Dictionary of Statistics*. London: George Routledge and Sons.

Multhauf, Robert P. 1978. *Neptune's Gift: A History of Common Salt*. Baltimore, MD: Johns Hopkins University Press.

Musson, A.E. 1975. "Joseph Whitworth and the Growth of Mass-Production Engineering." *Business History*, Vol. 17, No. 2 (July), pp. 109–49.

———. 1980. "The Engineering Industry." In Roy Church, ed., *The Dynamics of Victorian Business: Problems and Perspectives*. London: George Allen and Unwin, pp. 87–106.

Musson, A.E. and Robinson, Eric. 1969. *Science and Technology in the Industrial Revolution*. Manchester: Manchester University Press.

Nardinelli, Clark. 1980. "Child Labor and the Factory Acts." *Journal of Economic History*, Vol. 40, No. 4 (Dec.), pp. 739–55.

———. 1985. "The Successful Prosecution of the Factory Acts: A Suggested Explan ation." *Economic History Review*, New Series, Vol. 38, No. 3 (Aug.), pp. 428–30.

———. 1986. "Technology and Unemployment: The Case of the Handloom Weavers." *Southern Economic Journal*, Vol. 53, No. 1 (July), pp. 87–94.

Nasmyth, James. 1841. "Remarks on the Introduction of the Slide Principle in Tools and Machines Employed in the Production of Machines." Appendix B in Robertson Buchanan, *Practical Essays on Mill work and other Machinery*. 3rd edn., with additions by George Rennie. Vol. 2. London: J. Weale.

Neal, Larry. 1982. "Efficient Markets in the Eighteenth Century? Stock Exchanges in Amsterdam and London." *Business and Economic History*, Vol. 11, pp. 81–101.

———. 1990. *The Rise of Financial Capitalism: International Capital Markets in the Age of Reason*. Cambridge: Cambridge University Press.

———. 2004. "The Monetary, Financial and Political Architecture of Europe, 1648–1815." In Leandro Prados de la Escosura, ed., *Exceptionalism and Industrialization: Britain and its European Rivals, 1688–1815*. Cambridge: Cambridge University Press, pp. 173–90.

Needham, Joseph. 1970. *Clerks and Craftsmen in China and the West*. Cambridge: Cambridge University Press.

Nef, John U. 1933. *The Rise of the British Coal Industry*. 2 vols. London: G. Routledge and Sons.

Nelson, Richard R. 1973. "Recent Exercises in Growth Accounting: New Understanding or Dead End." *American Economic Review*, Vol. 63, No. 3 (June), pp. 462–68.

Nicholas, Stephen J. and Nicholas, Jacqueline M. 1992. "Male Literacy, 'Deskilling', and the Industrial Revolution." *Journal of Interdisciplinary History*, Vol. 23, No. 1 (summer), pp. 1–18.

Nicolini, Esteban A. 2007. "Was Malthus Right? A VAR Analysis of Economic and Demographic Interactions in Pre-industrial England." *European Review of Economic History*, Vol. 11, Part 1 (April), pp. 99–121.

Nordhaus, William D. 1997. "Do Real-Output and Real-Wage Measures Capture Reality? The History of Lighting Suggests Not." In Robert J. Gordon and Timothy Bresnahan, eds., *The Economics of New Goods*. Chicago: University of Chicago Press and NBER, pp. 29–65.

———. 2004. "Schumpeterian Profits in the American Economy: Theory and Measurement." Yale University, Cowles Foundation Discussion Paper No. 1457, April.

Norris, J.M. 1958. "Samuel Garbett and the Early Development of Industrial Lobbying in Great Britain." *Economic History Review*, Vol. 10, No. 3 (Aug.), pp. 450–60.

North, Douglass C. 1981. *Structure and Change in Economic History*. New York: Norton.

North, Douglass C. 2005. *Understanding the Process of Economic Change.* Princeton, NJ: Princeton University Press.

North, Douglass C. and Thomas, Robert P. 1973. *The Rise of the Western World: A New Economic History.* Cambridge: Cambridge University Press.

North, Douglass C. and Weingast, Barry. 1989. "Constitutions and Commitment: Evolution of Institutions Governing Public Choice in Seventeenth Century England." *Journal of Economic History,* Vol. 49, No. 4 (Dec.), pp. 803–32.

Nougaret, Pierre J-B. 1816. *Londres: La cour et les provinces d'Angleterre.* 2 vols. Paris: Chez Briand.

Nuvolari, Alessandro. 2004. "Collective Invention during the British Industrial Revolution: The Case of the Cornish Pumping Engine." *Cambridge Journal of Economics,* Vol. 28, No. 3 (May), pp. 347–63.

Nuvolari, Alessandro and Verspagen, Bart. 2008. "Technical Choice, Innovation and British Steam Engineering, 1800–1850." Unpublished ms., Eindhoven University of Technology.

Nye, John Vincent. 1991. "Lucky Fools and Cautious Businessmen: On Entrepreneurship and the Measurement of Entrepreneurial Failure." In Joel Mokyr, ed., *The Vital One: Essays in Honor of Jonathan R.T. Hughes. Research in Economic History,* Vol. 6, pp. 131–52.

———. 2007. *War, Wine, and Taxes: The Political Economy of Anglo-French Trade 1689–1900.* Princeton, NJ: Princeton University Press.

O'Brien, Patrick. K. 1988. "The Political Economy of British Taxation, 1660–1815." *Economic History Review,* Vol. 41, No. 1 (Feb.), pp. 1–32.

———. 1991. "The Mainsprings of Technological Progress in Europe, 1750–1850." In Peter Mathias and J.A. Davies, eds., *Innovation and Technology in Europe from the Eighteenth Century to the Present Day.* Oxford: Oxford University Press, pp. 6–17.

———. 1993a. "Modern Conceptions of the Industrial Revolution." In Patrick O'Brien and Roland Quinault, eds., *The Industrial Revolution and British Society.* Cambridge: Cambridge University Press, pp. 1–30.

———. 1993b. "Political Preconditions for the Industrial Revolution." In Patrick O'Brien and Roland Quinault, eds., *The Industrial Revolution and British Society.* Cambridge: Cambridge University Press, pp. 124–55.

———. 1994. "Central Government and the Economy." In Roderick C. Floud and D.N. McCloskey, eds., *The Economic History of Britain Since 1700,* 2nd edn. Cambridge: Cambridge University Press, Vol. 1, pp. 203–41.

———. 2002. "Fiscal Exceptionalism: Great Britain and its European Rivals from Civil War to Triumph at Trafalgar and Waterloo." In Donald Winch and Patrick O'Brien, eds., *The Political Economy of the British Historical Experience, 1688–1914.* Oxford: Oxford University Press, pp. 245–65.

———. 2006. "The Hanoverian State and the Defeat of the Continental System." In Ronald Findlay et al., eds., *Eli Heckscher, International Trade, and Economic History.* Cambridge, Mass.: MIT Press, pp. 373–406.

O'Brien, Patrick, Griffiths, Trevor, and Hunt, Philip. 1991. "Political Components of the Industrial Revolution: Parliament and the English Cotton Textile Industry, 1660–1774." *Economic History Review,* New Series, Vol. 44, No. 3 (Aug.), pp. 395–423.

O'Day, Rosemary. 1982. *Education and Society, 1500–1800.* London: Longmans.

Ó Gráda, Cormac. 1999. *Black '47 and Beyond: the Irish Famine in History, Economy, and Memory.* Princeton, NJ: Princeton University Press.

Oldham, James. 2004. "Murray, William, First Earl of Mansfield (1705–1793)." *Oxford Dictionary of National Biography.* Oxford: Oxford University Press.

Olson, Mancur. 1982. *The Rise and Decline of Nations.* New Haven, CT: Yale University Press.

Ormrod, David. 2003. *The Rise of Commercial Empires.* Cambridge: Cambridge University Press.

O'Rourke, Kevin, Rahman, Ahmed S. and Taylor, Alan M. 2007. "Trade, Knowledge, and the Industrial Revolution." Unpublished ms., University of California, Davis.

O'Rourke, Kevin and Williamson, Jeffrey G. 2002a. "After Columbus: Explaining Europe's Overseas Trade Boom, 1500–1820." *Journal of Economic History*, Vol. 62, No. 2 (June), pp. 417–56.

———. 2002b. "When did Globalization Begin?" *European Review of Economic History*, Vol. 6, No. 1 (April), pp. 23–50.

Overton, Mark. 1996a. "Re-establishing the English Agricultural Revolution." *Agricultural History Review*, Vol. 44, Part 1, pp. 1–20.

———. 1996b. *Agricultural Revolution in England: The Transformation of the Agrarian Economy, 1500–1850.* Cambridge: Cambridge University Press.

Owen, Robert. [1815], 1927. "Observations on the Effects of the Manufacturing System." In Robert Owen, *A New View of Society and Other Writings*, G.D.H. Cole, ed. London: Everyman's Library, pp. 93–104.

Palmer, Sarah. 1978. "Experience, Experiment and Economics: Factors in the Construction of Early Merchant Steamships." In Keith Matthews and Gerald Panting, eds., *Ships and Shipbuilding in the North Atlantic Regions.* St. John: Memorial University of Newfoundland, pp. 233–47.

Payne, Peter. 1978. "Industrial Entrepreneurship and Management in Great Britain." In Peter Mathias and M.M. Postan, eds., *The Cambridge Economic History of Europe.* Cambridge: Cambridge University Press, pp. 180–229.

Peacock, A.E. 1984. "The Successful Prosecution of the Factory Acts, 1833–55." *Economic History Review*, Vol. 37, No. 2 (May), pp. 197–210.

Pearson, Robin. 1990. "Thrift or Dissipation? The Business of Life Assurance in the Early Nineteenth Century." *Economic History Review*, Vol. 43, No. 2 (May), pp. 236–54.

———. 1991. "Collective Diversification: Manchester Cotton Merchants and the Insurance Business in the Early Nineteenth Century." *Business History Review*, Vol. 65, No. 2 (summer), pp. 379–414.

———. 1997. "Towards an Historical Model of Services Innovation: The Case of the Insurance Industry, 1700–1914." *Economic History Review*, Vol. 50, No. 2 (May), pp. 235–56.

———. 2005. *Insuring the Industrial Revolution.* Aldershot: Ashgate.

Pearson, Robin and Richardson, David. 2001. "Business Networking in the Industrial Revolution." *Economic History Review*, Vol. 54, No. 4 (Nov.), pp. 657–79.

Perkin, Harold J. 1969. *The Origins of Modern English Society, 1780–1880.* London: Routledge and Kegan Paul.

Persson, Gunnar. 2000. *Grain Markets in Europe, 1500–1900: Integration and Deregulation.* Cambridge: Cambridge University Press.

Petty, William. 1679. *A Treatise of Taxes and Contributions*. London: Obadiah Blagrave.

Philips, David. 1993. "Crime, Law, and Punishment in the Industrial Revolution." In Patrick O'Brien and Roland Quinault, eds., *The Industrial Revolution and British Society*. Cambridge: Cambridge University Press, pp. 156–82.

Phillips, Nicola. 2006. *Women in Business, 1700–1850*. Woodbridge, Suffolk: Boydell Press.

Pitt, William. 1808. *Speeches of the Right Honourable William Pitt in the House of Commons*. London: Printed for Longman, Hurst, Rees, and Orme.

Plumb, J.H. 1982. "The Acceptance of Modernity." In Neil McKendrick, John Brewer, and J.H. Plumb, eds., *The Birth of a Consumer Society: The Commercialization of Eighteenth-Century England*. Bloomington: Indiana University Press, pp. 316–34.

Polanyi, Karl. [1944], 1985. *The Great Transformation*. Boston: Beacon Press.

Polanyi, Michael. 1962. *Personal Knowledge: Towards a Post-Critical Philosophy*. Chicago: University of Chicago Press.

Pollard, Sidney. [1965], 1968. *The Genesis of Modern Management*. London: Penguin Books.

————. 1978. "Labour in Great Britain." In Peter Mathias and M.M. Postan, eds., *The Cambridge Economic History of Europe*, Vol. 6. Cambridge: Cambridge University Press, pp. 97–163.

Pollexfen, Henry. 1697. *A Discourse of Trade, Coyn, and Paper Credit*. London: Brabazon Aylmer.

Pomeranz, Kenneth. 2000. *The Great Divergence: China, Europe, and the Making of the Modern World Economy*. Princeton, NJ: Princeton University Press.

Porter, Roy. 1981. "The Enlightenment in England." In Roy Porter and Mikuláš Teich, eds., *The Enlightenment in National Context*. Cambridge: Cambridge University Press, pp. 1–18.

————. 1982. "Was There a Medical Enlightenment?" *British Journal for Eighteenth Century Studies*, Vol. 5, pp. 49–63.

————. 1990a. *English Society in the 18th Century*, 2nd edn. London: Penguin Books.

————. 1990b. *The Enlightenment*. Atlantic Highlands, NJ: Humanities Press International.

————. 1991. "Cleaning up the Great Wen: Public Health in Eighteenth-century London." In Roy Porter and W.F. Bynum, eds., *Living and Dying in London*. London: Wellcome Institute.

————. 1997. *The Greatest Benefit to Mankind: A Medical History of Humanity*. New York and London: W.W. Norton.

————. 2000. *The Creation of the Modern World: The Untold Story of the British Enlightenment*. New York: W.W. Norton.

Porter, Roy and Teich, Mikuláš. 1981. *The Enlightenment in National Context*. Cambridge: Cambridge University Press.

Posner, Eric A. 2000. *Law and Social Norms*. Cambridge, Mass.: Harvard University Press.

Post, John D. 1990. "The Mortality Crises of the Early 1770s and European Demographic Trends." *Journal of Interdisciplinary History*, Vol. 21, No. 1 (summer), pp. 29–62.

Postan, M.M. [1935], 1972. "Recent Trends in the Accumulation of Capital." *Economic History Review*, Vol. 6, No. 1 (Oct.). Reprinted in F. Crouzet, ed. 1972. *Capital Formation in the Industrial Revolution*. London: Methuen, pp. 70–83.

Postlethwayt, Malachy. 1774. *The Universal Dictionary of Trade and Commerce* [expanded translation of Jacques Savary des Brûlons' *Dictionnaire universel de commerce*], 4th edn. London: Printed for W. Strahan and others.

Pressnell, L.S. 1956. *Country Banking in the Industrial Revolution*. Oxford: Clarendon Press.

Price, Richard. 1785. *Observations on the Importance of the American Revolution, and the Means of Making it a Benefit to the World*. Dublin: Printed for L. White.

Priestley, Joseph. 1768. *An Essay on a Course of Liberal Education for Civil and Active Life*. London: J. Johnson.

———. 1769. *The History and Present State of Electricity, with Original Experiments*, 2nd edn, corrected and enlarged. London: J. Dodsley.

———. 1771. *An Essay on the First Principles of Government*. 2nd edn. London: J. Johnson.

———. 1787. *A Letter to the Right Honourable William Pitt, ... on the Subjects of Toleration and Church Establishments*. London: Printed for J. Johnson.

Puffert, Douglas J. 2009. *Tracks Across Continents, Paths through History: The Economic Dynamics of Standardization in Railway Gauge*. Chicago: University of Chicago Press.

Quinn, Stephen. 2001. "The Glorious Revolution's Effect on English Private Finance: A Microhistory, 1680–1705." *Journal of Economic History*, Vol. 61, No. 3 (Sept.), pp. 593–615.

Randall, Adrian J. 1986. "The Philosophy of Luddism: The Case of the West of England Workers, ca. 1790–1809." *Technology and Culture*, Vol. 27, No. 1 (Jan.), pp. 1–17.

———. 1989. "Work, Culture and Resistance to Machinery in the West of England Woollen Industry." In Pat Hudson, ed., *Regions and Industries: A Perspective on the Industrial Revolution in Britain*. Cambridge: Cambridge University Press, pp. 175–98.

———. 1991. *Before the Luddites*. Cambridge: Cambridge University Press.

Redford, Arthur. [1926], 1964. *Labour Migration in England, 1800–1850*. Manchester: Manchester University Press.

Reed, M.C. 1975. *Investment in Railways in Britain, 1820–1844*. Oxford: Oxford University Press.

Rees, Gareth. 1971. "Copper Sheathing: An Example of Technological Diffusion in the English Merchant Fleet." *Journal of Transport History*, 2nd Series, Vol. 1, No. 2 (Sept.), pp. 85–94.

Reid, Alastair J. 2004. *United We Stand: A History of British Trade Unions*. London: Penguin Books.

Reid, David. 2006. "For the Benefit of Knowledge: Charity, Access Costs, and Education in Pre-industrial Britain." Paper presented for the workshop on History, Technology, Economy. Appalachian State University.

Reilly, Robin. 1992. *Josiah Wedgwood*. London: Macmillan.

Reis, Jaime. 2005. "Economic Growth, Human Capital Formation and Consumption in Western Europe before 1800." In Robert C. Allen, Tommy Bengtsson, and Martin Dribe, eds., *Living Standards in the Past: New Perspectives on Well-being in Asia and Europe*. Oxford: Oxford University Press, pp. 195–225.

Repton, Humphry. 1840. *The Landscape Gardening and Landscape Architecture of the Late Humphry Repton*, ed. J.C. Loudon. London: Longman and Co.

Reynolds, Terry S. 1983. *Stronger than a Hundred Men: A History of the Vertical Water Wheel*. Baltimore MD.: Johns Hopkins University Press.

Richards, Eric. 1974. "Women in the British Economy Since About 1700: An Interpretation." *History*, Vol. 59, Issue 197 (Oct.), pp. 337–57.

Richardson, Gary and Bogart, Dan. 2008. "Institutional Adaptability and Economic Development: The Property Rights Revolution in Britain, 1700–1830." NBER Working Papers, 13757.

Riley, James C. 1987. *The Eighteenth-century Campaign to Avoid Disease*. New York: St. Martin's Press.

Robertson, John. 1997. "The Enlightenment above National Context: Political Economy in Eighteenth-century Scotland and Naples." *Historical Journal*, Vol. 40, No. 3, pp. 667–97.

————. 2000a. "Unenlightened England: A Review." *Prospect*, Dec. 21.

————. 2000b. "The Scottish Contribution to the Enlightenment." In Paul Wood, ed., *The Scottish Enlightenment: A Reinterpretation*. Rochester, NY: University of Rochester Press, pp. 37–62.

Robinson, Eric. 1962. "The Profession of Civil Engineer in the Eighteenth Century: A Portrait of Thomas Yeoman, F.R.S., 1704 (?)–1781." *Annals of Science*, Vol. 18, No. 4 (Dec.), pp. 195–215.

————. 1963. "Eighteenth-century Commerce and Fashion: Matthew Boulton's Marketing Techniques." *Economic History Review*, New Series, Vol. 16, No. 1 (Feb.), pp. 39–60.

————. 1964. "Matthew Boulton and the Art of Parliamentary Lobbying." *Historical Journal*, Vol. 7, No. 2, pp. 209–29.

————. 1972. "James Watt and the Law of Patents." *Technology and Culture*, Vol. 13, No. 2 (April), pp. 115–39.

Rochefoucauld, François, duc de la. [1784], 1988. *A Frenchman's Year in Suffolk: French Impressions of Suffolk Life in 1784,* trans. and ed. Norman Scarfe. Suffolk: Boydell Press.

Rodrik, Dani, Subramanian, Arvind, and Trebbi, Francesco. 2004. "Institutions Rule: The Primacy of Institutions over Geography and Integration in Economic Development." *Journal of Economic Growth*, Vol. 9, No. 2 (June), pp. 131–65.

Roll, Eric [1930], 1968. *An Early Experiment in Industrial Organization*. Reprint ed., New York: Augustus Kelley.

Rolt, L.T.C. 1970. *Victorian Engineering*. Stroud, Gloucestershire: Sutton Publishing.

Rorty, Richard. 2001. "The Continuity between the Enlightenment and 'Postmodernism'." In Keith Michael Baker and Peter Hanns Reill, eds., *What's Left of the Enlightenment?* Stanford, Calif.: Stanford University Press, pp. 19–36.

Rose, Mark. 1993. *Authors and Owners: The Invention of Copyright*. Cambridge, Mass.: Harvard University Press.

————. 2003. "Nine-tenths of the Law: The English Copyright Debates and the Rhetoric of the Public Domain." *Law and Contemporary Problems*, Vol. 66 (winter/spring), pp. 75–86.

Rosenberg, Nathan. 1976. *Perspectives on Technology*. Cambridge: Cambridge University Press.

Rosenthal, Jean-Laurent. 1992. *The Fruits of Revolution, Property Rights, Litigation and French Agriculture (1700–1860)*. New York: Cambridge University Press.

Ross, Ian Simpson. 1995. *The Life of Adam Smith*. Oxford: Clarendon Press.

————. 1998. *On the Wealth of Nations: Contemporary Responses to Adam Smith*. Bristol: Thoemmes Press.

Rothschild, Emma. 2001. *Economic Sentiments: Adam Smith, Condorcet, and the Enlightenment*. Cambridge, Mass.: Harvard University Press.

Rothschild, Emma. 2002. "The English *Kopf.* " In Donald Winch and Patrick O'Brien, eds., *The Political Economy of the British Historical Experience, 1688–1914*. Oxford: Oxford University Press, pp. 31–60.

Rowning, John. 1779. *A Compendious System of Natural Philosophy*, 8ᵗʰ edn., corrected, with additions. London: John Rivington, Jr.

Rubinstein, W.D. 1983. "The End of 'Old Corruption' in Britain 1780–1860." *Past and Present*, No. 101 (Nov.), pp. 55–86.

Ruggles, Steven. 1987. *Prolonged Connections: The Rise of the Extended Family in Nineteenth-century England and America*. Madison: University of Wisconsin Press.

Rule, John. 1988. "The Formative Years of British Trade Unionism." In John Rule, ed., *British Trade Unionism, 1750–1850: The Formative Years*. London: Longman, pp. 1–28.

Rumford, Count (William Thompson). 1876. *The Complete Works of Count Rumford*. London: The American Academy of Arts and Sciences and Macmillan.

Rushton, Peter. 1991. "The Matter in Variance: Adolescents and Domestic Conflict in the Pre–industrial Economy of Northeast England, 1600–1800." *Journal of Social History*, Vol. 25, No. 1 (autumn), pp. 89–107.

Rusnock, Andrea. 2002. *Vital Accounts: Quantifying Health and Population in Eighteenth-century England and France*. Cambridge: Cambridge University Press.

Ruttan, Vernon W. 2001. *Technology, Growth and Development: An Induced Innovation Perspective*. New York and Oxford: Oxford University Press.

Ryan-Johansson, Sheila. 2006. "Medics, Monarchs and the Knowledge Driven Health Transition in Europe, 1600–1800." Unpublished ms., Cambridge University.

Sargent Thomas J. and Velde, François R. 2002. *The Big Problem of Small Change*. Princeton, NJ: Princeton University Press.

Saussure, César de. [1726], 1902. *A Foreign View of England in the Reigns of George I. & George II. The Letters of Monsieur César de Saussure to his Family,* trans. and ed. Madame Van Muyden. London: J. Murray.

Say, Jean-Baptiste. [1803], 1821. *A Treatise on Political Economy*. 4ᵗʰ edn., Boston: Wells and Lilly.

Schmiechen, James A. 1984. *Sweated Industries and Sweated Labor*. Urbana: University of Illinois Press.

Schofield, Robert E. 1963. *The Lunar Society of Birmingham*. Oxford: Clarendon Press.

———. 1997. *The Enlightenment of Joseph Priestley*. Philadelphia, PA: University of Pennsylvania Press.

Schofield, Roger S. 1973. "Dimensions of Illiteracy, 1750–1850." *Explorations in Economic History*, Vol. 10, No. 4, pp. 437–54.

Schonhardt-Bailey, Cheryl. 1996. *Free Trade: The Repeal of the Corn Laws*. Bristol: Thoemmes Press.

Schumpeter, Joseph A. 1934. *The Theory of Economic Development*. Oxford: Oxford University Press.

Schwarz, L.D. 1992. *London in the Age of Industrialization: Entrepreneurs, Labour Force, and Living Conditions, 1700–1850*. Cambridge: Cambridge University Press.

Scott, H.M., ed. 1990. *Enlightened Absolutism: Reform and Reformers in Later Eighteenth-Century Europe*. Houndmills, Basingstoke: Palgrave Macmillan.

Selgin, George. 2008. *Good Money: Birmingham Button Makers, the Royal Mint, and the Beginnings of Modern Coinage, 1775–1821*. Ann Arbor: University of Michigan Press.

Sen, Amartya. 1987. *The Standard of Living.* Cambridge: Cambridge University Press.

Shammas, Carole. 1990. *The Pre-Industrial Consumer in England and America.* Oxford: Clarendon Press.

Shapin, Steven. 1994. *A Social History of Truth.* Chicago: University of Chicago Press.

Sharpe, Pamela. 1991. "Literally Spinsters: A New Interpretation of Local Economy and Demography in Colyton in the Seventeenth and Eighteenth Centuries." *Economic History Review*, New Series, Vol. 44, No. 1 (Feb.), pp. 46–65.

Shavell, Steven and Van Ypersele, Tanguy. 2001. "Rewards vs. Intellectual Property Rights." *Journal of Law and Economics*, Vol. 44, No. 2 (Oct.), pp. 525–47.

Sher, Richard B. 2000. "Science and Medicine in the Scottish Enlightenment: The Lessons of Book History." In Paul Wood, ed., *The Scottish Enlightenment: A Reinterpretation.* Rochester, NY: University of Rochester Press, pp. 99–156.

Sherwood, Joan. 1993. "The Milk Factor: The Ideology of Breast-feeding and Post-partum Illnesses, 1750–1850." *Canadian Bulletin of Medical History*, Vol. 10, No. 1, pp. 25–47.

Shleifer, Andrei and Vishny, Robert. 1998. *The Grabbing Hand: Government Pathologies and their Cures.* Cambridge, Mass.: Harvard University Press.

Shoemaker, Robert B. 1998. *Gender in English Society, 1650–1850: The Emergence of Separate Spheres.* Harlow, Essex: Pearson.

Shorter, Edward. 1971. "Illegitimacy, Sexual Revolution, and Social Change in Modern Europe." In Theodore K. Rabb and Robert I. Rotberg, eds., *The Family in History: Interdisciplinary Essays.* New York: Harper and Row, pp. 48–84.

Siddall, William R. 1969. "Railroad Gauges and Spatial Interaction." *Geographical Review*, Vol. 59, No. 1 (Jan.), pp. 29–57.

Simond, Louis. [1815], 1968. *An American in Regency England: The Journal of a Tour in 1810–1811*, ed. Christopher Hibbert. London: The History Book Club.

Skempton, A.W. et al., eds. 2002. *A Biographical Dictionary of Civil Engineers in Great Britain and Ireland, Vol. 1: 1500–1830.* London: Thomas Telford for the Institution of Civil Engineers.

Smail, John. 1994. *The Origins of Middle-class Culture: Halifax, Yorkshire, 1660–1780.* Ithaca, NY and London: Cornell University Press.

Smelser, Neil J. 1959. *Social Change in the Industrial Revolution.* Chicago: University of Chicago Press.

Smiles, Samuel. 1859. *Self Help.* Available on http://www.emotionalliteracyeducation.com/classic_books_online/selfh10.html

———. 1865. *Lives of Boulton and Watt.* Philadelphia, PA: J.B. Lippincott.

———. 1884. *Men of Invention and Industry.* London: J. Murray.

———. [1889], 1901. *Industrial Biography: Iron-workers and Tool Makers.* London: John Murray. Available at http://www.fullbooks.com/Industrial–Biography6.html

Smith, Adam. [1757], 1978. *Lectures on Jurisprudence*, eds. Ronald Meek et al. Oxford: Clarendon Press.

———. 1759. *Theory of Moral Sentiments.* London: A. Millar.

———. [1776], 1976. *The Wealth of Nations,* ed. Edwin Cannan. Chicago: University of Chicago Press.

Smith, Cyril Stanley. 1964. "The Discovery of Carbon in Steel." *Technology and Culture*, Vol. 5, No. 2 (spring, 1964), pp. 149–75.

Smout, T.C. 1969. *A History of the Scottish People, 1560–1830*. New York: Charles Scribner's and Sons.

Snell, K.D.M. 1985. *Annals of the Labouring Poor: Social Change and Agrarian England, 1660–1900*. Cambridge: Cambridge University Press.

———. 1991. "Pauper Settlement and the Right to Poor Relief in England and Wales." *Continuity and Change*, Vol. 6, No. 3, pp. 375–415.

Snooks, Graeme D. 1994. "New Perspectives on the Industrial Revolution." In Graeme Donald Snooks, ed., *Was the Industrial Revolution Necessary?* London: Routledge, pp. 1–26.

Sokoloff, Kenneth L. and Dollar, David. 1997. "Agricultural Seasonality and the Organization of Manufacturing in Early Industrial Economies: The Contrast Between England and the United States." *Journal of Economic History*, Vol. 57, No. 2 (June), pp. 288–321.

Solar, Peter. 1995. "Poor Relief and English Economic Development Before the Industrial Revolution." *Economic History Review*, New Series, Vol. 48, No. 1 (Feb.), pp. 1–22.

Souligné, M. de. 1706. *A Comparison between Old Rome in its Glory, as to the Extent and Populousness, and London as it is at Present. By a Person of Quality, a Native of France*. London: Printed and sold by John Nutt.

Spackman, William Frederick. 1845. *An Analysis of the Railway Interest of the United Kingdom*. London: Longman.

Spadafora, David. 1990. *The Idea of Progress in Eighteenth-century Britain*. New Haven, CT: Yale University Press.

Spagnolo, Giancarlo. 1999. "Social Relations and Cooperations in Organizations." *Journal of Economic Behavior and Organizations*, Vol. 38, No. 1 (Jan.), pp. 1–25.

Sprat, Thomas. [1667], 1702. *The History of the Royal Society of London, for the Improving of Natural Knowledge*. London: Printed for Rob. Scot, Ri. Chiswell, Tho. Chapman, and Geo. Sawbridge.

Stasavage, David. 2003. *Public Debt and the Birth of the Democratic State: France and Great Britain, 1688–1789*. Cambridge: Cambridge University Press.

Steckel, Richard. 1995. "Stature and the Standard of Living." *Journal of Economic Literature*, Vol. 33, No. 4 (Dec.), pp. 1903–40.

———. 2008. " Biological Measures of the Standard of Living." *Journal of Economic Perspectives*, Vol. 22, No. 1 (winter), pp. 129–52.

Stern, Philip. 2008. "'A Politie of Civil & Military Power': Political Thought and the Late Seventeenth-Century Foundations of the East India Company State." *Journal of British Studies*, Vol. 47, No. 2 (April), pp. 253–83.

Stewart, Dugald. 1854. *The Collected Works of Dugald Stewart*, ed. Sir William Hamilton, 11 vols. Edinburgh: Thomas Constable.

Stewart, Larry. 1992. *The Rise of Public Science*. Cambridge: Cambridge University Press.

———. 1998. "A Meaning for Machines: Modernity, Utility, and the Eighteenth-century British Public." *Journal of Modern History*, Vol. 70, No. 2 (June), pp. 259–94.

———. 2007. "Experimental Spaces and the Knowledge Economy." *History of Science*, Vol. 45, No. 148 (June), pp. 155–77.

Stewart, Larry. 2008. "Assistants to Enlightenment: William Lewis, Alexander Chisholm, and Invisible Technicians in the Industrial Revolution." *Notes and Records of the Royal Society*, Vol. 62, pp. 17–29.

Stone, Lawrence. 1983. "Interpersonal Violence in English Society 1300–1980." *Past and Present*, No. 101 (Nov.), pp. 22–33.

———. 1985. "The History of Violence in England: Some Observations—Rejoinder." *Past and Present*, No. 108 (August), pp. 216–24.

Styles, John. 1993. "Manufacturing, Consumption and Design in Eighteenth Century England." In John Brewer and Roy Porter, eds., *Consumption and the World of Goods*. London: Routledge, pp. 527–54.

Styles, P. 1963. "The Evolution of the Law of Settlement." *University of Birmingham Historical Journal*, Vol. 9, pp. 33–63.

Sullivan, Richard J. 1989. "England's 'Age of Invention': The Acceleration of Patents and Patentable Invention During the Industrial Revolution." *Explorations in Economic History*, Vol. 26, No. 4 (Oct.), pp. 424–52.

Sunderland, David. 2007. *Social Capital, Trust and the Industrial Revolution, 1780–1880*. London and New York: Routledge.

Sussman, Nathan and Yafeh, Yishay. 2006. "Institutional Reforms, Financial Development and Sovereign Debt: Britain 1690–1790." *Journal of Economic History*, Vol. 66, No. 4 (Dec.), pp. 906–35.

Szostak, Rick. 1989. "The Organization of Work: The Emergence of the Factory Revisited." *Journal of Economic Behavior and Organization*, Vol. 11, No. 3 (May), pp. 343–58.

———. 1991. *The Role of Transportation in the Industrial Revolution*. Montreal: McGill's-Queen's University Press.

Szreter, Simon and Mooney, G. 1998. "Urbanization, Mortality, and the Standard of Living Debate: New Estimates of the Expectation of Life at Birth in Nineteenth-century British Cities." *Economic History Review*, Vol. 51, No. 1 (Feb.), pp. 84–112.

Taine, Hippolyte. [1872], 1958. *Notes on England*, trans. with an introduction by Edward Hyams. Fair Lawn, NJ: Essential Books.

Tallis, John. 1852. *Tallis's History and Description of the Crystal Palace, and the Exhibition of the World's Industry in 1851*. London and New York: J. Tallis.

Taylor, Barbara. 1983. *Eve and the New Jerusalem*. New York: Pantheon Books.

Teich, Mikuláš and Porter, Roy, eds. 1996. *The Industrial Revolution in National Context*. Cambridge: Cambridge University Press.

Temin, Peter. 1997. "Two Views of the British Industrial Revolution." *Journal of Economic History*, Vol. 57, No. 1 (March), pp. 63–82.

Temin, Peter and Voth, Hans-Joachim. 2005. "Credit Rationing and Crowding out during the Industrial Revolution: Evidence from Hoare's Bank, 1702–1862." *Explorations in Economic History*, Vol. 41, No. 3 (July), pp. 325–48.

———. 2008a. "Interest Rate Restrictions in a Natural Experiment: Loan Allocations and the Change in the Usury Laws in 1714." *Economic Journal*, Vol. 118, Issue 528 (March), pp. 1–16.

———. 2008b. "Private Borrowing during the Financial Revolution: Hoare's Bank and its Customers, 1702–24." *Economic History Review*, Vol. 61, No. 3 (Aug.), pp. 541–64.

Thackray, Arnold. 1974. "Natural Knowledge in Cultural Context: The Manchester Model." *American Historical Review*, Vol. 79, No. 3 (June), pp. 672–709.

Thomas, Brinley. 1985. "Food Supply in the United Kingdom during the Industrial Revolution." In Joel Mokyr, ed., *The Economics of the Industrial Revolution.* Totowa, NJ: Rowman and Allanheld, pp. 137–50.

Thompson, E.P. 1963. *The Making of the English Working Class.* New York: Vintage Books.

————. 1967. "The Political Education of Henry Mayhew." *Victorian Studies,* Vol. 11, No. 1 (Sept.), pp. 41–62.

Thomson, Ross. 2009. *Structures of Change in the Mechanical Age.* Baltimore, MD: Johns Hopkins University Press.

Timmins, Geoffrey. 1998. *Made in Lancashire: A History of Regional Industrialization.* Manchester: Manchester University Press.

Tocqueville de, Alexis. 1958. *Journeys to England and Ireland,* trans. George Lawrence and K.P. Mayer. New Haven, CT: Yale University Press.

The Tradesman's Director or the London and Country Shopkeeper's Useful Companion. 1756. London: Printed for W. Owen. Tröhler, Ulrich. 2000. *"To Improve the Evidence of Medicine": The 18th Century British Origins of a Critical Approach.* Edinburgh: Royal College of Physicians of Edinburgh.

Tucker, Josiah. 1758. *Instructions for Travellers.* Dublin: Printed for William Watson at the Poets Head in Carpel Street.

————. 1763. *The Case of Going to War, for the Sake of Procuring, Enlarging, or Securing of Trade, Considered in a New Light.* London: printed for R. and J. Dodsley; and L. Hawes, W. Clarke, and R. Collins.

Turnbull, Gerard. 1987. "Canals, Coal and Regional Growth during the Industrial Revolution." *Economic History Review,* Vol. 40, No. 4 (Nov.), pp. 537–60.

Turner, Michael E. 1986. "English Open Fields and Enclosures: Retardation or Productivity Improvement?" *Journal of Economic History,* Vol. 46, No. 3 (Sept.), pp. 669–92.

Turner, Michael E. Beckett, J.V., and Afton B. 1997. *Agricultural Rent in England, 1690–1914.* Cambridge: Cambridge University Press.

————. 2001. *Farm Production in England 1700–1914.* Oxford: Oxford University Press.

Tuttle, Carolyn. 1999. *Hard at Work in Factories and Mines: The Economics of Child Labor during the British Industrial Revolution.* Boulder, Colo.: Westview Press.

Uglow, Jenny. 2002. *The Lunar Men: Five Friends whose Curiosity Changed the World.* New York: Farrar, Strauss and Giroux.

Ure, Andrew. 1835. *The Philosophy of Manufactures; or, An Exposition of the Scientific, Moral, and Commercial Economy of the Factory System of Great Britain.* London: C. Knight.

Van Bochove, Christiaan. 2008. *The Economic Consequences of the Dutch: Economic Integration around the North Sea, 1500–1800.* Ph. D. thesis, University of Utrecht.

Vanderlint, Jacob. 1734. *Money Answers all Things or, an Essay to Make Money Sufficiently Plentiful amongst all ranks of People, and Increase our Foreign and Domestick Trade.* London: Printed for T. Cox.

Van Zanden, Jan Luiten. 2009. *The Road to the Industrial Revolution: Institutions and Human Capital Formation in Europe in Global Perspective, 1000–1800.* Leiden: Brill.

Veneer, Leucha. 2006. "Provincial Geology and the Industrial Revolution." *Endeavour,* Vol. 30, No. 2 (June), pp. 76–80.

Vickery, Amanda. 1993. "Golden Age to Separate Spheres? A Review of the Categories and Chronology of English Women's History." *Historical Journal*, Vol. 36, No. 2 (June), pp. 383–414.

Voltaire. 1816. *Dictionnaire philosophique: dans lequel sont réunis les questions sur l'encylcopédie, l'opinion en alphabet, les articles insérés dans l'encyclopédie.* Paris: Didot.

Von Archenholz, Johann Wilhelm. [1785], 1797. *A Picture of England: Containing a Description of the Laws, Customs, and Manners of England.* London: Printed for the booksellers.

Von Tunzelmann, G. Nicholas. 1978. *Steam Power and British Industrialization to 1860.* Oxford: Oxford University Press.

———. 1985. "The Standard of Living Debate and Optimal Economic Growth." In Joel Mokyr, ed., *The Economics of the Industrial Revolution.* Totowa, NJ: Rowman and Allanheld, pp. 207–26.

———. 1994. "Technology in the Early Nineteenth Century." In Roderick C. Floud and D.N McCloskey, eds., *The Economic History of Britain since 1700.* 2nd edn., Vol. 1. Cambridge: Cambridge University Press, pp. 271–99.

Voth, Hans-Joachim. 1998. "Time and Work in Eighteenth Century London." *Journal of Economic History*, Vol. 58, No. 1 (March), pp. 29–58.

———. 2000. *Time and Work in England, 1750–1830.* Oxford: Oxford University Press.

———. 2004. "Living Standards and the Urban Environment." In Roderick C. Floud and Paul Johnson, eds., *The Cambridge Economic History of Britain, 1700–2000*, Vol. 1. Cambridge: Cambridge University Press, pp. 268–94.

Voth, Hans-Joachim and Leunig, Timothy. 1996. "Did Smallpox Reduce Height? Stature and the Standard of Living in London, 1770–1873." *Economic History Review*, New Series, Vol. 49, No. 3 (Aug.), pp. 541–60.

Wadsworth, A. P. and Mann, J. De Lacy. 1931. *The Cotton Trade and Industrial Lancashire.* Manchester: Manchester University Press.

Wahrman, Dror. 1995. *Imagining the Middle Class: The Political Representation of Class in Britain, c. 1780–1840.* Cambridge: Cambridge University Press.

Wallerstein, Immanuel. 1976. *The Modern World System: Capitalism, Agriculture and the Origins of the European World Economy in the Sixteenth Century.* New York: Academic Press.

———. 1980. *The Modern World System II: Mercantilism and the Consolidation of the European World-Economy, 1600–1750.* New York: Academic Press.

Wallis, Patrick. 2008. "Apprenticeship and Training in Premodern England." *Journal of Economic History*, Vol. 68, No. 3 (Sept.), pp. 832–61.

Wallis, P.J. 1963. "An Early Best-seller: Francis Walkingame's 'Tutor's Assistant'." *Mathematical Gazette*, Vol. 47, No. 361 (Oct.), pp. 199–208.

Walton, John R. 1984. "The Diffusion of the Improved Shorthorn Breed of Cattle in Britain during the Eighteenth and Nineteenth Centuries." *Transactions of the Institute of British Geographers*, New Series, Vol. 9, No. 1, pp. 22–36.

Ward, J.T. 1962. *The Factory Movement, 1830–1855.* London: Macmillan.

Wear, Andrew. 1993. "A History of Personal Hygiene." In W.F. Bynum and Roy Porter, eds., *Companion Encyclopedia of the History of Medicine*, Vol. 2. London: Routledge, pp. 1283–308.

Weatherill, Lorna. 1988. *Consumer Behaviour and Material Culture in Britain, 1660–1760.* New York: Routledge.

Weber, Max. [1923], 1961. *General Economic History.* New York: Collier Books.

Wedgwood, Josiah. 1973. *Letters of Josiah Wedgwood,* ed. Katherine Euphemia, [Lady Farrer], 3 vols. Manchester : E.J. Morten [for] the Trustees of the Wedgwood Museum.

Whatley, Christopher A. 1997. *The Industrial Revolution in Scotland.* Cambridge: Cambridge University Press.

White, Lynn. 1968. *Dynamo and Virgin Reconsidered.* Cambridge, Mass.: MIT Press.

Williams, Eric. 1944. *Capitalism and Slavery.* Chapel Hill: University of North Carolina Press.

Williams, Karel. 1981. *From Pauperism to Poverty.* London: Routledge and Kegan Paul.

Williams, Samantha. 2005. "Poor Relief, Labourers' Households, and Living Standards in Rural England, c. 1770–1834: A Bedfordshire Case Study." *Economic History Review,* Vol. 58, No. 3 (Aug.), pp. 485–519.

Williamson, Jeffrey G. 1984. "Why Was British Growth So Slow During the Industrial Revolution?" *Journal of Economic History,* Vol. 44, No. 3 (Sept.), pp. 687–712.

———. 1985. *Did British Capitalism Breed Inequality?* London: Allen and Unwin.

———. 1990. *Coping with City Growth During the British Industrial Revolution.* Cambridge: Cambridge University Press.

Williamson, Oliver. 1980. "The Organization of Work: A Comparative Institutional Assessment." *Journal of Economic Behavior and Organization,* Vol. 1, No. 1 (March), pp. 5–38.

Winchester, Simon. 2001. *The Map That Changed the World.* New York: Harper Collins.

Withers, Charles W.J. 2007. *Placing the Enlightenment: Thinking Geographically about the Age of Reason.* Chicago: University of Chicago Press.

Wohl, Anthony S. 1983. *Endangered Lives: Public Health in Victorian Britain.* Cambridge, Mass.: Harvard University Press.

Wood, Paul. 2003. "Science in the Scottish Enlightenment." In Alexander Broadie, ed., *The Cambridge Companion to the Scottish Enlightenment.* Cambridge: Cambridge University Press, pp. 94–116.

———. 2006. "Candide in Caledonia: The Culture of Science in the Scottish Universities, 1690–1805." In Mordechai Feingold and Victor Navarro-Brotons, eds., *Universities and Science in the Early Modern Period.* Dordrecht: Springer, pp. 183–99.

Wood, William. 1718. *A Survey of Trade. In Four Parts ... Together with Considerations on our Money and Bullion.* London: W. Wilkins for W. Hinchliffe.

Woods, Robert. 1985. "The Effects of Population Redistribution on the Level of Mortality in Nineteenth Century England and Wales." *Journal of Economic History,* Vol. 45, No. 3 (Sept.), pp. 645–51.

———. 2000. *The Demography of Victorian England and Wales.* New York: Cambridge University Press.

———. 2003. "Urban–Rural Mortality Differentials: An Unresolved Debate." *Population and Development Review,* Vol. 29, No. 1 (March), pp. 29–46.

Wrigley, E.A. 1967. "A Simple Model of London's Importance in Changing English Society and Economy, 1650–1750." *Past and Present,* No. 37, pp. 44–70.

———. 1987. *People, Cities, and Wealth.* Oxford: Blackwell.

———. 1988. *Continuity, Chance and Change: The Character of the Industrial Revolution in England.* New York: Cambridge University Press.

———. 2004a. "The Quest for the Industrial Revolution." In E.A. Wrigley, *Poverty, Progress, and Population.* Cambridge: Cambridge University Press, pp. 17–43.

Wrigley, E.A. 2004b. "The Divergence of England: The Growth of the English Economy in the Seventeenth and Eighteenth Centuries." In E. A. Wrigley, *Poverty, Progress, and Population*. Cambridge: Cambridge University Press, pp. 44–67.

———. 2009. *Opening Pandora's Box: Production and Reproduction between the Reigns of Elizabeth and Victoria*. Unpublished ms., Cambridge University.

Wrigley, E. A. and Schofield, Roger S. 1981. *The Population History of England, 1541–1871: A Reconstruction*. Cambridge: Cambridge University Press.

———. 1997. *English Population History from Family Reconstitution, 1580–1837*. Cambridge: Cambridge University Press.

Young, Arthur. 1771. *The Farmer's Kalendar, or, A Monthly Directory for All Sorts of Country Business*. London: Printed for Robinson and Roberts, and J. Knox.

———. 1772. *Political Essays concerning the Present State of the British Empire*. London: Printed for W. Strahan and T. Cadell.

———. [1790], 1929. *Travels in France During the Years 1787, 1788, and 1789*, ed. Constantia Maxwell. Cambridge: Cambridge University Press.

———. 1793. *The Example of France a Warning to Britain*, 2nd edn. London: Bury St. Edmund's.

———. 1794. *Travels during the Years 1787, 1788, & 1789*. 2nd edn. London: Printed for W. Richardson.

Zagorin, Perez. 1998. *Francis Bacon*. Princeton, NJ: Princeton University Press.

Index

steam engine (*cont'd*)
  high pressure 84, 87, 125, 213
  stationary 84
steam power 82, 102, 124
  impact on the economy 125
  in coastal shipping 211
  in textile industry 269
steamships 125
steam-jacketing 125
stearine 136
Steckel, Richard 463, 465
steel and steelmaking 9, 83, 132, 142
  crucible method 115
  pens 109, 453
Stephenson, George 55, 92, 139-141, 214, 215, 233, 251, 349, 386, 478
Stephenson, George and Robert 165 213, 362
Stephenson, Robert 55, 87, 233, 251
Stern, Philip 413
Steuart, James 275
Stewart, Dugald 59, 69–70, 480
  on the division of knowledge 59
Stewart, Larry 44, 50, 51, 57, 86, 346
stillbirths 281
Stillerman, Richard 94
stock exchange 231
  provincial 267
Stockport 127
Stockton and Darlington 213
Stone, Lawrence 374, 401
Stourbridge 251, 350
Strathclyde, University of 234
straw 196
straw plaiting and plaiters 320–21, 457
strikes 354
Strutt, Jedediah 85, 88, 320, 349, 359
Strutt, William 85
Stubs, Peter 138
Sturgeon, William 407
Styles, John 16, 376
Styles, P. 277
subcontracting 111, 353
subscriptions, private 381
Suffolk 180
Suffolk (horses) 190
sugar 146, 430, 454, 462
  colonies 161
Sullivan, Richard 84
sulphuric acid manufacture 88
Sunday schools 236

Sunderland, David 322, 370, 372, 375, 386
surface condenser 217
Surrey iron railway 213
surveyors 250
Sussman, Nathan 412
Sutton, Robert 244
swaddling 248
Swansea 213
sweated trades 321
Sweden 287
  iron ore imports from 162
Switzerland 102, 157, 165
Sydenham, Thomas 243, 248, 301
synthetic dyes 83
syphilis 280
Szostak, Rick 155, 203, 342
Szreter, Simon 299, 300

tacit knowledge 46, 60, 107
Taine, Hippolyte 370
Talfourd's Act 253
Tallis, John 477, 479
tallow 196
Tamboro volcano 176, 451
tariffs 20, 21, 149–54, 169–70, 193, 430 436–37
  fiscal purpose of 152
  impact of 170
  internal 11, 68
  legislation 193
  level of 166
  optimal 166
  purposes of 152
  reform 71
  see also commercial policy; free trade
taxes and taxation 68, 427, 429–33
  administration 432
  collection 437
  farming 412
  system, British 432
  income 430
Taylor, Alan M. 146, 347
Taylor, Barbara 327
Taylor, Frederick Winslow 44
Taylor, James 340
Taylor, John 339, 349
tea 453, 454, 462
  medicinal effects of 295
  tariff on 430
technological change and progress 124–44, 255–78